International Energy Markets

International Energy Markets

Understanding Pricing, Policies and Profits

Carol A. Dahl

Disclaimer

The recommendations, advice, descriptions, and the methods in this book are presented solely for educational purposes. The author and publisher assume no liability whatsoever for any loss or damage that results from the use of any of the material in this book. Use of the material in this book is solely at the risk of the user.

Copyright ©2004 by
PennWell Corporation
1421 S. Sheridan Road
Tulsa, Oklahoma 74112-6600 USA

800.752.9764
+1.918.831.9421
sales@pennwell.com
www.pennwellbooks.com
www.pennwell.com

Marketing Manager: Julie Simmons
National Account Executive: Barbara McGee
Managing Editor: Kirk Bjornsgaard
Book Design: Clark Bell
Cover Design: Ken Wood

Library of Congress Cataloging-in-Publication Data

Dahl, Carol A. (Carol Ann), 1947–
  International Energy Markets: Understanding Pricing, Policies and Profits
/ by Carol A. Dahl.
      p. cm.
Includes bibliographical references.
  ISBN 10: 0-87814-799-3
  ISBN 13: 978-0-87814-799-1
  1. Energy industries. 2. International economic relations. I. Title.

  HD9502.A2D335 2004
  333.79--dc22

                                                          2003022430

Printed in the United States of America.

7 8 9   12 11

To my mother, the first great love of my life,
and to all of those who followed.

Contents

Acknowledgments

The technical, political, and economic challenges of global energy industries and markets are fascinating!

My work has given me the privilege and joy of traveling all over the globe while observing, applying economic reasoning, and teaching about these industries. This book has evolved out of these experiences and my desire to share the fascination of these industries with my readers.

It has benefited immeasurably from the many gifted students, coauthors, and colleagues who have provided me with intellectual challenge through their questions, suggestions, answers, and comments on my thoughts and work over the years. I have learned much from them and for this I am grateful. Although too numerous to mention fully, I particularly want to thank the following professional colleagues, students, and assistants.

Colleagues

Professor Emeritus Morris Adelman, Massachusetts Institute of Technology
Professor Richard Baillie, Michigan State University
Professor Roy Boyd, University of Ohio, Athens
Professor Jean Thomas Bernard, Lavalle University
Linda Casey, Map LLC
Professor Janie Chermak, University of New Mexico
Professor Graham Davis, Colorado School of Mines
Dr. Dorothea El Mallakh, International Center for Energy and Economic Development
Dr. Eystein Gjelsvik, The Norwegian Confederation of Trade Unions
Professor Einar Hope, Norwegian School of Economics and Business Administration
Professor Emeritus Richard Gordon, Penn State University
Professor Lennart Hjalmarsson, Gothenberg University
Marianne Kah, ConocoPhillips
Professor G. S. Laumas, Illinois State University, Carbondale
Lanie Littlejohn, Littlejohn and Associates
Professor Robert Mabro, Oxford Institute for Energy Studies
Professor Emeritus Alan Manne, Stanford University
Professor Dennis O'Brien, University of Oklahoma
Professor Robert Patrick, Rutgers University
James Ragland, ARAMCO Services
Professor Douglas Reynolds, University of Alaska
Professor Luis Sosa, Colorado School of Mines
Professor Helen Tauchen, University of North Carolina
Professor John Tilton, Colorado School of Mines
Professor Geoffrey Turnbull, Georgia State University
Professor Thomas Sterner, University of Gothenberg
Dr. Campbell Watkins, University of Aberdeen
Professor Myrna Wooders, Warwick University
Dr. Mine Yücel, Federal Reserve Bank of Dallas

Students

Basil Al-Ajmi
Nasser Al-Dossary
Mansoor Al-Harthy
Ayed Al-Qahtani
Mohamed Al-Shami
Serhat Altun
Patricio Amuchastegui
Zauresh Atakhanova
Hamit Aydin
Felipe Azocar
Rafael Bacigalupo
Olivier Bardet
Alfred Bograh
Thitisake Boonpromote
Diego Bravo
Steve Brochu
Laura Burke
Jeffrey Campbell
Jili Cao
Daniel Celta
William John Decooman
Kevin Degeorge
David Domagala
Remi Duchateau
Thomas Duggan
Meftun Erdogan
Tsepho Falatsa
Luciano Ferreira Sa
Benjamin Freestone
Garcia, Alfonso Garcia
Benoit Gervais
Greta Goto

Detlef Hallerman
David Hammond
John Tyler Hodge
Peter Howie
Daniel Ingelido
Pirat Jaroonpattanapo
Javier Jativa
Hankyung Jhung
Eric Juan
Bo Jonsson
Mohamed Sami Kamel
Miharu Kanai
Shin Won Kang
DP Kar
Catherine Kesge-Handley
Jinwen Ko
Karlygash Kuralbayeva
Kurtubi Kurtubi
Ella Lein
Hermann Logsend
Alejandro Lombardia
Brice Ludognon
Pongkit Luksamepicheat
Marc Maestracci
Thomas Matson
Joe Mazumdar
Lisa McDonald
Remco Meeuwis
Agusto Mendonca
Sofia Pilar Morales
Gail Mosey
Damdinjav Munkbold
Precious Myeni
Balazs Nagy

Derek Ofori-Kuragu
Kehinde Ogunsekam
Takashi Ohoka
Yris Olaya
Javier Olivero Alvares
Fanyu Pei
Jan Pfeifer
Steven Piper
Kaibin Qiu
Alban Reboul-Salze
John Reinsma
Marc Rock
Patrick Rogers
Carlos Roman
Marcela Rosas
Theodore Royer
Sara Russell
Dedi Sadagori
Francisco Sanchez
Maria Sanchez
Jeff Sanders
Martha Sandia
Tayo Soyemi
Didier Strebelle
Baruno Subroto
Yohan Sumaiku
Agus Supriano
James Clay Terry
Robert E. Tucker
Claudio Valencia
Thorsten Viertel
Laura Vimmerstedt
Michael S. Wilson
Luky Yusgiantoro

I would also like to give special thanks to the following individuals who have helped me by being my teaching and research assistants.

Zauresh Atakhanova
Sofia Pilar Morales
Didier Strebelle

Leida Castillo
Maria Sanchez
Yohan Sumaiku

Karlygash Kuralbayeva
Aggei Semenov

Professor Carol Dahl, Director
CSM/IFP Petroleum Economics and Management
Division of Economics and Business
Colorado School of Mines
Golden, CO 80401 USA

List
of **Figures**

List
of **Tables**

1 Introduction

> *Energy economists want to get the price right. Politicians can't define obscene energy prices but know them when they see them. Energy traders believe that everything has a price and they know it, but if you outlaw price only outlaws will know it.*
>
> —Modified from Unknown Author

Whether you are an energy economist, a politician, an energy trader, or an energy consumer, energy and its price are of interest to you. Energy in all its forms can help us live easier and more comfortable lives. In the 1950s, it was touted that nuclear power would introduce an era when energy would be a non-scarce resource, and we would have "power too cheap to meter." (Today, we would call that a bear market with perpetually decreasing prices.) Alas, this prediction has not yet come to pass. Energy is still a limited natural resource that is occasionally scarce, with prices rising in a bull market. But whether the market is running with the bulls or hibernating with the bears, we must understand and use our energy resources wisely.

Since economics is the science of optimization under scarcity, it is a valuable tool to help us do so. Thus, the major goal of this text is to develop the economic fundamentals and technical and institutional knowledge needed to implement sound economic, business, and government policy decisions relating to energy industries.

Energy originates with the four fundamental forces of physics:

- Gravity, which holds the universe together.

- Electromagnetism, which is the attraction between oppositely charged particles and repulsion between like-charged particles. The electromagnetic force is transmitted by photons, which sometimes act like packets and sometimes like waves. From longest to shortest wavelengths, electromagnetic waves are radio, micro, infrared, light, ultraviolet, X-rays, and gamma rays. The shorter the wavelength, the higher the energy carried per photon. The electromagnetic force holds the atom together and is responsible for chemical reactions.

- Weak nuclear force, which governs radioactive decay. During radioactive decay, neutrons break into protons, electrons, and antineutrinos. The weak nuclear force is transmitted by vector bosons with positive, negative, and neutral charges

- Strong nuclear force, which holds the nucleus of the atom together. Energy is liberated when this force is broken by separating elements heavier than iron (fission). When this force is exploited to fuse together elements lighter than iron (fusion), energy is also liberated. However, separating lighter elements or fusing heavier elements than iron requires an input rather than a release of energy.

These four forces generate commercial energy in six familiar forms.

1. **Mechanical energy** is associated with motion. Falling water resulting from gravity can turn a grinder, wind resulting from temperature differentials can turn a wind turbine, and human and animal power can be used to move objects fueled by the chemical reaction of food.

2. **Chemical energy** is released when molecular bonds are broken or changed as in the combustion of fossil fuels—coal, oil, and natural gas. Such chemical energy may be turned into mechanical energy as in the internal combustion engine.

3. **Thermal energy** is the heat in the vibrations of molecules. It results from friction and may also be a product of the chemical energy of combustion. Geothermal energy, which is heat from within the Earth, may be heat stored from the formation of Earth supplemented with heating from pressure and radioactive decay.

4. **Radiant energy** is light and all forms of electromagnetic radiation. Solar energy is a critical source of radiant energy, and infrared is a radiant source of heat.

5. **Nuclear energy** from fusion and fission results from the strong nuclear force. It is changed to mechanical and other forms of energy in nuclear submarines, the explosions of nuclear weapons, and in nuclear power plants.

6. **Electrical energy** is movement of electrons caused by electromagnetic force. If electrons travel one way through a wire, we have direct current. If they continually reverse directions, we have the more common alternating current.

In any system, we can change energy from one form into another. For example, the mechanical energy of a stream can be turned into electricity by a hydro unit. The resulting electricity can be turned into heat and light in a home or can run a machine in a factory. With these changes, the first law of thermodynamics requires that the total amount of energy in an isolated system will always remain constant. Energy scarcity becomes a problem because of the second law of thermodynamics, which requires that when energy is converted, it is reduced in quality and its ability to do work. Thus, with each energy conversion, we have the same total amount of energy but less available energy to do work. For example, the generation of electricity produces both heat and electricity. However, the heat generated is generally at a temperature too low to be otherwise usefully captured for work. (Georgescu-Roegen, 1979) (Hinrichs, 1996).

An understanding of the economical use of energy is interdisciplinary. It involves knowledge of economics, tools of mathematical optimization, simulation, and forecasting along with institutional, engineering and technical information for energy production, transportation, transformation, and use. Hence, in this book, we will combine economics and mathematical analysis with institutional and technical information to better understand various energy markets.

Since the advent of the big bang, theorized to have occurred some 13 billion years ago, energy has remained a fundamental component of the universe. Humans, who arrived only a few million years ago, have consumed only a small portion of the vast supply of energy on this small planet. Part of the ascent of humans has been the process of learning how to use ever more of this energy to satisfy basic needs, along with space conditioning, transportation, and entertainment.

In chapter 2, we begin with the history of energy use and speculate upon future global energy production and consumption.

Economists often favor markets in a capitalist economy for allocating scarce resources. They feel that market discipline helps to create efficiencies and minimize costs. The lure of profits helps to attract capital to growing markets and away from those that are shrinking. Markets spur innovation and promote new products. With competition and decentralized decision-making, capitalist economies are more flexible and personal freedom is enhanced.

In chapter 3, we analyze energy markets past and future, focusing on competitive markets in a static framework with an application to the coal industry. Principles of demand and supply help us to understand how market prices are influenced. Demand and supply elasticities, which capture responsiveness to price, are developed and used to analyze market changes and price controls. In turn, elasticities can also be used to recreate demand and supply curves.

Energy resources are often publicly owned and considered basic wealth to a society. As such they are usually taxed—sometimes quite heavily. In chapter 3, we also consider energy taxes in the context of a static model. Who pays, or the incidence of the tax, depends on how responsive demanders and suppliers are to market price. Types of taxes and information on energy tax structure are presented.

Economists who favor markets and private ownership for the allocation of goods and services sometimes agree that markets fail and that room exists for the government to step in. One such case is a decreasing-cost industry in which the greater the production, the lower the unit costs, and the bigger the producer, the lower its average costs. Such industries are considered *natural monopolies.*

For many years, the electricity industry's huge capital costs and economies of scale had marked it as a natural monopoly. In such an industry, we prefer one producer on the grounds of greater efficiency. However, one private producer when left to his own devices will be able to monopolize the industry and make monopoly profits. In chapter 4, we consider the electricity industry, summarize the various technologies for generating electricity, and discuss how government ownership or price regulation have been used to try to control monopoly profits.

Alleged problems with government ownership and regulation, along with technical changes in electricity generation, have led to the current moves toward deregulation and privatization, which are discussed in chapter 5. Classic deregulation examples in New Zealand, the United Kingdom, and Scandinavia are considered along with the problems accompanying the restructuring of regulated markets in California.

If large producers have market power and are able to set prices, they can make monopoly profits. A classic example of this market failure is the Organization of Petroleum Exporting Countries (OPEC), which we discuss in chapter 6. We include both the history of OPEC as well as models to explain OPEC behavior. Since OPEC cannot control non-OPEC production, it will be treated as a dominant firm, rather than a monopoly; however, since OPEC is not a monolith but is comprised of 11 different countries, some of their differences will be noted as well.

With deregulation, institutional arrangements or governance structures in markets are likely to evolve. Such structures include spot purchases, long-term contracts, and vertical integration. Transaction-cost economics suggests that the market structure that survives is the one that minimizes transaction costs. Market governance is determined by a number of factors including the specificity of assets in the industry. For example, a pipeline is a very specific asset transporting a particular good from one predefined place to another, whereas a semi-truck is much less specific and can transport a variety of different goods to and from a variety of places. Market governance is also influenced by the amount of uncertainty and the frequency of transactions, all of which influence transaction costs. In chapter 7, we introduce transaction cost economics and apply it to changes in the U.S. natural gas markets.

Energy production, transport, and consumption produce a variety of pollutants. Often such pollutants affect others besides the producers of the pollutants. For example, when the Exxon Valdez went aground in Prince William Sound, Alaska, spilling millions of barrels of oil, Exxon lost money but wildlife, fishermen, and others external to the producers and consumers of the product were affected negatively as well. Thus, pollutants are called negative externalities. Since the producer or private decision-maker does not take into account these costs, which are external to them, private markets will not allocate energy efficiently. Therefore governments have stepped in with laws and policies that have been undertaken in response to externalities such as pollution. A review these policies will be presented in chapter 8.

Another externality comes from public goods: A good from which people cannot be excluded (*non-excludability*) and one person's consumption does not reduce another person's consumption (*non-rivalrous*). The classic example is a lighthouse: Anyone in the vicinity can look at it, and one person looking at it does not generally restrict the ability of another to look at it. If, in making a private decision to produce such a good, an individual only takes his own satisfaction or utility into account, too little of the good will likely be produced. Further, if one cannot be excluded from consumption, each consumer will want someone else to pay for the good (*the free-rider problem*). Both effects cause a public good to be under-provided by the private market.

In poorer countries, a significant amount of biomass is consumed to provide energy. This consumption, along with the associated land clearing and timber harvest, allegedly reduces the biodiversity on the planet, which might be considered a public good. In addition, the reduction in forest reduces the capacity of flora to absorb carbon dioxide (CO_2) while at the same time, the burning of fossil fuels (largely from industrial countries) increases the amount of CO_2 in the atmosphere. It is generally agreed that this buildup will cause global climate change, although when, where, and the exact effects of this buildup are more uncertain. Since everyone enjoys the benefits of biological diversity and lower levels of CO_2—but they are non-excludable and non-rivalrous—they have the characteristics of public goods. An analysis of the provision of such public goods as well as current policies towards global climate change will be considered in chapter 9.

Market power in the hands of either buyers or sellers leads to an inefficient allocation of resources. If there is only one buyer in a market, we refer to this market structure as *monopsony*. One buyer is able to depress the buying price and reap monopsony profits. A multinational company with exclusive rights to buy energy resources in a small developing country with a weak government would be an example of market power on the part of the buyer. With the so-called redline agreement in 1928, the multinational oil companies of the time carved up the Middle East and agreed not to compete with one another over resources, preserving their monopsony power. We develop the monopsony model in chapter 10 and apply it to Japan's purchases of liquefied natural gas (LNG) in the Asia Pacific market.

A single multinational company dealing with a strong government in an energy-rich developing country would be an example of a *bilateral monopoly*, which is a monopsonist buying from a monopolist. In such a case, the outcome is ambiguous and depends on the negotiation skills of the two players in the market. We conclude chapter 10 with pointers on negotiation along with "dirty tricks" to watch out for.

Few buyers or few sellers in a market constitute *oligopsony* and *oligopoly*, respectively. These models get more complicated as their outcome depends on the strategies of all the players in the market. We consider these market structures in the context of game theory with an application to the European natural gas market in chapter 11.

In chapters 2–11, we apply only static economic analysis to the allocation of energy resources. However, many energy sources—such as fossil fuels and uranium—are nonrenewable, depletable resources. For such a fuel, if we use the resource today it will not be available tomorrow, and dynamic analysis in which we maximize net present value of the resource is more appropriate. In chapter 12, we look at a basic two time-period model with applications to oil production and leasing.

Dynamic analysis also has applications in allocating capital costs over time. In a very capital-intensive industry such as energy, it is important to be able to allocate such costs across units of production or consumption. Capital cost allocation procedures are developed in chapter 13 and applied to the costs of electricity generation, energy transport, renewable energy production, and services from household appliances. These costs are important inputs to the many market models considered in this text, and have implications for energy supply. A case in point: Shell Oil Company expects that renewable energy sources will provide half of our energy needs by 2050. Which markets renewable sources penetrate—and how fast—will be strongly influenced by their characteristics and their costs.

If a problem can be modeled using linear equations, it is usually easy to solve—even if the model is quite large. In linear programming, we maximize or minimize a linear objective function subject to linear constraints. We apply this technique to oil refining and energy transportation in chapter 14.

In chapters 1–14, most of the analysis was done under the assumption of certainty. However, we face large uncertainties in most aspects of our lives and with uncertainty comes risk. Energy is no exception; it is a risky business. Government policies, the economy, and competition influence energy prices and costs, and all three can provide unpleasant surprises, threatening not only profits, but, in some instances, a company's very survival. Should we want to reduce risk, we have various choices, including organized futures markets with standardized contracts where parties do not know who is on the other side of the trade. With futures and options markets, discussed in chapter 15, we can lock in future prices for energy products that we want to buy or sell to reduce and manage risk.

Sometimes a player would rather provide a ceiling or a floor for the price of energy. A refinery might want to lock in a minimum price for its product and a maximum price for the crude oil it buys. To do so, it can buy or sell an option on a futures contract for these products. These standardized contracts, also discussed in chapter 15, give the buyer the right, but not the obligation, to buy or sell a futures contract depending on whether a call or put option has been purchased. If it is not profitable, the option is usually allowed to expire. However, if the option is "in the money," usually the buyer closes out an option for a cash settlement rather than taking delivery, as with futures contracts.

Energy is produced in a technically complex industry. Uranium requires sophisticated processing; coal is gouged out of the earth with huge equipment; refineries use complicated processes utilizing catalysts to break down oil and reshape it into the products we have come to depend upon. Natural gas is transported through complicated pipeline networks with computer systems to monitor and measure its location. With the information revolution, even more technical choices influence how firms are organized and how they function. Some of these technologies and how they are being used are considered in chapter 16.

Energy is a global business with many large national, multinational, and transnational companies involved in its production and distribution. It includes not only the economics and technology considered in this text—it also has a human face. To effectively compete in this highly competitive atmosphere requires a company to understand the culture of its employees and its customers. It is also important to develop a corporate culture that is compatible with both its own mission and vision statements, as well as with the national cultures with which the company does business. Chapter 17 concludes the book by considering aspects of national and corporate culture. Topics include how power is earned and distributed, people's views of themselves relative to others and to nature, and views on uncertainty and time.

2 Energy Lessons from the Past for the Future

Those who cannot remember the past are condemned to repeat it.

—George Santayana

Energy markets have and will continue to evolve. Influencing factors include energy resources, technology, population growth, demographics, climate change, costs, preferences, government policy and regulation, risk, and income. In this chapter, we will sum up this evolution and set the stage for the energy models in coming chapters.

Energy Geological History

Science tells us that the most cataclysmic energy event for the universe was at its beginning with the big bang and the following inflation of the universe some 13 billion years ago. These and other geological energy milestones are shown in Table 2–1.

Table 2–1 Cosmological and Geologic Milestones in Energy

Date	Event or Time Period	Comment
13 bya	Big bang	
5.5 bya	Sun formed	
4.6 bya	Earth formed	
4.5 to 0.544 bya	Precambrian	
4.5 to 3.8 bya	Hadean (Early)	Earth crust solidified
3.8 to 2.5 bya	Archaeozoic (Middle)	First life forms released oxygen to atmosphere
2.5 to 0.544 bya	Proterozoic (Late)	First multi-celled animals, one continent called Rodinia, oxygen build up, mass extinction
544 million years ago (mya to today)	Phanerozoic	
544 to 245 mya	Paleozoic Era	Invertebrates, primitive amphibians
544 to 505 mya	Cambrian	Age of trilobites, explosion of life, all phyla developed, 50% of animals went extinct, continents began to break up
505 to 440 mya	Ordovician	Primitive land plants and fish appear, N. America covered by shallow seas, glaciation kills many species
440 to 410 mya	Silurian	First fish with jaws, insects, vascular land plants
410 to 360 mya	Devonian	Age of fishes, first amphibians, new insects, many extinctions
360 to 286 mya	Carboniferous	Huge forests and many ferns reduced CO_2, global temperature cooled, atmospheric moisture increased, first winged insects and reptiles
286 to 245 mya	Permian	Age of amphibians, super continent Pangea, largest extinctions, earth's atmosphere approaches modern composition
245 to 65 mya	Mesozoic Era	Age of dinosaurs or reptiles
245 to 208 mya	Triassic	First dinosaurs, true flies, mammals, and many reptiles, minor extinctions allowed dinosaurs to flourish
208 to 146 mya	Jurassic	Many dinosaurs, first birds, first flowering plants, minor extinctions
146 to 65 mya	Cretaceous	Tectonic and volcanic activity high, first marsupials, butterflies, bees, ants, many dinosaurs, continents as today, large extinction from comet collision
65 mya to today	Cenozoic Era	Age of mammals
65 to 1.8 mya	Tertiary	Modern plants and invertebrates
65 to 54 mya	Paleocene	First large mammals and primates

Table 2–1 Cosmological and Geologic Milestones in Energy (cont'd)

Date	Event or Time Period	Comment
54 to 38 mya	Eocene	Lots of mammals, first rodents, and whales
38 to 23 mya	Oligocene	Many new mammals, grasses common
23 to 5 mya	Miocene	More mammals, horses, dogs, bears, modern birds, monkeys
5 to 1.8 mya	Pliocene	First hominids, modern whales
1.8 mya to today	Quaternary	Age of humans
1.8 mya to 11,000 years ago (ya)	Pleistocene	Appearance of humans, first mastodons, saber tooth tigers, giant sloths, mass extinction at 10,000 years ago ago from glaciation
1.8 mya to 6,000 ya	Stone Age	Dates vary from region to region. Hunters and gatherers chipped and flaked stone for tools for many uses—arrows, needles, axes, etc. Agriculture appeared. Pottery developed. Humans used fire to cook, heat, and ward off animals
400,000 ya	Discovery of Fire	
11,000 ya to today	Holocene	Human civilization, domestication of plants and animals
6,000 ya to 3,200 ya	Bronze Age	Dates vary from region to region. Bronze from heating tin and copper used for tools, ornaments and weapons.
3,200 ya	Iron Age	Dates vary from region to region. Iron formed by heating iron ore, charcoal, and limestone to form molten iron and slag. The iron could be heated and formed into horseshoes and many other products

bya=billion years ago, mya=million years ago, ya=years ago
Sources: http//www.scotese.com/earth.htm, http//www.kheper.auz.com/gaia/timescale/
geological_timescale.htm, http//www.zoomdinosaurs.com/subjects/Geologictime.html,
http//www.cnie.org/nle/eng-3.html, http//www.bergen.org/technology/

Around 5.5 billion years ago, our sun formed, which is still directly or indirectly the source for most of our usable supply of energy. Somewhat later, the earth formed with a core of iron. After a million years, the crust had solidified, although the interior still remains molten and is the source of our geothermal energy. After the earth's formation, water may have accumulated from comets hitting the earth's surface and melting.

Life formed in the oceans during the Precambrian period, more than half a billion years ago, and petroleum is known to have formed as early as this as well. From the Precambrian up through the Devonian Period, marine organisms (mostly plants such as algae, phytoplankton, and bacteria) probably served as the source for petroleum. The organisms were deposited in the absence of oxygen (anaerobic conditions), which prevented their decay. As sediment piled up, the material was subject to bacterial action forming kerogen. Heat and pressure eventually formed oil and gas. Oil forms under pressure at temperatures of about 60–120 degrees centigrade, while gas forms at temperatures of about 120–255 degrees centigrade.

The gas and oil migrated in interconnected porous rock to accumulate in pools, when stopped by impermeable cap rock. The world's largest oilfields and the time of their formation are shown in Table 2–2.

The reserves shown are the amount estimated from primary recovery or oil recovered from the natural pressure of the well. The amount of reserves that can be recovered can be increased by secondary recovery, which increases well pressure by injecting water, gas, steam, or other materials.

According to Tissot and Welte (1984), the Paleozoic, the Cretaceous, and the Tertiary periods account for the world's conventional oil and gas accumulations. Specifically, the Paleozoic period is credited with 14% of oil and 29% of gas, the Cretaceous is credited with 54% of oil and 44% of gas, and the Tertiary period is credited with 32% of oil and 27% of gas. During this time global temperatures except for occasional ice ages tended to be much hotter than today. (Fig. 2–1.)

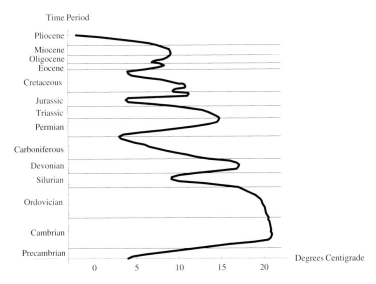

Fig. 2–1 Global Temperatures throughout Geological History
Source: Approximated from Brooks (1951), p 1007.

Table 2–2 The World's Largest Oilfields

Field	Country	Age of Reservoir	Primary Reserves* Billion Barrels
1. Ghawar	Saudi Arabia	Jurassic	83
2. Burgan	Kuwait	Cretaceous	72
3. Bolivar Coastal	Venezuela	Mio.[a]–Eoc.[b]	32
4. Safaniya-Khafji	Saudi Arabia/Neutral Zone	Cretaceous	30
5. Rumaila	Iraq	Cretaceous	20
6. Ahwaz	Iran	Oligo.[c]–Mio., Cret.[d]	17.5
7. Kirkuk	Iraq	Oligo. –Eoc., Cret.	16
8. Marun	Iran	Oligo.–Mio.	16
9. Gach Saran	Iran	Oligo.–Mio., Cret.	15.5
10. Agha Jari	Iran	Oligo.–Mio., Cret.	14
11. Samotlor	U.S.S.R.	Cretaceous	16
12. Abqaiq	Saudi Arabia	Jurassic	12.5
13. Romashkino	U.S.S.R.	Carb.[e]–Devon.[f]	14.3
14. Chicontepec	Mexico	Eoc.–Cret.	12.3
15. Berri	Saudi Arabia	Jurassic	12
16. Zakum	Abu Dhabi	Cretaceous	12
17. Manifa	Saudi Arabia	Cret.–Jurassic	11
18. Fereidoon-Marjan	Iran/Saudi Arabia	Cret.–Jurassic	10
19. Prudhoe Bay	U.S.	Cret.–Trias.[g] Miss.[h]	9.6
20. Bu Hasa	Abu Dhabi	Cretaceous	9
21. Qatif	Saudi Arabia	Jurassic	9
22. Khurais	Saudi Arabia	Jurassic	8.5
23. Zuluf	Saudi Arabia	Cretaceous	8.5
24. Cantarell	Mexico	Paleocene	8
25. Raudhatain	Kuwait	Cretaceous	7.7
26. Sarir	Libya	Cretaceous	7.5
27. Hassi Messaoud	Algeria	Camb.[i]–Ord.[j]	7.5
28. Shaybah	Saudi Arabia	Cretaceous	7
29. Abu Sa'fah	Saudi Arabia/Bahrain	Jurassic	6.6
30. Minas	Indonesia	Miocene	7
31. AJ Bermudez	Mexico	Jurassic	6.5
32. Asab	Abu Dhabi	Cretaceous	6
33. Bab	Abu Dhabi	Cretaceous	6
34. Taching	China	Cretaceous	6
35. East Texas	U.S.	Cretaceous	6.8
36. Umm Shaif	Abu Dhabi	Jurassic	5

Notes: * Primary reserves include estimated ultimately recoverable reserves (EUR) for primary recovery only.
[a]Miocene, [b]Eocene, [c]Oligocene, [d]Cretaceous, [e]Carboniferous, [f]Devonian, [g]Triassic, [h]Mississippian, [i]Cambrian, [j]Ordovician
Source: Tiratsoo, E. N., 1984, *Oilfields of the World, Third Edition*, Scientific Press Ltd. p 23.

Extra heavy oil deposits from 5° API to 15° API in the form of tar sands also contain vast amounts of hydrocarbons with reserves shown in Table 2–3. Oil deposits that have been degraded by the loss of lighter components generally form these reserves.

Table 2–3 Data on Some Major Oil Sands

Location	Age	In-place reserves millions of barrels
Albania		
Selenizza	Miocene	371
Canada		
Melville	Permian	50–100
Kindersley	Mississippian–L. Cretaceous	410
Athabaska		
Surface	L. Cretaceous	120,000
Subsurface	L. Cretaceous	505,000
Peace River	L. Cretaceous	50,000
Cold Lake	L. Cretaceous	164,000
Wabaska	L. Cretaceous	53,000
Malagasy		
Bemolanga	Triassic	1.75
Rumania		
Derna	Pliocene	25
Trinidad		
La Brea	Miocene	60
United States		
California	Miocene–Pliocene	200
Kansas	Pennsylvanian	750
Kentucky	Mississippian–Pennsylvanian	75
New Mexico	Triassic	57
Utah	Cretaceous–Oligocene	17,700–27,500
Azerbaijan		
Kobystan	Miocene	24
Venezuela		
Orinoco	Oligocene–Miocene	261,000

Source: Selley, Richard, 1997, *Elements of Petroleum Geology*, W.H. Freeman and Company New York, p. 421.

API gravity is an index measuring the density of oil products established by the American Petroleum Institute and the U.S. Bureau of Standards. It is equal to 141 divided by a product's specific gravity at 60°F minus 131.5. Water has an API gravity of 10° and a light crude oil has an API of more than 30°.

Some source rocks rich in kerogen and carbonate, but which have not been subject to enough heat and pressure, are known as oil shale. Vast amounts of hydrocarbons are locked up in oil shale with major deposits shown in Table 2–4.

Table 2–4 Estimation of the Main Oil Shale Reserves

Country	Million m³ potential oil
U.S.	264,000
Canada	7,000
Brazil	127,000
Italy	5,600
Russia	56,000
Jordan	7,800
Morocco	7,400
Zaire	16,000
China	4,400
Thailand	2,000
Other Countries	1,000
Total World	500,000

Note: m³ = cubic meters.

Source: Tissot, B.P. and Welte, D.H., 1984, p 264.

Although there have been shale oil industries in various countries, beginning in France in 1838, the high cost of extracting oil from the shale has caused much of this extraction to be phased out.

Coal was formed from higher plants in swampy areas beginning in the Devonian Period. It usually started out as peat. With increasing heat and pressure, the peat changed to brown coal, then hard coal, and eventually, anthracite, as the oxygen carbon ratio and the hydrogen carbon ratio fell. The major deposits of coal were formed in North America and Europe during the Carboniferous period. The periods of major coal deposits range from the Carboniferous to the Pliocene (Table 2–5).

Table 2–5 Major Eras of Coal Formation

Era	N. America	Europe	Far East	Southern Hemisphere
Cenozoic				
Pliocene	+ (Alaska)	+	-	-
Miocene	-	++	-	+ (Australia)
Eocene	++	+	++	+ (Australia)
Paleocene	++(Powder River Basin)			
Mesozoic				
Cretaceous	++	-	++(Japan,China)	++
Jurassic	-	+	++	++ (Australia)
Triassic	-	+	-	+ (Australia)
Paleozoic				
Permian	-	-	++(China)	++(All Gondwanaland)
Carboniferous	++	++	-	-
Pennsylvanian	++(U.S. Applachia & Midwest)			
Mississippian	-	++	-	-

++ coals very abundant, + abundant, - absent

Source: Tissot and Welte, 1984, p. 232 and Dr. Peter Howie, Kazakhstan Institute of Management, Economics, and Strategic Research.

Energy's Human History

When humans appeared, during or immediately after the formation of hydrocarbons, they were mostly unaware of the energy riches that had accumulated prior to human emergence. The sun warmed them, and wood rather than fossil fuels was their fuel source. Human muscle was the prime means of transportation. Humans learned much about their plant and animal food sources. They domesticated plants and animals to have a more stable food supply and more sources of energy. These domestications led to two different life styles—herding and sedimentary agriculture—around 11,000 years ago. With sedentary agriculture, slavery also developed as a source of energy, which was carried on in many areas until the 1800s.

By 3000 B.C., the Chinese are thought to have discovered magnetism, the force that now allows us to generate electricity. At the same time, Middle Easterners were using wind to push sails and primitive water wheels. Sometime after this, it was discovered that heating tin and copper could create bronze. Around 1200 B.C., humans discovered how to purify iron by heating iron ore in the presence of charcoal and oxygen. The carbon in the charcoal combined with the oxygen in the iron ore, leaving pure iron.

Around the same time, steel, which is similar but purer than iron with a higher carbon content, was discovered. The use of wood for building and to create charcoal for iron and steel production put a strain on the wood supply. In Greece and Italy, there were wood shortages as early as 500 B.C., while local shortages in England did not crop up until the 1300s.

The first crude oil used by humans was found in pools that seeped from the earth or was gathered with sponges from the sea. In ancient Egypt, oil was used to preserve mummies and as a lubricant on chariot wheels. The Assyrians and Babylonians mixed asphalt with sand and fibers to make building blocks, roads, and dams more than 5000 years ago and had a thriving petrochemical industry using petroleum for paints, water proofing, adhesive, and for insect and rodent repellent. In ancient China, petroleum was used to polish swords and armor. By 3000 B.C., the Chinese were using oil for lamps and cook stoves. When oil was not available on the surface, they drilled down and used bamboo pipes to bring it to the surface. They found that oil's quality could be improved by filtering it through cloth or sand. The Bible mentions the use of pitch for caulking ships, and the Greeks were known to pour oil on the sea and light it to thwart enemy ships.

Much later, the Mayans made an ointment for priests' bodies and burned it in religious rituals as well as using it for fuel in fires. Mongolians were reported to have used arrows dipped in oil to set fires during their military campaigns in Central Asia and the Middle East. American trappers received oil in trade from the Native Americans. They used it as a cure-all and for protecting the skin from the sun, wind, and rain. Although some of these uses, such as preserving mummies have been abandoned, products from crude oil are still used as lubricants, for lamps, for road building, and as petrochemical feedstocks.

The origins of natural gas use also date from long ago. But gas use has been neither as ubiquitous nor as continuous as oil use. The eternal fires of Baku had religious significance to local inhabitants and the nickname of Azerbaijan in the local Azeri language meant "land of fire." Before 1000 B.C., the Chinese drilled for natural gas and transported it through bamboo pipelines, using it for lighting, heating, and cooking. In the West, the first gas was "made" from coal and was called coal gas or town gas. The first English factory to use coal gas lighting did so in the early 1800s.

People in the Middle East first built windmills to grind grain around 800 A.D. This technology, along with water wheels, was brought back to Europe by the crusades. The *Domesday Book*, published in 1086, records data from an English census ordered by William the Conqueror and catalogues more than 5000 water mills in England. (For more information on the Domesday Book go to http://www.domesdaybook.co.uk/.) Both water and wind came to be used to grind corn, drive saws, and pump water. Around the same time or a bit later, the horse collar was brought from China. It too increased the energy supply, since the collar did not cut off a horse's wind, allowing it to pull five times as much weight. Horses could then replace the slower oxen as draft animals. Horseshoes and tandem harnesses further increased horsepower.

Wind powered the Polynesian outriggers when they settled the Pacific Islands between 2500 B.C. and 700 A.D., the Viking long boats from 790 to 1100 A.D., and the great European ages of exploration in the 15th and 16th centuries.

We know that about a thousand years ago, the Chinese burned coal, because Marco Polo brought back the knowledge of these burnable black stones in 1275 A.D. The Dutch subsequently discovered coal and exported it to England. However, the English soon overtook the Dutch in productive capacity and by 1660, the English were mining and exporting much of the world's supply. Coal was also responsible for an early but ineffective environmental regulation forbidding the burning of coal in London toward the end of the 14th century. In the early 1700s, Thomas Newcomen developed the steam engine to pump water from mines. This greatly increased the supply of coal. Abraham Darby replaced charcoal with coking coal, which greatly increased coal demand. A further improvement by James Watt in 1765 allowed the steam engine to run machines, which further promoted the industrial revolution. Steam engines allowed flexibility in siting plants, since they did not require running water. In the early 1800s, coal, along with the steam locomotive and steamboat, changed the face of transportation. Almost a century later, internal combustion engines were put in automobiles and aircraft. These innovations boosted the use of petroleum and had a profound impact on the 20th century.

The first oil well in North America was drilled in Oil Springs, Ontario, Canada, in about 1854. The modern oil era in the United States began with Colonel Drake in Titusville, Pennsylvania. He had been skimming oil off a creek to get kerosene but went bankrupt. In 1859, he decided to drill and struck oil at 69 feet. The discovery spawned the first U.S. oil boomtown. This and other important events in recent energy history are summarized in Table 2–6, many of which will be discussed later in this book.

One of the noteworthy things about the history of energy is the consistency of fuel and energy use even from the earliest times. They provided heat, light, lubrication, transportation, mechanical power, and materials for war. Thus, while many of the basic needs remain unchanged, the means of providing them have changed, as humans have sought better ways of satisfying these needs with increasingly sophisticated technologies. Most fuels, except for electricity and nuclear power, have been known for centuries. Which fuels have claimed dominance has evolved.

In Figure 2–2, Nakićenović summarizes how fuel use has changed since 1850 and speculates how it will continue to evolve during the coming century. In Figure 2–2, F is the share of energy supplied by a particular fuel. Thus, when coal supplied one half of the world market:

$$F/(1–F) = 0.5/0.5 = 1$$

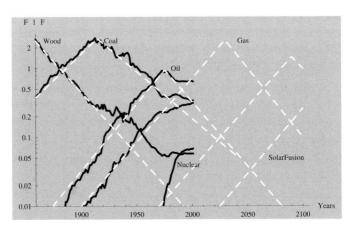

Fig. 2–2 World Primary Energy Substitution

Notes: Solfus = solar and fusion. The black line is actual consumption and the dotted white line is smoothed and projected consumption.

Sources: 1850–1994 was downloaded from ftp://ftp.iiasa.ac.at/pub/ecs/ ag_book/ w-energy.csv from data developed by Nakićenović (1984) and updated for use in Grübler (1998). These data are also available from Publications Department, International Institute for Applied Systems Analysis, Laxenburg, Austria. 1995–2001 updated from EIA/DOE *International Energy Annual*, 2001.

Table 2–6 Milestones in Recent Human Energy Use

Dates	Era or Event
1600s	Europeans started using gunpowder
1694	British patented oil extraction from oil shale
1709	Darby replaced charcoal with coking coal for iron production
1712	Newcomen used first coal steam engine to pump water
1750–1850	Industrial Revolution in England with dates varying for other industrial countries
1765	Watt steam engines could run machinery
early 1800s	Murdock lit a factory using coal gas lamps
early 1800s	Kerosene, called coal oil, was extracted from coal
1800	Volta invented the first battery
1804	First steam locomotive
1807	First steam boat by Fulton
1808	Davy built a battery powered arc lamp
1831	Faraday built a generator to produce electricity from electromagnetic force
1839	Becquerel developed first fuel cell
1846	First Russian oil well drilled in Bibi-Aybul
1854	First North America oil well drilled in Ontario, Canada
1859	Drake discovered oil in Pennsylvania while looking for a replacement for coal oil
1860	15 simple U.S. refineries in operation
1861	First suggestion that CO_2 build–up would cause global warming
1862	Lenoir created a two-stroke internal combustion engine
1870	Rockefeller began refining oil into kerosene in Cleveland
1873	Nobel family searched for oil in Baku, Azerbaijan
1877	Edison invented electric light bulb
1878	Otto improved the internal combustion engine
1880s	Mechanical coal stokers introduced in U.S.
	Coal mining equipment commonly used in U.S.
1881	French engineer d'Arsonval considered ocean thermal energy conversion (OTEC)
1882	First power plants in U.K. and U.S.
	First hydro power produced in U.S.
1885	Rothchilds produced oil in Russia
	Royal Dutch produced oil in Indonesia
	Daimler and Benz made first automobile
	U.S. coal consumption surpassed wood consumption
1890s	Diesel engine invented and used for ships and factories
	Machine built to undercut coal seams
1890	Danes constructed first modern windmills
1892	Shell oil tanker created to transport oil through Suez Canal
1901	Oil discovered in Iran (Persia) and Spindletop found in Texas
1903	Wright brothers' first airplane flight powered by internal combustion engine
1904	Geothermal electricity first generated in Italy
1907	Royal Dutch and Shell merged
1910s	U.S. coal mined with steam-powered stripping shovel
1910	Marland used geology in searching for oil
1911	U.S. government broke up Standard Oil
1913	Ford introduced first automobile assembly line
1917	American Association of Petroleum Geologists (AAPG) founded

Table 2–6 Milestones in Recent Human Energy Use (cont'd)

Dates	Era or Event
1918	Automatic oil burner created, reducing need to carry coal or wood in and ashes out
1920s	Thermal cracking invented
	Draglines introduced for surface coal mining
1921	Seismograph invented
1938	Mexico nationalized oil industry
1942	First nuclear chain reaction
1950s	U.S. railroads converted from coal to diesel
1951	U.S. oil consumption surpassed coal consumption
1952	Bell Labs constructed photovoltaic cell
1956	First nuclear reactor generated electricity in U.K.
1959	Mandatory U.S. oil import controls
1960s	U.S. railroads started to use unit trains
	Long wall coal mining used in U.S. mines
1960	OPEC formed
1968	Prudhoe Bay found in Alaska
	First tidal power station in France
1969	Oil found in the North Sea
1970s	Many U.S. environmental laws introduced
	U.S. oil production peaked
1971	OPEC first received 55% tax rate on oil
	Libya nationalized BP concession
1972	Libya negotiated a posted price increase
	Iraq nationalized the Iraq Petroleum Company
	Libya nationalized some foreign holdings
1973	Iran nationalized the Iranian Petroleum Consortium
	Some oil nationalized by Libya, Nigeria and Iraq
	U.S. implemented crude oil price controls
	Energy crisis from Arab oil embargo
1974	Kuwait, Qatar, Nigeria, Saudi Arabia, and Abu Dhabi all increased government participation in foreign oil holdings
	International Energy Agency formed
	Iraq completed nationalization of its oil industry
1975	Kuwait and companies agreed on nationalization terms
1976	Venezuela nationalized its oil industry
	Energy Policy and Conservation Act required the U.S. Strategic Petroleum Reserve (SPR)
1978	U.S. Natural Gas Policy Act passed
1979	Energy crisis from Iranian Revolution and oil production cuts
	Nuclear accident at Three Mile Island
1980	U.S. enacted Oil Windfall Profits tax
	Iran/Iraq war began
1981	U.S. domestic oil price controls lifted
1982	OPEC first established production quotas
1986	Oil price plummeted more than 50% when Saudi Arabia instituted netback pricing
	Nuclear accident at Chernobyl
1988	Iran/Iraq war ended
1989	Exxon Valdez spilled 11 million gallons of crude oil off Alaska

Table 2–6 Milestones in Recent Human Energy Use (cont'd)

Dates	Era or Event
1990	Iraq invaded Kuwait
1991	Gulf war ousted Iraq from Kuwait
	Collapse of U.S.S.R.
	U.S., Canada and Mexico signed North American Free Trade Agreement (NAFTA)
	Norwegian Consortium to deliver Norwegian Gas to Europe
1995	Venezuela allowed foreign investment in oil industry
	22-year ban on Alaska oil exports lifted
1996	Gabon withdrew from OPEC
	First Iraqi sales of oil for humanitarian purposes
1997	Qatar started exporting from world's largest LNG facility
	Caspian Pipeline Consortium agreed to build oil pipeline from Caspian to Russia's Black Sea Coast
	Kyoto Protocol to reduce greenhouse gases signed
	Asian financial crisis
1998	Caspian Sea area became exploration hot spot
	50-year moratorium on mining and oil exploration in the Antarctic ratified
	Korea deregulated oil refining sector
1999	BP Amoco merger
	Exxon Mobil merger
	Honduras privatized state electrical company
	ENI and Gazprom agree on Blue Stream Natural Gas Pipeline Russia to Turkey
	DaimlerChrysler and Ford to introduce hydrogen fuel cell cars by 2004
	Repsol acquired YPF
	Norsk Hydro purchased Saga
	Ecuador announced privatization of all downstream facilities
2000	Saudi Arabia became more open to foreign investors
	Germany announced plans to phase out nuclear power
	Chevron and Texaco agreed to merger
	First California electricity black outs from electricity restructuring problems
	Merger of TotalFina with Elf to become TotalFinaElf
2001	California purchased power financed by bond issue
	World's largest oil platform owned by Petrobras sunk offshore Brazil
	Oil pipeline completed from Tengiz field in Kazakhstan to Black Sea
	Korea began privatizing its electricity industry
	Norwegian government privatized 18% of Statoil
	Electricity interconnect began between Venezuela and Brazil
	Pacific Gas and Electric and Enron filed for bankruptcy
	German E.On received European Union approval to take over UK Powergen, which would create one of world's largest utilities
2002	Japan Arabian Oil Company's 40-year concession in the Neutral Zone between Kuwait and Saudi Arabia ended
	Japan National Oil Company is to be dissolved
	General Strike in Venezuela slows oil production and exports

Table 2–6 Milestones in Recent Human Energy Use (cont'd)

Dates	Era or Event
2002	U.S. royalty in kind used for SPR fill
	Tokyo Electric Power Company (TEPCO) was discovered to have falsified reactor inspection data leading to reactor shutdowns for reinspection
	Conoco and Phillips merged
2003	Most of PDVSA workers went on strike and many were fired
	Russia passed a law to break up electricity monopoly
	Nigerian oil production slowed from labor unrest
	U.S. and U.K. attacked Iraq, ousting Saddam Hussein, and setting up an interim government
	Russia's biggest and fifth largest oil companies, Yukos Oil Company and Sibneft, announced a merger that was later cancelled
	Tokyo Gas Company and Sakhalin Energy of Russia signed a 24 year agreement for LNG deliveries to begin 2007
	U.N. lifted most economic sanctions on Iraq
	BP and NIOC agreed to develop Rhum natural gas field in the North Sea

Sources: Jenkins (1989), http//www.bergen.org/technology/, http//www.swifty.com/apase/charlotte, *Coal Data, A Reference, International Energy Statistics Sourcebook*, http://www.eia.doe.gov, *Monthly Energy Chronology*, January 2001 to June 2003, *World Oil Market and Oil Price Chronology*, 1970–2002.

Figure 2–2 was produced two decades ago and shows how rapidly our perceptions about the future change. He forecasted that oil would never reach the ascendancy of either wood or coal in terms of market share in the coming century but that gas would. This forecast is still rather believable. However, the prominence of nuclear power now seems doubtful. One would guess that solar and other renewables, such as wind, will probably be more prominent in the coming decade. The president of the Shell Oil Group has predicted that renewables will be half of our energy supply by 2050. Since we have seen changing energy patterns in the past and can expect the changes to continue in the future, how might we predict for the future?

Energy Forecasting

Knowledge of future energy markets is a valuable commodity. It allows sellers to plan and develop the appropriate capacity, buyers to pick the appropriate mix of equipment and appliances to minimize the cost of producing energy services, government to make policy plans during peace (and contingency plans for war), and financial institutions to pick the projects to back and those to reject. Because of this value, considerable resources have been spent in energy forecasting, particularly during the late 1970s and early 1980s when increases in prices and shortages focused policy attention very heavily on energy availability and cost. A variety of techniques have been used for energy forecasting.

We'll briefly consider the following techniques:

- historical trends
- univariate time series
- multivariate time series
- econometric models
- judgment
- Bayesian estimation
- input-output
- energy balances
- end-use models
- engineering or process models
- optimization
- network models
- simulation
- game theory
- scenarios
- surveys

One of the simplest and longest-used tools for forecasting is historical trends or growth rates. In such a technique, if oil demand has been growing by 2.5% per annum, we assume that oil will continue to grow by this same rate. It is quite easy to represent such growth using an exponential function.

$$O_t = e^{rt}O_{t-1}$$

where

O_t is the consumption of oil in time period t

e is the exponential function

r is the growth rate of oil production

For small changes in t, we can represent ΔO by the derivative dO/dt and the growth rate by $(dO_t/dt)/O_t$. For the exponential function $dO/dt = re^{rt}O_{t-1}$ and $(dO_t/dt)/O_t = re^{rt}O_{t-1}/O_t = re^{rt}O_{t-1}/e^{rt}O_{t-1} = r$. Using this model, if current oil consumption was O_o, then next year's forecast, O_1, would be $O_1 = e^{0.025}O_o$ and the forecast 10 years from now would be $O_{10} = e^{0.025*10}O_o$. With this assumed constant growth rate, oil consumption would increase exponentially.

This technique works well when growth is constant and may be quite effective in the short run with a business-as-usual scenario. For example, in the United States during the 1960s and early 1970s, electricity consumption grew fairly consistently at 7% per year and electric utilities found it quite easy to plan for capacity expansion. This growth continued until the 1973 energy price increases, when electricity consumption growth fell considerably. The result was that electric utilities both in the United States and Europe found that they had built considerable excess capacity.

An early proponent of forecasting using an exponential growth rate was William Stanley Jevons, who forecast coal consumption for England. Writing in 1865, when British coal consumption was around 84 million tons per year, and using an exponential growth rate of 0.75%, he forecast coal consumption would exceed 2600 million tons by 1960. However, actual coal consumption for the entire United Kingdom was just under 200 million by the year 1960, falling to less than 60 million tons by 1999. Thus, historical extrapolation of trends does not predict turning points very well, and it can also be very misleading in the long run, as consumption seldom increases exponentially over the long haul.

A somewhat more sophisticated technique of historical extrapolation is univariate time series analysis. In this technique, the current value of an energy variable (X_t) is a function of past values of the same variable along with an error term to represent random events (ε_i) that affect this variable.

$$X_t = \Sigma_{i=1}^{n} \alpha_i X_{t-i} + \varepsilon_t$$

Statistical techniques applied to historical data are used to pick the unknown coefficients $(\alpha_i$'s) and n, which determines how many past values influence the current value of the variable. This technique is more general than the exponential extrapolation, since it does not require a fixed growth rate and can accommodate cyclical-type behavior as well as growth over time. (For the canonical reference on univariate time series, see Box and Jenkins 1970.) Time series may provide reasonably good short-term forecasts, but it does not forecast turning points very well.

Bopp and Neri (1978) found that univariate time series forecast month-ahead gasoline consumption better than more complicated multivariate techniques. However, univariate time series forecast 18 month-ahead consumption very poorly. Further, neither extrapolation nor univariate time series allows policy analysis because they do not typically include any policy instruments such as taxes or regulations as variables.

Sheik Zaki Yamani, Saudi Oil Minister 1962–1986, argues that politics may govern oil prices in the short run but economics governs oil prices in the long run (Yergin 1991). This is likely true for other energy sources as well. Thus, as we shall see later, the amount of energy consumption, its composition, and its costs are strongly influenced by underlying economic fundamentals, particularly in the long run. These fundamentals include income, interest rates, exchange rates, demographic trends, preferences, technologies, weather, environmental effects, quantity and quality of known energy reserves, and associated costs. Since these fundamentals change over time, they do not support models of exponential growth at a constant rate or models where current values of an energy variable are solely determined by past values.

However, time series can be expanded to incorporate these other variables and their lags. Suppose quantity demanded of oil (Q) is a function of its own price (P) as well as income (Y) and their lagged values. You can incorporate P and Y in a multivariate time series as follows:

$$Q_t = \Sigma_{i=1}^{n} \alpha_i Q_{t-i} + \Sigma_{i=1}^{m} \beta_i P_{t-i} + \Sigma_{i=1}^{k} \chi_i Y_{t-i} + \varepsilon_t$$

Again, statistical techniques and historical values are used to estimate the number of lags (n, m, k) and the unknown coefficients (α_i's, β_i's, χ_i's). (For a straightforward description of univariate and multivariate time series techniques, see Pindyck and Rubenfeld 1997.) Time series can help you determine the structure of the model or the variables to include and the length of the lags for variables. For example, let's suppose you are estimating the following model for the demand for gasoline:

$$Q_d = \alpha_1 + \alpha_2 P + \alpha_3 P_{transit} + \alpha_4 Y + \alpha_5 Y_{t-1} + \alpha_6 Y_{t-2} + \alpha_7 Y_{t-3} + \alpha_8 Y_{t-4} + \alpha_9 P_d + \varepsilon$$

Where

Q_d is the quantity purchased

P is the price of gasoline

Y_{t-i} is income lagged i periods

P_d is the price of diesel fuel

$P_{transit}$ is the price of transit

If the price of transit ($P_{transit}$) is not important, the estimates for its coefficient when you estimate the previous model should not be significantly different from zero and the variable can be excluded. Lags are often included in models because it takes time to adjust to changes in a variable. If your income increases, you may not immediately buy a new car that consumes more gasoline. Thus, consumers may still be responding today to income changes that took place in the past. How long the adjustment takes may be indicated by the coefficients on lagged variables. If the variable is not important after two periods, its coefficient on lags of-greater-than-two should not be significantly different from zero. In the above model, a_7 and a_8 would then not be significantly different from zero.

Time series analysis works best when you have lots of data over a consistent structural regime with lots of variation in the variables on right side of the equation. It works less well on short series or series where the structure is changing. In addition, series variables may move together or correlate with each other. If the price of gasoline and the price of diesel fuel move together in the previous model, the statistical techniques will have trouble distinguishing the separate effects of either variable.

Since economists often cannot generate their own data through experiments, their time series for a consistent regime may be relatively short. In such a case, econometric techniques may be applied instead of time series. Econometric techniques are similar to time series except more attention is paid to the variables that should be included in the model. The data that is used may also be cross-sectional, may represent variables at one point in time across various economic entities—e.g., households, states, provinces, firms, countries—or may be a combination of cross-section time series.

With short time series, the data may not have enough information to accurately choose the variables and lag structure for us. Thus, economic theory is relied upon more heavily to specify the model in econometric estimation, but the coefficients are still estimated on historical data using statistical techniques. Often, there is less emphasis on lagged variables in econometric than in time series work. In principle, both multivariate time series and econometric models should be better at forecasting turning points than univariate models, and both can incorporate policy instruments for better policy analysis. However, forecasting becomes more difficult because these multivariate techniques also require a forecast of right-side exogenous variables. For example, in the previous gasoline model:

$$Q_d = \alpha_1 + \alpha_2 P + \alpha_3 P_{transit} + \alpha_4 Y + \alpha_5 Y_{t-1} + \alpha_6 Y_{t-2} + \alpha_7 Y_{t-3} + \alpha_8 Y_{t-4} + \alpha_9 Pd + \varepsilon$$

You would need forecasts for the price of gasoline, the price of transit, income levels, and the price of diesel fuel to forecast gasoline consumption. (See Pindyck and Rubenfeld 1997 for more discussion of econometric techniques.)

Both time series and econometric estimates can be extended to multiple equations. For time series, the models are called vector auto regressions. (For more information on these models, see Hamilton 1994, chapter 11, or Lutkepohl 1993.)

For econometric series, there have been four main types of multi-equation models. There are models that investigate interfuel substitution using some kind of energy share or energy demand equations for a number of fuels. Structural models, as their name implies, represent the structure of a system. For example, there are models with equations describing purchase decisions and use of the stock of energy-using equipment. Models of the oil reserve discovery process include drilling equations, reserves found per successful well, and share of successful wells. Expenditure system models consider consumer expenditures on all goods simultaneously. Simultaneous systems models representing a particular market include supply and demand estimated simultaneously or estimating one equation in the model and taking other equations into account.

All of these models are explicitly based on historical information. However, sometimes we believe the future may not be like the past and we want to include more personal judgment and rationality in the model. Such a forecast can be purely judgmental with no formal model but with forecasters and analysts basing their forecast on what they *think* will happen. This judgment is likely based on the analyst's historical experience in the market along with speculation on what will happen in the future.

Judgment is often incorporated into other models. For example, in multivariate and econometric models, the forecaster picks the variables to include in the model. Bayesian analysis formally includes preconceived notions about the values of model parameters. This can be particularly useful if your sample is small but you have other information to include in the model. Suppose you have the following econometric model for the supply of coal from a particular mine:

$$Q_s = \alpha_o + \alpha_p P_c + \Sigma_{i=1}^n \beta_i X_i + \varepsilon$$

where

P_c is the price of coal

X_i is the other variable that you believe influences production from this mine

From long experience with this mine and knowledge of its costs you think that α_p is distributed as a normal variable with mean 2 and standard deviation 0.16. Bayesian analysis will allow you to incorporate these prior beliefs into your estimate. If your priors are correct, you will be able to get better estimates than you could from the data alone. (For more discussion and references on how to use Bayesian analysis, see Greene 2000, p. 402–412.)

Models can be developed from components called bottom-up or they can be built by looking down from an aggregate level called top-down. Bottom up models start with disaggregate data trying to look at an economic decision-maker or particular technology. For example, your may look at demand for coal for various electricity generators. The bottom-up model lacks comprehensiveness but contains more detail. To find out total demand by all generators you would need to aggregate over all generators. Top-down models typically look comprehensively at some energy system or subsystem but lack the intimate detail of the components of that system. You might estimate total end-use demand for energy and non-energy goods but disaggregate a top-down model demand into total production for energy and non-energy goods through input-output analysis.

The easiest way to demonstrate an input-output model is by simple example. Suppose you have an economy with two goods, energy (E) and "another good" (NE). Both goods are used as intermediate inputs and as final goods for end uses. Suppose it takes 0.1 unit of energy to produce a unit of E and 0.2 units of energy to produce a unit of NE. It takes 0.3 units of NE to produce a unit of E and 0.4 units of NE to produce a unit of NE. Suppose that we have a good forecast of end-use demand for E and NE from a top-down model of D_E = 80 and D_{NE} = 1200. We want to disaggregate to determine how much total production of E and NE are needed to satisfy this demand. Since both goods are used as end-use demand and intermediate goods, we know that production of E and NE will have to be larger than the end use demands for E and NE.

Let's start with total requirements for E. Since each unit of E requires 0.1 unit of E as an input, the demand for E in the energy sector will be 0.1E. Since each unit of NE requires 0.2 units of energy, the demand for E in the other sector will be 0.2E. The total requirement for E will be these intermediate requirements plus the end use demand or:

$$E = 0.1E + 0.2NE + D_E$$

Similarly, the total requirement for NE would be:

$$NE = 0.3E + 0.4NE + D_{NE}$$

Combining terms, the system of two equations to solve is:

$$0.9E - 0.2NE = D_E$$

$$-0.3E + 0.6NE = D_{NE}$$

Substituting in for end use demand, we have:

$$0.9E - 0.2NE = 80$$

$$-0.3E + 0.6NE = 1200$$

To solve, get E from the first equation and substitute into the second equation:

$$E = 80/0.9 + (0.2/0.9) \text{ NE} => E = 88.889 + 0.222NE$$

$$-0.3(88.889 + 0.222NE) + 0.6NE = 1200 => NE = 2300$$

Then:

$$0.9E - 0.2*2300 = 80 => E = 600$$

Matrix algebra solves this system as:

$$x = (I-A)^{-1}d$$

where

x   is the vector of total production

I   is the identity matrix, $I = \begin{bmatrix} 1 & 0 \\ 0 & 1 \end{bmatrix}$

A   contains the input output coefficients, $A = \begin{bmatrix} 0.1 & 0.2 \\ 0.3 & 0.4 \end{bmatrix}$

d   is the vector of final demands $d = \begin{bmatrix} D_E \\ D_{NE} \end{bmatrix} = \begin{bmatrix} 80 \\ 1200 \end{bmatrix}$

The superscript for (I-A) indicates that we take the inverse of (I-A). Matrix algebra and computer algorithms solve input-output models for hundreds of goods, which can be measured in either monetary or physical units.

Input-output models have also been used to hook models together. For example, end-use demands for energy services may be broken into components by an input-output model. These components may then be fed to a linear programming model discussed in chapter 14 that minimizes the cost of producing the end use services as in the Brookhaven model, BESOM. (Kydes 1980)

Input-output models are accounting models since they keep track of how inputs and outputs are related to each other. Another accounting-oriented model is the material or energy balance approach. In this system-wide model, independent estimates are compiled for each major energy end–use and its growth. Econometric models, tempered by expert judgment and institutional considerations, are often used to craft estimates. Independent estimates are also compiled of major energy supply sources. These supply components may come from engineering, econometric, geological, or combination models coupled with expert judgment.

Supplies and demands are then compiled and compared. Scenarios are built and assumptions challenged until supplies and demands are consistent. Often, the model is brought into balance by assuming that a back-up energy type will be available to fill the gap. For example, the National Petroleum Council in 1972 assumed that imported oil was the back-up source. Such analysis was especially popular after the 1973 "oil crisis" because division of labor allowed fairly comprehensive analysis in a short time frame. Examples of these studies include the World Energy Conference (1978), the Workshop on Alternative Energy Strategies (1977), the Organization for Economic Cooperation and Development (1977), and the U.S. Central Intelligence Agency (1977).

End-use and process models may be bottom-up models. An end-use model considers separately the decision of whether to own an appliance or piece of energy-using equipment and how much to use it. For example, utilities may focus research attention on end-use models in planning electricity expansions. Consumers who decide to buy an air conditioner will need to decide what size to buy and how much to run it. Both of these decisions will be influenced by economic variables including the price of air conditioners, the cost of electricity, and income as well as the weather.

Engineering process models consider the process of converting an energy product to an energy service. It could be as simple as a coefficient that represents the amount of gas required per kilowatt-hour of electricity; it might be a production function with output Q related to some set of inputs such a capital, labor, and energy, such as $Q = f(K,L,E)$; or it might be as complex as a large multi-equation energy optimization model. Such optimization models have often been used to model oil refining, energy transportation, and electricity systems.

For example, Deam (1981) developed a global refinery and crude allocation model that included 52 types of crude oil, 22 refining centers, and six types of tankers. His linear programming model covered 3500 rows and 13,500 columns. The model minimized cost with exogenous variables for the model that included product demand by region, refinery, transport technology, and refining cost. If you believe that economic agents optimize, and you have the correct objective function and constraints, you may do well using such models to forecast. More often, such models are used normatively to determine how economic agents should behave to optimize. Such optimization techniques include mathematical programming (linear, nonlinear, integer, and mixed integer), Lagrangean techniques, calculus of variation, and optimal control theory.

Simulation studies build models to represent the behavior of economic entities and interactions between entities to simulate outcomes. These outcomes can be forecasts, if the model and parameters are good representations of reality. More likely they are used to investigate various outcomes under different conditions to plan strategy. They are particularly useful in systems with a lot of interaction and feedback that cannot be easily otherwise seen. In the 1970s a variety of models were used to simulate OPEC to obtain world oil price paths under various assumptions. The most likely path was chosen. Examples are Kennedy's (1974) *World Oil Model* and United States Federal Energy Administration (1974).

Network models are optimization models similar to linear programming (LP) models with some computational advantages. They include nodes hooked together by arcs. Nodes may include demand centers, supply centers, and energy conversion centers with arcs representing transportation links. Debanne (1973) used a network flow model to minimize the total cost of providing end-use oil demands for North America. His model was extended to minimize total social costs including pollution for a multi-energy product case. Power plants are represented as transshipment nodes, while pollution control can be included as a transport cost. Energy resources are allocated optimally subject to minimum energy demands, producing capacity, transmission constraints, and costs. Debanne (1980, 1981a, 1981b) extended his pre-1973 network flow model to include coal, syncrude, nuclear, and renewable power, and combined it with a binary integer program to represent discrete variables such as technology options. For a textbook explanation of network modeling see Ahuja et al. (1993).

Dynamic system simulation, called System Dynamics, was developed at MIT in the 1950s to enable the models to be played much like a game. In some, decisions are made every period and the model simulates the results of the decisions. Thus, these models may incorporate feedback from decision-makers over many periods of play. An early system dynamic model, without feedback, is the *Limits to Growth* model of Meadows, et al. (1972) that tried to investigate whether the Earth's resources could provide sustainable growth rates into 21st century given predicted economic and population growth rates. Its use of exponential growth rates painted a bleak picture for future sustainability. Their simulations for 1900–2100 for population, industrial output per capita, food per capita, pollution, nonrenewable resources, crude birth rate, crude death rate, and services per capita are shown in Figure 2–3.

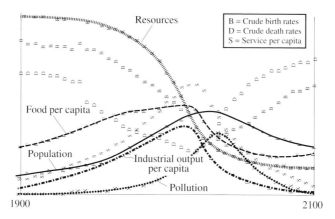

Fig. 2–3 Limits to Growth World Model Standard Run

Source: Recreated from diagram in Meadows et al. (1974) with permission of Dennis Meadows

Simulation models often follow equilibrium or optimization paths. However, game theory models, which are another form of simulation model, show interactions by a small number of players with a variety of options that affect the outcome of interest. A player's strategies are chosen to take into consideration the uncertainty of other player's actions, possible payoffs under different strategies, and the players' risk aversion. For example, the Norwegian government built game theory models of the European natural gas market to help decide when to add capacity when continental European natural gas import demand was to be satisfied by the three export countries—Norway, Russia, and Algeria. (See Tirole 1989 for a popular graduate textbook with game theory models applied to industry.)

A more forward-looking tool for forecasting is to conduct surveys that ask firms about their plans. Trade journals regularly conduct and publish surveys about ongoing and future investments. For example, PennWell's *Oil and Gas Journal* publishes information from a number of surveys that they collect annually or biannually. They include:

- *Worldwide Pipeline Construction* (usually early February)
- *Worldwide Construction Update* (usually early April and late October)
- *EOR Survey* (biannually, usually mid-April)

Another unique survey is the *International Energy Workshop* (IEW) conducted jointly by Stanford University's Energy Modeling Forum (EMF) (http://www.stanford.edu/group/ EMF/home/index.htm) and the International Institute for Applied System Analysis (http://www.iiasa.ac.at/). From 1981–1997,

IEW collected energy forecasts and analyzed why the forecasts differ. For information on the 2003 meeting of the IEW see http://www.iiasa.ac.at/Research/ECS/IEW2003/

The record for energy price forecasts, however, has not been promising. Figure 2–4 shows successive forecasts for increasing prices—all of which have been incorrect. This particular example for oil price forecasts is not unique and many other examples can be found in the post-1970 period.

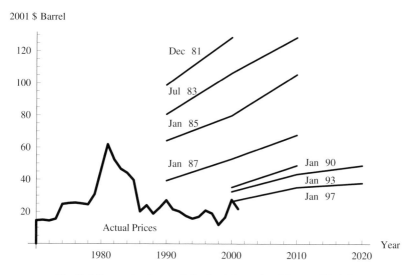

Fig. 2–4 Successive Forecasts by the International Energy Workshop

Source: Manne and Schrattenholzer (1988), International Energy Workshop and personal correspondence with Leo Schrattenholzer, IIASA, April 2003. Recreated with permission of Leo Schrattenholzer.

Another feature of forecasting is the phenomena noted by Robinson (1992) called forecast feedback. He notes that forecast results may be passively accepted, which might lead to one outcome, or that they might be vigorously opposed, which might lead to another outcome. Thus, forecasts can't necessarily be compared to reality to ascertain their validity. Hence, self-fulfilling prophecies would look good, whereas self-defeating ones would look bad. Forecasts of recession might lead to recession, whereas forecasts of high energy prices and shortages have been known to lead to surpluses and falling prices. Forecasts may also be used to affect an outcome, which Robinson calls the theory of deliberate feedback. An environmental group may forecast low electricity demand growth while opposing a new nuclear power plant, while the electricity industry planning the plant may forecast much higher electricity demand growth. These phenomena as well as the types of models used should be considered when interpreting forecasts.

The unreliability of forecasts decades or more into the future suggests another technique, called scenario planning. Scenarios are also useful when you think the future is unlikely to be like the past. This technique relies more on imagination and less on history. To build scenarios you imagine future possible events and circumstances, use logic to determine what the events and circumstances imply, and then plan for possible contingencies. It is desirable to have scenarios that are logically consistent and span the range of possibilities. Such a range of scenarios allows planners to recognize both opportunities and potential hazards.

Shell Oil has used this technique fairly extensively. (Skov et al. 1995) In the early 1980s, Shell was considering whether to develop the Giant Troll field in Norway. At the time, Soviet gas was politically limited to around 35% of the European market. Some of the scenario games included removing this limit, which was thought to be a possibility at the end of the Cold War and an invitation for foreign investment into the Soviet Union. At the time of these scenarios, *glasnost*, the breakup of the Soviet Union and the end to the Cold War were far off, but they were considered and possible responses entertained. More recently, Pacific Gas & Electric used scenarios to help prepare strategies after problems of cost run-ups with its Diablo Canyon nuclear power plant.

Schwartz (1991) argues that scenario building is best done in teams that include some high-level management, a broad range of functions and divisions within the company, and imaginative people. He summarizes the techniques and strategies of scenario building in eight steps.

1. **Identify the focal issue for the decision.** This could be to build a power plant, search for new oil reserves in a new province, or increase use of information technology.

2. **Identify local key forces.** They can be within your company or immediate markets.

3. **Identify macro driving forces.** These include social, technological, economic, political, and environmental. Identify those you have control over and those you don't. Quantify uncertainties if possible. Identify constraints.

4. **Rank the driving forces by importance and uncertainty.**

5. **Develop plots for your scenarios.** Limit them to four or so. Develop several criteria by which to rank scenarios or parts of scenarios. Develop a worst-case, a best case, an expected or desired case, an environmentally optimal case, and a government intervention case. Best and worst cases depend on who is making the scenario. For producers, low price might be a worse case, whereas for consumers it would be a best case. Categorize and score the ideas and pick the best to assemble your scenarios. Save all ideas in case you need to come back and reconsider any of them later.

6. **Fill in scenario details and driving forces from a variety of sources.** Look for perception-changing events that might engage cultural pressure for change. For example, publication of Rachel Carson's *Silent Spring* in 1962 heralded the environmental movement; accidents at Chernobyl and Three Mile Island generated opposition to nuclear power; problems with California's power market restructuring put a damper on deregulation.

7. **Develop the implications of the scenarios.** If your scenario is glasnost, decide what this will do to the European gas market. (e.g. increased Russian supplies to the continent, changes to gas imports and prices, how you will respond to these changes.)

8. **Develop leading indicators and signposts for your scenarios.** What sorts of things will indicate that a scenario is likely to come to pass? Review old scenarios to see what you can learn from them.

So, what sorts of scenarios might we envision for the coming decades? Possibilities to consider include the major driving force of population growth. Demographic shifts and elongation of human life span are likely to change work and leisure patterns, and, consequently, fuel use. A second major consideration is income growth. Will the industrial countries be able to continue their high lifestyles? Will developing countries continue to catch up? If so, will energy and natural resources or environmental carrying capacity become a constraint? If income continues to grow, how will the new income be spent? Will people want more goods, more services, or more leisure?

Environmental concerns, both local and global, will also influence fuel use. As we learn to sequester carbon so that fossil fuels pose less of a threat, then coal will remain a feasible long-term fuel. We could continue to use fossil fuels and move on to gas-to-liquids, gas hydrates, tar sands, and shale oils for an extended fossil fuel age. If fossil fuels remain important, how will depletion and technological improvement change their relative prices?

Alternatively, environmental constraints and/or technology may move us to cleaner, more sustainable energy sources. Buildings and homes could be the main energy generators in a distributive utility approach. Power could be derived from solar, wind, fuel cells or some hybrid and be stored in new and better batteries. Biomass waste could become a fuel instead of a nuisance. Efficiency could improve with appliances and other energy-using equipment employing intelligent sensors for power control. Fusion could become our mainstay in a centralized electricity grid. Indeed, we could even see a renaissance of fission, if issues such as waste storage and proliferation can be mastered and smaller, safer technologies evolve.

Energy market structure could influence the shape of our energy future. An OPEC that keeps oil prices high could hasten the transition out of fossil fuels; decreasing regulation could mean a movement towards cheaper fuels and higher fuel use. Government intervention to internalize the negative affects of fossil fuels could promote a cleaner world sooner.

Around a quarter of total energy consumption in the Organization for Economic Cooperation and Development (OECD) countries goes for transportation; almost 20% of energy consumption in developing countries does so. Travel includes moving freight, commuting, recreation and tourism, socializing, shopping, other services, and industry travel. However, information technology might affect fuel use by streamlining traffic patterns and telecommuting, tele-visiting, e-commerce, and changing geographical settlement patterns could change how many miles people and freight travel.

Technology will clearly influence all these uses and the amount of investment capital available will affect its growth. Technological change will also influence the price and availability of various fuels. As technical change helps to conserve energy, less energy will be consumed per unit of energy service output. However, this conservation will make the energy service cheaper and possibly increase the demand for the energy service, causing a rebound effect, which cancels some of the decrease in energy use. For example, increasing miles per gallon would decrease gasoline consumption; at higher miles per gallon, it's cheaper to drive a mile and people may drive more.

Thus, a variety of economic, political, cultural, and technological issues will shape fuel use in the coming century. How? Forecasting in the short run is difficult, forecasting in the long run is more difficult yet. But what of the long-long run?

Summary

From the big bang until the Quaternary (the age of humans), energy has had a pervasive influence on the evolution of the Universe. In the future, energy will provide for the same needs as in the past—heat, light, cooling, lubrication, transportation, communication, mechanical power, and materials for war. How much will be needed and how it will be provided will vary. Predicting these needs so that they can be satisfied is a job for forecasters. Accurate knowledge of prices and energy needs will allow producers to have capacity available, consumers to invest in the appropriate capital stock, banks to finance the best technologies, and governments to design optimal policies.

A number of techniques have been used including extrapolating historical trends, univariate time series, multivariate time series, econometric models, Bayesian estimation, judgment, surveys, input-output, energy balances, end-use models, engineering or process models, optimization, network models, simulation, game theory, survey, and scenarios.

Forecasting is fraught with difficulty, as a variety of economic, political, cultural and technological issues influence the evolution of energy markets. All these issues are shrouded in uncertainty making the forecaster's job difficult. In addition, the forecasts themselves may influence the outcome. A good forecast may be believed and actions may be taken to cause it to come true—a self-fulfilling prophecy. A bad forecast may be resisted and actions may be taken to cause it to not come true—a self-defeating prophecy.

Although we would expect technological change that increases energy efficiency to reduce energy consumption, it may not, because of the rebound effect. An increase in energy efficiency will have two effects. As it lowers the amount of energy used to provide each unit of energy service, it will lower the cost of energy services and increase the amount of energy services purchased.

Forecasting typically becomes more difficult, the further out you are trying to forecast. Long-long run forecasts are difficult, as well. Once the sun winks out, humans—if they are still around—will probably have moved on or they will have to find an alternative source of energy. But in the meantime we have lots of energy and the analytical tools to learn how to use it wisely.

3 Perfect Competition and the Coal Industry

All of us form models of the world in our heads, which help us to understand what happens around us.

—Professor Marji Lines, Department of Statistical Science, University of Udine, Italy

Introduction

Coal is the world's most abundant and widely distributed fossil fuel. It has a long and venerable history. It may have been used in households and industry in China 2000 years ago, with its industry becoming very well developed by the 12th century A.D. While oil was not yet even a twinkle in some wildcatter's eye, coal was fueling the industrial revolution in England.

In the middle 1800s, Great Britain produced just more than 60% of the world's coal from around 3000 mines or collieries. It exported around 15% of its production. The United States and Russia together accounted for another

20% of world production (Fig. 3–1). By 1900, the United States had surpassed the United Kingdom in coal production, and in the 1920s the United States consumed about half of the world's coal.

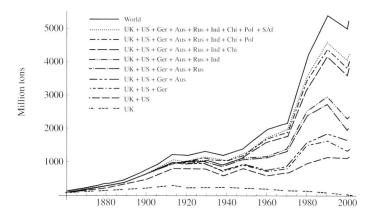

Fig. 3–1 World Historical Coal Production by Major Country

Notes: UK = Great Britain then the United Kingdom; Ger = Prussia, then Saxony, then Germany; Aus = Australia; Rus = the Russian Empire, then USSR, then Russia; Ind = India; Chi = China; Pol = Poland; SAf = South Africa.
Sources: Jevons (1965), Gordon (1987), EIA/DOE International Energy Annual, 2001.

Coal consumption has always been strongly tied to industrial production and we see its sensitivity to war and to the economic cycle. Thus, coal consumption fell from 1913 to 1920, largely as a result of falling consumption in the economic downturn in Germany after World War I and in Russia after the revolution. During the Great Depression, consumption fell once again, with the United States the hardest hit. Germany by then was re-arming and showed modest increases in consumption, while Russia's economy, rather isolated from the rest of the world under Stalin, was rapidly industrializing. During this time, Russian coal production increased an average of 12% per year. Almost 70% of world reduction in the 1990s was in the Former Soviet Union (FSU), where coal consumption fell by half as their economies crashed. Germany's consumption fell by somewhat less than half as the country phased out high-cost mines and dirty lignite production in the former East for environmental reasons. The current production shares of the world's more prominent coal producers are shown in Figure 3–2.

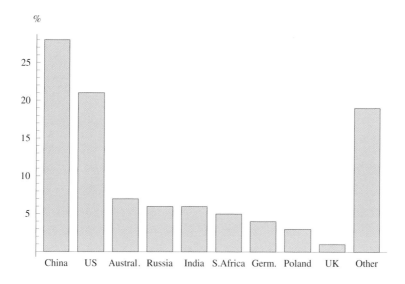

Fig 3–2 Coal Production in Major Countries

Notes: Austral. = Australia, S. Africa = South Africa, Germ. = Germany.
Source: EIA/DOE *International Energy Annual*, 2001.

Growth rates of coal production have varied over time, as well. They averaged more than 4% per year from 1860 to 1913; but with a world war and a world recession, coal production in 1938 had not regained its prewar level of 1913. World production increased more than fourfold from 1938 to 1990, but it never regained its pre-1913 growth rates except in the 1970s, when the oil crisis and surging oil prices caused industry and electric utilities to switch to cheaper and politically safer coal. Coal consumption fell during the 1990s for the reasons stated. Coal prices have fluctuated rather dramatically as shown by U.S. anthracite prices since 1800 (Fig. 3–3).

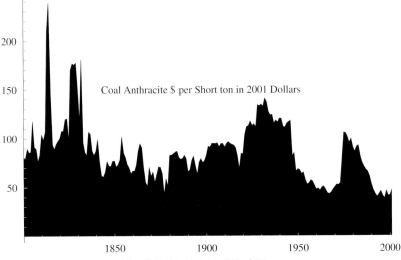

Fig. 3–3 U.S. Historical Coal Prices

Sources: Variable is anthracite price deflated by consumer price index. For 1800–1969, U.S. Department of Commerce, *Historical Statistics of United States Colonial Times to 1970.* For anthracite prices for1970–2001, EIA/DOE, *Annual Energy Review*, 2002. For consumer price index 1970–2001, U.S. Council of Economic Advisers, *Economic Report of the President*, 2002.

Price, which has been adjusted for inflation, has averaged $86.58 per short ton over the last 200 years and has varied from a minimum of $38.75 during the latter part of the 1990s when environmental concerns increasingly disadvantaged coal to a maximum of $238.88 per short ton in 1814 (the last year of the U.S. War of 1812). The average deviation around the mean is measured by the standard deviation:

$$\sigma = \sqrt{\sum_{i=1}^{T}(P_i - \overline{P})/^2(T\text{-}1)} = \$31.47$$

where

P$_i$ is the price in year i

T   is the sample size 201

$\overline{P}$ is the average price $= \sum_{i}^{T}(P_i)/T = \$86.58$

Anthracite prices are used instead of prices for the more widely consumed bituminous coal, since a longer time series is available. The price of lower quality bituminous coal in the United States has been between 50% and 80% that of anthracite since World War II.

These prices are the result of all the economic forces that have impinged on the coal market including the strength of the economy, the prices of factors of production, and the price of other goods related to coal and technology. To help us better understand how production and coal prices have evolved, we turn to our first economic model.

Coal industry

The fundamental challenge in economics is to allocate scarce resources across competing uses. A consumer with a restricted budget may have to choose between buying gasoline or blue jeans. A wealthy consumer may have to choose between driving to a movie and ordering Pay Per View, where time rather than cost is the constraint. An underground coal mine's owner may choose between long wall and room-and-pillar mining. A government may decide to allocate more research and development funds to clean coal technologies or to renewable resources. In each case, the decision-maker will want to make an optimal allocation.

Such allocations are typically done either by the private sector through markets or by the government. Economists tend to favor the private sector for such allocation when the market is perfectly competitive, property rights are well defined, externalities are few, and the subject industry does not have decreasing average costs as production increases. We will see why this is the case in this and subsequent chapters. To begin, let us build a competitive model for the coal industry.

In such a model, we first assume there is free entry into and exit from the industry and sufficient buyers and sellers so that no one of them can set the price. Thus, each buyer and seller must take the market price as given. Free entry and exit assures that no buyer or seller can develop and maintain market power. This is probably not an unreasonable assumption for the United States. As we can see in Table 3–1, the top 10 coal companies control only just more than half of the U.S. coal production. The government owns about 20% of U.S. coal reserves, which it leases to companies for production. These leases are administered by the U.S. Bureau of Land Management. In nearly all other countries, coal and all other primary energy resources are owned exclusively by the government.

Table 3–1 10 Largest U.S. Coal Producers, 2001

Company Name	Production (thousand short tons)	Website
Peabody Coal Sales Co.	146,132	http://www.peabodyenergy.com
Arch Coal, Inc.	116,462	http://www.archcoal.com
Kennecott Energy & Coal Co.	112,656	http://www.kenergy.com/
Consol Energy Inc.	70,299	http://www.consolenergy.com/
RAG American Coal Holding, Inc.	65,131	http://www.rag-american.com/
Horizon Natural Resources Inc. (Previously AEI Resources Inc.)	47,457	http://www.horizonnr.com
A.T. Massey Coal Co., Inc.	43,400	http://www.masseyenergyco.com/
Vulcan Partners, L.P.	43,049	NA
North American Coal Corp.	26,728	http://www.nacoal.com
TXU Corp.	22,814	http://www.txucorp.com
Subtotal	694,128	
U.S. Total	1,127,689	

Notes: 1 short ton = 2000 pounds = 0.9072 metric tons = 0.8929 long tons.
Source: EIA/DOE, *Annual Coal Report* 2001, Table 11,
http://www.eia.doe.gov/cneaf/coal/page/acr/acr.pdf

Although not every coal consumer is able to buy from every coal producer because of transportation costs, excessive profits in one mining area are likely to bring new entrants in the form of other coal producers or other energy sources. This threat of entry by other producers is referred to as *market contestability*. As the coal industry is a global industry and coal is the second largest product by weight to be traded internationally, this contestability can come from large foreign producers as well as other domestic companies. Such international contestability may have increased in recent years as transportation costs have decreased. Examples of large coal companies worldwide are given in Table 3–2. The largest two of these are owned by governments—China National Coal Company and Coal India, Limited.

In addition, a competitive market is homogeneous—each unit of the product is just like every other. For coal, we know this is not quite true. Coal varies by energy content and impurities. For example, in the United States, eastern coal has about 24 million British Thermal Units per short ton (MMBTU/s.ton); central coal about 22 MMBTU/s.ton; western coal about 18 MMBTU/s.ton, while lignite in the Dakotas and Texas has more moisture with a still lower heat content. The ranges of energy content by general coal type are shown in Table 3–3.

Table 3–2 World Coal Producers

Company	Coal Production in Million Metric Tons (MMT)	Year 2000	Website	Country
595 mines for China's key state-owned companies are to be consolidated into 1 or 2 companies producing more than 100 million tons and 5 or 6 companies producing more than 50 million tons by 2005.	536	2000	na	China
China National Coal Industry Import & Export (Group) Corporation (CNCIEC)	25	2001	http://www.chinacoal.com	China
Coal India Ltd and 7 Subsidiaries	280	2001	http://www.coalindia.nic.in/vscoalindia/	India
Seven State–Owned Coal Holding Companies	151	2001		Poland
Rio Tinto	134	2000	http://www.riotinto.com	U.K.
Ukrainian Coal Industry Ministry	77	2000		Ukraine
BHP Billiton	87	2001	http://www.bhpbilliton.com/bb/home/home.jsp	U.K./Australia
RWE Rheinbraun AG	270	2001	http://www.rwe.com/de/de.jsp	Germany
RAG Coal International	66	2000	http://www.rag-coalinter.de/	Germany
Amcoal	63	1999	http://angloamerican.co.uk	U.K.
Sasol	51	2001	http://www.sasol.com	South Africa
UK Coal	20	2000	http://www.ukcoal.com	U.K.
Xtrata	44	2002	http://www.xstrata.com/	Switzerland
Luscar, Ltd.	36	2001	http://www.luscar.com/	Canada
Elk Valley Coal Partnership	<22.4	2001		Canada
Kumba Resources	16.8	2001	http://www.kumbaresources.com/	South Africa
Cerrejon Coal Company (Equally owned by BHP, Anglo, Xstrata)	20.4	2002	www.cerrejoncoal.com	Colombia
Krasnoyarskugol	37.5	2002		Russia
Kuzbassrazrezugol	34.6	2002		Russia
Kuzbassugol (79.7% state owned)	16.7	2002		Russia
Adaro	18	2001	http://www.ptadaro.com/	Indonesia

Notes: For other coal company links see http://www.wci-coal.com/web/content.php?menu_id=5.11.1 One metric ton = 1.1023 short ton = 0.9842 long tons. < indicates less than.
Sources: Company home pages, *Coal International* 2002, "Asian Giants," Sept/Oct: 212-216, "South African Developments," Jul/Aug: 177-81. *Coal International* 2003 "Russian Coal: A Drama in Five Acts," Jan/Feb: 31, Coal Association of Canada, http://www.coal.ca/about.html, U.S. EIA/DOE Country Briefs, http://www.eia.doe.gov/emeu/cabs/contents.html

Table 3–3 Energy Content by Coal Type

Coal Type	% Carbon	1000 BTU/Short ton Range	
Lignite	30	10,000	15,000
Subbituminous	40	16,000	20,000
Bituminous	50–70	22,000	30,000
Anthracite	90	28,000	

Source: Hinrichs (1996)

This same variation in quality can be seen in Table 3–4, where we present coal production, consumption, reserves, and energy content of the world's most important coal producers and consumers.

Table 3–4 World Coal Production, Consumption, and Reserves, 2000

Region/ Country	Prod	Cons	Net Exports	Recoverable Coal			Heat content
				Anthracite/ Bituminous	Lignite/ Subbituminous	Total	
	Trillion BTU			Million Short Tons			1000 BTU/ST
North America							
Canada	1,819	1,593	301	3,826	3,425	7,251	23,863
Mexico	213	270	-69	948	387	1,335	17,012
United States	22,623	22,657	1,149	126,804	146,852	273,656	17,012
Total	**24,655**	**24,520**	**1,381**	**131,579**	**150,866**	**282,444**	
Central & South America							
Brazil	78	529	-457	0	13,149	13,149	14,363
Colombia	1,033	115	969	6,908	420	7,328	24,568
Other	258	214	50	1,622	1,878	3,500	
Total	**1,370**	**858**	**563**	**8,530**	**15,448**	**23,977**	
Western Europe							
Germany	2,374	3,236	-750	25,353	47,399	72,753	10,541
Greece	355	390	-32	0	3,168	3,168	5,046
Spain	294	752	-454	220	507	728	11,378
Turkey	518	781	-261	306	3,760	4,066	7,437
United Kingdom	767	1,464	-587	1,102	551	1,653	22,727
Yugoslavia	305	308	-3	71	17,849	17,919	8,048
Other	377	2,860	-2,490	30,592	82,263	112,856	104,188
Total	**4,990**	**9,791**	**-4,578**	**27,650**	**73,693**	**101,343**	

Table 3–4 World Coal Production, Consumption, and Reserves, 2000 (cont'd)

Region/ Country	Prod	Cons	Net Exports	Recoverable Coal			Heat content
				Anthracite/ Bituminous	Lignite/ Subbituminous	Total	
	Trillion BTU			Million Short Tons			1000 BTU/ST
Eastern Europe & Former USSR							
Bulgaria	264	358	-101	14	2,974	2,988	8,087
Czech Republic	847	799	147	2,330	3,929	6,259	11,795
Poland	2,846	2,410	588	22,377	2,050	24,427	15,964
Romania	234	293	-58	1	1,605	1,606	7,254
Russia	5,147	4,880	320	54,110	118,964	173,074	18,438
Ukraine	1,751	1,843	-92	17,939	19,708	37,647	19,406
Other	1,503	1,031	181	35,274	8,908	44,182	
Total	**12,359**	**11,613**	**1,043**	**132,046**	**158,138**	**290,183**	
Middle East							
Total	**36**	**337**	**-284**	**1,885**	**0**	**1,885**	**23,245**
Africa							
South Africa	5,292	3,396	1,890	54,586	0	54,586	21,302
Other	165	331	-162	6,229	216	6,445	
Total	**5,457**	**3,726**	**1,728**	**60,816**	**216**	**61,032**	
Asia & Oceania							
Australia	6,664	2,098	4,522	46,903	43,585	90,489	19,704
China	24,333	23,606	1,551	90,826	2,205	93,031	18,512
India	6,065	6,483	-511	871	5,049	5,919	17,699
Indonesia	1,963	570	1,420	852	0	852	23,245
Japan	68	3,543	-3,485	331	331	661	20,826
Korea, N	2,457	2,455	2	86	0	86	23,245
Korea, S	78	1,604	-1,541	4	0	4	17,009
Philippines	27	210	-183	0	366	366	18,120
Taiwan	2	1,309	-1,326	1	0	1	23,434
Thailand	215	325	-112	0	1,398	1,398	10,961
Vietnam	232	151	80	165	0	165	21,166
Other	198	450	-247	68,680	60,742	129,421	
Total	**42,302**	**42,805**	**170**	**208,719**	**113,675**	**322,394**	
World	**91,168**	**93,649**	**25**	**571,224**	**512,035**	**1,083,259**	

Notes: Prod=Production, Cons=Consumption, Net exports = Exports - Imports, BTU/ST = British Thermal Unit per short ton. Production minus consumption equals exports minus imports plus stock changes.

To convert to Kilocalories/metric ton multiply BTU/ST by 0.2285.

Source: EIA/DOE, Feb 2003, *International Energy Annual,* 2001.

http://www.eia.doe.gov/iea/

We also assume that market participants know prices and other information relating to their market decision. For instance, coal sellers have information on coal mining technologies, factor prices, and output prices. Coal buyers—57% of which are electricity generators worldwide—employ technologies that produce electricity and process heat from coal and from other fuels and technologies. (See Table 3–5 for coal used for electricity generation. See chapter 4 for a discussion of electricity generation from coal and other sources.)

Table 3–5 World Gross Energy Consumption for Electricity Generation

Country or Region	Oil	Natural Gas	Coal	Nuclear	Renewables	Total
U.S.	1.2	6	18.1	7.5	3	38.6
Industrial Countries*	4.9	14.7	30.9	22.4	16.7	89.6
Eastern Europe/FSU	1.3	8.0	6.0	4.1	3.2	22.6
Developing Countries	5.3	6.5	15.1	2.7	11.7	41.2
Total World #	**11.5**	**29.2**	**52.0**	**29.1**	**31.6**	**153.4**

Notes: all amounts are in quadrillion BTUs. *Industrial countries consumption includes that for the U.S. #Components may not add perfectly to total because of rounding errors. A quadrillion BTUs is about 293 terawatts, 293,000 gigawatts, 293,000,000 megawatts or 293,000,000,000 kilowatts. U.S. values are converted from net to gross generation figures using EIA heat rates of 10,201 BTU/kWh for hydro, wood, wind, solar waste, 21,017 BTU/KWh for geothermal, and 10,623 for nuclear.
Sources: EIA/DOE, *International Energy Outlook*, 2003
ftp://ftp.eia.doe.gov/pub/pdf/international/0484(2003).pdf and *Annual Energy Review*, 2001
http://www.eia.doe.gov/aer

For purposes of our perfect-competition model, we assume that property rights for coal are well defined, there are no externalities, and coal mining is not a decreasing cost industry. With well-defined property rights, coal producers have exclusive rights to the coal reserves they own or lease; there are no external costs or benefits that accrue to others as the result of coal production or consumption. Again, we know this is a simplification. Both coal production and consumption produce pollution—a negative externality—as will be discussed in chapter 8. If an industry has decreasing costs, unit costs fall as the size of the firm increases. In such an industry, monopolies will have a tendency to develop as will be discussed in chapter 4.

Energy Demand and Supply

To develop our competitive model, we divide the coal market into two groups. Buyers are represented by a demand equation and sellers by a supply equation.

Demand. The quantity purchased as a factor of production by one buyer will be influenced by the following:

- the price of coal (P_c),
- the price of substitutes to coal (P_{sb}), such as oil and natural gas,
- the price of complements to coal (P_{cm}), such as coal boilers,
- technology for coal use (T),
- the price of the output produced (P_{ot}), and
- energy policy (P_{ol}).

The quantity purchased by all buyers (Q_d) will also be influenced by the number of buyers (#buy).

Thus, we can write market demand as:

$$Q_d = f(P_c\text{-}, P_{sb}\text{+}, P_{cm}\text{-}, T\text{+/-}, P_{ot}\text{+}, P_{ol}\text{+/-}, \#buy\text{+}) \qquad (3.1)$$

The signs in parenthesis to the right of the variables indicate the direction of the effect that the variable will have on coal purchases or the sign of the partial derivative of coal purchases with respect to that variable. For example, $\partial Q_d/\partial P_c$ tells us how much coal consumption changes for a change in the price of coal. This value may change depending on the price before the change. (For a review of derivatives and partial derivatives, see any standard calculus text. For a review of calculus applied to economic modeling, see Dowling 1980 or Chiang 1984).

We expect that $\partial Q_d/\partial P_c$ would be negative. As the price of coal increases, electric generators and other users would try to economize on coal use and switch to other fuel sources, and this effect might be very small in the short run but much larger in the long run. $\partial Q_d/\partial P_{sb}$ should be positive. If the price of a substitute (such as natural gas) increases, we would expect a shift toward coal use. $\partial Q_d/\partial P_{cm}$ should be negative. If the price of coal boilers increases, coal becomes a less desirable fuel and buyers may switch to competing fuels.

The sign of $\partial Q_d/\partial T$ is uncertain. It depends on the type of technological change taking place. If the technology raises the productivity of coal relative to other fuels, there may be a shift toward coal from other fuels. Alternatively, if the technology raises the productivity of other fuels, there may be a shift away from coal toward alternative fuels. The sign of $\partial Q_d/\partial P_{ot}$ should be positive. If the price of output goes up, we will want to increase production and we will need more coal.

Instead of the price of output, the quantity of output or some measure of economic activity is often used, which we will designate as Y. This is particularly appropriate if the buyer is a consumer rather than someone using the energy as a factor of production, since consumers will consider their income in making consumption decisions. The sign on $\partial Q_d / \partial P_{ol}$ depends on the policy.

For example, United States energy law forbade new under-the-boiler use of natural gas in 1978 and Germany's coal price subsidies increased coal consumption; more recent environmental regulations are more likely to decrease coal use. The sign of $\partial Q_d / \partial \#buy$ should be positive, since more buyers will increase coal consumption or the quantity of coal demanded.

Supply. We represent suppliers by an equation in which we write quantity supplied (Q_s) as a function of:

- the price of coal (P_c)
- the price of factors of production for coal, such as labor and capital (P_f)
- the price of similar goods that coal miners could produce (P_{sim})
- the price of byproducts of coal production (P_b)
- coal production technology (T)
- government coal policies (P_{ol})
- the number of sellers (#sel)

Thus, we can write the supply of coal as:

$$Q_s = f(P_c+, P_f-, P_{sim}-, T+, P_b+, P_{ol} +/-, \#sel+) \qquad (3.2)$$

In equation 3.2, we expect $\partial Q_s / \partial P_c$ would be positive: As the price of coal increases, coal producers will want to produce and sell more coal. $\partial Q_s / \partial P_f$ should be negative. As the prices of factors of production increase, suppliers will produce less coal. $\partial Q_s / \partial P_{sim}$ should be negative. If the price of a similar good that coal producers could produce goes up, they might switch to the similar good. For example, they could acquire other property and switch to mining other minerals or producing gravel. The sign of $\partial Q_s / \partial T$ should be positive. Technical change should reduce costs and increase coal production.

The sign on $\partial Q_s / \partial P_{ol}$ depends on the policy. For example, laws that have been passed to improve mine safety and reclamation have increased costs and decreased production, whereas policies that have encouraged research and development in coal mining have increased production. The sign of $\partial Q_s / \partial P_b$ should be positive. If the price of byproducts that are complements to coal production increase, profits from coal mining increase and coal production should increase. The sign of $\partial Q_s / \partial \#sel$ should be positive since more sellers will increase coal production.

Equilibrium price and quantity. To show how markets work let's develop an example. Let demand and supply be equal to the following linear functions.

$$Q_d = 75 - 2P_c + P_{sb} - 2P_{cm} + 0.1Y$$

$$Q_s = 6 + P_c - 1P_k - 0.2P_l - 0.4P_{nr} - 1.5P_{sm}$$

where

P_c is the price of coal

P_{cm} is a complement to coal consumption such as a boiler, set $= 10$

P_k is the price of capital, set $= 2$

P_l is the price of labor, set $= 3$

P_{nr} is the price of other natural resources used in production of coal, set $= 5$

P_{sb} is the price of a substitute to coal, such as natural gas, set $= 1$

P_{sm} is the price of similar products which a coal producer could produce, set $= 4$

Y is a measure of economic activity, set $= 100$

Standard procedure in economics requires that we hold all variables but price and quantity constant (called *ceteris paribus* or all else equal) and develop demand and supply equations as follows. First, fix the ceteris paribus values in each equation and you will get:

$$Q_d = 75 - 2P_c + 1 - 2*10 + 0.1*100 = 66 - 2P_c$$

$$Q_s = -4.6 + 1P_c$$

(For a review of the algebra needed to solve linear equations, go to any standard algebra book or Speigel 1995.) Next, invert the above demand and supply curves, or solve for price as a function of quantity.

$$\textbf{Demand } Q_d = 66\text{-}2P_c => 2P_c = 66\text{-}Q_d =>$$

$$P_c = 66/2 - 1/2Q_d = 33 - 0.5Q_d$$

$$\textbf{Supply } P_c = 4.6 + Q_s$$

To graph the above demand and supply curves, note that they are both linear functions. When $Q_d = 0$, $P_c = 33$ and when $P_c = 0$, $Q_d = 66$. We can graph these two points and connect them as seen in Figure 3–4. We can employ the same procedure to graph supply.

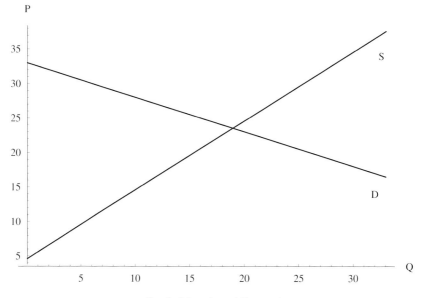

Fig. 3–4 Supply and Demand

To forecast equilibrium price and quantity in this model, we would find where quantity demanded equaled quantity supplied. The graph shows equilibrium to be at a price and a quantity near 20. To be more precise, we use our functions setting $Q_s = Q_d$ and solving:

$$Q_d = 66 - 2P_c = Q_s = -4.6 + 1P_c$$

$$66 + 4.6 = 1P_c + 2P_c$$

$$70.6 = 3P_c$$

$$P_c = 70.6/3 = 23.5$$

We can solve for equilibrium Q using either the demand or supply equation:

$$Q_d = 66 - 2(23.5) = 18.9 \text{ or } Q_s = -4.6 + 23.5 = 18.9.$$

To check whether this is likely to be a stable equilibrium, suppose that the price is 30. If the price were 30, quantity demanded would be $66 - 2*30 = 6$ and quantity supplied would be $-4.6 + 30 = 25.4$. There is excess quantity supplied and coal price is likely to fall. A similar argument can be used to show that equilibrium is stable from below as well.

Shifts in supply and demand. Now suppose that one of our ceteris paribus variables (those variables held constant) changes. Let the price of natural gas go to 15. With gas more expensive, electricity generators might run their gas turbines less and their coal generators more. This would shift our demand curve to the right as in Figure 3–5, making the demand curve $Q_d = 80 - 2P_c$. We call this a change in demand, since it shifts the whole demand curve. This shift would move us along the supply curve to a higher price and quantity. This movement along the supply curve to a different quantity in response to a higher price, we call a change in quantity supplied.

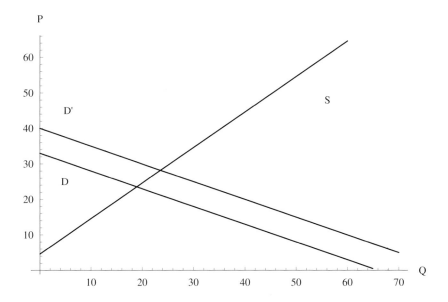

Fig. 3–5 Increase in Demand

Sometimes we don't know the magnitude of variable changes or the specific functions and can only do qualitative analysis. If Exxon develops large coal deposits in Colombia, we expect supply to shift out, lowering price and raising quantity. If a financial crisis in Asia reduces demand, it lowers price and quantity. Higher interest rates might shift demand away from coal toward other less capital-intensive fuels, which would lower price and quantity; higher interest rates would also raise the costs to suppliers and reduce supply, thus raising the price and lowering quantity. Since both of these effects would lower quantity, we would expect quantity to fall. However, since the reduction in demand lowers price and the decrease in supply raises price, the change in price would depend on which effect were larger.

Often more than one event at a time impinges on a market. For example, in 1973 and again in 1979 oil prices increased dramatically. We would expect this to increase the demand for coal as in Figure 3–5 and increase price and quantity of coal consumed. However, during this same period coal mine productivity decreased from 2.20 to 1.82 short tons per miner hour. (U.S. Department of Energy/Energy Information Administration (DOE/EIA) *Annual Energy Review*, http://www.eia.doe.gov/historic.html) We would expect this to decrease the supply of coal to *S'* (Fig. 3–6). At any given price, less coal would be supplied and supply would move left, which would increase price and decrease quantity.

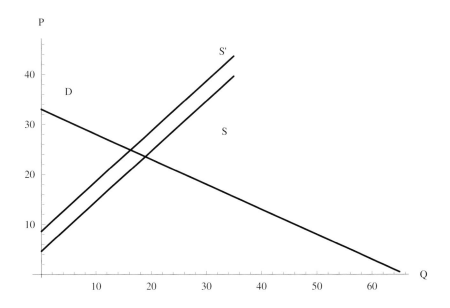

Fig. 3–6 Decrease in Supply

What is the net effect of these two market changes? Since both increase coal price, we conclude that coal price will increase. The increase in demand increases quantity while the decrease in supply decreases quantity. The net effect would depend upon which effect is larger, so the change in price is positive and the change in quantity is uncertain. Subsequent to 1979, coal mine productivity has shown dramatic improvements with production per miner hour increasing to 7.02 tons per miner hour by 2000. (U.S. National Mining Association, http://www.nma.org/)

Government policy

Coal price supports. Governments often seek to influence in markets. For example, after World War II, the European coal industry was contracting. To protect the industry and to protect jobs in the coal mines, the British, Belgium, Spanish, and West German governments all subsidized the industry. Although these subsidies have been reduced over time, at the turn of the century, they still amounted to more than $6 billion for Germany, Britain, Spain, Belgium, and Japan. (Table 3–6) (For a report on energy subsidies, see the *Earth Council Report on Subsidies*. To track events in the coal industry, refer to coal periodicals such as *Coal Outlook and Coal Daily*.)

Table **3–6** European Coal Subsidies, 2001

Country	Total million U.S.$	Subsidy/ton U.S.$
Germany	4,643	144
Spain	1,194	75
France	1,073	494
U.K.	91	3

Source: EAI/DOE, *International Energy Outlook 2003*, p. 84, May, http://ftp.eia.doe.gov/pub/pdf/international/0484(2003).pdf

One way of subsidizing the industry is to buy up coal in order to keep its price up. Suppose that Figure 3–7 represents the West German coal industry. The market price with no interference is $23.50. Suppose the German government wanted the domestic coal price to be a minimum of $28. The government could buy enough coal to artificially inflate the price to $28. In Figure 3–7, P_{mn} is the minimum price of $28. At that price, note that quantity demanded is less than quantity supplied.

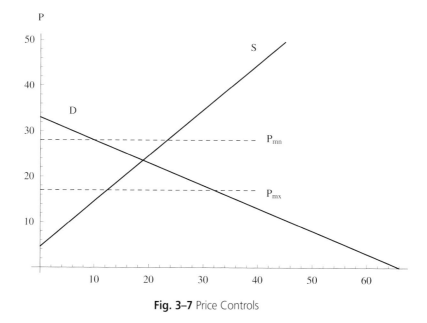

Fig. 3–7 Price Controls

Another way governments sometimes affect markets is by setting maximum prices. If they set the P_{mx} in Figure 3–7, note that quantity demand would be greater than quantity supply and a shortage might develop. Since demanders are willing to pay more and suppliers are willing to produce more in such a case, a black market might develop.

Demand and Supply Elasticities

Often we want to measure how responsive quantities demanded and supplied are to prices and/or other variables to help design energy plans and policy. For example, if coal demand in Asia is very responsive to income growth and income rises or falls sharply, there will be a large effect on the coal market. If coal demand and supply are very responsive to price, only a small change in price will be needed to bring about equilibrium after demand or supply shocks hit the coal market. Economists use elasticities to provide such a measure of responsiveness. For example, price elasticity of demand is the percentage change in quantity divided by the percentage change in price. We write this as:

$$\varepsilon d = \frac{\% \text{ change quantity}}{\% \text{ change in price}} = \frac{\dfrac{\Delta Q_d}{Q_d}}{\dfrac{\Delta P_d}{P_d}} \qquad (3.3)$$

If the price elasticity is –0.5, and price goes up by 100%, quantity demanded falls by 50%. Often for convenience, we write the price elasticity as:

$$\varepsilon_d = \frac{\Delta Q_d \, P_d}{\Delta P_d \, Q_d}$$

If we take very small changes in price or take the limit as ΔP_d goes to zero, then we can rewrite the previous elasticity in terms of partial derivatives or:

$$\varepsilon_d = \frac{\partial Q_d \, P_d}{\partial P_d \, Q_d}$$

∂Q_d represents a change in Q_d for a small change in P_d (∂P_d). To compute elasticities, go back to the original demand and supply equations.

$$Q_d = 75 - 2P_c + P_{sb} - 2P_{cm} + 0.1Y$$

$$Q_s = 6 + P_c - 1P_k - 0.2P_l - 0.4P_{nr} - 1.5P_{sim}$$

The price elasticity of demand is $(\partial Q_d/\partial P_d)(P_d/Q_d)$. In this example "price" is the price of coal represented by P_c, so the demand elasticity is $(\partial Q_d/\partial P_c)(P_c/Q_d) = -2(P_c/Q_d)$. This elasticity varies as P_c and Q_d vary. Thus, to evaluate this elasticity, we need to pick a price and values for our other right-side variables and compute a Q_d. Let $P_c = \$20$ and our other right-side variables are as above. Then at $P_c = 20$, $Q_d = 66 - 2P_c = 66 - 2*20 = 26$ and the elasticity $= -2*20/26 = -1.5$. This suggests that if price declines 1%, then quantity demanded goes up by 1.5%.

If the demand elasticity is less than –1, quantity responds by a larger percent than the percent price change and we call the demand price elastic. If the demand elasticity is between –1 and 0, the quantity responds by a percentage smaller than the percent price change, and we call the demand price inelastic.

If price changes, we can use the demand elasticity to compute what would happen to sales. If a coal tax raised coal price 10%, and the demand elasticity were –0.2 in the short run, then $\Delta Q_d/Q_d = \varepsilon_d * \Delta P_c/P_c = -0.2*0.1 = -0.02$. Coal demand would fall by 2%. If coal demand were 500 million tons before the price change, consumption after the price change would be $(1+\Delta Q_d/Q_d)*$original demand $= (1 - 0.02)*500 = 490$.

Price elasticities reveal the relationship between price changes and total revenues for the good sold. We know that total revenue equals price times quantity sold and that the demand elasticity is:

$$\varepsilon_d = \frac{\%\text{ change quantity}}{\%\text{ change in price}} = \frac{\dfrac{\Delta Q_d}{Q_d}}{\dfrac{\Delta P_d}{P_d}}$$

Suppose that this elasticity equals −2 for coal. If price decreases 10%, quantity demanded increases by −2*(0.10) = 0.2 or 20%. The price decrease causes revenue to decrease, but the quantity increase causes revenue to increase. Since the numerator or quantity effect is larger, total revenues increase. We can see this same effect for different elasticities in Table 3–7. When price falls from 50 to 45 (a 10% decrease at an elasticity of −2), the quantity demanded increases by 20% to 9.6. Revenues increase from 400 to 432. Alternatively, if demand is inelastic with elasticity −0.5, a 10% decrease in price raises quantity by only 5% and revenues fall to 378.

Table 3–7 Revenues Related to Elasticities

Elasticity	P	Q	P*Q
-2	50	8	400
	45	9.6	432
-0.5	50	8	400
	45	8.4	378

Income elasticity of demand (ε_y) tells us how sensitive sales are to income changes.

$$\varepsilon_y = \frac{\%\text{ change quantity}}{\%\text{ change in income}} = \frac{\dfrac{\Delta Q_d}{Q_d}}{\dfrac{\Delta Y}{Y}}$$

If $\varepsilon_y > 1$, demand is income elastic and we have a luxury good. For a luxury good, sales increase at a faster percentage rate than income. If $0 < \varepsilon_y < 1$, demand is income inelastic, and sales increase at a slower percentage rate than income. If $\varepsilon_y > 0$, we have a normal good, but if $\varepsilon_y < 0$, we have an inferior good. For example, coal for household heating use has been an inferior good. As households got richer, they used less coal and substituted natural gas, fuel oil, and electricity for coal heating. Although coal is used for household heating in developing countries, very little coal is used in this sector anymore in the industrialized countries.

Income elasticity also tells us how sensitive demand is to the business cycle. In industrial countries, income tends to change cyclically. At times income is growing, but at other times we have recessions and income falls. Figure 3–8 shows a representative business cycle.

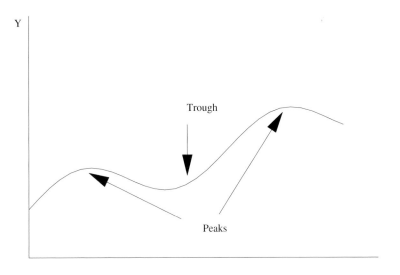

Fig. 3–8 Representative Business Cycle

When income increases, it is said we are "going up the cycle," and when income falls, it is said we are "going down the cycle." A peak is the point where income growth changes from positive to negative. A trough is the point where income growth changes from negative to positive. A business cycle would be from one peak to the next peak, or one trough to the next trough. In the post World War II era until the 1990s, U.S. business cycles tended to average 8 to 10 years. We can discern these cycles in Figure 3–9.

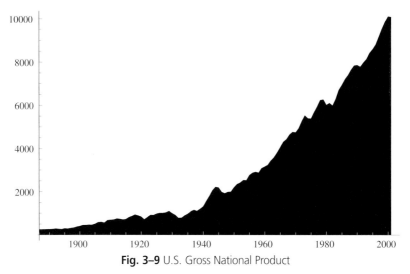

Fig. 3–9 U.S. Gross National Product

Source: Computed from information in *Historical Statistics of the United States, Colonial Times to 1970* and *Economic Report of the President,* 2003.

Activities that increase spending during peaks and decrease spending during troughs are said to be pro-cyclical. That is, they tend to increase the cycle. Activities that decrease spending during peaks and increase spending during troughs are said to be anti-cyclical. That is they tend to moderate or decrease the cycle by lowering the peak and raising the trough. If $\varepsilon_y > 1$, we have a luxury good and sales are very sensitive to the business cycle or sales are pro-cyclical. If $0 < \varepsilon_y < 1$, we have a normal good with income inelastic demand. If $\varepsilon_y < 0$, when income increases, we buy less of the good. Such a good is called an inferior good and sales of the good are anti-cyclical.

A cross-price elasticity (ε_{cross}) tells us how the quantity demanded of one good changes when the price of another good (P_o) changes.

$$\varepsilon_{cross} = \frac{\%\text{ change quantity}}{\%\text{ change in price of another good}} = \frac{\dfrac{\Delta Q_d}{Q_d}}{\dfrac{\Delta P_o}{P_o}}$$

For example, if the cross price elasticity of demand for coal with respect to natural gas is 0.5, then $\Delta Q_d/Q_d = 0.5(\Delta P_o/P_o)$. If the gas price goes up 10%, the percentage change in coal demand is $\Delta Q_d/Q_d = 0.5(\Delta P_o/P_o) = 0.5(0.10) = 0.05$ or

5%. Such a positive cross–price elasticity of demand indicates that the two goods are substitutes in demand. When the price of one good goes up, consumers switch to the other substitute good. If the cross–price elasticity of coal demand with respect to coal boilers is -1.2, then if the price of coal boilers falls 20%, the percentage demand for coal boilers is $\Delta Q_d/Q_d = -1.2(-0.2) = -0.24$ or -24%. Such a negative cross-price elasticity of demand indicates the two goods are complements. If the price of one of the goods goes up, people consume less of that good and also less of the complement good.

Supply elasticities

The responsiveness of quantity supplied to a variable is called the elasticity of supply with respect to that variable. It is the percentage change in quantity divided by the percentage change in the variable. We can write the elasticity of supply with respect to price (P) as:

$$\varepsilon_s = \frac{\% \text{ change } Q_s}{\% \text{ change P}} = \frac{\dfrac{\Delta Q_s}{Q_s}}{\dfrac{\Delta P}{P}}$$

Where Δ represents a discrete change in the variable. If the supply price elasticity of coal is 0.89, then when the price of coal increases by 1%, the percentage quantity of coal supplied is $\Delta Q_s/Q_s = 0.89(0.01) = 0.0089$ or 0.89%.

As with demand, the cross-elasticity of supply indicates how quantity supplied is related to another price. For example, if the cross-price elasticity of gasoline supply with respect to the price of distillate is –0.2, then if the price of distillate increases 1%, the quantity of gasoline produced decreases 0.2%. This negative cross-price elasticity indicates the two goods are similar in production. If the price of one goes up, the supplier shifts to producing this higher-priced product and reduces production of the other. If the cross-price elasticity of supply were positive, when the price of one goes up, we produce more of both implying the two goods are complements in supply. For example, if the price of methane goes up, it might stimulate production of coal bed methane from certain deposits as well as the coal itself.

The time period over which we measure supply and demand elasticities influences the size of the elasticity. In the short run, if the price of coal goes up, coal mines may only be able to increase production a small amount. Since coal mining is very capital intensive, using specialized equipment, it takes time to buy new equipment, and it typically takes four to seven years to open a new mine. Thus, the short-run elasticity may be quite low. However, in the long run—the amount of time required to totally adjust to a price change—production may change much more, and the long-run elasticity is likely to be much larger than the short-run elasticity. The more capital intensive the industry, and the longer lived the capital stock, the greater the difference between long- and short-run elasticities. The same is true for demand elasticities.

Although the long run may vary from product to product, it is fairly well defined. It is simply the time required for total adjustment to take place. The short run is less well defined and typically depends on the period of interest and is most often a year or less. If you are doing statistical analysis on real data, the short run is often the periodicity of the data (e.g., daily or weekly energy prices, monthly data for natural gas in storage, quarterly data on economic indicators, or annual data for oil consumption). If your analysis were on monthly data for coal supply, the short run would be a month. If your analysis were on annual data, the short run would be a year, and you would expect the annual response to be larger than the monthly response. The long-run elasticities in both cases should be the same but would be more elastic than the short run. For example, Labys et al. (1979) found that the underground supply of U.S. coal over the period 1955–1973 had a short-run annual elasticity of 0.07 and a long-run elasticity of 1.31. Thus, with time to adapt, coal producers were many times as price responsive as they were in a year.

Using elasticities to forecast supply

Supply elasticities are quite useful for policy and planning as shown in the following examples. Suppose the world price of coal goes up. Government planners in Australia will want to know what will happen to domestic coal production. Because Australia is a large coal exporter, coal production will have implications for employment, gross national product (GNP), tax revenues, balance of payments, and demand for mining equipment. Likewise, competitors in South Africa and the United States will want such information for their own and their competitor's production. Let coal price go from $20 per metric ton to $22 per metric ton. Suppose that the short-run (one year) supply elasticity is 0.10, and the long-run supply elasticity is 1.1. Since:

$$\varepsilon_s = \frac{\Delta Q_s / Q_s}{\Delta P / P}$$

In the short run:

$$\Delta Q_s / Q_s = \varepsilon_s (\Delta P / P) = 0.10 * 2 / 20 = 0.01$$

Thus, Australian production would go up 0.01 or 1%. Australian production was 345.664 million metric tons in 1998, so production would increase $0.01 * 345.664 = 3.456$ million metric tons.

In the long run, the increase would be $\Delta Q_s/Q_s = \mathcal{E}_s(\Delta P/P) = 1.1 \times 2/20 = 11\%$ for an increase of $0.11 \times 345.664 = 38.023$ million metric tons.

Price changes from a supply disruption

Labor relations in coal mining have often been turbulent. If these strikes lead to a supply disruption, elasticities can tell us what happens to price. We know that:

$$\mathcal{E}_d = (\Delta Q_d/Q_d)/(\Delta P_d/P_d)$$

Implying that:

$$(\Delta P_d/P_d) = (\Delta Q_d/Q_d)/\mathcal{E}_d$$

Suppose a long strike reduces supply to world markets by 6%. What price change would we need to reduce demand by this same amount? If the short-run price elasticity of demand were –0.20, then world coal prices would increase by:

$$(\Delta P_d/P_d) = (-0.06)/(-0.20) = 0.3 \text{ or } 30\%.$$

With supply disruptions, a significant quantity is taken off the market in a very short time. Since elasticities tend to be very small over very short periods of time, the price spike may be rather large in the short run. However, in the long run, demand is more elastic. If the long-run demand elasticity were –0.50, the price would fall in the future until it was only $(-0.06)/(-0.50) = 0.12$ or 12% more than current price.

Cross-elasticities of demand and supply tell us something about the relationship between goods. If the demand cross-price elasticity is positive, an increase in the price of one good increases the demand for another, suggesting the two goods are substitutes. For example, in econometric studies of household energy demand for natural gas, an increase in the price of natural gas raises the demand for electricity. Since gas and electricity are both used for household heating, cooking, and water heating, an increase in the price of one causes some households to shift to the other fuel.

Creating demand and supply from elasticities

Elasticities tell us how responsive quantity demanded and quantity supplied are to various economic variables. They can also be used to create demand and supply equations for modeling and for forecasting. Suppose you have the following elasticities for the demand for gasoline. Let's create a linear demand equation around the following values:

- Price Elasticity ε_p = -0.80
- Income Elasticity ε_y = 1.40
- Price per gallon = $1.15
- Consumption in millions of barrels per day = 8.00
- Income in trillions of U.S. dollars = 5.40

To create a linear demand equation, let:

$$Q_d = a + bP + cY$$

We know that:

$-0.8 = \varepsilon_d = \partial Q/\partial P*(P/Q) = b*(P/Q)$ **or** $-0.8 = b*(1.15/8)$. **Solve for b = −5.57.**

Similarly for income:

$1.40 = \varepsilon_y = c*(Y/Q)$ **or** $1.40 = c(5.4/8)$. **Solve for c = 2.07.**

Use b and c and current Q, P and Y to solve for a:

$a = Q - bP - cY = 8 - (-5.57)*1.15 - 2.07*5.4$. **Solve for a = 3.23.**

Substitute into demand to get:

$$Q_d = 3.23 - 5.57P_d + 2.07Y_d$$

If you want to forecast when only price changes, you would use the same procedure but only create a function $Q = a - bP$. If you want to forecast for price, income, and cross-price changes you would create a function with $Q = a - bP + cY + dP_{cross}$.

Energy Taxation

Governments have various reasons for taxing energy, and such taxes will influence energy markets. An energy-producing country or state may find energy taxation a politically expedient source of revenues, particularly if a large part of the output is exported. They may tax an energy source to provide a public good related to energy consumption such as gasoline taxes that are collected to fund roadways. They may use taxes to discourage energy use such as passing a carbon tax to discourage the use of high-carbon fossil fuels, which may cause global climate change. They may use differential taxes on energy products to influence industrial behavior such as Europe's high import taxes on oil products and low import taxes on crude oil imports to encourage refineries to be built in Europe rather than in the oil producing countries.

Alternately, governments may subsidize rather than tax an energy product to encourage use, such as California subsidies on solar energy panels, or to protect a domestic industry and employment, such as Germany's subsidies to protect its domestic coal industry. Governments may subsidize energy products as part of an income redistribution scheme, such as Indonesian subsidies on kerosene to help poor residents who use kerosene for cooking and lighting.

No matter what the reason for their adoption, energy taxes and subsidies are likely to distort prices and production in energy markets. Such distortions may decrease efficiency in efficient markets, or they may increase efficiency in inefficient markets.

Types of taxes

Often energy and natural resources are subject to taxes beyond corporate taxes. Energy and mineral producing states in the United States often have special taxes on natural resources called severance taxes, which are taxes on producing the resource or "severing it" from the earth. Total tax revenues from severance taxes were 3.3% of state tax revenues in 1985 when energy prices were higher, particularly for oil. By the early 1990s, severance taxes accounted for around 1.3% of total state tax revenues. These taxes tend to more often be *ad valorem* taxes, which are taxed as a percent of price rather than a unit tax of a constant amount per unit. Thus, a natural gas tax of $0.10 per 1000 cubic feet (Mcf) would be a unit tax, while tax of 10% on natural gas price would be an ad valorem tax. The ad valorem tax would be $0.10 per Mcf if natural gas were $1 per Mcf but would be $0.30 if natural gas were $3 per Mcf.

The top eight energy-producing states ranked by the value of their energy production are Texas, Louisiana, Wyoming, Alaska, Kentucky, West Virginia,

Oklahoma, and California. All these states have oil and gas, while Wyoming, Kentucky, and West Virginia are the largest domestic coal producers. In 1993, severance taxes provided 4.3% of the revenue of these states. However, state dependence on energy severance taxes varies considerably. Alaska gets almost half of its government revenues from oil and gas, Wyoming gets 40% from oil, gas, and coal, while most other states get no more than 10% (U.S. EIA/DOE 1997). Severance tax rates for selected states are given in Table 3–8.

Table 3–8 Severance Tax Rates for the 10 Largest Energy Producing States, 2002

State	Oil % or $/bbl	Gas % or $/MCF	Coal % or $/s-ton
Alaska			
1st five years	12.25%	10%	
After five years	15%	6%	On profits
Min. after five years	$0.80	$0.06	
California	$0.0422	$0.0042	
Kentucky	4.50%	4.50%	4.50%
Louisiana	12.50%	$0.199	
New Mexico	3.75%	4%, 3.75% for new wells	
Oklahoma			
Oil price ≥ $17/bbl	7%	7%	
17≥oil price ≥$14	4%	4%	
Oil price ≤$14	1%	1%	
West Virginia	5%	5%	5% with $0.75 minimum
Wyoming	6%	6%	
Surface Coal		7%	
Underground			2%
Maximum surface coal			$0.80

Notes: bbl is barrels, MCF is 1000 cubic feet, and s-ton is short ton.
Source: State Income Tax Forms. Links to these forms can be found at Society of Petroleum Evaluation Engineers, http://www.spee.org under SPEE Oil & Gas Production Taxes, Section 29 and COPAS.

Private owners of a resource receive a royalty if they lease their mineral rights to someone else to produce, as does the U.S. government, when it owns the energy and mineral resources and leases them, as in the U.S. offshore and national forests. The U.S. situation with private ownership of mineral rights is unique; in most of the rest of the world, the mineral rights are owned by the government and the share the government takes is highly variable.

Figure 3–10 compares the percent of per barrel retained by the government relative to the company's share for a variety of countries. For example, in Yemen in 1995 the government received more than 90% of profits, whereas the companies received less than 10% in the first contract. The majority of countries received more than half the oil profits, while the most generous countries in this particular grouping were the United Kingdom and Ireland, which were the only governments to take less than 40% of the profits. State percentage on gas tends to be lower than on oil.

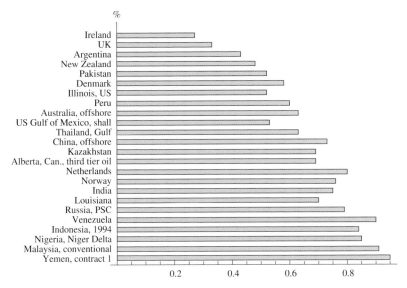

Fig. 3–10 Government Share per Barrel of Oil, 1995

Source: OGJ 7/14/97:30.

Note that rates vary considerably across countries. However, to be competitive, countries with poorer quality, more expensive, less well-known reserves, or countries whose situation is less desirable in any way or more risky, are likely to levy lower taxes to be able to attract investment.

Severance taxes are applied at the production level but energy taxes are also applied as tariffs when energy is traded across borders and as excise taxes when energy is sold to final consumers, such as the gasoline tax you pay at the pump. The most heavily taxed energy sources are oil products. To illustrate the extent of this taxation, note the wide variation in price for oil products in Table 3–9. Although some of the price differences reflect different transport, exchange rates, and distribution costs, much of the difference is from varying tax rates. The top rows of Table 3–9 include wholesale prices of premium gasoline and light fuel oil (called distillate in the United States and gas oil in other places) at three world oil market centers—New York harbor, Rotterdam, and Singapore. These three prices illustrate the small difference in wholesale prices before tax across the world's local markets.

All these excise taxes distort markets, and in the next section we will see how.

Table 3–9 World Survey of Selected Petroleum Product Prices, Including Taxes

Region Country	Premium Gasoline#	Diesel Fuel	Residential Fuels Light Fuel Oil	Kerosene	LPG	Industrial Fuels Light Fuel Oil	Heavy Fuel Oil
			U.S. $ per Gallon			U.S. $ per Barrel	
Wholesale Prices							
NY Harbor	49.33	--	--	--	--	48.98	--
Rotterdam	47.31	--	--	--	--	48.19	--
Singapore	46.79	--	--	--	--	46.31	--
North America							
Canada	1.73	1.43	1.10	--	--	28.48	23.41
Mexico	2.63	1.53	--	--	--	29.35	13.77
United States	1.29	1.15	1.10	0.98	0.38	26.71	18.65
Central & South America							
Argentina	1.62	1.14	0.68	0.77	0.57	--	--
Brazil	2.39	1.30	0.50	0.72	1.83	--	--
Chile	2.09	1.26	0.84	1.14	1.35	--	--
Colombia	1.80	1.03	0.62	0.93	0.70	--	--
Ecuador	1.46	0.90	0.53	--	0.23	--	--
Venezuela	0.23	0.14	0.14	0.33	0.35	--	--
Western Europe							
France	3.31	2.47	1.13	--	--	39.88	24.30
Germany	3.49	2.73	1.08	--	--	39.03	22.05
Italy	3.34	2.78	2.72	--	--	95.10	26.10
Netherlands	3.87	2.55	1.72	--	--	--	25.89
Norway	3.85	3.42	2.05	--	--	65.33	61.81
Spain	2.57	2.15	1.16	--	--	41.93	28.56
United Kingdom	4.16	3.94	0.78	--	--	34.84	24.77
Eastern Europe & Former USSR							
Kazakhstan	1.06	--	0.76	--	--	28.80	11.15
Poland	3.01	2.31	1.31	--	--	37.76	15.62
Middle East							
Iran*	1.31	0.26	0.14	0.26	--	--	--
Kuwait*	0.77	0.67	0.22	0.67	--	--	--
Qatar*	0.70	0.62	--	0.42	--	--	--
Saudi Arabia*	0.91	0.37	0.15	0.44	--	--	--
United Arab Emirates*	0.90	0.83	0.58	0.85	--	--	--
Africa							
Algeria*	1.04	0.61	0.48	0.23	--	--	--
Libya*	0.78	0.70	0.08	0.46	--	--	--
Nigeria*	0.75	0.71	0.41	0.58	--	--	--
South Africa*	1.59	1.37	--	--	--	--	--
Far East & Oceania							
Australia	1.65	1.72	--	--	--	--	--
China*	1.19	1.20	--	--	--	--	--

Table 3–9 World Survey of Selected Petroleum Product Prices, Including Taxes (cont'd)

Region Country	Premium Gasoline#	Diesel Fuel	Residential Fuels				Industrial Fuels	
			Light Fuel Oil	Kerosene	LPG		Light Fuel Oil	Heavy Fuel Oil
	U.S. $ per Gallon						U.S. $ per Barrel	
India*	2.54	1.66	0.61	--	--		--	--
Indonesia*	0.48	0.28	0.24	0.14	--		--	--
Japan	2.94	2.39	1.29	--	--		35.70	26.46
Korea, South	3.52	1.73	1.46	--	--		61.01	38.40
New Zealand	1.64	0.98	--	--	--		39.27	42.76
Taiwan*	2.13	1.43	--	--	--		36.37	30.77
Thailand*	1.32	1.15	1.33	--	--		--	31.73

Notes: # indicates conventional gasoline which is leaded gasoline in Singapore.
 -- indicates data is unavailable.
*All prices are from some time period in 2001, except * entries which are from 2001.
Source: EIA/DOE, *Weekly Petroleum Status Report,*
http://www.eia.doe.gov/oil_gas/petroleum/data_publications/weekly_petroleum_status_report/wpsr.html

Modeling taxes in a competitive market

Let us go back to our competitive model. Let demand and supply in the lignite market be calculated as follows:

$$Q_d = 18 - 2P_d$$

$$Q_s = -6 + P_s$$

If we want price in terms of quantity, we can invert as follows:

$$P_d = 9 - 0.5Q_d$$

and

$$P_s = 6 + Q_s$$

We can see equilibrium in this market in Figure 3–11. Solving for the price that makes supply equal to demand $18 - 2P = -6 + P =>$ equilibrium $P = 8$ and $Q = 2$.

Now suppose that we put a unit tax of one on this product. The demand price will have to include the payment to the supplier plus the tax. The easiest way to see the intuition of the tax is to add tax to the supply price as in Figure 3–12. Where this new function crosses demand is where demand price equals supply price (plus the tax). Both suppliers and demanders are happy with the quantity at their price.

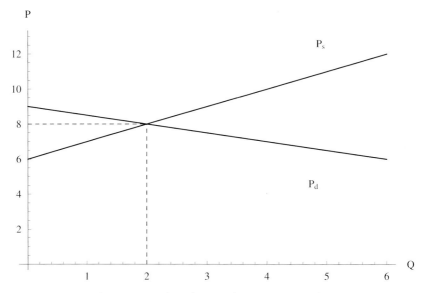

Fig. 3–11 Supply and Demand in an Energy Market

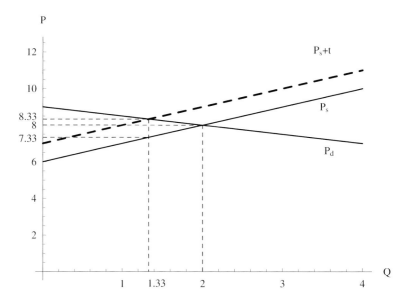

Fig. 3–12 Supply and Demand With a Unit Tax

From the diagram, we can see that if we added the tax at the original quantity two, demanders would not want to buy two at the supply price plus the tax. At the new higher demand price, there would be excess quantity supplied, which would push supply price down. Supply price would keep falling until the demand price equaled the supply price plus tax, and demanders and suppliers wanted to exchange the same quantity. This would be at a quantity of 1.33, a demand price of 8.33, and a supply price of 7.33. To see how to determine those prices and quantities, go back to the model. If we invert the demand and supply curves and set $P_d = t + P_s$, we get:

$$P_d = P_s + t$$

and

$$P_d = 9 - 0.5Q_d = P_s + 1 = 6 + Q_s + 1$$

At equilibrium $Q_d = Q_s = Q_e$, so:

$$9 - 0.5Q_e = 6 + Q_e + 1$$

Solving for equilibrium Q_e:

$$Q_e = 1.33$$

To get the demand price substitute Q_e back into the inverse demand to get:

$$P_d = 9 - 0.5 * 1.33 = 8.33.$$

To get supply price, substitute Q_e back into the inverse supply to get:

$$P_s = 6 + 1.33 = 7.33$$

The above solution matches the economic "intuition" of how a tax would work in a competitive market.

An alternative solution technique would be to substitute the relationship $P_d = P_s + t$ into the direct demand curve and solve:

$$Q_d = 18 - 2(P_s + t) = -6 + P_s$$

This will yield the same solution as above.

Who pays this tax? As demand price goes up from $8 to $8.33, so consumers of this energy product pay $0.33 of the tax. Supply price falls from $8 to $7.33 so producers pay $0.67 of the tax. Government revenues from the tax equal $Q*t = \$1.33*1 = \$1.33$.

Suppose that we collect the entire tax from the consumer. The consumer pays the tax, and what the consumer is willing to pay to the supplier is $P_d - t$. We represent $P_d - t$ in Figure 3–13. It is easy to see that the effect would be the same. Thus, it does not matter whether the tax is collected from the consumer or producer provided the costs of collecting the tax are similar. (Fig. 3–13)

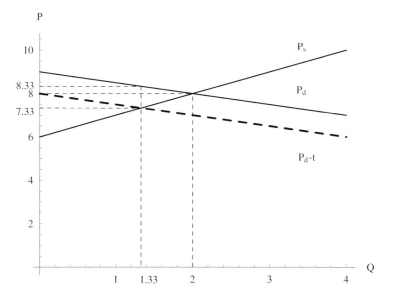

Fig. 3–13 Supply and Demand with Tax on the Consumer

Incidence of tax depends on demand and supply elasticities

Who pays the tax, or tax incidence, depends on the shape of demand and supply. For example, note the very elastic demand curve to the left of Figure 3–14. At the initial equilibrium (Q_c), demand price (P_d) equals supply price (P_s). The demander won't pay a higher price. When tax is added (S'), the demand price after the tax (P_d') is the same but the new supply price P_s' has fallen and the supplier pays the whole tax. Note for the perfectly inelastic demand curve to the right of Figure 3–14, the consumer will not reduce quantity and so pays the whole tax.

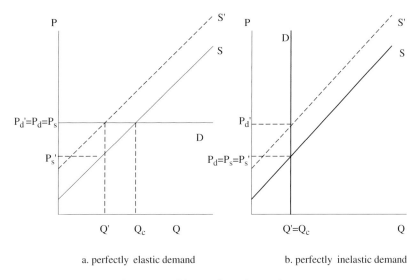

Fig. **3–14** Incidence of a Unit or Volume Tax

Figure 3–14 illustrates that the more responsive the demanders, the more they can pass the tax on to suppliers. Similarly, you will find that the more responsive the suppliers, the more they can pass on the tax to demanders.

Consumer and producer surplus show deadweight loss from a tax

The above analysis tells us that in most cases energy taxes decrease quantity consumed, increase demand price, and decrease supply price, causing a market distortion. To measure this distortion we consider two measures of social welfare—consumer and producer surplus. To illustrate these concepts, consider the market equilibrium in Figure 3–15. Assume there are no externalities in this market. Thus, neither the production nor the consumption of this energy product causes costs or benefits outside of this market. The demand and supply curves are those given earlier:

$$Q_d = 18 - 2P_d$$

$$Q_s = -6 + P_s$$

We can think of the demand curve as a marginal benefit curve. For example, if the demand price is $8.5, we sell $Q_d = 18 - 2*8.5 = 1$ unit. Someone must value that first unit by at least $8.5. If the price is $8, we can sell $Q_d = 18 - 2*8 = 2$ units. Someone must value that second unit by at least $8, and so on. At the market price of $8, the person who values that first unit at $8.5 is getting it at $8 and is getting a surplus of $0.50. Thus, consumer surplus is the difference between what a consumer is willing to pay and what he actually pays. In the continuous case, we measure it as the area under the demand curve and above the price. This would be the triangle abc in Figure 3–15, which is equal to $(9-8)*2*0.5 = 1$.

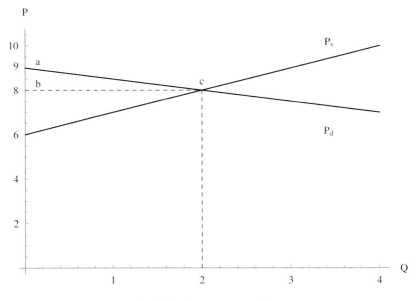

Fig. 3–15 Consumer Surplus

On the supply side, suppose that we have a competitive market in which firms maximize profits. In such a market, each firm is so small that they take the price as given. Suppose their production costs are a function of their output, or $C = f(Q)$. Then profits (π) for the competitive supplier are revenues minus costs:

$$\pi = PQ - C(Q)$$

If the competitor chooses the Q that maximizes profits, first-order conditions are:

$$\partial \pi / \partial Q = P - \partial C(Q) / \partial Q = 0$$

Since $\partial C(Q)/\partial Q$ is marginal cost, the first-order condition tells us that the supplier should produce up to the point where price equals marginal cost. Second-order conditions for a maximum are:

$$-\partial^2 C(Q)/\partial Q^2 < 0$$

This implies that:

$$\partial^2 C(Q)/\partial Q^2 > 0$$

Since $\partial^2 C(Q)/\partial Q^2$ is the slope of the marginal cost, second-order conditions are that marginal cost should slope up or increase (Fig. 3–16).

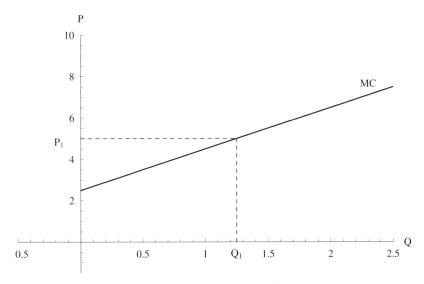

Fig. 3–16 Supply Equals Marginal Cost in a Competitive Market

If price is P_1, the producer makes profits on all units up to Q_1. Beyond Q_1, the producer loses money on the last or marginal unit and so should not produce beyond Q_1. Thus, in a competitive firm, maximizing profit, the supply curve is the marginal cost curve. For the total market in the short run, we get a supply curve at any point in time by adding together the production of all suppliers. (In the long run, firms can enter and exit, giving us a somewhat different supply curve, but one that still relates to costs.) Thus, the market supply curve is represented by the marginal cost curve for the whole industry.

To consider supplier welfare, take the supply curve or the marginal cost curve to be $MC = P = 6 + Q_s$. In Figure 3–17, the marginal cost of the first unit $MC = 6 + 1 = 7$, MC of the second unit $= 6 + 2 = \$8$, and so on. At equilibrium, two units are sold at \$8. However, the first unit only cost \$7 to produce leaving that supplier with a surplus of \$1. In the continuous case, we measure this producer surplus by the triangle bcd. Thus, producer surplus at equilibrium in this market equals $(8-6)*2*0.5 = 2$. The sum of producer plus consumer surplus $= 3$, which is the area adc in Figure 3–17.

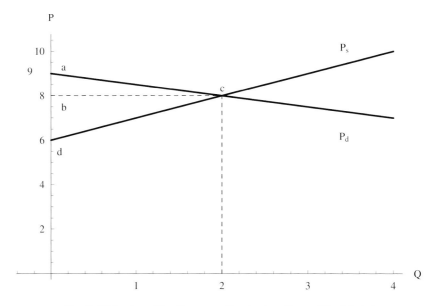

Fig. 3–17 Producer Plus Consumer Surplus in a Competitive Market

We use the concept of consumer-plus-producer surplus to measure the distortion from a tax. In Figure 3–18, the tax is represented. The loss in consumer surplus in the market from the tax is hbcg. The loss in producer surplus is gcdf. Part of the consumer and producer surplus goes to the government as revenues hbdf. We consider this a transfer. It is not lost; whoever benefits from the government gets this amount. What no one gets is the area bdc. This area we call the deadweight loss or the welfare loss from the tax, which is equal to $(2 - 1.33)*1*0.5 = 0.335$ in this case. It is because of this distortion that unit and ad valorem taxes are thought to be less efficient than income taxes. Taxes with smaller deadweight losses are considered more efficient.

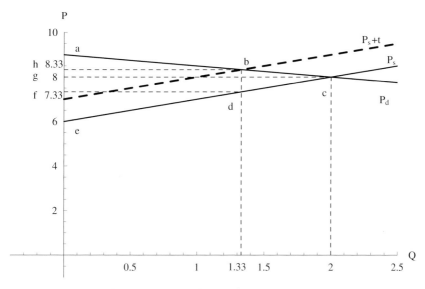

Fig. 3–18 Deadweight Loss from an Energy Tax

Energy subsidies

The opposite of an energy tax would be an energy subsidy. The analysis for a subsidy would be similar, but instead of adding the tax to supply you would subtract it. Thus, consumers would pay a lower price than suppliers receive. Alternatively, instead of subtracting a tax from demand you would add the subsidy to demand. In addition, the government would pay out the subsidies instead of receiving tax revenues.

Summary

Coal is our most abundant fossil fuel, and it fueled the industrial revolution. The competitive market model demonstrates how coal was first surpassed by oil and more recently by gas. Although highly stylized, this powerful model can also give us clues as to how newer fuel sources will penetrate and supplant fossil fuels. In a competitive market, we assume many buyers and sellers, a homogenous product, both buyers and sellers with information relating to market transactions, and free entry into and exit out of the industry.

In addition, we assume that property rights are well defined, there are no externalities, and coal mining is not a decreasing cost industry, to ensure that a competitive market allocates resources efficiently. (We will relax many of these assumptions in coming chapters.)

In our competitive model, coal buyers are represented by a demand curve and coal sellers by a supply curve. Movements along these curves as the result of a coal price change are called changes in quantity demanded or supplied. Shifts of the whole curve, from other variables changing, are called changes in demand and supply. By using basic demand and supply analysis, we improve business decisions by analyzing the effects of many events on market price and quantity including business cycles, changes in the prices of related goods, and government price supports.

Quantity of coal demanded is positively related to the number of buyers, the price of substitutes such as oil or gas, and income or industrial activity. It is negatively related to the price of coal and complement goods such as capital. The quantity of coal supplied is positively related to the number of sellers (producers), the price of coal, the price of byproducts of coal production, and the price of output produced using coal. It is negatively related to the price of factors of production for coal such as labor and capital and the price of any similar product to which coal producers could switch. Technology and government policies also affect coal demand and supply with the type of effect depending on the specific policy or technology.

Elasticities (the percentage change in quantity divided by the percentage change in another variable) measure how responsive quantity demanded and quantity supplied are to prices and other variables. Demand price elasticities indicate relations between price changes and revenues; income elasticities also tell us how sensitive the demand is to the business cycle, while cross-price elasticities indicate whether goods are substitutes or complements. Elasticities are important indicators of how markets behave and can also be used to create demand and supply curves for forecasting and policy analysis.

Governments have various reasons for taxing products with the most predominant being to collect revenues. Energy and natural resources are often subject to special taxes beyond corporate taxes. Severance taxes are taxes on the production of energy, while royalties are payments to the owner of the resource for exploiting it. In the United States, this owner may be a private citizen or the government. In most other countries, the government owns the mineral rights, and the share the government takes is highly variable.

Energy taxes are also applied as tariffs when energy is traded across borders and as excise taxes when energy is sold to final consumers. Most governments tax energy products, with petroleum products (particularly gasoline) typically being the most heavily taxed.

Excise taxes and subsidies have distribution effects, which include who pays the tax (also called the incidence of the tax) and how much revenue the government collects. The elasticities of demand and supply determine who pays the tax with the more price elastic side of the market paying less of the tax. Excise taxes in general are inefficient because they distort economic decisions creating losses in welfare referred to as deadweight losses. The deadweight losses may be losses in consumer or producer surplus or both.

4 Natural Monopoly and Electric Generation

Communism is socialism plus electricity.

—V.I. Lenin

Introduction

Ever since the first electric power plant became operational in London in 1879, electricity use has grown to make our lives increasingly comfortable and interesting. We can see this growth in the United States since 1949 in Figure 4–1.

Historically in the United States, electricity consumption roughly doubled every decade (e.g. $1.07^{10} = 1.97$) until the 1950s. Through the 1960s, it grew on average 7% a year or more. However, with higher fuel prices in the 1970s and early 1980s, electricity markets maturing, and the service sector becoming an increasing share of the economy, these growth rates slowed to an average of 4.1% per year in the 1970s, 2.6% in the 1980s, and 2.1% in the 1990s.

Billions of Kwh

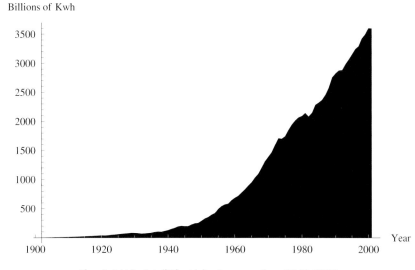

Fig. 4–1 U.S. Retail Electricity Consumption, 1949–2001

Sources: 1902–1948, U.S. Department of Commerce, *Historical Statistics of United States Colonial Times to 1970*, 1949–2001, DOE/EIA, *Annual Energy Review*, downloaded from www.eia.doe.gov/emeu/aer/txt/tab0708.htm

Electricity was not only important to the development of the United States and other developed capitalist countries but also was a cornerstone of the development strategy in the FSU, as demonstrated by the quote at the beginning of this chapter. It is equally important in the current plans for the developing countries. We can see current electricity consumption by major region of the world along with population in Figure 4–2.

North America is clearly the most electricity intensive region of the world with each consumer averaging more than 10,000 kilowatt-hours (kWh) or 10 megawatt-hours (MWh) per year. European average consumption is roughly half of that, with Eastern Europe (EE) and the FSU somewhat less. However, electricity consumption has fallen in EE/FSU. In 1989, their per capita consumption was very similar to that of Western Europe, showing the emphasis these previously socialist economies placed on electricity. Other developing areas consume considerably less electricity per capita, especially Africa.

Table 4–1 contains average annual growth rates for electricity for the 1980s and 1990s among other electricity statistics. Note that the developing world has higher growth rates in electricity than the industrial world.

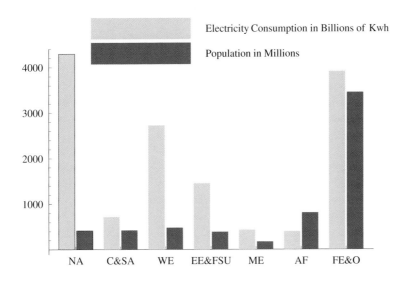

Fig. 4–2 Electricity Consumption and Population by Major World Regions

Notes: NA=North America, C&SA=Central and South America, WE=Western
Europe, EE&FSU=Eastern Europe and Former Soviet Untion, ME=Middle East,
AF=Africa, FE&O=Far East and Oceania
Source: EIA/DOE, *International Energy Annual,* 2001

The Far East has the highest rates of growth. If we include only the developing
countries for this region, rates of growth have been 7% or better since the 1980s,
matching earlier growth rates in the United States. Both the Middle East and South
America are now near the average per capita consumption levels of the United
States in 1950 but the Far East and Africa are at a lower average level.

Most electricity is produced from chemical reactions from burning coal, oil,
and natural gas to produce thermal energy; from nuclear sources; or from
gravitational sources like hydropower. The shares from each of these sources for the
United States and the world are shown in Figure 4–3. Small amounts of power in
the United States now come from other renewables—geothermal, wind, biomass,
and solar—and these sources are likely to increase if fossil fuels get scarcer and
worries of global climate change continue.

Table 4–1 Net Electricity Consumption, Growth, and Population

Region	Electricity 2001 consumption	Population 2001	Consumption Per capita	Electricity consumption	
				Total growth	
	Billion kWh	**Millions**	**Thousand KWh**	**1980– 1989**	**1990– 2001**
North America	4,294.03	416.93	10.30	25.26%	21.53%
Central and South America	719.95	426.20	1.69	36.67%	35.83%
Western Europe	2,726.82	482.42	5.65	20.37%	19.61%
EE & FSU	1,453.66	386.25	3.76	20.18%	-26.12%
Middle East	430.35	171.21	2.51	57.95%	50.54%
Africa	396.03	811.69	0.49	36.37%	27.70%
Asia and Oceania	3,913.24	3,450.11	1.13	41.75%	44.04%
World Total	13,934.09	6,144.81	2.27	28.03%	24.32%

Source: EIA/DOE, Feb 2003, *International Energy Annual, 2001.*
http://www.eia.doe.gov/iea/

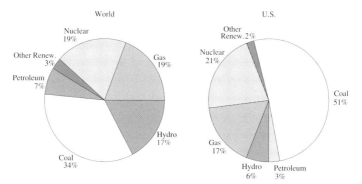

Fig. 4–3 U.S. and World Electricity Production by Fuel Type, 2001

Sources: EIA/DOE, *Annual Energy Review* 2001, EIA/DOE, *International Energy Annual 2001*, and *International Energy Outlook 2003.*

In the United States, the largest portion of electricity is generated by coal, followed by nuclear and gas. Table 4–2 compares regional electricity generation patterns for the world. Thermal electricity, which uses the heat generated from the burning of fossil fuels, dominates generation in all major regions except South and Central America where hydropower accounts for almost 75% of generation. The Middle East with its huge reserves of oil and gas is the most heavily dependent on thermal power and has the least diversified power supply by source. North America has a higher proportion of electricity coming from other renewables than other regions, whereas Western Europe has a higher proportion of nuclear generation than other regions.

Table 4–2 World Net Electricity Generation by Type, 2000

Region	Thermal	Hydro	Nuclear	Geothermal and Other	Total
			(Billion kWh)		
North America	2,997.1	657.6	830.4	99	4584
Central & South America	204.1	545	10.9	17.4	777.4
Western Europe	1,365.4	557.5	849.4	74.8	2,847.1
EE & FSU	1,043.7	253.5	265.7	3.9	1,566.9
Middle East	425.3	13.8	0	0	439.1
Africa	333.7	69.8	13	0.4	416.9
Asia & Oceania	2,949.2	528.7	464.7	43.1	3,985.7
World Total	9,318.4	2,625.8	2,434.2	238.7	14,617

Source: EIA/DOE, Feb 2003, *International Energy Annual*, 2001. http://www.eia.doe.gov/iea/

Modeling Electricity Markets

Costs. To model electricity markets, begin with production costs. Total cost is composed of fixed cost, which is not related to electricity production and must be paid whether we produce or not and variable costs which are related to quantity of production. Fixed costs can include leases on office space, insurance premiums, and equipment that we have already paid for, such as an electric generator or a stack gas scrubber to remove sulfur dioxide. Fixed costs are often referred to as sunk costs and tend to be large in capital-intensive industries such as energy.

Power plants have typically been large and have required infrastructure to acquire fuel and to deliver power to end-use customers. These capital costs are typically fixed in the short run, since such equipment has a long life. Plant life for an electric power plant is considered to be 40 years. However, in the long run, we can mothball or sell any piece of equipment or even the whole plant, and we do not have to replace them. Thus, in the long run, all costs are variable.

Suppose the following equation represents costs for electricity generation:

$$TC = FC + VC(Q)$$

where

TC	is total cost
FC	is fixed cost
Q	is quantity of production
VC	is variable cost
VC(Q)	is variable cost which is a function of Q

These costs should include both out-of-pocket costs and opportunity costs. For example, if a generator invests his own funds in building a new unit, the cost of these funds is the value of the funds in their next best alternative. For a hydro unit, the out-of-pocket cost of the water might be zero, but the true opportunity cost of the water would be the foregone value of the water in its next best alternative. If the next best use is for irrigation, revenue you could have earned from selling the water for irrigation would be the opportunity cost for the water.

The above is our total cost outlay. We may also want to know what unit production costs are. There are two unit production costs that are of interest to us—average cost and marginal cost.

Consider average cost first. If we want to know what it costs to produce one unit on average, then we use average cost, which we get by dividing total cost by output:

$$TC/Q = FC/Q + VC(Q)/Q$$

Average total cost (TC/Q) equals average fixed cost (FC/Q) plus average variable cost $(VC(Q)/Q)$. Average fixed cost (which is just a constant divided by Q) has a consistent structure. Average variable costs, however, may take on a variety of structures depending on the production process. Knowing your variable cost structure is critical for making sound business decisions. In what follows we will consider some of the possibilities.

Suppose a power plant owns a coal deposit of 1000 tons that has a fixed cost of $1000 and costs $10 per ton to produce. Our total costs are $TC = 1,000 + 10Q$, and our average costs are $TC/Q = 1,000/Q + 10$. In this case, average variable cost is constant, but average fixed cost and average total cost decrease as production increases until Q is 1000. However, at 1000 variable cost jumps to infinity since we can produce no more coal at any cost. What happens to average cost in the above equation as Q increases? We know that FC/Q decreases over time. Since average variable costs are constant, average total cost falls as Q increases until the mine runs out of reserves. (Fig. 4–4.)

Changing our variable costs to $Q^{0.5}$ would change our average variable costs to $Q^{0.5}/Q = Q^{-0.5}$. In this case, as we scale up production we become more efficient, and both our average variable costs, and our fixed costs fall. Alternately, some of the reserves could be low-cost, and others could be high-cost as we deplete our reserves. To represent this case, suppose that fixed costs are still $1000 but variable costs are $Q^{1.5}$. Then:

$$TC = 1000 + Q^{1.5}$$

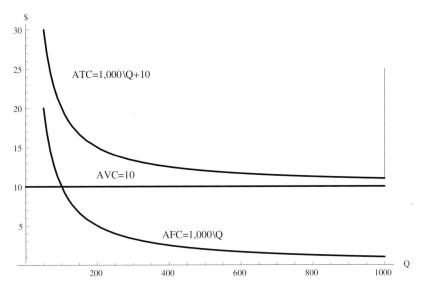

Fig. 4–4 Decreasing Average Costs

Average costs are:

$$TC/Q = 1000/Q + Q^{1.5}/Q = 1000/Q + Q^{0.5}$$

In this case, average fixed cost falls as Q increases, and average variable cost rises as Q increases. Since fixed costs are large relative to variable costs, average total cost falls until about 160 and then rises. (Fig. 4–5.)

Changing variable costs to Q^2 would give us yet another cost structure. In this case, average variable costs would rise fast enough so that average total costs would rise as production increased.

Average costs are a useful measure of the average resources needed to produce products. We can easily determine our total costs if we know our average costs by multiplying average total costs by output. (TC = ATC*Q = (TC/Q)*Q). Thus, if average cost is 15, and we produce 20 units, our total cost is $300.

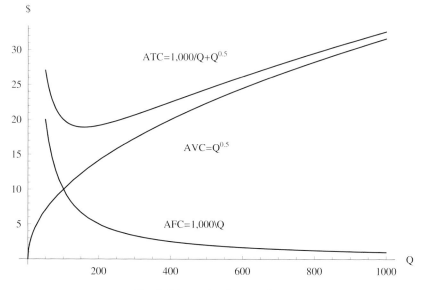

$$ATC=1{,}000/Q+Q^{0.5}$$

$$AVC=Q^{0.5}$$

$$AFC=1{,}000\backslash Q$$

Fig. 4–5 Increasing Average Costs

A second important unit cost to know in determining good economic decisions is the cost of the last unit, which economists call marginal cost. This, along with marginal revenue, will help us determine whether a particular unit should be produced or not. Marginal cost in the above example is:

$$dTC/dQ = dFC/dQ + dVC(Q)/dQ$$

Where dTC/dQ is the derivative of total cost with respect to Q or it is the change in total cost divided by the change in total quantity. Also, dFC/dQ is the derivative of total cost with respect to output and dVC(Q)/dQ is the derivative of total cost with respect to output.

Since FC is constant (dFC/dQ = 0). Thus, marginal cost comes from changes in variable cost as we change production, and its sign depends on whether we have decreasing, constant, or increasing economies of scale for our short-run variable costs. For example, the bulk of coal used by utilities is transported by rail. If railroads give lower rates per ton of coal moved to a utility for large shipments than for small shipments, marginal costs may fall when the utility produces more electricity.

The cost curve is expressed as TC = $1000 + 10Q^{1.5}$ then marginal cost is $\partial TC/\partial Q = 15 \cdot Q^{0.5}$. Thus, marginal cost increases as Q increases, and we dip into our higher costs reserves. This can also be seen by measuring marginal cost at two output levels rounded to the nearest cent. If output is 5, our variable cost is

10*5$^{1.5}$ = 111.8. If production is 6 our variable cost is 10*6$^{1.5}$ = 146.9. Our marginal cost for the 6th unit is the dTC/dQ = (146.9 – 111.8)/(6–5) = \$35.1/1 = \$35.1.

Marginal costs are important for determining whether we should produce a given unit or not. We won't decide based on average costs of all units but rather on the costs for that particular unit. (See Fig. 4–6 for average and marginal costs curves for the TC = 1000 + 10Q$^{1.5}$.) Notice that the marginal cost is above the average cost curve, and the average cost curve is rising. Since producing an additional unit costs more than the average, it is pulling up the average.

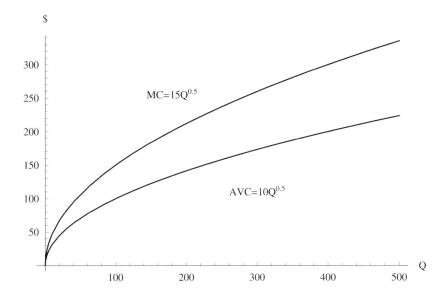

Fig. 4–6 Average Variable Cost and Marginal Cost

Load cycle. Costs may vary throughout the day and the year as the load cycle for electricity varies. Daily peak production tends to occur during the day, shoulder production occurs early in the morning and later in the evening, and off-peak during the night. Figure 4–7 shows typical daily load curves for Israel, Jordan, and Egypt. Israel—the most developed country of the three—shows peak during the day as is common in industrial countries; Jordan and Egypt, which are less industrialized, show peak load during the evening hours.

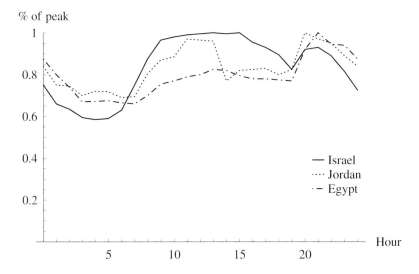

Fig. 4–7 Typical Daily Electric Load Curves for Israel, Jordan, and Egypt

Source: Used with the permission of Professor Amnon Einav. Downloaded May 2001 from http://magnet.consortia.org.il/ConSolar/SunDaySymp/Einav/Einav4.html.

Electricity consumption also varies seasonally. In the United States, the summer air conditioning season is the peak season as seen in Figure 4–8. In parts of Canada, where summers are cooler, and a higher percentage of homes are heated with electricity than in the United States, the peak season is the winter heating season. In other parts of the world, the load curve depends on the climate, how much electricity is used for heating and cooling, and whether commercial and industrial activity follows a seasonal pattern or not.

To satisfy electricity demand, utilities use their most-efficient, least-cost plants—usually coal, nuclear, and hydro—for baseload supply. Baseload plants tend to run at all times except when offline for maintenance and repair. During peak periods, less efficient reserve capacity is used, such as gas turbines, which have lower capital costs but higher fuel costs, or pumped storage (water pumped up into a reservoir during off peak to be released to produce energy during peak times). Older, dirtier, higher-cost plants are also held in reserve. Thus, during peak periods, the variable cost increases as we produce more electricity.

Billion Kilowatthours

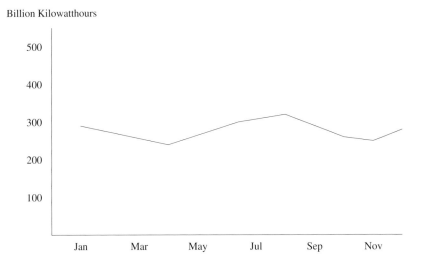

Fig. 4–8 U.S. 2000 Net Electricity Consumption by Month

Source: EIA/DOE (2001), *Monthly Energy Review,* March.

Monopoly in a decreasing cost industry

If average costs decrease over a wide range of values, we call such industries decreasing cost industries. (Fig. 4–9.)

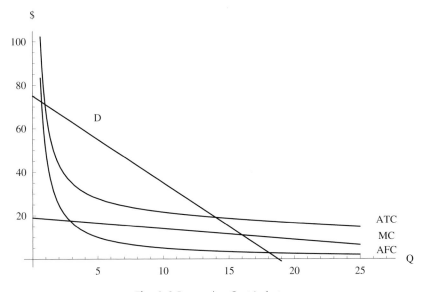

Fig. 4–9 Decreasing Cost Industry

Suppose Figure 4–9 shows the annual demand and cost curves for electricity in a village.

In this case, P is measured in cents per kWh and Q is measured in kWh per year. The demand and total cost curve for this example are:

$$P = 75 - 4Q$$

$$TC = 50 + 19Q - 0.25Q^2$$

$$FC = 50$$

$$VC = 19Q - 0.25Q^2$$

$$AFC = FC/Q = 50/Q$$

$$AVC = VC/Q = 19 - 0.25Q$$

$$MC = 19 - 0.50Q$$

Total cost for producing 20 units is:

$$TC = 50 + 19*20 - 0.25(20)^2 = 330 \text{ cents or } \$3.30$$

Average fixed and variable costs for 20 units are:

$$AFC = 50/20 = 2.5 \text{ cents}$$

$$AVC = 19 - 0.25Q = 19 - 0.25*20 = 14 \text{ cents}$$

The marginal cost of the 20th unit is:

$$MC = 19 - 0.50Q = 19 - 0.5*20 = 9 \text{ cents}$$

Note that there are economies of scale. Thus, as we produce more, average unit costs fall. Since unit costs are falling, marginal cost (or the cost of the last unit) must be below the average, pulling the average down. Such cost curves also imply that the largest producer of electricity will have the cheapest unit cost and will be able to undercut producers with smaller generating units. In such an instance, a monopoly is likely to evolve.

If the producer is a monopolist, she enjoys the whole market demand. Instead of competing, she picks the point on the demand curve that she likes the best—usually, the one that maximizes profits. We can easily work out what that quantity would be. Let the inverse demand curve be $P = P(Q)$, which slopes downward ($P'<0$). In other words, if you reduce quantity, you can sell at a higher price. Let the monopolist's output be Q and the monopolist's cost be $TC(Q)$. We assume that *TC* slopes upward ($TC'>0$), which means that marginal costs are positive, but $TC''<0$, which means that marginal costs are decreasing. The monopolist's profits are total revenues minus total costs or:

$$\pi = P(Q)^{\ast}Q - TC(Q)$$

To maximize profits with respect to output, take the first derivative of the function with respect to output, and set it equal to zero. First-order conditions for profit maximization are:

$$d\pi/dQ = P + (dP/dQ)^{\ast}Q - dTC/dQ = 0$$

The first two terms on the right side of the equation are $P + (dP/dQ)^{\ast}Q$ [also written as $(P + P'^{\ast}Q)$] and constitute marginal revenue (MR). *P* is the demand curve, or the average price at each quantity. To price we add dP/dQ (the slope of the demand curve) times output. dP/dQ is the reduction in price required to sell an extra unit of output. Since this reduction is for all units, we multiply the reduction times the number of units sold, *Q*. Thus what we get for an additional unit is the price minus the revenue reduction on all previous units. Thus, marginal revenue is less than or below the demand curve. The third term dTC/dQ, which is also written as TC', is the marginal cost curve (MC). Thus, the first order condition suggests that the monopolist is to produce where:

$$MR - MC = 0 \qquad\qquad (4.1)$$

Or where:

$$MR = MC$$

Second-order conditions confirm whether we have a maximum or not. Taking the derivative of Eq. 4.1 with respect to Q we get:

$$dMR/dQ - dMC/dQ < 0$$

Since the first expression above is the slope of marginal revenue, and the second is the slope of marginal cost, the second order condition requires that:

slope MR < slope of MC

Since the slope of MR and MC are both negative this result means that the MC curve must be less steep than the MR curve.

Before we apply this result to the above problem, let's develop one additional general result that will be useful. Suppose we face an inverse linear demand curve $P = a - bQ$. Total revenue for this demand curve is:

$$TR = P{*}Q = (a - bQ){*}Q = aQ - bQ^2$$

Marginal revenue equals:

$$dTR/dQ = a - 2bQ$$

Thus, marginal revenue is downward sloping and is twice as steep as the demand curve.

We are now ready to work out how much the monopolist should produce in the above example to maximize profits. (Fig. 4–10.) We represent the monopoly market, including marginal revenue, which in this case is linear and twice as steep as the demand curve. Thus, it bisects the Q axis halfway between zero and where the demand crosses the Q axis.

The monopolist would produce Q_m, which is where marginal revenue equals marginal cost, and sell at a price of P_m. Monopoly profits would be $(P_m - AC_m)Q_m$. For the above example, the numerical solution for P_m and Q_m can be computed as follows:

$$TR = (75 - 4Q){*}Q = 75Q - 4Q^2$$

$$\text{Then } MR = \partial TR/\partial Q = 75 - 8Q$$

Setting marginal revenue equal to marginal cost and solving for Q:

$$MR = 75 - 8Q = MC = 19 - 0.5Q => Q = 7.467$$

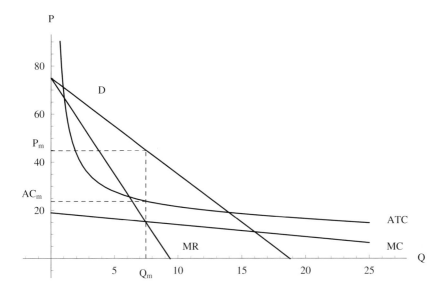

Fig. 4–10 Monopoly Producer

Second order conditions are:

$$\partial MR/\partial Q - \partial MC/\partial Q = -8 - (-0.5) < 0$$

So, we have a maximum:

$$P_m = 75 - 4(7.467) = 45.132$$

$$\pi = PQ - TC = 7.467*(45.132) - 50\text{-}19*(7.467) + 0.25*(7.467)^2$$

$$= 159.067$$

Since the price people are willing to pay at that point is greater than the marginal cost at Q_m, there are social losses associated with monopoly output. Remember from chapter 3 that we represent society's welfare by the sum of producer plus consumer surplus. Using this definition we measure the social optimum by again turning to calculus.

The sum of consumer surplus plus producer surplus can be represented by the area below demand and above price plus the area above marginal cost and below price. We can represent these areas in integral notation as:

$$W = \int_0^Q P(Q)dQ - PQ + PQ - \int_0^Q MC(Q)dQ = \int_0^Q P(Q)dQ - \int_0^Q MC(Q)dQ$$

We are in effect maximizing the area between D and MC in Figure 4–10. If we integrate or add up marginal costs, we get total variable costs, so consumer surplus can also be written as:

$$W = \int_0^Q P(Q)dQ - TVC$$

Optimizing this function with respect to output Q gives us:

$$\partial W / \partial Q = \partial(\int_0^Q P(Q)dQ - TVC(Q))/\partial Q = P(Q) - MC(Q) = 0$$

The calculus tells us we should operate where the price equals marginal cost or where the demand curve crosses the marginal cost curve. We can also see this result in Figure 4–11. At outputs less than Q_s, price is above MC so we can increase social welfare by increasing output. However, producing outputs more than Q_s, price is below marginal costs or people value the extra output by less than the cost of the extra output and welfare is diminished.

Using the above example, we can solve for P_s and Q_s:

$$P = 75 - 4Q = MC = 19 - 0.50Q => Q = 16$$

$$P = 75 - 4(16) = 11$$

Notice that at Q_s, average total costs are above price, and the utility would lose money. The amount lost would be:

$$\pi = PQ - TC = 11*16 - 50 - 19(16) + 0.25(16)^2 = -\$114$$

Calculus does not tell us how to allocate fixed costs—only how to price the product.

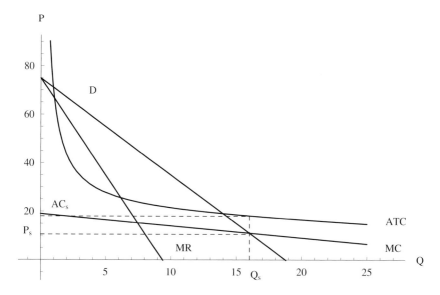

Fig. 4–11 Social Optimum in a Natural Monopoly Market

Government Policy for a Natural Monopoly

Since the social optimum in a decreasing-cost industry is at a loss-making quantity, it would not be sustainable in a competitive market. Also, without intervention in such a market, we would expect a monopoly to evolve. In such a case, economists think there is room for government intervention. From the time it was generally agreed that electric utilities were natural monopolies, governments have historically responded with government ownership or regulation. Outside the United States, most public utilities have historically been publicly owned. In the United States, the majority of electricity is produced by privately owned utilities (referred to as investor owned utilities or IOUs). Since 1907, these utilities have been subject to price regulation by regulatory commissions. The early agencies had a vague mandate to "maintain just and reasonable prices" and to limit price discrimination that was unrelated to variation in cost. When a utility wanted a rate increase, it would present a case to the commission in the state in which it operated. Prices would be set in these rate cases and would generally be fixed until the next case. The benefits of such regulation are the avoided social losses associated with monopoly, while the costs are those associated with running the regulatory agencies and any other unintended side effects of the regulation.

A U.S. legal decision in 1944 established that regulated prices should cover costs including a return so that utilities could attract capital and compensate investors for risks. In this section, we will consider three regulatory price models: rate of return, fully distributed cost, and peak-load pricing.

Rate of return regulation

In rate of return regulations, the utility is allowed to earn a rate of return that is calculated on its capital stock or rate base, represented as RB in the following equations. Because of economies of scope, suppose the firm produces n products $(q_1, q_2, q_3, \ldots q_n)$ and charges a price (p_i) for the "ith" product. (Economies of scope arise if unit costs fall when more than one type of product is produced.) Total revenue is $\Sigma_{i=1}^{n} p_i q_i$. The firm is allowed to charge p_i such that it covers its non-capital expenses and earns a normal rate of return (s) on its rate base. The basic accounting equation for rate of return regulation is:

$$\Sigma_1^n \ p_i q_i = \text{expenses} + s(\text{RB})$$

where:

p_i	is the price of the ith service class
q_i	is the quantity of the ith service class
n	is the number of service classes
s	is the allowable or "fair" rate of return
RB	is the rate base of the regulated firm's investment

The procedure requires that the company's revenues equal its costs including a normal rate of return. Economic profits are zero, but there is no requirement for economically efficient prices.

Suppose that a utility has a rate base of $2000. It expects to sell 4000 kWh to industrial customers and 2500 kWh to residential customers. Operating costs are $200. The regulator believes that 10% is a normal rate of return for the utility. The utility has asked the public utility commission for a rate increase to $0.05 per kWh for industrial users and to $0.10 per kWh for residential users. Should the commission approve the rate increase?

The utility's revenues would be 0.05*4000 + 0.10*2500 = $450. Its expenses plus return on capital would be 200 + 0.10*2000 = $400. Since revenues are larger than expenses, the commission would not approve the rate increase.

Problems with rate of return regulation

There are a number of difficulties in implementing rate of return regulation. For the most part, it is straightforward to compute expenses. There may be some difficulties with transfer prices, which are prices at which one part of a company sells products to another. For example, if a utility owned a coalmine and sold itself coal, the book or accounting value recorded may be distorted for tax or rate of return regulation purposes. Thus, the value of the coal may not represent an arms-length transaction from one independent firm to another. Such cost distortions may arise from tax laws as well as from cost pass-through. Since costs can be passed on to the ratepayers, there may be less incentive to hold the line on costs than in a competitive industry.

There is also controversy over the normal rate of return and the rate base. A normal rate of return is what is required to attract capital to the market. Rates on capital depend on how the investment is financed. Suppose the utility finances using the three conventional sources—bonds, preferred stocks, and common stocks—in the proportions shown in Table 4–3. One could compute the required rate of return (s) as the weighted average of the three financing sources.

Table 4–3 Financing for a Representative Utility

	% of capitalization	Required Return as a %
Bonds	48	8.22
Pref. Stocks	14	9.34
Common Stocks	38	12.5

Weighted average: 0.48*8.22+0.14*9.34+0.38*12.5=10.0%

Annual rates of return for a bond are quite easy to compute. A utility bond usually pays coupons quarterly as are stipulated on the bond. The rate of return for a long-term bond is approximately the annual coupon divided by the bond price. For example, suppose the utility sells you a bond for $1000 and pays four quarterly coupons of 25 cents each. If you hold the bond for a very long time, then the rate of return on the bond can be approximated by (25*4)/1000 = 100/1000 = 0.10 or 10%.

The rate of return will be influenced by other rates of return in the market. For example, suppose that the Fed tightened monetary policy to reduce inflation, and the market interest rate went up to 20% on items of risk similar to the utility bond. Now the utility bond would not look very attractive if it only paid 10%. If you wanted to sell the bond, you would have to lower the price so that it paid the same rate as other similar assets. Thus, for a bond that will be held for a very long time, the equation $100/P = 0.20$ holds approximately. This equation implies that the price of the bond would have to fall to $P = 100/0.20 = 500$ for the bond to be competitive.

For preferred stocks, it is equally easy to compute a rate of return. Preferred stocks pay a maximum rate of return or maximum dividend. Companies do not have to pay dividends on preferred stock but if they pay any dividends on common stock, they must pay the maximum value on preferred stock. Since companies typically pay dividends on preferred stock (unless they're in financial duress), their rate of return for a preferred stock is approximately the annual dividend payment divided by the issue price for preferred stocks that are held for a very long time.

Computing rate of return on common stocks poses more of a problem. Stocks represent equity or ownership, and dividends may vary as economic conditions change. We can observe the price paid when the utility issues the stock; however, we are uncertain of the dividends that will be paid out in the future.

Valuing Money across Time

Suppose we know the future flow of dividends and the stock price at issue. To see how to develop a precise measure of rate of return, let us first review how to value money across time.

You have \$1 today. The interest rate at the bank is 5%, and the bank compounds interest annually. After one year you will start to receive interest on the interest accrued. If you put the money in the bank you will have $(1 + 0.05)*\$1 = \$1.05$ at the end of the year. If you leave this \$1.05 in the bank for another year, you now get interest on the principle and the interest so at the end of two years you will have $(1.05)(1.05)*\$1 = 1.1025$. If you hold it for t years you will have $(1.05)^t*\$1$. If you have A dollars and the interest rate is r, at the end of t years you will have $(1+r)^t*\$A$.

Similarly, we can see what money in the future is worth today. If I offer you a dollar in a year, what is it worth to you today? In other words, how much money (B) would you have to have today to put in the bank to have a dollar at the end of the year? The answer depends on the interest rate and compounding. If the interest rate is 5%, then we know that $B*(1.05) = 1$, the dollar I am offering you in a year. Solving for B, we get $B = 1/1.05 = \$0.9524$. We call this process discounting future income and the value today is called the present value or discounted cash flow.

What is the present value of \$1 in two years, if the interest rate is 5% and interest is compounded annually? $(1.05)^2*B = 1$, so $B = 1/(1.05)^2$. The present value of \$1 in t years $= 1/(1.05)^t$. The present value of D_t dollars in t years at an interest rate of r is $D_t/(1+r)^t$.

We can now value a stream of income quite easily. If I offer you D_1 dollars at the end of one year and D_2 at the end of two years, the present value of this stream of income with interest rate r is the sum of the present values of each amount or:

$$PV = D_1/(1+r) + D_2/(1+r)^2$$

If I offer you a stream of income D_t from time period $t = 1...T$, its present value (PV) is:

$$PV = \Sigma_{t=1}^{T}\{D_t/(1+r)^t\}$$

If you have a future flow of income (D_t) and a future flow of costs (C_t), the present value of your net cash flow (also called your discounted cash flow or DCF) is the present value of your income minus the present value of your cost or:

$$PV = \Sigma_{t=1}^{T}\{D_t/(1+r)^t\} - \Sigma_{t=1}^{T}\{C_t/(1+r)^t\} = \Sigma_{t=1}^{T}\{D_t - C_t)/(1+r)^t\}$$

Utility rate of return on a stock

Discounting enables us to compute a utility's rate of return (also called internal rate of return or IRR) on a stock. To do so, note that the stock's price should be equal to the discounted cash flow of its future dividends or:

$$P = \Sigma_{t=1}^{T} \{D_t/(1 + k)^t\} \qquad (4.2)$$

where

P   is the current cost of the stock

D_t is the expected dividend in year t

k   is the cost of equity capital with similar risk characteristics

T   is the period over which the company pays dividends

The discounted cash flow of the future income is what the future flow of income is worth today if it pays you the required return or discount rate, which is generally your opportunity cost plus any adjustment for risk. If the project is risky you will require a higher rate of return; if it is less risky, you will need a lower rate of return.

To illustrate that an asset price should be equal to its DCF, take a simple example of a project that lasts a year. Suppose the project pays $100 in a year. Other projects that are equally risky pay 10%. The DCF = 100/1.10 = $90.91. Thus, if you have $90.91 now and invest it for a year, you would have $100. If you invested your $90.91 in another equally risky asset with the same cash flow you would also have $100. Now suppose you only have to pay $85 for this asset. This would be a good buy since it would pay $100 at the end of a year, whereas other projects that yielded $100 would cost $90.91. Because this is a desirable project, everyone would want to buy it instead of the other more expensive assets, and they would switch out of more costly assets into this one. As more people bid on this asset, its price would increase until it was equally desirable or its price was equal to its DCF.

Notice that k in Eq. 4.2 (the equity cost of capital) is the rate of return required by investors. Its value depends on how risky the firm is. Here risk is taken to mean variability in profits from the capital or investment. The causes of the risk include business as well as regulatory risk. The more risky the firm, the higher k investors will demand to invest in the firm.

Now let's compute k from stock price and dividend information. If a stock sold for $98 today and paid $56 in dividends at the end of the year for two years, the formula to solve for k would be:

$$98 = 56/(1 + k) + 56/(1 + k)^2$$

Solving:

$$(1 + k)^2 98 = (1 + k)^2 56/(1 + k) + (1 + k)^2 56/(1 + k)^2$$

$$(1 + 2k + k^2)98 = 56(1 + k) + 56$$

Simplifying:

$$98k^2 + 140k - 14 = 0$$

The solution for k in the above equation can be found using the quadratic formula:

$$k= (-140 +/-(140^2 - 4*98*(-14))^{0.5})/2*98)$$

The solution for the positive root is:

$$k = (-140 + (19600 + 5488)^{0.5})/196 = 0.0939 \text{ or about } 9.4\%$$

The solution for the negative root is:

$$k = (-140 - (19600 + 5488)^{0.5})/196 = -1.522 \text{ or about } -152.2\%$$

Although this second root makes mathematical sense, it does not make economic sense, and we ignore this root.

The problem with computing the IRR is that future D_ts are hard to measure. Our choices are to turn to an electricity market analyst to estimate D_t or use some historical value, such as the last value in the market or some average over time. If we can come up with good estimates for the D_ts, and we have computed the rates of return on stocks, bonds, and preferred stocks and their shares of financing, then we can compute s, the required rate of return, to be able to raise capital.

Utility rate base

The last thing we need for rate of return regulation is the rate base (RB). It is usually original cost minus depreciation, but this value understates actual investment if inflation has occurred. To see why, consider how to convert values measured in one year's dollars to those measured in another. Suppose you purchased your plant in 1980 for 500 million 1980 dollars. You depreciate the plant over 40 years, so that annual depreciation is 500/40 = 12.5. Let's compute the rate base in 2000. RB (2000) = 500 – 20*12.5 = 250 million. However, if prices have doubled from 1980 to 2000, the rate base related to 2000 dollars would be 2*250 = 500 million. Original cost understates the rate base.

We can easily adjust the rate base, if we have the appropriate index. For example, suppose we have capital stock (K) measured in 1985 dollars, and we want to know the value in 2000 dollars. We need an index that captures the value of a dollar in 2000 divided by the value of a dollar in year 1985. Call this index I2000$/1985$. The denominator is called the base year. The index is computed by dividing the value of a basket of goods in year 2000 by the value of the same basket of goods in 1985. For example, if the basket of goods cost $200 in 1985 and cost $350 in 2000, the I2000$/1985$ = (350/200) = 1.75. This index tells us that prices for the goods in the basket in 2000 are 1.75 times higher than their prices in 1985. To use our index to inflate 1985 dollars up to 2000 dollars, multiply by our 1985 capital stock, or:

$$K(in1985\$)*(I2000\$/1985\$) = K(\ in\ 2000\$)$$

For example, if we paid $200 for a piece of capital in 1985, and the wholesale price index for year 2000 with base year 1985 = (I2000$/1985$) = 1.75, the price of capital in 2000$ is 200*(1.75) = 350. Alternatively, if we bought capital in 2000, and wanted to deflate these 2000 dollars back to 1985$, we would divide by the index in decimal form or:

$$K(in\ 2000\$)/(I2000\$/1985\$) = K(in\ 1985\$)$$

Remember to divide by a fraction invert and multiply.

A piece of capital purchased for $350 in 2000 would be worth 350/(175/100) = $200 (in 1985$)

What if we need to know the index I2000$/1985$ with base year 1985 but only have indices with base year 1990? Use the index I1985$/1990$ and the index I2000$/1990$ to construct the appropriate index as follows:

$$(I2000\$/1990\$)/(I1985\$/1990\$) = I2000\$/1985\$$$

Thus, if the wholesale price index for year 2000 with base year 1990 = (I2000$/1990$) = 1.61, and the wholesale price index for the year 1980 with base year 1990 = (I1985$/1990$) = 0.92, then the wholesale price index for year 2000 in 1985 dollars is (1.61/0.92) = 1.75. When indices are reported in the literature, they are usually reported in percents, which means the above numbers would have to be multiplied by 100. Thus, (I1985$/1990$) = 0.92 would be reported at 92. However, to use the indices to deflate or inflate, you would need to divide them by 100.

The financial approach to valuing the utility's capital would be to ascertain the value of the company's stocks and bonds. However, this is not an independent value. It depends on s, the allowed rate of return. To see why, take a simple example. Suppose that our allowed rate of return is 0.10, we have stocks equal to $100 and no bonds. Thus, our dividends are $10. If equally risky alternatives in the market paid 9%, then our stock would look like a good investment. People would keep buying our stock, bidding up the price until it was paying only 9% as well. The new price would be such that:

Dividend/Price = 0.09 = 10/P

Solving, we get:

P = 10/0.09 = $111.11

If the rate of return changed, the price would change.

Rate of return regulation usually has a regulatory lag. Once a utility decides that its prices are too low, it must present a case and get the rate increased by the public utility commission. These new prices stay fixed until the next approved rate case. The utility then has an incentive to reduce costs through technical improvement, since it gets to keep the extra savings until the next rate case.

Rate of return regulation does not dictate a rate structure but approves a suggested rate structure. Most utilities price discriminate and charge different prices to different customer classes. As an example, U.S. average prices and consumption per customer class in 2002 are shown in Table 4–4.

Table 4–4 U.S. Average Electricity Prices and Consumption by Customer Class

Sectors	Electricity Prices (cents/kWh)	Sectors	Electricity Sales (billion kWh)
Residential	8.43	Residential	109.0
Commercial	7.93	Commercial	87.7
Industrial	4.84	Industrial	78.4

Source: EIA/DOE *Electric Power Monthly*, March 2003, Table 52, Table 45.
http://www.eia.doe.gov/cneaf/electricity/epm/epm.pdf

Since utilities are only allowed a nominal rate of return on their capital, they may have a tendency to overinvest in capital relative to the least-cost input mix of production. This tendency has come to be known as the Aversch-Johnson (AJ) effect. (For a mathematical analysis of how this might distort the choice of inputs go to Crew1 at http://dahl.mines.edu.)

Although economic theory leads us to suspect an AJ effect, empirical studies investigating the issue have found mixed results. If the AJ affect exists, it is raising the costs of generating electricity.

Utility cost allocation

Utilities typically are multi-product firms supplying different customer classes. For example, they supply high- and low-voltage customers as well as peak and off-peak services. A utility's fixed cost may contribute to services for more than one product or customer class. Fully distributed cost (FDC) deals with the issue of how to distribute these fixed costs over customer or product classes.

One way to allocate fixed costs is to distribute them in the price across all consumers. This, however, distorts consumption decisions and causes losses in social welfare, since price will no longer be equal to marginal cost. Since markets with less elastic demand will cut consumption the least, it will be more economically efficient to allocate more costs to consumers with less elastic demand. For more information on allocating cost in this way, known as Ramsey pricing, see Viscusi, et al. (1996).

The more efficient way to allocate fixed costs is in the form of fixed charges. As long as you do not drive consumers out of the market by charging them more than their consumer surplus, you can allocate fixed costs over consumer groups in any way you like, and it will be economically efficient. For more information on distributing costs as fixed charges and issues of fairness, again, see Viscusi, et al. (1996).

Peak-load pricing

Peak-load pricing means charging different prices for electricity depending on the load factor. Since it is expensive to store electricity, capacity is usually made large enough to satisfy the peak demand. This means, however, that during much of the time some capital is sitting idle.

In the example of Duke Power Company, given in Viscusi, et al. (1995), Duke produces 55 billion kWh per year. Its average single-customer demand is 6300 megawatts (MW), peak demand is 11,145 (MW), and installed capacity is 13,234 (MW), with the extra needed as a mandated reliability margin. If a utility can move some of the peak demand to off-peak, it can decrease the amount of total capital needed and use existing capital more intensely, reducing costs.

To develop the efficiency criteria for peak load pricing, we use a simple model. Suppose daily demand at peak is D_{pk} and at off-peak demand is D_{op}. Demands are independent, so the price in peak period does not affect the quantity demanded in the off-peak period and vice versa. (Fig. 4–12.)

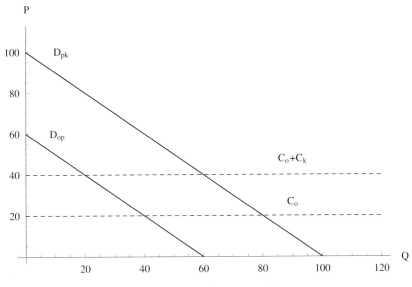

Fig. 4–12 Peak Load Model

Operating costs are constant for both peak and off-peak at C_o. Capital costs per unit are constant at C_k, and we assume capital can be added in small increments. We want to pick prices in the two markets (peak and off-peak) to maximize social welfare. We know that the social welfare is the area under the demand curve minus cost. We can use either prices or quantities as our choice variable, since choosing one determines the other. It is easiest to optimize in terms of quantity. Capacity will be assumed to be at the peak with no margin for safety. Total consumer benefits (area under the demand curve) minus total cost or social welfare for this case is:

$$SW = \int_0^{Q_{pk}} P_{pk}(Q_{pk})dQ_{pk} + \int_0^{Q_{op}} P_{op}(Q_{op})dQ_{op} - c_o Q_{pk} - c_o Q_{op} - c_k Q_{pk}$$

First-order conditions are:

$$SW_{pk} = P_{pk} - c_o - c_k = 0 => P_{pk} = c_o + c_k$$

$$SW_{op} = P_{op} - c_o = 0 => P_{op} = c_o$$

The above first-order conditions require that peak load pays operating plus capital costs, but off-peak only pays operating costs. Since off-peak has idle capacity, we increase welfare by increasing consumption off-peak as long as we are covering our variable costs. However, before such a scheme is implemented it is necessary to ensure that costs of metering do not negate the gains from peak-load pricing.

Summary

Electricity is produced from a variety of sources including fossil fuels, nuclear, and renewable sources. Fossil fuels tend to dominate power production worldwide but fuel sources vary considerably across countries and regions. Coal dominates in the United States; hydropower accounts for 75% of generation in Latin America; Europe has a higher proportion of nuclear power than elsewhere; the Middle East is the most heavily dependent on oil and gas.

North America remains the most electricity intensive region of the world, followed by Europe, the FSU, and the industrial countries of Asia and Oceania. The developing countries trail far behind, especially Africa. The developing countries, however, are eager to catch up and provide very promising markets for new generation capacity.

Costs are an important consideration in determining which fuels to use to generate electricity and how much electricity to generate. Total costs include fixed costs, which are unrelated to production, and variable costs, which are related to how much is produced. In the long run all costs are variable, but in the short run existing plant and equipment, leases, and insurance are all fixed (or sunk) costs. Average unit cost tells us what it costs us to produce a unit on average and is useful in helping us compute total costs and total profits. Marginal cost tells us what the last unit costs to produce and is an important input in deciding how much to produce.

We also see that through the day and the year, the load cycle for electricity varies. We have daily peak and off-peak demand. Peak tends to occur during the day and early evening; shoulder production, early in the morning and later in the evening. Off-peak occurs during the night. There are also seasonal peaks and off-peaks depending on the climate and daylight hours. To satisfy electricity demand, utilities use their most efficient, least-cost or baseload plants—usually coal, nuclear, and hydro all the time. During peak periods, less efficient reserve capacity is used, such as turbines with lower capital costs but higher fuel cost or pumped storage and older plants. Thus, during peak periods, the variable cost is usually higher.

Revenues are also an important factor in deciding how much electricity to produce. Price is the average revenue for each unit and is important in determining profits. Marginal revenue is the revenue from the last unit and is important in helping determine how much to produce. If a plant has market or pricing power, its marginal revenue will be below its price.

Historically, increasing economies of scale gave the largest plant the lowest marginal cost. This largest, most efficient plant is referred to as a natural monopoly. It would be able to drive other plants out of business. If it became sole producer, it could maximize profits where marginal revenue equaled marginal costs and make monopoly profit. However, the social optimum would be at the larger output, where price equals marginal cost. The resulting social losses from monopoly have historically caused governments to intervene in this market to either regulate or produce the electricity themselves.

We considered three different types of regulatory approach to regulating prices—rate of return, fully distributed cost, and peak load. Under rate of return regulation, revenues must cover variable costs plus a fixed rate of return on capital necessary to attract the appropriate amount of capital to the industry. This required rate depends on the rates of return on the bonds, common stock, and preferred stock used to finance capital and may be difficult to compute. Valuing the rate base is also fraught with difficulties. Inflation means that using original cost may understate the rate base, whereas using the current cost is likely to overstate the rate base. Rate of return regulation may cause utilities to invest in too much capital and may not be efficient.

Economic efficiency requires that price be set equal to marginal cost. This leaves the problem of allocating the fixed costs across consumer classes. If we are constrained to allocating the costs across each unit of production, we will not have the economically efficient outcome, but economic theory says social losses are smaller if we allocate more costs to groups with less elastic demand.

If we maximize social welfare, we should set price equal to marginal cost in each customer class and allocate the fixed costs as fixed charges rather than dividing them up into price. Efficiency criteria do not tell us how to allocate the fixed charges, except that the charges should not distort consumer decisions on the margin. Thus, no fixed charge should be greater than the consumer surplus in that market.

If the consumer classes are peak and off-peak, and there is no peak shifting, then theory indicates that the most efficient way to price electricity is to charge all capital costs to the peak users and only marginal costs to the off peak users.

5 Deregulation and Privatization of Electricity Generation

As has long been noted, the key resource of government is the power to coerce. Regulation is the use of this power for the purpose of restricting the decisions of economic agents.

—Viscusi et al. (1996)

Introduction

Natural monopoly arguments traditionally led most governments to either regulate or produce electricity themselves in vertically integrated monopolies. Thus, the publicly or privately owned companies owned the generation, the high-voltage transmission lines, and the local distribution companies. They were responsible for all aspects of the power market. They built and maintained generating facilities and assured the quality of the electricity supply. They built and maintained the transportation network, making sure that power was dispatched and transported when and where it was needed. They built and maintained local distribution companies, distributed power, and billed customers.

Problems with regulated and government-owned utilities

Regulation can invite the dangers of regulatory capture, where the regulator tends to take the point of view of the regulated industry. Often regulators retire from government and move into the regulated industry in a process referred to as a revolving door. The AJ effect may raise costs; guaranteed rates of return may not be conducive to cost minimization, and regulators may get rates wrong.

In the case of government ownership you may get what Leibenstein calls "X-inefficiency," or higher costs than would prevail in a competitive market with cost minimization. Governments may also have other goals than cost minimization. For example, in New Zealand before privatization, the government-owned electricity monopoly employed far more people, and at higher costs than privately owned utilities—presumably a government employment policy. In developing countries electricity prices are often held low to subsidize development, while costs are often high, resulting from poor management, electricity theft, and corruption. This leads to capital shortages for developing new generation capacity with the result that in many poor countries, electricity brownouts and blackouts are routine occurrences.

As markets have gotten larger and technical changes have lowered costs for smaller generators, economists have also questioned whether the electricity market is really a natural monopoly, particularly at the generation level. Hunt and Shuttleworth (1996) note that the optimal electricity generation plant size has fallen from 1,000 MW to approximately 100 MW in the last 30 years. All these changes have led to new work that considers how to transform the electricity supply sector into a competitive industry with minimal regulation.

Models for the electricity sector

We will consider four electricity models combining the model types from Hunt and Shuttleworth (1996) and Tenenbaum, Lock and Barker (1992). The models are distinguished by the type of competition at each stage in the supply chain rather than by ownership.

- **Model One:** No competition at any stage or monopoly as we have known it in the past. Often these companies are vertically integrated and they may be publicly or privately owned.

- **Model Two:** Model one but with competition in generation. A single buyer such as a distribution company may buy from a number of different producers to encourage competition in generation. The United States started moving to this model with the Public Utilities Regulatory Policy Act (PURPA, 1978) that required U.S. utilities to purchase output from independent power producers (IPPs) at avoided costs. Avoided costs are the costs of generating a utility avoids by buying power from an IPP.

- **Model Three:** Model two but with common or contract carriage of high voltage transmission lines offered to all wholesale sellers and buyers. Often distribution companies (DISCOS) own the distribution wires and can choose their suppliers with competition in generation and in the wholesale supply.

- **Model Four:** Model three but retail customers also choose their suppliers in full retail competition. There is open access in both transmission and distribution. In the British model, there is also complete separation of generation, transmission, and distribution with an independent company owning the high voltage transmission and perform the dispatch function.

The important differences in these models are whether there is competition among generators, whether retailers or distribution companies can choose the generator to buy from, and whether the final consumer can choose who to buy their power from. The United Kingdom and New Zealand have model four as their goal. Hunt and Shuttleworth (1996) argue that model four is the most economically efficient if there are

- a well-established electricity retailing system,
- mature market institutions,
- constant vigilance against market power, and
- appropriate methods of dispatch.

With privatization and restructuring, the need for dispatch and coordination becomes crucial, particularly where formerly vertically integrated companies have been broken up. Often an independent system operator (ISO) coordinates the whole physical system based on a wholesale market for electricity or a power pool. (For more information on ISOs in the United States, go to http://www.eia.doe.gov/cneaf/electricity/wholesale/wholesalelinks.html.)

The majority of U.S. steam electric generation involves fossil fuels burned to heat a boiler for steam. The share of capital costs are typically:

- 44% for electricity production
- 22% for transmission
- 34% local distribution

The shares of operating cost are typically:

- 89% production and fuel
- 3% transmission
- 8% local distribution

Gas can also be used to run a turbine with the heated air running the turbine rather than heating water. Although this takes less capital, it is typically less fuel efficient. The efficiency of the process is typically 25% for the gas turbine instead of the 35% efficiency of steam. Combined-cycle, which takes the exhaust from the gas turbine and also uses it to generate steam, can raise efficiencies to more than 40%.

Examples of Electricity Restructuring

One of the early moves toward restructuring electricity markets in the United States, PURPA, allowed small producers using renewables and combined heat and power facilities to access the grid. The Energy Policy Act of 1992 opened up the wholesale market even further in the United States.

Freed (1997) has summarized restructuring in the United Kingdom, Norway, Sweden, and New Zealand—all of which were early entrants into electricity restructuring. Their changes have been significant over time, and all programs have provided lessons for later restructuring efforts. The latter three are unusual for industrial countries because more than half their generation capacity is hydro, not fossil fuels. Because inexpensive fuel prices result from hydro, these countries have reasonably cheap electricity prices, though they have relatively high electricity taxes. (Table 5–1.)

Table 5–1 Electricity Prices and Taxes

	New Zealand		Norway		Sweden		U.K.		U.S.*
	Price $/kWh	Tax %	Price $/kWh	Tax %	Price $/kWh	Tax %	Price $/kWh	Tax %	Price $/kWh
	2002	2002	2002	2002	1997	1997	2000	2000	2002
Industrial	0.033	0.0	0.027	19.4	0.034	0.0	0.055	0.0	0.049
Household	0.058	11.1	3.202	37.1	0.064	36.4	0.108	4.8	0.084

Note: *Tax % unavailable for the U.S.
Source: IEA, *Energy Prices and Taxes*, 1st Quarter 2002, Converted to U.S. $ using annual exchanges rates from the Federal Reserve Bank of New York as compiled by the Nebraska Department of Economic Development at http://international.neded.org/exchrate.htm

Total trade in electricity for these for countries (Table 5–2) represents a higher proportion of consumption in Norway and Sweden, which are in the Scandinavian power pool with Denmark and Finland, but is non-existent for isolated New Zealand.

Each of these four countries began its deregulation under a different set of circumstances.

Table 5–2 Electricity Trade in TWh, 2000

Trade With	Norway				Sweden					U.K.
	Denm.	Finl.	Sweden	Russia	Denm.	Finl.	Germ.	Norway	Poland	France
Imports	0.15	0.17	0.92	0.24	1.62	0.83	0.08	15.74	0.05	14.3
Exports	4.63	0.13	15.74	0.00	3.39	8.23	0.66	0.92	0.43	0.13

Notes: Denm. = Denmark, Finl = Finland, Germ. = Germany
Source: IEA, *Electricity Information*, 2002.

United Kingdom

U.K. electricity restructuring began with the Electricity Act of 1983, aimed at the three vertically integrated national companies in Northern Ireland, Scotland, and England and Wales. England and Wales are connected by a high voltage direct current (HVDC) link and have seen the most extensive reforms. The Act was part of the Thatcher revolution to remove government controls and ownership and to move toward a more competitive environment.

The Electricity Act sought to eschew rate of return regulation, direct government control, and monopoly in the electricity market. IPPs were allowed open access to the national grid with their power purchased by the Central Electric Generating Board (CEGB) at avoided costs. However, CEGB's low interest rate (5% real) kept IPPs from entering.

Prior to restructuring, the English & Welsh electricity supply industry (ESI) had a publicly owned CEGB with a vertically integrated monopoly over generation and transmission. CEGB supplied 12 area boards that held local monopolies over distribution. Both CEGB and the area boards were allowed to pass on costs to captive consumers. ESI's mandate was to operate for the public good with autonomy over the electricity industry. However, it was often called upon to alter plans in the interest of wider economic policy, including reducing price increases to lower inflation, ordering plants ahead of time to stimulate employment, limiting gas use (because it was considered a premium fuel), buying British nuclear generators to support the local nuclear industry, and supporting the local coal industry. Since it was unable to keep a lid on investment costs, CEGB power stations took longer to build with costs up to 100% higher than similar privately owned systems.

In 1988, the government began its massive restructuring with a two-year goal to set up a structure for privatization along with accompanying regulatory and licensing schemes. It sought to protect its nuclear industry and have a successful public share offering synonymous with rising electricity supply industry share prices. It proposed a horizontal and vertical de-integration of the industry. The area boards, called Regional Electricity Companies (RECs), would each be sold off intact. CEGB would be split into three companies. The National Grid Company (NGC) owned by the RECs would operate the high-voltage transmission grid and a new power pool.

On April 1, 1990, called Vesting Day, generation went to two new companies, National Power and PowerGen, except for pumped storage, which went to NGC's First Hydro subsidiary. Nuclear power went to the larger of the two companies, National Power. Its size was thought to enable it to absorb this higher cost portion of the industry but the economics of the nuclear facilities were weak from higher private sector discount rates and uncertainty about possible liabilities and decommissioning costs. This led the government to require distributors to buy a certain percent of electricity not produced by fossil fuel through a non-fossil fuel obligation (NFFO). Nuclear power also received support from a 10% fossil fuel levy (FFL) on power sales. Nuclear power was ultimately not privatized but transferred to a new state-owned entity called Nuclear Electric.

The power pool was to have been based on bidding from both sides of the market to construct demand and supply schedules. However, because of software constraints prior to Vesting Day, CEGB's one-sided dispatching algorithm was used. The first bidders in the pool were Power Gen, National Power, National Grid Company, Eléctricité de France (EdF) and the Scottish generators. In this process, demand by half-hour periods is forecast from models, while suppliers bid their marginal costs. From the cost bids, a system marginal cost is constructed. Dispatch is then made based on the marginal costs and transmission constraints.

For example, suppose that forecast demand is 100 kW for the next hour. There are bids from five generators as follows:

- National Power bids $0.05 per kWh for 75 kWh
- Power Gen bids $0.06 per kWh for 25 kWh
- The Scottish utility bids $0.07 per kWh for 50 kWh
- EdF bids $0.075 per kWh for 10 kWh
- National Grid bids $0.08 per kWh for 50 kWh

There is a current transmission capacity constraint of 65 kW from National Power to market but no other constraints. In this case you would dispatch 65 kW from National Power, 25 kW from Power Gen, and 10 kW from the Scottish utility. The System Marginal Price (SMP) for this case is $0.07. All generators who bid SMP or lower will be paid the pool purchase price (PPP) equal to this SMP plus a capacity charge (CC). The CC signals how much need there is for new generation capacity.

Demanders pay the pool-selling price (PSP) equal to PPP plus an uplift charge. The uplift charge is used to recover costs from unforeseen transmission constraints and demand forecast errors. For example, if a plant is dispatched 10 kW, but there is no market for the power, the plant must still be paid.

Since Vesting Day, more than a dozen new generators have come on the market. About half are owned by generators that already existed and the rest by new companies. Most of the new generators are affiliated with the RECS, which are allowed to self-generate up to 15% of their power needs. Much of the new capacity is provided with combined-cycle gas turbines (CCGT). This flurry of construction has been dubbed the dash for gas.

The Director General (DG) is a regulator who heads up the Office of Electricity Regulation (Offer). His task is to make sure demand is satisfied, encourage competition, protect customer interests, issue licenses to generators and RECs, and regulate transmission and distribution using the price-cap methodology. The price-cap(RPI-X) is the rate of inflation(RPI) minus the target productivity factor X. X is reset only every four to five years. This lag is to encourage utilities to reduce costs, since they are allowed to keep any savings greater than X. Utilities are free to choose how to reduce costs. Disagreements between the regulator and regulated companies are referred to the Monopolies and Mergers Commission (MMC).

At Vesting Day, large customers with maximum demand exceeding 1 MW (30% of total demand) could disengage from local RECs and choose their supplier. More than half did so. Beginning in April 1994, consumers with maximum demand more than 100 kW (20% of total demand) could choose their supplier. To reduce market power, the DG ordered National Power and PowerGen to dispose of about 15% of their capacity, and the DG has discouraged attempts of generators to buy RECs. First Hydro was also sold to a new generator. In 1995, the National Power Grid was separated from the RECs. Full retail competition was implemented in 1998.

The older Magnox nuclear plants in England and Wales have remained in government ownership, while the newer plants in England and Scotland were privatized in 1996 and came together in 1998 to form British Energy Corporation. Since 1995, there has been a flurry of takeovers and mergers of the RECs, largely by British and American interests. During 2001, electricity distribution and supply were disintegrated into separate companies as required by the Utility Act of 2001. Electricity price was totally deregulated in April, 2001. In July of 2002, German based E.on took over Powergen to become the largest energy service provider in the world.

New Zealand

A second early electricity industry restructuring took place in New Zealand. It too arose out of a desire to reduce government involvement in the economy. In the 1980s, New Zealand went from one of the most heavily regulated industrial economies in the world to one of the least. The impetus for this change was a weak economy, unemployment, inflation, and balance of payments problems. The major reforms began with the 1986 Commerce Act aimed at the removal of price controls and making SOEs, such as electricity, as efficient as they would be in the private sector. It prohibited activities that restricted competition.

Prior to 1987, the central government owned most of the generation and transmission system with local governmental Electricity Supply Authorities (ESAs) owning local distribution and retailing. In 1987, New Zealand's government chose not to privatize but to corporatize government generation and transmission into the Electricity Corporation of New Zealand (ECNZ). The government owned the corporate shares. ECNZ had to pay taxes and was to be governed by commercial rather than political considerations. Others were allowed to enter generation but transmission was still considered a natural monopoly. However, excess capacity prevented new generation from coming on line for many years. Transpower was set up in 1988 as a subsidiary of ECNZ to run the transmission grid.

The Electricity Act of 1992 required information disclosure and removed the monopoly franchises, first for small and then for large customers of the 61 ESAs. The ESAs were allowed to compete with each other. Obligation to supply was to be phased out, and electricity distribution was to be ring fenced from other activities. (Ring fencing is to have separate financial accounts for distribution and other non-regulated activities. It is required to prevent a regulated sector from subsidizing a non-regulated sector of the business.) Appointed directors replaced elected officials to make the ESAs more commercial. Community trusts for each ESA, the directors, and the Ministry of Energy were to decide the future ownership of the ESAs. Most distribution companies are still owned by trusts, and none have yet been privatized.

In 1993, the Electricity Marketing Company (EMCO), now owned by Rand Merchant Bank and called M-co, was set up by the electricity industry to develop a market for wholesale trading. In 1994, Transpower was set up as a separate crown corporation with requirements for disclosure. In 1996, a competitive wholesale market commenced. EMCO, as market manager, set prices to clear the market, and Transpower dispatched the power. As in the U.K. case, the marginal price is paid to all bidders who are dispatched into the market. Nodal pricing is practiced, in which half-hour prices are made at 244 grid connection points or nodes. These prices, which reflect available electricity, transmission losses, and grid constraints, should provide signals to potential investors. There was no price cap and prices were based on bids and offers. The government was no longer responsible for setting bulk tariff. Contact Energy was broken off from ECNZ to provide more competition in generation, and restrictions were placed on ECNZ until its market share fell below 45%.

The Electricity Industry Reform Act of 1998 mandated that distribution be separated from retailing and generation. It also allowed for the regulation of prices to domestic and rural customers. In 1999 the government sold Contact Energy to the private sector, ECNZ was broken into three companies, and EMCO was sold to the Rand Merchant Bank.

The winter of 2001 (June, July, August) was one of the coldest and driest on record, which led to a reduction of hydropower production. At the same time, demand was high, which brought price increases. This led the government to study whether it should require generators to offer hedge contracts (fixed price contracts). As of May 2003, a commission has been formed that can require generators to offer long-term hedge contracts.

Regulation in New Zealand has not taken the form of price caps as in England and Wales but has been light-handed, with the Commerce Commission seeking to restrict anti-competitive behavior by being allowed to award damages or implement temporary price controls. In addition, information disclosure rules require that information such as prices, energy and line charges, and condition of supply be made available to customers and investors. More information must be divulged by the natural monopoly sectors—transmission and distribution—than the more competitive—generation and retailing sectors.

Norway

Norway's electricity reforms began in 1991 and have not been accompanied by the same degree of economic reform as in either England or New Zealand. However, they are probably only second to the United Kingdom in Europe in their moves to promote more competition. They also occurred in a very different setting. Ninety-nine percent of Norway's electricity is hydropower, with more than 90 producers and 200 distributors/suppliers who retail electricity. Ownership is mixed, allowing yardstick comparison between public and private companies. Thus, the private firms, which had to compete, or other best practice firms were the yardstick and public performance was compared to these benchmark firms. If the public sector did not do as well as the benchmark firms, they were pressured to do better.

The largest generator, the Norwegian State Power Board (Statkraft), produces 30% of the total. Another 30% is produced by county and municipal governments. The second largest generator, Norsk Hydro, is a private company. Between 80% and 90% of distribution is by publicly owned companies. Half have long-term contracts with wholesalers, and half are vertically integrated utilities.

Prior to 1991, Statkraft was part of a government ministry. It was the price leader, owning 80% of the transmission network and maintaining an import-export monopoly. Price regulation was light, with prices approved by Parliament under a principle of marginal cost pricing with a rate of return constraint. There was a 20-year-old power pool operated by the Norwegian Power Pool (NPP). The market was voluntary, with buy and sell bids used to set the price on a weekly basis. Statkraft voluntarily acted as swing producer to balance supply and demand when the market did not clear.

During the reorganization, Statkraft was incorporated as a generating company although the government still guaranteed its debt, and the transmission network was transferred to a new SOE, Statnett. Its subsidiary, Statnett Marked, now runs the spot and an up to six-month futures market, and it can lease the part of the grid it does not own. Bids and offers are aggregated, and prices in the spot market are made for the following day at hourly intervals, determining a system price. If there are transport capacity constraints, separate prices are computed within respective areas based on the local bids and offers. This will lower price in the surplus areas and raise the price in deficit areas.

Since there is third-party access (TPA) for all networks, anyone is allowed to buy in the spot market—even households. Generation must be ring fenced from distribution for any vertically integrated utilities. Brokers, traders, and domestic importers and exporters can bid into the pool. The Norwegian Electricity Council and the Norwegian Price and Cartel Board grant licenses for operation, provide regulatory oversight of the transmission and distribution networks, set principles for transmission and distribution access charges, investigate monopoly power, and mediate network price disputes. Network services (considered the natural monopoly element of the system) are under income frame regulation, which is a combination of rate of return, price cap, and yardstick regulation.

Sweden

With the energy intensity of Swedish industry and high per-capita electricity consumption, the Swedish government felt that electricity restructuring would stimulate a weak economy, and adopted a competitive electricity market in 1992.

Sweden had a much more concentrated industry than Norway. Prior to restructuring, the Swedish State Power Board, Vattenfall, a state-owned limited liability company, produced half of Swedish power and owned and operated the high-voltage transmission grid. The next nine largest companies produced another 40%. The two largest—Vattenfall and Sydkraft—dominated the import-export trade. Ownership of distribution was mixed, with 60% municipally owned, 22% privately owned, 14% owned by Vattenfall, and 4% owned by cooperatives. Sweden's power pool was less open than Norway's and was more like an exchange, with bilateral contracts. Prices in the pool were set halfway between the marginal cost of the buying and the selling firms. Weak price regulation existed. Vattenfall was required to break even using the government bond rate.

In generation, Vattenfall was the price leader and yardstick. Competition pressured private firms to keep prices in line. Yardstick competition was also used to keep distributor prices in line between areas and municipalities, which were not permitted to earn a profit on electricity distribution.

With reform, generation was separated from the transmission and international interconnection network. These network activities were transferred from Vattenfall to a new SOE, Svenska Kraftnät, with more transparent network prices. Wholesale and retail wheeling were allowed. In 1994, the government slowed liberalization over concerns that it would discourage a planned nuclear plant phase-out and increase rural prices. Liberalization was resumed in 1996 with third-party access to the network and Sweden joining Norway's power pool, Nord Pool. Nord Pool is half-owned by Statnett of Norway and half by Svenska Kraftnät. Nord Pool included Finland in 1998, part of Denmark in 1999, and the rest of Denmark in 2000.

Local distribution companies (LDCs) have an obligation to supply existing customers but customers can switch suppliers. Distribution is ring fenced from transmission and generation, and there are no formal price controls. Since reform, there has been consolidation among distributors, with large local and foreign power producers buying municipal distributors and municipals combining into intermunicipals. For more information on power pools see http://www.analyticalq.com/energy/powerpools.htm

Freed (1997) evaluated these reforms along the following five lines:

1. efficiency in investments
2. efficiency in pricing
3. market power and barriers to entry
4. regulation
5. ownership

Cost overruns in investment were prevalent in government-owned utilities in New Zealand and the United Kingdom prior to reform but were relatively rare in Sweden and Norway due to their mix of public and private ownership and yardstick comparisons across utilities. Overruns in the former countries occurred because of government-designated contractors and design. For example, when Sweden allowed nuclear generators to choose their own technology, they chose boiling water and pressurized water reactors and experienced low-cost nuclear power relative to the United Kingdom and its Magnox plants.

Other cost overruns included the use of public rather than private sector discount rates and cost pass-through that left all the risk with captive customers. With privatization, these reasons have been eliminated, as demonstrated by the prevalence of new U.K. generators choosing combined-cycle gas turbines, which can be built in less than two years, over coal or nuclear.

Efficient electricity pricing requires that prices reflect costs by time and location to send appropriate signals to producers and consumers. Generally, costs are higher for sparsely populated areas than for those that are more densely populated, for smaller users than for larger consumers, and for peak use than for off-peak consumption. However, prices have not often reflected such costs. Prior to deregulation, cross-subsidization was prevalent in three of the four countries. New Zealand subsidized household and rural consumers from business and urban consumers. Norway subsidized electricity-intensive heavy industry such as aluminum production. The United Kingdom subsidized the largest consumers. With competition, third-party access, and ring fencing, it is hard to maintain such cross-subsidization. There is evidence that prices in New Zealand and the United Kingdom have been realigned.

In the past, prices were not subject to competition and were usually set at average costs. Half-hour to hourly bids also mean that, at least for large customers, where hourly metering costs are not prohibitive, prices should reflect marginal costs. For example, hourly metering costs in the United Kingdom are estimated at £400 per customer per year (Green 1995). In principle, prices should send the appropriate signals to producers and consumers about when and where to consume electricity or put in new capacity. However, in practice there has been concern in the United Kingdom whether there will be enough mid-merit, also called shoulder, and peaking capacity, since all new capacity has been baseload.

Efficiency in the electric power market after the reforms is contingent upon creating competition in those sectors that are not to be subject to regulation. Free entry or at least contestability is needed for a market to be competitive. Barriers to entry and market power remain a concern in all four of the early reforming countries. Excess capacity and the dominance of hydro generation in New Zealand by ECNZ and Contact led to barriers to entry in that market. National Power and PowerGen in England and Wales have manipulated SMP by bidding their low-cost plants at low levels to ensure they run and bidding their high-cost plants at costs higher than marginal costs to ensure high SMPs to earn rents on all their production. Governments have responded in both of these cases by further breaking up company size to improve competition.

One simple measure of concentration in an industry is Herfindahl's index of concentration:

$$H = \Sigma_{i=1}^{n} \alpha_i$$

where

α_i is market share of the ith producer

If there is one participant or a monopoly in the industry, its market share is 100%. Its $\alpha=1$ and $H = 1^2 = 1$. If there are two equal sized firms in the industry, then market share is $\frac{1}{2}$ each and $H = (1/2)^2 + (1/2)^2 = \frac{1}{2}$.

Perfect competition would be represented by:

$$\lim_{a \to 0} H = 0$$

Thus the closer to zero, the more competition we would expect, and the closer to one, the more market power we would expect.

With recent divestitures in England and Wales, H has fallen from 0.3 to 0.16, which would be roughly equivalent to going from three to six equal-sized firms. Vattenfall's large share of the Swedish electricity market (H equals roughly 0.33) and its virtual monopoly on gas imports have been a cause of concern and will need monitoring.

Norway would seem to have the structure most conducive to competition, but even Norway has environmental barriers to entry for new hydro power plants and production externalities for new entrants on water courses with existing plants. These externalities exist because one plant's use of water output will affect that of another plant downstream. There are ways for distribution in vertically integrated utilities to subsidize production, and there has been occasional collusion and supply manipulation in the power pool.

Regulatory instability can also bar entry because companies unsure of what a regulator will do may hesitate to enter a market. Here the Swedish policy to phase out their nuclear plants earlier than their expected life is a source of instability, since the government could change its mind, leaving existing capacity higher than anticipated. The United Kingdom, having the DG as sole regulator, means a director change could lead to major consequences in the regulatory regime.

Cross-country trade can be a source of new competition and barriers to such trade seem to be falling in all four of the countries except New Zealand, where geography prohibits international trade. Nord Pool is tying four Scandinavian countries ever closer; linkages within the United Kingdom and between the United Kingdom and Ireland and between England and France are increasing.

Deregulation requires that regulation be revamped for the natural monopoly elements of the system—transmission and distribution—and that regulators keep a watchful eye on generation and retailing where competition is thought to be the most economically efficient form of organization. This requires ring fencing of competitive operations from the natural monopoly elements and an independent regulator with access to current and accurate information to make sure that no one is cheating. Regulatory approaches vary and it remains to be seen whether the U.K.'s price cap, Norway and Sweden's yardstick performance-based regulation, or New Zealand's light-handed approach will prove the most effective.

Ownership is another issue to be considered when deregulating the electricity supply industry. Three types of ownership have been prominent around the world:

1. direct government ownership, usually run by a ministry, often with a mix of political and economic goals

2. a government-owned corporation, where the company has separate accounts but all shares are owned by the government

3. private ownership

Each of our four countries started from a different point, and each has followed a different pattern of change. All now allow private ownership. The United Kingdom and New Zealand started at direct government ownership. The United Kingdom attempted to jump from direct government ownership to private ownership as quickly as possible. New Zealand gradually moved to a government-owned corporation and then toward private ownership in generation. Norway was a mix of the first and third choices and Sweden a mix of all three. Norway corporatized its state-owned generation and transmission but there has not been a strong push to privatize at any level. Sweden has seen a bit of privatization with large power companies, both domestic and foreign, purchasing municipal and pension-owned distribution systems.

In principle, publicly owned companies should perform as well as privately owned companies. However, it appears that they often do not. For example, Kumbhakar & Hjalmarsson (1994) found private electricity distributors to be significantly more economically efficient than municipalities. There are a variety of reasons why publicly owned companies may be less efficient:

- the government may guarantee their debt, providing escape hatches
- combining ownership and regulation may create a conflict of interest
- a public rather than private rate of return may distort investment and production decisions
- procurement and hiring rules may be more stringent than for the private sector
- there may be added political objectives not faced by private sector plants
- there may be less incentive for profit maximization and cost minimization than in the private sector because of the lack of discipline from shareholder pressure and the stock and debt markets

Although the countries profiled in this chapter show early representative examples of restructuring, they are not unique. Electricity restructuring is ongoing in many areas—including the United States. In 1996, the U.S. Federal Energy Regulatory Commission (FERC) issued Orders 888 and 889 to encourage competition in the interstate wholesale power market by requiring nondiscriminatory open access. This requirement has spawned activity at the state level, which is summarized in Figure 5–1.

Fig. 5–1 Deregulation in the U.S. Electricity Sector, 2003

Source: US DOE/EIA "Status of State Electric Industry Restructuring Activity as of February 2003" http://www.eia.doe.gov/cneaf/electricty/chg_str/regmap.html

The European Union (EU) issued an Electricity Directive in 1996 requiring full competition in generation by 2003, with some exceptions. It requires consumer choice of supplier, unbundling, and breaking up of then-current monopolies. Deregulation is also required for new membership into the EU. The goal in deregulation is integration of power markets into an overall single market. Within the continental EU, Germany has probably moved the furthest toward unregulated markets; France had probably advanced the least.

There are no formal EU requirements for real (power pools or exchanges) or financial markets (futures and options), but a number of them have been developing. Nord Pool is the oldest international trading platform having started in 1996. It offers both spot and futures trading. (See www.nordpool.com for more information.) The U.K. Power Exchange was launched in May of 2000 at www.ukpx.com. Germany had two spot power exchanges—Leipzig and EEX—both launched in June of 2000. They merged in 2002 and began offering futures trading in July of 2002 at www.eex.de. Scandinavia, the United Kingdom, and Germany, the three most open electricity markets in Europe, account for more than 90% of the power trading in the EU. Other exchanges include Amsterdam Power Exchange launched in May of 1999, www.apx.nl, Austrian Power Exchange launched in March of 2002, www.exaa.at, and France's Powernext launched in November of 2001, www.powernext.fr.

California

The most notorious restructuring has been in California, the fourth largest economy in the world. Throughout the 1990s, its economy grew quite rapidly with the boom in information technologies. In 1996, at the beginning of the restructuring, California electricity prices were one-third above the U.S. average and among the highest in the country.

To help correct high rates, which were at least partially blamed on rate-of-return regulation, California passed a law to go into effect during March 1998. Its goal was model four from earlier in this chapter—beginning with competition in the wholesale market followed by full retail competition after investor owned utilities had divested themselves of generating capacity.

With restructuring and opening up generation to new producers and consumer choice, existing higher cost plants are driven out of business. Since generators put in these higher cost assets (called stranded costs) in good faith with a guaranteed rate of return, they asked to be compensated for these now non-competitive assets. Each state that restructures must decide who pays the costs for these stranded assets—generators, rate payers, or tax payers.

In California, stranded costs were handled through a Competitive Transition Charge (CTC) charged on all retail service accompanied by a rate freeze for larger consumers and a 10% rate reduction on small consumers until the stranded costs were recovered. With the rate reduction, few small consumers switched suppliers. Utilities were allowed to fund the freeze and rate reduction by tax free bonds, which means that the interest on the bonds are not taxable and are being subsidized by the government. To see how other states are handling stranded costs go to http://www.eia.doe.gov/electricity/chg_str_issu/chg_str_iss_rpt/table17.htm.

The California law required mandatory nondiscriminatory open access to transmission and distribution with the existing utilities owning the grid. The California Power Exchange (CalPX), formed for the wholesale power market, was run by a nonprofit independent system operator (ISO), which was in turn governed by representatives of stakeholders including customers, government, independent power producers (IPPs), and environmentalists. Since stakeholders managed, rather than owned, the asset, they battled over distribution instead of wealth generation. The utilities originally had to buy from the exchange on the day-ahead spot market and they could not enter into long-term contracts. The IPPs could use the exchange on a voluntary basis.

All worked well until June 2000, when shortages began to appear. Between 1990 and 1999 electricity demand had increased 11.3%, while aggregate capacity had fallen by 1.7%. Environmental agitation had caused early decommissioning of two nuclear generators and no new power plant applications were filed from 1994–1998. Power production increased in California by using existing capacity more intensively with the shortfall of power, as in the past, made up by imports. Natural gas provided more than a third of California's power.

This was an economical arrangement from 1985 to 1999, since U.S. gas prices fell in real terms. Gas demand remained relatively flat from 1995 to 1999 and gas stocks were relatively low entering the winter of 1999–2000, which turned out to be cold. An explosion on the El Paso natural gas line from Texas to California further exacerbated the gas shortage. Spot gas prices, which had been around $2.25 per Mcf, shot up to $10 per Mcf by late 2000. (A $1 per Mcf increase in natural gas price translates into roughly a $10 per MWh increase in electricity prices.) *Wash trading*, in which a company buys and sells power simultaneously to the same client, is suspected to have increased electric prices as well. Another source of cost increase was the cost of NO_x emission credits in the Los Angeles basin. As fossil fuel generation increased, the permits increased from $6 to $45 per pound, adding almost another $40 to the cost per MWh.

Drier weather and salmon management restrictions reduced hydropower in California and the Pacific Northwest. The hot summer of 2000 increased power needs.

At the same time, there were transmission constraints from neighboring regions as well as constraints between Northern and Southern California. Forest fires reduced transmission capacity in Western States and schedule outages in British Columbia reduced power exports to California. Such constraints take time to ease as it takes six years to install new transmission lines in California—three years to plan and site and three years to build. Also, more than half of California's plants are more than 20 years old. During 2000 when these older plants were being run hard, sometimes up to 10 GW of power was out during high demand periods

With high demand and restricted supply, wholesale prices, normally set by the cost of the marginal producer in a competitive market, shot up. Capacity constraints gave more market power to the generators allowing them to set prices even higher than the cost of the marginal producer. At the same time retail prices remained capped. In addition, generators who weren't being paid stopped deliveries leaving a mismatch between the retail and wholesale market. The California Public Utility Commission (CPUC), which regulates the California electricity market, put on a wholesale price cap of $500 per MWh at the end of June 2000, then reduced it to $250 by August.

Brownouts and blackouts were the result. In December of 2000, the U.S. Department of Energy ordered some generators and marketers to supply power to the California market if there was a danger of an outage, and FERC eliminated the requirement that the three large utilities buy their power on the spot market through the CalPX, which subsequently ceased operation in January of 2001. By January of 2001, wholesale power prices in California remained higher than those elsewhere in the country. They were $313 MWh in California compared to $74 in the New England Power Pool (NEPOOL), $53 in the New York Power Pool (NYPP), and $39 in the Pennsylvania, New Jersey, and Maryland power pool (PJM).

When the lights went out, blame started to fly. Californian Governor Davis blamed deregulation and greedy power generators and traders. The conservatives blamed environmentalists and antigrowth groups, the prohibition of long-term contracts, and a centralized spot market that discouraged investment. The power generators blamed CPUC, residential customers blamed the government, and the CPUC blamed the Federal Energy Regulatory Commission (FERC), which did not allow utilities to obtain capacity at avoided cost.

So why were prices so much higher in California than in the rest of the country? One important factor was differences in fuel costs. In California, gas fired plants were approaching half of the generation capacity, whereas in NEPOOL, NYPP, and PJM the share was only 19%, 18%, and 4%, respectively. The much higher dependence on nuclear and coal for East Coast generators helped shield them from the gas price run ups. Further, they allowed fuel cost pass through provisions, so prices went up rather than the lights going out.

The three Eastern power pools had installed capacity requirements. For example NYPP had a penalty of three times the cost of peaking capacity, if peak power needs were not met. Thus, utilities in these power pools had strong incentives to make sure there was enough peaking capacity. The result of such regulation is likely to make average prices higher and peak prices lower but may be inefficient since peak supply is increased rather than reducing peak demand.

California and Ontario both allowed peak wholesale price changes to ration demand with no capacity requirements. However, California subsequently put on price caps in the wholesale market. Further, retail prices were also capped and there was no peak load pricing. Thus, except briefly for SDG&E's customers, consumers did not see any power price increases during the periods of shortages. Other states also have had shortages, but of a lesser magnitude and they have allowed rates to go up. To illustrate the two different cases—one where price is allowed to increase and the other where it is constrained and shortages develop, see Figure 5–2.

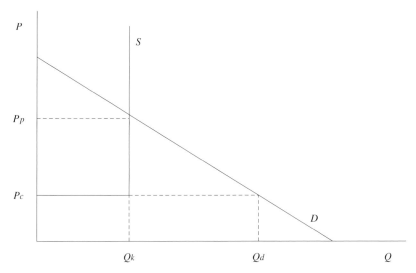

Fig. 5–2 Peak Load Demand and Supply

Suppose the diagram represents the summer peak load market in California. Assume supply is perfectly elastic until capacity is reached at Q_k. If price is allowed to allocate this capacity, the price will jump up to P_p. There will be no shortages but existing generators will make rents of $P_p - P_c$. Thus, there will be a transfer of wealth from consumers to producers. However, if the price is constrained at P_c, there will be excess demand of $Q_d - Q_k$. Forced blackouts will occur, and there will be political fights over the outputs.

Although in this case, there will be no wealth transfer, it sends the wrong signals to both consumers, who will try to over consume, and to producers, who won't see the advantage of putting in capacity with high fixed and low marginal cost that will only operate during peak periods. An alternative is to put a price control on existing capacity but not on new capacity. This gives more incentive to invest but signals that producers won't receive rents during shortages as in a normal non-regulated market.

If prices are allowed to run up and a region is interconnected to other regions, power will flow into the shortage region. Let's see how prices should be related across markets. The U.S. lower 48 is divided into 10 National Electricity Reliability Councils (NERC regions). For more information and a map of the NERC regions see http://www.nerc.com/regional/. They are nonprofit organizations responsible for overall security and planning for the grid within their regions. They are connected to adjacent regions for power trading and each of these regions is also included in three larger regions with more limited connections between them—the Western Interconnect, the Texas Interconnect, and the Eastern Interconnect. The Interconnects also contain parts of Canada, Alaska, and Mexico. The Texas

Interconnect, only connected to the other two interconnects by high voltage direct current, also known as the Electricity Reliability Council of Texas (ERCOT), does not include any other state within its confines and, hence, is free of Federal regulation within its borders.

With connections between the reliability regions, prices should be the same after adjustments for transportation costs unless there are transportation constraints. For example, suppose that wholesale electric power prices are $P_e = \$150$ MWh in California but only $P_e = \$75$ in ERCOT with transport costs and losses from ERCOT to California of $10. If you are buying in the wholesale market in California, your cost of power is $150, but if you buy from ERCOT it will cost you $75 + $10. Since it is cheaper to buy from ERCOT and transport it, a buyer will want to buy from ERCOT instead of California. If the market is open and there are no transport constraints, consumers will buy from ERCOT. As more power is bought from ERCOT and less from California producers, the price will increase in ERCOT and decrease in California. The power purchases will continue to shift until the cost of purchasing from California or from ERCOT will become the same on the margin or when $P_e + \$10 = P_c$.

Throughout 2001, both the CPUC and FERC moved to ease the shortage situation. In the first part of the year, CPUC allowed retail rate increases for PG&E and SCE and the State of California's Department of Water was authorized to sign long-term power contracts with generators for resale to cash strapped PG&E and SCE. These long-term contracts allocate the risk from consumers to generators. Bids for non-peak 3- to 10-year contracts were expected to be $55 per MWh but were almost $70 per MWh. Peak price bids were around $250 per MWh with exact contracted prices not known. These prices may be higher for the state because of risk that the state may renege on the contract, if electricity prices fall later.

In addition, bills were passed to shorten permitting times for new power plants in California and ease environmental requirements. Another move that put the state squarely in the power business was the purchase of SCE's transmission grid to ease SCE's financial difficulties. This move, along with subsidies for energy conservation, the authority to build and operate electricity facilities, and the suspension of retail choice, signaled that California's power reform was far from turning the market over to the private sector.

Meanwhile in the first half of 2001, FERC improved market signals in the wholesale power market by allowing more fuel cost pass through, better data reporting, simplified regulation for the wholesale power market, and easier permitting for new natural gas transport projects. In addition, the Western Area Power Administration (managed by DOE) is increasing electricity transportation capacity on Path 15 from Southern to Northern California.

Although the summer of 2001 was as hot as the summer of 2000, peak demands were approximately 10% less than for the previous summer from higher prices, media attention, and a weaker economy. By October of 2001, 2236 MW of new generation capacity had become available and the Bonneville Power Administration had increased hydro output. By July of 2003, 4470 MW of new generation capacity was available. This evidence suggests that the crisis has been averted at least for the time being.

So is government ownership and regulation the answer? Some say it is and cite the evidence of the Los Angeles Department of Water and Power, which is a government owned utility. It did not suffer the shortages of the other three large investor owned utilities. However, it was not required to buy on the spot market, and it had excess coal-fired capacity and hydropower under long-term contracts, which it sold on the spot market, using the profits to lower rates to existing customers. Also, the state of California now has long-term power under contracts, which helped increase power supplies in the summer of 2001. However, one can question the wisdom of those contracts, which were locked in at high rates in a crisis setting. By late fall of 2001 California was beginning to have power surpluses. And indeed, California as of August 2002 was trying to renegotiate these high priced power contracts claiming the prices set were "unjust and unreasonable." As of June 2003, a number of these contracts had been renegotiated.

Economists are inclined to dislike government ownership and recommend letting the market operate except where market failures are persistent. They generally favor eliminating price caps for generating, provided there are not barriers to entry and providing for real time metering, so that the market provides consumers and producers with the proper signals. However, markets will not work if regulatory restraints and uncertainty prevent entry and exit from the industry and proper price signals from being sent. Although both transmission and distribution are thought to be natural monopolies, the operation of the grid should be returned to the utilities and governed by economic principals rather than political wrangling. Here open access and some sort of rate control for grid usage is likely to be warranted.

Summary

Natural monopoly considerations have led most governments to either regulate or produce electricity themselves in vertically integrated monopolies. However, regulatory inefficiency, government inefficiency, changes in economies of scale, and changes in market size have led many governments to consider restructuring their markets. Industrial countries are often doing so in the interests of reducing electricity prices and promoting economic efficiency, whereas developing countries are often doing so to attract much needed capital to provide adequate electricity for their population.

A number of issues must be considered when restructuring: where we allow competition, where we require regulation, allowed market structure, and ownership. We can allow competition at three levels.

1. We can allow new generators to enter the market for given distributors, which means the new suppliers have to have access to the distributors transmission network.

2. We can have a wholesale market that allows distributors to choose their supplier from across the entire gird and suppliers to choose their distributor from across the entire grid, which requires access to the entire transmission system. This level of competition requires some efficient way of pricing and dispatching electricity across the transmission grid such as a power pool and an independent system operator. It often allows large customers to bypass the distribution companies if they wish.

3. The most extensive form of competition is full retail competition, in which large and small consumers can choose suppliers. In such an environment, there needs to be open access to the distribution network as well as the transmission network. Thus, we need unbundling, in which a distributor can sell you power that includes distribution costs, or consumers can buy power from someone else and only pay distribution costs to the local distributor.

Five examples—the United Kingdom, New Zealand, Norway, Sweden, and California—show how restructuring evolves and how it depends on the political and economic climate within the country and the existing structure of the electricity supply industry. Each case is unique and there is as yet no compelling evidence on the optimal structure. There are, however, some common threads and lessons:

- transmission and distribution are often still considered natural monopolies with some sort of regulatory restraint or oversight
- price regulation may take varying forms—rate of return, price cap, light handed, and yardstick being the most prominent
- generators, marketers, and retailers are typically considered potentially competitive, and these are the areas gradually being opened up
- usually generation is opened up first
- with opening up, existing generators, which had been monopolies, often have a fair degree of market power. Such power has caused governments to intervene to promote more competition
- open access to transmission is used to allow generators, wholesalers, and retailers to compete

The extent of vertical integration is another important issue. With some parts of the supply chain competitive and other parts natural monopolies, it is pretty clear that the competitive activities should be ring fenced or otherwise separated from the monopoly portions. In our four examples, all have separated or ring-fenced various activities.

Ownership structure is a last important issue to be considered in restructuring. The three most prominent types of ownership are government ownership, a government-owned corporation, and private ownership. Some believe that a competitive model doesn't depend on ownership, but rather on the degree of competition at each stage of the supply chain. However, with a drive for economic efficiency, government ownership appears to be losing favor to government-owned corporations or privatization. Government-owned corporations are less economically efficient for several reasons:

- government debt guarantees provide barriers to exits
- public rather than private interest rates and required rates of return distort decisions
- political objectives may conflict with economic objectives
- without discipline from the market there is less incentive to maximize profits and minimize costs

Although the majority of economists would likely argue that private corporations are more economically efficient than government corporations, three of the four example countries have opted to not wholly privatize but to keep parts of their system as public corporations. Whether these will outperform the many utilities worldwide that are privatizing remains to be seen.

The California power crisis, in particular, provides us some interesting lessons. This extreme case with brownouts and blackouts gained world attention and probably slowed electricity reform in many countries. In California, power consumption increased over the course of the 1990s but capacity did not keep up. By the hot summer of 2000, there was not enough capacity to meet peak demand. High gas prices, high priced NO_x emission credits, dry weather that reduced hydro-power production, outages from old plants, difficulties in siting new plants, and transmission constraints all exacerbated the shortage and raised wholesale electricity prices dramatically. The three large investor owned utilities were required to buy power on the spot market where prices were not controlled and resell on the retail markets, where prices were controlled. This caused financial hardships for the IOUs and the bankruptcy of PG&E. Payment failures and wholesale price caps further aggravated the problem since the independent power producers did not want to deliver power to the IOUs.

The state eventually bought power on long-term contracts to resell to the IOUs, bought the transmission system of SCE, was authorized to build its own power projects, allowed retail price increases, promoted conservation efforts, and sped up the power project permitting. The federal government also moved to apply more economic principles to the wholesale market, require more information disclosure, simplify regulation for the wholesale power market, ease permitting for new natural gas transport projects, and increase transport capacity between Southern and Northern California. By the summer of 2001 the crisis had passed, electricity consumption was down despite a hot summer, and electricity production was up. By fall of that year, there were electricity surpluses in California. Capacity increases appear to be adequate to keep up with demand increases for the moment.

An important lesson from California is that provision must be made to ensure adequate capacity. If market prices are to allocate electricity and signal the need for more capacity, they must be allowed to do so. Prices should be varied by time of day to reflect the real level of scarcity. If prices are not to allocate electricity, then some other means must be developed to develop capacity requirements.

6 Monopoly, Dominant Firm, and OPEC

Go directly to jail. Do not pass go. Do not collect $200.

—From the game Monopoly created by
Charles Brace Darrow in 1931,
quoted from *Colombia World of Quotations*

Introduction

In chapter 3, we saw a perfectly competitive energy market with many small buyers and sellers taking the market price as given. The marginal cost curve is then the supply curve. In the absence of externalities, economists believe that such a market is efficient because it maximizes social welfare as measured by consumer plus producer surplus as shown in Figure 6–1.

Such a situation may approximately prevail in the coal market or in the market for windmills, but not in all energy and energy equipment markets. In chapter 4, we considered how electricity markets for many years were considered natural monopolies and typically regulated or government-owned. Now generation is considered amenable to competition and many countries are moving toward competition in this sector. Oil is another market where monopolies are found.

John D. Rockefeller developed the first monopoly out of the oil boom pandemonium that began with the initial U.S. oil strike in Titusville, Pennsylvania, in 1859. After establishing the Standard Oil Company in Cleveland, Ohio, in 1870, he proceeded to swallow up competitors or drive them out of business. By 1880, he controlled about 90% of the U.S. oil product market.

Rockefeller was followed by the "Seven Sisters," a term coined for the seven large Anglo-American multinational oil companies (Esso, Gulf, Texaco, Mobil, Socal, BP, and RD Shell), the Texas Railroad Commission, and, more recently, OPEC. All of these entities display examples of market power in the oil industry. Unlike the case for natural monopolies, these monopolies seem to wax and wane.

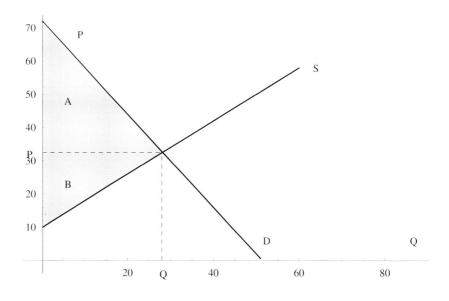

Fig. 6–1 Social Welfare in a Competitive Market

Note: A is consumer surplus in a competitive market, B is producer surplus in a competitive market, D is the demand curve, P is price, Q is quantity, and S is the market supply curve.

Monopoly Model

Let's see how monopolists can maximize profits with market power. We begin with the most extreme case, assuming one producer faces the whole market demand. Instead of competing, he picks the point on the demand curve that he likes the best, which maximizes his profits. Let the inverse demand curve be $P = P(Q)$ which slopes downward or $dP/dQ < 0$.

In other words, if you reduce quantity, you can sell at a higher price. Let the monopolist's output be Q and the monopolist's cost be TC(Q). We assume that TC slopes upward or $dTC/dQ > 0$, which means that marginal costs are positive, and $d^2TC/dQ^2 > 0$, which means that marginal costs are increasing. Remember from chapter 4 that monopolists' profits are total revenue minus total costs or:

$$\pi = P(Q)Q - TC(Q)$$

To maximize profits with respect to output, we take the first derivative of the function with respect to output and set it equal to zero. First order conditions for profit maximization are:

$$d\pi/dQ = P + (dP/dQ)^*Q - dTC/dQ = 0$$

As we saw in chapter 4, marginal revenue is the price plus the change in price resulting from selling additional units (dP/dQ) times the sales (Q). Thus, when we sell an additional unit, we get its price. However, we have to lower the price on all the previous units to sell more. The second expression shows the losses from the sales on these additional units.

The above expression can be written as:

$$\text{MR} - \text{MC} = 0 => \text{MR} = \text{MC.} \qquad\qquad (6.1)$$

Second order conditions confirm whether we have a maximum or not. Taking the derivative of Equation 6.1 with respect to Q we find:

$$dMR/dQ - dMC/dQ < 0 => \text{slope MR} < \text{slope of MC}$$

A useful result for monopoly, which relates price to the demand price elasticity, is easily developed. Start with the first order condition.

$$P + (dP/dQ)Q - MC = 0$$

Rearrange this expression to:

$$P[1 + (dP/dQ)(Q/P)] = MC$$

Note that the second expression inside the parentheses can be rewritten as:

$$(dP/dQ)(Q/P) = 1/\varepsilon_p$$

Thus:

$$P(1 + 1/\varepsilon_p) = MC$$

Since it is easier to relate to positive elasticities than negative elasticities, we take the absolute value of ε_p and change the + sign in the parenthesis to –, and then rearrange to get:

$$P = MC/(1 - 1/|\varepsilon_q|)$$

Suppose you are Rockefeller and you have managed to monopolize the petroleum product market. You face the linear demand in Figure 6–2. Marginal cost slopes up as assumed in the above example; marginal revenue is linear and twice as steep as the demand curve. Thus, it bisects the Q axis halfway between the intercept and where the demand crosses the Q axis.

In Figure 6–2, we can see that MR crosses MC at Q_m. It is easy to see that this is a maximum. If we produce less than Q_m, the marginal revenue is greater than marginal cost. Thus, it is profitable to produce extra units until we get to Q_m. After that point, the marginal cost, or the cost of an extra unit, is greater than the marginal revenue, and increasing production decreases profits. Also, since the slope of the marginal revenue is negative and the slope of the marginal cost is positive, the second order conditions are satisfied, which also confirms that we have a maximum. The price that relates to Q_m is P_m, which can be read off of the demand curve.

Economists include a normal rate of return as part of the economic costs. Thus, any excess of profits over economic costs is called monopoly profit. Monopoly profit can be shown in the above diagram as the area $(P_m - AC_m)Q_m$.

Now let's do a numerical example. Let the demand curve be:

$$Q_d = 97.56 - 1.22P$$

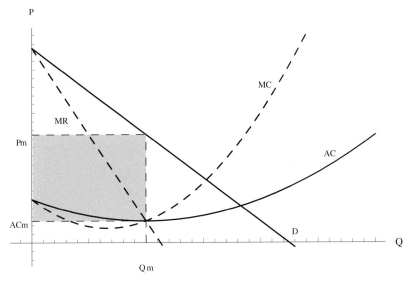

Fig. 6–2 Monopoly Producer

Note: AC = average cost, D = demand, MC = marginal cost, and MR = marginal revenue.

Q is measured in barrels, and price is measured in dollars per barrel. The inverse demand curve is:

$$P = 80 - 0.82Q$$

Let the total cost curve be:

$$TC = 0.15Q^2 + 75$$

Then profits are:

$$\pi = PQ - TC = (80 - 0.82Q)^{\star}Q - (0.15Q^2 + 75)$$

$$= 80Q - 0.82\,Q^2 - 0.15\,Q^2 - 75$$

First order conditions are:

$$d\pi/dQ = -1.94Q + 80 = 0$$

Solving, we find that Q = 41.24 barrels.

Checking second order conditions, we find:

$$d^2\pi/dQ^2 = -1.94 < 0$$

So, we have a maximum. Substituting production back into the inverse demand curve gives us the monopolist's price of:

$$P = 80 - 0.82*41.24 = \$46.19$$

Cost, average cost, and monopoly profit at the optimal output are:

$$TC = 0.15Q^2 + 75 = 0.15(41.24)^2 + 75 = \$330.11$$

$$\textbf{Average Cost} = AC = TC/Q = 0.15Q + 75/Q$$

$$= 0.15(41.24) + 75/41.24 = \$8.01$$

$$\textbf{Monopoly Profits} = (P - AC)*Q = (46.19 - 8.01)*41.24 = \$1,574.54$$

This is the shaded area in Figure 6–3.

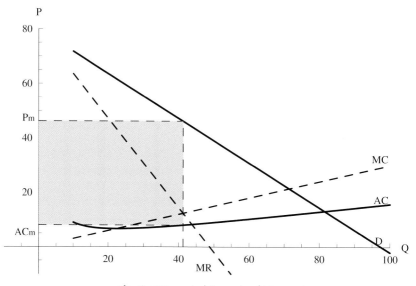

Fig. 6–3 Numerical Example of Monopoly

Monopoly Compared to Competition

How does the previous result compare to the results in a competitive example? It depends on the cost curves for all the additional firms that enter the market. Suppose the cost curves are the same for each additional firm and there are no barriers to entry. If a monopoly existed in this market and the monopolist was maximizing profits, he would be making excess profits as shown above. This would cause other firms to enter into the industry. See AC_2 in Figure 6–4.

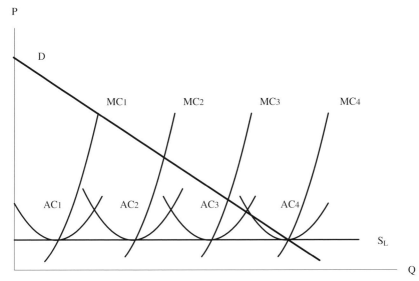

Fig. 6–4 Competitive Supply in a Constant Cost Industry

If another firm entered and the two firms did not collude, the short-run supply curve would be the horizontal sum of the two marginal cost curves as in MC_2. As there would still be profits in the industry, more firms would enter. For this constant-cost industry, notice that with the entry and exit of identical firms, a horizontal long-run supply curve is traced out, S_L as seen in Figure 6–4. There would be four firms in the industry in long-run equilibrium. The social losses in this market from monopoly power would then be the area under the demand curve and above the supply between the monopoly output and the competitive output – area fde—as shown in Figure 6–5.

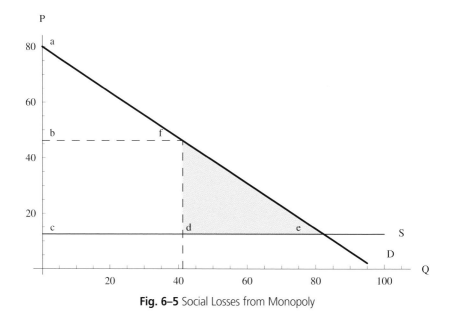

Fig. 6–5 Social Losses from Monopoly

If you have market power, you can optimize profits if you exploit it. Thus, the monopolist makes more money, because he can pick the price or the quantity and does not have to accept the market price as in the competitive case. However, note that the monopolist can pick price or quantity but not both. If he picks the price, the market dictates the quantity. If he picks the quantity, the market dictates the price.

Price Controls in a Monopoly Market

A policy that governments might consider in the monopoly case is price controls. It is easiest to see the effect of price controls by considering Figure 6–6 (a) and 6–6 (b). If we set the maximum price at the dotted line, P_1, the monopolist's new marginal revenue curve becomes the dotted line until it crosses the demand curve; below that price the demand curve would prevail along with its associated marginal revenue. The monopolist would still produce at Q_m and change P_m.

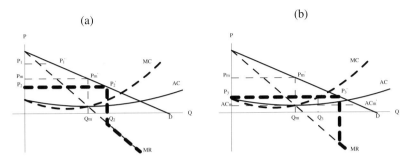

Figs. 6–6 (a) and 6–6 (b) Monopolist and Price Controls

Now pick a price between P_m and where MC crosses the demand. For example, let's see what happens at P_2. The new marginal revenue curve becomes the bold dotted line in Figure 6–6.a, $P_2P_2'Q_2MR$. Marginal revenue now crosses marginal cost in the vertical portion of marginal revenue above Q_2. In this case, demand is satisfied and the monopolist is producing more (Q_2) at a lower price (P_2) than in the monopoly case.

Now take a price P_3, which is between the price where demand crosses the marginal cost curve and the minimum of the average cost curve (AC_m). Now the marginal revenue curve (bold dotted line in Figure 6–6.b) crosses marginal cost to the left of the demand curve. Although the monopolist produces more than at his desired price of P_m and charges a lower price, there is excess quantity demanded in the market or a shortage. If a price control even lower than AC_m were implemented, the monopolist could not cover costs and would go out of business in the long run. Thus, a price control would improve the monopoly allocation by lowering price and raising output, but in some cases it could cause a shortage in the market. For this reason, price-controlled public utilities with monopoly franchises, discussed in chapter 4, were required to satisfy market demand at the controlled price.

Antitrust laws

Although price controls would lower the price, they would not give us the socially optimal amount of output in the case of monopoly. As a result, the United States and many other governments have relied on antitrust laws. The most famous of these laws is the U.S. Sherman Antitrust Act of 1890, which made monopoly and restraint of trade illegal. It was under this act that the most famous energy antitrust case in the U.S. was conducted—against the Standard Oil Trust. This case led to the break up of Standard Oil in 1911. (Table 6–1.) In 1914, the Clayton Act supplemented the Sherman Act and made mergers to restrain competition illegal. The Federal Trade Commission (FTC) Act prohibited unfair competition and set up the FTC to supervise trade and enforce the antitrust laws.

Table 6–1 Major Oil Company Mergers and Acquisitions, 1910–2003

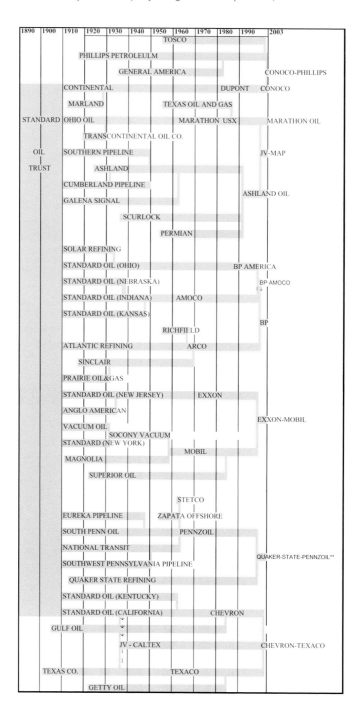

Table 6–1 Major Oil Company Mergers and Acquisitions, 1910–2003 (cont'd)

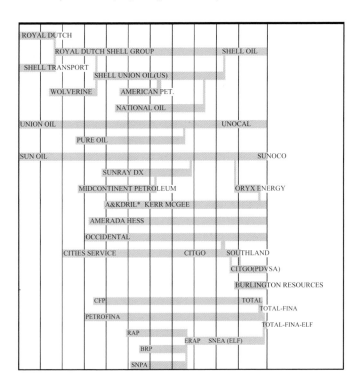

Notes: *A&KDRIL = Anderson and Kerr Drilling. **Taken over by Shell U.S. in 2002, # Ashland bought the Permian Company and merged with Scurlock Oil Company. See http://www.virginia.edu/igpr/apagoilhistory.html for histories of numerous oil companies. *Source*: Updated from Berger and Anderson, 1992, with company homepages, other Internet sources and personal correspondence with Linda Casey, MAPLLC.

Another possible policy is nationalizing the industry. In this case, the company would probably remain big, since many small companies would be less manageable for the government. However, there is no economic rationale for having one big company as in the case of a natural monopoly. With no competition and no discipline from the market to control cost, we might expect X-inefficiency and costs to go up. The current solution is to promote competition with antitrust (or threats of antitrust), and to regulate where competition is not feasible.

Brief History of OPEC

These monopoly theories can be used to analyze OPEC and the world oil market. Before doing so, let's briefly consider the history of the oil market. For more detailed information see Yergin (1991) or Sampson (1975); for a more complete chronology of recent events go to http://www.eia.doe.gov/).

From its inception, the boom and bust of the oil market saw prices fall from more than $100 per barrel in 1860 (measured in 2001 dollars) to less than $10 in 1861 as drillers produced as fast as possible. Such rapid exploitation largely resulted from the law of capture, which is relatively unique to the United States. Whoever drilled down and pumped out the oil got to keep it, even if the pool of oil lay under more than one owner's well. Unless producers were colluding, they had incentive to capture as much as possible to block drillers on neighboring plots. In a competitive foray, once they put in their well and it was a sunk cost, drillers had an incentive to produce up to the point where the price equaled their marginal cost, which was relatively low in this capital-intensive industry.

Rockefeller consolidated control over the U.S. product market to stabilize it, and he did so by fair means and foul. Meanwhile, half a world away, Royal Dutch made oil finds in Indonesia beginning in the 1890s, while Shell Transport and Trading commissioned its first tanker to transport kerosene from Russia to the Far East in 1892. These two companies came together in 1907 to become the Shell Group.

Oil production in the United States was concentrated in Appalachia until 1901, when the huge Spindletop well in East Texas came in and Texaco and Gulf Oil were born. Prior to the turn of the century, Standard Oil and Shell were the major players on the world oil scene. The Nobels and the Rothchilds soon joined them producing oil in Baku, Azerbaijan, then part of Russia. Standard Oil was broken up by antitrust in 1911, and the Nobels and Rothschilds lost out with the Russian revolution in 1917. During World War I, a need for oil to fuel the British fleet induced that country to buy a controlling share in Anglo-Persian (later British Petroleum).

By 1920, post-war oil prices had slumped. Attempts by Standard Oil of New Jersey (later Exxon), Royal Dutch Shell (RD Shell), and Anglo-Persian to shore up prices were thwarted by newcomers Gulf and Texaco, along with two other oil companies out of the old Standard Trust, which evolved into Chevron and Mobil. These are the seven companies that came to be pejoratively called the Seven Sisters. They later managed to stabilize world oil prices for many years.

Executives of three of the "sisters" (Anglo Persian, RD Shell, and Jersey Standard) met at Achnacarry, Scotland, in 1928 and agreed to share world markets. In the same year, RD Shell, Anglo Persian, Companie Française Petrole, Exxon, Mobil, Amoco, Gulbenkian, and others agreed to cooperate through the Turkish Petroleum Company in much of the old Ottoman Empire. This cartel-like agreement, which came to be known as the Red Line Agreement, took its name from the Red Line used to mark the area covered by the agreement on a map.

By the end of World War II, the Seven Sisters controlled world crude oil trade. Markets in the United States were more competitive; state oil commissions responded to devastating waste and over-production in the West Texas fields of the early 1930s with prorationing, which dictated how much could be produced from each well. Other controls—well spacing and restrictions on transporting "hot" oil (i.e., oil over prorationed amounts) across state borders—helped enforce prorationing. The most famous of these state bodies was the Texas Railroad Commission, which instituted monthly production allowances from wells in the state of Texas.

During the 1950s, new companies such as Getty and Occidental produced oil in North Africa, again putting downward pressure on world oil prices. Taxes levied on the companies were set at 50%, which had been initially established in Venezuela and had spread to all the major producing countries. Oil companies paid these taxes to the countries based on posted prices but did not immediately reduce posted prices. Falling demand from a European recession and rising world supply caused the major multinationals to cut market and posted prices in the late 1950s. This reduced taxes paid to producing countries and prompted Venezuela, Iran, Iraq, Kuwait, and Saudi Arabia to form OPEC in September 1960. Qatar joined in 1961, Libya and Indonesia in 1962, UAE in 1967, Algeria in 1969, and Nigeria in 1971. Two other countries were members for a time—Ecuador from 1973 to 1992 and Gabon from 1975 to 1994—leaving current OPEC membership at 11.

OPEC did not manage to increase prices in the 1960s, but it did manage to hold the line on taxes. However, when oil production in the United States peaked in 1970 and markets tightened, OPEC was able to raise prices during the Yom Kippur war of 1973. Prices rose again in 1979 after the Iranian revolution. These rapid price increases are seen in Figure 6–7. They caused a reduction in oil consumption and an increase in production outside of OPEC. OPEC's production fell by about a third between 1973 and 1985, and OPEC's share of world oil markets fell from more than 55% to about 30%. In 1983, it reduced posted prices from $34 per barrel to $29 per barrel and moved to a quota system, which has been in place since. OPEC's share has rebounded somewhat since 1985.

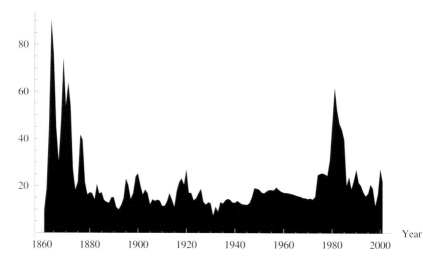

Fig. 6–7 U.S. Oil Prices, 1861–2001 (2001 dollars)

Source: American Petroleum Institute (API), 1959 EIA/DOE, 2003, Annual Energy Review. Converted to real 2001 dollars using the consumer price index from Department of Commerce(1975) and Council of Economic Advisers, 2003.

Saudi Arabia, in particular, took a large hit, with production falling from a peak of more than 9 million barrels a day in the late 1970s and early 1980s to less than 3.5 million barrels a day in 1985. As a result, in late 1985, it began using *netback pricing,* and in 1986, it raised production to more than 4.5 million barrels a day. Netback pricing means that the Saudis charged companies an oil price equal to the value of product from a barrel of oil minus transport and refinery cost. As a result, world prices plummeted, with West Texas Intermediate falling from $24.06 to $12.66 per barrel through 1987, according to EIA statistics at http://www.eia.doe.gov.

Oil prices remained at lower levels with a slight downward trend, except for the Gulf War blip in 1990 and 1991. At lower prices, demand increased and non-OPEC production decreased. OPEC sales climbed as did its share of world oil production. Oil demand growth remained strong, and discipline within OPEC remained reasonably good until after 1996. Continued growth in production in 1997 and early 1998 was largely the result of quota violation. Venezuela overproduced the most (Table 6–2 and Fig. 6–8).

Table 6–2 OPEC Average Production and Quotas, 1984–2003

Quota Dates Month/Year	OPEC* Prod.	Quota	Algeria Prod.	Quota	Indonesia Prod.	Quota	Iran Prod.	Quota	Iraq Prod.	Quota	Kuwait Prod.	Quota
04/82–03/83	15,117	17,150	998	650	1,250	1,300	2,592	1,200	881	1,200	852	800
04/83–10/84	16,756	17,150	1,004	725	1,422	1,300	2,270	2,400	1,124	1,200	1,159	1,050
11/84–10/86	17,347	15,680	995	663	1,354	1,189	2,179	2,300	1,540	1,200	1,195	900
11/86	17,822	14,580	993	669	1,356	1,193	2,166	2,317	1,542	0	1,201	921
12/86	18,005	14,658	989	669	1,359	1,193	2,156	2,317	1,551	0	1,211	999
01/87–06/87	18,224	15,438	1,010	635	1,311	1,133	2,368	2,255	1,803	1,466	1,342	948
07/87–12/87	19,287	16,220	1,085	667	1,374	1,190	2,226	2,369	2,350	1,540	1,824	996
01/88–12/88	23,375	14,680	1,040	667	1,341	1,190	2,239	2,369	2,685	0	1,491	996
01/89–06/89	22,042	18,104	1,085	695	1,401	1,240	2,789	2,640	2,763	2,640	1,615	1,037
07/89–09/89	22,660	19,083	1,105	733	1,401	1,307	2,830	2,783	2,994	2,783	1,885	1,093
10/89–12/89	23,959	20,062	1,105	771	1,434	1,374	2,830	2,926	3,063	2,926	2,009	1,149
01/90–07/90	23,841	21,616	1,160	827	1,393	1,374	2,993	3,140	3,099	3,140	1,961	1,500
08/90–03/91	22,808	22,021	1,209	827	1,576	1,374	3,242	3,140	388	3,140	60	1,500
04/91–09/91	23,082	21,740	1,230	827	1,608	1,443	3,311	3,217	358	0	124	0
10/91–01/92	24,815	23,650	1,230	na	1,552	na	3,383	na	420	na	509	na
02/92–09/92	24,945	22,436	1,218	760	1,571	1,374	3,350	3,184	450	505	946	812
10/92–12/92	25,645	24,200	1,210	na	1,550	na	3,617	na	450	na	1,402	na
01/93–02/93	26,000	24,289	1,210	764	1,562	1,374	3,700	3,490	500	500	1,770	1,500
03/93–09/93	25,636	23,301	1,191	732	1,525	1,317	3,636	3,340	504	400	1,827	1,600
10/93–06/96	26,359	24,233	1,196	750	1,513	1,330	3,643	3,600	553	400	2,044	2,000
07/96–12/97	27,468	25,033	1,269	750	1,532	1,330	3,670	3,600	972	400	2,078	2,000
01/98–03/98	29,408	27,500	1,290	909	1,520	1,456	3,635	3,942	1,596	0	2,212	2,190
07/98–03/99	26,177	24,387	1,228	788	1,514	1,280	3,644	3,318	2,492	1,314	2,010	1,980
04/98–06/98	26,662	26,255	1,253	859	1,510	1,386	3,768	3,802	2,050	0	2,108	2,065
04/99–03/00	25,299	22,976	1,191	731	1,447	1,187	3,666	3,359	2,461	0	1,898	1,836
04/00–06/00	22,406	21,069	1,245	788	1,437	1,280	3,729	0	2,758	0	2,117	1,980
07/00–09/00	27,341	25,400	1,258	811	1,446	1,317	1,275	3,727	2,798	0	2,171	2,037
10/00	29,135	26,200	1,275	837	1,275	1,359	3,874	3,844	1,275	0	1,275	2,101
10/00–01/01	27,367	26,700	1,278	853	1,418	1,385	3,810	3,917	1,968	0	2,208	2,141
02/01–03/01	27,040	25,201	1,250	805	1,418	1,307	3,783	3,698	2,525	0	2,115	2,021
04/01–08/01	26,432	24,201	1,263	773	1,365	1,255	3,554	3,552	2,392	0	2,018	1,941
09/01–12/01	24,128	23,201	1,240	741	1,335	1,203	3,554	3,406	2,604	0	1,950	1,861
01/02–12/02	26,338	21,700	1,291	693	1,267	1,125	3,444	3,186		0	2,023	1,741
01/03	23,279	23,000	1,045	735	1,080	1,192	1,192	3,377	2,550	0	1,990	1,845
02/03–03/03	25,517	24,574	1,075	782	1,063	1,270	3,695	3,597	1,918	0	2,225	1,966
04/03–05/03	26,685	na	1,200	na	1,030	na	3,750	na	125	na	2,400	na
06/03		25,400		811		1,317		3,729		0		2,038

Table 6–2 OPEC Average Production and Quotas, 1984–2003 (cont'd)

Month/Year	Libya Prod.	Libya Quota	Nigeria Prod.	Nigeria Quota	Qatar Prod.	Qatar Quota	Saudi Arabia Prod.	Saudi Arabia Quota	UAE Prod.	UAE Quota	Venezuela Prod.	Venezuela Quota
04/82–03/83	1,253	750	1,185	1,300	303	300	5,640	7,150	1,177	1,000	1,913	1,500
04/83–10/84	1,122	1,100	1,364	1,300	363	300	5,089	5,000	1,162	1,100	1,791	1,675
11/84–10/86	1,045	990	1,502	1,300	308	280	3,985	4,353	1,252	950	1,726	1,555
11/86	1,044	999	1,495	1,304	307	300	4,020	4,353	1,253	950	1,727	1,574
12/86	1,044	999	1,485	1,304	303	300	4,061	4,353	1,256	950	1,727	1,574
01/87–06/87	926	948	1,285	1,238	234	285	4,094	4,133	1,216	902	1,739	1,495
07/87–12/87	1,017	996	1,395	1,301	349	299	4,522	4,343	1,780	948	1,782	1,571
01/88–12/88	1,175	996	1,450	1,301	339	299	4,913	4,343	1,530	948	1,875	1,571
01/89–06/89	1,128	1,037	1,618	1,355	370	312	5,116	4,524	1,681	988	1,898	1,636
07/89–09/89	1,154	1,093	1,812	1,428	395	329	4,923	4,769	1,853	1,041	1,905	1,724
10/89–12/89	1,189	1,149	1,812	1,501	382	346	5,412	5,014	2,141	1,094	1,960	1,812
01/90–07/90	1,288	1,233	1,746	1,611	398	371	5,616	5,380	2,095	1,095	2,038	1,945
08/90–03/91	1,492	1,233	1,902	1,611	405	371	7,436	5,380	2,242	1,500	2,269	1,945
04/91–09/91	1,458	1,425	1,890	1,840	407	399	7,918	8,034	2,366	2,320	2,354	2,235
10/91–01/92	1,538	na	1,905	na	381	na	8,414	na	2,381	na	2,396	na
02/92–09/92	1,469	1,395	1,950	1,751	375	377	8,404	7,887	2,333	2,244	2,290	2,147
10/92–12/92	1,500	na	2,067	na	435	na	8,485	na	2,312	na	2,423	na
01/93–02/93	1,453	1,409	2,115	1,857	448	380	8,538	8,395	2,274	2,260	2,450	2,360
03/93–09/93	1,356	1,350	2,024	1,780	416	364	8,211	8,000	2,196	2,161	2,434	2,257
10/93–06/96	1,386	1,390	1,978	1,865	438	378	8,165	8,000	2,217	2,161	2,673	2,359
07/96–12/97	1,431	1,390	2,224	1,865	594	378	8,433	8,000	2,303	2,161	3,180	2,359
01/98–03/98	1,463	1,522	2,287	2,042	718	414	8,750	8,761	2,393	2,366	3,447	2,583
04/98–06/98	1,358	1,323	2,062	2,033	676	640	8,192	8,023	2,291	2,157	3,033	2,845
07/98–03/99	1,385	1,442	2,226	1,917	715	384	8,557	8,461	2,410	2,241	3,297	2,383
04/99–03/00	1,321	1,227	2,121	1,885	671	593	7,793	7,438	2,167	2,000	2,795	2,720
04/00–06/00	1,407	1,323	2,130	2,033	718	640	8,055	8,023	2,373	2,157	2,893	2,845
07/00–09/00	1,425	1,361	2,150	2,091	748	658	8,488	8,253	2,346	2,219	2,967	2,926
10/00	1,275	1,404	1,275	2,157	1,275	679	1,275	8,512	1,275	2,289	1,275	3,019
10/00–01/01	1,445	1,431	2,270	2,198	763	692	8,833	8,674	2,436	2,333	3,060	3,077
02/01–03/01	1,395	1,350	2,270	2,075	755	653	8,510	8,189	2,410	2,201	3,065	2,902
04/01–08/01	1,374	1,296	2,180	1,993	729	627	8,110	7,865	2,305	2,113	2,920	2,786
09/01–12/01	1,323	1,242	2,338	1,911	690	601	7,803	7,541	2,154	2,025	2,773	2,670
01/02–12/02	1,319	1,162	2,118	1,787	679	562	7,634	7,053	2,062	1,894	2,606	2,497
01/03	1,375	1,232	2,150	1,894	725	596	8,570	7,476	2,100	2,007	620	2,647
02/03–03/03	1,403	1,312	2,035	2,092	750	635	9,185	7,963	2,225	2,138	1,863	2,819
04/03–05/03	1,430	na	1,920	na	750	na	9,600	na	2,300	na	2,550	na
06/03	na	1,360	na	2,092	na	658	na	8,256	na	2,217	na	2,923

Notes: A zero quota indicates the country was not in the production agreement during that period. Total OPEC production includes only those countries in the production agreement at the time. na under quota indicates that there was not a quota agreement at the time. na under production indicates the numbers were not available at the time table was compiled.

Sources: Quotas taken from OPEC *Annual Statistical Bulletin* and OPEC press releases downloaded from http://www.opec.org. Production numbers compiled from EIA/DOE *International Petroleum Supply*, downloaded from http://www.eia.doe.gov/emeu/international/petroleu.html#IntlProduction. Downloaded 08/03.

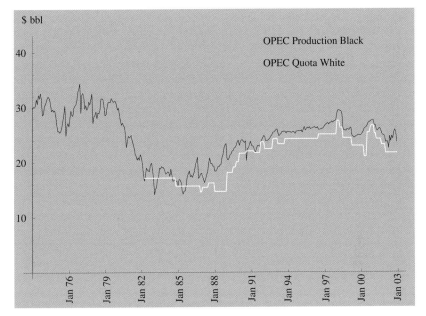

Fig. 6–8 OPEC Production and Quotas
January–December 2003

Sources: Quotas taken from OPEC *Annual Statistical Bulletin* and OPEC press releases downloaded from http://www.opec.org. Production numbers compiled from EIA/DOE *International Petroleum Supply*, downloaded from http://www.eia.doe.gov/emeu/international/petroleu.html#IntlProduction. Downloaded 08/03.

Throughout the 1990s, OPEC exceeded its production ceiling by more than 1 million barrels a day. This, along with the decrease in the world demand for oil from the Asian financial crisis and other reasons, caused prices again to fall below $12 per barrel during 1998, leaving large budget deficits and a need for funds. In early 1999, the tide started to turn, as a new president was elected in Venezuela, and, under his leadership, OPEC pulled together to reduce production. Gradually, the Asian economy picked up. Low oil prices had taken their toll on higher-cost producers. The market tightened, pushing oil prices to more than $20 per barrel during 2000 with an average of around $30. The U.S. economy was weaker in 2001 than in 2000, and oil prices posted at more than $25 for most of the first part of the year. They fell below $25 after the U.S. World Trade Centers in New York were attacked on September 11, and third-quarter U.S. gross domestic product (GDP) fell. Prices averaged around $26 for the year.

Figure 6–7 reflects these events in real U.S. oil prices. Initially, turbulent prices stabilized when Rockefeller gained monopoly power, and they remained stable when the Seven Sisters and Texas Railroad Commission reigned, from 1930 to 1970. There was turbulence as OPEC took over until 1986, when market pressures moved OPEC to a quota system and prices reverted to historic levels. Currently, OPEC is riding high, but weathering the Asian crisis may not be enough. Global warming concerns and ensuing regulations may be just around the corner to provide further challenges.

Multiplant Monopoly Model

How should OPEC behave to maximize its profits? First, OPEC is not one country but 11, so we use a multiplant monopoly model. If OPEC wants to maximize profits as a group, it must find its combined marginal cost and demand function. The monopolist's costs depend on costs in each of the countries. To see how, consider marginal costs in the following diagrams.

To simplify the exposition, we assume that OPEC consists of two countries, a lower-cost and a higher-cost country, whose costs are represented by the two MC curves on the left in Figure 6–9.

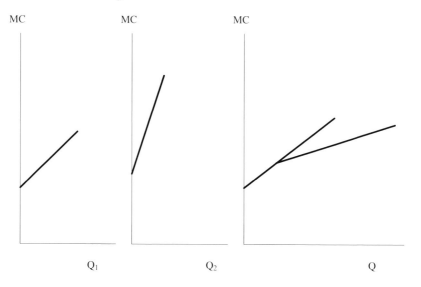

Fig. 6–9 Marginal Cost for a Two-Country OPEC

Their total marginal cost curve is the horizontal sum of the separate cost curves. We can think of this summation as adding up Q's for a given marginal cost. For example, suppose the two marginal cost functions are:

$$MC_1 = 1 + Q_1 \text{ and}$$

$$MC_2 = 2 + 2Q_2$$

For market prices below $2, only country one can afford to produce, so the group's MC curve would coincide with country one's curve. At prices above $2, country two would enter the market and OPEC's marginal cost curve would be the horizontal sum of the two curves. Since we have to sum quantities for a given marginal cost, we need to invert these two functions, which gives us:

$$Q_1 = -1 + MC_1 \text{ and}$$

$$Q_2 = -1 + (1/2)MC_2$$

Summing the right side, we see market quantity:

$$Q = -1 + MC_1 + (-1 + (1/2)MC_2)$$

OPEC should allocate production so that $MC_1 = MC_2 = MC$. Otherwise it should reallocate production to the country where it is cheaper to produce. Substituting in MC for MC_1 and MC_2, yields:

$$Q = -2 + 1.5MC$$

Inverting gives us marginal cost after the kink. We solve it as:

$$MC = 4/3 + (2/3)Q$$

Next we need the demand curve for OPEC oil. Since OPEC has a large share of oil reserves, it has market power and its demand curve is downward sloping. We know that the monopolist should produce where marginal revenue equals marginal cost. If demand is as in Figure 6–10, the optimal production for OPEC is Q_o at a price of P_o. To see how much each OPEC producer should produce, look to Figure 6–11, where each individual country must be operating at MC'.

To create a numerical example, let the demand for OPEC's oil be:

$$Q = 10 - 2P => P = 5 - (1/2)Q$$

Then total revenues are:

$$TR = PQ = (5 - (1/2)Q)Q$$

And marginal revenues are:

$$MR = \partial TR / \partial Q = 5 - Q$$

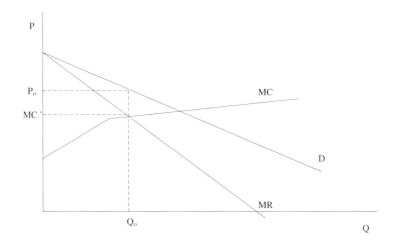

Fig. 6–10 OPEC's Optimal Production

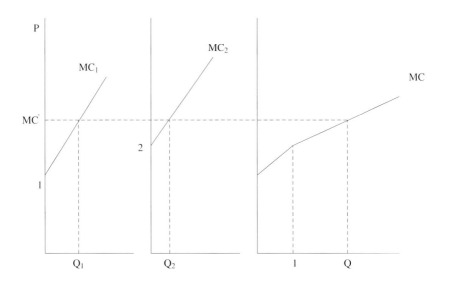

Fig. 6–11 Allocating Optimal Production Across OPEC Countries

Setting marginal revenues equal to marginal cost:

$$5 - Q = 4/3 + (2/3)Q$$

Solving yields:

$$Q = 2.2$$

We need to check that we are assessing the portion where both countries are producing. Since Q is greater than one, both countries are producing. If Q were less than one, only the low-cost country would be producing and we would have to use the marginal cost curve to the right of the kink to solve for Q. We solve for market price by substituting Q into the demand equation:

$$P = 5 - (1/2)Q = 5 - 0.5*2.2 = 3.9$$

See the solution in Figure 6–12.

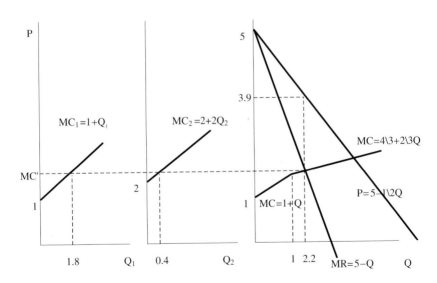

Fig. 6–12 Multi-Plant Monopoly Numerical Example

How much does each country produce?

$$MR = 5 - Q = 5 - 2.2 = 2.8 = MC$$

$$Q_1 = -1 + MC_1 = -1 + 2.8 = 1.8$$

$$Q_2 = -1 + (1/2)MC_2 = -1 + 0.5{*}2.8 = 0.4$$

Thus, the high-cost country is producing much less than the low-cost country. Only if costs are very similar should each country get a similar production quota. Right away, we can see political problems would evolve trying to allocate production across producers.

OPEC's demand curve and marginal revenue curve

In the above example, we assumed a demand curve for OPEC. To derive a demand curve for OPEC, we divide the world into two groups—OPEC, the dominant firm, and the rest of the world, which we call the competitive fringe (its supply curve is equal to its marginal cost curve). Let world demand and the fringe supply be as seen in Figure 6–13.

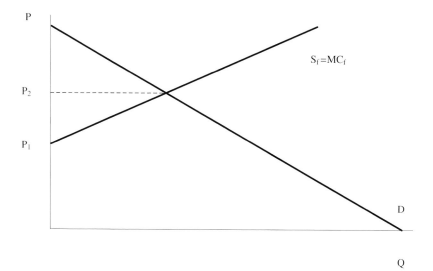

Fig. 6–13 Developing Demand for OPEC's Oil

In this model, if oil prices are below P_1, the fringe does not produce and OPEC faces the whole world demand curve. If price is P_2 or above, the fringe satisfies the whole market, and OPEC does not produce. At any price between P_1 and P_2, OPEC demand is world demand minus the production of the fringe.

We represent OPEC demand as a bold kinked line in Figure 6–14. To develop the marginal revenue curve for OPEC's oil, we need the marginal revenue for the two parts of the demand curve. For the flatter portion of the demand curve to the left of the kink line, we need to take the marginal revenue from the flatter portion, which is world demand minus the fringe supply. For the steeper portion of OPEC demand to the right of the kink line, we need to take the marginal revenue curve from the steeper portion, which is the total world demand. This yields the discontinuous dotted marginal revenue function as pictured in Figure 6–14. Once we have MC and MR for OPEC, the optimum is the quantity where marginal cost equals marginal revenue. The price is then the price on the demand for OPEC's oil—the broken-line demand.

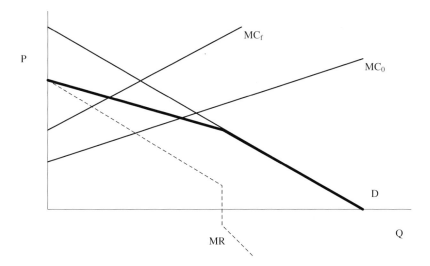

Fig. 6–14 Dominant Firm Example

To better see how this works, let's walk through a numerical example shown in Figure 6–15. Let world demand, marginal cost of the fringe, and marginal cost of OPEC be:

$$Q_w = 25 - (1/2)P => P = 50 - 2Q_w$$

$$MC_f = 5 + Q_f$$

$$MC_o = 1 + Q_o$$

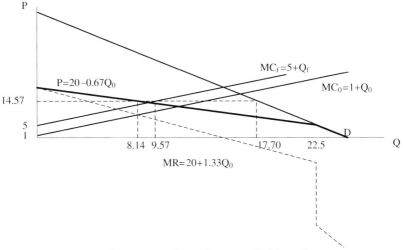

Fig. 6–15 Dominant Firm Numerical Example

The first step is to find the demand for OPEC's oil, which is world demand minus supply of the fringe. To get Q_f of the fringe, we know that fringe supply is equal to its marginal cost curve. Thus:

$$MC_f = 5 + Q_f => Q_f = -5 + MC_f$$

For $P = MC$ we can write:

$$Q_f = -5 + MC = -5 + P$$

The kink in demand is where the fringe doesn't produce or where:

$$Q_f = 0 = -5 + P$$

$$P = 5$$

So the fringe produces nothing when price is five or lower. At this price world demand is:

$$Q_w = 25 - 0.5(5) = 22.50$$

For any given price above the kink, the demand for OPEC's oil is world demand minus the fringe or:

$$Q_o = Q_w - Q_f$$

We have world demand from above. OPEC demand to the left of the kink is:

$$Q_o = Q_w - Q_f = 25 - (1/2)P + 5 - P$$

$$Q_o = 30 - (3/2)P$$

Inverting this demand yields:

$$P = 20 - (2/3)Q_o$$

Marginal revenue for this demand curve can be derived as follows:

$$TR = P*Q = (20 - (2/3)Q_o)*Q_o$$

$$MR = \partial TR/\partial Q = 20 - (4/3)Q_o$$

Remember, it has the same intercept but is twice as steep as the inverse demand curve.

As shown in chapter 4, this is always the case for a linear demand. For any price below the kink, we are to the right of the kink and on the world demand and world marginal revenue curves, which are:

$$P = 50 - 2Q$$

$$MR = 50 - 4Q$$

We know that MC_o could cross the MR to right or left of the kink. First, we'll try to the left. Setting marginal revenue equal to marginal cost:

$$20 - 4/3Q = 1 + Q$$

$$19 = (7/3)Q$$

$$Q_o = 8.14$$

The solution is to the left of 22.5, so MC crosses MR before the kink. (If Q had been greater than 22.5 we would have been on the wrong MR curve and would need to go back to MR for world demand and resolve). Now that we know OPEC's optimal quantity, we can get price from the demand for OPEC's oil to the left of the kink, which is:

$$P = 20 - (2/3)Q_o = 20 - (2/3)(8.14) = \$14.57$$

The quantity supplied by the fringe easily follows from its supply curve:

$$Q_f = -5 + P = -5 + 14.57 = 9.57$$

OPEC's and the fringe's monopoly profits are:

$$\pi_o = P^*Q_o - \int_0^{Qo} MC_o dQ = 14.57^*8.14 - 8.14 - 8.14^2/2 = \$77.33$$

$$\pi_f = P^*Q_f - \int_0^{Qf} MC_f dQ = 14.57^*9.57 - 9.57^*5 - 9.57^2/2 = \$45.77$$

Price elasticity of demand for OPEC's oil

We can also relate the optimal price to price elasticities in the above dominant firm model, but derivation is a bit more complicated. From the monopoly example, we have the well known result that:

$$P = MC /(1 - 1/|\mathcal{E}_p|).$$

So, what is $\mathcal{E}_p$ for the dominant firm? We know that OPEC demand is world demand minus supply of the fringe or:

$$Q_o = Q_w - Q_f$$

Taking the derivative with respect to P, we get:

$$\frac{\partial Q_o}{\partial P} = \frac{\partial Q_w}{\partial P} - \frac{\partial Q_f}{\partial P}$$

Multiply by P/Q_o to get OPEC's elasticity, ε_o:

$$\varepsilon_o = \frac{\partial Q_o P}{\partial P Q_o} = \frac{\partial Q_w P}{\partial P Q_o} - \frac{\partial Q_f P}{\partial P Q_o}$$

Which we can rewrite as:

$$\varepsilon_o = \frac{\partial Q_o P}{\partial P Q_o} = \frac{\partial Q_w P Q_w}{\partial P Q_o Q_w} - \frac{\partial Q_f P Q_f}{\partial P Q_o Q_f}$$

Remember that world price elasticity of demand, ε_w, and fringe price elasticity of supply, ε_f, are

$$\varepsilon_w = \frac{\partial Q_w P}{\partial P Q_w} \text{ and } \varepsilon_f = \frac{\partial Q_f P}{\partial P Q_f}$$

Using these two definitions, OPEC's elasticity can be rewritten as:

$$\varepsilon_o = \varepsilon_w \frac{Q_w}{Q_o} - \varepsilon_f \frac{Q_f}{Q_o}$$

This equation tells us that OPEC's price elasticity of demand is the world price elasticity of demand weighted by world production divided by OPEC production (Q_w/Q_o), minus the fringe price elasticity of supply weighted by fringe production divided by OPEC production (Q_f/Q_o).

Now let's investigate the elasticity for one country within OPEC, if it is the only country to change price. Let's say Venezuela changes its price and the rest do not. Suppose that Venezuela has α percent of the market $(0<\alpha<1)$ or Venezuelan production is $Q_v = \alpha Q_o$. Then Venezuela's price elasticity is:

$$\varepsilon_v = \frac{\partial Q_v P}{\partial P Q_v} = \frac{\partial Q_v P}{\partial P \alpha Q_o}$$

But if only Venezuela lowers price, Venezuela gets the entire increase in OPEC demand.

Writing the total change in output in partial differential notation, we get $\partial Q_v = \partial Q_o$. Substituting this result into Venezuela's elasticity above we find that Venezuela's elasticity can be rewritten as:

$$\varepsilon_v = \frac{\partial Q_o P}{\partial P Q_o \alpha} = \frac{\varepsilon_o}{\alpha}$$

The above shows that the smaller the share, the more elastic (more negative) the demand. We know that the greater the elasticity, the lower the price. Thus, the smaller the country's market share, the more tempting it is to cheat by producing over quota. Also, the smaller the country's share, the less likely the country will be caught if it cheats.

Alternatively, all countries could follow Venezuela's lead and lower their prices. In that case, it is likely that Venezuela would get its normal share of the increase, or $\partial Q_v = \alpha \partial Q_o$, substituting into Venezuela's elasticity:

$$\varepsilon_v = \frac{\partial \alpha Q_o P}{\partial P Q_o \alpha} = \varepsilon_o$$

Thus, Venezuela's elasticity is the same as OPEC's elasticity.

From the equation $P = MC/(1 - 1/|\varepsilon_p|)$, you can conclude that higher cost producers want higher prices by restricting production, and smaller countries with more elastic demand will put downward pressure on prices. Thus, some of the tension within OPEC comes from different reserve amounts and oil costs.

Non-profit maximization goals for OPEC

Profit maximization may not be the only goal for OPEC. With development in mind, Cremer and Isfahani (1980) suggest that some countries may have a target revenue that they want to use to invest in domestic industry. To see how countries might behave under this goal, take a simple example. Assume that all oil revenues are used for investment purposes. Suppose that we have two types of OPEC countries depending on the quantity of investment funds they are able to absorb and invest—high absorbers with low income and large populations, such as Indonesia and Nigeria, and low absorbers with high income and low populations such as Kuwait and the United Arab Emirates (UAE). The high absorbers may have a larger target revenue for investment than the low absorbers.

To see how an OPEC country might choose such an investment target revenue, suppose that curve MEI_L in Figure 6–16 represents the marginal efficiency of investment curve for a low absorber like the UAE, and MEI_H represents the marginal efficiency of investment for a high-absorber country like Nigeria. Note the marginal efficiency of investment is the rate of return on the last unit of investment.

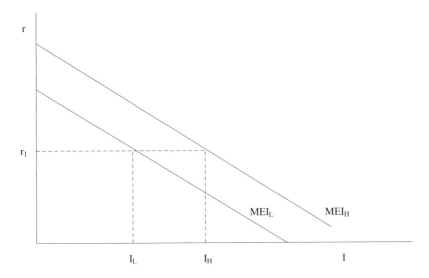

Fig. 6–16 Marginal Social Efficiency of Investment

Assuming that the social discount or interest rate in both countries is r_1, then the UAE would want to invest I_L, since investment up to that point brings in a higher social return than it costs. The high-absorber country with a large population, Nigeria, has a higher marginal efficiency of investment and, consequently, a higher target revenue for investment, I_H. If each country wants to raise target investment revenues from its oil industry, then investment expenditure must equal oil revenues or $I_L = P_L Q_L$ and $I_H = P_H Q_H$. Graphing these two functions along with oil demand gives us the hyperbolae in Figure 6–17.

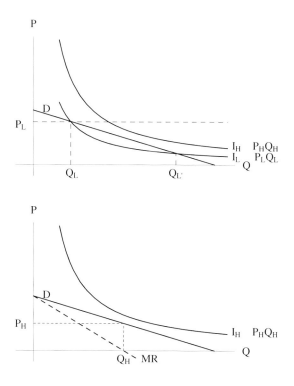

Fig. 6–17 Target Revenues and Output for Low- and High-Absorber Countries

Let D in this same graph be the demand for oil for each group, which is assumed to be identical for easier comparison. We can see that for the UAE, a variety of points on the demand curve—Q_L to Q_L^*—would satisfy or more than satisfy their investment demand. However, Nigeria would never be satisfied along this demand curve. So UAE would likely want to sell Q_L but Nigeria would want to maximize revenues to get as close to I_2 as possible. We assume zero marginal costs for Nigeria to keep the diagram less cluttered and show these two solutions in Figure 6–17. At the top is UAE It initially sells at P_L and Q_L. On the bottom is Nigeria who originally wants to sell where marginal revenue equals marginal cost at P_H and Q_H.

Now suppose that demand shifts out to D' for both countries as shown in Figure 6–18. The low absorber will want to remain on I_L and would likely want a higher price (P_L') and a lower output (Q_L'). Since it wants to produce less at a higher price, it has a downward sloping supply curve. The high absorber would want to move closer yet to I_2 and should maximize profits. According to the figure, Nigeria would want to sell Q_H' at P_H' or it would want to sell more at a higher price.

Since the high absorber increases output as price increases, it has an upward sloping supply curve. It would like to increase output even more, but the market cannot absorb that output at the given price.

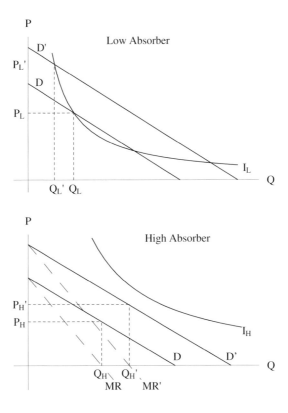

Fig. 6–18 Target Revenues and Price Increase for Low- and High-Absorber Countries

Another factor that might influence an OPEC member's long-run views on prices is the quantity of its reserve. High-reserve Gulf countries have a longer-run interest in reserves and are more worried that oil substitutes will be found. This, and the fact that high-reserve countries often have lower costs, lead them to prefer lower prices. Thus, population, revenue needs, production costs, and reserves may influence a member country's preference for oil price. Table 6–3 shows such variables for OPEC countries.

Table 6–3 OPEC Petroleum, Income, and Population Statistics for 2000

Country	Production (P) 1,000 b/d	Reserves (R) Billions	R/P	Well Depth Feet	Wells (W)	Production Share	Population in Million	P/W/d	Per Capita GDP
Algeria	802	9.2	31.4	8777	1281	2.84	32.6	626	1480
Indonesia	1290	5.0	10.6	4080	8457	4.57	224.8	153	698
Iran	3700	89.7	66.4	7620	1120	13.12	65.6	3304	939
Iraq	2570	112.5	119.9	6875	1685	9.11	22.7	1525	678
Kuwait	2200	96.5	120.2	7350	790	7.80	2.0	2785	15,850
Libya	1410	29.5	57.3	6825	1470	5.00	5.6	959	7071
Nigeria	2000	22.5	30.8	9363	2374	7.09	123.3	842	375
Qatar	659	3.7	15.4	5513	379	2.34	0.7	1739	13,831
S. Arabia	8400	259.0	84.5	6909	1560	29.79	22.7	5385	7225
UAE	2270	97.8	118.0	8677	1592	8.05	2.4	1426	26,333
Venezuela	2900	76.8	72.6	8302	15580	10.28	23.5	186	4660

Notes: b/d = barrels per day, R/P = Reserves over production, P/W/d = barrels of production per well per day.
Source: Country Analysis Briefs/ OPEC Fact Sheet, 08/08/2001, http://www.eia.doe.gov OGJ 12/18/00:122–123

Summary

Market power has been a dominant feature of the global oil market since its inception. High capital costs and low operating costs have led to price instability as the market lurched from boom to bust. Economies of scale were prevalent and led to large firms with an incentive to collude. Governments highly dependent on oil revenues have also sought to stabilize and support higher prices.

With market power, firms should operate where marginal revenue equals marginal costs. They will produce less than is socially optimal and charge a higher price. A price control should reduce social losses but is likely to encourage a shortage in the market unless the control is set where marginal cost crosses the demand curve.

A monopolist will make more profit than in the competitive case with the total loss in consumer-plus-producer surplus being greater than the monopolist's gain in profits. This net loss is called a deadweight loss and is why many governments try to prevent monopoly.

The most famous antitrust case in energy is the break up of the Standard Oil Trust in 1911. Recent oil company mergers, including Exxon-Mobil, BP-Amoco-ARCO, Total-Fina-Elf, Chevron-Texaco, and Conoco-Phillips, were scrutinized by governments in the United States and Europe before they were allowed. Alternatively, other governments have national oil companies, which are some of the largest oil companies in the world. However, as with electricity, there are moves afoot to privatize some of the national oil companies. Earlier, Canada and the United Kingdom privatized their national oil companies. More recently Argentina has privatized and China and Indonesia are considering it.

If OPEC's 11 members want to maximize total revenue, they should behave as a dominant firm, multiplant monopolist. Its demand curve is world demand minus the supply of the competitive fringe, and its marginal cost curve is the horizontal summation of all 11 members' marginal cost. As with any producer with market power, it should operate where marginal revenue equals marginal cost. Each member country would produce where its marginal cost was equal to OPEC's marginal revenue, so high-cost countries would produce less than low-cost countries. A monopolist should price where $P = MC/(1 - 1/|\varepsilon_p|)$. Thus, the higher the marginal cost or lower the price elasticity, the higher the price. OPEC's overall price elasticity is:

$$\varepsilon_o = \varepsilon_w \frac{Q_w}{Q_o} - \varepsilon_f \frac{Q_f}{Q_o}$$

Thus, the more elastic world demand is or the more elastic the fringe supply is, the more elastic the demand for OPEC's oil and the lower the desired price. If one OPEC country with market share α changes its price and no other country changes its price, then that country's elasticity is ε_o/α. Smaller countries, therefore, have higher price elasticities and a bigger incentive to lower prices.

However, if all countries change their prices, then each is likely to have OPEC's elasticity. Revenue needs, costs, and reserves vary from country to country and may cause them to desire different pricing patterns. Yet, despite the economic and cultural differences, OPEC has managed to stay together, often influencing prices in its own interests.

7 Market Structure, Transaction Cost Economics and U.S. Natural Gas Markets

The choice between the firm and market organization is neither given nor largely determined by technology but mainly reflects efforts to economize on transaction costs; the study of transaction costs is preeminently a comparative institutional undertaking; and this very same comparative contractual approach applies to the study of economic organization quite generally—including hybrid forms of economic organization, externalities, and regulation.

—Oliver Williamson, Edgar F. Kaiser Professor of Business Administration, Professor of Economics, Professor of Law, University of California Berkeley

Introduction

Market structure is an important determinant of how firms behave. The market structures of various energy industries have evolved in different ways across time and countries. The coal industry in the United States and in world markets has remained fairly competitive, with the majority of coal sold under long-term contracting, which is the predominant form of market governance. Electricity has evolved in a far different way. Once private or government-owned, vertically integrated monopolistic firms were the predominant form of market organization, but they are now privatizing and deregulating, particularly at the generation level.

Oil seems to have gone from cartel to cartel, with each cartel acting as a dominant firm until new suppliers weakened cartel hold on the market. The Texas Railroad Commission, the Seven Sisters, and OPEC have all had formal or informal agreements at one time or another to restrict output to maintain price.

Natural gas has evolved in different ways in different markets. In this chapter, we will broadly survey world natural gas markets, including consumption, production, reserves, and natural gas production technology. We will then use transaction cost economics to look more specifically at the evolution of U.S. natural gas markets. In chapters 10 and 11, game theory techniques will be applied to the European natural gas market and the Asia-Pacific LNG market. Information technology that affects transaction costs in energy markets will be considered in chapter 16.

Natural Gas Consumption and Production Worldwide

Since 1980, natural gas has experienced the fastest consumption growth of all fossil fuels, averaging 2.5% a year, compared to 1.4% per year for coal and less than 1% a year for oil. Of the major energy sources, only primary electricity production in the form of hydroelectric, nuclear, geothermal, and other renewable sources has seen faster annual growth, averaging 4.1% over this same period. The net result is that by 2001 gas constituted about 23% of global commercial energy consumption, coal a slightly higher 24%, oil 39.0%, and primary electricity most of the rest. (EIA/DOE, *International Energy Annual,* 2002)

Figure 7–1 is a regional summary of natural gas production and consumption. For example, North America is the largest producer and consumer of natural gas followed by the FSU. The western hemisphere (North, Central, and South America) is almost self-sufficient in natural gas except for small amounts of LNG imports to the United States from Algeria, Australia, and the UAE. The FSU and Africa are net exporters to Europe, while Asia supplements internal consumption with relatively small shipments of LNG from Alaska and the Middle East.

To see how this gas consumption is distributed across countries, see Table 7–1, which contains a summary of natural gas production and consumption by major region and for some selected countries.

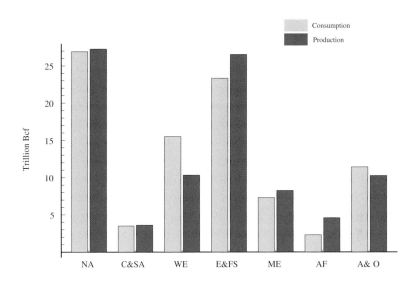

Fig. 7–1 Natural Gas World Consumption and Production, 2001

Notes: measured in trillion cubic feet (tcf).
Source: DOE/EIA, 2003, *International Energy Annual,* 2001, http://www.eia.doe.gov/
emeu/iea/table41.html and "International Dry Natural Gas Consumption
Information", http://www.eia.doe.gov/emeu/international/gas.html#IntlConsumption.
Last accessed 08/03.

Table 7–1 World Dry Natural Gas Consumption and Production

Region/Country	Consumption			Dry Gas Production			Heat content
	1980	1990	2000	1980	1990	2000	BTU/MCF
North America							
Canada	1,883	2,378	3,283	2,759	3,849	6,469	1,020
Mexico	908	946	1,380	1,010	944	1,315	1,057
United States	19,877	18,716	23,455	19,403	17,810	18,987	1,025
Total	**22,668**	**22,040**	**28,117**	**23,172**	**22,603**	**26,771**	
Central & South America							
Argentina	359	717	1,173	280	630	1,321	1,045
Bolivia	14	30	44	79	107	117	1,043
Brazil	42	97	333	42	97	257	1,040
Chile	85	66	184	85	66	40	1,050
Colombia	99	151	201	99	151	201	929
Ecuador	3	4	5	3	4	5	1,300
Peru	40	19	12	40	19	12	929
Trinidad and Tobago	81	177	354	81	177	493	1,191
Venezuela	517	761	961	517	761	961	1,045
Total	**1,241**	**2,024**	**3,304**	**1,277**	**2,014**	**3,430**	

Table 7–1 World Dry Natural Gas Consumption and Production (cont'd)

Region/Country	Consumption			Dry Gas Production			Heat content
	1980	1990	2000	1980	1990	2000	BTU/MCF
Western Europe							
Austria	167	215	272	67	45	64	1,058
Belgium	419	341	554	2	0	0	1,065
France	1,006	1,022	1,420	280	101	66	1,086
Germany	2,621	2,669	3,195	925	715	779	981
Italy	973	1,672	2,498	443	611	587	1,023
Netherlands	1,493	1,538	1,725	3,398	2,693	2,559	894
Norway	35	80	140	917	976	1,867	1,083
Spain	56	192	588	0	49	6	1,140
Turkey	0	122	524	0	7	23	1,045
United Kingdom	1,702	2,059	3,373	1,323	1,754	3,826	1,057
Total	**8,593**	**10,272**	**15,241**	**7,387**	**7,151**	**10,186**	
Eastern Europe & FSU							
Czech Republic	325	532	326	18	25	8	1,013
Hungary	353	396	425	210	174	113	999
Poland	412	413	470	224	137	184	937
Romania	1,251	1,261	600	1,200	1,001	480	998
Armenia	0	0	50	0	0	0	1,047
Azerbaijan	0	0	200	0	0	200	1,047
Belarus	0	0	692	0	0	7	1,037
Estonia	0	0	40	0	0	0	1,001
Georgia	0	0	43	0	0	2	1,047
Kazakhstan	0	0	491	0	0	314	1,047
Kyrgyzstan	0	0	68	0	0	0	1,047
Latvia	0	0	57	0	0	0	1,000
Lithuania	0	0	92	0	0	0	1,001
Moldova	0	0	75	0	0	0	1,064
Russia	0	0	14,130	0	0	20,631	1,009
Tajikistan	0	0	44	0	0	1	1,047
Turkmenistan	0	0	261	0	0	1,642	1,047
Ukraine	0	0	2,779	0	0	636	1,047
Uzbekistan	0	0	1,511	0	0	1,992	1,017
FSU	13,328	24,961	20,115	15,370	28,782	15,370	
Total	**16,419**	**27,569**	**22,800**	**16,801**	**29,757**	**26,220**	
Middle East							
Bahrain	100	205	303	100	205	303	1,047
Iran	232	837	2,221	250	387	2,127	1,056
Iraq	62	77	111	62	148	111	1,047
Kuwait	244	256	339	244	185	339	1,047
Oman	28	99	221	28	99	322	1,047
Qatar	184	276	532	184	276	1,028	1,047
Saudi Arabia	334	1,077	1,759	334	1,077	1,759	1,047
Syria	17	103	215	17	103	215	962
United Arab Emirates	105	663	1,110	200	780	1,355	1,047
Total	**1,311**	**3,599**	**6,822**	**1,424**	**3,716**	**7,570**	

Table 7–1 World Dry Natural Gas Consumption and Production (cont'd)

Region/Country	Consumption			Dry Gas Production			Heat content
	1980	1990	2000	1980	1990	2000	BTU/MCF
Africa							
Algeria	460	681	726	411	1,787	2,940	1,127
Egypt	30	286	646	30	286	646	1,047
Libya	180	175	184	180	219	212	1,047
Nigeria	38	131	238	38	131	440	1,047
South Africa	0	0	58	0	0	58	1,047
Tunisia	13	54	109	13	12	66	1,143
Total	**735**	**1,351**	**2,038**	**686**	**2,459**	**4,440**	
Asia & Oceania							
Afghanistan	2	67	8	60	104	8	1,047
Australia	325	625	796	325	723	1,155	1,069
Bangladesh	50	162	343	50	162	343	979
Brunei	60	46	39	316	318	349	1,154
Burma	11	38	66	11	38	120	1,054
China	505	508	957	505	508	957	1,162
India	51	399	795	51	399	795	1,034
Indonesia	195	547	1,081	630	1,525	2,359	1,090
Japan	903	1,851	2,753	78	72	87	1,045
Korea, South	0	116	669	0	0	0	1,119
Malaysia	56	315	722	56	654	1,498	1,053
New Zealand	47	170	214	47	170	214	1,040
Pakistan	286	482	856	268	428	856	934
Taiwan	43	80	243	43	80	31	1,000
Thailand	0	208	705	0	208	658	977
Total	**2,534**	**5,615**	**10,367**	**2,458**	**5,444**	**9,475**	
World Total	**53,068**	**72,961**	**88,688**	**53,455**	**73,609**	**88,093**	

Notes: bcf=billion cubic feet.

Source: EIA/DOE, Feb 2003, *International Energy Annual,* 2001. http://www.eia.doe.gov/iea/

With higher transportation costs, natural gas trade patterns tend to be more regionally oriented than those seen in oil. Canada exports to the United States; Argentina exports to Chile, Brazil, and Uruguay; Bolivia exports to Brazil. Major suppliers to Western Europe are the Netherlands, Norway, Russia, and Algeria, with small amounts of LNG from Africa and the Middle East. The European market will be more completely discussed in chapter 11. Russia supplies Eastern and Western Europe as well as FSU countries. Turkmenistan and Uzbekistan also supply gas to other FSU countries. All of the gas trade in the Asia Pacific region is in the form of LNG imports to Japan, South Korea, and Taiwan. The LNG market will be discussed more completely in chapter 10. Gas transportation will be more completely discussed in chapter 14.

Natural gas conversions

As with oil, natural gas is measured in various ways. In the United States, the volumetric measure is cubic foot (cf or ft^3), 1000 cubic feet (Mcf), million cubic feet (MMcf), billion cubic feet (bcf) and trillion cubic feet (tcf) usually measured at a pressure of 1 atmosphere = 14.73 pounds per square inch. The energy unit measure is BTU. One BTU is roughly the amount of energy emitted by burning one kitchen match. Sometimes BTUs are aggregated in units of 100,000 called *therms* (in the United Kingdom) or in units of 10^{15} called *quads* (for quadrillion BTUs). In the rest of the world, the volume measure is cubic meters and the energy unit tends to be *kilocalories* or *kilojoules*.

Natural gas is composed primarily of methane (CH_4), which contains 1012 BTU/cf. Natural gas also contains small amounts of heavier hydrocarbon gases: ethane (C_2H_6), propane (C_3H_8), and butane (C_4H_{10}), which raise the energy content. It can also contain other gases such as CO_2, nitrogen, helium, and sulfur dioxide (SO_2), which lower the energy content.

Table 7–1 includes representative energy contents for natural gas from various countries. Energy content for gas varies from a low of 894 BTU/cf in Netherlands to 1300 BTU/cf in Ecuador. Russia, which is the largest producer and exporter of natural gas, has gas averaging 1009 BTU/cf. The United States, which is the second largest producer, has gas with a slightly higher energy content, averaging 1025 BTU/cf. Where precise values are not needed, the energy content is often rounded to a more convenient 1000 BTU/cf or 1,000,000 BTUs per Mcf. Other major exporters, except for the Netherlands, tend to have gas of a bit higher energy content than the United States or Russia.

Four sectors consume the bulk of U.S. natural gas:

- residential (R)
- commercial (C)
- industrial (I)
- electricity (E)

Their historical demands are shown in Figure 7–2. Industry has traditionally been the largest consumer in the United States and remains so today. It has also seen the most volatility in its consumption.

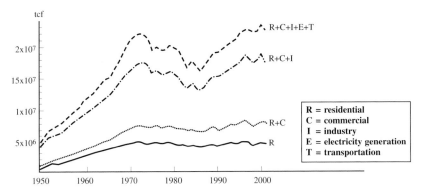

Fig. 7–2 Historical Natural Gas Consumption in the U.S. by Major Sector

Source: Compiled from information in EIA/DOE *Annual Energy Review 2001*. Downloaded from http://www.eia.doe.gov/emeu/aer/natgas/html

Natural gas reserves

Gas is a fairly clean fuel. When burned, it produces less CO_2 and nitrogen oxide (NO_x) than the other fossil fuels, little SO_2, and no particulate matter. Its current known reserves, shown in Table 7–2 by regions and for selected countries, suggest that it is more plentiful than oil on the basis of energy content. Oil and gas are both found at shallow depths. However, the greater heat and pressure at lower depths breaks down the hydrocarbons into smaller molecules like methane. This suggests that natural gas is likely to become relatively more plentiful as our exploration takes our search deeper within the earth. Russia contains a third of proven reserves of natural gas and the Middle East contains another third. All other continents contain proven reserves but they are relatively small by comparison.

Table 7–2 World Natural Gas Reserves

Region/Country	Tcf	Region/Country	Tcf
		Natural Gas Reserves	
North America		**Middle East**	
Canada	59.733	Bahrain	3.249
Mexico	29.505	Iran	812.300
United States	183.46	Iraq	109.800
Total	**272.698**	Kuwait	52.700
		Oman	29.280
Central & South America		Qatar	508.540
Argentina	27.46	Saudi Arabia	219.500
Bolivia	24	Syria	8.500
Brazil	7.805	United Arab Emirates	212.100
Chile	3.46	Yemen	16.900
Colombia	4.322	**Total**	**1,974.569**
Peru	8.655		
Trinidad and Tobago	23.45	**Africa**	
Venezuela	147.585	Algeria	159.700
Total	**253.021**	Egypt	35.180
		Gabon	1.200
Western Europe		Libya	46.400
Germany	12.088	Nigeria	124.000
Italy	8.072	**Total**	**394.846**
Netherlands	62.542		
Norway	44.037	**Asia & Oceania**	
United Kingdom	25.956	Australia	90.000
Total	**160.715**	Bangladesh	10.615
		Brunei	13.800
Eastern Europe & FSU		Burma	10.000
Hungary	1.282	China	48.300
Poland	5.119	India	22.865
Romania	3.556	Indonesia	92.500
Kazakhstan	65	Malaysia	75.000
Russia	1,680	Pakistan	25.078
Turkmenistan	101	Philippines	3.693
Ukraine	39.6	Thailand	12.705
Uzbekistan	66.2	**Total**	**433.313**
Total	**1,967.937**	**World Total**	**5,457.099**

Source: EIA/DOE, Feb 2003, *International Energy Annual*, 2001. http://www.eia.doe.gov/iea/

Evolution of Natural Gas Market Structure

Neoclassical economics views the corporation as a production function with output as a function of the various inputs, which include capital, labor, and materials. It has paid little attention to such philosophical questions as, "Why do corporations exist?" or "What determines their function and their relationship to each other?"

Transaction-cost economics focuses on these more fundamental issues. It suggests that corporations are the integrating force for the increasing complexity and division of labor—the market structure evolves that minimizes transaction costs between entities. After a brief discussion of transaction cost economics in the next section, we will consider how the U.S. natural gas market has evolved historically in response to changes in transaction costs.

Transaction-cost economics

Cost is an extremely important parameter in optimal economic decision-making. The costs we have considered so far in this book are production costs or what we pay for all the resources used in transforming inputs into outputs. They should include both direct and opportunity costs. Total costs can be written as $\sum_{i=1}^{n} p_i q_i$, where p_i and q_i are the price and purchase of the ith factor. Price can be either the market price of purchased resources or the opportunity cost of owned factors of production, and n is the number of factors used. Looking at costs in this way helps us choose the appropriate factor mix. Another way to consider costs is to break total costs into fixed and variable costs to help make short- and long-run economic decisions.

In macroeconomics, costs are viewed in a somewhat different way. When goods are produced, their costs are payments to factors but they also generate income for these factors. If we tally the costs of all end-use products, we get a measure of total income. Aggregate income (Y) represents both the supply of goods available and the income generated. Thus, sufficient income is generated to buy back all goods produced.

In a simple Keynes model, the economy is divided into consumers, business, government, and the foreign sector. Purchases of goods from each of these sectors, respectively, is represented by C = consumption, I = investment, G = government, and Ex - Im = net exports or exports minus imports. Equilibrium in this model comes when income equals purchases:

$$Y = C + I + G + (Ex - Im)$$

Looking at costs in this framework will help in forecasting macro aggregates—an important input into business decision-making.

Once goods are produced, most are exchanged in a modern capitalist economy, which leads to transaction costs—the costs of conducting such exchange. Coase divides them into:

- search costs
- information costs
- bargaining costs
- decision costs
- policing costs
- enforcement costs

The institutional arrangements that govern such transactions are the governance structure. Transaction-cost economics considers four models of transaction governance. From the least to the most formal they are:

- trading in a spot market (*market governance*)
- trading using long-term contracts (*bilateral governance*)
- trading with long-term contracts with a third party helping facilitate the transaction (*trilateral governance*)
- vertical integration (*unified governance*) with transactions that are internal to the company

Survival of the fittest suggests that the chosen mode of governance should minimize transaction costs.

Underlying these costs are some basic economic realities. Economic agents have bounded rationality, and they may be opportunistic. Bounded rationality assumes that agents can't acquire, assimilate, and use all information, nor can they anticipate all future contingencies in a contractual relationship. Opportunism assumes that some agents may take advantage of information asymmetries and make promises they do not intend to keep or may be intentionally misleading in their economic dealings for personal advantage.

Given these two facets of economic behavior, termed *bounded rationality* and *opportunism*, transaction-cost economics focuses on three institutional factors—uncertainty, asset specificity, and frequency of transactions—how they influence transaction costs, and the choice among the four alternative modes of governance. Uncertainty comes from not being able to predict volatility in future states of the world and from complexity, which bounded rationality may prevent us from understanding. If we can't anticipate the future and mitigate opportunism, we need an adaptive, sequential decision-making process to handle new situations as they occur. Complexity requires the flexibility to respond efficiently to possibly conflicting stimuli. An increase in uncertainty will raise bargaining or noncompliance costs as opportunistic parties employ strategic behavior to their advantage.

Asset specificity refers to investment in relationship-specific assets, which may be physical, locational, dedicated, or human. A *non-specific asset* is a piece of standard equipment that can be used in many applications and places by many different operators. A general utility van is a nonspecific asset. A *mixed asset* is more specific and could be a piece of equipment that is not totally specific but is customized in some way. A utility van that has been modified to carry radioactive waste would be a mixed asset. An *idiosyncratic investment* is very specific to a particular transaction. A conveyor belt from a mine to a power plant in an isolated region would be an idiosyncratic investment. For an idiosyncratic investment, the value or opportunity cost of the asset in its next-best use is often quite low and may even be zero. For example, it might be quite expensive to tear up the conveyor belt and move it to another mine.

Now, if you owned the conveyor belt with high sunken costs and were selling to an unscrupulous power plant owner, she might be able to push the price for your services below your total costs. For example, if your total cost for conveying coal is $0.50 per ton, your variable costs are $0.05 per ton, and the conveyor has no alternate value, then the price (P) for conveying coal would have to be greater than $0.05 for you to keep producing in the short run. Any amount above what you require to produce is called a *rent* (R), which would be R = P − $0.05. If price were $0.25, your rents would be R = $0.25 − $0.05 = $0.20.

In the long run, price would have to be greater than $0.50 per ton for you to keep producing. (Your rents would be P − $0.50 for P > $0.50.) At prices less than $0.50, you would not be willing to produce as you would not be making avoidable losses, and you would shut down.

Thus, a return to cover your fixed cost that is not required in the short run is considered rent; if it is required in the long run, it would not be considered a rent in the long run. Such a return is called *quasi-rent.* If price were $0.75 in the short run, then total rents would be $0.75 − 0.05, but $0.50 − $0.05 = $0.45 (the amount of fixed costs) would be quasi-rents. If the price is $0.45 in the short run, you would make quasi rents of $0.45 − 0.05, but no long-run rents—only losses. The difference between rent and quasi-rent is shown in Table 7–3.

Table 7–3 Rents and Quasi-Rents

Long Run	
P<ATC	shut down
ATC <P	total rent = P - ATC
Example	
Short Run	
AVC =0.05	ATC = 0.50
0<P<0.05	shut down
0.05<P<0.50	quasi-rent = P - 0.05
0.50<P	total rent = P - 0.05
Long Run	
0<P<0.50	shut down
0.50<P	total rent = P - 0.50

Now complicate the problem a bit: Suppose you can sell the conveyor at any time for an equivalent return of $0.10 per ton of coal. Now your variable costs are your variable production costs of $0.05 per ton plus your opportunity cost of $0.10 per ton. In the short run, your rents would now be R = $P – $0.05 – $0.10. Quasi-rents would be those rents that would disappear in the long run. They would be $0.50 – $0.15, if P > $0.50, but P – $0.15 for $0.15 < P < $0.50.

Although quasi-rents are required in the long run, in the short-run quasi-rent may be lessened through strategic bargaining, or *hold–up*, if assets are very specific. For example, suppose that you own a pipeline and are selling gas to a single power plant. Your fixed costs are $0.50 per Mcf, your variable costs are $0.75 per Mcf, and your total costs are $1.25. Your pipeline is far from any other buyer. Suppose the power plant refuses to pay you more than $0.80 per Mcf. You can refuse to sell, but with no recourse you are better off getting $0.80 than nothing. With $0.80 you are paying variable costs and have $0.05 towards your fixed costs, so you are losing $0.45 per Mcf. If you stop selling you have nothing towards your fixed cost and are losing $0.50. In the long run, however, you would not replace the pipeline unless you were reimbursed for your total costs. With such idiosyncratic investment and the threat of hold-up, there is a need to establish formal guidelines for the relationship.

The frequency of transactions refers to how often transactions take place. The purchases may be recurrent or occasional. For example, food for the cafeteria may be purchased weekly or even more often, but paper and supplies may be purchased less often, perhaps monthly or quarterly. Large capital equipment may be purchased every decade or even less often. Frequent transactions of non-specific assets in a competitive market are likely to be governed by the market. If someone acts opportunistically in one period, they may be hurt in the next transaction, which should discourage opportunism. With frequent transactions, informational asymmetries are less likely. If uncertainty is low in such a case, there is little incentive to lock in transaction arrangements by more formal forms of governance. If uncertainty is very high, there is the fear of locking in transaction provisions that may be disadvantageous as market conditions change. However, infrequent transactions are more likely to require more formal governance, especially when the assets are very specialized.

Market governance, represented by a spot market, is adequate for transactions involving generalized or nonspecific assets, regardless of transaction frequency, when there are alternative trading partners available to protect against opportunism by either party.

With bilateral governance, two parties contract with each other but remain separate entities, as is the case with long-term natural gas contracts. This is appropriate when recurring transactions involve medium to high degrees of asset specificity, information asymmetries, and there are few buyers and sellers in the market. Products are more likely to be customized with a medium level of uncertainty in the market. Transactions are now frequent enough to recover the contract setup cost. The degree of specificity increases the length and comprehensiveness of contracts, while uncertainty may decrease the length of the contract or cause the inclusion of clauses that allow for specified contract changes as market conditions change. Thus, many natural gas contracts have price escalation clauses, where price is tied to fuel oil or some other energy product. Bargaining typically sets prices under bilateral governance.

Trilateral governance is a slightly different form of governance between two firms. In such a case, two firms trade with each other, but a third firm may be involved in the transaction to make sure one firm does not take unfair advantage of the other. When firms provide for mandatory arbitration by an impartial third party in cases of dispute, there is trilateral governance. Although contracts hold parties to particular activities, it may be expensive to enforce contracts through the courts. When assets are mixed, and transactions are only occasional, trilateral governance may be desirable to reduce the cost of enforcing contracts. With frequent transactions and mixed assets there is less need for a third party in the transaction and bilateral governance may suffice. Neither side is likely to try to take advantage of the other since they know that such behavior may jeopardize future transactions. An example of trilateral governance was the U.S. Export–Import Bank's threat to call in loan guarantees to pressure arbitration between Enron and the Government of India over the unfinished Dabhol power plant project.

Unified governance, also called *vertical integration*, may be appropriate with highly specific assets or idiosyncratic purchases, large information asymmetries, and complex customized products. For example, labor, which often becomes very specific to the firm, is likely to be hired rather than purchased under long-term contract. The choice between unified and other forms of governance for purchasing inputs is termed the *make-or-buy decision*. Purchasing a service that was formerly performed in-house is referred to as *outsourcing*. With unified governance, the need for adaptive, sequential decisions as a result of uncertainty is satisfied without the cost of involving another party by removing the transaction from the market. However, internal transaction or control costs also exist and influence the choice of governance. With infrequent idiosyncratic transactions, there are less likely to be scale economics to unified governance, and firms that go to the market use trilateral governance to insure against hold-up.

Williamson (1993) summarizes the likely types of governance depending on specialization of the assets and frequency of transactions as shown in Table 7–4.

Table 7–4 Likely Governance Structure Matrix

Frequency of Transaction	Non-Specific Assets	Mixed Assets	Idiosyncratic Assets
Occasional	Market	Trilateral	Trilateral
Frequent	Market	Bilateral	Unified

Source: Williamson 1993

The predominant form of governance in the natural gas industry has evolved in response to the market and government interventions. Governance was a competitive spot market at the turn of the century but became unregulated vertical integration in the 1920s. Long-term contracts dominated a highly regulated environment beginning in the 1930s. Deregulation returned it to a competitive spot market in the 1980s and somewhat longer contracts in a more competitive environment in the 1990s with the rise of marketers and market hubs. The decline of physical asset specificity, behavioral uncertainty, and the introduction of systems effects have been responsible for this evolution. We consider this evolution later in this text. Since we focus on transactions that are conducted with regularity, frequency of transactions will not be considered.

Evolution of the U.S. Natural Gas Industry

The U.S. natural gas industry has adapted as regulatory frameworks have changed. In its infancy, the natural gas industry inherited the regulatory structure of the existing town gas (also called coal gas) systems. In the 1800s, distributors of synthetic gas, which was produced from coal, actively sought municipal and state assistance and protection of their investment in coal gasifiers and distribution lines in the form of eminent domain and franchises. Lacking incorporation laws, corporate status was granted on a case-by-case basis in the form of charters. Local rate regulation was practiced until out-of-town natural gas supplies became available, which resulted in the formation of state public utility commissions (PUC).

Short-term contracting was common in the first quarter of the 20th century because the natural gas fields were relatively close to markets. Investment in the specialized assets needed to transport gas to market was fairly low and the existence of multiple pipelines allowed competition. Uncertainty came from the capability of individual wells to sustain production, encouraging the use of a spot market where buyers could switch suppliers as necessary.

The development of welded steel pipelines allowed the long-distance transmission of natural gas. These pipelines introduced the industry into interstate commerce and required a large investment in specialized assets. State regulators were not allowed to control matters beyond their borders but no federal regulatory authority was able to grant monopoly status to protect investments from competition. Therefore, vertical integration was adopted as the common governance structure: Groups of producers and distributors combined into holding companies to build pipelines to bring the gas to market, thereby internalizing the transactions. Fear that these holding companies would abuse their market power— as they eventually did—led to enactment of the Public Utilities Holding Company Act (PUHCA) in 1935. PUHCA allowed only two layers of integration, largely splitting off distribution from production and transportation. Such a breakup was less common in the intrastate market.

The Natural Gas Act (NGA) of 1938 required the Federal Power Commission (FPC) to control interstate transport and sale-for-resale of natural gas. Interstate natural gas pipeline companies were then subject to federal oversight of their rates. Although interstate oil pipeline companies were common carriers controlled by the Interstate Commerce Commission (ICC) to prevent monopolies, gas pipeline companies were allowed to remain private carriers. Common carriers are required by law to provide transportation on a nondiscriminatory basis, whereas a private carrier can restrict carriage to its own products. Common carriage is often called *third-party access.*

Gas purchased from others was recognized at cost or the price paid. However, affiliated producing companies were regulated on the same basis as the pipeline company using original cost of capital and a regulated rate of return. Therefore, vertical integration was discouraged by regulation. There was little competition in the early history of the interstate transportation of natural gas, and regulation rather than vertical integration may have curbed opportunistic behavior. Private regulated monopoly pipeline companies purchased gas from producers and sold gas to distributors under long-term contracts. These contracts, which were for 20 years and longer, tended to be longer than the more typical five-year contracts in non-regulated industries of similar capital intensities. Since the right to abandon sales was typically not granted by regulators, sellers had no reason to request shorter contracts. Since prices were typically the highest allowable by law, neither producers nor pipelines saw any advantages to shorter-term contracts. Regulatory stability also reduced uncertainty and lengthened contracts.

Long-term contracts contained provisions relating to payment, pricing changes, and dedication of reserves, such as:

- take-or-pay clauses that guaranteed payment by pipeline companies to producers of a contracted payment whether product was taken or not
- minimum-billing clauses that obligated local distribution companies (LDCs) to take or pay for contracted volumes made available to them
- most-favored-nation clauses gave the producer the right to the highest price paid by the purchaser within a specified geographic area
- price renegotiation was allowed on specified dates or under certain conditions
- automatic price adjustments were either at specified intervals or triggered by specific events
- exclusivity or sole-source clauses included such things as the dedication of reserves

Embedded in their regulated rates were all the products and services associated with the merchant function, including the commodity, transportation, storage, and all complementary goods. Pipelines bundled these services and were required by certificate and contract obligations to maintain sales capacity and provide it on demand without notice.

Regulation from wellhead to burnertip

It is debatable whether gas producers had monopoly power that would have required price regulation except in isolated fields with few producers. Nevertheless, beginning in 1954, all producer sales-for-resale transactions put into the interstate market were regulated. This regulation disrupted economic allocation by distorting the signaling function of market-determined prices. The result was supply shortages when controlled natural gas prices were depressed below market clearing levels. Supply shortages in the interstate market in the early 1970s prompted the Federal Power Commission (FPC) to raise price ceilings for producers. Continued shortages encouraged industrial users and utilities to develop dual-fuel burning capability, allowing them to switch between gas and other sources such as fuel oil.

In 1977, the U.S. Federal Energy Regulatory Commission (FERC) replaced the FPC in regulating interstate gas pipelines. To increase gas going into the interstate market, the Natural Gas Policy Act (NGPA) of 1978 instituted a phased decontrol of prices for new gas and extended price controls to gas sold in the intrastate market. With uncertain supplies and expected high demand growth, interstate pipelines negotiated high-priced contracts with producers. The contracts contained more stringent than usual take-or-pay provisions.

The worldwide recession of 1981, energy conservation, and fuel switching spurred by high energy prices reduced the demand for oil and gas, which caused oil product prices to fall sharply. However, inflexible pricing provisions in long-term contracts, price regulations, and large take-or-pay obligations on higher-priced gas prevented gas prices from falling to compete with oil products. Pipelines took expensive take-or-pay gas at the expense of lower cost gas with the anomalous result that prices rose in a surplus market. Producers shut in gas supplies, and pressure for political reform mounted.

In 1983, FERC authorized special marketing programs (SMPs) to allow producers to deal directly with end-users, who could switch to competing fuels. This lower-cost gas prevented the further loss of market share, increased the throughput on pipelines, and opened the door for contract carriage and the development of a spot market in natural gas. Some pipeline companies began reneging on their take-or-pay obligations, and producers filed suit against them. However, producers faced prospects of long court battles with no revenue in the interim, and so regulation by court order was found not to be an effective means of enforcement. In response, FERC Order 380 (1984) offered regulatory relief for pipeline customers by eliminating the minimum bill (LDC take-or-pay obligations to the pipeline companies), which put the cost burden on pipeline companies, particularly those with take-or-pay obligations with producers. Minimum billing had allowed pipeline companies to transfer risk associated with their investment in physical assets to their customers. Price risk was also passed on to residential and commercial users by purchased gas adjustment (PGA) rules at the state level, which allowed the cost of gas to the LDC to be passed to the consumer.

The new economic burdens on pipeline companies led them to attempt renegotiation of contract terms with producers. However, uncertainty of supply and demand, limited court precedents, and potential regulatory relief made this a difficult process in the existing institutional environment. After this period of uncertain supply, demand, and regulatory interventions, contracts in the mid-1980s were generally no longer than three years.

Open access: Development of a spot market

The courts found SMPs discriminated against non fuel-switchable end-users. In 1985, FERC Order 436 allowed interstate pipelines to voluntarily offer nondiscriminatory open access transportation capacity. Pipeline customers were allowed to convert their bundled, firm-contract sales volumes to firm (i.e., non-interruptible) transportation. Contract carriage reduced asset specificity and the need for long-term contracts, and the spot market rose from 4% of consumption in 1983 to more than 70% of the gas market in 1987 and 1988. Pipelines challenged Order 436 because it did not reduce their take-or-pay liabilities. These challenges resulted in Order 500 in 1989, which allowed pipeline companies to offset take-or-pay liabilities with the transportation of gas. Sales and transportation were becoming separate economic activities.

The growth of intermediaries

The breakup of the pipeline merchant function and switch to open access left a void in the institutional environment and raised transaction costs. Firms that desired to buy or sell their own gas faced a learning curve. Companies with low sales volumes could not realize economies of scale and were not always perceived as reliable suppliers. Marketers sprang up to pool supply and demand, taking advantage of margins up to 25 cents per MMBtu in the early days of open access. They made money from price volatility, poor pricing signals, discovering new markets, and taking advantage of information asymmetries. These new markets raised transaction costs by introducing performance uncertainty including *nondelivery* (in which a buyer turns back its purchase obligation for better terms elsewhere), long-term sales commitments not backed by long-term purchases, and the bankruptcies of a few large marketers in late 1992 and early 1993. The concern over nonperformance accelerated the consolidation of marketers into affiliation with companies large enough to guarantee contractual performance. As the spot market matured, consolidation took place and margins were down to about 1 cent per MMBtu by 1993.

As marketers gained experience and network effects increased, assets became more specific. A number of marketers have moved toward more vertical and horizontal integration within the industry. There were only about 50 marketers in 1986 that purchased gas for resale. They increased rapidly to more than 350 companies in 1991 before falling back to about 260 in 1995, which is more or less the same number of marketers as in 2000. In 1993, the top 20 marketers moved 46.2 bcf/d. In 1996, they moved 84.8 bcf/d but by the second quarter of 2001, they moved 168.9 bcf/d. Many of the large marketers shown in Table 7–5 are affiliated with gas producers, pipelines, or gathering-processing-marketing companies.

There has also been a strong consolidation among interstate pipelines, particularly since 1997, with some of the largest companies acquiring systems that span much of the United States. The top 10 interstate pipeline-owning companies have almost 90% of the market and the majority have a marketing affiliate as well. (Table 7–6.)

Table 7–5 Top 11 Natural Gas Marketers, First Quarter 2003

Company	1Q03 Bcf/d
BP	20.10
Mirant	14.10
Coral	9.90
Sempra	9.45
ConocoPhillips	8.80
El Paso	5.50
Cinergy	4.17
ChevronTexaco	4.01
Reliant	4.00
Williams	3.50
Oneok	3.50
Total	87.03

Source: NGI Intelligence Press, Inc., http://intelligencepress.com/features/rankings/gas/

Table 7–6 Top 10 Interstate Pipeline Companies, 2001

Company	Pipeline Mileage	# M&A from 1997–2001	Marketing Affiliate
El Paso	45,805	6	El Paso Merchant Function
Williams	27,002	3	Williams Energy Services
Enron*	23,372	0	Enron Online Trading*
Kinder Morgan	18,694	4	KM Gas Services Division
NiSource	15,620	2	
Duke	14,596	3	Duke Energy Trading
CMS	11,071	3	CMS-MST
Dominion	9,950	1	
Reliant	8,204	0	Reliant Energy Wholesale Group
Koch	7,278	1	Koch Energy Trading
Other	24,408		

Notes: #M&A = Number of Mergers and Acquisitions. *Enron filed for bankruptcy in December of 2001.

Source: EIA/DOE, 2001, *Natural Gas Transportation – Infrastructure Issues and Trends*, p 20.

Seasonal demand causes a variation in production under fixed prices but a variation in prices under a spot market. Price volatility (Fig. 7–3) prompted the creation of an organized futures market for natural gas on the New York Mercantile Exchange (NYMEX) in April of 1990 for delivery at Henry Hub, Louisiana. By buying or selling a futures contract, you can essentially lock in a price for your product and avoid risk. (We will consider how futures contract and hedging work in chapter 15). In 1993, NYMEX increased access to futures markets by instituting after-hours electronic trading with NYMEX Access.

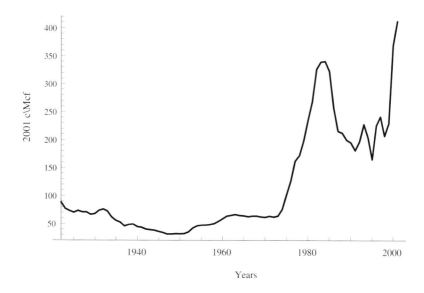

Fig. 7–3 Historical Natural Gas Prices, 1920–2001

Source: 1922–1948, *Twentieth Century Petroleum Statistics,* Degolyer McNaughton, page 99; 1949–2001, EIA/DOE Annual Energy Review 2001, 2002, downloaded from http://www.eia.doe.gov/emeu/aer/

Buyers and sellers hesitated to use the futures market because of the additional skills required, and so marketers have increasingly taken over this risk management. By 1995, gas marketers hedged almost half of their sales. They held almost 70% of gas futures contracts in 2000, while gas producers held less than 10%. However, more recently some independent gas producers have hedged around 20% of their production to lock in high prices. (*OGJ*, 8/13/2001:22)

Pipelines have phased out their gas sales in favor of transportation sales as required by law. Firm transportation, a complementary good to natural gas, has increased as open access has grown. Between 1990 and 1998, 18 new pipeline systems were built. In addition, laterals, looping, and compression capacity have increased daily deliverabilities. From 1990 to 2000, system capacity increased more than 25% while average deliveries increased less than 20%.

Industry restructuring

FERC Order 636, issued in 1992, carried on the deregulation that started with the NGPA. It essentially restructured the pipeline industry by mandating contract carriage, including storage in the definition of transportation, unbundling transportation from sales, and generally encouraging a more competitive atmosphere based on private contracts. Competition was to play a major role in the conduct of business with regulation used only where competition was not present.

Market hubs developed quite rapidly, usually around areas where a number of gas pipelines came together or where storage was available. Prior to 1994, 12 gas market hubs existed in the United States and Canada. As of 1996, 39 market hubs were operational with six more proposed. By 2000, EnronOnline was quoting prices at more than 100 market points. Gas loans, along with balancing and parking services are now offered at many market hubs, which help avoid imbalance penalties and improve reliability. Prices of these and other services, such as title transfer and real time tracking, are market-based. However, transportation and storage services are open access at controlled prices unless given special dispensation to operate in an environment that FERC considers competitive. Figure 7–4 shows some of the most prominent market hubs.

Fig. 7–4 Prominent U.S. Gas Market Hubs

Reliability is one of the desirable features of the traditional merchant function, but it was eroded by restructuring. Buyers became responsible for obtaining their own gas supplies. For some buyers, particularly industrial, commercial, and electric generators who were buying interruptible gas prior to deregulation, this has not been a problem. Fuel switching allows them to absorb the costs of interruption, and they prefer the cheaper spot prices in off-peak periods and the cheaper transport prices that interruptible transportation provides. Interruptible supply, which was 20 to 30% of the market in 1985, had returned to this share in 1995 and is likely to remain in the spot market with interruptible transportation.

Released capacity is transportation capacity that was under long-term contracts that have expired. If contracts were not resigned, the released capacity could be purchased in the market. The combination of released capacity and interruptible transportation capacity approximately amounts to former interruptible capacity. The ability to shift fuels during peak transportation periods has been very advantageous. The largest decreases in transportation costs have been for the electricity generation sector followed by the industrial sector, both of which have traditionally used the bulk of this interruptible service.

In the past, pipelines took possession of gas and then resold it. These sales have been phased out as mandated. Some of the capacity devoted to pipeline-owned gas became *no-notice transportation*, which means shippers can have the capacity on demand. This category is similar to the service provided to non-interruptible customers when pipelines were merchants and transporters. Firm transportation means that the buyer pays for the capacity. This category has increased as marketers and pipelines have stepped in to provide firm gas service as the pipelines had done in the past.

On-system consumers are those that still buy in the traditional way from the local distribution companies, whereas *off-system consumers* are those that have left the old system. Off-system customers do not buy from LDCs but may buy from marketers or even producers. On-system commercial and residential customers have not fared as well because they do not use much interruptible service. Residential and on-system commercial customers saw a decline in gas transportation plus distribution costs of 9% from 1990 to 1995. Off-system commercial, industrial, and electricity generators saw larger declines. Part of the off-system price declines resulted from the change from modified fixed variable transportation rates, in which all customers share in paying the fixed costs, to straight fixed variable rates, in which peak customers pay all of the fixed costs as discussed in chapter 4. However, the price differentials narrowed somewhat with the price run-ups in 2000, as the advantages of interruptible contracts and spot purchases were much lower in a tight market.

Residential, small commercial, and industrial customers have stayed on-system. These customers are often using gas for heating and require reliable peaking service. No-notice delivery under Order 636 allows these users the kind of pipeline service previously provided to firm sales customers. Capacity release of firm transportation also encouraged this movement as it has made firm transportation cheaper and further spurred a gray market, in which reliability is being offered by the bundling of sales, transportation, and storage. This ability to bundle recreates some asset specificity not realized in the separate markets. (Fig. 7–5.)

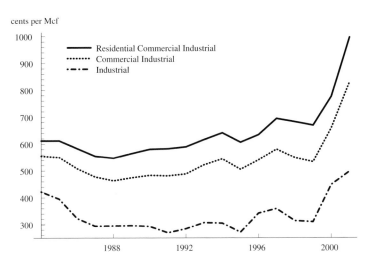

Fig 7–5 Natural Gas Prices by Sector, 1984–2000

Source: EIA/DOE *Annual Energy Review 2001, 2002,* downloaded from
http://www.eia.doe.gov/emeu/aer/

Storage is a complementary good to interruptible transportation and sales. If you have gas stored, an interruption in gas or transportation can be filled by gas from storage. Storage is therefore a substitute for firm transportation. If your gas deliveries are secure, you do not need storage. Earlier marketers did not have access to storage or firm transportation, hence, their reliance on interruptible services. With Order 636, storage also received open access status, in 1993. Open access, along with recent and planned increases in storage services, allow marketers to package gas in ways similar to traditional pipelines.

Straight fixed variable pricing of transportation services increased differences in cost between firm and interruptible transportation and increased the production of working gas storage capacity by 6% from 1992 to 2000. The Gas Research Institute of Chicago forecasts 5% increase in storage from 2000 to 2015. (*OGJ* 5/22/00)

A more open market stimulated the need for information. Order 636 mandated that capacity release on pipelines be made through electronic bulletin boards. The first electronic trading of natural gas began in 1994. By 1996, 16 market hubs had electronic trading and another 17 had electronic bulletin boards, which provided information but no capacity for trading. In late 1996, three major transmission companies—KN Energy (now part of Kinder Morgan), Enron (now under Chapter 11), and Transco (now part of Williams Companies, Inc.)—began posting bulletin board information on the Internet. Early complaints of a lack of uniform standards on the bulletin boards for dispatching, nominating, and monitoring gas sales were resolved by the Gas Industry Standards Board's (GISB) standards for electronic transfer in gas marketing and transportation. These standards were approved by FERC in the summer of 1996 and introduced in the following year. Transportation service companies were required to have internet home pages by August 1, 1997.

While the many market changes outlined above had reintroduced some degree of asset specificity, these information standards have been reducing it. FERC subsequently required that pipelines use Internet compatible messaging and business formats. GISB was renamed the North American Energy Standards Board in 2001 (www.naesb.org), and its standards have been gaining widespread acceptance in the U.S. gas and electricity industries. We will discuss electronic commerce and protocols more completely in chapter 16.

Contracts

Contracting practices have been evolving along with the changes in the natural gas industry. The fixed natural gas prices of pre-regulation days are over. Natural gas prices have become twice as volatile as those for crude oil and four times as volatile as the stock market. In Figure 7–6, it is easy to observe the large price spike in winter of 2000 and 2001 that resulted from cold weather and low volumes of gas in storage, which also contributed to the California power crisis. High storage costs, seasonally related swings in demand, and storage distance from the market contribute to this volatility, thereby shortening contract lengths in the marketing segment. Figure 7–6 shows how price and storage changes have been inversely related since 1990.

The 20-year contracts of pre-deregulation days are no longer the norm but an anomaly, with long-term contracts now defined as a year or more. Spot market sales made up more than half the market from 1987 to 1994 but fell to around 10% or less in 1998 as regulatory uncertainties fell. There has been a tendency for marketers to buy more on the spot market than they sell there, but to sell more on the intermediate and long-term market than they buy there, thus repackaging gas into somewhat longer-term commitments. Players tend to hold portfolios of gas and transportation with contracts of varying lengths.

Contracts used in the spot market have been streamlined and standardized to include quantity, contract term, price, delivery point, payment schedule, and performance obligations. This has lowered transaction costs by saving time on confirmation of verbal agreements and lessening the potential for misunderstanding. In response to the problem of buyers defaulting if they can get a better price, marketers began to include language about nonperformance. For example, if prices fell, and the buyer turned back the gas, then the buyer would owe the difference in price to the original seller. A similar penalty would be invoked if prices rose and the seller would not deliver.

Initially, there was no standard long-term contract for gas marketing and contractual relationships were highly personalized. However, with huge increases in volume, long-term gas contracts have become more standardized, and since the market demands flexibility in pricing, few contracts contain fixed prices. By 1995, 90% of marketers' purchase contracts were indexed; just over 80% of their sales contracts were. To maintain allocative efficiency, these prices are usually indexed to factors that reflect current market conditions, such as NYMEX natural gas futures prices or published spot price indexes.

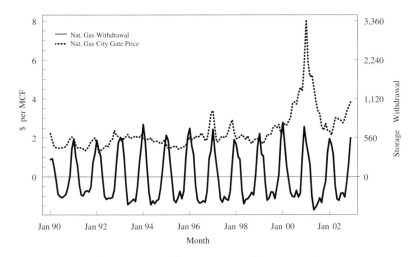

Fig. 7–6 U.S. Gas from Storage and Gas Spot Prices

Source: DOE/EIA *Natural Gas Monthly*, various issues. Downloaded from www.eia.doe.gov

Open access, the increasing interconnectedness of the natural gas grid, and increased storage suggest reduced asset specificity for existing pipelines. This reduction in specificity, along with regulated rates, provides some degree of protection from opportunism, and this, along with increased uncertainty in the natural gas industry and shorter contracts in the marketing of gas, also lead us to expect a reduction in the length of transportation contracts. The Interstate Natural Gas Association of America (INGAA) agrees that 20-year contracts are disappearing. In its post-636 survey of 289 contracts, fewer than 7% ran 20 years or more. The same phenomenon is occurring in intrastate markets, where 20-year transportation contracts, once the norm, are being reduced. In Canada, export permits that required long-term contracts now allow short-term contracts. Short-term exports to the United States became greater than long-term exports beginning in 1995.

For a pipeline relatively isolated from the rest of the network—implying more asset specificity—or where markets are more stable, we expect contracts to be longer. Where new gas assets are being built, we expect contracts to be longer. FERC requires proof of a 10-year commitment for new projects. Traditional funding of large capital projects is highly leveraged, which also requires that contracts be very long. For example, cogeneration facilities often require a firm fuel source, and long-term contracts average 15 years.

Shorter contracts, on average, appear to be here to stay. However, we can expect a wide variation in contract lengths with longer contracts for new or more specific assets and shorter-term contracts where uncertainty is greater. The days of fixed prices appear to be over, as well. If the oil industry is an indicator, indexing and hedging will be primary methods for allocating price risk rather than fixed prices.

Shorter-term contracts make gas prices more volatile, but in a world where prices are indexed, contract length is irrelevant to volatility. In a competitive world, even fixed-price contracts do not ensure stable prices, as shown by the take-or-pay debacles of the 1980s. If we move from governance-by-regulation to governance-by-market, we can expect to see price volatility continue. Ultimately, increased price volatility is the cost of the improved efficiency flowing from increased competition. For those who do not want to take on this price risk, futures and options markets have evolved for the devolution of short-term risk.

New Directions: Electricity Deregulation and Information Technologies

What do we expect for the future? Interruptible gas supplies should clearly stay in the spot market with interruptible transportation. Some gas—supplies in the heating market, where reliability is important—will stay in longer-term commitments with few contracts as long as in the days of regulation. One-to-five year contracts are becoming the norm. As long as prices are highly volatile, we can expect contracts to be shorter and indexed. New capacity may require longer-term contracts to attract financing, as will more isolated capacity that is subject to holdup. A wild card, however, is the pace of electricity deregulation.

As gas marketers enter the free market foray, the terms one-stop energy shopping, BTU marketers, and BTU convergence are heard. There have been numerous mergers between and among gas and electric companies (PanEnergy/Duke Power, Enron/Portland General, Pacific Enterprises/Enova, Houston Industries/NorAm, and Texas Utilities/Enserch, among others). Speculation suggests that other retailers, including telecommunication companies, bankers, and credit card companies are potential entrants to the market. Who finally ends up at the top of the BTU heap will depend heavily on who has the lowest transaction costs.

Another new force is the information revolution, including e-commerce and e-business, which is dramatically changing cost structures and may require new management and business techniques. Such changes will influence transactions across and within companies. In chapter 16 we consider some of the changes that are occurring in information technologies.

Summary

Since 1980, natural gas has exhibited the fastest consumption growth of all fossil fuels, averaging 2.5% per year. It currently constitutes just over 22% of global energy consumption. Natural gas is a fairly clean fuel and more plentiful than oil on the basis of energy content.

North America is the largest producer and consumer of natural gas followed by the FSU. Russia contains one-third of the world's proven reserves of natural gas; the Middle East holds another third. The Western hemisphere (Americas) is almost self-sufficient in natural gas except for small amounts of LNG imported from Algeria, Australia, and the UAE. The FSU and Africa are net exporters to Europe, while Asia receives small shipments of LNG from Alaska and the Middle East.

Various techniques are used to help find the most promising places to look for oil and gas, such as subsurface geologic interpretation, satellite imaging, seismic imaging including 3D seismic, and land and airborne magnetic studies. Produced natural gas is separated from water and other impurities, while heavier, more valuable products, such as ethane, propane, and butane, are extracted and sold separately. Methane and some ethane are sent through pipelines, while propane and butane are typically liquefied under pressure and sold as liquid petroleum gases (LPG). They are removed from the gas and used for heating and cooking, for petrochemical feedstock, and as engine fuel. Natural gas is transported by pipeline, shipped by tanker, and/or stored underground in depleted reservoirs, aquifers, and salt caverns to be used in periods of peak demand.

With higher transportation costs than oil, natural gas trade patterns tend to be more regionally oriented, with regional markets in North America, South America, and Western Europe. Natural gas traded in the Asia-Pacific region takes the form of LNG imports into Japan, South Korea, and Taiwan. In the United States, industry remains the largest—and most volatile—consumer of natural gas.

Transaction and transportation costs have influenced the evolution of the natural gas industry. Transaction-cost economics assumes bounded rationality and opportunism. Given these assumptions, transaction-cost economics focuses on three institutional factors that influence costs: uncertainty, asset specificity, and frequency of transactions; and four types of governance: spot market, bilateral, trilateral, and unified governance. With nonspecific assets, spot markets are likely to dominate. More idiosyncratic assets, coupled with more uncertainty and less-frequent transactions, mean it is more likely that unified governance will occur. Less idiosyncratic assets, coupled with more uncertainty and more frequent transactions, mean it is more likely that spot market governance will occur.

Although frequency-of-transactions has not changed much over the history of the natural gas market, uncertainty and asset specificity *have* changed as markets, technologies, and regulations have evolved. Early production of natural gas tended to occur close to end-use markets. Transportation assets were inexpensive and often regulated at the state level. Supply uncertainty and short-term contracts were common. With the development of welded pipe and distribution systems, assets became more specific and companies moved into the unregulated interstate market. They adopted vertical integration to protect against hold-up in supply to the market. PUHCA intended to split off distribution from production and transportation, while the NGA required the FPC to regulate rates for interstate transport and sale-for-resale. To avoid regulation of gas production, companies separated production from transportation and dismantled vertically integrated systems.

As many pipeline companies became merchants, they bought gas from producers, resold the gas to local distribution companies, and provided all services required in between. Regulatory stability reduced uncertainty, and 20-year contracts developed as the norm. Federal price controls implemented on natural gas sold into the interstate market in 1954 proved to be problematic: the FPC lacked the resources to set prices for the multitude of natural gas wells in existence, and price controls caused shortages in the interstate market by the 1970s. Energy shortages caused the passage of the NGPA in 1978. It phased out price controls on natural gas, but in the meantime created a variety of price categories for natural gas. Pipelines expecting high prices and demand growth became locked into high-priced new gas with take-or-pay contracts. When slow economic growth and energy conservation reduced gas demand in the early 1980s, pipelines took contracted high-price gas and shut in lower-priced old gas.

Prices rose in a surplus market. In 1983, FERC allowed producers to sell surplus gas directly to special customers through SMPs instead of to interstate pipelines, and the gas spot market was born. FERC allowed some distribution companies out of their minimum-billing obligations and pipelines began to renege on take-or-pay obligations. Pipelines tried to renegotiate contracts, but with lots of regulatory, supply, and price uncertainty, contract lengths fell to three years or less.

By 1989, FERC had allowed the pipelines to convert take-or-pay liabilities to open-access firm transportation. Open access reduced asset specificity, and the spot market increased. New marketers entering the business performed many of the functions that had previously been supplied by the pipelines. As the market has matured, and margins have fallen, the number of marketers has continuously been consolidated. Currently, most of them are affiliated with gas producers, pipelines, or gathering-processing-marketing companies. With more uncertainty in the markets, there has also been a strong consolidation amongst interstate pipelines with the top 10 companies now holding almost 90% of the market and most of them having a marketing affiliate.

High-price volatility led to the development of a gas futures market to moderate price uncertainty, and marketers handled much of their risk management this way. FERC Order 636 mandated contract carriage and unbundled sales from transportation and other services. Pipeline transport prices remained regulated. By the late 1990s, firm and no-notice transportation, along with firm gas sales, represented approximately 65% of the market. Interruptible gas and spot sales constituted 32% of the market—roughly equal to interruptible and release capacity for transportation. Market hubs developed rapidly to provide services formerly offered by the pipelines, and storage increased to help provide reliable service that pipelines had formerly offered.

Residential, small commercial, and small industrial customers have stayed on the system and have not seen the degree of price reduction in transportation that large users that could take advantage of interruptible service have seen.

A more open market stimulated the need for information. FERC Order 636 mandated that capacity release on pipelines be made public through electronic bulletin boards, and more recently, through the Internet. GISB standards implemented to make information flow easier between parties in the gas industry have successfully reduced asset specificity and have also made inroads into the electricity business. Contracts have been streamlined and standardized to some extent, although contract lengths vary considerably. Decreased asset specificity and increased uncertainty have led to much shorter contracts than the pre-deregulation standard of 20 years, with current contracts of a year or more considered to be long term and contracts with a term from 30 days to a year considered short term. Less than 10% of gas sales are made in the spot market on terms of 30 days or less. Price uncertainty is being handled by indexing price in some way, usually to some market basket. This basket could include the Henry Hub near-term future price, gas prices at another hub, averages of two or three hubs, and/or fuel oil prices.

Electricity deregulation appears to be creating some convergence between the electricity and natural gas markets. Numerous mergers have joined gas and electric power producers. More than half of the top 20 power marketers at the turn of the 21st century were also in the top 20 for natural gas marketing. Some states have programs to promulgate retail choice, which will encourage further changes in the electric and gas industries. In addition, information technologies are increasingly being applied to the natural gas industry. How these technologies change transaction costs and economies of scale and economies of scope may profoundly influence the natural gas and other energy industries.

8 Externalities and Energy Pollution

An external cost exists when…an activity by one agent causes a loss of welfare to another agent and the loss of welfare is uncompensated.

—David W. Pearce and R. Kerry Turner

Introduction

The extraction, conversion, and consumption of energy may pollute the air and water, create solid wastes that are toxic (or non-toxic), emit unusable heat into the air and water, degrade the land, and possibly contribute to global climate change. Such issues have real impacts on any economic analysis of energy, no matter what one's politics may be.

An important source of air pollution is the burning of fossil fuels. CO_2, NO_x, Sulfur Dioxide (SO_4), carbon monoxide (CO), and particulates are all the result of this process. For example, when we burn methane (CH_4), the most common component of natural gas, which is the cleanest burning fossil fuel, we have the following reaction:

$$CH_4 + 2O_2 => CO_2 + 2H_2O + energy$$

Thus, we add oxygen and methane and get CO_2, water (H_2O), and energy. None of the products of this combustion are toxic. However, the CO_2 build up is thought to cause global climate change when it causes the Earth's atmosphere to absorb more heat and reflect less, much the same as a greenhouse traps heat.

A molecule with more carbon is heavier and emits more CO_2 when burned. For example, when the heavier natural gas molecule ethane (C_2H_6) is burned, it emits twice as much CO_2 as methane but not twice as much energy. This chemical reaction would be:

$$6C_2H_6 + 30O_2 => 12CO_2 + 36H_2O + energy$$

The lightest hydrocarbons are gaseous. With more carbon, the hydrocarbons move to liquid and finally to solid states. Thus, crude oil, which is a mixture of liquid and gaseous hydrocarbon compounds, emits more carbon than natural gas, and coal, which is a solid, emits more carbon than oil. Heavier hydrocarbons contain more energy but their energy content does not increase in the same proportion as their CO_2 emissions. Thus, heavier hydrocarbons emit more CO_2 per unit of energy. For example, hard coal emits around 27.9 tons of CO_2/billion BTUs, oil emits around 23.9 tons of CO_2/billion BTUs, and natural gas emits around 14.4 tons of CO_2/billion BTUs.

Energy is not the only source of greenhouse gases such as carbon dioxide, but it is the predominant source. Other sources include methane from natural leakages, animal flatulence, and decaying hydrocarbons, along with nitrous oxide (N_2O), ozone (O_3) and chlorofluorocarbons (CFCs) from aerosols and refrigeration units. CFCs have been shown to contribute to the deterioration of stratospheric O_3 and are being phased out of use.

With incomplete combustion, results are somewhat different. For example, suppose methane is burned in the following chemical reaction:

$$5CH_4 + 9O_2 => 2CO + 3CO_2 + 10H_2O + energy$$

In this case, the ratio of carbon to oxygen is lower than in the first case, and we end up with toxic CO. Incomplete combustion is the reason that oxygenated fuels are required in some air pollution non-attainment areas of the United States at certain times. Leaner mixtures with more oxygen burn hotter and more completely. If combustion temperatures are very hot (>1000° C or > 1832° F), it is less likely that there is incomplete combustion. However, the heat causes the nitrogen in the air to bond with the oxygen to create nitrogen oxides:

$$N_2 + O_2 => 2NO$$

$$2NO + O_2 => 2NO_2$$

Nitric oxide (NO) is clean, colorless, and non-toxic but unstable and soon reacts and turns to other compounds. If you add water to nitric oxide or nitrogen dioxide (the combination of such nitrogen compounds are usually abbreviated NO_x), you form nitrous and nitric acid in the following reactions:

$$4NO + 2H_2O + O_2 => 4HNO_2$$

$$4NO_2 + 2H_2O + O_2 => 4HNO_3$$

Hydrocarbons often contain impurities. For example, suppose you have sour gas, which is methane with some sulfur. This can be represented by the following combustion:

$$4CH_4 + 5S + 13O_2 => 5SO_2 + 4CO_2 + 8H_2O + energy$$

In addition to CO_2 and H_2O, you also get SO_2. When SO_2 interacts in the atmosphere, with H_2O and oxygen, you get sulfurous and sulfuric acid as follows:

$$SO_2 + H_2O => H_2SO_3$$

$$2SO_2 + 2H_2O + O_2 => 2H_2SO_4$$

When these acids fall with the rain, they can cause damage to the flora and fauna of closed water systems, land vegetation, forests, and buildings. The acid rain increases acidity in the water, dissolving heavy metals such as lead out of the soil and proving detrimental to fish and vegetation in the lakes. It also reduces organic decomposition, washes nutrients out of the soil, and can damage plant leaves and needles.

Heavier hydrocarbons produce additional pollutants including particulates, unburned hydrocarbons, and ash. Volatile organic compounds, which are produced from incomplete combustion of hydrocarbons and from evaporation of organic-based liquids such as gasoline, solvents, paint thinners, and cleaning solutions, react with NO_x in the presence of sunlight to produce O_3. The majority of urban smog consists of this ground-level (tropospheric) O_3.

Examples of solid wastes from energy production include overburden from coal mining, radioactive solid waste from nuclear electricity generation, and drilling muds from oil exploration. Drilling muds are typically not harmful to the environment, since they are mainly made up of water and bentonite, which is a product of pure clay. Nuclear power plant thermal emissions can change the ecosystem of a body of water. Coalmine run-off and crude oil spills are also problematic (Table 8–1).

Table 8–1 World's Largest Oil Spills

When	What
1978	The Amoco Cadiz wreck spilled about 1,600,000 barrels of crude oil (the world's largest tanker spill), significantly damaging the Brittany coast of France.
1979	Mexico's Ixtoc I blew out and spilled about 3,350,000 barrels of crude oil into the Gulf of Mexico.
1989	U.S. tanker Exxon Valdez spilled about 260,000 barrels of crude oil (the largest U.S. oil spill), significantly damaging Prince William Sound, Alaska.
1989	Iranian supertanker Kharg 5 ruptured and spilled about 450,000 barrels, creating a 100-square-mile oil slick in the Atlantic.
1991	Iraq damaged Kuwaiti wells and about 11,000,000 barrels of crude oil spilled into the Persian Gulf during the Gulf War.
1994	A damaged pipeline spilled about 50,000 barrels of crude oil at Milford Haven, Wales.
1996	The supertanker Sea Empress ran aground and spilled more than 600,000 barrels of oil at Milford Haven, Wales.
1999	The Maltese tanker Erika sank and spilled about 3,000,000 gallons of oil off of Brittany.
2000	Petrobras, the Brazilian national oil company, had a ruptured pipeline off Rio de Janeiro that spilled 340,000 gallons of heavy oil into Guanabara Bay.
2000	The oil tanker Westchester ran aground near Port Sulphur, Louisiana, and spilled about 567,000 gallons of crude oil into the lower Mississippi River.

Source: http://www.infoplease.com/ipa/A0001451.html8.1

Pollution as a Negative Externality

To understand how energy pollution affects energy economic policies, we begin our analysis with Figure 8–1.

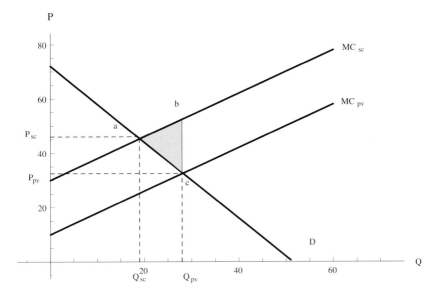

Fig. 8–1 Supply and Demand in a Market with Negative Externalities

D equals the demand or the marginal benefits in the oil market. MC_{pv} represents the private marginal costs of the private supply curve. We assume that the production and transportation of oil creates oil spills and other pollution. With the included external costs of such pollution, the supply curve representing private and external costs or all social costs would be MC_{sc}. The private market allocation in this market would be at P_{pv} and Q_{pv}. At the private market solution, Q_p, the true social costs are greater than the benefits, with the area abc representing the social losses in this case.

If we could internalize the externality, then the social costs would equal the private costs and the market price and quantity would be P_{sc} and Q_{sc}. If we knew the social costs, we could internalize this cost with a tax equal to bc in this market. That would put the market price equal to the social optimum and would put us at the price and quantity that maximized social welfare (i.e., producer plus consumer surplus). In chapter 2, we noted that taxes can distort the market and cause social losses. However, in this case, the tax corrects a social loss and makes the market more efficient. If a tax is taken off another product or service where it is causing inefficiencies and put on energy to correct inefficiency, we get what is called a *double dividend*. We remove social losses in two markets at the same time.

Optimal Level of Pollution

Another interesting way to look at externalities focuses on the pollutant itself and considers its costs—and benefits. Costs include health costs, property damage, and aesthetic costs. The benefit of pollution is the savings from not having to clean up the environment, which has been used as a waste repository free of charge. Suppose the costs and benefits for a water pollutant are as they are shown in Figure 8–2.

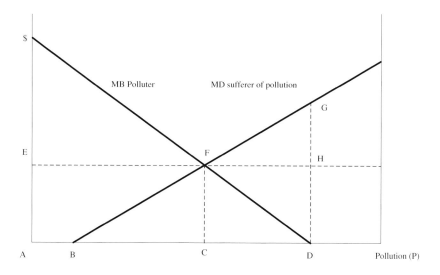

Fig. 8–2 Costs and Benefits of Water Pollution

A small amount of pollution may cause no damage if the natural environment is able to absorb it. However, as pollution increases, we exceed the environment's carrying capacity, and marginal damage (or the damage of the last unit of pollution) gets larger as the pollution increases. Thus, the environment becomes less able to cope as pollution increases. On the benefit side, we note that marginal benefits are high for the first units of pollution suggesting it is very difficult to emit almost no pollution. However, as the amount of pollution increases it becomes increasingly easier to not emit or clean up the pollution. For example, if you have a stack gas scrubber at an electric power plant, it takes out about 96% of the SO_2. Further reductions would require another scrubber to catch the exhaust from the first scrubber to take out 96% of the last 4%, or 3.84%. This next 3.84% is then very expensive to abate.

In Figure 8–2, if those who suffer the damages of pollution have rights to the water, pollution will be at B. With less pollution than B, they will suffer no damage. When there is more pollution than B, they will suffer damages. If polluters have rights to the water, then the pollution level will be at D. Since they don't benefit from pollution beyond D, they will not pollute more than D. Since there are benefits for all units when pollution is less than D, they will pollute up to point D.

Alternatively, if property rights are not well defined, the pollution level would likely be at D, as well, as those having no recourse will not be able to stop the pollution. From an economic point of view, the optimal level of pollution—what economists would call an efficient level of pollution—is at point C. At pollution levels less than C, the benefits of pollution are greater than costs, so society benefits from pollution. After C, costs are greater than the benefits, so society loses if we pollute more than C.

If the polluter is large and the group suffering damages is also large, the two are likely to get together and negotiate an optimal solution. For example, suppose the polluter is a coal mine with runoff that makes a local river more acidic. A refinery downstream uses the water in its processes. Acidic water has to be cleaned up or it corrodes the refinery equipment. Suppose that initially the coalmine has the property rights and pollution is at D. For the last unit of pollution, the refinery would be better off if it paid anything less than GD to get the coal mine not to pollute. Similarly, for the next-to-last unit of pollution there is some payment from the refinery to the coal mine to not pollute that would make both the refinery and the coal mine better off. Through negotiation, the firms could come to some payment schedule that would make them both better off until we reach point C. For less pollution, there is no payment between them that would make them both better off. We could start at B and make the same arguments why the firms should end up at C.

This result was first arrived at by Coase, who noted that given well-defined property rights and the absence of transaction costs, an optimal level of pollution is derived by bargaining between polluter and sufferer, no matter who holds the original property rights. Transaction costs in this context include money costs as well as the time and effort required to conduct the transaction.

However, transaction costs are often very high. Take the example of a refinery polluting a low-income neighborhood. Although the residents as a whole may suffer more damages than the refinery gains by polluting, it may be difficult and costly to organize and negotiate a better solution with the refinery. Further, they may not have access to any market where they can convert the health damages they will suffer into the cash to make payments to the refinery. In such a case we think markets will fail, and most economists agree that the government should intervene.

Four different policies could be implemented in this case. The government could:

1. set a pollution standard permitting pollution at level C
2. set a tax on pollution of AE
3. sell pollution permits equal to AC
4. subsidize clean up or abatement of AE

Setting standards and enforcing them tends to be how U.S. environmental policy has been implemented. It is called command and control. If the regulation were obeyed, the firm would pollute C and abate or no longer pollute amount CD. The polluter's losses would be the cost of abatement or area CFD in Figure 8–2.

The last three, more market-oriented policies are often called incentive-based policies. They include a tax on pollution, selling pollution permits, or offering a subsidy to help abate pollution. In Figure 8–2, if a tax equal to AE were set, then the optimal level of pollution would also occur.

For pollution before C, the benefits are greater than the tax; it is beneficial to pollute and pay the tax. After C, the benefits of pollution are less than the tax, and the facility is better off not polluting. The distribution effects of the policy indicate the gains and losses from the policy. The total tax the polluter would pay would equal AEFC, and the cost of abatement would be CFD. If pollution had been at D before the policy, the benefits to society would be equal to FGD. The government would have revenues of AEFC, which would be more than enough to compensate for the losses from pollution of BFC.

The government would have to give out or sell pollution permits equal to AC. If the government auctioned off permits, firms would have to buy them in order to pollute. If the price of a permit was less than AE, then firms would want to pollute more than AC. There would not be enough permits, and the price of permits would be bid up. Similarly, if the price of permits were higher than AE, there would be forces pushing the price down. The cost of permits to the polluters should be the same as in the tax case.

A subsidy on abatement would have to be equal to AE. Then for any pollution after C, the benefits to pollution would be less than the subsidy. It would be better to take the subsidy and abate. However, before C, the benefits to pollution are higher than the subsidy. The polluter is better off polluting than taking the subsidy and abating. In this case the polluter gets a total subsidy of CFHD, but abatement only costs CFD for a net profit of FHD.

Economists do not favor a subsidy policy, believing it forces victims to pay to reduce pollution. Most recommend the polluter-pays principle. Making victims or the government pay to reduce pollution could in principle get us to a social optimum but economists believe that making the polluter pay is likely to be more efficient for a couple of reasons. Victims are usually a more diverse group than polluters. Thus, collecting fees from them has higher transaction costs and incentives exist for each victim to want a free ride, and let others pay. Also, if either the government or victims pay polluters to not pollute, it could cause polluters to exaggerate how much they would like to pollute to increase their payments. It could also lower costs for polluting industries and so encourage entry into the industry by more of them, further raising levels of pollution and subsidy costs to the taxpayers. Having the polluter pay also appeals to society's sense of fairness. The higher costs will be reflected in higher goods prices in polluting industry, causing consumers to pay the full cost of the product.

Regional differences in optimal pollution levels

When it comes to standards, the government often picks a technology, which it applies uniformly across regions and firms. Economists are skeptical of standards for three reasons. First, it is unclear whether policymakers are better at picking cleanup technology than the more decentralized market. Second, it is not true that pollution damages or costs are uniform across regions. Third, the benefits of pollution are hardly uniform across firms.

In terms of the second reason—that pollution costs vary across regions—automobile emissions in the middle of Wyoming may cause far less damage than those in the middle of Manhattan. In Figure 8–3, suppose that MC_1 equals marginal cost or marginal damage in Manhattan while MC_2 equals marginal cost or damage from pollution in Wyoming. From an economic efficiency point of view, the amount of pollution should be P_2 in Manhattan and P_1 in Wyoming.

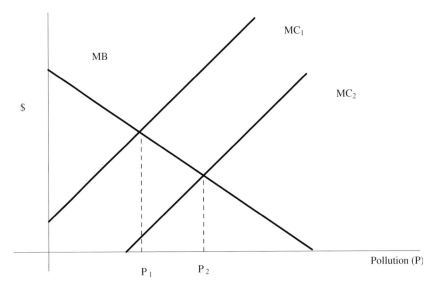

Fig. 8–3 Varying Marginal Costs by Area

The third reason economists don't favor standards is that pollution control benefits are not the same for all polluters. Remember that the benefits of pollution are the benefits of not cleaning up pollution or the costs of abatement. For example, let the benefits of pollution above be $MB_p = 10 - 2P$. The optimal level of pollution (P) from the firm's point of view would be where the marginal benefits of pollution would be $0 = 10 - 2P$ or $P = 5$. If the firm abates (A) then amount of pollution would be $P = 5 - A$. Since the cost of abatement is the benefit from not polluting $MB_A = 10 - 2P = 10 - 2(5\text{-}A) = 2A$.

Now, let's look at control from a different angle, and focus on these costs of abatement across two firms. Let the amount we need to abate be the distance CD from Figure 8-2. Suppose that Figure 8–4 represents the costs of SO_2 abatement for two electric power producers. The costs of abatement are the costs of stack gas scrubbers and other pollution control devices and any foregone output that results from abatement. These costs are a reflection of the benefits of pollution in the above model. In the figure, read the amount abated for firm one from the left hand axis and the amount abated for firm two from the right hand axis. The horizontal axis represents the amount that the law requires to be abated and is the optimal amount of abatement or the amount CD from Figure 8–2.

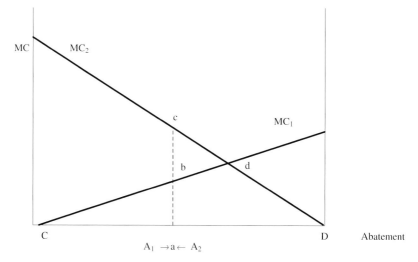

Fig. 8–4 Marginal Abatement Costs for Two Firms

Suppose the allocation of abatement is at point a with firm one abating A_1 and firm two abating A_2. Notice that at this allocation, the cost for firm one to abate is ab, and for firm two it is ac. It would be cheaper for society if firm one abated more, and firm two abated less. This would be true until we arrived at the point where MC_1 crossed MC_2. Beyond that point it would be more expensive for firm one to abate than firm two. Thus, from a social point of view, if the government set the same standard for both firms at a, the losses would be cbd.

The government could set each firm's abatement rate, with firm one required to abate more than firm two, or if it knew cost, it could pick a tax rate to achieve the optimal level of abatement for each. This would, however, require that the government know the cost situation for each firm. Since such information is proprietary, it is unlikely that the government would get the targets or the taxes right. Each firm has an incentive to exaggerate abatement costs to be required to abate less. In addition, it would seem politically difficult to impose different standards on different firms.

For these reasons, economists tend to most often favor marketable permits. Such permits require that the government make a decision on the optimal level of pollution. Once that is decided, pollution permits are auctioned. If the price of permits is too low, firms will want to pollute too much, resulting in a shortage of permits and their price will be bid up. Similarly, too high a price will result in a surplus of permits. The market will determine the price of the permit and then firms with low abatement costs will abate more, and firms with high abatement costs will abate less, as is socially efficient.

Early U.S. pollution regulations favored pollution standards or the command-and-control approach. However, with the high cost of this approach and at the urging of economists, more and more market incentives have been introduced into the regulations. A convincing argument for using marketable permits comes from the SO_2 regulations in the Clean Air Act Amendments of 1990. These regulations set up a market in SO_2 emission permits beginning in 1995. Before the regulations were passed, estimates of compliance cost, which would determine permit price, were between $170 and $1000 dollars a ton with a few even higher. Once implemented in 1995, permits averaged around $80 per ton. (*Economic Report of the President*, 1997). Thus, by allowing firms to decide on their own abatement strategy, the costs of the program were much lower than expected. This result is illustrated in Figure 8–5. The 441 electricity generating units in the sample were ranked by their emissions in 2000 after the permit system had been in effect for several years. The rising white line measures their emissions. The solid vertical black lines are emissions in 1985. Note that there is no pattern to which polluters reduced emissions most. Some highly emitting firms are still highly emitting and buying permits, while other firms that were highly emitting before have found it cheaper to abate. These results are one of the reasons that the United States is strongly in favor of tradable CO_2 permits. The average pollution in 1985 for all units was 1.58 lbs/MMBTU, which fell to 0.95 lbs/MMBTU in 2000.

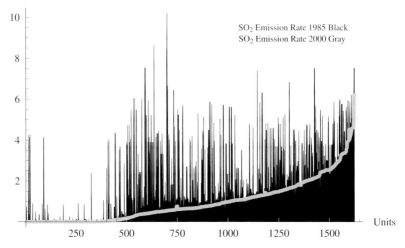

Fig. 8–5 SO_2 Emissions Rate Reductions for 441 Generating Units, 1985 and 2000

Difficulties Measuring Costs and Benefits of Pollution

In theory, we can derive the optimal amount of pollution from energy sources. In practice, however, we need accurate estimates of both costs and benefits. Determining the marginal benefit of pollution is probably easier than determining the marginal cost. The marginal benefit is the opportunity cost of pollution, or the cheapest way not to produce that pollution, whether it comes from reducing production of final product, buying abatement equipment, or using different production materials. If the abatement is a standard process, one can use market prices to estimate costs. For new processes, the costs will be less reliable and have to be derived from engineering estimates of equipment and production costs.

Some damages are easier to measure than others. For economic damages, we can go to markets. If we want to measure the damage of acid rain on timber, we can go to biologists and get measures of reduced growth and lost harvest and multiply this lost harvest by market prices. If particulate matter makes our clothes dirtier, we may be able to monetize the change by measuring extra cleaning bills.

Other damages are harder to measure because there are no markets for them. For example, CO has health effects of increasing morbidity (sickness) and mortality. Although we may be able to use medical evidence to quantify statistical days of illness and death, it is not easy to change these into monetary measures. A number of ways have been devised to try to measure such non-market costs. One direct approach is contingent valuation, in which surveys determine either willingness to pay to avoid something unpleasant or willingness to accept a payment to put up with an unpleasantness.

An indirect approach would include *hedonic pricing*. This is pricing that would fit a function on empirical data (e.g., the price of a house as a function of the house's characteristics such as area, number of bathrooms, or local amenities, along with air quality or other pollution factors). The decrease in housing price from each negative externality would be a measure of how the market values the externality.

The value of a life (V) can be measured by the value people seem to place on their lives as measured in the market place. For example, suppose that people are willing to increase the risk of death in a given year by 1 in 10,000 for a $500 higher salary. If they die, their loss is V and if they live their loss is zero. Their expected loss (L) is:

$$L = 0.0001*V + 0*0.9999$$

Remember the expected value of a random variable is $\sum_{i=1}^{n} X_i P(X_i)$, where X_i is the value assigned to an event, and $P(X_i)$ is the probability of the event occurring, n is the number of events that can occur, and $\sum_{i=1}^{n} P(X_i) = 1$. If they are willing to take the above expected loss for $500, they are setting their expected loss equal to $500 or:

$$0.0001*V + 0*0.9999 = \$500$$

Solving for V gives the implicit value (V) they are giving to their life or:

$$V = \$500/0.0001 = \$5,000,000$$

Summary

Energy production, transportation, conversion, and consumption are all significant sources of pollution. Since pollution is a negative externality, it creates costs that consumers and producers do not directly account for and respond to in their production and consumption decisions. This failure to directly observe negative externalities leads to overconsumption of energy services and social losses.

From an economic point of view, the socially optimal level of pollution is not a zero level of pollution but one that maximizes the net benefits of pollution. The net benefits of pollution equal total benefits, which are the savings from not having to use scarce resources to clean up the mess, minus total costs, which include the damage to health, property, and recreation resulting from pollution. With decreasing marginal benefits of pollution and increasing marginal cost of pollution, the optimal level of pollution is where marginal benefits are equal to marginal costs. This optimal level may vary across regions.

There are various ways to determine a socially optimal level of pollution. If transaction costs are low, no party has disproportionate market power, and the parties are well informed, the Coase theorem suggests that private parties might negotiate an optimal level of pollution regardless of who has the property rights to the environment. However, when there are many parties and transaction costs are high, the government needs to step in. If the government is well informed, it can determine the optimal level of pollution and policies to obtain that level. The government could use command and control by setting pollution standards, and it may even dictate the technology. Alternatively, the government could use more market-based economic approaches and subsidize polluters to clean up, tax or charge for pollution, or issue marketable pollution permits.

Economists favor the polluter-pays principle and marketable pollution permits. Subsidizing abatement, rather than charging for pollution, may encourage firms to exaggerate the amount of pollution they would produce without the subsidy and inflate the cost of abatement. With marketable permits, those firms with cheaper abatement will abate more and those with higher abatement costs will abate less. The market will set the costs of the permit to be the marginal cost of the last unit abated, which should be the same across all polluters.

Determining the optimal level of pollution requires knowledge of the benefits and damages from pollution. The benefits of pollution are measured by abatement costs. These costs can be determined by market prices for well-developed abatement technologies but must be estimated from engineering estimates for new technologies. Damages include those that have market measures and those that do not. For non-market costs, contingent valuation and hedonic pricing may be used, and life may be valued by using the amount of compensation needed for people to work in riskier occupations.

9 Public Goods and **Global Climate Change**

The parties should protect the climate system for the benefit of present and future generations of humankind, on the basis of equity and in accordance with their common but differentiated responsibilities and respective capabilities.

—Global Climate Convention, Rio de Janeiro, 1992

Introduction to Public Goods

As we have seen, build up of CO_2 is considered an externality, since emissions from one source affect others. But abatement in this case has the special characteristics of a *public good*. A public good is one in which one person's consumption of the good does not influence or reduce another person's consumption of it, or there is non-rivalry in consumption. With public goods, you may also not be able to exclude someone from benefiting. For example, you cannot stop someone from looking at a lighthouse as they sail by. Cost-of-production is independent of the scale of use. Once produced, marginal costs of an extra unit of consumption of a public good may be zero.

In the environmental context, examples of public goods include control of global pollutants, such as CO_2, to prevent global warming, maintenance of biodiversity, and control of chemicals that damage stratospheric O_3 levels. If CO_2 build up is decreased, many benefit because the climate is not disrupted. If biodiversity is preserved, everyone benefits from new medicines developed or genetic material that can be used for agriculture. If we phase out CFCs and stop destroying the stratospheric ozone that protects us from harmful ultraviolet radiation, we all benefit from lessened risks of blindness and skin cancer. In these cases, we expect the market to misallocate and produce too little of the public good from an economic efficiency point of view. Therefore, the private market would be likely to produce too little biodiversity and too little control of CFCs and CO_2.

To see why, consider an ecosystem with two consumers—coastal dweller, Clarence, and inland dweller, Ingrid. Their demands for CO_2 control, which are their marginal benefits of abatement, are shown in Figure 9–1. Assume that the benefits of abatement are higher for the coastal dweller, because global warming would raise the sea level and flood the coast. To make life simple, assume that CO_2 control is a constant-cost industry and that the marginal cost of removing or abating an additional ton of CO_2 from current emissions is constant at MC. Let abatement be the number of tons of CO_2 removed.

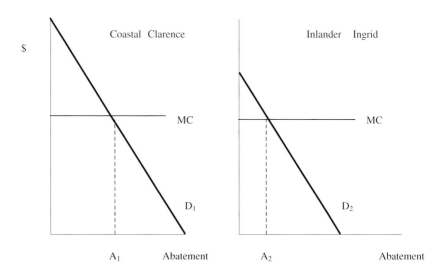

Fig. 9–1 Coastal and Inland Demand for CO_2 Abatement

The demand for abatement represents the marginal benefit of abatement or the expected gain from less climate change. If the world consisted only of Clarence, he would maximize the net benefits of CO_2 abatement by abating A_1. If the world consisted only of Ingrid, she would abate A_2. With both persons, Ingrid would like Clarence to abate A_1, and she would like to have a free ride and spend nothing on abatement. Clarence would prefer that Ingrid abates A_2, so he could have a free ride and only abate $A_1 - A_2$. The fact that you can't exclude anyone makes both individuals want to spend less than they would in the absence of the other person and have a potential free ride. Thus, we would expect to get less of the public good than would be the optimum for either person alone.

A second problem with the market allocation of public goods is that there is a positive externality for the other group for each ton of CO_2 abated. Thus, the total social benefit of a ton of CO_2 abated is the sum of the benefits from the inland and the coastal person (D_s). We can represent the total social benefits of abatement as the vertical sum of the two benefit curves as shown in Figure 9–2.

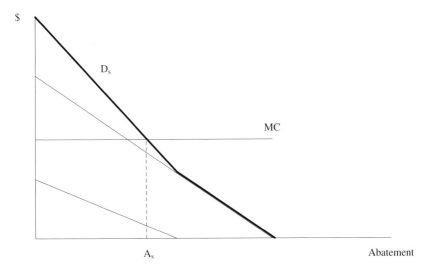

Fig. 9–2 Total Social Benefits and Social Optimum for CO_2 Abatement

Figure 9–2 shows the optimal level of abatement is A_s, which is higher than the private optimal level for either the coastal or inland person. However, due to externalities and the effects of free riding, the market is unlikely to produce A_s. The social losses in a private market depend on how much public good is produced. For example, if the private market produced A_p as in Figure 9–3, then the social losses would be the area abc.

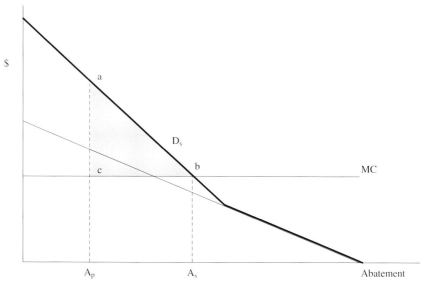

Fig. 9–3 Social Losses for Private Market Production of Public Goods

Now let's do a numerical example that is represented in Figure 9–4.

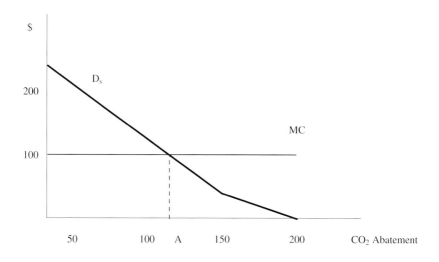

Fig. 9–4 Social Optimum for a Public Good

Suppose the marginal benefit for CO_2 abatement for our two consumers are as follows:

$$MB_1 = 150 - A_1$$

$$MB_2 = 100 - 0.5A_2$$

If the marginal cost of abatement is 70, then the coastal dweller's (1) optimum would be:

$$MB_1 = 150 - A_1 = 70 => A_1 = 80$$

The inland dweller's (2) optimum would be:

$$MB_2 = 100 - 0.5A_2 = 70 => A_2 = 60$$

However, two would want one to abate 80, leaving two to abate nothing, whereas one would want two to abate 60 leaving one to abate only 20. Free riding creates pressures to produce less than the individual optimums of either 60 or 80. In addition, the social optimum may be greater than either individual's optimum. To see this, compute the social optimum. First, vertically sum the two marginal benefit curves. For each level of abatement, vertically sum the marginal benefits. This vertical summation is:

$$MB_1 + MB_2 = 150 - A + 100 - 0.5A = 250 - 1.5A$$

Notice that this is the marginal benefit curve for $0 < A < 150$. After that, the marginal benefit for one becomes zero and total benefits are only the benefits accruing to two. Thus, the kink in the social marginal benefit curve is at $A = 150$, since only consumer two benefits from more than 150 units of abatement.

The social optimum is computed from:

$$250 - 1.5A = 70 => A = 120$$

Since $A_s = 120$, we are to the left of the kink and this is the social optimum. If A_s had been to the right of the social optimum, we would have to re-compute the social optimum using the marginal benefit from two, since two constitutes the whole benefit curve to the right of the kink.

From a social point of view, we should abate 120. Since the private sector is unlikely to provide this amount of abatement, we need government to step in to accomplish abatement. Who pays for the abatement is an issue that will have to be solved politically.

Our first policy has been to set marginal social benefits equal to marginal costs. However, these cases all assume that costs and benefits are known with certainty, which is not the case; there are large uncertainties in measuring the benefits of CO_2 abatement as noted by Hinrichs (1996), because we do not totally understand the process of global warming. So how should we proceed? We could do nothing and just wait and see. If we can quantify the uncertainties, we might proceed as above. For example, suppose scientific evidence suggests two possible scenarios. The first has a 75% probability and the second has a 25% probability. The two scenarios have the following global marginal benefit functions for CO_2 abatement.

$$MB_1 = 100 - A$$

$$MB_2 = 50 - 0.2A$$

Marginal abatement cost = 27.5. With such information, we can maximize the expected value of abatement. (Remember the expected value of a random variable $= \sum_{i=1}^{n} X_i P(X_i)$, where X_i is value assigned to an event, $P(X_i)$ is the probability of the event occurring, n is the number of events that can occur, and $\sum_{i=1}^{n} P(X_i) = 1$.) Then, the expected marginal benefit of abatement is:

$$E(MB) = \sum_{z=1}^{n} MB_i * P(MB_i) = MB_1 * 0.75 + MB_2 * 0.25$$

$$= (100 - A) * 0.75 + (50 - 0.2A) * 0.25 = 87.5 - 0.8\,A$$

To maximize the net benefits of abatement, we set the expected marginal benefit of abatement equal to the marginal cost:

$$MC = E(MB) = 27.5 = 87.5 - 0.8A$$

And solve for:

$$A = 75$$

Abatement Policies

Since abatement costs money, members of local industry are often worried that environmental protection will make them noncompetitive in global markets. However, Porter (1990) argues that strong environmental regulations that require abatement may actually produce net savings by stimulating new processes that save resources. He offers anecdotal evidence from the nonferrous metals industry. Economists tend to be a bit skeptical of his arguments. If all these cost savings are lying about, wouldn't profit-maximizing firms be likely to snatch them up in the absence of regulation?

Consider three economic approaches to setting abatement policy:

1. the economically efficient policy
2. the no-regrets policy
3. the minimaxing regrets policy

The economically efficient policy sets marginal cost of abatement equal to marginal benefits. The no-regrets policy has us undertake activities that help remove existing market distortions and work to mitigate global warming as well.

For example, current subsidies to fossil fuel industries cause market distortions. Removing these subsidies would raise costs in these industries and help reduce CO_2 emissions. Automobiles cause local air-pollution problems as well as traffic congestion. Policies to reduce the amount of driving and amount of fuel used would help solve these problems plus contribute to CO_2 reductions. Taxing parking subsidies given to employees by businesses would reduce a market distortion, increase the cost of driving to work, and cause some to switch to mass transit. Encouraging bicycling and walking to work could improve health in countries such as the United States, where obesity is a problem. These policies would all help solve existing problems with certainty, so we would have no regrets if we implemented them, even if global warming turned out to not be a problem. Reducing taxes in markets without externalities and increasing them in energy markets to reduce both local and global pollutants are said to have a double dividend since they reduce distortions in both markets.

Energy Conservation and Its Cost

Providing information on cost-effective conservation for households would conserve energy and save on consumer energy bills. Such information has some aspects of a public good. There is non-rivalry in consumption—my consumption of it does not preclude someone else from also consuming it. It is transferable—if I teach you, then we both know it.

The marginal cost of an extra user is minimal, particularly with new information technologies. These pubic good attributes suggest that the market may under-produce information, and there may be room for the government to produce and disseminate information about effective conservation measures.

Is conservation cost-effective? To determine the answer to this question, we need to compare capital and operating costs per unit of energy service for traditional versus an energy conserving technology. For example, a 75-watt incandescent bulb ($75/1000 = 0.075$ kW) lasts about 600 hours. However, an incandescent light is very inefficient, with about 90% of the energy lost to heat. A 20-watt ($20/1000 = 0.020$ kW) compact fluorescent bulb will produce the same amount of light, will last around 8400 hours, and usually costs less after operating expenses are factored in. Suppose the lights will run 1200 hours per year and electricity costs $0.07 per kWh. The interest rate is 10% and interest is compounded monthly. The hourly operating cost for the incandescent bulb (c_i) is the number of kW per bulb times the cost per kWh = (kW/bulb)*(cost/kWh) = cost/(bulb*h) = the cost of operating the bulb for an hour = $(0.075)*0.07 = \$0.00525$ per hour. Similarly, the hourly operating cost (c_f) for the fluorescent is $(0.020)*0.07 = \$0.0014$ per hour.

The capital cost per unit of output—called the *levelized cost* for each bulb—is a bit harder to compute. Since we have to pay for the bulb up front but get the services spread out over time, we must allocate the capital cost across output and across time. To see how, let X be the monthly output of light (1200/12) that begins immediately and lasts for n years. K is the initial capital cost. You pay your bill monthly. We assume output is spread equally over the year. Let $ be the unit cost per kWh—the levelized cost—that would make the net present value of the future flow of service equal to the purchase price.

$$K = \frac{\$X}{1 + \frac{r}{12}} + \frac{\$X}{(1 + \frac{r}{12})^2} + \ldots + \frac{\$X}{(1 + \frac{r}{12})^{n*12}}$$

Then:

$$K = \$X \sum_{i=1}^{12n} \frac{1}{(1+\frac{r}{12})^i}$$

Solving for:

$$\$ = \frac{K}{X} \Big/ \sum_{i=1}^{12n} \frac{1}{(1+\frac{r}{12})^i}$$

The package of incandescent bulbs costing K = \$1.40 would last n = one year and would run X = 100 hours per month. Applying the above formula to the incandescent life, we get:

$$\$ = \frac{\frac{1.40}{100}}{\sum_{i=1}^{12*1} \frac{1}{(1+\frac{0.10}{12})^i}} = \frac{\frac{1.40}{100}}{11.375} = \$0.0012$$

Capital cost per unit of light is lower than operating cost for the incandescent.

The compact fluorescent costing K = \$14.50 would last n = 7 years and would run X = 100 hours per month. Applying the above formula, we find:

$$\$ = \frac{\frac{14.50}{100}}{\sum_{i=1}^{12*7} \frac{1}{(1+\frac{0.10}{12})^i}} = \frac{\frac{14.50}{100}}{60.237} = \$0.0024$$

For the compact fluorescent, operating costs are lower than capital costs. Adding capital and operating costs means that:

- total incandescent costs are $\$_i + c_i$ = \$0.0012 + \$0.00525 = \$0.00675 per kWh
- total compact fluorescent costs are $\$_f + c_f$ = \$0.0024 + \$0.0014 = \$0.0038 per kWh

Thus, the compact fluorescent is just under half the cost of the incandescent. However, as the interest rate goes up, and electricity price goes down, the fluorescents have less of a cost advantage over the incandescent bulbs.

Is the above computation is totally accurate when we are comparing a bulb that produces for a year with a bulb that lasts for seven years? To provide a more valid comparison, we should compare light production over the same periods of time and for the same profile of light production. Thus, we could compare the fluorescent with 14 incandescent bulbs bought sequentially to provide light for seven years. Now, the fluorescent and the incandescents would produce the same flow of light service. The present cost of the fluorescent purchased now is \$14.50. The present value of the 14 bulbs purchased two at a time at the beginning of the year for the next six years is:

$$K = \sum_{i=0}^{6} \frac{140}{(1 + \frac{0.10}{12})^{12*i}} = \$7.41$$

Distributing this cost over the flow of services from the incandescent lights to get the unit capital cost of the incandescent ($\$_i$) over 7 years, we need:

$$\$_i = \frac{K}{X} \Bigg/ \sum_{i=1}^{12n} \frac{1}{(1 + \frac{r}{12})^i} = \frac{\frac{7.41}{100}}{60.237} = \$0.0012$$

Interestingly, this estimate on comparable light production profiles produces the exact same values as the earlier comparison.

A second way to compare the two options would be to look at the present value of costs providing a similar amount of electricity. Thus, the present value of seven years of electricity for the fluorescent would be:

$$PV_f = 14.50 + 100 * 0.0014 * \sum_{i=1}^{12*7} \frac{1}{(1 + 0.1/12)^i}$$

$$= 14.50 + 100 * 0.0014 * 60.237 = \$22.93$$

The present value of seven years of electricity for the incandescent would be:

$$PV_i = \sum_{i=0}^{6} (1.40/(1 + 0.1)^i) + 100 * 0.00525 * \sum_{i=1}^{12*7} (1/(1 + 0.1/12)^i)$$

$$= 7.41 + 100 * 0.00525 * 60.237 = \$39.034$$

Again, we can see the much higher cost of the incandescent.

These examples are especially relevant because lighting accounts for about 22% of U.S. electricity use. The Rocky Mountain Institute estimates cost-effective technology exists to reduce this use by 50%, reducing CO_2 emissions by 20 million tons per year or more.

Passive solar, which requires positioning new buildings to take advantage of solar heat, may not cost extra. In the Northern temperate zone, windows on the south side with eaves provide shade in summer but let in light and heat in winter when sun is lower on the horizon. Trees used as a windbreak can reduce heat loss in the winter.

Insulation is another area where it may be cost-effective to conserve. The amount of heat flow measured in BTU/hour through a wall or window is directly related to the area (A), which is measured in feet squared, and the temperature difference on the two sides (ΔT), measured in degrees Fahrenheit and inversely related to the resistivity of the material (R) measured in ft^{2}*hour*Δ/BTU. The formula for this flow is:

$$\frac{BTU}{hr} = \frac{A^{*}\Delta T}{R}$$

Table 9–1 offers a resistivity index (R) for some common building and insulation materials.

Table 9–1 Resistivity Measures for Various Construction Materials

Material	R (ft^{2}*hour*ΔT/BTU)
Hardwood, 1"	0.91
Softwood, 1"	1.25
Concrete Block, 8"	1.04
Brick, 1"	0.62
Flat glass, 1/8"	0.88
Cellulose Insulation, 1"	3.70
Insulation glass, 1/4" air space	1.54
Insulation glass, 1/2" air space	1.72
Nylon carpet, 1"	2.00
Fiber glass insulation, 6"	19.00

Source: Hinrichs 1996

Industry is another area where conservation and process changes may be cost-effective. Examples come from the three most energy intensive industries—steel, cement, and aluminum. In the steel industry, you can reduce coke and energy use through better fuel preparation and injection, continuous casting and rolling, and using hot metal directly from the blast furnace so you don't have to reheat. Mini mills relying on electric furnaces also conserve energy. In the cement industry, replacing a wet process with a dry process has conserved energy. In the aluminum industry, electricity use has been reduced through use of improved electrodes and their spacing, improved anodes, the addition of lithium, no reheating for fabrication, and better insulation. Again, however, the higher interest rates and lower energy costs mean it is less likely that investments to change processes will be economical.

In fact, opportunities for energy conservation may not always be undertaken. Some of the hurdles to financing energy conservation include:

- high real interest rates
- risky expected return
- greater uncertainty for long term investment and more innovative projects
- high information and transaction costs discouraging small businesses and consumers
- lenders' lack of experience with energy efficiency investments

Integrated resource planning (IRP) might also be considered a no-regrets policy. IRP is designed to aid in providing minimum-cost energy services. With IRP, all environmental and social costs and benefits must be considered with equal emphasis on demand- and supply-side alternatives. Thus, if it costs less to improve the efficiency of energy production using capital than to produce more energy, the efficiency option would be undertaken. Cost savings can be accomplished through demand-side management (DSM) or through more traditional, least-cost planning (LCP). DSM cost-savings come from reducing resource consumption through increased efficiency.

Such an increase may come from conservation or from producing the same services with less energy intensive resource use or by changing the timing of consumption (called *load management*) to require less capital. LCP would require looking at the supply options and selecting the least-cost method of increasing supply. DSM would include deciding whether to build more power or decrease power demand. Thus, if the Nepalese electricity authority is applying IRP to decide how best to supply light to customers, it needs to compare four costs:

1. the full social cost of adding new generation capacity (LCP), which requires choosing the cheapest generating alternative
2. the full social cost of reducing generating and transmission losses (estimated to be 26% in 1994)
3. the full social cost of converting to compact fluorescent lights (DSM), which consume considerably less electricity than incandescent lights
4. the full cost of switching some load to off-peak hours so existing generation can supply lighting needs

IRP was developed in North America in the mid-1970s by state and provincial regulators of private electric utilities with monopoly franchises. Regulatory commissions pressed electricity utilities to adopt IRP to improve electricity efficiency on the demand side. These polices were designed to reduce energy use and electricity service costs. By 1991, 31 U.S. states required utilities to implement IRP. Further, the U.S. National Energy Policy Act of 1992 requires that all state PUCs design, implement, and evaluate IRP programs for all electric utilities.

So, why did regulators encourage IRP rather than just let the market operate? If energy efficiency was cheaper than energy supply, why didn't consumers invest in energy efficiency rather than buying electricity? In an increasing-cost, competitive world with marginal-cost pricing, no externalities, perfect information, and perfect capital markets, we believe that markets would allocate energy efficiently. If DSM is more efficient, consumers will reduce demand rather than increase supply. However, we live far from such an ideal world.

For example, electricity generation often uses average-cost pricing. During peak periods, marginal cost is typically much higher than average cost. During off-peak times, costs are less, which leads consumers to over consume electricity during peak periods and under-consume electricity in off-peak periods. Thus, capital is idle during off-peak periods. If load could be shifted from peak to off-peak or even shoulder-peak periods, even if total consumption of electricity were the same, it would still promote efficiency. Off-peak generating capacity would be used more intensively with less generating capacity needed during the peak load period. Load shifting can be accomplished by three means—changing the electricity tariff structure, direct load control, and changing technologies of energy using equipment.

Changing a tariff structure to include higher peak-load pricing would encourage a shift from peak to off-peak consumption. EdF, the French state electricity company, has one of the longest and most extensive policies concerning peak-load pricing. The evidence suggests that peak-load pricing has been a very effective load management tool in France and that many French industries including cement, ferro-alloys, iron and steel, electrometallurgy, electrochemical, water-pumping, petroleum pipelines, and cold storage have more ideal load curves than those elsewhere. Interruptible contracts are a popular alternative in the industrial sector to provide for direct load control. Introducing specific energy-efficient technologies would include automatic timers to run appliances in off-peak periods.

A third approach to abatement policy aims to minimize regrets. This option can be represented in the following game theoretic framework, which is a slight adaptation from an example from Pearce and Turner (1990). In this example, we need to quantify the possibilities: there is global warming (GW) or there is no global warming (NGW). We can respond in two ways: we can do nothing (N) or we can mitigate (M). Represent this choice set as:

	GW	NGW
Do Nothing	R_{gw-n}	R_{ngw-n}
Mitigate	R_{gw-m}	R_{ngw-m}

The R-values inside the matrix indicate the regrets, which are the costs of each strategy. For example, R_{gw-n} would be the cost or regret of doing nothing, if global warming was occurring. The minimize-regret strategy would include choosing the option that minimizes the maximum losses. Thus, we would look at the maximum loss for the global warming scenario and for the non-global warming scenario and then take the option with the minimum/maximum loss.

For example:

	GW	NGW
Do Nothing	700	0
Mitigate	400	200

In the above scenario, if we do nothing, our maximum losses are 700; if we mitigate, our maximum losses are 400. The policy that would minimax our regrets or losses is to mitigate. Another option would be to adapt rather than mitigate.

With adaptation, carbon emissions would be allowed to increase, but we would adapt to the consequences. Now, if we decide by one criteria or another that we want to mitigate or abate CO_2, we know that in the case of a public good such as CO_2 reduction, we do not expect the market to produce the economically efficient amount. Countries contribute different amounts to the problem and each country would prefer that other countries bear the burden of the reductions, while they receive the benefits. We can see the different contributions to the problem in Table 9–2, which shows historical global carbon emissions from 1980 through 1999.

The table also shows income and income per capita. Incomes are converted to U.S. dollars by exchange rates. For example, if the original income was 20,000 lira and the exchange rate is 1000 lira per dollar, then the dollar amount equals:

$$\text{lira/(exchange rate)} = \text{lira/(lira/dollar)} = \text{lira*dollar/lira} = \text{dollar} = 20000/1000 = \$20$$

The exchange rates are the result of demands and supplies of currencies that reflect imports, exports, short and long term capital flows, and other forces.

As was seen in Table 9–1, industrialized countries produce more than half of the world's CO_2 and considerably more CO_2 per capita. Third-world countries

Table 9–2 World Carbon Emissions and GDP Statistics

Country	Emissions Million Metric Tons of Carbon Equivalent (CE)			Population, Million 2001 USD	GDP Billion 2001 USD	GDP per capita	CE per capita
	1980	1990	2001	2001	2001	2001	2001
Canada	125.56	130.03	156.19	31.08	835	26,851	5.03
Mexico	64.67	83.96	96.05	101.75	433	4,253	0.94
United States	1,293.37	1,365.73	1,565.31	283.97	10,505	36,991	5.51
North America	**1,483.80**	**1,579.97**	**1,817.88**	**416.93**			
Argentina	25.93	28.39	34.85	37.52	325	8,674	0.93
Brazil	51.96	68.90	95.77	172.39	896	5,200	0.56
Venezuela	25.24	30.06	38.55	24.63	95	3,873	1.57
Central and South America	**174.21**	**197.89**	**268.27**	**426.20**			
Belgium	37.43	33.89	39.36	10.26	374	36,422	3.84
France	136.02	102.00	108.13	59.19	2,106	35,582	1.83
Germany	0.00	0.00	223.24	82.36	3,140	38,123	2.71
Germany, East	82.57	78.61					
Germany, West	208.63	192.75					
Italy	103.31	113.24	121.50	57.95	1,424	24,576	2.10
Netherlands	53.96	57.64	67.52	16.04	584	36,411	4.21
Spain	59.24	61.80	82.72	40.27	840	20,871	2.05
Turkey	18.02	35.26	50.07	68.61	222	3,238	0.73
United Kingdom	168.16	163.66	154.33	59.54	1,551	26,054	2.59
Western Europe	**1,025.23**	**1,007.07**	**1,023.87**	**482.42**			**2.12**
Czech Republic			29.01	10.29	66	6,447	2.82
Former Czechoslovakia	89.12	80.20					
Former U.S.S.R.	837.21	1,037.47					
Hungary	22.88	18.41	15.52	9.92	66	6,615	1.56
Poland	115.92	89.27	78.61	38.64	192	4,970	2.03
Romania	46.94	47.69	25.97	22.41	41	1,811	1.16
Russia			440.26	144.40	426	2,953	3.05
Ukraine			96.58	49.11	42	862	1.97
Uzbekistan			30.16	25.56	15	582	1.18
EE & FSU	**1,143.13**	**1,297.73**	**830.67**	**386.25**			
Iran	33.13	55.67	90.12	64.53	148	2,289	1.40
Saudi Arabia	49.12	58.52	84.56	21.03	167	7,951	4.02
UAE	8.26	21.48	35.28	2.65	57	21,653	13.31
Middle East	**137.80**	**202.63**	**312.07**	**171.21**			
Egypt	11.72	25.54	34.29	67.89	94	1,383	0.51
Nigeria	18.91	22.48	23.52	116.93	128	1,095	0.20
South Africa	64.15	80.88	105.18	44.33	204	4,611	2.37
Africa	**147.21**	**197.79**	**246.92**	**811.69**			

Table 9–2 World Carbon Emissions and GDP Statistics cont'd

Country	Emissions Million Metric Tons of Carbon Equivalent (CE)			Population, Million 2001 USD	GDP Billion 2001 USD	GDP per capita	CE per capita
	1980	1990	2001	2001	2001	2001	2001
Australia	54.67	72.37	99.03	19.49	527	27,025	5.08
China	394.01	616.89	831.74	1,285.00	1,294	1,007	0.65
India	82.67	155.66	251.33	1,017.54	588	577	0.25
Indonesia	23.49	41.43	87.13	214.84	251	1,168	0.41
Japan	261.18	269.14	315.83	127.34	6,567	51,574	2.48
Korea, North	29.06	67.84	67.19	22.30			3.01
Korea, South	35.16	63.82	120.80	47.34	743	15,692	2.55
Taiwan	20.22	32.00	71.23	22.41	386	17,249	3.18
Thailand	9.77	23.02	48.49	62.91	203	3,232	0.77
Asia and Oceania	975.17	1,445.51	2,068.14	3,450.11			
World Total	5,086.55	5,928.59	6,567.82	6,144.81			

Notes: Carbon equivalent is total greenhouse gas emissions standardized into carbon dioxide equivalent units. USD is U.S. dollars.
Source: EIA/DOE, International Energy Annual 2001, from http://www.eia.doe.gov/iea/

believe that the first-world countries have benefited from cheap fossil fuels and have largely caused the problem, thus they should solve the problem. The industrialized countries, while conceding they have caused the bulk of the problem, note that as third-world countries with high population growth continue to grow and develop, their CO_2 will soon surpass that of the developed countries. As would be expected, each side wants the other side to pay more. Taking action against global warming will clearly require global cooperation.

We have noted that with public goods, markets fail to allocate properly and we need governments to step in. However, governments can also fail. In regulating pollution, governments have imperfect information. For the global warming issue, there are large uncertainties in available scientific information. We do not yet completely understand the carbon cycle, nor its effect on the weather. In quantifying costs of abatement, often the government does not have the in-house expertise and must rely on the industry being regulated for abatement costs. (Goodstein 1999)

For example, suppose you are in a polluting industry and know you are going to have to buy permits to pollute. If the control authority is going to choose the number of issued permits by computing where marginal benefits of pollution (abatement costs) are equal to the marginal damages of pollution, you will have an incentive to overstate your costs or the marginal benefits of pollution (Fig. 9–5). If the true control costs are MB_1, but you can convince the control authorities the costs are MB_2, then more permits will be issued (P_2 instead of P_1), they will cost less to buy, and the firm can profitably emit more pollutants.

Alternatively, if you know a tax is going to be set, you would want to understate your compliance cost. In the above figure, if your compliance costs were really MB_2, but you could convince the control authorities that they were MB_1, then your tax would be lower, and you could profitably pollute more, P_3 instead of P_2, than if the tax reflected your true abatement cost (C_2 instead of C_1).

Other government failures can include small but well-focused groups that can influence the decision process through lobbying, votes, publicity campaigns, and dollars.

Typically, environmentalists are better at getting votes and mustering popular opinion, but industry has more dollars to spend and can make campaign contributions and hire lobbyists and lawyers and commission expensive studies. Goodstein says this tends to lead to tough environmental laws that are poorly enforced.

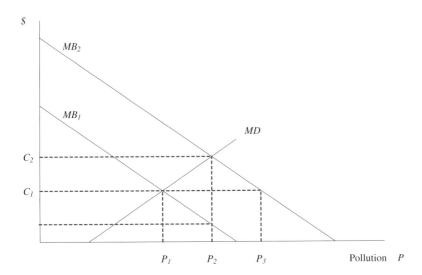

Fig. 9–5 Permits Issued Under Different Abatement Cost Scenarios

Summary

Public goods provide a classic example of poorly defined property rights because of non-rivalry in consumption. In such a case, one person's consumption of the good does not influence or reduce another person's consumption. No one can be excluded from consumption of a true public good, such as mitigation of CO_2 to prevent global warming. If CO_2 is reduced, many benefit, whether they contribute to mitigation or not. Free riding becomes a strong temptation and a less-than-efficient reduction of CO_2 may be attained. Therefore, governments need to step in to determine the optimal level of CO_2 reduction and to initiate policies to attain this optimal level. The optimal level is the point where marginal benefits of reduction equal marginal costs. Because of non-rivalry of consumption, the total benefits of a unit of mitigation are the sum of benefits to all who are affected by mitigation, while the costs should include the direct costs as well as any opportunity costs such as foregone output.

Although there is still some disagreement regarding the extent and timing of global warming and feedback effects, many scientists are concluding that the build-up of CO_2 and other greenhouse gases is likely to trap heat in the lower atmosphere and warm the Earth's surface. With this disagreement, some economist endorse a no-regrets policy, which would implement policies to correct other market distortions and help address the problem of CO_2 build up.

An alternate way to deal with uncertainties is to maximize the expected value of net benefits, where X_i is the expected benefit in the ith scenario and $P(X_i)$ is the probability of the ith scenario, then the expected benefit is $\sum_{i=1}^{n} X_i P(X_i)$. A further way to incorporate uncertainty is to pick the policy that minimizes regrets.

To evaluate new technologies that conserve on energy, both operating and capital costs need to be distributed over the life of the project. Compact fluorescent lighting, passive solar, trees for windbreaks, insulation, and continuous processes are all possibilities for economically efficient conservation techniques. High interest rates, uncertainty, and high transaction costs are all barriers to conservation. IRP complements DSM such as conservation with least-cost supply planning. All environmental and social costs and benefits are considered with equal emphasis on demand- and supply-side alternatives.

Whether conservation projects are economically efficient depends on the amount of energy saved, the cost of capital, and the interest rate. When comparing different conservation projects, the most valid comparison is for a similar production profile of services. With similar services, levelized costs per unit are valid comparisons.

Industrial countries contribute about half of the world's CO_2 emissions, the transitional economies emit around 14%, and developing countries are responsible for the remainder. It is relatively straightforward to compare carbon emissions across countries. Measuring income across countries is more difficult. Exchange rates provide the most direct and transparent mechanisms. However, since exchange rates are influenced by currency flows for goods and services and financial transfers that fluctuate on a daily basis, they do not always provide a consistent and reliable measure of relative value.

International agreements are difficult when we suffer private market failures. We can also see government regulatory failure to introduce correct regulation because of the lack of information, misinformation, and pressure from interest groups. Firms may misrepresent costs to the government. Small but well-focused groups may influence the decision-making process through lobbying, votes, publicity, campaigns, and dollars.

10 Monopsony: Japan and the Asia Pacific LNG Market

Introduction

The vast majority of the world's natural gas is transported to market through long-distance pipelines. However, if gas is far from its market, and/or its market is across an ocean, it is cheaper to transport the gas as LNG.

The first commercial shipments of LNG traveled from Algeria to the United Kingdom in 1964. Although it has relatively small share of the natural gas market, recent LNG growth rates have been higher than for piped gas. Lowered gas exploration and production costs, along with new storage tank design, larger compressors, and larger LNG trains have decreased costs, making this fuel more competitive. It is technically feasible to produce, store, and offload LNG from floating platforms, and then move to another field. Such offshore production of LNG may further enhance this market by making smaller and remote gas fields economically viable.

Typically, the gas used in an LNG project is relatively cheap, since it often has no alternative markets. For example, much of the LNG that came on stream from Bonny Island in Nigeria in 1999 had previously been flared. Capital costs, on the other hand, are quite high—usually in the billions of dollars. This is because liquefaction and regasification equipment and special LNG ships, which are made of special alloy steel that is resistant to low temperatures, have to be built. Estimated costs for the Bonny Island liquefaction facilities are $3.6 billion for a 5.2 million metric ton per year capacity.

LNG is normally measured in metric tons. 1 ton = 2.47 cubic meters of LNG = 87.2 cubic feet of LNG. One cubic meter of LNG = around 590 cubic meters of gas at 20° C.

Reserves must be large enough to produce for at least 20 years to justify the high up-front investment. Often long-term contracts must be in place to avoid any possibilities of hold-up.

A checklist of items bankers and financiers may consider before granting a loan for an LNG project—or other large scale energy project—are contained in Figure 10–1.

Information for Your Banker

I. Loan request
    A. Amount and type
    B. Term: long run/short run
    C. Purpose
        1. Working capital, inventory, equipment, real estate
        2. Merger/acquisition, refinancing
    D. Project plan and what it will accomplish
    E. Collateral
        1. Accounts receivable, inventory
        2. Fixed assets, real estate
        3. Marketable securities
        4. Guarantor
        5. Letters of credit
    F. Demonstrate credit worthiness and when and how the money will be repaid

II. Business information
    A. Purpose of business and when established

Fig. 10–1 Financing Energy Projects

B. Number of employees
C. Accountant/insurance agent/attorney
D. Years at present location—own/lease
E. Ownership and other commitment of funds

III. Management
A. Names/Credentials/Responsibilities
B. Compensation
C. Hierarchy
D. Reporting policies
E. Role of board of directors
F. Bank access to board and management

IV. Environmental
A. Philosophy
B. Real or potential liabilities
C. Accident response preparedness
D. Precautions when purchasing new properties
E. Environmental reports

V. For oil and gas reserves
A. How do you add
   1. Exploration, development
   2. Reservoir management
   3. Acquisitions (properties or companies)
B. Your inventory of reserves and replacement ratios
C. Performance statistics
   1. Finding costs
   2. Replacement ratios (find vs. acquire vs. extensions)
   3. Level of effort (LOE)
D. Three years of engineering reports
E. Reserve breakdown by
   1. Proved developed producing reserves (PDP)
   2. Proved developed nonproducing reserves (PDNP)
   3. Proved undeveloped reserves (PUD)
F. Major fields

VI. Financial information and controls
A. Your bank and credit relations
B. Fiscal statements for the last three years
   1. Balance sheet/profit and loss/cash flow
   2. External audit report
   3. Federal tax returns
   4. State and local tax returns

Fig. 10–1 Financing Energy Projects (cont'd)

C. Your dividend policy
D. Contingent liabilities
    1. Lawsuits
    2. Tax audits
    3. Pension fund commitments
    4. Environmental liabilities
E. Any history of bankruptcy
F. Implementation and control of hedging strategies
G. Organizational agreement
    1. Articles of incorporation
    2. Partnership agreement
    3. Trust agreement
H. Information on affiliates and off balance sheet activities

VII. Performance statistics and plans
    A. Production costs
    B. General and administration costs (G&A)
    C. History of stock trading prices
    D. Forecast of three-year cash flow with all planned investments
    E. Brief history of your company
    F. Analysis of the market and business outlook
    G. Your competition
    H. Future drivers in your industry

Fig. 10–1 Financing Energy Projects (cont'd)

LNG Technologies

A liquefaction facility would normally include a gas processing plant to remove natural gas liquids and condensate that are stored and sold separately; a liquefaction facility, called an LNG train; highly insulated, double-hulled, spherical-shaped storage facilities, and an LNG loading jetty. The LNG train cools the natural gas to −161.5° Centigrade. (Remember the conversion from Centigrade to Fahrenheit is F = 32 + (9/5)C.) This reduces the volume of the gas at atmospheric pressure to 1/600 of its original volume, making it more economical to transport. About 8 to 9% of the gas delivered to the plant is used as fuel to liquefy the rest.

LNG is shipped in highly insulated, specially designed ships with cargo capacities most often measured in cubic meters. Vessels ranging from 120,000 to 135,000 cubic meters (m^3) are typical. The gas is maintained at a constant temperature by using the LNG boil-off to run the vessel's cooling system, using 0.15 to 0.25 percent of the cargo a day. The number of ships per project depends on the size of the contract, distance to market, speed of the ship, expected down time, and desired safety margins, among other things.

A receiving and unloading terminal, a re-gasification plant (which is less capital-intensive than a liquefaction plant), and storage facilities are also necessary at the LNG delivery point. The re-gasification process uses another 2.5% of the delivered gas. A study by Andersen et al. (1997) for the DOE suggested that costs for a typical LNG project might be $0.50/MMBTU for gas production, $2.50/MMBTU for gas liquefaction, $0.75 for shipping, and $0.56 re-gasification for a total of $4.31/MMBTU. By comparison, the average U.S. city gas price in 1998 was $3.19/MMBTU, the average residential price was $6.54/MMBTU, the average commercial price was $5.54/MMBTU, the average industrial price was $3.40/MMBTU, and the electrical utility price was $2.57/MMBTU.

LNG Production and Trade

A number of countries currently produce and export LNG. Algeria, the first to export commercial quantities of LNG, still has the largest number of liquefaction trains, but it no longer has the largest capacity—Indonesia does. The size of trains has steadily increased in time, so that Indonesia can deliver more LNG with fewer trains. Asia/Pacific has the largest amount of regional capacity and is also the largest purchaser of LNG.

Just as trains are increasing, so is the number of greenfield projects—totally new projects, not additions to existing projects—that have been completed or are nearing completion. Shipments of LNG from Trinidad–Tobago commenced in April of 1999, shipments from Nigeria's Bonny Island commenced in 1999, shipments from Oman commenced in 2000 and shipments from Yemen were expected to commence sometime after that but seem to have been put on hold for the time being. Other projects that are in various stages of planning or are under consideration include liquefaction facilities in Egypt, Argentina, Sakhalin, and Canada, plus expansions in Australia, Indonesia, Qatar, Nigeria, and Alaska's North Slope. Countries considering putting in LNG receiving terminals include Brazil, Thailand, India, and China.

Given the huge capital costs for LNG projects, they are often undertaken by a consortium of companies and contracts tend to be long-term—on the order of 20 to 25 years. Take-or-pay clauses are often included, which mean that you pay for the gas whether you take it or not. Prices are usually indexed to some benchmark crude oil or crude oil products price, often with minimum price provisions. Although projects are not typically vertically integrated from gas production through to final consumers, buyers often take a stake in the liquefaction facilities.

Table 10–1 shows world LNG trade patterns as of 2001. Japan, with almost 60% of the world's LNG market at that time, remains the world's largest LNG importer. It has the most diversified sources of supply and it constitutes more than half of the market for every country from which it imports LNG. Although a number of electricity and natural gas companies buy the LNG, the contracts were negotiated through the Ministry of Economy, Trade, and Industry (METI), formerly known as MITI—the Japanese Ministry of International Trade and Industry.

This suggests that Japan might have some market or monopsony power as a buyer. A strict monopsonist—one buyer in a market—is the counterpart of a monopolist, which is one seller in a market.

Japan has had three types of energy policies at various times since World War II. Prior to 1973 in the pre-oil crisis period, energy policy focused on acquiring energy supplies to fuel economic growth. In the second period, which lasted from post-energy crisis to just before 1986, policy focused on energy security and diversifying out of oil. In the third period, after the Chernobyl nuclear plant disaster in 1986, policy focused on environmental safety. These last two periods have seen the build-up of the LNG trade.

LNG Monopsony on Input Market, Competitor on Output Market

To analyze how Japan should behave if it were the only buyer of LNG in the Asia Pacific market, consider the following monopsony model. Assume that suppliers of LNG to Japan are competitive, that Japanese companies are competitors on their output market, but they band together through METI to become a monopsonist. About 75% of Japan's LNG purchases go to produce electric power and the rest goes to LDCs for the residential sector. Since both gas and electric utilities have been regulated until recently, assume that the regulations simulate what would happen in a competitive output market. To make the exposition easier, assume that all of Japan's LNG(L) goes to produce electricity and that LNG is the only input into the production of electricity for these plants. If Japan maximizes profits, its objective function would be:

$$\pi = P_e E(L) - P_L(L)*L$$

where

P_e = the price of their output or the price of electricity

$E(L)$ = the production function for electricity as a function of liquefied natural gas

$P_L(L)$ = the supply of LNG which should be the combined marginal cost curve for the competitive producers of LNG

Table 10–1 LNG Exporting Countries, 2001

	From							
To	USA	Trinidad & Tobago	Oman	Qatar	UAE	Algeria	Libya	Nigeria
North America								
U.S.	-	2.62	0.34	0.64	-	1.84	-	1.08
South & Central America								
Puerto Rico	0.58	0.05	-	-	-	-	-	
Europe								
Belgium	-	-	-	-	-	2.32	-	0.08
France	-	-	-	0.15	-	9.80	-	0.50
Greece	-	-	-	-	-	0.50	-	-
Italy	-	-	-	-	-	2.25	-	3.00
Portugal	-	-	-	-	-	-	-	0.26
Spain	-	0.45	0.91	0.78	0.02	5.20	0.77	1.71
Turkey	-	-	-	-	-	3.63	-	1.20
Asia Pacific								
Japan	1.79	-	0.83	8.30	6.89	-	-	-
S. Korea	-	-	5.30	6.67	0.17	-	-	-
Taiwan	-	-	-	-	-	-	-	-
Total Exports	**1.79**	**3.65**	**7.43**	**16.54**	**7.08**	**25.54**	**0.77**	**7.83**

	From					
To	Australia	Brunei	Indonesia	Malaysia	Taiwan	Total imports
North America						
U.S.	0.07	-	-	-	-	**6.59**
South & Central America						
Puerto Rico	-	-	-	-	-	**0.63**
Europe						
Belgium	-	-	-	-	-	**2.40**
France	-	-	-	-	-	**10.45**
Greece	-	-	-	-	-	**0.50**
Italy	-	-	-	-	-	**5.25**
Portugal	-	-	-	-	-	**0.26**
Spain	-	-	-	-	-	**9.84**
Turkey	-	-	-	-	-	**4.83**
Asia Pacific						
Japan	10.05	8.20	22.74	15.27	-	**74.07**
S. Korea	0.08	0.80	5.36	3.04	0.41	**21.83**
Taiwan	-	-	3.70	2.60	-	**6.30**
Total Exports	**10.20**	**9.00**	**31.80**	**20.91**	**0.41**	**142.95**

Note: All amounts in billion cubic meters.

Source: Cedigas quoted from BP *Statistical Review of World Energy 2002*, http://www.bp.com/centres/energy2002/2001inreview.asp)

First order conditions for Japan's optimization problem are:

$$\partial\pi/\partial L = P_e(\partial E/\partial L) - P_L - (\partial P_L/\partial L)^*L = 0 =>$$

$$P_e(\partial E/\partial L) = P_L + (\partial P_L/\partial L)^*L$$

The previous expression has price of output or electricity times the extra electricity produced by an extra unit of LNG (the marginal product of LNG) on the left. The whole expression represents the extra revenue gained from buying an additional ton of LNG and is referred to as the *marginal revenue product* of LNG (MRP_L). To understand this expression, take a simple example. Suppose regulators set the price of electricity at P_e = $0.11, and you can sell all you want at that price. Let the thermal efficiency for the power plants that burn LNG be about 0.35 (for every 100 BTUs of energy input there is an output of 35 BTUs of electricity). Assume constant marginal product up to generation capacity of 150,000 kWh. Suppose one Mcf of gas has 1,012,000 BTUs and one kWh of electricity has 3412 BTUs. Then one Mcf=1,012,000/3412=296.6 kWh.

At this thermal efficiency, the marginal product of 1 Mcf of gas = 296.6*0.35= or about 103.8 kWh/Mcf. The revenue per Mcf is then 0.11*103.8 = $11.418. Gas use at capacity Mcf = 150,000/103.8 or about 1445 Mcf. Once you reach capacity, the MRP falls to zero, since you can produce no more electricity. This MRP_L is shown later in Figure 10–2.

In the optimization equation, the right represents the extra cost of buying an additional unit of LNG, referred to as the *marginal factor cost* of LNG (MFC_L). It is equal to the price of LNG, which is a function of LNG. It is the competitive supply curve for LNG and also the average cost for LNG. The third expression is the slope of the supply curve for LNG (or the change in price for a given change in quantity) times the quantity of LNG purchased. It represents the increase in cost for all previous units consumed. Thus, as we move up the supply curve, we pay a higher average price not just for the last unit but for all units. The marginal price is then the average price, which we pay for the last unit, plus the extra cost of all other units sold.

It is easy to see the relationship of marginal factor cost to price by taking a simple supply function. Suppose that supply of LNG is L = –20 +100P_L. When the price of LNG is 5, then 480 units of LNG are supplied. When the price of LNG is 5.25, then 505 units of LNG are supplied and so on as shown in Table 10–2.

Table 10–2 Developing Marginal Factor Cost for LNG Supply Function

P_L	$L = -20 + 100P_L$	$TFC = P_L*L$	$MFC = \Delta(TFC)/\Delta L$
5.00	480	2,400.00	
5.25	505	2,651.25	$(2651.25 - 2400)/(505 - 480) = \$10.05$
5.50	530	2,915.00	10.55
5.75	555	3,191.25	11.05
6.00	580	3,480.00	11.55

The total LNG bill, or total factor cost (TFC) at any point on the supply curve, is the price of LNG times the amount purchased ($P_L L$) as seen in the third column in Table 10–2. Now, as we move up the supply curve, it is easy to see MFC = $\partial(TFC)/\partial L$. In a discrete problem, we can approximate $\partial(TFC)/\partial L$ by $\Delta(TFC)/\Delta L$ as seen in Table 10–2, column 4. For example, the change in total factor cost when going from price \$5 to \$5.25 is (2651.25 - 2400) and the change in L when going from price \$5 to \$5.25 is (505 - 480). Then $\Delta(TFC)/\Delta L$ = (2651.25 - 2400)/(505 - 480) = \$10.05.

So at a price of \$5.25, the average factor cost is \$5.25 but the marginal factor cost is \$10.05. Though we pay \$5.25 for each of the 505 units, on the margin we are paying more since we pay \$5.25 not only for the additional 25 units but also for each of the first 480 units, for which we only paid \$5 when we bought only 480 units.

The first-order conditions tell us that Japan should buy LNG up to the point where the marginal revenue product equals marginal factor cost. Since marginal revenue product is \$11.42, we can see from Table 10–2 that it crosses MFC somewhere between a price of \$5.75 and \$6.00. We can solve for the exact amount using the continuous functions, MFC = $\partial(TCF)/\partial L$.

First we need total factor cost TCF = $P_L L$. To get P_L, invert the above supply curve L = -20 + 100L to get P_L = 0.2 + 0.01*L. Then:

$$P_L L = (0.2 + 0.01*L)*L = 0.2*L + 0.01*L^2$$

To get MFC for a change in LNG take the derivative:

$$MFC = \partial(P_L L)/\partial L = \partial(0.2*L + 0.01*L^2)/\partial L = 0.2 + 2*0.01*L$$

Note that when the supply curve is linear, the MFC has the same intercept but is twice as steep as the supply curve. The units of measurement for MFC are measured in \$/Mcf. This must be set equal to the marginal revenue product of LNG, which is equal to the price of electricity times the marginal product of LNG, or:

$$\$11.418 = 0.2 + 0.02*LNG$$

Solving for LNG yields:

$$L = 561 \text{ Mcf}$$

To buy 561 Mcf, the generator will need a price of $P_L = 0.2 + 0.01 * 561 = \$5.81$. This solution can be seen in Figure 10–2.

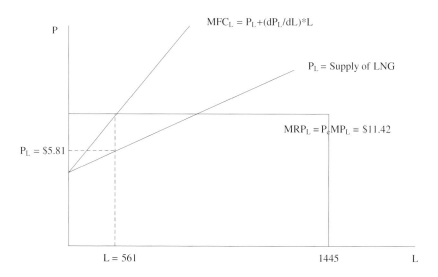

Fig. 10–2 Monopsony Purchase of Inputs for Competitive Constant Output Market and Constant Marginal Product up to Generating Capacity

Now let's sum up what we have learned about pricing power on the demand side of the market.

As with all economic decisions, we need to look at the marginal benefits and costs of undertaking an activity. In this market, the benefits are the extra revenues brought in by another unit of the factor, and the marginal costs are the extra payments we need to hire an additional unit of the factor. With pricing power in demand, the costs of an extra unit are higher than the average cost, which is measured on the supply curve. We buy the factor up to the point where the MRP is equal to the MFC.

In a more realistic example, a utility may be large enough to face a downward, sloping demand of $P_e(E)$ instead of a fixed price. In addition, if the utility has more than one plant, with some plants more efficient than others, the marginal product of LNG may fall with increased LNG use. You use your most efficient plants first; as you increase electricity production, you may need to move to less-efficient plants with less electricity output per unit of fuel. In Figure 10–3, L is the amount of LNG purchase that equates MRP_L and MFC_L. For this amount of purchase, the monopsonist has to pay the amount on the supply curve P_L.

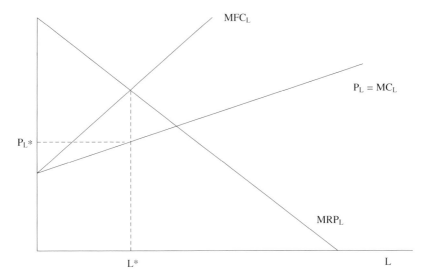

Fig. 10–3 Monopsony Purchases of LNG

Monopsony Model Compared to Competitive Model

Suppose that METI no longer bargains for the utilities, so utilities lose their monopsony power and must compete for natural gas. To see the value of monopsony power, compare the above result to a competitive case. In the monopsony case, the optimization conditions are:

$$\partial \pi / \partial L = P_e(\partial E / \partial L) - P_L - (\partial P_L / \partial L) * L = 0$$

In the competitive case, the utilities do not have any pricing power, so $(\partial P_L / \partial L) = 0$ and the competitive solution is:

$$\partial \pi / \partial L = P_e(\partial E / \partial L) - P_L = 0$$

Note this is where marginal revenue product equals price. Thus the demand for the factor is the marginal revenue product curve, and the new equilibrium is where the marginal revenue product curve crosses the supply curve.

Monopsony model with price discrimination

In the above examples, we have assumed that each supplier receives the same price. However, contract prices are not usually public information. If each supplier does not know what other suppliers are receiving, it might be possible to pay each supplier a different price. In such a case, Japan should pay each supplier its reservation price, which is the lowest price the supplier would be willing to accept. At a price lower than the reservation price, suppliers should drop out of the market. We represent this situation in Figure 10–4.

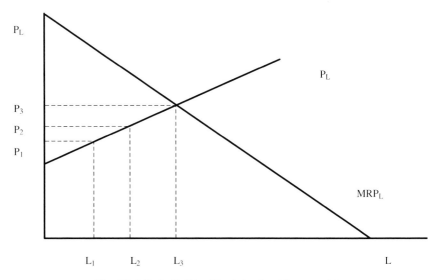

Fig. 10–4 Perfectly Price-Discriminating Monopsonist

Japan pays the first supplier P_1 for L_1 units of output. It pays P_2 for $L_2 - L_1$ units and P_3 for $L_3 - L_2$ units. If Japan can perfectly price discriminate and pay the second supplier a higher price than the first and the third a higher price than the first two, the marginal factor cost is not above the supply curve. The marginal cost of a factor is just its price. In this case, Japan should buy L_3 units and pay each supplier its reservation price. The marginal price, or the highest price paid, would be the same as in a competitive market but Japan would be able to garner the entire producer surplus.

Monopoly and bilateral monopoly

If Japan has more competitors, it will not have as much market power and the LNG suppliers will do better with higher prices and larger quantities. Another way for LNG suppliers to counteract monopsony power would be for them to band together and behave as a monopolist. Let's see what would happen in such a case.

Assume that Indonesia, the largest seller of LNG, organizes a cartel called the Organization of LNG Exporting Countries. (OLEC) Assume that they are selling to a competitive market of buyers. In a competitive buyer market, the monopoly exporter or seller should sell up to the point where marginal revenue equals marginal cost. The demand for LNG in Japan is the marginal revenue product of LNG, while the marginal revenue for LNG exporters is below this demand if exporters have market power. The solution is L_o in Figure 10–5.

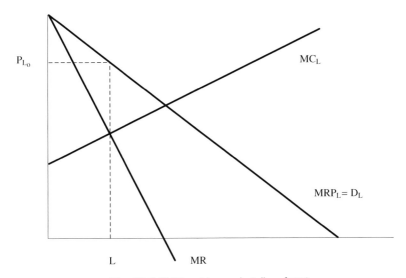

Fig. 10–5 OLEC as Monopoly Seller of LNG

Compare this to Figure 10–3: Price for LNG is considerably higher when the supplier has the market power than when Japan has it. Whether quantity is larger or smaller is uncertain and depends on the slope of the MRP and the MC curves.

Now put the two markets together into a bilateral monopoly as in Figure 10–6. To simplify the explanation and exposition, assume that both players want the same quantity of LNG. Both players desiring the same quantity would happen if the slope of the marginal revenue product is equal in absolute value to the slope of the marginal cost curve.

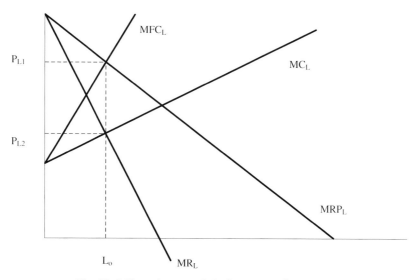

Fig. 10–6 Bilateral Monopoly in the Asia-Pacific LNG Market

The seller wants to receive P_{L1} and the buyer wants to pay P_{L2}. Where the price settles depends on the bargaining power of the two parties. We can, however, determine the range in which we might expect the price to fall. First the absolute minimum price a monopoly seller would be willing to accept would be the point at which they received no producer surplus or are just covering all their costs. (Remember that an economist includes in cost a normal rate of return.) Thus, the absolute minimum price for the quantity L_o would be somewhat below P_{L2} in Fig. 10–6. Mathematically, it would be:

$$\textbf{Producer Surplus} = \textbf{P}_{\textbf{min}}\textbf{L}_{\textbf{o}} - \int_{o}^{Lo} MC(L)dL = 0$$

Solving yields:

$$\textbf{P}_{\textbf{min}} = \int_{o}^{Lo} MC(L)dL/\textbf{L}_{\textbf{o}}$$

At this point, losses on the last units just cancel the economic profits on the first units sold.

The absolute maximum price that the consumer would be willing to pay is where consumer surplus is 0. This would be a price somewhat above P_{L1}. Mathematically, consumer surplus is the area under the demand curve minus the total amount paid, which is price times quantity. The maximum price they would pay is where this value is zero or:

$$\text{Consumer Surplus} = \int_{o}^{Lo} MRP(L)dL - P_{max}L_o = 0$$

Solving yields:

$$P_{max} = \int_{o}^{Lo} MRP(L)dL/L_o$$

At this price, the consumer's surplus gains on the first units just cancel out the consumer's surplus losses on the last units sold. Price must fall below P_{max} and above P_{min}, but its exact location is determined by the party with the stronger bargaining power.

Bargaining and Negotiation

Bargaining and negotiation skills are important for success in your personal and professional life, since there is no shortage of disputes. However, it is necessary to have some mechanism for solving disputes. Institutions that can settle disputes include traditions, regulations, and courts. More decentralized methods of settling disputes include markets and negotiations. Honing your negotiating and bargaining skills improves the chances that disputes will be settled in your favor.

In *distributive games*, the negotiation is over how payments are distributed between the players. Negotiating over the purchase of an item is the classic distributive game. In distributive games, if the players are too greedy, a bargain may not be made. A person's reservation price is his opportunity cost. If you do not meet or exceed the other side's reservation price, they walk away. However, sometimes parties walk away strategically hoping you will make a better offer. In other cases, when you have not met their reservation price, they may walk away for good.

In *distributive negotiations*, an unreasonable offer with concessions tends to work better than a reasonable offer with no concessions. It is also better to get your opponent to make the first offer. This tends to be good advice in most types of negotiation. Caution is advised in choosing your opening offer. If you are too conservative, you may give away too much. If you are too extreme, you may insult your opponent, and he may walk away. If your opponent makes an extreme first offer, either break off or quickly counter. Remember that the point midway between the bids often becomes a focal point. The pattern of concessions usually gets smaller as parties approach their aspirations or their reservation price. The smaller the zone of agreement in distributive, as in other games, the longer it takes to come to an agreement.

What are some of the normative ethics of negotiation? Disputants often fare poorly if they act greedily and deceptively. In many negotiations, there are joint gains. Those that often fare best are those who seek to enlarge the pie and then to get a fair share of gains. Others may use less than ethical tactics.

Summary

Natural gas, although an environmentally desirable fuel, has the drawback of high transportation costs relative to oil. Because of these higher costs, natural gas markets tend to be more regional, and large suppliers and consumers may have market power. Where gas is far from its customers and over deep oceans, gas maybe liquefied by chilling to -161.5° C, shipped to customers, then re-gasified, as is the case in the Asia Pacific LNG market.

LNG projects typically require cheap natural gas supplies and large up-front capital investment. For banks to supply such funds, they will require a variety of information about the company involved, including the company's mission and management, environmental philosophy and record, investment strategies, financial information and performance, and risk management strategies.

Traditional LNG suppliers include Algeria, Libya, Australia, Brunei, Indonesia, Malaysia, Abu Dhabi, Qatar, and the United States. More recently, Nigeria and Trinidad have been added to the list. Asia/Pacific has the largest amount of regional capacity and also the largest purchases of LNG. Given the large capital costs, projects are often owned by a consortium of companies and contracts are typically for 20 years or longer.

Japan is the largest importer of LNG, and, because it negotiates contracts through METI, it has monopsony or buyer market power. Japan faces a supply curve rather than a given world price and can minimize its costs for LNG by buying where MFC is equal to MRP. Compared to a competitive solution, Japan will pay a lower price for LNG and buy less. If Japan is able to price discriminate and pay each supplier its reservation price, Japan can reduce its costs even more.

If sellers are able to cooperate with each other, they will have some monopoly power on the selling side of the market and we have a bilateral monopoly with a monopolist selling to a monopsonist. We can determine the reservation price of each player, but the negotiating skills and bargaining power of the two players in the market will determine the exact price.

A negotiation can be thought of as a game, which will be played differently depending on whether parties are monolithic, whether the game is repetitive, whether the negotiation is stand-alone, whether the issues are quantitative or qualitative, whether negotiations are conducted in person or on the phone, the complexity of the negotiation, and the normal bargaining conventions for such a negotiation.

It is always safest to document details of the agreement. It is wise to separate your aspirations, or what you would like to receive, from your reservation price, which is the minimum you must receive to reach an agreement. At the end of the negotiation, take a moment to consider whether there might still be any gains for both sides.

When parties can't agree, there are four common types of third party interveners. A facilitator brings parties together for a negotiation. A rules manipulator provides the negotiating rules. A mediator helps in the negotiation. An arbitrator helps in the decision. The goal of all parties should be an efficient negotiation where the negotiators don't leave the table if another agreement that improves the deal for both parties could be made.

In distributive games, an unreasonable offer with concessions typically seems to work better than a reasonable offer with no concessions. It is best to get your opponent to make the first offer. The focal point will be midway between the first pair of bids, with concessions getting smaller as parties approach their reservation price.

11 Game Theory and the Western European Natural Gas Market

The problem faced by each participant is to lay his plans so as to take account of the actions of his opponents, each of whom, of course, is laying his own plans so as to take account of the first participant's actions.

—Dorfman, Samuelson, Solow, 1958

Introduction

Western Europe's natural gas market has steadily grown since the end of World War II. Table 11–1 shows total primary energy consumption and the variety of consumption patterns for this region in this period. Fossil fuels are all primary energy sources, whereas electricity generated from fossil fuels is considered a secondary energy source. Primary electricity includes all non-fossil generation—nuclear, hydropower and other renewables. Consumption has been converted to billions of cubic meters (bcm = 10^9 m^3), since the focus of this chapter is on natural gas. Conversion assumes that 1 m^3 of natural gas equals 36,000 BTU.

In the 1950s, most of the countries we analyze in this chapter received more than half of their energy from coal. (Greece, Italy, Norway, Portugal, Sweden, and Switzerland did not.) Oil accounted for much of the rest of consumption. Primary electricity in the form of hydropower was a small share in a few countries but constituted more than 25% of energy consumption in Norway and Switzerland.

Table 11–1 Relative Share of Energy Consumption from Major Sources

Country	Year	Pop 10^6	Per Capita 1000 m^3	Total (bcm)	Solid	Liquid	Gas	Elec.
Austria	53	6.93	2569.35	17.81	35.21%	6.88%	3.60%	54.31%
Austria	63	7.17	2532.46	18.16	40.81%	30.01%	10.81%	18.38%
Austria	73	7.53	3988.62	30.02	17.54%	47.75%	15.63%	19.08%
Austria	83	7.55	3852.56	29.09	12.32%	41.49%	16.29%	29.90%
Austria	93	7.99	4291.58	34.29	9.29%	39.01%	20.28%	31.42%
Austria	01	8.08	4872.05	39.37	10.07%	38.78%	20.69%	30.46%
Belgium	53	8.78	3281.98	28.81	84.74%	14.69%	0.47%	0.11%
Belgium	63	9.29	4091.98	38.01	65.36%	34.18%	0.46%	0.00%
Belgium	73	9.74	5811.76	56.60	27.09%	52.35%	20.57%	0.00%
Belgium	83	9.86	5117.17	50.46	21.76%	47.39%	17.41%	13.44%
Belgium	93	10.08	6151.52	62.01	15.12%	47.20%	18.66%	19.03%
Belgium	01	10.26	7252.66	74.41	13.50%	47.04%	21.76%	17.70%
Denmark	53	4.37	1659.89	7.25	66.78%	31.91%	0.00%	1.32%
Denmark	63	4.68	2883.06	13.50	34.67%	64.34%	0.00%	0.99%
Denmark	73	5.02	4346.40	21.84	12.59%	87.41%	0.00%	0.00%
Denmark	83	5.11	3722.41	19.02	32.29%	67.29%	0.32%	0.09%
Denmark	93	5.19	4479.76	23.25	35.62%	49.52%	12.76%	2.10%
Denmark	01	5.33	4696.78	25.03	19.08%	50.48%	23.38%	7.06%
Finland	53	4.14	939.98	3.89	40.63%	21.97%	0.00%	37.39%
Finland	63	4.52	1988.09	8.99	24.10%	47.83%	0.00%	28.07%
Finland	73	4.66	4574.45	21.30	14.21%	65.51%	0.00%	20.29%
Finland	83	4.86	5063.45	24.61	12.09%	49.91%	2.65%	35.34%
Finland	93	5.07	6130.25	31.08	15.52%	39.68%	9.75%	35.06%
Finland	01	5.19	6542.71	33.96	13.92%	36.11%	13.36%	36.61%
France	53	42.67	1671.48	71.32	75.60%	21.91%	0.37%	2.12%
France	63	47.85	2723.86	130.34	49.07%	35.93%	4.20%	10.80%
France	73	52.16	4045.06	211.01	17.75%	64.49%	8.96%	8.80%
France	83	54.73	4058.06	222.10	13.95%	47.37%	12.18%	26.50%
France	93	57.65	4824.06	278.11	5.88%	38.49%	12.54%	43.09%
France	01	59.19	5271.50	312.02	4.29%	37.38%	14.34%	43.98%

Table 11–1 Relative Share of Energy Consumption from Major Sources (cont'd)

Country	Year	Pop 10^6	Per Capita 1000 m³	Total (bcm)	% Fuel Shares			
					Solid	Liquid	Gas	Elec.
FRG	53	51.39	2370.16	121.79	92.04%	5.16%	0.18%	2.61%
FRG	63	57.61	3434.36	197.85	67.04%	29.78%	0.91%	2.26%
FRG	73	61.96	4934.98	305.79	31.84%	52.14%	12.32%	3.69%
FRG	83	61.38	4744.56	291.22	28.90%	46.04%	16.12%	8.94%
GDR	53	17.00	2929.40	49.80	98.41%	1.30%	0.00%	0.29%
GDR	63	17.16	4203.60	72.12	96.33%	3.29%	0.15%	0.23%
GDR	73	16.98	5338.53	90.64	74.93%	15.69%	9.07%	0.31%
GDR	83	16.70	5900.68	98.54	70.47%	20.01%	5.36%	4.16%
Germany	93	81.19	4805.38	390.15	27.10%	42.52%	18.01%	12.36%
Germany	01	82.36	4839.44	398.58	21.94%	40.58%	22.79%	14.70%
Greece	53	7.82	249.05	1.95	20.26%	79.16%	0.00%	0.58%
Greece	63	8.48	559.39	4.74	27.63%	66.56%	0.00%	5.81%
Greece	73	8.93	1971.53	17.61	26.15%	69.41%	0.00%	4.44%
Greece	83	9.85	2089.79	20.58	29.96%	66.35%	0.41%	3.27%
Greece	93	10.38	2900.55	30.11	31.24%	66.09%	0.38%	2.29%
Greece	01	10.60	3582.80	37.98	30.07%	62.43%	5.40%	2.10%
Ireland	53	2.95	1226.49	3.62	74.66%	21.39%	0.00%	3.95%
Ireland	63	2.85	1611.95	4.59	58.99%	37.19%	0.00%	3.82%
Ireland	73	3.03	2376.19	7.20	26.91%	70.18%	0.00%	2.92%
Ireland	83	3.44	2420.75	8.33	13.91%	57.43%	25.96%	2.69%
Ireland	93	3.57	3136.82	11.20	20.69%	53.71%	23.57%	2.02%
Ireland	01	3.84	4426.06	17.00	13.00%	59.54%	25.84%	1.62%
Italy	53	47.57	579.49	27.56	31.57%	26.06%	9.10%	33.27%
Italy	63	51.17	1500.86	76.80	13.89%	55.49%	10.41%	20.21%
Italy	73	54.92	2735.46	150.23	6.43%	71.66%	12.51%	9.40%
Italy	83	56.84	2803.80	159.37	8.21%	64.92%	17.21%	9.66%
Italy	93	57.05	3234.61	184.53	6.31%	58.24%	27.84%	7.61%
Italy	01	57.95	3646.61	211.32	7.03%	50.98%	33.80%	8.18%
Netherlands	53	10.49	1647.63	17.29	79.27%	20.57%	0.16%	0.00%
Netherlands	63	11.97	2525.24	30.22	46.23%	51.58%	2.15%	0.05%
Netherlands	73	13.44	5164.03	69.39	4.86%	36.24%	58.90%	0.00%
Netherlands	83	14.36	5426.92	77.93	7.46%	44.90%	46.29%	1.35%
Netherlands	93	15.29	6353.27	97.14	9.36%	45.22%	43.81%	1.61%
Netherlands	01	16.04	7016.00	112.54	12.67%	46.36%	38.74%	2.23%

Table 11–1 Relative Share of Energy Consumption from Major Sources (cont'd)

Country	Year	Pop 10^6	Per Capita 1000 m³	Total (bcm)	% Fuel Shares Solid	Liquid	Gas	Elec.
Norway	53	3.36	2851.78	9.58	12.84%	25.04%	0.00%	62.12%
Norway	63	3.67	4870.60	17.86	4.72%	26.89%	0.00%	68.38%
Norway	73	3.96	7883.10	31.23	3.34%	27.75%	0.00%	68.91%
Norway	83	4.13	10110.46	41.76	2.40%	21.85%	3.31%	72.44%
Norway	93	4.31	11169.11	48.14	1.95%	21.36%	5.71%	70.99%
Norway	01	4.51	11509.45	51.91	3.49%	21.56%	8.35%	66.60%
Portugal	53	8.53	261.66	2.23	38.01%	47.22%	0.00%	14.77%
Portugal	63	8.77	520.85	4.57	22.50%	49.04%	0.00%	28.45%
Portugal	73	8.57	1221.51	10.46	7.04%	69.83%	0.00%	23.14%
Portugal	83	9.88	1394.40	13.78	3.63%	79.00%	0.00%	17.37%
Portugal	93	9.88	2175.10	21.49	15.84%	71.62%	0.00%	12.54%
Portugal	01	10.02	3009.17	30.15	11.04%	64.69%	9.11%	15.16%
Spain	53	28.72	711.46	20.43	70.49%	15.35%	0.00%	14.16%
Spain	63	31.39	1072.64	33.67	46.28%	30.45%	0.01%	23.26%
Spain	73	34.85	2294.60	79.97	20.01%	61.73%	1.77%	16.49%
Spain	83	38.16	2577.38	98.35	26.29%	59.95%	2.46%	11.31%
Spain	93	39.09	2861.21	111.84	19.54%	54.23%	6.37%	19.87%
Spain	01	40.27	3906.57	157.32	11.99%	55.26%	12.76%	19.99%
Sweden	53	7.17	2463.72	17.67	28.08%	36.61%	0.00%	35.31%
Sweden	63	7.60	4201.02	31.94	8.72%	55.93%	0.00%	35.36%
Sweden	73	8.14	6476.17	52.70	3.35%	61.24%	0.00%	35.41%
Sweden	83	8.33	6378.84	53.14	4.13%	40.36%	0.00%	55.51%
Sweden	93	8.72	6948.88	60.59	4.38%	31.00%	1.37%	63.25%
Sweden	01	8.83	7226.95	63.81	3.93%	29.07%	1.44%	65.56%
Switzerland	53	4.89	1613.42	7.89	25.49%	20.71%	0.00%	53.80%
Switzerland	63	5.79	3154.29	18.26	13.97%	47.26%	0.00%	38.76%
Switzerland	73	6.45	4800.03	30.97	1.38%	63.03%	0.76%	34.84%
Switzerland	83	6.42	4839.93	31.07	1.77%	47.82%	4.28%	46.13%
Switzerland	93	6.94	5084.85	35.29	0.58%	44.56%	7.01%	47.85%
Switzerland	01	7.23	5429.87	39.26	0.44%	42.02%	7.90%	49.64%
Turkey	53	22.46	395.91	8.89	73.68%	25.87%	0.00%	0.45%
Turkey	63	29.68	533.22	15.82	51.43%	40.33%	0.00%	8.24%
Turkey	73	37.37	1051.41	39.29	26.18%	69.69%	0.00%	4.13%
Turkey	83	47.86	661.31	31.65	26.51%	63.10%	0.23%	10.16%
Turkey	93	58.51	1106.75	64.76	27.10%	49.79%	8.02%	15.09%
Turkey	01	68.61	1153.28	79.13	26.66%	43.80%	20.70%	8.84%

Table 11–1 Relative Share of Energy Consumption from Major Sources (cont'd)

Country	Year	Pop 10^6	Per Capita 1000 m^3	Total (bcm)	% Fuel Shares			
					Solid	Liquid	Gas	Elec.
U.K.	53	50.97	3842.35	195.85	89.12%	10.58%	0.00%	0.30%
U.K.	63	53.80	4178.62	224.79	71.31%	27.15%	0.08%	1.46%
U.K.	73	56.06	4608.14	258.32	41.67%	44.46%	12.59%	1.28%
U.K.	83	56.35	4143.34	233.48	33.03%	37.40%	22.26%	7.31%
U.K.	93	58.19	4525.27	263.33	23.00%	38.98%	26.44%	11.58%
U.K.	01	59.54	4526.33	269.50	16.79%	35.56%	35.72%	11.93%
U.S.	83	234.31	8360.79	1959.02	22.52%	42.61%	24.61%	10.26%
U.S.	93	257.78	9217.76	2376.15	23.22%	39.56%	24.96%	12.26%
U.S.	01	283.97	9278.74	2634.88	23.16%	40.41%	24.48%	11.94%
Europe 19	53	330.22	1858.33	613.66	78.58%	13.36%	0.62%	7.45%
Europe 19	63	363.44	2592.55	942.24	55.72%	33.31%	1.95%	9.02%
Europe 19	73	393.76	3770.19	1484.56	26.04%	53.63%	11.79%	8.54%
Europe 19	83	415.81	3618.15	1504.46	23.27%	46.50%	14.39%	15.85%
Europe 19	93	439.10	3979.28	1747.30	16.45%	44.21%	17.99%	21.35%
Europe 19	01	457.85	4266.18	1953.27	13.32%	42.52%	22.30%	21.87%

Notes: *FRG = Federal Republic of Germany = W. Germany, and GDR = the German Democratic Republic = E. Germany. The information for Germany 1953, 1963, and 1973 is divided between FRG and GDR. Measured in billions of cubic meters(bcm) unless otherwise indicated. One m^3 = 36,000 Btu = 9068 Kcal. Oil includes all liquid petroleum fuel. Electricity is gross consumption and production. Years prior to 1983 are estimated by prorating 1983 numbers using the earlier U.N. statistics.
Sources: 1950–70: U.N., 1978, *World Energy Supplies 1950–1974*,
1980–2001: EIA/DOE, 2003, *International Energy Annual 2001*.

Between 1947 and 1956 energy shortages were the chief energy policy concern. In 1951, Belgium, France, Italy, Luxembourg, the Netherlands, and West Germany (FRG) signed the Treaty of Paris, which created the European Coal and Steel Community (ECSC) to cooperate on energy supply. In this first step at economic integration, members agreed to promote free trade in coal and steel within the community.

The first gas used in Europe was town gas made from coal in the following chemical reactions:

$$C + O_2 \Rightarrow CO_2$$

$$CO_2 + C \Rightarrow 2CO$$

$$C + H_2O \Rightarrow CO + H_2$$

Typical output was 12% hydrogen, 25% CO, 7% CO_2, and 56% nitrogen. Town gas was potentially dangerous because of the high amount of CO. The Lurgi process occurs under higher pressure and in two additional reactions to get rid of the CO and create methane. These reactions are:

$$C + 2H_2 \Rightarrow CH_4$$

$$CO + 3H_2 \Rightarrow CH_4 + H_2O$$

(James Plambeck, 1995, University of Alberta, http://www.psigate.ac.uk/newsite/reference/plambeck/chem1/p01264a.htm)

This town gas is less toxic, and the methane can be further processed to liquid. Gas-to-liquids technology (GTL), based on the Fischer Tropsch process, may also be used for natural gas in remote areas where it is too expensive to transport in the gaseous form or as LNG.

Town gas was not as economical as natural gas; equipment to burn town gas had to be modified to accommodate the higher heat content of natural gas. It was replaced whenever natural gas became available. Only Austria and Italy had significant natural gas consumption in 1953, all from local production. When a huge natural gas field was discovered in Groningen, Holland, in 1961 this gas was fed into existing networks, displacing the more expensive town gas. By 1963, the Netherlands and France had also begun to use natural gas from local production. Rapid development of the gas grid in Europe followed, to supply Dutch gas to Belgium, France, and FRG.

The first LNG shipments reached the Canvey terminal in the United Kingdom from Algeria in 1964. Later, gas from Norway and the Soviet Union and LNG from Libya supplied the growing European gas network.

From 1957 to 1972, energy was no longer an issue for Western Europe. Coal shortages of the early 1950s turned into a coal surplus by 1959, as cheap Middle Eastern oil increasingly displaced coal. By 1973, coal's share had decreased for all countries in Table 11–1 except Greece falling to less than a third of consumption for all but the German Democratic Republic and the United Kingdom. Oil use continued to increase and by 1973 it supplied more than half the energy consumption in these countries except for Austria, the German Democratic Republic, Netherlands, Norway, and the United Kingdom.

In 1957, European economic integration was further enhanced when the Treaty of Rome joined the countries in the ECSC into the European Economic Community (EEC)—the common market. The EEC's goal was to abolish all barriers to the flow of goods, services, people, and capital within the common market and to establish common customs barriers to all non-members. The European Atomic Energy Commission was set up at the same time. The EEC added Great Britain, Ireland, and Denmark (1971), Greece (1981), Spain and Portugal (1986), and Turkey (1996).

The oil embargo of 1973, along with the Iranian revolution of 1979 and the accompanying dramatic oil price increases, considerably altered consumption patterns. Energy consumption fell in about a third of these countries. There was diversification out of oil, with oil's share falling in all Western European countries except the Netherlands and Portugal, and falling below 50% in eight of the countries. Oil's share did not fall in the German Democratic Republic (GDR), which was supplied by Russia. The GDR was also a member of the Council for Mutual Economic Assistance (COMECON), along with the Soviet Union, Bulgaria, Czechoslovakia, Hungary, Poland, and Romania.

Considerable diversity marked what energy source was substituted for oil. Coal substitution dominated in Denmark, Greece, and Spain. Electricity substitution was important in Austria, Belgium, France, FRG, Norway, Sweden, and Switzerland, while gas substitution was found in FRG, Ireland, Italy, and the United Kingdom.

Between 1973 and 1985, the focus turned to security of supplies and prices. There was a diversification away from OPEC energy supplies. Whereas OPEC supplied more than 93% of Western European consumption in 1973, by 1983 that share had fallen to 63% and total oil imports had fallen by 45%. The largest gainers from this substitution were the North Sea, Mexico, and the Soviet Union.

With the fall of the Berlin Wall in 1989, German re-unification, the founding of the European Bank for Reconstruction and Development (EBRD) in 1990 for the financial support of transition economies of Central and Eastern European countries, and creation of the European Union (EU) in 1992, Europe committed to closer political union and to a European Monetary Union (EMU). In 1993, the Single-Market Act reduced non-tariff barriers to trade within the EU and created a single EU market.

The EU initially consisted of the 12 EEC members, joined by Austria, Sweden, and Finland, in 1995. (Norway has repeatedly voted down attempts to join the EU.) Turkey is in the customs union but not in the EU. Closer political union within the EU is based on adoption of a common foreign and security policy and cooperating on justice and home affairs. The EMU is based around a European central bank, a system of branch banks, and a common currency. In 1999, the new currency, the Euro, was accepted by 11 of the 15 EU countries, and currency and coins were adopted by all but the United Kingdom, Sweden, and Denmark on January 1, 2002.

Energy policy (after the oil price decreases of 1985) focused on the three most popular policy areas—environment, competition, and Eastern Bloc reforms. Environmental concerns favored gas. Between 1983 and 1998, all of the countries but the Netherlands increased their share of gas consumption. The Netherlands—with the highest gas share of all—diversified out of gas and toward coal and electricity. Overall, coal's share of the market was lower in 1998 than in 1983 for the majority of Western European countries.

The push for increased competition in energy markets with the Single-Market Act had major ramifications in the energy sector. Downstream oil was already reasonably competitive in many countries and the European Commission pushed for liberalization in places where it did not exist, such as Spain, Portugal, and Greece. For coal, there was continued pressure to enforce the subsidy reduction policies. Gas and electricity, which were highly concentrated, came under even more pressure: The price transparency directive for gas and electricity required pricing and consumption information be supplied to the EEC Statistical Office on a regular basis. Third-party transit rights were implemented for electricity in 1991 and for natural gas in 1992.

More recently, the Electricity and Natural Gas Directives have sought to reduce monopoly power by opening up the EU markets. The Electricity Directive required EU member countries to deregulate 23% of their electricity market by 1999. The Natural Gas Directive required that 20% of the gas market be opened to competition by 1999 and 33% in 2008 with all power companies having the right to choose their suppliers.

The European Energy Charter Treaty (EECT), signed in 1994, aimed at supporting energy reform in the former Eastern Bloc countries and assuring safe energy supplies from those areas. The 49 signatory nations included all countries of the FSU, Western Europe, all of Eastern Europe except Serbia, along with Australia and Japan. The United States and Canada signed the earlier non-binding Energy Charter but declined to sign the binding treaty. The treaty contains provisions for the energy sector on:

- trade and commerce
- competition
- energy transit
- transfer of technology
- access to capital
- investment promotion and protection
- recognition of state sovereignty over energy resources
- environmental protection
- transparency of laws and regulations
- taxation
- state enterprises
- economies in transition to market economies
- dispute settlement and institutional arrangements

The treaty has the goal of encouraging free and nondiscriminatory trade and investment. Other provisions encourage transit at nondiscriminatory and reasonable rates. The investment criteria promotes investment provisions for non-nationals under the same conditions as prevail for nationals. Each signatory is obliged to advance competition and is encouraged to promote technology transfer and environmental goals.

The environmental provisions, although non-binding, request that signatories prevent energy-related pollution that affects other states through a polluter-pays principle. Although the EECT provisions that govern competition law are not as encompassing as those of the EU, they do promote lower barriers to competition, the free movement of goods within internal markets, and price transparency within the gas and electricity markets.

A rich diversity in fossil fuel use across European countries has been influenced by both market conditions and government policy. Energy endowments for the countries have also varied considerably. (Table 11–2.) (Note: Negative net imports are net exports.) On the supply side, we note a fairly high dependence on energy imports: more than half the European countries imported more than 45% of their energy needs in 1953; and by 1973, all but East Germany, and the United Kingdom imported that much. Between 1973 and 1983, imported energy's share fell for all but Italy, Netherlands and Portugal, while Norway and the United Kingdom became net energy exporters.

Coal remained the dominant fuel produced in Western Europe until 1983, when total production fell by almost half and coal's production share fell to just under one-third of primary energy production. By 1993, oil, gas, and electricity had all surpassed coal production in Western Europe.

Fewer than half of the European countries had oil production of any significance in 1953, with oil making up less than 10% of energy production for all but Austria. Countries with little or no production over this period included Belgium, Ireland, Portugal, Sweden, and Switzerland. Oil production held a very small share of Western European energy production until the North Sea finds. Ekofisk in Norwegian waters was the first North Sea oil field to be discovered. Since 1975, Ekofisk oil has landed in Teesside, England.

Statfjord, the largest oil field in the North Sea with considerable gas reserves, was discovered in 1974 and is expected to produce through 2020. It is owned 15% by Britain with the remainder owned by Norway. Oil is transported from the field by shuttle tankers. The bulk of Western European oil is produced by Norway and the United Kingdom from the North Sea with small amounts from the Netherlands, Denmark, and Germany. Primary electricity production (nuclear and hydropower) has continued to increase in Western Europe, reaching almost half of all electricity production in the 1980s.

Table 11–2 Energy Production and Imports in Western Europe

Country	Year	Production (bcm)	Net Imports as % of Consumption	% Fuel Shares Coal	Oil	Gas	Elec.
Austria	53	10.73	39.73%	27.22%	43.70%	6.82%	22.25%
Austria	63	13.60	25.10%	22.80%	28.08%	16.48%	32.63%
Austria	73	15.67	47.80%	11.49%	23.96%	19.12%	45.43%
Austria	83	15.97	45.11%	6.12%	9.83%	29.58%	54.47%
Austria	93	19.64	42.72%	2.47%	6.91%	35.36%	55.27%
Austria	01	21.64	45.03%	1.69%	5.67%	37.23%	55.42%
Belgium	53	40.30	-39.89%	99.40%	0.00%	0.49%	0.11%
Belgium	63	28.89	23.99%	98.79%	0.00%	0.89%	0.32%
Belgium	73	12.33	78.22%	95.58%	0.00%	1.59%	2.83%
Belgium	83	21.42	57.55%	26.83%	0.00%	41.50%	31.67%
Belgium	93	23.97	61.34%	2.12%	0.00%	48.67%	49.22%
Belgium	01	29.42	60.47%	0.45%	0.00%	54.77%	44.78%
Denmark	53	0.23	96.81%	95.57%	0.00%	0.00%	4.43%
Denmark	63	0.71	94.77%	98.91%	0.00%	0.00%	1.09%
Denmark	73	0.09	99.59%	0.00%	91.39%	0.00%	8.61%
Denmark	83	2.61	86.29%	0.00%	99.34%	0.00%	0.66%
Denmark	93	13.57	41.65%	0.00%	73.87%	22.52%	3.60%
Denmark	01	27.53	-9.96%	0.00%	72.39%	21.19%	6.42%
Finland	53	1.43	63.29%	2.41%	0.00%	0.00%	97.59%
Finland	63	2.35	73.82%	1.27%	0.00%	0.00%	98.73%
Finland	73	2.93	86.23%	0.61%	0.00%	0.00%	99.39%
Finland	83	9.25	62.40%	0.00%	0.00%	6.00%	94.00%
Finland	93	13.95	55.11%	0.00%	0.00%	21.90%	78.10%
Finland	01	16.87	50.31%	0.00%	0.00%	26.34%	73.66%
France	53	59.22	16.97%	85.97%	0.92%	0.50%	12.62%
France	63	72.72	44.21%	64.40%	5.78%	8.43%	21.39%
France	73	60.72	71.22%	43.37%	4.98%	15.68%	35.97%
France	83	103.57	53.37%	14.30%	2.87%	26.01%	56.82%
France	93	165.98	40.32%	4.38%	2.33%	21.09%	72.21%
France	01	185.53	40.54%	0.87%	1.06%	24.11%	73.97%
FRG	53	163.40	-34.16%	96.01%	1.83%	0.16%	2.00%
FRG	63	180.41	8.81%	90.82%	5.62%	1.15%	2.40%
FRG	73	166.90	45.42%	74.29%	5.45%	14.56%	5.70%
FRG	83	165.68	43.11%	53.01%	2.94%	28.33%	15.72%
GDR	53	42.79	14.08%	99.69%	0.00%	0.00%	0.31%
GDR	63	61.98	14.05%	99.51%	0.06%	0.17%	0.26%
GDR	73	66.31	26.84%	88.14%	0.11%	11.03%	0.72%
GDR	83	74.46	24.44%	87.33%	0.08%	7.09%	5.50%

Table 11–2 Energy Production and Imports in Western Europe (cont'd)

Country	Year	Production (bcm)	Net Imports as % of Consumption	% Fuel Shares			
				Coal	Oil	Gas	Elec.
Germany	93	215.76	44.70%	43.39%	1.69%	32.57%	22.35%
Germany	01	216.06	45.79%	29.04%	1.80%	42.04%	27.12%
Greece	53	0.14	92.94%	92.34%	0.00%	0.00%	7.66%
Greece	63	1.28	72.94%	79.68%	0.00%	0.00%	20.32%
Greece	73	4.46	74.67%	83.88%	0.00%	0.00%	16.12%
Greece	83	7.30	64.55%	69.88%	20.89%	0.00%	9.23%
Greece	93	9.66	67.91%	85.81%	7.04%	0.00%	7.15%
Greece	01	13.52	64.39%	77.20%	2.52%	14.38%	5.90%
Ireland	53	1.23	66.12%	91.47%	0.00%	0.00%	8.53%
Ireland	63	1.39	69.85%	90.75%	0.00%	0.00%	9.25%
Ireland	73	1.18	83.54%	87.18%	0.00%	0.00%	12.82%
Ireland	83	2.50	69.94%	2.27%	0.00%	88.77%	8.96%
Ireland	93	3.01	73.17%	0.02%	0.00%	92.44%	7.54%
Ireland	01	4.72	72.23%	0.00%	0.00%	94.15%	5.85%
Italy	53	18.48	32.94%	8.48%	1.34%	19.34%	70.84%
Italy	63	37.41	51.29%	3.39%	8.54%	30.46%	57.62%
Italy	73	46.24	69.22%	1.20%	4.13%	51.97%	42.70%
Italy	83	46.23	70.99%	1.05%	6.17%	59.49%	33.29%
Italy	93	70.80	61.63%	0.25%	7.34%	72.58%	19.83%
Italy	01	93.58	55.72%	0.00%	5.23%	76.29%	18.48%
Netherlands	53	5.03	70.89%	90.90%	8.85%	0.24%	0.00%
Netherlands	63	5.76	80.95%	73.94%	20.92%	5.15%	0.00%
Netherlands	73	36.51	47.38%	1.74%	2.31%	95.53%	0.42%
Netherlands	83	40.87	47.56%	0.00%	9.07%	88.36%	2.57%
Netherlands	93	47.93	50.66%	0.00%	8.05%	88.68%	3.27%
Netherlands	01	48.63	56.78%	0.00%	5.18%	89.67%	5.15%
Norway	53	4.39	54.24%	5.54%	0.00%	0.00%	94.46%
Norway	63	8.59	51.92%	2.59%	0.00%	0.00%	97.41%
Norway	73	17.08	45.30%	1.37%	7.71%	0.00%	90.92%
Norway	83	68.67	-64.46%	0.54%	53.39%	2.02%	44.05%
Norway	93	175.46	-264.49%	0.11%	78.83%	1.58%	19.48%
Norway	01	230.63	-344.31%	0.51%	82.58%	1.93%	14.99%
Portugal	53	0.68	69.48%	57.82%	0.00%	0.00%	42.18%
Portugal	63	1.52	66.67%	24.51%	0.00%	0.00%	75.49%
Portugal	73	2.28	78.17%	7.42%	0.00%	0.00%	92.58%
Portugal	83	2.48	82.03%	3.38%	0.00%	0.00%	96.62%
Portugal	93	2.77	87.11%	2.72%	0.00%	0.00%	97.28%
Portugal	01	7.35	75.63%	0.00%	0.00%	37.80%	62.20%

Table 11–2 Energy Production and Imports in Western Europe (cont'd)

Country	Year	Production (bcm)	Net Imports as % of Consumption	Coal	Oil	Gas	Elec.
Spain	53	15.75	22.93%	82.21%	0.14%	0.00%	17.65%
Spain	63	21.29	36.77%	62.73%	0.45%	0.01%	36.81%
Spain	73	25.84	67.69%	43.94%	4.30%	0.00%	51.76%
Spain	83	38.06	61.31%	55.28%	8.93%	6.57%	29.22%
Spain	93	43.72	60.91%	29.62%	3.04%	16.52%	50.82%
Spain	01	59.76	62.01%	13.22%	0.70%	33.47%	52.61%
Sweden	53	6.30	64.35%	3.41%	1.16%	0.00%	95.43%
Sweden	63	10.88	65.94%	0.69%	0.80%	0.00%	98.51%
Sweden	73	17.52	66.76%	0.00%	0.00%	0.00%	100.00%
Sweden	83	29.53	44.42%	0.03%	0.08%	0.00%	99.89%
Sweden	93	39.16	35.37%	0.01%	0.00%	2.13%	97.86%
Sweden	01	42.67	33.14%	0.00%	0.00%	1.95%	98.05%
Switzerland	53	4.23	46.38%	0.00%	0.00%	0.00%	100.00%
Switzerland	63	6.84	62.52%	0.00%	0.00%	0.00%	100.00%
Switzerland	73	10.96	64.61%	0.00%	0.00%	0.00%	100.00%
Switzerland	83	15.72	49.40%	0.00%	0.00%	8.83%	91.17%
Switzerland	93	19.38	45.07%	0.00%	0.00%	12.90%	87.10%
Switzerland	01	22.54	42.57%	0.00%	0.00%	13.55%	86.45%
Turkey	53	2.77	68.85%	98.41%	0.99%	0.00%	0.60%
Turkey	63	4.66	70.58%	72.21%	16.16%	0.00%	11.63%
Turkey	73	8.60	78.12%	49.91%	42.26%	0.00%	7.83%
Turkey	83	13.14	58.47%	55.25%	20.28%	0.00%	24.46%
Turkey	93	32.69	49.51%	39.85%	14.13%	16.14%	29.88%
Turkey	01	41.29	47.82%	36.31%	7.04%	39.70%	16.95%
U.K.	53	196.40	-0.28%	99.58%	0.10%	0.00%	0.31%
U.K.	63	176.08	21.67%	97.85%	0.09%	0.10%	1.95%
U.K.	73	157.38	39.08%	71.96%	0.33%	21.03%	6.68%
U.K.	83	291.95	-25.05%	28.46%	47.90%	17.79%	5.84%
U.K.	93	264.10	-0.29%	16.48%	45.57%	26.40%	11.54%
U.K.	01	296.52	-10.03%	7.40%	49.25%	32.51%	10.84%
U.S.	83	1723.52	12.02%	27.80%	33.16%	27.98%	11.06%
U.S.	93	1910.04	19.62%	29.45%	24.58%	31.05%	14.92%
U.S.	01	2018.38	23.40%	32.26%	20.41%	31.96%	15.37%

Table 11–2 Energy Production and Imports in Western Europe (cont'd)

Country	Year	Production (bcm)	Net Imports as % of Consumption	% Fuel Shares			
				Coal	Oil	Gas	Elec.
Europe 19	53	573.50	6.54%	89.48%	1.61%	0.88%	8.02%
Europe 19	63	636.37	32.46%	78.92%	3.72%	3.57%	13.79%
Europe 19	73	653.01	56.01%	54.77%	3.88%	20.88%	20.47%
Europe 19	83	949.41	36.89%	30.74%	21.35%	22.79%	25.11%
Europe 19	93	1161.56	33.52%	15.51%	25.25%	27.12%	32.13%
Europe 19	01	1358.26	30.46%	8.93%	27.58%	32.05%	31.44%

Notes: *FRG = Federal Republic of Germany = W. Germany, and GDR = the German Democratic Republic = E. Germany. The information for Germany 1953, 1963, and 1973 is divided between FRG and DDR. Measured in bcm unless otherwise indicated. One m^3 = 36,000 Btu = 9068 Kcal. Oil includes all liquid petroleum fuel. Years prior to 1983 are estimated by prorating 1983 numbers using the earlier U.N. statistics. Electricity is gross consumption and production. Negative net imports are net exports.
Sources: 1950–70: U.N., 1978, *World Energy Supplies 1950–1974*, 1980–2001: EIA/DOE, 2003, *International Energy Statistics 2001*.

Nuclear power, first produced in the United Kingdom in 1956, has constantly increased in use. Only Austria, Denmark, Greece, Ireland, Italy, Norway, Portugal, and Turkey have no nuclear power. Belgium, France, and Sweden have the strongest commitment to nuclear power with well more than a third of their electricity generated by nuclear facilities since 1983. They are models of how quickly a nuclear power industry can develop with government promotion. However, Europe's nuclear power is uncertain with the current phase out in Germany and Sweden.

Natural gas production expanded and diversified in the post-WWII period. In 1953, Italy and Austria produced and consumed more than 83% of Western European natural gas; by 1963, Italy, France, and Austria produced 87%. In the mid-to-late 1960s, the Netherlands began exports from its huge Groningen field. The European pipeline network continually developed. By 1973, the Netherlands, the United Kingdom, the FRG, and Italy produced 85% of the region's natural gas; by 1983, the top five producers—the Netherlands, the United Kingdom, Norway, the FRG, and Italy—produced 76%. The USSR began to export gas to Austria via Czechoslovakia in 1968 from Orenburg through the Soyuz gas line.

After 1973, brisk development marked the gas trade, with more than 25% of imported gas coming from outside Western Europe by 1983. Norway began to supply the continent with gas in 1977, from Ekofisk to the continent and from Frigg to St. Fergus, Scotland. Norwegian gas from Statfjord came through Emden, Germany, through the Stat/Norpipe system, while British gas landed in Scotland by pipeline through the Brent field. Agreements to sell Norwegian gas from Statfjord, Gullfaks, and Heimdal were signed in 1981 with deliveries of 15 billion m^3 a year in 1985 to Belgium, the FRG, France, and the Netherlands.

The Troll field, discovered in the early 1980s, is the largest Norwegian gas field and the largest offshore gas field in the world. The Troll contract, signed in the late 1980s, brought a doubling of Norwegian exports. The contract was unique because volumes were contracted without requirements that the gas come from specific fields. (Although much of the gas will come from Troll, other fields can be used to fulfill the contract.) The contract requires three new pipelines to the continent: Zeepipe to Belgium, which began making deliveries in 1993; Europipe, which began making deliveries to Germany in 1995; and Nor/Fra pipe, which began making deliveries to France in 1996, allowing deliveries to Spain and Italy. The Troll A platform, which started production in 1996, is the tallest man-made structure in the world and was built to last 70 years. Production from Troll was 20 X 10^9 m^3 in 1998.

The interconnector pipeline from Bacton, England, to Zeebrugge, Belgium, was completed in 1998. The gas flows from the United Kingdom to the continent, but the pipeline was designed so gas can flow back if conditions require it. Zeebrugge is a major gas hub with throughput capacity of 40 billion m^3 per year. Its LNG terminal and Zeepipe terminal receive Norwegian gas from the Troll field. Because of its strategic position, six major gas companies—Enron, Mobil, Gaz de France, Ruhrgas, BP Amoco, and Distrigas—developed a gas trading contract based in Zeebrugge.

France and the United Kingdom began LNG imports from Algeria in the mid-1960s. Spain began in the mid-1970s. Italy and Spain began importing LNG from Libya in the early 1970s. Deliveries of Algerian gas through the 667-mile Trans-Mediterranean pipeline to Italy began in 1983. The Maghreb-Europe pipeline from Algeria to Spain began transporting gas to Spain in 1996 and to Portugal in 1997.

Politics and a Pipeline

The Soviet Yamal pipeline was to have originated in the Yamal Peninsula in Siberia, but when contract volumes were less than expected, it was built from Urengoi, which was closer and had easier access. U.S. opposition to this project took the form of trade sanctions in effect from December 1981 to November 1982. The Soviets proved much better at laying pipe than building compressor stations, which slowed the construction because the suppliers John Brown of Edinburgh, AEG Kanis of Western Germany, and Nuovo Pignone of Italy normally imported required rotor shafts and gas turbines from U.S.-based General Electric.

Initially, five countries took contracts to buy Soviet gas. (Table 11–3) Belgium, Spain, and Holland had also been considering buying Soviet gas but decided against it. No pipeline business went to Belgium or the Netherlands, which may have influenced their decisions to cancel their contracts. The Soviets requested an amortization period of 8 to 10 years and an interest rate between 7.8 and 8.5 %, which was estimated by Adelman to provide a subsidy of approximately $7 per million m^3.

Table 11–3 Soviet Gas Contracts

Country	Amount of Gas	Starting	Length
France	7,999	1984	25 years
Germany	10,499	1984	25 years
Italy	7,985	1984	25 years
Switzerland	446	1988	20 years
Austria	1,501	1984	25 years

Note: Gas amounts are millions of cubic meters
Sources: *Wall Street Journal* (1/25/82–22;1), (11/23/81–31;1), (1/25/82–22;1), (1/29/82–33;2), (5/14/82–28;1), (6/24/82–32;1).

This agreement for Soviet gas involved building a 2760-mile pipeline from the Urengoi gas field, just north of the Arctic Circle, to the Czechoslovakian border. Part of the pipeline was an extension of the Northern Lights pipeline. The Yamal pipeline, a 1.42-meter (56-inch) high-pressure pipeline formed the fourth of seven pipelines from the Urengoi gas field, which was discovered in 1966 and came on stream in 1978.

The Yamal pipe was completed in 1983—ahead of schedule—and deliveries began in 1984 to Austria, West Germany, and France. These deliveries, however, were rumored to not have come from Urengoi but rather to have been diverted from Southern USSR. The pipeline crosses permafrost, mountains, dense forests, and some 700 rivers and is estimated to have cost $15 billion (U.S. currency). It has 40 compressor stations at intervals of 100 to 120 km. Urengoi produced 288 X 10^9 m^3/y in 1990 but production has fallen since then (*OGJ* 10/18/93:41).

Six 56-inch pipelines from Yamburg to European Russia were completed by 1993. Yamburg is the second largest gas field in Western Siberia. The most recent agreement for the Yamal-Europe pipeline will eventually connect the Yamal Peninsula—a nearby area with large gas reserves—with the Western European gas grid through Belarus and Poland. The pipeline is being built from west to east; at this writing, the Polish and German sections are complete. The Russian portion will be completed via extensions of lines in Russia and will not be connected to the Yamal peninsula until the gas is needed. Initial capacity will be for 30 X 10^9 m^3 with planned expansions to 60 X 10^9 m^3. The Russians are especially keen to complete this pipeline to be able to bypass Ukraine, which has accounted for more than 90% of Russian exports to the west, since Ukrainian gas thefts and lack of payment have been a problem.

Russian gas potential for export remains impressive. It is estimated to have more than a third of the world's explored reserves, which may exceed the energy equivalent of Saudi oil reserves. It has 9 of the world's 15 largest gas fields and more than an 80-year supply of gas at its 1999 production rate. Three-quarters of these reserves are in Western Siberia. Urengoi, the largest gas field in the world, had initial reserves of 7.76 trillion cubic meters (10^{12} m^3). Other super fields in the area are Yamburg, 4.75 X 10^{12} m^3; Bovanenkovskoye, 4.15 X 10^{12} m^3; Zapolyarnoye, 2.67 X 10^{12} m^3; Medvezhye, 1.55 X 10^{12} m^3; and Kharasavei, 1.27 X 10^{12} m^3.

Europe's early concern with these contracts was their degree of dependence on Soviet energy sources. However, the Soviets—and subsequently, the Russians— have proven to be fairly reliable trade partners, although weather and disputes with the Ukraine have for short times interrupted supplies. Dependence on Soviet energy supplies, as well as the degree of concentration of energy from other suppliers, is reported in Table 11–4, which shows recent imports by origin.

Table 11–4 Europe Pipeline Natural Gas Imports

Exports To	Imports From							
	Denm	Germ	Neth	Norw	U.K.	Russian Fed.	Alge	Total
Austria	-	0.32	-	0.50	-	5.22	-	6.04
Belgium	-	0.19	7.60	5.12	0.31	-	-	13.22
Finland	-	-	-	-	-	4.54	-	4.54
France	-	-	5.80	12.87	1.29	11.18	-	31.14
Germany	2.20	-	20.20	19.89	3.26	33.20	-	78.75
Greece	-	-	-	-	-	1.48	-	1.48
Ireland	-	-	-	-	3.42	-	-	3.42
Italy	-	-	7.10	1.10	-	19.50	21.85	49.55
Luxembourg	-	0.40	0.40	-	-	-	-	0.80
Netherlands	-	-	-	5.50	7.50	0.13	-	13.13
Portugal	-	-	-	-	-	-	2.20	2.20
Spain	-	-	-	1.22	-	-	6.54	7.76
Sweden	0.90	-	-	-	-	-	-	0.90
Switzerland	-	1.75	0.60	-	-	0.40	-	2.75
United Kingdom	-	-	0.50	2.20	-		-	2.70
Sum	3.10	2.66	42.2	48.4	15.78	75.65	30.50	218.38

Note: Imports by Selected Country, 2001, in 10^9 m^3.
Source: BP Statistical Review of World Energy, June 2002, http://www.bpamoco.com/worldenergy

This statistical survey shows that European energy markets have undergone a dramatic transition, particularly since 1973. This period has demonstrated a flexibility and speed of adjustment unexpected at the time of the oil embargo in 1973. Diversification has been out of oil and into coal, nuclear, and natural gas. The biggest adjustment out of oil came at the expense of heavy fuel oil and refineries adapted to produce more of the lighter fuels.

Energy production and distribution tends to be characterized by large firms. In 1999, more than 10% of the world's 100 largest corporations (measured by sales) were involved in the oil, gas, coal, or electricity industry. (*Fortune,* http://www.fortune.com.) In Europe, the percentage of large companies in the gas industry was even higher: Through the early 1980s, gas distribution and transmission was usually under government control or ownership, while production was a mix of public and private. In Germany and Switzerland, the gas industry was largely privately owned by large oil, gas, coal, and utility companies, which were responsible for the production, transmission, importation, and distribution of gas. Private companies produced Dutch gas but they sold the gas to Gasunie, which the government half-owned.

The Belgium transmission company, Distrigas, was one-third government owned; wholly government-owned companies (OMV Ag, Neste Oy, Gaz du France, Snam, Bord Gais Eireann, Statoil, INH, and British Gas) in Austria, Finland, France, Italy, Ireland, Norway, Spain and the United Kingdom, respectively, were all heavily involved in the gas industry in their respective countries. More recently, many of these state companies have been or are being privatized.

Newer markets for gas (Greece, Denmark, Portugal, and Turkey) all have state involvement in the industry. Given the EU gas directive, we can expect more entrants from the private sector. Large companies involved in the European gas market are noted in Table 11–5.

Table 11–5 Major Gas Companies in Western Europe

	Country	Major Gas Companies	Internet Homepage	Business	Major Stock Holders
EU	Austria	Österreichische Mineralölverwaltung (ÖMV)	http://www.omv.com/	P, T, D	State (35%),Abu Dhabi Intl. Petroleum Investment (19.4%)
EU	Belgium	Distrigaz	http://www.distrigas.be/	T	Tractebel (43.625%), Belgian Shell (16.67%), Publigas (24.995%), State (1 share)
EU	Denmark	Danish Oil & Natural Gas Company (Dong)	http://www.dong.dk/		State(100%)
EU	Finland	Gasum Oy	http://www.gasum.fi/ frindex_eng.htm	T, D	Fortum Oyj (25%), OAO Gazprom (25%), Ruhrgas (20%), State (24%)
EU	France	Gaz de France	http://www.gdf.fr/	P, T, D	State(100%)
EU	Germany	Ruhrgas	http://www.ruhrgas.de/		BEB (25%), Schubert KG(15%), Bergemann GmbH (58.76%)
		Thyssengas	http://www.thyssengas.de/	T	Shell(25%), PWR Power AG. (75%)
		Wingaz	http:/www/wingas.de	T	Wintershall Ag. (65%), Gazprom (35%)
		BEB	http:.www.beb.de	P, T, D	Esso (50%), Shell (50%)
EU	Greece	DEPA	http://www.depa.gr/	T,D	85% owned by Greek State
EU	Ireland	Bord Gais Eireann	http://www.bge.ie/	T,D	State (100%)

Table 11–5 Major Gas Companies in Western Europe (cont'd)

	Country	Major Gas Companies	Internet Homepage	Business	Major Stock Holders
EU	Italy	Snam (subsidiary of ENI)	http://www.snam.it/	P, T, D	ENI - State(36%)
EU	Netherlands	Gasunie	http://www.gasunie.nl/	T, D	Energie Beheer Nederland B.V. (40%), ESSO (25%), Shell (25%), State (10%)
		Nederlandse Aardolie Maatschappij (NAM)	http://www.nam.nl/	P	Shell (50%), Esso (50%)
	Norway	Statoil	http://www.statoil.com/	P, T	State (100%)
		Norsk Hydro	http://www.hydro.com/	P, T	State (44%)
EU	Portugal	Petroleos e Gas de Portugal (GALP)	www.galp.pt	T, D	State(34.81%), ENI (33.34%), EDP (14.27%), Caixa GD (13.50%)
EU	Spain	Enagas	http://www.enagas.es/	T, D	Repsol (45.3%), la Caixa (26.1%).
EU	Sweden	Vattenfalls Naturgas AB	http://www.vattenfallnaturgas.com/		
		Sydgas	http://www.sydgas.se/		Part of E.ON
	Switzerland	Swissgas		T	Union Bank of Switzerland (20%), Crédit Suisse (10%), Swiss Natural Gas Industry Association (16.45%), Erdgas Ostschweiz AG (16.45%), Gasverbund Mitteland of Arlesheim (16.45%), Société pour l'approvisionnement et le transport du gaz naturel en Suisse romande (16.45%), Erdgaz Zentralschweiz of Lucerne (4.2%)
EU	UK	British Gas Group	http://www.bgplc.com/	P, T, D	
		Centrica	http://www.centrica.co.uk/	P, D	
		Transco	http://www.transco.uk.com/	T	

Notes: P = production, T= transmission, D = distribution

No Western European economy has ever had an open market for gas, although the German market appears to be one of the more open, given the number of companies involved in importation and distribution. International gas contracts required government approval and were very complex because of the large infrastructure involved: A typical contract was 20 years in length and often had provisions for contract revision with prices typically tied to some grade of fuel oil.

Germany, the most dependent on Soviet gas, today operates a sophisticated grid through which gas from several sources can be distributed by means of gas blending stations. (It is sometimes difficult to tell the ultimate destination of natural gas after it enters a country.) Austria's gas field at Baumgarten is a safeguard against minor variations. France and Italy are most vulnerable to a Soviet supply reduction because they follow Austria and Germany on the pipeline grid. However, they have relatively large underground storage. (Table 11–6.)

Table 11–6 Gas Storage in the European Union, 2001

Country	Volume billion m³	% of 2000 Demand	Withdrawal capacity million m³/day
Austria	2.30	31.60	24.0
Belgium	0.68	4.20	19.0
Denmark	0.81	17.60	25.0
France	11.10	26.20	180.0
Finland	0.00	0.00	0.0
Germany	18.56	22.30	425.0
Greece	0.08	3.80	5.0
Ireland	0.00	0.00	0.0
Italy	15.10	22.00	265.0
Luxembourg	0.00	0.00	0.0
Netherlands	2.50	6.10	145.0
Portugal	0.00	0.00	0.0
Spain	1.00	5.50	8.0
Sweden	0.00	0.00	0.0
U.K.	3.58	3.70	137.0
EU-15	55.69	14.20	1,233.0

Source: Commission of the European Communities, Brussels, November 9, 2002, Communication from the Commission to the European, Parliament and the Council, *The Internal Market in Energy: Coordinated Measures on the Security of Energy Supply,* http://europa.eu.int/comm/energy/home/internal_market/oil_gaz/doc/com_2002_488_final_en.pdf

Russia is the most significant exporter to the European gas market by pipeline followed by Norway. Germany is the largest importer followed by Italy and France. Norway consumes almost no natural gas domestically whereas the Netherlands is a large gas consumer and exports somewhat more than half of its production. These markets have tended to be dominated by a few large players—huge exporters negotiating with large transmission and distribution companies in the importing countries, usually with natural monopoly status. There historically was heavy government involvement in the negotiations as well as the markets.

The three major exporters into the continental European market—Norway, Russia, and Algeria—had state companies that heavily or exclusively directed the export of natural gas: Statoil, Gasprom, and Sonatrach. These exporters sold to large importers that were often at least partially state owned—Gas de France, Distrigas in Belgium, ENI in Italy, Ruhrgas in Western Germany, and GasUnie in the Netherlands. These large importers in turn often owned or jointly owned the long distance transportation networks.

Cournot Duopoly

To analyze such a market, we turn to game theory models, beginning with duopoly theory, in which two sellers face competitive buyers. We will consider three models in this framework:

1. a Cournot model, in which each firm chooses quantity to maximize profits based on the other firm's output

2. a Stackleberg model, in which one firm is a leader in the market and sets quantity knowing how the other firm will react

3. a Bertrand model, in which the two firms set price instead of quantity.

We begin with a Cournot model with two players. Suppose that Norway (country one) and Russia (country two) are the only two gas exporters to Germany. The inverse demand function in this market is:

$$P = 100 - 0.5(q_1 + q_2)$$

Where P is price and q_1 and q_2 are the outputs for firms one and two, respectively. Costs are:

$$C_1 = 0.5q_1^2 \text{ and } C_2 = 5q_2$$

Where C_1 and C_2 are the total costs for firms one and two.

Profit functions for the two firms, using the other firm's output, are price times quantity minus cost or:

$$\pi_1 = (100 - 0.5(q_1 + q_2))q_1 - 0.5q_1^2$$

$$\pi_2 = (100 - 0.5(q_1 + q_2))q_2 - 5q_2$$

First-order conditions for profit maximization for firm one are:

$$\partial\pi_1/\partial q_1 = 100 - 0.5(q_1 + q_2) - 0.5q_1 - q_1 = 0$$

This equation can be rearranged to:

$$\partial\pi_1/\partial q_1 = 100 - 0.5q_2 - 2q_1 = 0$$

Solving for q_1 gives us firm one's reaction function. This function shows the profit maximizing quantity for firm one, given firm two's output:

$$q_1 = 100/2 - (0.5/2)q_2 = 50 - 0.25q_2$$

First order conditions for profit maximization for firm two are:

$$\partial\pi_2/\partial q_2 = (100 - 0.5(q_1 + q_2)) - 0.5q_2 - 5 = 0$$

This equation can be rearranged to:

$$\partial\pi_2/\partial q_2 = 95 - 0.5q_1 - q_2 = 0$$

Solving for q_1 gives us firm two's reaction function. This function shows the profit maximizing quantity for firm two, given firm one's output.

$$q_2 = 95 - 0.5q_1$$

These two reaction functions are shown in Figure 11–1.

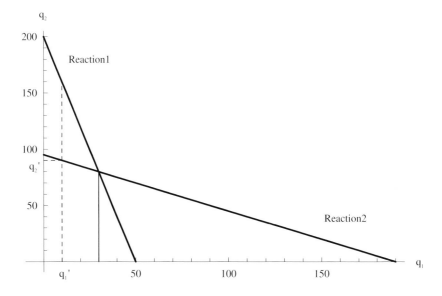

Fig. 11–1 Reaction Function for a Duopoly

For this model to be in equilibrium the firms have to be on their reaction function. For example: Assuming firm one is at q_1', then if firm two is on its reaction function and knew that firm one was producing q_1', firm two would be at q_2'. But for firm one to be at q_1', it must think that firm two is producing more than it is. This implies that there is excess demand in the market. When firm one finds out the actual quantity of q_2 it will move back onto its reaction function at a larger output. Firm two will react with a lower output, and so on, until they reach equilibrium. Equilibrium is found where both firms are on their reaction function or at the solution to the following system of equations:

$$q_1 = 50 - 0.25q_2$$

$$q_2 = 95 - 0.5q_1$$

One way of solving this equation is by substituting the first equation into the second.

$$q_2 = 95 - 0.5(50 - 0.25q_2) = 95 - 25 + 0.125q_2 = 70 + 0.125q_2$$

$$q_2 - 0.125q_2 = 70$$

$$q_2(1 - 0.125) = q_2{}^*0.875 = 70$$

$$q_2 = 70/(0.875) = 80$$

We find q_1 by substituting q_2 back into q_1's reaction function:

$$q_1 = 50 - 0.25*80 = 30$$

We find the price in the market by substituting q_1 and q_2 back into the demand equation or:

$$P = 100 - 0.5(30 + 80) = 45$$

We can find profits for the players by substituting their respective prices and quantities back into their profit functions:

$$\pi_1 = Pq_1 - C_1 = 45*(30) - 0.5*30^2 = 900$$
$$\pi_2 = Pq_2 - C_2 = 45*(80) - 5*80 = 3200$$

We know that we need marginal cost to be less than price to be producing, so we check whether or not the firms should shut down.

$$MC_1 = \partial C/\partial q_1 = \partial(0.5q_1^2)/\partial q_1 = 2*0.5q_1 = q_1 = 30$$
$$MC_2 = \partial C/\partial q_2 = \partial(5q_2)/\partial q_2 = 5$$

MC is smaller than price in both cases so the firms should produce.

If this model is extended to more suppliers, then each player would have a reaction function that depended on the production of the other players. For example, the Norwegian Central Bureau of Statistics has modeled the European gas market with Norway, Russia, and Algeria as the major players in order to work out optimal gas development plans. (Bjerkholt et al. 1990)

Duopoly Compared to Competitive Market

In the previous example, the firms are taking advantage of the fact that they have some pricing power and are facing a downward sloping demand instead of taking price as given. Let's compare this to the case in which each player behaves in a competitive manner and operates where price is equal to marginal cost.

In a competitive market, the supply curve equals the horizontal sum of the marginal cost curves. For the above example, the cost curves are:

$$C_1 = 0.5q_1^2 \text{ and } C_2 = 5q_2$$

The marginal cost curves are:

$$MC_1 = q_1$$

$$MC_2 = 5$$

These curves are represented in Figure 11–2. Horizontally summing the two marginal cost curves gives the marginal cost or the competitive market supply curve in Figure 11–3.

Demand crosses supply where:

$$P = 5 = 100 - 0.5(q_1 + q_2)$$

Solving for market quantity at five we find:

$$q_1 + q_2 = 190$$

Marginal cost must be equal to price for both suppliers so that:

$$MC_1 = P = 5 = q_1$$

$$q_1 = 5$$

$$q_2 = 190 - 5 = 185$$

Firm one has economic profits of:

$$\pi_1 = 5*5 - 0.5*(5^2) = 12.5$$

Profits for firm two are:

$$\pi_2 = 185*5 - 5(185) = 0$$

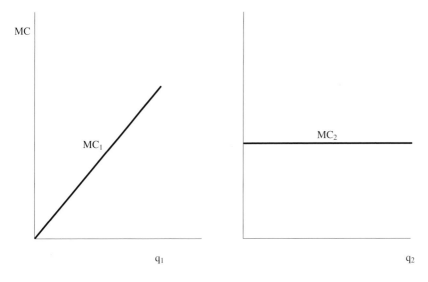

Fig. 11–2 Marginal Cost Curves for Producer 1 and 2

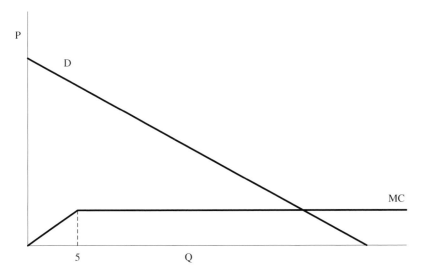

Fig. 11–3 Market Supply and Demand in a Competitive Market

Firm two has no monopoly rents but is making a normal rate of return. Firm one's profits are called Ricardian rents: These rents results because firm one has lower costs or better resources and not because firm one has monopoly power. The profits in this example are much lower than in the duopoly case above, where the two firms exploit their market power.

Monopoly Compared to Competitive and Duopoly Market

A third case for these two gas producers would be to have the two producers get together and monopolize the market. In this case, the producers should operate where marginal revenue equals marginal cost as in Figure 11–4.

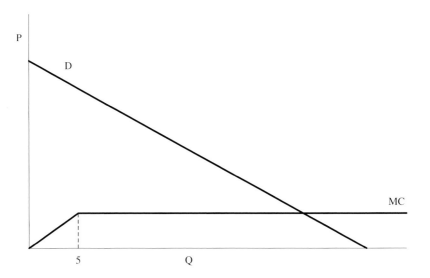

Fig. 11–4 Two Gas Producers Acting as a Monopolist

Setting marginal revenue equal to marginal cost and solving yields:

$$MR = 100 - (q_1 + q_2) = 5$$

$$q_1 + q_2 = 95$$

Now they produce half of what they would produce together in a competitive market. To maximize profits they should behave as a multiplant monopoly and each should produce where MR of five equals MC. Firm one should produce:

$$MC_1 = 5 = q_1$$

$$q_1 = 5$$

Or the same amount as in the competitive case, while firm two should satisfy the remainder of the market.

$$q_2 = 95 - q_1 = 95 - 5 = 90$$

Price in this market and profits are substantially higher than in the competitive case at:

$$P = 100 - 0.5(95) = 52.5$$

$$\pi_1 = 5*52.5 - 0.5*(5^2) = 250$$

$$\pi_2 = 90*52.5 - 5(90) = 4275$$

Bertrand Model

In all of the previous examples, we assumed the firms picked quantity. In the Bertrand duopoly, it is assumed that one firm sets price assuming the other firm holds price constant. To see what might happen in this case, suppose that firm one sets the price at P_1. If $P_1 < P_2$, then firm one has no market, and if $P_1 > P_2$, then firm one has the whole market. Each has an incentive to lower price to get the whole market until the competitive solution is reached.

Limit Pricing Model

A last model suggests the effect of potential entrants and is called the limit pricing model.

Demand in Figure 11–5 is for an energy service that can be satisfied by a fossil fuel or some more expensive but unlimited backstop fuel. The backstop is some source that has yet to be developed on any large scale, such as photovoltaic, micro-hydro, or hydrogen fuel cells. In this model, we assume that the low-cost fossil fuel supplier is a monopolist in the fossil fuel market. The higher-cost backstop (with costs as shown by AC_b in Fig. 11–5) is a potential competitor. Without the backstop, the monopolist should operate where marginal revenue (MR_m) equals marginal cost (MC_m) charging P_m and producing Q_m. However, at this price the backstop would have an incentive to enter. An alternative would be to charge a price that is equal to the minimum of the average cost curve for the backstop or slightly below this competitive price (P_c) to discourage entry.

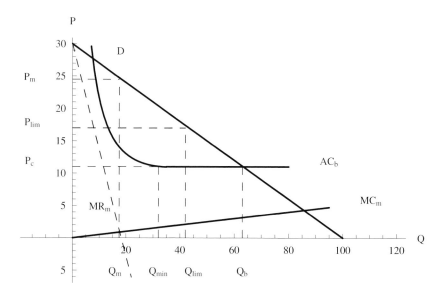

Fig. 11–5 Limit Pricing Model

However, the monopolist may be able to do better than price at the long run minimum of the backstop. To see how, consider the following argument.

Note that Q_{min} is the smallest output that gives the backstop maximum economies of scale. If the monopolist picked a quantity Q_{lim} such that $Q_{min} + Q_{lim}$ would drive price below the long-run minimum average cost, and the backstop would not want to enter the market. The limit quantity would be $Q_{lim} = Q_b - Q_{min}$ and the price charged would be P_{lim}.

Thus, a monopolist threatened with a lower-cost backstop may still be able to charge a higher price. Here the threat of increasing production should discourage the discerning entrant. However, the monopolist needs to be careful that the price charged is not so high as to encourage entrants that may subsequently be protected under antitrust or other legislation.

Summary

Energy use has changed substantially in Western Europe in the decades since World War II. Coal was king in 1950 with postwar shortages, but cheap Middle Eastern and North African oil, then Dutch gas, and then North Sea oil turned coal shortages into a coal glut. With the oil price run-ups in the 1970s and the political uncertainties of secure oil supplies, Europe diversified into nuclear and gas. Long-distance pipelines from Norway, Algeria, and the Soviet Union have continued to expand and bring in gas from further and further away to a hungry European market. Since the 1990s, economic union and a monetary union are knitting Western Europe ever closer together.

Large companies have dominated the Western European gas industry, often with monopoly control over parts of the industry in their respective countries, particularly for transmission and distribution. In such an oligopoly market, large companies and governments negotiate for long-term international contracts. Game theory is a useful technique for studying strategic interaction in these types of small-number bargaining situations.

The Cournot model is a non-cooperative game in which each player maximizes profits taking the other player's output as given. In this model, players are competing with quantities and the optimization problem gives each player a reaction function. Equilibrium in the market is solved from the system of reaction functions. Cournot players will make more profits than competitive players but will make fewer profits jointly than if they collude and act as a monopolist. As we add Cournot players to the market, we will approach a competitive price and quantity.

The Bertrand model is a non-cooperative game, with market participants competing on price. An important application of this model is auctions. Interestingly, the Bertrand solution is the same as the competitive solution: When firms compete based on price they bid away monopoly profits.

As fossil fuels are depleted, we expect to move on to higher-cost renewable fuels, which are often called backstop fuels. The limit pricing model suggests that current low cost suppliers with monopoly power may not charge the monopoly price for fear of entrance of the backstop fuels. However, the monopolist may not have to come down to the backstop price. The mere threat that price could be driven below the backstop's cost may be enough to prevent the backstop from entering the market.

12 Allocating Fossil Fuel Production Over Time and Oil Leasing

"Drill for oil? You mean drill in the ground to try and find oil? You're crazy!"

> —Drillers who Edwin L. Drake tried to enlist to his project to drill for oil in 1859 downloaded from http//:www.freemaninstitute.com/quotes.htm

Introduction

Many energy decisions are dynamic because what we decide today influences energy markets tomorrow. If we sign a long-term contract (such as an oil lease) today, it binds our activities over the life of the contact. If we invest in long-lived capital that uses or produces energy, it influences energy markets for years to come. Industrial capital often lasts more than 20 years, while many consumer durables last more than 10. Table 12–1 lists the typical lives of a variety of energy-using capital.

For renewable energy resources (such as tree plantations) and nonrenewable energy resources (such as fossil fuels) the timing of their use matters. When we cut trees influences total yield; use of a nonrenewable resource today negates its use tomorrow. In such instances—when economic decisions today influence what happens tomorrow—the economic decision-maker must consider these inter-temporal effects. Economic decision-making should be dynamic, optimizing across time rather than optimizing for one point in time (static). In this chapter, we focus on dynamic analysis with applications to fossil fuel production patterns and oil leasing. We begin our analysis with fossil fuel reserves.

Table 12–1 Typical Lives for Various Equipment and Appliances

Equipment	Years
Power Plant	40
Pipeline	25–30
Boiler	20
Household Appliances	
Gas ranges	18
Electric ranges	15
Gas clothes dryer	14
Refrigerator	14
Electric clothes dryer	13
Washing machine	13
Dishwasher	11
Microwave	10
Vacuum cleaner	10
Air conditioner	9
Blender	8
Color television	8

Source: Household Appliance Data, *Consumer Reports*.

Reserves and reserve-over-production ratios

Table 12–2 shows current proven crude oil reserves by region and by major reserve holders in the world. Reserves are very concentrated, with roughly two-thirds of them found in the Middle East. Other major areas have between 4% and 10% of the reserves with the exception of Europe, which is particularly poorly endowed with oil. Gas reserves are also concentrated but not as much as for oil. The FSU and the Middle East share about 70% of the world's proven gas reserves. The reserve-over-production ratio (R/P) indicates how many years of production these reserves provide if production stays at the current level.

Global R/P for oil is pegged at about 40 years, gas at about 50 years, and coal more than 200 years. These numbers suggest that at current production rates, oil is the scarcest resource and coal is the most abundant.

Table 12–2 Proven Coal, Oil, and Gas Reserves and Production, 2001

Region/ Country	Production			Reserves			Reserves/ Production		
	Oil Billion Barrels	Gas Tcf	Coal Million s.tons	Oil Billion Barrels	Gas Tcf	Coal Million s.tons	Oil Years	Gas Years	Coal Years
North America									
Canada	1.03	6.60	77.68	4.86	59.73	7,251.00	4.7	9.1	93.3
Mexico	1.32	1.30	12.81	26.94	29.51	1,334.90	20.4	22.7	104.2
United States	3.27	19.36	1,121.33	22.45	183.46	273,656.49	6.9	9.5	244.0
Total	**5.61**	**27.25**	**1,211.82**	**54.25**	**272.70**	**282,444.12**			
Central & South America									
Argentina	0.30	1.31	0.21	2.97	27.46	473.99	9.8	20.9	2,311.8
Brazil	0.57	0.21	4.53	8.46	7.81	13,149.47	14.7	37.1	2,903.5
Colombia	0.22	0.20	47.89	1.75	4.32	7,328.17	7.8	21.5	153.0
Venezuela	1.13	1.12	8.36	77.69	147.59	528.00	68.7	131.8	63.1
Total	**2.53**	**3.61**	**61.67**	**95.97**	**253.02**	**23,977.48**			
Western Europe									
Netherlands	0.03	2.75	0.00	0.11	62.54	100547.85	3.7	22.8	
Norway	1.25	1.93	1.66	9.45	44.04	1.10	7.6	22.8	0.7
United Kingdom	0.94	3.74	34.74	4.93	25.96	1,653.47	5.2	6.9	47.6
Total	**2.54**	**10.31**	**500.55**	**17.30**	**160.72**	**101,343.20**			
EE and FSU									
Kazakhstan	0.29	0.36	88.52	5.42	65.00	37,478.59	18.6	182.6	423.4
Russia	2.66	20.51	299.50	48.57	1,680.00	173,073.91	18.3	81.9	577.9
Turkmenistan	0.06	1.70	0.00	0.55	101.00	nr	9.2	59.3	
Ukraine	0.03	0.64	90.06	0.40	39.60	37,647.24	12.5	61.6	418.0
Uzbekistan	0.05	2.23	2.94	0.59	66.20	4,409.25	11.4	29.7	1,498.1
Total	**3.30**	**26.48**	**817.65**	**58.39**	**1,967.94**	**290,183.47**			
Middle East									
Iran	1.39	2.17	1.54	89.70	812.30	1,884.95	64.4	374.0	1,221.4
Iraq	0.90	0.10	0.00	112.50	109.80	nr	125.6	1,126.5	
Kuwait	0.77	0.34	0.00	96.50	52.70	nr	124.6	157.1	
Oman	0.35	0.49	0.00	5.51	29.28	nr	15.7	60.2	
Qatar	0.32	1.14	0.00	15.21	508.54	nr	48.2	444.4	
Saudi Arabia	3.18	1.90	0.00	261.75	219.50	nr	82.2	115.8	
UAE	0.94	1.59	0.00	97.80	212.10	nr	104.3	133.6	
Total	**8.22**	**8.25**	**1.54**	**685.59**	**1,974.57**	**1,884.95**	**83.4**	**239.4**	**1,221.4**
Africa									
Algeria	0.56	2.84	0.03	9.20	159.70	44.09	16.6	56.3	1,666.7
Egypt	0.30	0.75	0.00	2.95	35.18	24.25	9.9	47.0	
Libya	0.52	0.22	0.00	29.50	46.40	2.20	56.6	212.6	
Nigeria	0.83	0.55	0.07	24.00	124.00	209.44	29.1	223.9	3,064.5
Total	**2.97**	**4.58**	**257.26**	**76.68**	**394.85**	**61,031.67**			

Table 12–2 Proven Coal, Oil, and Gas Reserves and Production, 2001 (cont'd)

Region/ Country	Production			Reserves			Reserves/ Production		
	Oil Billion Barrels	Gas Tcf	Coal Million s.tons	Oil Billion Barrels	Gas Tcf	Coal Million s.tons	Oil Years	Gas Years	Coal Years
Asia & Oceania									
Australia	0.27	1.17	356.85	3.50	90.00	90,488.74	12.9	77.0	253.6
China	1.20	1.07	1,459.02	24.00	48.30	126,214.65	19.9	45.1	86.5
Indonesia	0.53	2.44	99.64	5.00	92.50	5,919.41	9.5	38.0	59.4
Malaysia	0.27	1.90	0.39	3.00	75.00	4.41	11.3	39.6	11.4
Total	**2.95**	**10.24**	**2,415.53**	**43.78**	**433.31**	**322,394.11**			
World Total	**28.12**	**90.72**	**5,266.01**	**1,031.96**	**5,457.10**	**1,083,258.99**			

Notes: Oil includes crude oil, natural gas plant liquids, other liquids, and refinery processing gain. nr = not reported. Oil and gas reserves are from the *Oil and Gas Journal*. Countries included have crude oil reserves greater than 5 billion barrels or natural gas reserves greater than 24 tcf. Totals include all countries listed and not listed, b/d = barrels per day. (*) There are about 35.3 cubic feet per cubic meter. There are usually 7 to 8 barrels of oil per metric ton depending on the grade of the oil. For example, U.S. and Saudi oil average about 7.3 barrels per metric ton whereas light North Sea oil tends to average more than 7.5 barrels per metric ton. EIA/DOE *International Energy Annual* contains these and numerous other energy conversions. http://www.eia.doe.gov/iea/convheat.html

Source: EIA/DOE, Feb. 2003, *International Energy Annual*, 2001.

R/P for U.S. oil and gas is around 10 years. Does this mean that in 10 years the United States will be out of oil and gas and will be importing all its supplies? Probably not. To see why not, consider Figure 12–1. In 1900, the United States had about 40 years of oil reserves and by 1940 it still had more than 13 years of oil left. This was despite the fact that production in 1940 was considerably higher than production in 1900. By 1980, the United States still had more than nine years remaining, which was even a bit higher by 2000. Thus, an R/P of 10 years in the United States really means that the oil industry has a developed inventory of 10 years of oil reserves at current production levels and assuming that as reserves deplete, the industry will find and develop new reserves. However, the fact the R/P has fallen from 40 years in 1900 to 10 years in 2001, suggests that oil is getting relatively scarcer in the United States.

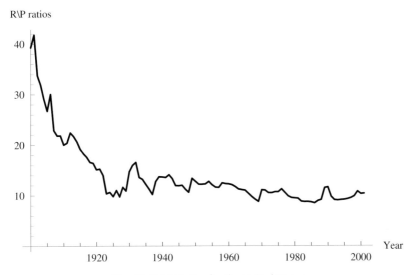

Fig. 12–1 R/P Ratios for the United States

Source: American Petroleum Institue.

Dynamic Two-Period Competitive Optimization Models Without Costs

To understand how reserves (R) should best be produced over time, we begin with a simple two-period model with competitive markets and no production costs. The goal of the producer is to choose the production over the two periods (Q_0, Q_1) that maximizes present value of reserves from production. P_0 is equal to the price in the current period and P_1 is the price in the future period. The present value of production over the two years is:

$$PV = P_0 Q_0 + \frac{P_1 Q_1}{(1+r)}$$

We maximize this result subject to our resource constraint:

$$R = Q_0 + Q_1$$

In this model, we disallow any new reserves to be discoveries and maximize the value of existing reserves. To do this, we use the Lagrange multiplier technique, which gives our optimizing function as:

$$\mathcal{J} = P_0 Q_0 + \frac{P_1 Q_1}{(1+r)} + \lambda(R - Q_0 - Q_1)$$

The Lagrange multiplier in front of the constraint incorporates the constraint into the optimization. The interpretation of the multiplier is interesting: Mathematically it is $\lambda = \partial\mathcal{J}/\partial R$. Along the constraint, $\mathcal{J}$ is equal to the present value of our reserves. Thus, $\partial\mathcal{J}/\partial R$ is the change in the present value of reserves when we change reserves and is a measure of the present value of an additional unit of reserves. In a general Lagrangian problem, λ is called the shadow value of the constraint, and it represents the change in the value of our objective function for a change in the constraint. Here, it is the shadow value of an additional unit of reserves or the present value of an additional unit of reserves.

In such a problem, we treat λ as a choice variable, just as we do with our other choice variables. Then first order conditions for a maximum are:

$$\mathcal{J}_\lambda = R - Q_0 - Q_1 = 0 \qquad (12.1)$$

$$\mathcal{J}_{Q0} = P_0 - \lambda = 0 \qquad (12.2)$$

$$\mathcal{J}_{Q1} = \frac{P_1}{(1+r)} - \lambda = 0 \qquad (12.3)$$

Note that $\mathcal{J}_\lambda = 0$ merely forces us to be on the constraint. Rearranging (12.2) and (12.3) we get:

$$P_0 = \lambda \qquad (12.4)$$

$$\frac{P_1}{(1+r)} = \lambda \qquad (12.5)$$

Setting (12.4) equal to (12.5) we get:

$$P_0 = \frac{P_1}{(1+r)}$$

Or alternatively:

$$P_1 = (1+r)P_0 \qquad (12.6)$$

Equation (12.6) requires that the price increases at the interest rate. To see the intuition of this mathematical result or why this condition maximizes present value of reserves, suppose that price does not go up at the interest rate. Let oil price go up slower than the interest rate or:

$$P_1 < P_0(1+r)$$

In this case, money in the bank is worth more than oil in the ground: It is better to produce more oil now, sell for P_0, and put the money in the bank to collect interest. We can easily see this with a numerical example.

Suppose the interest rate is $r = 0.1$, $P_0 = 20$, and $P_1 = 21$. Then $P_1 < (1+r)P_0$ or $21 < (1.1)*20 = 22$. If you leave oil in the ground, it will be worth $21 in a year. But if you sell the oil for $20 and put the money in the bank, you will have $(1.1)*20 = 22 in a year. Thus, you should produce more oil now and put the money in the bank. However, if everyone produces more now and less next period, price P_0 will fall and P_1 will increase until the price goes up at the rate of interest. Alternatively, if the price goes up faster than the interest rate, oil in the ground is worth more than money in the bank. Producers should produce less now, leaving more oil in the ground, and produce more in the next period. Such a production change will drive oil prices up in this period and down in the next period. Production should be reallocated until price increases by the interest rate. Thus, if producers dynamically optimize in this simple model, market forces should cause price to go up at the interest rate.

Some simple two-period examples will better illustrate the intuition of dynamic modeling.

Model One (Base Model: No Costs, No Income Growth)

Suppose demand is:

$$Q = 50 - 2.5P + 1Y$$

$$\text{Reserves (R)} = 60$$

$$MC = 0$$

$$\text{Income (Y)} = 50$$

Demand at the above income in the current period is:

$$Q_0 = 50 - 2.5P_0 + 1(50) = 100 - 2.5P_0$$

Inverse demand is:

$$P_0 = 40 - 0.4Q_0$$

This demand is graphed in Figure 12–2, with Q_0 varying from 0 to our total reserves of 60 as we move from left to right. If we assume that income does not grow, then demand in the next period is:

$$P_1 = 40 - 0.4Q_1$$

To include this demand, we graph it from right to left.

Figure 12–3 shows both demand curves. The top horizontal axis labels under the graph show consumption in the current period, Q_0. The bottom labels under the graph show consumption during the second period, Q_1. For example, if we consume all reserves in these two periods and Q_0 is 0, then Q_1 is 60. When $Q_0 = 20$, then $Q_1 = 40$. The graph allows us to easily compare the price received in each period. For example, when $Q_0 = 20$ and $Q_1 = 40$, P_0 is greater than P_1. When $Q_0 = 30$ and $Q_1 = 30$, the price is equal in the two periods. If Q_0 is greater than 30 and Q_1 is less than 30, then P_0 is less than P_1.

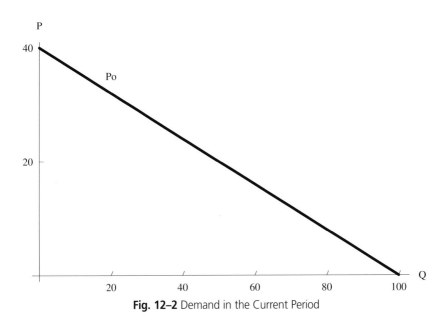

Fig. 12–2 Demand in the Current Period

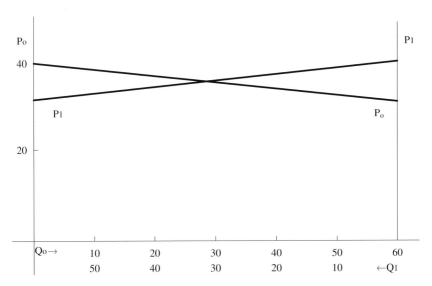

Fig. 12–3 Demand for Oil

We are now almost ready to make our economic choice. As economists, we always want to consider our return in each period and sell where we get the best price. But since a dollar in the second period is not equal to a dollar in the first period, we have to discount the second period. We discount the price in the second period by dividing by $(1+r)$ for an $r = 20\%$. (Fig. 12–4.) This is a fairly high interest rate but makes it easier to visualize the changes on the diagrams.

Note that discounted price in period 1 is not parallel to the non-discounted price in period 1 and moves further from the non-discounted price as price increases. The graph shows Q_0 and Q_1 are the optimal allocation. Before Q_0, selling more in the current period yields a higher return, since $P_0 > P_1/(1+r)$. After Q_0, however, we are better off selling in the next period, since $P_0 < P_1/(1+r)$. At the optimal allocation Q_0 and Q_1, prices in the two periods are P_0' and P_1'.

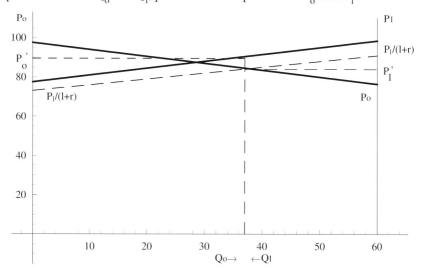

Fig. 12–4 Optimal Allocation of a Resource in a Two-Period Model

We can also solve this model numerically to get a more precise solution. At the optimal allocation Q_0 and Q_1, prices in the two periods are P_0 and P_1. First-order conditions require that we should set:

$$P_0 = P_1/(1+r)$$

For $r = 20\%$; then:

$$40 - 0.4Q_0 = (40 - 0.4Q_1)/1.2 \qquad (12.7)$$

The reserve constraint tells us that:

$$Q_o + Q_1 = 60 \qquad\qquad (12.8)$$

Solve (12.8) for Q_1 and substitute into (12.7) to get:

$$40 - 0.4Q_o = (40 - 0.4\,(60 - Q_o))/1.2$$

Solve for quantities in the two periods to get:

$$Q_o = 36.36$$

$$Q_1 = 60 - Q_o = 60 - 36.36 = 23.64$$

Substituting quantities into the inverse demand equation, we get prices in the two periods as:

$$P_o = 40 - 0.4 * 36.36 = 25.456$$

$$P_1 = 40 - 0.4 * (23.64) = 30.544$$

The price that the producer receives, minus his marginal economic costs, was called the producer surplus in our earlier competitive static models. This surplus (often referred to as Ricardian rent) occurs because some units have lower costs than others, whereas all units receive the price of the marginal unit. In a dynamic problem, even marginal producers may receive more than their marginal cost as the result of scarcity. This scarcity-induced surplus—referred to as Hotelling rents—is the difference between price and marginal cost for the marginal producer. In this contrived problem with no economic costs, the whole price is rent. The present value of these rents is:

$$PV_r = P_o Q_o + \frac{P_1 Q_1}{(1.2)}$$

$$= 25.456 * 36.36 + [(30.544 * 23.64)/1.2]$$

$$= 1{,}527.36$$

We can also represent the present value of consumer surplus in this example as the area below demand in period zero plus the area below the discounted demand in period one minus discounted rents (PV_r).

$$PV_{cs} = \int_0^{36.36} P_o dQ_o + (\int_0^{23.64} P_1 dQ_1)/1.2 - PV_r$$

$$= (40Q_o - (0.4/2)Q_o^2)|_0^{36.36} + (40Q_1 - (0.4/2)Q_1^2)|_0^{23.64}/1.2 - 1{,}527.3$$

$$= 357.5$$

This is the gray area abcde in Figure 12–5.

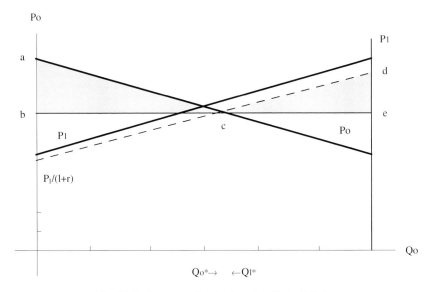

Fig. 12–5 Consumer Surplus in a Two-Period Model

With a linear demand, consumer surplus can be even more easily computed by using Figure 12–5's triangles abc+cde as (abc = $0.5*(40-25.456)*36.36 = 264.4$; cde = $0.5*(33.33-25.456)*23.64 = 93.04$).

With no externalities in this market, this competitive solution maximizes the present value of social welfare, which is the present value of consumer surplus plus the present value of producer surplus or Hotelling rents. In Figure 12–6, at the competitive optimum, the present value of social welfare (producer plus consumer surplus) is the area above zero and below aeh. If we move to another allocation, the social welfare is reduced. For example, if the allocation is at point d, then the present value of social welfare is the area above zero and below abch, and we lose the area bce.

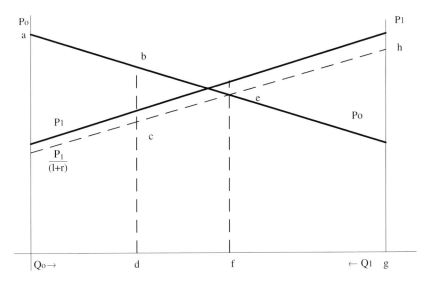

Fig. 12–6 Dynamic Competitive Solution Maximizes NPV of Social Welfare

Model Two
(Base Model:
No Costs but Income Growth)

Now, suppose that in Model Two income grows at 10%, increasing demand in the later period. (Fig. 12–7) The income change is exaggerated to more clearly show what happens. Discounted future price crosses the present demand at a lower current consumption (at m instead of n). The model tells us that less is consumed now and more in the future. With higher income in the future, future demand is higher, bidding up price and moving consumption to the second period. Note that the price is higher in both periods in this scenario than with no income growth.

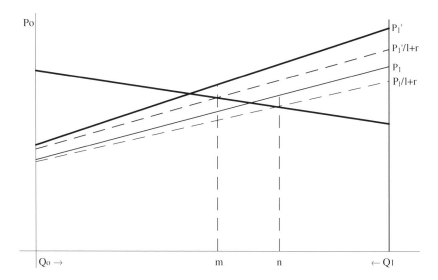

Fig. 12–7 Change in Resource Allocation Over Time with Income Growth

Model Three
(Base Model: No Costs,
No Income Growth but Lower
Interest Rate)

If in Model One (no income growth, no cost model) the federal reserve loosens monetary policy and the interest rate falls to 5% to give us Model Three's lower interest rate (Fig. 12–8), the interest rate change is exaggerated to make it easier to see what happens.

Figure 12–8 suggests that we should consume at m instead of n—less now and more in the future. With a lower discount rate, we discount the future less, making the resource relatively more valuable in the future and thus shifting consumption forward.

Increasing reserves

As we search for new reserves and as technology improves, total known reserves may increase. For example, U.S. reserves jumped from 29.6 billion barrels in 1970 to 39.6 billion barrels in 1971 with finds in Alaska; Western European reserves jumped from 3.7 billion barrels in 1971 to 14.2 billion barrels in 1972 with finds in the North Sea. If we increase reserves—stretching out the above graph—we expect prices to fall in both periods. However, if reserves increased to 250, we could get the situation shown in Figure 12–9.

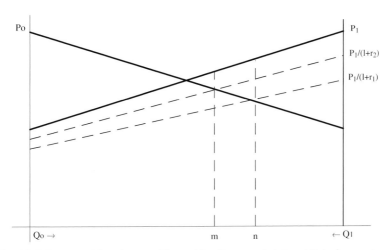

Fig. 12–8 Resource Allocation over Time with a Decrease in Interest Rate from r_1 to r_2

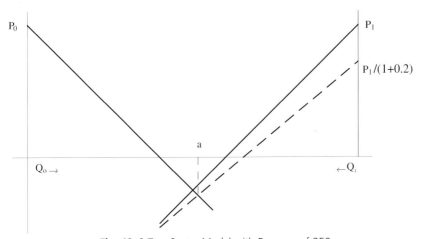

Fig. 12–9 Two-Sector Model with Reserves of 250

There are so many reserves, that to consume them all we need to drive the price down to negative amounts. In such a market, there is no scarcity across time: We can consume all we want now and in the future period and still have reserves. In such a case, we do not need to dynamically optimize, since there is no scarcity across time. We should operate in each period where price equals marginal cost, bringing us back to the static optimum. In this case, price would be zero and the demand in the two periods would be:

$$P_0 = 0 = 40 - 0.4Q_0 = 0 => Q_0 = 100$$

$$P_1 = 0 = 40 - 0.4Q_1 = 0 => Q_1 = 100$$

In this case, there is no producer rent: price is zero, but consumer surplus is quite high since consumers get the oil for nothing.

$$CS = (0.5*40*100) + (0.5*33.33*100) = 3,666.5$$

Model Four
(Base Model:
No Income Growth but With Costs)

Model Four is made more realistic by adding costs to model one. Now the benefits in each period are Hotelling rents (P – MC). The new optimization condition is then:

$$P_0 - MC_0 = \frac{P_1 - MC_1}{(1+r)} \qquad (12.9)$$

The first-order conditions tell us to set the present value of Hotelling rent (or user cost) equal on the margin across time. This Hotelling rent is not required in order to entice a supplier to produce, since marginal costs include a normal rate of return. However, if Hotelling rent is maximized, it helps the market allocate scarce resources efficiently across time. To see why, use the same arguments for this more stylized model above without costs. If the user cost in the current period is greater than the present value of user cost in the next period:

$$P_0 - MC_0 > \frac{(P_1 - MC_1)}{(1+r)}$$

Here, money in the bank is more valuable than oil in the ground: It is better to produce the oil now, sell it, and put the money in the bank. Producing more oil now and less in the next period would lower the price now and raise it in the next period. We should keep producing more until oil in the ground and money in the bank are equal in value.

The same mathematical techniques show that the condition in equation 12.9 also provides the socially optimal allocation. We can conclude that if there are no externalities in the market (demand and cost curves represent true social costs), if property rights are well defined so the producer is assured of having property rights in both periods, and if the interest rate represents the social discount rate, then the private competitive market maximizes social welfare.

In the simpler model (with no costs), price rose at the interest rate. To see how price increases in this case, begin with the optimizing condition:

$$P - MC_0 = \frac{(P_1 - MC_1)}{(1+r)}$$

Rearranging this condition, we have:

$$P_1 - MC_1 = (1+r)(P_0 - MC_0)$$

This suggests that user cost goes up at the interest rate. Solving for P_1, we have:

$$P_1 = (1+r)(P_0 - MC_0) + MC_1 = (1+r)(P_0) + MC_1 - (1+r)MC_0$$

If marginal costs rise faster than the interest rate $(MC_1 - (1+r)MC_0 > 0)$, then P rises faster than the interest rate. If marginal cost goes up exactly at the interest rate $(MC_1 - (1+r)MC_0 = 0)$, then the price rises at the interest rate. If marginal cost rises slower than the interest rate, then P rises slower than the interest rate. If marginal cost falls enough, then prices could even fall in this model.

Adelman (1993) argues that petroleum resource costs are determined by a race between depletion and technology: Depletion tends to increase costs and technology lowers them. Falling prices would be a case of technology winning. In the last decades, important technical changes have reduced oil-finding and production costs.

To continue our cost analysis, we model marginal cost as constant across production and time, which implies the race between depletion and technology is a tie. Assume model one (constant income and interest rate) with constant marginal costs of 20, as seen in Figure 12–10. Our optimization conditions tell us to first subtract a constant marginal cost from each demand to get user costs and then discount the future period user cost to find the optimal allocation.

Including costs in the model delays consumption. Optimal consumption is at b rather than a. By including costs, you decrease current consumption and increase future consumption. If you can't see this result from the picture, work out the optimum. First-order conditions are:

$$P_0 - MC_0 = \frac{P_1 - MC_1}{(1+r)}$$

$$40 - 0.4Q_0 - 20 = \frac{(40 - 0.4Q_1 - 20)}{(1 + 0.2)}$$

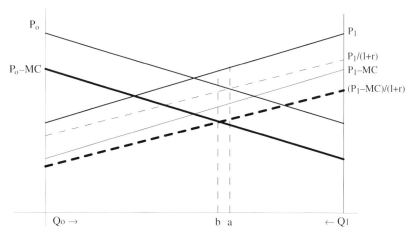

Fig. 12–10 Allocation in Two-Period Dynamic Model with Constant Marginal Cost

Substitute in the constraint:

$$40 - 0.4Q_o - 20 = (40 - 0.4(60 - Q_o) - 20)/(1 + 0.2)$$

Solving yields:

$$Q_o = 31.82, Q_1 = 28.18, P_o = 27.27, P_1 = 28.73, PV_r = 436.36$$

Compare these results to model one, which is the same but without costs. Including costs in the model delays consumption. Optimal consumption is at b rather than a. Future costs do not reduce future revenue as much as today's cost reduce today's revenue, making the future relatively more desirable.

In the earlier models (without costs), we saw that as interest rates rise the future becomes less valuable, and we consume more today. Let's see what happens in the model when we add costs and the interest rate goes to infinity. At an interest rate of infinity, or:

$$\lim_{r \to \infty} \left[P_o - MC_o = \frac{P_1 - MC_1}{(1+r)} \right] \to P_o - MC_o = 0$$

Thus, we want to operate where price equals marginal cost. In this case, the future is totally discounted—it is worth nothing to us. With an infinite discount rate, we are back to the static solution:

- an oil firm in danger of being nationalized in an oil-producing country might totally discount the future and produce where price equals marginal cost

- a government with high deficits and a threatened political future might also produce where price equals marginal cost to try to survive since revenues spent on social programs today might be used to ensure that there will be a political tomorrow.

Technical change has been an important factor reducing costs in the more mature oil-producing areas in the world such as the United States. Continued technical change will be required to keep these higher-cost areas viable.

Model Five (Base Model: No Income Growth with Backstop Technology)

As oil prices increase over time, we gradually switch away from oil to other renewable or more abundant products (commonly called backstops) and leave high-cost reserves in the ground. This view—that we will never totally deplete our oil resources—is most strongly put by Adelman (1993): "Minerals are inexhaustible and will never be depleted….How much was in the ground at the start and how much will be left at the end are unknown and irrelevant."

What we expect to happen is that we will gradually move to renewables and other energy sources that are currently too expensive to be exploited. Sweeney (1989) computed backstop technologies for gasoline and their costs using a 10% discount rate. (Table 12–3.) However, the existence of backstops does not mean we should completely ignore time in our decision process. If we use up low-cost reserves now, we will not have them in the future. Time is still an element in the process of deciding when to shift to backstop technologies.

Table 12–3 Costs for Gasoline and Backstop Technologies

Product	$/bbl
Gasoline	$37.68
Natural gas to methanol	$53.82
Coal to methanol	$62.20
Wood to methanol	$87.31
Compressed natural gas	$39.47
Corn to ethanol	$77.75
Oil Shale	$50.24
Tar sands	$49.04

Notes: Prices in 2001 U.S. dollars per barrel. Computed using a 10% discount rate.
Source: Sweeney (1989)

In our model, the backstop is more expensive to produce than all of our low-cost reserves, is abundant, and can be produced at a constant cost (P_{bk} = $30). Since any reserves at prices higher than $30 per unit will be left in the ground, the backstop price puts an upper limit on the price we can charge for our product and replaces the existing demand for all prices above $30. (Fig. 12–11.)

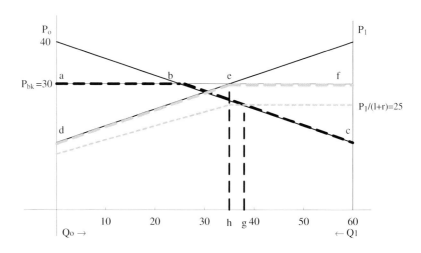

Fig. 12–11 Two-Period Model with a Backstop Fuel of $30

Demand in the current period (P_0) becomes the curve abc and demand in period one (P_1) becomes def. Using these new truncated demands we find $P_1/1+r = P_0$. P_1 = $30 is the price that we would charge in the second period. If the current price is P_0 = $30, we will want to produce all the reserves now and put the money in the bank to produce interest instead of waiting until next period to get the $30. This will drive reserve prices down in the current period until:

$$P_0 = 30/1.2 = \$25$$

At a price of $25:

$$Q_0 = g = 100 - 2.5*25 = 37.50$$

This leaves reserves of g to 60 = 22.50. At a price of $30, demand in period one is:

$$Q_1 = \text{the distance from h to } 60 = 100 - 2.5*30 = 25$$

The remaining reserves of 22.50 are consumed along with distance h to g = 2.5 of the backstop.

The same analysis can be done for a price control as for a backstop. In the price-controlled case, the ultimate price is the controlled price, and the excess demand in the future period is a shortage instead of being filled by the backstop.

Dynamic Multi-Period Models

All of the above examples are for only two periods—a current and a future period. Although a simple model, it gives us the basic intuition about how to optimize over time: We always need to compare the price today with the discounted opportunity cost in other periods; if we produce today, we give up the opportunity to produce in another period. More realistically, our reserves will last many years through many periods.

Suppose we have n periods. By the same reasoning as above, the discounted present value of all prices should be equal across time.

$$P_0 = \frac{P_1}{(1+r)} = \frac{P_2}{(1+r)^2} = \dots = \frac{P_n}{(1+r)^n}$$

All our reserves will be gone after n periods so:

$$Q_0 + Q_1 + Q_2 + \dots + Q_n = R$$

Since we do not know n, typically such models will be solved iteratively (by computer) to choose the optimal n.

Dynamic Models with Market Imperfections

So far we have also assumed that markets behave well. However, we also have market imperfections in dynamic optimization just as we have in static optimization. We will briefly consider four such problems:

1. negative externalities
2. private interest rate unequal to social interest rate
3. property rights not well defined as in the United States under the law of capture
4. firms with monopoly power

You can use the previous examples to understand the effect of negative externalities on optimal allocation. Suppose that energy production creates pollution so that private costs are lower than social costs. Comparing Model One and Model Four shows how the market would misallocate: When we added costs to the model, we decreased current output and shifted consumption to the future. Thus, ignoring or using costs which are too low to do the optimizing would cause us to consume too much today.

Earlier in this chapter, we argued that if the private market is competitive—there are no externalities, property rights are well defined, and producers dynamically optimize—then social welfare is maximized, as well. This result requires producers to respond to the correct discount rate, which is the one that represents society's rather than producer's opportunity cost. If the private rate is higher, then our earlier modeling demonstrates that the resource would be exploited too rapidly. If the private rate is lower, the resource would be exploited too slowly.

In our discussion, we have used a discount rate that reflects the rate of return on an asset put into the bank. In reality, the discount rate should be the opportunity cost of capital. This could be money in the bank or another investment if that were the next best alternative. To determine when private and social rates diverge, we note that the cost of capital for a firm is composed of a risk-free rate (often represented by a safe government bond rate) plus a risk premium. This risk premium compensates capital owners for the fact that actual returns may differ from expected returns—the riskier the industry, the higher the required risk premium. If risks are higher for individual companies than for society as a whole, then private decision-makers will require a higher risk premium and the social and the private discount rate would diverge. This divergence would cause a misallocation of resources with too much oil produced in the present and too little saved for the future.

Alternatively, in a society that is very dependent on oil sales, the risks of dependency on one product may be higher for society than for an integrated oil company. An integrated company's oil-producing division may do well when prices are high, but the product sales division may do better when oil prices are low, demonstrating the cyclical nature of the industry. In the event that the social discount rate is higher than the private discount rate, the private market will produce too little oil today and save too much for the future when compared to the social optimum.

Absence of well-defined property rights can cause problems as well. A well-defined property right typically entitles the owner to the use and proceeds of an asset over time. If it is exclusive and enforceable, the owner can effectively exclude others from the use and proceeds. Further, if it is divisible and transferable, the owner can divide and sell it whole or piecemeal. Poorly defined property rights can cause a misallocation of resources. For example, in the early years of the U.S. oil industry, the law of capture prevailed: If A drilled into a pool of oil and the oil came out of A's well, it was A's. If B drilled into the same pool and the oil came out of B's well, it was B's. In such a case, property rights were poorly defined. If you did not produce the oil and another did, you lost the rights to the oil. You did not have exclusive use of the oil, even though it was under your property. In such a situation, producers had incentive to produce as much as possible for fear they would lose the oil. Price was driven down until it equaled marginal cost because producers infinitely discounted the future. As a society, we lost the Hotelling rents that well-defined property rights would be more likely to provide.

Two solutions to this problem have been utilized. In the United States, state commissions regulate oil production and well spacing. Elsewhere, fields are more often government-owned and fields are *unitized*, which means the field is operated as one unit and each owner or lessee gets a share of the profits, no matter when it is produced, and no matter which well brought it to the surface. Such a policy encourages producers to maximize the overall value of the field over time since they will then maximize the present value of their share.

The last market imperfection that we will consider in a dynamic context is a monopoly producer. The monopolist has pricing power and would consider the whole demand curve P(Q)—not just the price. Since the monopolist always looks at marginal revenue instead of price, the optimizing condition for a two-period model is:

$$MR_0 = \frac{MR_1}{(1+r)}$$

For the monopolist, marginal revenue, not price, goes up at the interest rate. (Fig. 12–13) The optimal level of production for the monopolist is at b. Price in the two periods are P_0' and P_1', respectively.

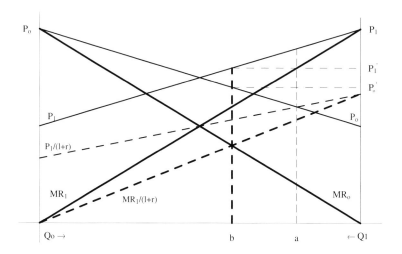

Fig. 12–12 A Monopoly Producer in a Two-Period Model

How does b compare to a competitive allocation? If you discount price, the discounted price curve shifts down in a steeper manner than when you discount the lower marginal revenue. Thus, the monopolist will produce less in the first period than competitors who should produce at a. (It is sometimes said that the monopolist is the conservationist's best friend, since he produces less now and puts off production to the future causing the resource to last longer.) Adding costs to the monopoly model brings expected results: The monopolist would produce where marginal revenue minus marginal cost in the current period is equal to discounted marginal revenue minus marginal cost in the next period.

So, what does our analysis thus far tell us about how oil prices will evolve? It tells us that evolution depends on a shifting mélange of forces in the market, influenced by market structure; myopic behavior of firms; political decisions of producing and consuming governments; costs; available reserves; short-run capacity; and interest rates.

Table 12–4 Companies with Significant Oil or Gas Production or Refinery Capacity

Company	Production Liquids Mil B/D 2001	Reserves Liquids Mil Bbl 2001	Production Gas Bcf 2001	Reserves Gas Bcf 2001	Refinery Capacity b/cd 2001	% Gov't Owned 2001
OPEC–National Oil Companies						
Petroleos de Venezuela (PDVSA)	3.267	77,783.0	1,493.9	148,295.0	2.656	100.0
http://www.pdvsa.com/						
National Iranian Oil (NIOC)	3.794	99,060.0	11,011.2	938,300.0	1.484	100.0
http://www.neda.net/niordc/						
Sonatrach (Algeria)	0.782	9,200.0	2,310.8	159,700.0	0.450	100.0
http://www.sonatrach-dz.com/						
Libyan National Oil	1.360	29,500.0	215.6	46,400.0	0.343	100.0
Nigerian National Oil	2.100	24,000.0	123.7	124,000.0	0.439	100.0
http://www.nigerianoil-gas.com/ upstream/nnpc.htm						
Abu Dhabi National Oil (ADNOC)	1.555	92,200.0	1,000.0	196,100.0	0.234	100.0
http://www.adnoc.co.ae/						
Dubai National Oil	0.230	4,000.0	60.0	4,100.0		100.0
www.enoc.com						
Iraq National Oil	1.960	112,500.0	242.8	109,800.0	0.418	100.0
Kuwait Petroleum Corp. (KPC)	2.042	96,500.0	249.4	54,983.9	0.966	100.0
http://www.kpc.com.kw/						
Saudi Arabian Oil Co. (Aramco)	8.372	259,300.0	1,940.0	224,200.0	1.991	100.0
http://www.saudiaramco.com/ cgi-bin/bvsm/home.jsp						
Pertamina (Indonesia)	1.200	5,000.0	2,619.1	92,500.0	0.993	100.0
http://www.pertamina.com/english/						
Qatar Petroleum Corp.	0.436	15,207.0	727.6	508,540.0	0.058	100.0
http://www.qp.com.qa/						
Other National Oil Companies						
Petroleum Development Oman	0.903	5,524.5	139.2	33,400.0	0.085	60.0
http://www.pdo.co.om/						
PetroChina Co. Ltd.	2.092	10,959.1	726.8	36,102.6	1.763	100.0
http://www.cnpc.com.cn/						
Sonangol (Angola)	0.685	5,412.0	20.4	1,620.0	0.039	100.0
http://mbendi.co.za/cosg.htm						
Egyptian General Petroleum Corp.	0.755	2,947.6	470.6	35,180.0	0.726	100.0
http://www.egpc.com.eg/						
Oil and Natural Gas Corp. Ltd (India)	0.535	15,393.0	895.6	1,000.0	1.502	84.1
http://www.ongcindia.com/						
Petronas (Malaysia)	0.682	4,492.0	1,608.0	82,520.0	0.230	50.0
http://www.petronas.com.my/ indexcorp.htm						
ENI (Italy)	0.857	3,948.0	1,093.0	17,072.0	0.814	30.0
http://www.eni.it/english/home.html						
Petroleos Mexicanos (Pemex)	3.559	25,425.0	1,646.0	28,151.0	1.692	100.0
http://www.pemex.com/						

Table 12–4 Companies with Significant Oil or Gas Production or Refinery Capacity (cont'd)

Company	Production Liquids Mil B/D 2001	Reserves Liquids Mil Bbl 2001	Production Gas Bcf 2001	Reserves Gas Bcf 2001	Refinery Capacity b/cd 2001	% Gov't Owned 2001
Petroleo Brasileiro SA (Petrobas) http://www2.petrobras.com.br/ portugues/index.asp	1.331	7,748.8	474.6	9,047.5	1.832	100.0
Ecopetrol (Colombia) http://www.ecopetrol.com.co/	0.396	727.1	113.9	4,507.0	0.286	100.0
Sinopec http://www.sinopec.com/	N/A	N/A	N/A	N/A	2.665	100.0
Chinese Petroleum Co (Taiwan)	0.007	4.0	30.3	2,700.0	0.770	100.0
OAO Lukoil (Russia) http://www.lukoil.com/	1.560	14,243.0	176.6	3,625.0	0.489	13.5
Norsk Hydro ASA (Norway) http://www.hydro.com/en/	0.329	1,018.0	191.0	5,986.0		43.8
Statoil ASA (Norway) http://www.statoil.com/	0.734	1,963.0	538.0	12,985.0	0.200	80.8
Repsol YPF SA (Spain) http://www.repsol-ypf.com/ home00.asp	0.645	2,294.9	757.3	18,592.6	1.150	32.4
OAO Gazprom http://www.gazprom.ru/	0.200	N/A	19,422.7	1,659,100.0	0.163	38.0
Large Private Oil Companies						
Royal Dutch Shell http://www.shell.com/royal-en/	2.219	9,469.0	3,288.0	55,829.0	3.889	0.0
Burlington Resources Inc. http://www.br-inc.com/	0.189	1,119.3	1,038.0	12,817.0		0.0
Unocal Corp http://www.unocal.com/	0.247	923.0	1,157.0	8,758.0		0.0
El Paso Corp http://www.elpaso.com/	0.077	311.1	1,152.0	11,329.0		0.0
TotalFinaElf (France/Belgium?) http://www.totalfinaelf.com/ ho/fr/index.htm	1.454	6,961.0	1,482.3	21,929.0	2.498	0.0
BP http://www.bp.com/index.asp	1.855	7,217.0	3,151.0	42,959.0	3.163	0.0
OAO Sibneft (Russia) http://www.sibneft.ru/	0.408	4,646.2	57.9	1,442.3	0.378	0.0
OAO Yukos (Russia) http://www.yukos.com/	0.992	9,630.0	50.0	2,512.0	0.607	0.0
ExxonMobil http://www2.exxonmobil.com/ corporate/	3.038	14,519.0	5,272.0	68,678.0	5.308	0.0

Table 12–4 Companies with Significant Oil or Gas Production or Refinery Capacity (cont'd)

Company	Production Liquids Mil B/D 2001	Reserves Liquids Mil Bbl 2001	Production Gas Bcf 2001	Reserves Gas Bcf 2001	Refinery Capacity b/cd 2001	% Gov't Owned 2001
ChevronTexaco http://www.chevron.com/ index.html	2.570	10,825.0	2,601.0	26,797.0	2.950	0.0
Phillips-Conoco www.conoco.com	1.548	8,039.0	2,004.0	25,765.0	2.580	0.0
Anadarko www.anadarko.com	0.364	1,605.0	1,268.0	12,683.0	0.000	0.0
Occidental http://www.oxy.com/	0.381	1,501.0	503.0	3,698.0	0.000	0.0
Amerada Hess http://www.hess.com/	0.381	1,096.0	458.0	3,892.0	0.458	0.0
Kerr-McGee http://www.kerr-mcgee.com/	0.274	1,158.0	413.0	6,952.0	0.000	0.0
Total These Companies	**58.364**	**1,005,369.6**	**74,193.3**	**4,864,547.9**	**46.267**	
Total World	**66.692**	**1,031,553.5**	**87,642.5**	**5,451,065.0**	**81.300**	

Sources: OGJ, 9/09/02, pp. 75–89, 3/11/02, p. 86, 12/24/01, pp. 68, 82–120, 127, Company Homepages

Taxing and Bidding Decisions

In most areas of the world, the government owns the mineral wealth. Government oil companies develop and produce the minerals, though the private sector is often involved. (Table 12–4.)

Private companies often bid for the right to search for oil and gas reserves and may pay taxes and royalties on the oil they produce from their leases. Private companies may be hired to develop and produce the governments' reserves. Our modeling thus far has implications for taxing and bidding systems for these governments' leasing, development, and production decisions for their petroleum properties.

Typically, a national oil company, a government ministry—or both—represent a government. Their goal should be to provide private-sector companies with the minimum rate of return required to enable them to develop and produce the mineral and to garnish the scarcity or Hotelling rents for the government. Two types of agreements are entered into: concessions and production sharing. If the government grants a concession (as in the United Kingdom), it is granting an ownership right (often called a lease) to the company, which in turn pays taxes and royalties. If the government enters into a production sharing agreement (PSA), it retains ownership. The company receives a share of production for providing services to the government (or a cash payment) rather than a portion of production as seen in a service contract. (Johnston, 1994) PSAs were begun in 1966, with Pertamina of Indonesia, and samples of their production-sharing terms can be found at http://www.pertamina.com. Despite philosophical distinctions about ownership between concessions and production-sharing agreements, they can be designed to be identical in economic impact.

Leasing and taxation systems vary considerably across countries, across time, and even within countries. We will consider five policies in the leasing taxation context and their effect on production profiles and economic efficiency:

1. unit tax (t_u)
2. royalty on price (ad valorem) (t_a)
3. user cost or rent tax (t_r)
4. bonus bidding (T)
5. work bidding (W)

A unit tax would affect production in the same way that costs affect production (as in model four). That is: the tax would decrease current consumption and push production off to the future. However, since taxes are not true costs—they are considered transfers by economists—a unit tax would distort the market.

Under the concessionary system, governments usually charge a royalty on the price of oil, equivalent to an ad valorem tax (t_a). The objective function for a resource producer under such a tax would be to maximize the after tax profit or:

Maximize: $$PV = (1 - t_a)P_oQ_o - TC(Q_o) + \frac{[(1-t_a)P_1Q_1 - TC(Q_1)]}{(1+r)}$$

Subject to the resource constraint $R = Q_o + Q_1$

The Lagrangian is:

$$\mathcal{J} = (1-t_a)P_oQ_o - TC(Q_o) + \frac{[(1-t_a)P_1Q_1 - TC(Q_1)]}{(1+r)} + \lambda(R - Q_o - Q_1)$$

First-order conditions are:

$$\mathcal{J}_\lambda = R - Q_0 - Q_1 = 0$$

$$\mathcal{J}_{Q0} = (1-t_a)P_0 - MC_0 - \lambda = 0$$

$$\mathcal{J}_{Q1} = \frac{[(1-t_a)P_1 - MC_1]}{(1+r)} - \lambda = 0$$

Since these are dissimilar from first-order conditions for the socially optimal production derived previously, a royalty levied on price alone distorts the market and gives us deadweight losses.

The easiest way to track the direction of the distortion is to understand that the tax shifts down the demand curve, with the shift wider at higher prices. Deducting marginal cost from this lower price and discounting the lower $[(1 - t_a)P_1 - MC]$ causes a smaller shift in the future period than in the case of no tax and calls for less consumption in the current period and more in the future period. However, a percentage tax (t_r) on user costs or rents does not distort the market. This can be seen as follows. The Lagrangian is:

$$\mathcal{J} = (1-t_r)(P_0 Q_0 - TC(Q_0)) + \frac{[(1-t_r)(P_1 Q_1 - TC(Q_1))]}{(1+r)} + \lambda(R - Q_0 - Q_1)$$

Where TC is the total cost including any opportunity costs.

First-order conditions are:

$$\mathcal{J}_\lambda = R - Q_0 - Q_1 = 0$$

$$\mathcal{J}_{Q0} = (1-t_r)(P_0 - MC_0) - \lambda = 0$$

$$\mathcal{J}_{Q1} = (1-t_r)\frac{(P_1 - MC_1)}{(1+r)} - \lambda = 0$$

These conditions can be rearranged to be:

$$(1-t_r)(P_0 - MC_0) = \frac{(1-t_r)(P_1 - MC_1)}{(1+r)}$$

Cancel $(1-t_r)$ from both sides and you are left with:

$$P_o - MC_o = \frac{(P_1 - MC_1)}{(1+r)}$$

This is the same allocation as without a tax. Thus, a rent tax would not distort the allocation of the resource over time. However, rent taxes are usually levied on accounting profits rather than on economic profits or Hotelling rents. Businesses are not allowed to deduct their opportunity costs, which we would do to compute rents. Thus, the tax is on: $(P_o Q_o - TC(Q_o) + \text{opportunity cost})$.

Bonus bidding requires that firms pay money up front for the right to search for oil. Since this is a fixed, up-front payment, it would not distort the production profile. If the bidding is competitive, we expect companies to bid away excess profits or rents and only make a normal rate of return. Thus, economists typically favor bonus bidding so that the government or society receives the rents rather than the producers.

Critics of this policy argue that large upfront costs may prevent some firms from bidding, thus making the market less competitive. This has led to some governments allowing smaller companies to make joint bids. Mead (1994) argues that lowering U.S. restrictions on foreign firms bidding on acreage would also increase competition.

Another argument against this type of bidding is called the *winner's curse.* When bidding for acreage, bidders do not know the actual hydrocarbon potential. Capen, Clapp, and Campbell (1971) argue that under bonus bidding, firms that consistently overestimate resource potential usually win the bids. But by overestimating potential, they make less than a normal rate of return and pay the resource owner more than the rents for the property. Although popular with engineers and geologists, economists discount this argument. Firms that consistently made incorrect bids and profits lower than normal would not stay in business. They would have to learn from incorrect bids to curb their wild-eyed optimism to survive.

Some governments use work bidding, which is typically measured in kilometers of seismic run and wells drilled. Work bidding may also be done in conjunction with other types of bidding. In strict work bidding, the company that promises to do the most drilling or develop the most amount of the resource quickly receives the bid. Often, this type of bidding is used by a government with a political goal of increasing employment or gaining revenue, which will be satisfied quicker if the oil is developed sooner. With competitive work bidding, the winning company will bid away the entire rent, whereas in an optimal production profile, producers should equalize the present value of the rents over the life of the project.

Of the five types of policies outlined, economists prefer competitive bonus bidding as the most likely to promote economic efficiency while garnishing the maximum rents for the government. Mead (1994) sums up empirical research on bonus bidding that supports this conjecture.

Summary

Around two-thirds of the world's proven oil reserves lie in the Middle East, while two-thirds of the world's gas reserves lie in the Middle East and the FSU. Reserve-over-production ratios for these countries are often many decades, and when used in conjunction with reserve figures can indicate the relative abundance of the resource in particular countries. Since production today influences production tomorrow for non-renewable resources, economic efficiency requires dynamic optimization of resources.

We considered two-period and multi-period models to illustrate the basic principle of allocating these resources efficiently across time. Theory suggests that in a competitive discrete model—fixed resources, no externalities, and well-defined property rights and no costs—the price of the resource would go up at the interest rate. Higher income growth in the future will raise prices and shift production to the future.

If we add costs to the model, then the user cost (or price minus marginal cost) should rise at the interest rate and production shifts towards the future. This user cost (or Hotelling rent) helps allocate the resource efficiently across time. To the extent possible, opportunity costs should be considered both across projects and across time for a better resource allocation.

Raising the interest rate discounts the future and shifts production to the present. However, if the interest rate goes to infinity, we are back to the familiar competitive case of price equal to marginal cost. Marginal costs may be a function of production if there are economies or diseconomies of scale. They may rise with depletion and fall with technical change. In the model with costs, prices can fall over time if cost falls fast enough.

Adelman argues that although oil and gas reserves are technically finite, we will continue to use them until they become too expensive, and we switch to alternative energy sources. Often we call such alternatives backstops or backstop technologies. Modeling suggests that if we do not interfere in markets and producers dynamically optimize, oil and gas prices should gradually approach the price of these backstops.

Market failures can cause markets to allocate inefficiently in dynamic models just as they do in static models. Negative externalities will cause the market to produce too much in the current period; for example, when the private interest rate is larger than the social interest rate. Poorly defined property rights that do not enable a producer to exclude another from its reserves are also likely to cause too much production today. Unitized production and pro-rationing have both been used to alleviate this problem.

Our last market failure example has the opposite effect: In a monopoly case, marginal revenue minus marginal cost increases at the interest rate. Monopoly firms tend to restrict output now and shift output to the future. By allocating production over a longer time horizon, they are able to keep prices high and extract more of the rents for themselves.

We have considered both competitive and monopoly models in earlier chapters where static optimization was accomplished. The first-order conditions for dynamic models compared to static models are summarized as follows:

Static Perfectly Competitive $\quad$ $P = MC$

Dynamic Perfectly Competitive $\quad$ $P_0 - MC_0 = \dfrac{(P_1 - MC_1)}{(1+r)}$

Static Monopoly $\quad$ $MR = MC$

Dynamic Monopoly $\quad$ $MR_0 - MC_0 = \dfrac{(MR_1 - MC_1)}{(1+r)}$

Most of the world's mineral resources are owned by governments, which allow development and production by national oil companies or through production-sharing or concessionary systems. A government's goal should be to allow companies a competitive rate of return while reserving the rents for its economy. In considering five leasing taxation systems for their efficiency effects, we saw that unit taxes, royalties on price, taxes on accounting profit, and work bidding all distort the optimal production profile. A tax on Hotelling rents would not distort the profile but may be difficult to implement; user costs or rents are hard to measure.

Conventional profit tax schemes typically do not allow companies to deduct opportunity costs, while companies have an incentive to inflate cost numbers to reduce their tax obligation. Theory and studies suggest that competitive bonus bidding would not distort the production profile and would be most likely to transfer the rent to the government. However, if high-cost, high-risk acreage is so expensive that only very large firms can enter, there may be some danger that the bidding may not be competitive. In such a case, allowing joint bids from smaller firms and international bidding can provide a more competitive playing field.

Another potential problem is the winner's curse: firms that more often overestimate reserves and overbid are more often the winners, yielding the government more than the Hotelling rents. However, such firms cannot stay in business in the long run. Therefore, as with other loss-making activities, economists expect the market to correct this behavior in the long run.

13. Supply and Costs Curves

Some Common Pitfalls in Decision Making…
Ignoring Opportunity Costs…
Failing to Ignore Sunk Costs.

—Robert H. Frank, Professor at Cornell University.
Frank (1991)

Introduction

As we have seen, energy comes from a variety of sources, with the majority from fossil fuels and the remainder from nuclear energy and renewables.

Primary energy consumption is measured at point of first consumption, whether fossil fuels are used directly to produce heat or are used to produce electricity. Electricity generated from fossil fuels has already been counted as primary energy consumption; if we counted both the fossil fuel and the fossil-generated electricity, we would be double counting energy. The same situation would occur if we counted both crude oil consumed by refineries and product consumption made from crude oil. Primary electricity is that generated from nuclear power and renewables, then, since they have not already been counted.

Another issue is how to measure primary and secondary electricity. If a country generates electricity from 1000 BTUs of coal at a 33% efficiency rate, it generates 333 BTUs of electricity and measures energy consumption at 1000 BTUs. Electricity generated from primary sources is usually measured by output: If another country generates 333 BTUs of electricity by nuclear power, the end-use of electricity would be the same but it would appear that the first country consumed three times as much electricity as the second. For this reason, we may measure gross electricity consumption for primary sources as the energy content of an equivalent amount of fossil fuels. Thus, for the second country, net electricity consumption would be 333 BTUs but gross consumption would be 1000 BTUs.

Primary and secondary energy consumption patterns have evolved, influenced by both the properties of the various energy sources and their costs. In this chapter, we first consider supplies from these sources and their characteristics and then how to "cost" different energy sources.

Commercial energy is energy purchased in a market. Oil, gas, and nuclear energy are examples of commercial energy. Wood, dung, or other biofuels that are gathered rather than purchased are not commercial energies. The supply of commercial primary energy to the world in 2000 was 397.48 quadrillion (10^{15}) BTUs with almost one quarter of this consumed in the United States. Figure 13–1 shows the breakdown of commercial energy consumption by supply sources and the prominence of fossil fuels.

Coal, discussed in chapter 2, constitutes almost a quarter of world energy supply. Steam coal is used as an energy source, burned to create steam, while coking coal is used in iron and steel production.

Natural gas constitutes only a slightly larger share of energy consumption than coal. *Non-associated natural* gas is found alone, while *associated natural gas* is found with oil. In the United States, about 80% of gas reserves are non-associated. As natural gas is produced, pentanes (C_5H_{12}) and heavier hydrocarbons condense with pressure and a temperature drop at the surface and are taken out at the wellhead. The remainder, called *wet natural gas*, is sent to gas processing plants, where natural gas liquids are extracted, leaving *dry natural gas*. In the United States, about 4% of wet natural gas is natural gas liquids (NGLs). Worldwide, total wet gas production in the late 1990s was almost 100 quads, of which around 81% was dry, 4% was NGLs, 4% was flared, and 11% was re-injected into gas wells to increase well pressure.

Crude oil and other liquid hydrocarbons (labeled "oil" in Fig. 13–1) provide the highest amount of energy of any source, at 38.7% of world primary energy use.

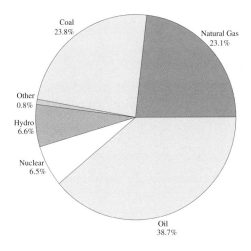

Fig. 13–1 Gross World Primary Energy Consumption, 2001

Source: EIA/DOE, 2003, *International Energy Outlook 2003*, EIA/DOE, 2003, *International Energy Annual 2003*

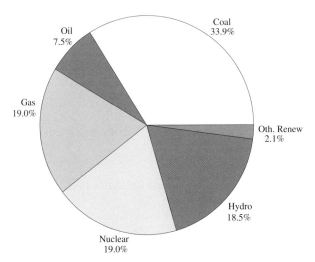

Fig. 13–2 Fuel Sources for World Electricity Consumption, 2001

Sources: EIA/DOE 2003, *International Energy Annual 2003*, EIA/DOE, 2003, *International Energy Outlook 2003*

Just over half of this use is for global transportation in the form of gasoline, diesel, and jet fuel. In North America, transport use of oil is even higher, estimated at more than 60%.

The other significant global energy supply is the 13% that comes from primary electricity. Most of this energy comes from nuclear and hydropower, which together provide more than 35% of the world's electricity. (Fig. 13–2.)

Nuclear fuels

Nuclear energy provides more than 5% of gross primary commercial energy worldwide, 19% of total electricity production, and a bit more than half of primary electricity supply. Uranium is the fuel source for the bulk of nuclear power, with small amounts from recycled plutonium. Just more than half of the world's current needs for uranium are supplied from mining with the rest coming from recycling of spent fuel, former military weapons, and stockpiles. Significant producers are shown in Table 13–1.

Table 13–1 Uranium Production and Resources, 2000

Country	Production	Reserves
Australia	7,720	622,000
Canada	12,520	331,000
Kazakhstan*	2,018	439,200
Namibia	2,239	156,120
Niger	3,096	69,960
Russia*	2,000	145,000
U.S.	1,000	110,000
Uzbekistan	2,400	66,210
Other	2,774	306,940
Total	35,767	2,246,430

Notes: *World Nuclear Association Estimate. # Resources at costs < $80 per kg. Production and reserves are measured in metric tons.
Sources: Reserves in 2000 from World Nuclear Association, 2000
http://www.world-nuclear.org/. Production 2001,
Uranium Information Centre, Ltd. http://www.uic.com.au/nip41.htm

The world uranium industry has been consolidating. According to the World Nuclear Association, eight companies accounted for 80% of world production in 1999. (Table 13–2.)

Cameco of Canada and Cogema of France—both partly owned by their governments—dominate production of uranium in the West with more than 60% of western capacity. There is a predominance of government control of uranium production in the FSU countries, although there has been some opening up in Kazakhstan and Uzbekistan, with their national companies initiating joint ventures

Table 13–2 Largest Uranium Producers in the World

Company	Headquarters	Tons of U 2001	Contact	Major Stockholders*
Cameco	Canada	7,218	http://www.cameco.com	Govt Saskatchewan (10.3%)
Cogema	France	6,643	http://www.cogema.fr	CEA-Industrie – Commissariat à l'Énergie Atomique, French Gov't., (74.7%), TotalFinaElf (14.5%), Erap (7.6%), Technip (3.2%)
Energy Resources of Australia	Australia	3,564	http://www.energyres.com.au	North Limited (68.39%), Japan Australia Uranium Resources Development Co Ltd. (10%), Cameco (6.45%), Urangesellschaft (6.2%)
Western Mining Corporation	U.S.	3,693	http://www.wmc.com	
Rossing	Namibia	2,293	http://www.rossing.com	Rio Tinto (68.6%), Industrial Development Corp of S. Africa Ltd. (10%), Gov't. Iran (10%)
Navoi Mining and Chemicals	Uzbekistan	2,400	http://www.antenna.nl/wise/uranium/ucnav.html	Government (100%)
Priargunsky Mining and Metallurgical	Russia	2000	http://www.x-atom.ru/minatom/min_eng.html	Minatom, Gov't., (51%)
KazAtomprom	Kazakhstan	2,018	http://www.kazatomprom.com	Government (100%)
Other		5,992		
World Total		35,767		

Notes: *Stockholders with more than 5% ownership. For a much longer list of companies, see http://www.antenna.nl/wise/uranium/.
Sources: Production from Uranium Information Centre, Ltd.
http://www.uic.com.au/nip41.htm, major stockholders from World Information Service on Energy, http://www.antenna.nl/wise/uranium/

with western companies (Kazatomprom in Kazakhstan with Cameco and Cogema; Navoi in Uzbekistan with Cogema). About 45% of world mining production comes from underground mining; 27% from open pit, 19% from in situ leaching, and 9% as a by-product in 2001.

Uranium ore is crushed and chemicals are used to leach out the uranium oxide (U_3O_8). The U_3O_8 is milled to a khaki-colored product called yellow cake, which is about 80% U_3O_8. Other metals—nickel, cobalt, or molybdenum—may be joint products and can also be extracted. Yellow cake is converted to uranium hexa-fluoride (UF_6), which allows enrichment of the fissionable U235 to 3 to 5%. Most commercial nuclear power plants require enriched fuel. Exceptions are the Canadian CANDU and the British Magnox reactors. The enriched UF_6 is changed into uranium dioxide (UO_2), which is made into ceramic pellets and inserted into metal fuel rods.

Uranium conversion is also fairly concentrated, with only seven companies converting yellow cake to UF_6. (Table 13–3.) Nine countries and eight companies currently enrich uranium. (Table 13–4.) Approximately 60% of the capacity is gaseous diffusion and the rest is centrifuge.

Table 13–3 Facilities for Conversion of Yellow Cake to UF_6

Country	Company	# of Plants	Annual Capacity Million Metric Tons U	Contact Information
Brazil	IPEN	1	90	http://www.ipen.br
Canada	Cameco	2	10,500	http://www.cameco.com
China	CNNC	1	400	http://www.cnnc.com.cn
France	Cogema	1	14,350	http://www.cogema.fr
Russia	Minatom	2	24,000	http://www.x-atom.ru/minatom/min_eng.html
U.K.	British Nuclear Fuels, Ltd.	1	6,000	http://www.bnfl.co.uk
U.S.	Converdyn	1	14,000	http://www.converdyn.com
World Total			**69,340**	

Source: Antenna Foundation, World Information Service on Energy Uranium Project http://www.antenna.nl/wise/uranium/efac.html

Table 13–4 World Uranium Enrichment Facilities by Country

Country	Company	% World Capacity	Contact
China	CNNC	3.6%	http://www.cnnc.com.cn/
France	Eurodif	20.6%	http:/antenna.nl/wise/uranium/eceud.html
U.S.	U.S. Enrichment Corp.	35.6%	www.usec.com
Germany	Urenco	2.5%	http://www.urenco.com/group.htm
Japan	JNC & JNFL	2.4%	http://www.jnfl.co.jp/index-e.html http://www.jnc.go.jp/
Netherlands	Urenco	2.9%	http://www.urenco.com/group.htm
Pakistan	Pakistan Atomic Energy Commission	0.0001%	
Russia	Minatom	28.6%	http://www.x-atom.ru/minatom/min_eng.html
U.K.	Urenco	2.5%	http://www.urenco.com/group.htm

Source: Antenna Foundation, World Information Service on Energy Uranium Project http://www.antenna.nl/wise/uranium/efac.html

Nuclear waste disposal is an ongoing problem, and a number of countries have opted for reprocessing spent fuel. Plutonium and uranium are extracted and mixed with new fuel to create mixed-oxide fuel (MOX). Other countries dispose of fuel without reprocessing. Table 13–5 lists countries that produce nuclear power, their capacity, and (where known) which reprocess.

Table 13–5 Operating Nuclear Electricity Capacity, 2001

Country	Number of Operating Units	MW Net	Spent Fuel Plans as of late 1990s
Argentina	2	945	Undecided
Armenia	1	376	
Belgium	7	5,713	Reprocess
Brazil	2	1,871	Undecided
Bulgaria	6	3,526	Reprocess under review
Canada	14	10,298	Disposal
China	3	2,100	
Czech Repub.	4	1,648	Reprocess under review
Finland	4	2,650	Disposal
France	59	63,173	Reprocess
Germany	19	21,044	Reprocess under review
Hungary	4	1,720	Reprocess under review
India	14	2,599	Reprocess
Japan	52	43,249	Reprocess
Korea, S	16	12,990	Undecided
Lithuania	2	2,500	Disposal
Mexico	2	1,308	Undecided
Netherlands	1	449	Reprocess
Pakistan	2	425	Undecided
Romania	1	630	Disposal
Russia	29	19,843	Reprocess
Slovakia	6	2,430	Reprocess under review
Slovenia	1	620	Undecided
South Africa	2	1,840	Disposal
Spain	9	7,730	Disposal
Sweden	11	9,325	Disposal
Switzerland	5	3,184	Reprocess
Taiwan	6	4,884	
U.K.	35	12,996	Reprocess
Ukraine	13	11,228	Reprocess under Review
U.S.	103	96,185	Disposal
Total	435	349,479	

Source: Information on plants and capacity: www.world-nuclear.org/info/reactors.htm, spent fuel plans: International Atomic Energy Agency, http://www.iaea.or.at/worldatom/inforesource/bulletin/bull401/article6.html

Hydroelectricity

Hydroelectricity produces slightly less power than nuclear worldwide. (EIA/DOE *International Energy Annual,* 2001) One-fourth of the world's countries get more than 50% of their power from hydro sources. (http://www.damsreport.org/) Canada, the United States, Brazil, China, and Russia (in order of capacity) are the largest producers with just more than half of total world capacity.

To generate hydroelectricity, water turns a bladed wheel inside a turbine. The amount of electricity produced depends on the water flow per unit of time and the *head*, which is the turbine distance from the surface of the water. If the flow (F) is measured in cubic meters per second and the head (H) is measured in meters, then an approximation of the power created (P) in kW is:

$$P = 5.9HF \quad \text{(http://www.iclei.org/efacts/hydroele.htm)}$$

If the turbine is 10 meters from the top surface of the water and if 20 m^3 flow through the turbine per second, then the capacity = 5.9*10*20 = 1180 kW. If run for an hour, it would produce 1180 kWh.

Since a higher head produces more power, one function of dams is to raise the water height. (Fig. 13–3.) Dam storage also allows for better control of water flow for measured power output (releasing water in dry years and storing it in wet years). Hydropower installations vary tremendously in size from run-of-river plants (no dam) with a capacity of less than 1 MW to multiple turbines at huge dams with capacities of thousands of MW. (Table 13–6.)

Hydropower has little carbon emissions and no fuel costs, but power supply depends on rainfall and may fall when rainfall is low. The dams provide flood control, the lakes behind them provide recreational boating and fishing and water for irrigation. However, changes in ecosystems are associated with large dams. Upstream areas flooded to create the reservoir mean that downstream areas can suffer water reductions; fish may not be able to migrate to spawning grounds over the dams.

Table 13–6 Some of the World's Largest Hydro Capacity Dams

Name	River	Country	Capacity (MW)
Itaipu	Parana	Brazil/Paraguay	12,600
Guri	Caroni	Venezuela	10,300
Sayano-Shushensk	Yenisei	Russia	6,400
Grand Coulee	Columbia	U.S.	6,180
Krasnoyarsk	Yenisei	Russia	6,000
Church Falls	Churchill	Canada	5,428
La Grande 2	LaGrande	Canada	5,328
Bratsk	Angara	Russia	4,500
Ust-Ilim	Angara	Russia	4,320
Tucurui	Tocantins	Brazil	3,960
Tarbela	Indus river	Pakistan	3,478
Ertan	Upper Yangzte	China	2,300
Kariba	Zambezi	Zambia/Zimbabwe	1,320
Three Gorges*	Yangzte	China	18,200

*Project under construction, planned completion 2010.
Source: Stanford University, National Performance of Dams Program, http://npdp.stanford.edu/dampower.html, downloaded August 2003. Embassy of the Peoples Republic of China, The Three Gorges Project, http://www.chinaembassy.org/eng/c2718.html, downloaded August 2003.

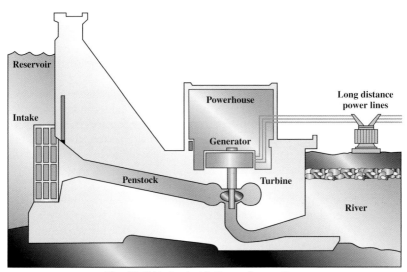

Fig. 13–3 Hydroelectric Power from a Dam

Source: http://www.tva.gov/power/hydroart.htm

Other renewable energy sources

Other renewable energy sources include biomass, wind, solar, and geothermal.

Biomass is fuel derived from living organisms. It once heated huts and castles and is still an important source of energy in the developing world in the forms of wood and dung. Solar energy has provided heat and light from the dawn of human history and is also the energy source for biomass and wind. Geothermal has heated baths for centuries, while the first use of geothermal for a power plant was in Italy in 1903. Even waves and tides created by the gravity between the earth, sun, and moon have energy potential, and two experimental tidal plants exist—a 20 MW plant in the Bay of Fundy, Canada, completed in 1984, and a 240 MW plant in St. Malo, France, completed in 1966.

As countries develop, they typically move away from renewable energy sources toward more concentrated, convenient, and efficient commercial fuels (crude oil products, natural gas, and electricity). However, more recently, environmental concerns about global warming and technical advances have improved the long-term outlook for renewables. Some experts are now estimating that renewables may constitute up to half of our commercial energy sources by the middle of the 21st century.

Biomass is currently about 10% of energy use worldwide but is estimated to be one-third of total energy use in Asia and almost a quarter in Africa. (IEA Fact Sheet, http://www.eia.org/techno/renew/index.htm) High use of biomass fuels in poorer countries can cause deforestation and erosion; using dung for fuel instead of fertilizer may have repercussions on food production. Thus, interest remains in moving to other energy sources, using biomass more efficiently, and/or generating more biomass through the use of energy plantations.

In industrial countries, increases in solid wastes and concerns for global warming have spawned interest in generating power from garbage and waste from wood, agricultural crops, food processing, and animals. In 2001, the United States got about 3% of its energy from biofuels—more than three quarters from wood and wood wastes and 19% from municipal and other solid wastes.

Wind is currently considered the most promising new renewable source for electricity generation. About 0.1% of the world's electricity is currently generated this way. (Wind power is really a form of solar power, as the uneven heating of the earth's surface causes the winds to blow, while the earth's rotation, water bodies, vegetation, and terrain modify the wind patterns.) Windmills—popular in the American plains to pump water for cattle—were first used to generate electricity in Ohio in 1888. Small turbines were put to use in the 1920s.

Unit or Levelized Costs of Wind Electricity

Currently, a typical wind turbine has three fiberglass blades, a standard gearbox, and a generator to turn mechanical energy into electrical power. A typical 600-kW turbine costs between $400,000 and $500,000. Installation costs are another $100,000 to $150,000 and the turbine lasts about 20 years. If we know how much power such a turbine will produce in a year, we can convert these up-front capital costs into a per-unit electricity cost. Since electricity is produced over time and capital costs are expended up front, we need to calculate levelized costs by using discounting to distribute our costs over the production profile for electricity.

Suppose that at the turbine installation site, the wind allows the turbine to run at full capacity 25% of the time. Assume that the turbine is totally idle the rest of the time. The turbine then generates 600*24*365*0.25 = 1,314,000 kWh per year. Let the generator last 20 years and stop producing at the beginning of year 21 with no down time. Ignore initial construction time, and assume that power is paid for at the beginning of the year and that the real discount (or interest) rate is 10%. Take the initial cost to be the midpoint of the above estimates (or $450,000 + $125,000 = $575,000). The real capital cost per kWh ($\$_k$) is the amount we would need to charge per kWh over time to recoup our capital costs. $\$_k$ can be computed from the following equation:

$$\$575,000 = \sum_{i=0}^{20} \$_k * 1,314,000/(1 + 0.10)^i =>$$

Solving for $\$_k$, we get:

$$\$_k = (575,000/1,314,000)/\left(\sum_{i=0}^{20} 1/(1 + 0.10)^i\right) = \$0.047 \text{ per kWh}$$

Solar energy

Solar power can be used to generate heat passively or through the use of solar panels, which can be either flat or concentrating. Passive solar water heaters and cookers can be built quite inexpensively—the cookers for as little as $10, using an insulated box and a reflector.

Concentrated solar heat can be used to generate steam to run a power plant. Two 10 MW experimental solar plants have been built in Barstow, California, by the U.S. government and a consortium of companies. Problems included designing mirrors to track the sun and a medium for power storage. Solar One, which operated from 1982 to 1988 used water as a receiver in the tower and as a storage and transmission mechanism. Solar Two, which operated from 1996 to 1999, used molten nitrate salt, which stored heat better and allowed more continuous power generation. Currently, U.S. companies are planning a commercial version called Solar Three to be built in Spain. It will be three times the size of the demonstration plants and will use the molten salt for storage. Spain was chosen because it is a sunny area of the world and sunnier areas are, of course, better candidates for solar electricity.

Alternatively, electricity can be generated by use of a photovoltaic cell (PV). PVs are typically made from two layers of silicon material, or other semiconductors that have added impurities. When sunshine strikes the cell, it interacts with electrons that set up a direct current. (Fig. 13–4.)

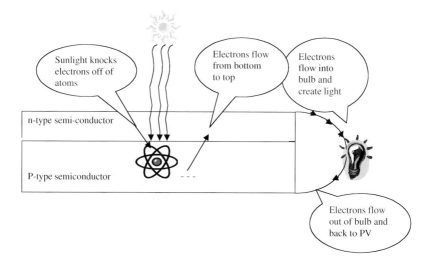

Fig. 13–4 Diagram of a Photovoltaic Device

Sources: Created from diagrams and information at http://www.sunrayce.com/ now American Solar Challenge and University of Central Florida, Internet and Science Technology Fair, http://www.cat.pinellas.k12fl.us/istf/02-549/glossary.html.

Because solar energy is widely spread around the world, it often matches population and energy use patterns. Disadvantages are cost—typically $0.18 to $0.50 per kWh. It is intermittent, requiring storage or alternative power sources, and is diffuse: A typical household in the U.S. would require 430 square feet of collecting surface to operate.

Geothermal Energy

Geothermal energy—heat from the earth's center—is tapped by drilling wells that are 1000 to 10,000 feet deep. It is accessible near active tectonic plate margins (e.g., El Salvador, Italy, Iceland, Indonesia, Japan, Mexico, New Zealand, Philippines, and the United States). Geothermal commands only a slightly higher share of electricity generation than wind. But, like wind, the potential for increase exists, and it proves competitive in some instances when current generation costs from five to seven cents/kWh. Estimates put geothermal potential at 8.3% of the world's electricity. Some 20 countries generate power from geothermal. The U.S. possesses around 25% of the world's capacity, followed by the Philippines, Mexico, and Italy.

Geothermal source temperature less than 300° F can be used for direct heat; if more than 300° F, it can be used for power generation. If hot water is produced from the well, a binary-cycle plant is used. (Fig. 13–5.) A heat exchanger raises the temperature of the water to steam, which runs the turbine. If steam is produced from the well, a flash power plant (Fig. 13–6.) is used. This is somewhat cheaper since the steam can be used to run the turbine directly.

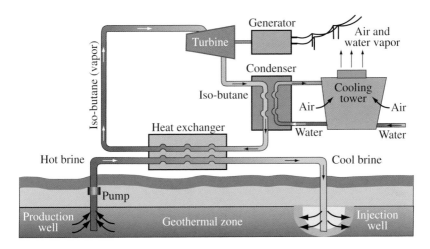

Fig. 13–5 Binary Cycle Power Plant

Sources: Idaho National Engineering and Environmental Laboratory, What is Geothermal Energy? http://geothermal.inel.gov/what-is.shtml. Last Accessed 08/03.

Again: Nuclear, hydroelectric, and renewable sources of electricity are considered primary; and electricity from fossil fuels is considered secondary. Some comparative electricity generating cost projections for years 2005–2010 for primary electricity from nuclear, and secondary electricity from coal and gas, are shown in Table 13–7. Capital costs can be computed for each of these sources as we've seen for wind energy. For the countries listed, different fuels are more economical.

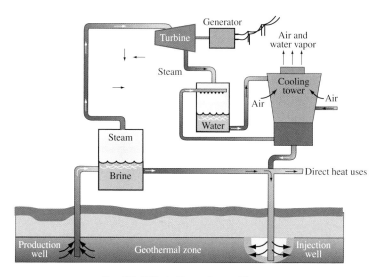

Fig. 13–6 Flash Steam Power Plant

Sources: Idaho National Engineering and Environmental Laboratory, What is Geothermal Energy? http://geothermal.inel.gov/what-is.shtml. Last Accessed 08/03.

Table 13–7 Comparative Electricity Generation Cost including Capital

	Nuclear	**Coal**	**Gas**
France	5.3	6.5	5.8
Russia	5.1	6.0	4.2
Japan	8.7	8.3	9.1
Korea	5.2	4.9	5.1
Spain	7.0	6.0	5.9
U.S.	4.3	3.8	2.9
Canada	4.3	25.8	3.6
China	4.2	4.3	
	Wind	**PV**	**Fuel Cells**
U.S.	5.7	36.9	10.0

Notes: Costs are in 2001 cents/kWh. Paffenbarger et al. (1998) cost estimates for coal, gas, and nuclear are forecasts for 2005. Assumptions are: discount rate of 10%, 40-year plant lifetime, 75% load factor. Coal prices varied by country from a low of $1.06 per Gigajoule in the U.S. to a high of $2.64 in France. Natural gas prices varied from a low of $1.58 per Gigajoule in the U.S. to $4.95 in Japan. $/million BTU = $/Gigajoule*1.054. Macauley et al. do not report their assumptions but make them available upon request.

Sources: Conventional power data, Paffenbarger et al. (1998), renewable power data, Macauley et al (2000).

Enlarging on this, Figure 13–7 shows historic changes for U.S. electricity operating costs. Similar operating costs command coal and nuclear. Thus, the higher total costs for nuclear in Table 13–7 are the result of higher capital costs for this more capital-intensive primary source. According to Resource Data International, three quarters of total nuclear costs are for capital, whereas only one quarter are capital costs for coal, and gas and oil have an even lesser capital cost share than coal. Costs decreased for oil and gas as fuel prices generally fell from the mid-1980s until the price and cost spikes in 2000 and 2001. Neither nuclear nor coal costs followed the oil and gas cost run-ups. Operating costs are consistently higher for gas than for coal, but lower capital costs made it competitive in many cases prior to 2000. Also, combined-cycle gas power plants have increased efficiency, which lowers costs. Gas accounted for around a third of new power generation from 1990 to 2001, as gas generation can be built quickly to take advantage of market opportunities and it can be ramped up and down quickly to follow the load curve. (Chambers et al 2001) As of 2001, even with gas price increases, gas generation was still slated to provide more than 90% of new planned capacity. (EIA/DOE, *Electric Power Annual* 2001, http://www.eia.doe.gov/cneaf/electricity/epa/epat2p4.html, downloaded August 2003.)

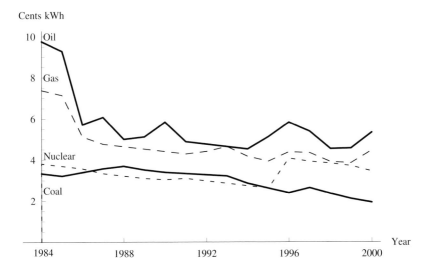

Fig. 13–7 U.S. Electricity Production Costs

Source: Uranium Information Centre Ltd, Nuclear Electricity, (Seventh edition, 2003), http://www.uic.com.au/ne2.htm, downloaded August 2003.

Above-Ground Costs for Gas and Oil

Costs are computed for oil or gas, in two ways. To compute above-ground costs, we take into account the production profile for oil, typically represented by an exponential decline curve. In such a curve, production at time t equals $Q_t = \alpha R_o e^{-\alpha t}$, where the decline rate is α per year. For example, if initial reserves R_o equal 100, the decline rate is 10% (α equals 0.10, and production follows an exponential decline, then at the beginning of production (year zero) a well would produce:

$$Q_o = 0.1*100*e^{-0.1*0} = 10$$

In a year, production would have declined to:

$$Q_1 = 0.1*100*e^{-0.1*1} = 9.05$$

After two years the production would be:

$$Q_2 = 0.1*100*e^{-0.1*2} = 8.2$$

And so on.

Once we have the production profile, we also need to be able to discount the value of that production. In chapter 4, we reviewed how to discount with annual compounding. A dollars in n years, discounted with interest rate r, is equal to $A/(1+r)^n$ today. If we compounded c times per year the formula becomes $A/(1+r/c)^{c*n}$. For example, the present value of $20 in 10 years with quarterly compounding at 15% is:

$$PV = \frac{\$20}{(1+0.15/4)^{4*10}} = \$4.59$$

Compounding tells us how often we receive interest on the interest we have earned but in oil production, it is more convenient to be able to discount continuously, which tells us that we receive interest on our interest immediately. Mathematically, this can be represented as:

$$\lim_{c \uparrow \ge} = \frac{A}{(1+r/c)^{c*n}} = Ae^{-r*n}$$

For example, the net present value today of $100 in 20 years with continuous discounting at a 15% interest rate is $100 * e^{-0.15 * 20} = \$4.99$. (If we have $4.99 today and hold it for 20 years with continuous compounding, we would have $100.) The continuous compounding case is the more realistic when we receive a flow of income with costs spread out over a year, which is most often the case. However, if you find discrete computations easier or have tables to do the computations, you can easily convert the rate so the discrete computation gives you the same present value as the more accurate continuous procedure. To do so, you just find the discrete rate with annual compounding that would give the same present value as the continuous rate.

Suppose you want to look at a continuous rate of r_c but want to approximate using a discrete rate r_d. The r_d rate you would need would be that rate, such that:

$$\exp(-r_c t) = (1/(1+r_d)^t$$

Solve this equation for r_d. Since the natural log is the inverse of the exponential function, first take the natural log of both sides of the equation:

$$\ln(\exp(-r_c t)) = \ln(1/(1+r_d)^t)$$

Then:

$$-r_c t = \ln(1) - t\ln(1+r_d)$$

Since $\ln(1)$ is zero, we can rewrite as:

$$-r_c t = -t\ln(1+r_d)$$

Cancel -t from both sides:

$$r_c = \ln(1+r_d)$$

Take the exponential of each side:

$$\exp(r_c) = 1 + r_d$$

Solve for r_d:

$$r_d = \exp(r_c) - 1$$

Thus, if you want to approximate a continuous rate of 0.08 with a discrete annual compounding rate you would use:

$$r_d = \exp(0.08) - 1 = 1.083 - 1 = 0.083$$

Suppose you produce oil over the next 20 years at an annual rate of $Q_1, Q_2, Q_3, Q_4, \ldots Q_n$ that sells for $P_1, P_2, \ldots P_n$. Q_1 is the amount you produce in the first year, Q_2 the amount in the second year, and so forth. You produce continuously over the year and are paid c times per year beginning at time 1/c years. The amount you are paid at 1/c, 2/c, 3/c is $(P_1Q_1)/c$. The amount you are paid at (i+1)/c, (i+2)/c, (i+3)/c is $(P_iQ_i)/c$. Income is compounded at the rate of c per year. To compute the net present value, you must determine when each payment is made and discount each payment back to the correct number of periods and sum them up. Then the net present value of this discrete stream of income is:

$$PV = \Sigma_o^{cn} \; P_iQ_i/(1+r/c)^i$$

If the income stream is a constant PQ every year, the formula simplifies to:

$$PV = PQ \; \Sigma_o^{cn} \; 1/(1+r/c)^i$$

With continuous compounding—taking the limit of the above two expression as c goes to ∞—the net present value of the above income flow for n periods for the variable income case would be:

$$NPV = \int_o^n P_tQ_t e^{-r^*t} dt$$

And for the constant income case:

$$NPV = PQ\int_o^n e^{-r^*t} dt$$

In order to value an income stream for crude production, we need to know the production profile. Often a reasonable approximation for production is to assume a constant decline rate of α so that $Q_t = \alpha R_o e^{-\alpha*t}$. To distribute costs over future production, we want to compute a unit cost ($\$_o$). Cost at time t will be production times unit cost or $\$_o \alpha R_o e^{-\alpha*t}$. If we want the present value of cost incurred at time t, multiply by e^{-rt} to get $\$_o \alpha R_o e^{-\alpha*t}$. The present value of all our future costs can be computed by summing up all these future costs. In a continuous case, this sum is the integral of costs over the production profile or $\int_o^n \$_o \alpha R_o e^{-\alpha*t} e^{-r*t} dt$. Unit costs will then be the amount $\$_o$, which makes the discounted present value of total future costs equal to the initial capital costs for development or:

$$K = \int_o^n \$_o \alpha R_o e^{-\alpha*t} e^{-r*t} dt = \int_o^n \$_o \alpha R_o e^{(-\alpha-r)*t} dt$$

Solving for $\$_o$ gives us:

$$\$_o = \frac{\frac{K}{R_o \alpha}}{\int_o^n e^{(-\alpha-r)*t} dt}$$

We can integrate the denominator to be:

$$(e^{(-\alpha-r)*t}/(-\alpha-r)|_o^n = [(e^{(-\alpha-r)*n}/(-\alpha-r) - e^{(-\alpha-r)0}/(-\alpha-r)]$$

$$= [(e^{(-\alpha-r)*n})/(-\alpha-r) - (1)/(-\alpha-r)]$$

$$= [(1)/(\alpha+r) - (e^{(-\alpha-r)*n})/(\alpha+r)]$$

Then:

$$\$_o = \frac{\frac{K}{R_o \alpha}}{\left(\frac{1-e^{(-\alpha-r)*n}}{\alpha+r}\right)} \qquad (13.1)$$

For easier comparison of this case to the case with no decline (which we will do in the next section) remember that αR_o is initial production from the field designated by Q_o. Then the formula becomes:

$$\$_o = \frac{\frac{K}{Q_o}}{\left(\frac{1-e^{(-\alpha-r)*n}}{\alpha+r}\right)} \qquad (13.2)$$

Often a reasonable approximation for production is to assume a constant decline rate forever so that n approaches infinity. We know that no oil well lasts forever; production eventually slows as we get far out in the production profile; but we can safely include production to ∞ without much loss of accuracy. Taking the limit of the above denominator as n goes to infinity we get:

$$\lim t\text{->}\infty[\ (1 - e^{(-\alpha - r)*n})\ /(\alpha + r)] = 1/(\alpha + r)$$

Substituting this denominator back into the solution for the unit cost in equations 13.1 and 13.2, we get:

$$\$_o = \frac{\dfrac{K}{\alpha R_o}}{\dfrac{1}{\alpha + r}} = \frac{K}{R_o}\frac{(\alpha + r)}{\alpha} = \frac{K}{Q_o}(\alpha + r) \qquad (\mathbf{13.3})$$

The next-to-last expression in equation 13.3 is the quickest and easiest approximate conversion of in-ground to above-ground costs. It is interpreted as follows: K/R_o is the average cost per barrel of reserves in the ground. To wait many years to produce all of the oil and get reimbursed means that the above-ground cost $\$_o$ is higher than the in-ground costs. To adjust, multiply the in-ground costs by the sum of the discount and decline rate divided by the decline rate.

Suppose you find a new field in the Norwegian North Sea. Its decline rate is $\alpha = 0.13$ and the discount rate is $r = 0.10$. The field costs K = $1 billion to develop and has reserves of R_o = 200 million barrels. Your in-ground costs are K/R_o = 1,000,000,000/200,000,000 = $5.00. However, this in-ground cost does not take into account a required rate of return for holding oil and producing it over many years. Including these holding costs, we can compute the approximate above ground costs from equation 13.3 using $(\alpha + r)/\alpha$:

$$\$_o = (1,000,000,000/200,000,000)*(0.13 + 0.10)/0.13 = 5*(0.23/0.13) = \$8.85\ (\mathbf{unit\ costs})$$

Thus, in-ground costs are $5 per barrel but above-ground costs are approximately $8.85.

Unit Costs with No Decline Rate

This same technique applies to transporting the oil. Suppose that as production from your field decreases, you are able to find and develop nearby fields to keep the flow in the pipeline constant at Q. You pay for the pipeline immediately and it lasts n periods. Again, we distribute this capital cost over the barrels transported over the life of the project. The unit capital costs for transporting oil is computed by finding $\$_t$ (the rate charged per unit of oil that will just cover the capital costs K). We compute $\$_t$ with the formula:

$$K = \int_0^n \$_t Q e^{-rt} dt$$

Solving for $\$_t$, we get:

$$\$_t = (K/Q)/\int_0^n e^{-r^*t} dt$$

Here, K/Q is referred to as capacity cost (the capital cost per barrel of oil transported per year). Integrating the denominator, we get:

$$\$_t = \left.\frac{\frac{K}{Q}}{\frac{-e^{-r^*t}}{r}}\right|_0^n = \left.\frac{\frac{K}{Q}}{\frac{1 - e^{-r^*n}}{r}}\right. = \left.\frac{\frac{K}{Q}}{\frac{1-e^{-r^*n}}{r}}\right. \quad (13.4)$$

Note that this resembles equation 13.2, with $\alpha = 0$ and initial production Q_0 replaced with the constant flow of production over the life of the project Q. If we approximate our problem with an infinite horizon, the denominator simply becomes 1/r. However, with continuous production, aggregate production after period n would not be trivial and we may not get a good approximation if we integrate to ∞, but the higher the discount rate and the longer the project life, the better the infinite approximation. This is because the higher the discount rate and the longer the life of the project, the less production beyond n is worth when discounted back to the present. For example, a dollar in 30 years at a 10% discount rate is worth less than a nickel now.

Now suppose you send 130 million barrels per year through a pipeline that lasts 30 years and costs 40 million dollars to build. Your capacity cost would be K/Q = ($40 million)/(130 million barrels) = $0.308 per barrel and your transportation cost per barrel would be:

$$\$_t = 0.308/((1 - e^{-(0.1*30)}/0.1) = \$0.032$$

Note that if you used the infinite approximation, the unit transport costs would be very close at:

$$\$_t = 0.308/((1/0.1) = \$0.031$$

With a discrete decline rate ($Q_t = (1 - \alpha)^t Q_o$) and annual compounding, these formulas for production costs (with constant decline ($0 < \alpha < 1$) and without a decline rate ($\alpha = 0$) are:

$$\$_t = \frac{K}{Q_o} \Bigg/ \sum_{t=0}^{n} \left\{\frac{1-\alpha}{1+r}\right\}^t = \frac{K}{Q_o} \Bigg/ \frac{1-\left\{\frac{1-\alpha}{1+r}\right\}^{n+1}}{\frac{r+\alpha}{1+r}} = \frac{K}{Q_o} \Bigg/ \left(1-\left\{\frac{1-\alpha}{1+r}\right\}^{n+1}\right)\frac{1+r}{r+\alpha}$$

$$\$_o = \frac{K}{Q_o} \Bigg/ \sum_{t=0}^{n} \left\{\frac{1}{1+r}\right\}^t = \frac{K}{Q_o} \Bigg/ \frac{1-\left\{\frac{1}{1+r}\right\}^{n+1}}{\frac{r}{1+r}} = \frac{K}{Q_o} \Bigg/ \left(1-\left\{\frac{1}{1+r}\right\}^{n+1}\right)\frac{1+r}{r}$$

If $r > 0$ and $n \rightarrow \infty$, the denominators can be simplified to $(1+r)/(r+\alpha)$ and $(1+r)/r$, respectively.

Operating costs

Production and transportation costs include operating as well as capital costs. But operating costs (C_t) are not spent up front; they are distributed over the production profile (Q_t). We compute unit operating cost in year t as:

$$\$_{op} = C_t/Q_t$$

Developing Cost Data

When we do not know the costs of putting in a large piece of capital, we may need to approximate them from other projects of similar nature.

For example, Adelman and Shahi (1989) developed capital costs for extracting oil in different countries around the world but needed a value for in-ground costs (K/R_o) to start with. (K is the costs of finding and developing reserves and R_o is the amount of reserves found and developed.) They had reasonably good estimates for the number of oil wells drilled, the number of dry wells (W_d), and average well depth but insufficient estimates on the costs of these wells. Thus, they approximated costs as follows.

They started with U.S. well drilling costs (C_w), which are available by depth, and multiplied by 1.66, which is an estimate of the other costs over-and-above drilling costs. This provided them with the ability to find and develop reserves based on U.S. statistics. They multiplied this cost-per-well times the number of wells drilled that struck oil (W_o) plus the number of dry wells (W_d). Their above-ground cost findings are then:

$$K/R_o = C_w(W_o + W_d)*1.66/R_o$$

Where they had information indicating well costs might be higher because of complex geology—such as Iran or Nigeria, or for offshore areas—they added a correction factor. Since they were interested only in real physical economic costs, they did not include taxes in their computations. (A company would certainly include taxes as part of its costs, but from a social point of view, taxes are transfer payments that do not reflect real physical costs of production.)

Because they believed that reserve figures were not accurate for many countries—and that production figures were more accurate—they estimated current reserve finding and development (R_o) as equal to current production divided by the decline rate $= Q_t/\alpha$. However, since $Q_t = \alpha(R_e + R_o)$ is a combination of earlier development (R_e) and current development (R_o), this modification means that $Q_t/\alpha = R_e + R_o$, which will overstate reserves that are developed by current wells drilled and understate costs. The slower that reserves are added and the larger is R_e relative to R_o, the more it should understate costs.

Adelman and Shahi adjusted their costs to above-ground costs using equation 13.3, or:

$$\$_o = \frac{K}{R_o} \frac{\alpha + r}{\alpha} = \frac{C_w(W_o + W_d)1.66}{R_o} \frac{\alpha + r}{\alpha}$$

Gas costs can be similarly computed, since oil and gas production costs include finding reserves (exploration costs) as well as development and operating costs. Coal development costs can be computed using the same technique, except that there may be no decline rate in production. Also, coal resources are generally known, so exploration costs may be trivial. Coal costs depend on the size of deposit, thickness of seam, depth, amount of overlying soil, amount of tectonic disturbance of the seam, angle of the seam, inflow of water and ethane, and heterogeneity of the deposit.

Although these unit costs indicate capital cost relative to operating cost for various energy projects, they do not provide the most reliable measure for comparisons across projects, unless production profiles and cost streams are identical across the projects. For project evaluation and decision-making, it is more reliable to rank projects by net present value and then undertake them; if capital is constrained, you undertake the portfolio of possible projects within your budget constraint with the highest net present value. (See Stermole and Stermole (2000) for very detailed descriptions of project analysis.)

Estimating Total Energy Resources

How fossil fuel costs evolve depends upon the total resource base and the success of discovery efforts. Oil is most often used to measure a resource base with two popular approaches represented by Hubbert (1962) and the U.S. Geological Survey (USGS) from 1993. Hubbert was a geologist, who used a logistics model to estimate U.S. reserves, where cumulative oil production at time t (Q_t) is represented by the logistic function:

$$Q_t = \frac{Q_\infty}{[1+\alpha e^{-\beta(t-t_o)}]}$$

Q_∞ is estimated total reserves and α and β are parameters that are all estimated statistically from historical data; t_o is the date of first production. Such a curve for cumulative production has the shape shown in Figure 13–8. The production curve would take the familiar bell-shaped curve.

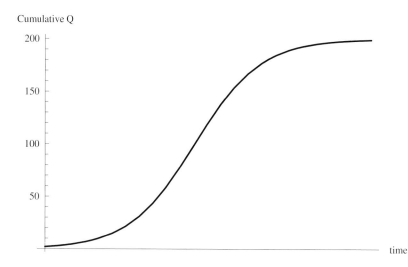

Fig. 13–8 Hubbert Curve for Oil and Gas Reserves

From his forecast curve for oil, Hubbert concluded that U.S. production would peak in 1970—which it did. His estimate of total U.S. reserves was $Q_\infty = 170$ billion barrels. Since U.S. cumulative production as of 1998 was 162.8 billion barrels, and the 1998 estimate of proven reserves was more than 20 billion barrels, his estimates of total reserves were clearly too low. More recent applications of Hubbert's techniques forecast world oil production to peak between 2000 and 2010. (Ivanhoe 1997)

Economists—typically more optimistic than geologists—criticize Hubbert's model because it does not incorporate oil prices or technological change into reserve estimates. It also does not include nonconventional oil reserves (tar sands and heavy oil deposits), which are estimated to be 10 times conventional reserves. (American Petroleum Institute (API), http://www.api.org/edu/oilsup.htm) Despite these critiques, Hubbert retains his supporters, and papers that debate oil reserves—often with a Hubbert slant—can be found at the M. King Hubbert Center (http://hubbert.mines.edu/).

The USGS publishes periodic reserve and resource assessments. Its last complete assessment as of this writing, in 2000, is more optimistic than Hubbert followers in their estimates. USGS characterizes the world's oil resource base by category. Identified reserves (proven reserves) are typically those that have been found and are expected to be produced under current costs and operating conditions. The USGS resource base category (essentially unidentified reserves) is more uncertain. USGS estimates a probability distribution for the total remaining world resources by using geological information on sedimentary basins and probabilities from past discoveries, while taking into account minimum economic sizes. The mean, 95%, and 5% level for their probability distribution are reviewed in Table 13–8.

Thus, for North America, proven reserves are 40 billion barrels; the mean for additional resources is 146.1 billion barrels. The USGS estimated probability that additional resources are greater than 67 billion barrels is 95% and estimated probability that additional resources are greater than 252 billion barrels is 5%. In all cases but for North America, USGS estimates proven reserves to be larger than cumulative production, suggesting that we have not yet produced half of world oil reserves.

Table 13–8 World Proven Reserves and Undiscovered Resources

Region	Oil – Millions of Barrels Proven Reserves	Undiscovered Resources F95	F5	Mean
U.S.	22,446	60,500	94,700	75,600
North America	40,268	67,302	252,190	146,091
FSU	77,832	35,601	225,654	115,985
Middle East and North Africa	699,464	73,286	432,178	229,882
Asia Pacific	32,978	8,726	58,653	29,780
South Asia	5,735	1,032	6,957	3,580
Central and South America	98,551	20,090	230,727	105,106
Sub-Saharan Africa and Antarctica	64,529	26,783	124,447	71,512
Europe	18,704	6,339	45,407	22,292
Total World	1,038,060	239,159	1,376,213	724,228

Region	Gas – Bcf Proven Reserves	Undiscovered Resources F95	F5	Mean
U.S.	183,460	392,600	697,600	526,900
North America	252,354	413,044	1,051,199	681,399
FSU	1,956,130	429,164	3,246,740	1,611,262
Middle East and North Africa	2,206,175	425,371	2,607,896	1,369,933
Asia Pacific	377,954	109,068	746,044	379,339
South Asia	63,923	30,518	248,647	119,610
Central and South America	250,083	96,168	1,087,521	487,190
Sub-Saharan Africa and Antarctica	199,962	83,474	439,436	235,290
Europe	194,843.0	44,706	733,412	312,365
Total World	5,501,424	1,631,513	10,160,895	5,196,388

Region	Natural Gas Liquids – Millions of barrels Undiscovered Resources F95	F5	Mean
U.S.	6,500	9,900	8,000
North America	7,397	29,057	15,853
FSU	13,491	117,260	54,806
Middle East and North Africa	23,976	162,673	81,747
Asia Pacific	4,023	32,153	15,379
South Asia	606	5,845	2,604
Central and South America	3,561	47,788	20,196
Sub-Saharan Africa and Antarctica	3,778	20,564	10,766
Europe	1,584	34,233	13,667
Total World	58,416	449,573	215,018

Notes: Proven reserves have been found and are economical at current prices. Undiscovered reserves are estimates of reserves that could be discovered in the next 30 years. F5 indicates that 5% of the time we would expect reserves to be found to be higher than this amount. F95 indicates that 95% of the time we would expect reserves found to be higher than this amount. Mean indicates that 50% of the time we would expect reserves to be higher than this amount.

Sources: Proven Reserves, *OGJ*, Worldwide Report Issue, 12/23/02:114-115. Undiscovered Resources: USGS *World Petroleum Assessment 2000*.

Summary

Energy comes from a variety of sources—fossil fuels, nuclear energy, and renewables. About 40% of the world's commercial energy comes from oil, another quarter from coal, somewhat less than a quarter from gas, and the remainder from nuclear and hydro with a dab of renewables thrown in. Hydropower—around half of primary electricity—is used in many countries, ranging in size from small, run-of-river generators to huge dam complexes that are the largest electrical facilities in the world.

Nuclear power represents the other half of primary electricity. Nuclear fuel reserves and processing are fairly concentrated, while nuclear power generation is more widespread. Significant government involvement and oversight protects us from environmental consequences.

Other renewables (biomass, wind, solar, and geothermal) have a long history of use but constitute a small share of commercial energy consumption. They are likely to continue to grow as environmental effects for non-renewables come under increasing scrutiny and increasing non-renewable scarcity raises their costs.

Fuel choices and how these choices will evolve in the future depend both on the fuel's properties and their relative costs of production, transportation, and transformation. These costs include capital costs and operating costs per unit of output. Capital costs are usually concentrated at the beginning of a long-lived energy project while the flow of product or service occurs over many years. To evaluate the profitability of energy projects, costs and benefits must be discounted to the same time period to determine whether project benefits outweigh costs and the project should be undertaken. In chapter 4, we considered the net present value of projects for discrete production profiles; in this chapter, we extend our analysis to the more realistic continuous production profile case, which requires continuous compounding. Thus, to discount income at time t, $(P_t Q_t)$ back to the present with discrete compounding c times per year, compute:

$$PV_0 = P_t Q_t / (1 + r/c)^{ct}$$

With continuous compounding, take the limit of the above equation as t goes to infinity and the present value is:

$$PV_0 = P_t Q_t e^{-rt}$$

If you are more comfortable using annual discrete compounding, convert a continuous rate (r_c) to a discrete rate (r_d) using the equation:

$$r_d = \exp(r_c) - 1$$

Then use discrete compounding.

These formulas can be extended to give the present value of a flow of income for discrete annual compounding and continuous annual discounting as follows:

$$PV = \Sigma_o^n \, P_i Q_i / (1+r)^i$$

$$PV = \int_o^n P_t Q_t e^{-r^*t} dt$$

Again, the more realistic continuous rate computations can be converted to a discrete rate and the discrete formula can be applied.

Energy capacity costs—up-front capital costs (K) divided by the capacity put in (Q) or K/Q—can be the cost per MW for a power plant, the cost per initial barrel produced for an oil well, or the cost per Mcf transported by a gas pipeline. Up-front capital costs are often distributed over the life of the project into what are called levelized costs, which is the cost that would have to be charged for each unit when sold to just cover the initial capital costs at the required rate of return (r). These levelized costs are computed by solving the following equations for $\$_k$ in the discrete and continuous case:

$$\text{Discrete: } K = \sum_{t=o}^{n} \frac{\$_k Q_t}{(1+r)^t} \Rightarrow \$_k = \frac{K}{\displaystyle\sum_{t=o}^{n} \frac{Q_t}{(1+r)^t}}$$

$$\text{Continuous: } K = \int_{t=o}^{n} \$_k Q_t e^{-r^*t} dt \Rightarrow \$_k = \frac{K}{\displaystyle\int_{t=o}^{n} Q_t e^{-r^*t} dt}$$

For initial production of Q_0 and a constant decline rate of $\alpha > 0$, these formulas further simplify:

$$\text{Discrete: } \$_k = \frac{K}{Q_0} \left/ \frac{1 - \left\{ \frac{1-\alpha}{1+r} \right\}^{n+1}}{\frac{\alpha+r}{1+r}} \right.$$

$$\text{Continuous} = \$_k = \frac{K}{Q_0} \left/ \left(\frac{1 - e^{(-\alpha-r)*n}}{\alpha+r} \right) \right.$$

When $\alpha = 0$, in the above equations you have a zero decline rate project. These computations are sometimes simplified by assuming an infinite-lived project. The formulas for $n \Rightarrow \infty$ are:

$$\text{Discrete: } \$_k = \frac{K}{Q_0} \left/ \frac{1}{\frac{r+\alpha}{1+r}} \right. = \frac{K}{Q_0} \frac{1+r}{r+\alpha}$$

$$\text{Continuous} = \$_k = \frac{K}{Q_0} \left/ \left(\frac{1}{\alpha+r} \right) \right. = \frac{K}{Q_0} \alpha+r$$

These approximations as $n \Rightarrow \infty$ are better; the higher the interest rate, the longer the project life and the higher the decline rate.

For a constant decline rate for oil or gas, the above equations can also be rewritten in terms of initial reserves by substituting for $Q_0 = (\alpha R_0)$ as:

$$\$_k = \frac{K}{R_0} \frac{(\alpha + r)}{\alpha}$$

In this equation in-ground reserve costs (K/R_0) are easily adjusted to above-ground reserves by multiplying them by $(\alpha+r)/\alpha$.

Oil and gas costs also include the resources necessary to find them. The ultimate resource base influences these exploration costs. Measurements of ultimate resource base have followed two popular methodologies: Hubbert's technology fits a logistic curve to a cumulative production profile, while the USGS uses measurement of the world's sedimentary basins along with probability distributions of known reserves to estimate the probability of reserves in unexplored areas.

14. Linear Programming, Refining and Energy Transportation

[Linear programming] is used to allocate resources, plan production, schedule workers, plan investment portfolios and formulate marketing (and military) strategies. The versatility and economic impact of linear programming in today's industrial world is truly awesome.

—Professor Eugene Lawler, Computer Science Division, University of California-Berkeley, 1980

Introduction

Frankel (1969) sums up many of the important properties of oil in his classic, *Fundamentals of Petroleum*. Oil is neither a final product nor a capital good, he says, but is needed to enjoy other goods. Since it is "a matter of life in peace and death in war," all possible means—including financial investment, political influence, and military action—are undertaken to ensure access to it. The fact that it is liquid, volatile, and a compound of hydrocarbons determines how it is handled and processed.

Exploration and drilling are expensive; production is cheap. Oil transportation and refining are most capital intensive of all. Its capital-intensive nature makes it a cyclical industry with big units working to capacity. During boom periods, it takes time to put in new equipment and take advantage of the good times; shortages make profits soar. During bust periods, companies produce as long as they cover their average variable cost; excess production causes profits to plummet. The petroleum industry's small and highly skilled labor force means that labor relations tend to be good. Petroleum is exhaustible, fugacious, and concealed; success in drilling requires luck and daring, whereas success in refining requires technical ability and organization. Refineries are located based on transport considerations and tax incidence. For example, in Europe, high tariffs on products (but not on crude oil) suggested incentives to develop refineries close to markets.

Crude Oil Refining

Crude oil is a mix of chemical compounds. Refining separates the mix into products with various useful characteristics. Kerosene and fuel oil give light and heat; gasoline and diesel fuel transportation; lubricating oil protects moving metal surfaces; lighter products are building blocks for the petrochemical industry, and asphalt provides tough road surfaces.

Refineries take in crude oil of varying quality and produce this variety of products using a mixture of processes. Sophisticated U.S. refineries produce light virgin or straight-run naphtha, heavy virgin naphtha, heavy naphtha, light naphtha, light vacuum oils, heavy vacuum oils, coker gas oil, and light gas oil. These products can be further treated and blended to produce kerosene, jet fuel, gasoline, diesel fuel, distillate (gas oil), and residual fuel oil.

Figure 14–1 shows oil product consumption by major product for major world regions. The first column for each region is production (P); the second is consumption (C). North America and Asia Pacific are the largest net importers and the E. Europe/FSU, the Middle East, and Central and South America are the largest net exporters. Figure 14–1 also shows a large variation in product use: North America consumes a higher share of gasoline and jet fuel but less residual than other areas; Europe and Asia consume a higher share of gas oil/diesel and a lower share of residuel. Kerosene is a larger share in Asia, the Middle East and Africa where the poor use it for heat and light. Trade patterns also vary: All net importers are net exporters of some products. Thus each region uses trade to balance their refinery slate with their consumption patterns.

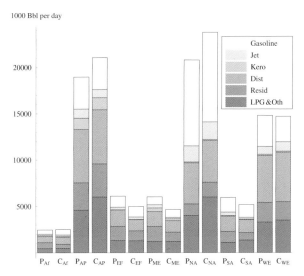

Fig. 14–1 Consumption and Production of Oil Products by World Region, 2000

Notes: Products measured in thousands of barrels per day. P=production and C= consumption. Af=Africa, AP=Asia Pacific, EF=Eastern Europe/FSU, ME=Middle East, NA=North America, SA=South America, WE=West Europe. Source: DOE/EIA, *International Energy Annual 2001*
http://www.eia.doe.gov/emeu/international/total.html#IntlConsumption

Given these variations in consumption patterns, refineries around the world have been adapted to provide the product slates for their domestic and export markets. Various processes that can be employed to do so include:

- *alkylation, polymerization, isomerization,* all of which take lighter hydrocarbons and put them together to produce heavier hydrocarbons
- *thermal cracking, catalytic cracking, and hydrocracking,* all of which crack heavier hydrocarbons into lighter products
- *coking,* which converts very heavy products into coke and much lighter products
- *hydrotreating,* which cleans sulfur from products
- *reforming,* which raises the octane of gasoline

For more details on refining, see Leffler (2000) and Mushrush and Speight (1995).

The refining process begins with distillation. As the crude oil is heated, various fractions boil off, beginning with the lighter products. (Table 14–1.) The *cut points* for the various products—the temperatures at which oil is changed into the next product, shown in Table 14–1, have some slack and can be adjusted. For example, if the cut point for naphtha were changed to 315 from 310, then more kerosene and less naphtha would be produced.

Table 14–1 Boiling Ranges for Petroleum Products

Degrees F	Product
< 90	Butane and Lighter
90–220	Straight Run Gasoline
220–315	Naphtha
315–450	Kerosene
450–650	Light Gas Oil
650–800	Heavy Gas Oil
> 800	Straight Run Residue

Source: Leffler (2000)

The heavier the crude (the more carbon), the lower its quality and the higher the proportion of heavy products that are produced from it. Specific gravity is the weight of a compound divided by the weight of water; crude oil is measured by its API gravity, which is equal to $[(141.5/\text{specific gravity}) - 131.5]$. The specific gravity of water is 1 and its API gravity is 10 degrees. The higher is the API gravity the lighter the crude oil. Gasoline has a specific gravity around 60 degrees while distillate's is around 32 degrees. Sample crude API gravities and their prices are given in Table 14–2.

Table 14–2 Sample Crude API's and Prices, 2003

Crude Oil	API	Price/bbl
U.K. – Brent	38	$24.56
Russia – Urals	32	$21.56
Saudi Light	34	$22.93
Dubai Fateh	32	$23.36
Algeria Saharan	44	$25.07
Nigeria Bonny Light	37	$24.93
Indonesia – Minas	34	$30.90
Venezuela – Tia Juana Light	31	$24.91
Mexico – Isthmus	33	$25.16
Alaska North Slope	27	$29.97
Louisiana Light	40	$22.25
California – Kern River	13	$19.50
West Texas Sour	34	$18.00
West Texas Intermediate	40	$23.00
Oklahoma Sweet	40	$23.00

Source: OGJ, 5/5/03, p.100.

In addition to API gravity of crude oil, the amount of sulfur is an important determinant of quality. A high-sulfur crude (> 2.5% sulfur content) is called a *sour crude*, and a low-sulfur crude (< 0.05% sulfur content) is called *sweet crude*. In-between crudes are called *intermediate*. The various fractions in a barrel of crude have different economic values, all of which determine the overall value of the crude. The fractions within a barrel can be seen from a crude's assay report. Sample assays are shown in Table 14–3.

Table 14–3 Sample Crude Assays

	West Texas Intermediate, U.S.	Saudi Arabian Light (Berri)	Brent, U.K. North Sea	Sahara Blend Algeria	U.S. Alaska North Slope	BCF24 La Salina, Venezuela
°API	40.80	37.8	38.16	45.5	27.5	23.5
Sulfur, wt %	0.34	1.19	0.26	0.053	1.11	1.85
Boiling Range Product Volume %						
°F	C1–C5	68–212	C5–85	C1–160	C5–68	82–200
vol%	4.35	10.1	7.5	9.9	2.37	3.8
°F	68–347	212–302	85–165	160–290	68–347	200–300
vol%	32.39	8.7	17.7	14.9	17.01	5
°F	347–563	302–455	165–235	290–390	347–563	300–350
vol%	23.50	18.7	13.5	14.5	20.16	2.82
°F	563–650	455–650	235–300	390–500	563–650	350–400
vol%	8.10	21.2	12.9	13.4	9.7	3.14
°F	650–1,049	650–1,049	300–350	500–635	650+	400–500
vol%	24.30	30.3	9.2	12.8	51.5	7.53
°F	650–1,500	650+	350+	635–775		500–550
vol%	33.30	39.3	36.5	14.3		4.55
°F	761–1,500	1,049+		775–932		550–650
vol%	25.30	9.0		10		9.73
°F	878–1,500			932+		650+
vol%	17.95			10.2		61.91
°F	1,049–1,500					
vol%	9.00					

Source: OGJ Databook, 2002, "Crude Oil Assays," p. 273–349.

A distillation curve (Fig. 14–2) shows how much of a given crude oil boils off at various temperatures, resulting in a gain in volume as products are separated. Light products expand and take up more room when they are separated. At temperatures higher than 750° F, the heavier products will separate, or crack, into lighter products. To prevent uncontrolled cracking of the heavier products, they are sent from the distillation unit to a vacuum flasher. The flasher's reduced pressure allows heavier products to separate without cracking at lower temperatures.

Since we want and need more gasoline than comes out of the distillation process, the heavier products may be cracked to make more gasoline. The most popular type of cracking is the fluid catalytic cracking (FCC) process. Feedstocks that boil from 650 to 1100° F are heated along with a catalyst introduced in the form of small particles. Resulting products range from light to heavy hydrocarbons and are, again, taken off in a fractionation tower. The heavy products may be sent to a thermal cracker, the light gas oil may be blended into distillate, and the cracked gasoline is blended into gasoline. By adjusting the process between gas oil and gasoline, refiners increase distillate production for the winter heating season and increase gasoline production for the summer driving season.

Gases coming out of the various processes are separated in gas processing units. Isobutane can be combined with propylene or butylene using a high-pressure, low-temperature process and a catalyst to form alkylate. High-octane alkylate is a valuable blending agent for gasoline. Naphtha, which lacks a high enough octane to make a good gasoline blending component, is reformed to raise its octane number by using heat and pressure in the presence of a platinum catalyst.

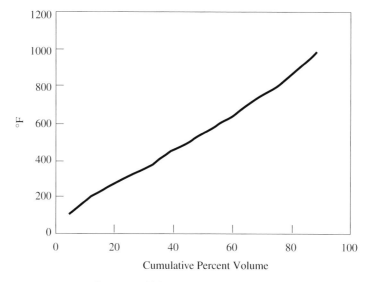

Fig. 14–2 Oklahoma Sweet Distillation Curve

Source: Leffler (2000)

The residual material at the bottom of the barrel is typically processed further using high temperatures to break it into lighter products. A vacuum flasher separates out heavier products without cracking them. The most intense process is coking, which breaks down all feedstocks into lighter products and coke. *Coke*—a solid, more difficult product to handle—can be used as a refinery fuel or sold for the manufacture of electrodes, anodes, carbides, and graphite.

Hydrocracking is catalytic cracking in the presence of hydrogen. It has the advantage of producing only light products such as light distillates, gasoline, and gases. In addition to lightening the barrel, hydrocrackers are used as hydrotreaters to remove sulfur and other impurities from heavier products. These units add considerable economic flexibility to a refinery allowing it to change yields of gasoline, distillate, and jet fuel as market conditions require and enabling it to run heavier, sour crudes. World capacities for these various processes are summarized in Table 14–4. For more information on refining, the *Oil & Gas Journal* publishes a worldwide report, usually every third week of December.

Table 14–4 World Refinery Capacity by Region

Region	No. of refineries	Crude distillation b/cd	Vacuum distillation b/cd	Catalytic cracking b/cd
Africa	45	3,213,262	491,844	195,000
Asia	202	20,204,810	3,841,586	2,720,395
Eastern Europe	95	10,617,099	3,649,826	894,334
Middle East	46	6,318,615	1,873,695	371,500
North America	160	20,290,751	8,857,554	6,546,810
South America	69	6,650,364	2,798,066	1,301,020
Western Europe	105	14,582,745	5,164,683	2,166,460
Total	722	81,877,646	26,677,254	14,195,519

Region	Catalytic reforming b/cd	Catalytic hydrocracking b/cd	Catalytic hydrotreating b/cd	Coke tons/day
Africa	387,273	28,708	835,449	781
Asia	2,019,390	782,173	8,244,163	12,810
Eastern Europe	1,476,831	212,090	4,061,323	12,498
Middle East	599,049	603,810	1,853,210	3,100
North America	4,145,437	1,754,360	13,006,745	115,993
South America	418,662	165,000	1,827,352	15,877
Western Europe	2,139,209	891,148	8,506,925	10,731
Total	11,185,851	4,437,289	38,335,167	171,790

Notes: b/cd = barrels per calendar day.
Source: OGJ, 12/23/02:6.

One way to measure refinery complexity is as follows. Assign each process unit a complexity factor based on its cost relative to the cost of a distillation unit. For example, an FCC unit costs about six times more than a distillation unit per barrel, so the distillation unit is assigned a complexity factor of one and the "cat cracker," a complexity factor of six. All barrels of crude go through the distillation unit, but usually only fractions of the barrel go through other process units. Suppose there are n process units after distillation. The share of crude going to process unit i is α_i and the complexity of process i is C_i. Then the overall complexity of a refinery C is the weighted average of all non-distillation process units complexity factors, C_i's, with the weights being the share of crude going to each process or:

$$C = \Sigma_1^n \alpha_i C_i$$

Gasoline blending

Two important qualities of gasoline are the vapor pressure and the octane number.

Fuel vapor pressure must be high enough so that at low temperatures enough fuel gets into the cylinder but not so high that oxygen cannot enter the cylinder when the engine is warm. At higher elevations, vapor pressure must not be so high that fuel vaporizes in the fuel system, causing vapor lock. Reid Vapor Pressure (RVP) is a measure of how quickly a fuel evaporates and varies from 5 to 15 for gasoline. RVP needs to be higher for cold weather than hot weather use.

The octane number of the fuel indicates whether a fuel is likely to self-ignite. Lower octanes than required will result in self-ignition and cause "knocking." Higher octanes than required cause no such problems but do not improve engine performance and so add an unnecessary expense. Lead tetraethyl—now illegal in the United States and in an increasing number of countries worldwide—was once used extensively as a cheap additive to prevent self-ignition and to raise octane.

Gasolines are blends of various components that meet the required specifications for these two gasoline qualities. For example, butane and isobutane have high vapor pressures while straight-run naphtha has a low vapor pressure. To see how blending works, take the following example from Leffler (2000). Your goal is to have a gasoline with a RVP of 10 and you have the blending stocks in Table 14–5. How much normal butane do you need to blend?

Table 14–5 Reid Vapor Pressure Blending Problem

Component	Barrels	RVP	Motor Octane
Straight Run Gasoline	4,000	1.0	61.6
Reformate	6,000	2.8	84.4
Light Hydrocrackate	1,000	4.6	73.7
Cat Cracked Gasoline	8,000	4.4	76.8
Normal Butane	x	52.0	92.0

Source: Leffler (2000)

RVP is a simple weighted average of the RVP's for all the blending stocks. Or:

$$\text{Gasoline RVP} = \sum_{i=1}^{n} (RPV_i)(B_i) / \sum_{i=1}^{n} B_i$$

where

RVP$_i$ is the Reid Vapor Pressure of product i

B$_i$ is the number of barrels of product i blended in

n is the number of products blended.

For the gasoline products blended in Table 14–5, the gasoline:

$$RVP = \frac{4000*1+6000*2.8+1000*4.6+8000*4.4+x*52}{(4000+6000+1000+8000+x)} = 10$$

Or:

$$60,600 + 52x = 10*(19,000 + x)$$

Solving the above equation, we find that the required quantity of normal butane is x = 3081 barrels. Total gasoline production would be 19,000 + x = 19,000 + 3081 = 22,081 barrels. Blending for octane requirements can be done in the same way. Blending for both RVP and octane at the same time would require two equations to be solved simultaneously.

Isobutane, isopentane, and isohexane have higher octane numbers than butane, pentane, and hexane, but they are more expensive. However, refiners that have trouble meeting their octane requirements may convert butane, pentane, and hexane to their "iso" equivalents through a process called isomerization. Additionally, polymerization is used to convert gases to liquid fuels.

In some large U.S. cities, the federal government requires that oxygen be added to gasoline so that CO_2 rather than CO is exhausted. The two most common blending agents to raise oxygen levels are ethanol and methyl tertiary butyl ether (MTBE).

Unlike gasoline, diesel fuel is required to be self-igniting. The *cetane rating* is a measure of the self-ignition properties of a fuel (the ignition delay). The shorter the delay, the better. As with octane numbers, cetane ratings can be increased through the blending of products.

Furnace oil—also called gas oil and number two distillate—is very similar to diesel but has more latitude in specification, since it does not have to meet cetane requirements.

Residual fuel oil (resid) is the heavy bottom end of the barrel. It must be heated before it can be transported and typically contains contaminants like sulfur and heavy metals. Hydrotreating can be used to remove sulfur, nitrogen, and metals to make resid more environmentally acceptable. Typically the hydrogen used in this process is a by-product of a reformer.

Linear Programming to Optimize Refinery Profits

A typical refinery uses many of these processes and varying crude types to produce a wide range of products. The goal of the refinery is to pick a crude oil and product slate that maximizes profits subject to a variety of capacity and quality constraints on inputs and outputs. Often the objective and constraints can be represented as linear functions, and we can apply linear programming to their solution. Symonds (1955) first modeled refineries in a linear programming framework but to see how linear programming works, let's begin with a simple blending problem from Kaplan (1983).

In this example, two processes produce two grades of gasoline. Process one produces straight-run gasoline u_1 with a maximum capacity of 100,000 and process two produces cracked gasoline u_2 with a maximum capacity of 140,000. The two products (u_1 and u_2) can be blended into two grades of gasoline (X_1 and X_2). The blending process can be represented by the following Leontief-fixed coefficient production functions:

$$\text{Grade one: } X_1 = 2.5 \min(u_1, u_2/2)$$

$$\text{Grade two: } X_2 = 1.75(u_1, u_2)$$

Thus, if $u_1 = 1$ and $u_2 = 2$, we get $2.5 * \min(1, 2/2) = 2.5$ gallons of grade X_1. However, if we add two more units of u_2 without any more u_1, we will not get any more of grade one gasoline, or we must blend in a ratio of one to two. We can represent these production functions by *isoquants*—lines that represent equal quantities. For example, two isoquants for grade one gasoline are shown in Figure 14–3. I_1 represents 2.5 gallons of grade one gasoline everywhere along it. I_2 represents the sets of inputs that will produce 5 gallons of grade two gasoline everywhere along it.

In Figure 14–3, start at $u_1 = 1$ and $u_2 = 2$. Note that adding more u_1 without any u_2 leaves us on the same isoquant; similarly, adding more u_2 without any more u_1 also leaves us on the same isoquant.

If profits for grade one gasoline are $\pi_1 = \$0.08$/gallon and for grade two are $\pi_2 = \$0.09$/gallon, then the objective function is to maximize total profits, or:

$$\pi = \$0.08 * X_1 + \$0.09 * X_2$$

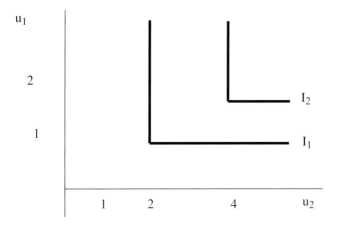

Fig. 14–3 Isoquants for the Leontief Production Function $X_1 = 2.5 \min (u_1, u_2/2)$

This objective function is maximized subject to the capacity constraints for our two blending agents u_1 and u_2. To develop these constraints, note that 2.5 gallons of grade X_1 requires 1 gallon of u_1. To get the gallons of u_1 per gallon of X_1 use u_1/X_1 = 1/2.5 = 0.4. Similarly for X_2, we know that 1.75 gallons of grade X_2 use 1 gallon of u_1. To get the gallons of u_1 per gallon of X_2, divide u_1/X_2 = 1/1.75 = 0.57143. Total requirements of u_1 for X_1 and X_2 have to be less than 100,000, giving the u_1 constraint as $0.4*X_1 + 0.57*X_2 < 100,000$. The whole optimization problem is to:

Maximize $\qquad \pi = \$0.08*X_1 + \$0.09*X_2$

Subject to $\qquad 0.4*X_1 + 0.57143*X_2 < 100,000 \qquad$ (straight run)

$\qquad\qquad\quad\ 0.8*X_1 + 0.57143*X_2 < 140,000 \qquad$ (cracked)

The easiest way to see the solution to this problem is to graph it in $X_1 X_2$ space. Since the constraints are linear, we can find two points for each function and connect them.

For constraint one, we have:

$$X_1 = 0 => X_2 = 175,000$$

$$X_2 = 0 => X_1 = 250,000$$

For constraint two, we have:

$$X_1 = 0, X_2 = 245,000$$

$$X_2 = 0, X_1 = 175,000$$

The graphs for these two functions are shown in Figure 14–4. The constraint set for this problem is 0ABC. We need to find where in this set profits are highest. Our profit function is:

$$\pi = 0.08{*}X_1 + 0.09{*}X_2$$

We can rewrite this as:

$$X_2 = \pi/0.09 - (0.08/0.09){*}X_1 = \pi/0.09 - (0.8888){*}X_1$$

We need to find the line with the above slope that is further from the origin but still is in the constraint set 0ABC. In other words: find the highest line with slope $dX_2/dX_1 = -0.8888$ that touches one of the points A, B, C.

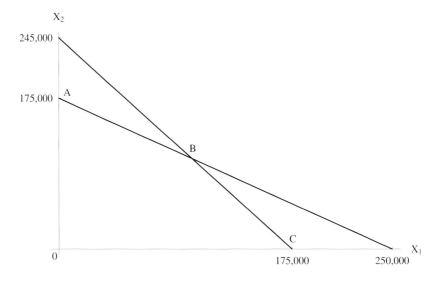

Fig. 14–4 Diagram for Gasoline Blending Problem

One way of solving this problem is to check the profits at each point. Profits at points A and C are:

$$\pi_A = 0.08 \cdot X_1 + 0.09 \cdot X_2 = 0.08 \cdot (0) + 0.09 \cdot (175,000) = 15,750$$

$$\pi_C = 0.08 \cdot X_1 + 0.09 \cdot X_2 = 0.08 \cdot (175,000) + 0.09 \cdot (0) = 14,000$$

To find profits at B, we need to solve for the values of X_1 and X_2 or solve the two constraints simultaneously.

$$0.4 \cdot X_1 + 0.57143 \cdot X_2 = 100,000$$

$$0.8 \cdot X_1 + 0.57143 \cdot X_2 = 140,000$$

Subtracting the second equation from the first yields:

$$-0.4 \cdot X_1 = -40,000$$

Solving for X_1 gives us:

$$X_1 = 100,000$$

From the second constraint, we can solve for X_2 to be:

$$X_2 = 140,000/0.57143 - 0.8 \cdot X_1/0.57143 = 244,999.3875 - 1.3999965 \cdot X_1$$

Substituting in the value for X_1 gives us:

$$X_2 = 244,999.3875 - 1.3999965 \cdot (100,000) = 105,000$$

Alternatively, by linear algebra, this system can be written as:

$$\begin{pmatrix} 0.4 & 0.57143 \\ 0.8 & 0.57143 \end{pmatrix} \begin{pmatrix} X_1 \\ X_2 \end{pmatrix} = \begin{pmatrix} 100000 \\ 140000 \end{pmatrix}$$

The solution:

$$\begin{pmatrix} X_1 \\ X_2 \end{pmatrix} = \begin{pmatrix} 0.4 & 0.57143 \\ 0.8 & 0.57143 \end{pmatrix}^{-1} \begin{pmatrix} 100000 \\ 140000 \end{pmatrix} = \begin{pmatrix} -2.5 & 2.5 \\ 3.49999 & -1.75 \end{pmatrix} \begin{pmatrix} 100000 \\ 140000 \end{pmatrix} = \begin{pmatrix} 100000 \\ 105000 \end{pmatrix}$$

So profits at solution point B are:

$$\pi_B = 0.08*(100,000) + 0.09*(105,000)$$

$$= 17,450$$

Since these profits at B are higher than at points A and C, we would want to produce 100,000 gallons of grade one and 105,000 gallons of grade two.

To see how much u_1 is used in each grade, go back to constraint one for straight-run gasoline and substitute in the quantities for each grade produced.

$$0.40*(100,000) + 0.57143*(105,000) = 100,000$$

The first term in the above constraint is the amount of straight-run gasoline used in grade one and the second term is the amount of straight-run gasoline used in grade two. Then, we know that:

$$u_1 = 40,000 \text{ for grade one and } 60,000 \text{ for grade two}$$

Substituting the grade amounts into the constraint for cracked gasoline, we get:

$$0.8*(100,000) + 0.57143*(105,000) = 140,000$$

The first term in the above expression is the amount of cracked gasoline used in grade one gasoline and the second term is the amount of cracked gasoline used in grade two gasoline. Therefore:

$$u_2 = 80,000 \text{ for grade one and } 60,000 \text{ for grade two}$$

These techniques can be extended to more complicated problems that involve running processes and blending as in the following problem from Symonds (1955).

Suppose that a refinery has four crude oils available—A, B, C, D—available in quantities of 100, 100, 200, 100. Crude C can be run in process C_1 to produce gasoline (G), heating oil (H) and fuel oils (F) and in process C_2 to produce G, H, F, and lubes (L). The four products G, H, F, L are required in the following quantities, 170, 85, 85, 20. Profits on crudes A, B, C_1, C_2 and D are 10, 20, 15, 25, and 7.

Table 14–6 Summary of Refinery Problem

| | Type of Crude or Process | | | | | Product |
	A	B	C_1	C_2	D	Demand
Profits on Crudes	10	20	15	25	7	
Products	Product Slate for Crude or Process					
G	0.6	0.5	0.4	0.4	0.3	170
H	0.2	0.2	0.3	0.1	0.3	85
F	0.1	0.2	0.2	0.2	0.3	85
L	0.0	0.0	0.0	0.2	0.0	20
Total Crude	100	100	$C_1+C_2 = 200$		100	

Thus, a barrel of crude A yields 0.6 barrels of gasoline, 0.2 barrels of heating oil, etc. The product slates for a barrel of each crude oil and process are given in Table 14–6.

The objective function—to maximize for this problem—comes from multiplying each product by its profits and summing up:

$$\pi = 10{*}A + 20{*}B + 15{*}C_1 + 25{*}C_2 + 7{*}D$$

Total amount of gasoline from crude A is $0.6{*}A$, from B it is $0.5{*}B$, etc. To make sure we satisfy the gasoline market, our gasoline constraint must be:

$$170 < 0.6{*}A + 0.5{*}B + 0.4{*}C_1 + 0.4{*}C_2 + 0.3{*}D$$

Similarly, our constraints for heating oil, fuel oil, and lubricants are:

$$85 < 0.2{*}A + 0.2{*}B + 0.3{*}C_1 + 0.1{*}C_2 + 0.3{*}D$$

$$85 < 0.1{*}A + 0.2{*}B + 0.2{*}C_1 + 0.2{*}C_2 + 0.3{*}D$$

$$20 < 0.2{*}C_2$$

In addition, because we cannot use more crude oil than we have at our disposal, the crude oil constraints are:

$$A < 100$$

$$B < 100$$

$$C_1 + C_2 < 200$$

$$D < 100$$

All variables must also be constrained to be non-negative. To see how to solve such a problem using Excel solver go to http://dahl.mines.edu and click on "Solving a Refinery Problm with Excel Solver" under Chapter 14.

Energy Transportation

Energy is transported by a variety of means over the earth's surface. Most electric power is transported in overhead insulated copper or aluminum power lines or in buried cables. Usually, grid interconnects under the sea use submarine cables. Since line losses are less at higher voltages and increasing and decreasing voltage is relatively inexpensive, voltage is increased for long distance transport. More than 99% of high-voltage lines worldwide had used alternating current (HVAC). In the United States, they are rated at around 400 kV, which is also a common voltage worldwide. (Higher voltages are also used. For example, the lines from Churchill Falls, Newfoundland, to Quebec are a whopping 735 kV.) There are some instances of direct current (DC), which has lower line loses than those for AC. However, to transport power by DC it must be converted at the power plant from AC to DC with a rectifier and then converted back with an inverter before it can be used. The conversions eat up the transport gains of DC for distances of less than around 300 miles overland or 30 miles in submarine cables for a 400 kV line. Total world high-voltage DC (HVDC) capacity as of 1993 was only 58 GW. (http://www.greentie.org/index.php, downloaded Jan 2001) However, increases in the bulk power market as well as DC generation from renewable sources are making HVDC more attractive.

Oil has a long history of transport by water: in 1861, oil was first shipped in barrels on a sailing ship from Philadelphia to London. Oil was loaded in barrels and shipped by horse and wagon on land. This early form of measurement has lingered to the present day, although oil is no longer shipped in barrels. Originally, barrels held 50 gallons but contracts were designated as 42 gallons/barrel to allow for spillage. This anachronism, has stuck as well.

The first bulk crude ocean carrier began commercial life in 1863. Such carriers require bulkheads (tanks) to separate oil to keep it from sloshing and destabilizing the vessel. After World War II, tankers up to 30,000 deadweight tons (dwt) were built. (Dwt, the most often used commercial measure for a tanker, indicates total tonnage including cargo, fuel, provisions, and crew and is usually measured in metric tons.) Since surface area increases as a square and volume goes up as a cube, there are significant economies of scale in tankers and so tanker size continued to increase. (For pipelines, the volume increases as the square of the radius.)

After 1956 and a shift to longer voyages, the size of tankers rapidly escalated. By 1966, the largest tanker was 210,000 dwt with plans for tankers up to 500,000 dwt. Currently tankers between 200,000 and 320,000 dwt are designated as very large crude carriers (VLCC) and those over 320,000 dwt are designated ultra large crude carriers (ULCC). The largest tanker in the world is a Norwegian Ship, the Viking Jahre, at 564,763 dwt and 1504 feet long. Its gross registered tons or cargo space is 260,851 dwt. Table 14–7 shows recent world tanker tonnage by size. (Lloyds Register, www.lr.org, has numerous publications on various aspects of shipping.)

Table 14–7 World Tanker Fleet by Size, 2001

Vessel Size	# Vessels	Total tonnage Million dwt
> 200,000 dwt (VLCC, ULCC)	442	129.4
Suezmax (120,000–200,000 dwt)	283	41.2
Aframax (80,000–200,000 dwt)	533	51.2
Average age for tankers >200,000 dwt is more than 20 years.		

Source: International Petroleum Encyclopedia, 2002, p. 193.

Since super tankers require super ports, ports in many parts of the world have been deepened or new ones built to accommodate these large ships. Because deepwater ports for VLCC and ULCC require expensive special conditions and equipment, numerous single-point mooring systems have also been set up. IMODCO-SBM, now a member of the IHC CALLAND Group, has installed about 75% of these systems worldwide since 1956. (http://www.sbmimodco.com) These anchored buoys, held in place by anchor chains, hold ships further out to sea while hoses deliver oil to shore. This system can accommodate larger tankers than many ports can handle. It's economical because ships remain in open waters and do not require jetties and breakwaters. Tankers can moor and still move 360 degrees around these buoys. Thus, tankers can maneuver more easily than in a fixed dock and are less likely to spill oil.

The only U.S. port that can take VLCC/ULCC carriers is the Louisiana Offshore Oil Port (LOOP) 18 miles offshore from Grand Isle. In 2002, an average of 685,000 barrels per day were offloaded. This oil represented about 11% of U.S imports. Offloading has increased since then. LOOP can take ships up to 700,000 dwt and is connected to a pipeline system that can take crude oil to refineries representing almost one-third of U.S refining capacity, in Louisiana, Texas, and the Midwest.

When limited by port size, another alternative is to transship—load oil onto large ships for long distances and then offload onto smaller ships before reaching the final destination. Deepwater ports in the Caribbean such as at Trinidad and the Bahamas have been popular transshipment points for crude oil going into shallower U.S. ports.

At this writing, about 60% of the world's oil is transported in tankers. Figure 14–5 shows the global trade patterns for oil as well as for coal and gas.

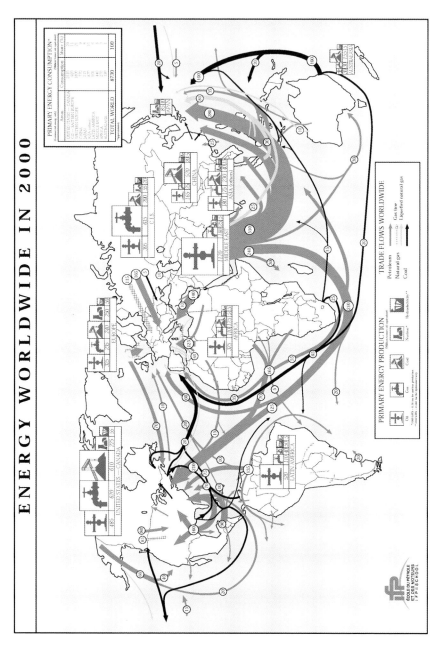

Fig. 14–5 Energy Transport Worldwide

Bottlenecks remain a problem in shipping lanes—areas where traffic jams affect movement of energy products. The estimated annual volumes of oil passing through the six major world bottlenecks at the turn of the century and their locations are as follows:

- 15.5 million b/d through the Straits of Hormuz between Oman and Iran, which connects the Gulf of Aden and the Arabian Sea

- 10.3 million b/d through the Straits of Malacca below Singapore, which connects the Indian Ocean and the South China Sea

- 3.25 million b/d through Bab el-Mandab between Africa and Yemen, which connects the Red Sea with the Gulf of Aden and the Arabian Sea

- 3.05 million b/d through the Suez Canal and Sumed Pipeline, which connect the Red Sea with the Gulf of Suez

- 1.6 million b/d through the Bosporus/Turkish Straits, which connects the Black Sea and the Mediterranean

- 0.5 million b/d through the Panama Canal which connects the Caribbean Sea with the Pacific Ocean

In addition, oil pipelines from Russia to Western Europe are reaching capacity. More than 500,000 b/d goes through Rotterdam Harbor to inland refineries along the Rhine river.

Oil companies own tankers and also charter tankers to move their oil. Around 80% of the world's tanker capacity is owned by independent tanker owners. This way, if an oil company does not need a tanker, it does not sit idle. The independents absorb the market fluctuation and spread the tankers over other users. Independents may also have other shipping interests to offset a lull in tanker use. For more information on independent tanker owners, go to International Association of Independent Tanker Owners (INTERTANKO) web site at http://www.intertanko.com/.

Charter rates are typically quoted in an index called Worldscale. These rates, published annually, list the cost per ton to carry oil between designated ports in a 19,500 dwt tanker traveling at 14 knots. The base rate is designated as Worldscale 100. A larger ship can transport crude more cheaply than a smaller one, so its rate will be some percent of Worldscale. For example, "Worldscale 45" indicates that the price per barrel is 45% of the published Worldscale rate. Rates vary with the size of the ship and market conditions. Rates will be lower when the tanker market is weak than when it is tight.

Table 14–8 shows recent weighted average freight rates for some long haul crude.

Table 14–8 Tanker Freight Rates (% of Worldscale), January 2003

Route	Dirty Tanker
Arabian Gulf to West	105
Arabian Gulf to East	140.5
Mediterranean to U.S. Atlantic Coast	193.5
	Clean Tanker
Mediterranean to NW Europe	271.5
Mediterranean to U.S. Atlantic Coast	261.5

Note: For more information on Worldscale and the history of tanker rate schedules go to http://www.worldscale.co.uk

Source: *Bloomberg Oil Buyers' Guide, Petroleum Intelligence Weekly*, quoted from the *Petroleum Economist*, 03/03.

For example, freight rates from the Arabian Gulf to the West averaged 105% of Worldscale for *dirty tankers*, those carrying black cargoes such as crude and resid. Dirty tankers do not require as much cleaning between voyages as *clean tankers*, which carry so-called white product, encompassing the lighter, more valuable products. White cargoes are more expensive to transport because contamination must be avoided and because much smaller ships typically carry these products. LPG (butane and propane) and ethylene must be transported in high-pressure containers and are not included in the designation of clean or dirty tankers.

Tankers sometimes sail under flags of convenience, which means they are registered in a country where tax rates, operating standards and environmental requirements are more lax than the home country of the chartering company. The two most popular flags of convenience are Liberia and Panama. Each officially has an estimated 10% of world tankers (U.S. CIA, *Factbook*, 1999) but because these tankers are generally larger ships, their tonnage probably represents an even larger percent of world tanker tonnage. For information on other countries that offer flags of convenience see http://www.flagsofconvenience.com.

Inland transportation of oil and products includes pipelines, rail, and truck. Water transport consists of self-propelled vessels and barges, which are moved by tug or push boats. Oil barges were the first to use the U.S. Gulf Intracoastal Waterway, which runs from Texas to Florida. Transportation of crude oil and products is shown in Table 14–9.

Receiving points for crude oil and petroleum products have large tanks for temporary storage, called tank farms, where crude and products are segregated by owners. Various grades of crude and products must also be segregated into batches in the pipeline. Scheduling and dispatching of batches is done by computer with a single batch having a minimum volume. Unless products are physically separated (sometimes batches are separated by huge rubber balls),

Table 14–9 Transport of U.S. Crude Oil and Products by Mode

Crude Oil	Billions of ton miles	Percent	Oil Products	Percent
Pipelines	321.1	75.9%	296.6	60.5%
Water Carriers	100	23.6%	147.5	30.1%
Motor Carriers	1.4	0.3%	27.6	5.6%
Railroad	0.5	0.1%	18.2	3.7%
Total	423	100.0%	489.9	100.0%

Source: U.S. Bureau of Transportation Statistics, *National Transportation Statistics*, 2001, downloaded from http://www.bts.gov/publications/nts/

there is some mixing at the interfaces. If product specification is not too tight, the products at the interfaces can be used; otherwise, they need to be reprocessed. (Van Dyke 1997)

Pipelines are manufactured in various standard sizes up to 56 inches in diameter. Pumping stations keep the crude moving. For example, along the 48-inch, 800-mile Alaska pipeline from the North Slope to Valdez, there are currently nine operating pumping stations. The oil travels at 5.4 mph and takes almost six days to reach the terminal at Valdez. The highest throughput was more than 2 million barrels per day in 1989. With falling production, throughput has fallen, as well, and is currently less than 1.5 million barrels per day. (http://www.alyeska-pipe.com/factbook/)

To increase throughput, you increase the diameter of the pipe or increase the power of the pumping station. Table 14–10 shows the sizes of recently laid pipe in the United States along with throughput for 10,000 and 20,000 horse-power of pumping capacity. Pumping equipment represents between 3 and 5% of new pipeline costs in the United States while pumping stations are an additional 21 to 23%. (*OGJ* 8/23/99, p.56)

Both oil and its products play a large role in international trade. Half of the world's oil production is exported, and product exports are about 40 % as large as crude oil exports. The world's largest exporters and importers of oil products are shown in Table 14–11.

A number of these countries have set up export refinery industries, with exports greater than the amount they supply to their domestic markets. They include Kuwait, Venezuela, Algeria and the U.S. Virgin Islands.

Natural gas is transported primarily by pipeline with small amounts transported as LNG. World trade in natural gas was shown in Figure 14–5. Gas transportation costs are considerably higher than for oil, and vary considerably by distance and conditions. (Fig. 14–6.)

Table 14–10 Pipeline Diameters, Average Cost, and Capacities

Inner Diameter Inches	Cost per Mile	Throughput b/d 10,000 hp	Throughput b/d with 20,000 hp
8	206,675	na	na
12	342,267	47,000	60,000
16	832,063	75,000	100,000
20	925,511	120,000	150,000
22	na	145,000	180,000
24	1,642,715	160,000	210,000
26	na	185,000	245,000
30	1,536,435	247,000	310,000
36	1,963,228	na	na
42	1,525,558	na	na

Notes: Capacities computed for 1,000 miles, oil at 34 API, 5% terrain variation, one-quarter inch thick pipe. na = data not available.

Source: Throughput from Cookenboo (1980). Diameters of recently laid pipe are from *OGJ*, Pipeline Economics Issue, 9/16/02, pp. 62–63.

Table 14–11 World's Largest Net Exporters and Importers of Refined Petroleum Products in 2000

Rank	Net Exporters	Exports (1000 Barrels/day)	Net Exports as % of Domestic Product Consumption	Net Importers	Imports (1000 Barrels/day)	Net Imports as % of Domestic Product Consumption
1.	Saudi Arabia	1,255	88.3%	United States	1,398	7.1%
2.	Russia	1,061	41.1%	Japan	1,245	22.5%
3.	Venezuela	793	158.7%	Germany	520	18.7%
4.	Kuwait	609	230.2%	China	346	7.2%
5.	Canada	586	28.3%	Mexico	338	17.0%
6.	Algeria	523	253.9%	Spain	267	18.3%
7.	UAE	392	130.3%	Hong Kong*	248	101.1%
8.	Virgin Islands, U.S.	353	533.5%	Brazil	221	10.2%
9.	Iran	260	20.6%	Turkey	194	29.3%
10.	Bahrain	255	848.5%	Pakistan	186	50.9%
11.	Netherlands	246	28.9%	Vietnam	171	97.2%
12.	Korea, South	231	10.8%	Switzerland	155	56.6%
13.	United Kingdom	200	11.6%	Taiwan	150	15.9%
14.	Norway	194	98.2%	Nigeria	143	58.2%
15.	Netherlands Antilles	166	234.0%	France	133	6.6%
16.	Libya	142	67.6%	Puerto Rico	122	60.6%
17.	Trinidad and Tobago	142	573.5%	Cuba	112	69.7%
18.	Argentina	125	24.6%	Lebanon	106	100.0%
19.	Belgium	111	19.0%	Dominican Republic	92	73.3%
20.	South Africa	107	23.5%	Portugal	90	27.1%

Notes: Hong Kong importing more than 100% of consumption indicates an increase in product stocks.

Source: Computed from information in EIA/DOE, *International Energy Annual, 2001* at http://www.eia.doe.gov/iea/pet.html, downloaded August 2003.)

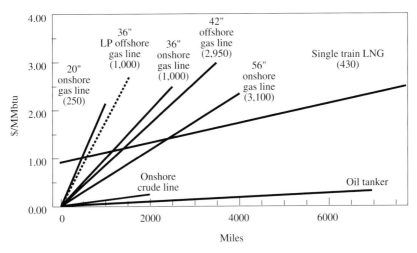

Fig. 14–6 Illustrative Gas and Oil Transportation Costs

Source: Used with permission of James Jensen, Jensen Associated, Inc. Presented at the U.S./International Association for Energy Economics 21st Annual North American Meeting, Philadelphia, Pennsylvania, September 24–27, 2000.
Notes: Numbers in parentheses are gas deliverability in millions of cubic feet per day (MMcdf), LP = low presure.

In Figure 14–6, the left-hand axis represents transport costs in dollars per MMBTU transported.

Oil tankers are the cheapest method of transport, followed by oil pipelines. To convert oil transport costs to per-barrel costs, multiply by 5.8. Gas onshore is cheaper than gas offshore and gas transport costs are, of course, cheaper as pipeline diameters increase. Shipping LNG becomes relatively cheaper than shipping natural gas by high-pressure pipeline at around 1500 miles, and becomes competitive with large onshore pipelines at around 2500 miles.

Because of these high transport costs, gas that is far from market, particularly small-scale finds, may not be commercial. For this reason, around 3% of gross natural gas production worldwide was vented or flared in 2000 and another 11% was re-injected to maintain pressure in oil wells. Around 5% of the gas in the Middle East was vented or flared and another 22% was injected. Nigeria vented or flared almost half of its gas and injected another 11%, which is down somewhat because of a large LNG project that came on-stream in 1999. Cameroon, a relatively new oil producer, flared or vented all of its natural gas production.

There are three types of gas transportation in the United States. At the field, small gathering pipelines transport gas to long-distance transportation pipelines. Distribution pipelines then transport gas from large, long-distance pipelines to the end user. The United States has 1,045,919 miles of distribution pipelines, 263,347 miles of transmission pipeline, and 36,115 miles of field and gathering pipelines. (http://www.bts.gov/publications/nts/html/table_01_08.html. National Transportation Statistics 2001)

Gas pipelines require compressor stations. As with all pipelines, more gas can be transported by increasing pipe diameters or by increasing the horsepower of the compressors. In the Netherlands, for example, gas may travel at 5 kilometers per hour (km/hr) during slack summer months and more than 50 km/hr in peak winter periods. Gas can also be stored in pipelines by increasing line pack. Compressor stations built in the United States range in size from 310–30,000 horsepower with cost running between $236 and $4,849 per horsepower. (*OGJ*, Pipeline Economics Issue, 9/16/03, p.64)

More than half of the world's coal is used to produce electricity and more than 60% of this utility use is located within 38.5 miles (60 km) of the mine mouth. (World Coal Institute, http://www.wci-coal.com) Nevertheless coal transport is still big business. Seaborn's transport of coal was the world's largest dry cargo, estimated at more than 500 million tons a year in 2001, with steam coal about 65% of the total. Crude oil and petroleum products are about 40% of total world shipping tonnage and steam coal is about a quarter of oil shipments by tonnage. (OECD, *Maritime Transport Statistics*, 1999 http://www.oecd.org/linklist/0,2678,en_2649_34367_2307973_1_1_1_1,00.html, downloaded August 2003, and World Coal Institute, *Transport and Storage – Shipping*, http://www.wci-coal.com/web/content.php?menu_id=2.6.2, downloaded August 2003.) Major shipping routes for coal can also be seen in Figure 14–5. As in the independent tanker trade, independent bulk cargo shippers have no fixed schedule but go where needed with deals typically set up by brokers.

Coal is shipped not only by bulk cargo ship, but also by rail, barge, truck, and conveyor. The majority of domestically used U.S. coal is transported by rail, accounting for more than 20% of freight revenue for American railroads and an even higher percentage of rail ton miles. (Table 14–12.)

Table 14–12 U.S Domestic Distribution of Coal by Transportation Method, 2001

Units	Railroad	Truck	Great Lakes	Conveyor	Other Water
1000 short tons	665,000	109,000	12,000	92,000	139,000
Percent	65.4%	10.7%	1.2%	9%	13.7%

Source: National Mining Association, Distribution of Coal by Transportation Method—1990–2001, http://www.nma.org/pdf/c_distribution.pdf, downloaded August 2003.

The cheapest way to transport coal by rail is by dedicated unit train. These trains often have more than 100 cars with capacities of 100 short tons each. They move back and forth between a mine and a power plant without uncoupling; rather, they are loaded by moving under a chute and simply drop the coal out the bottom at their destination.

Another 15% of U.S. coal moves through the Great Lakes, along inland waterways, or along the coasts. The Jones Act, passed in 1920 to protect U.S. shipping, requires that this coal, as well as all other goods shipped between U.S. ports, must be transported on U.S. built and owned vessels. Since U.S. vessels tend to be more expensive, this act raises the cost of water borne shipping within the United States and gives a slight transport cost advantage to foreign coal.

Conveyor belts and tramways, most often between the mine and a mine-mouth power plant, transport another 9% of U.S. coal. A somewhat higher percentage is transported by trucks, usually from mine mouth to preparation plants, to mine-mouth power plants, or to loading points for transfer to rail or water.

When a company decides among the various transport modes discussed above, they must consider costs along with transportation requirements and constraints. Linear programming is useful for minimizing transport costs while taking into account transport constraints. Symonds (1955) demonstrates another use for linear programming, which is to minimize transport costs for a crude oil problem. Suppose that you have m oil supply points with X_i being the quantity of oil available at the ith point. You have n refineries with Y_j being the oil requirements at the jth refinery. Let A_{ij} be the amount of oil transferred from supply point i to refinery j and C_{ij} be the unit cost to transfer a barrel of oil from i to j. This unit cost can be computed using the levelized costs from chapter 13 plus operating costs.

The objective function is total transport costs, which can be easily computed. Total cost for transferring oil from supply point one to refinery one is $C_{11}*A_{11}$, or cost per barrel times the number of barrels transported. Similarly, total cost for transferring oil from supply point i to refinery j is $C_{ij}*A_{ij}$. Total transport cost (TTC) is the sum of all costs from each supply point to each refinery of:

$$TTC = \sum_{i=1}^{m}\sum_{j=1}^{n} C_{ij}*A_{ij}$$

The constraints for this problem are that no supply point can ship more than they have available:

$$\sum_{j=1}^{n} A_{ij} < Y_i$$

And that each refinery must satisfy its crude oil requirements:

$$\sum_{i=1}^{m} A_{ij} = X_j$$

Such problems can be solved by computer programs solely dedicated to linear programming, which can handle models with hundreds and even thousands of constraints. (e.g., Gams, Lindo) For a survey of other packages, see http://lionhrtpub.com/orms/surveys/LP/lp1.html0. Free codes can be found at http://www-unix.mcs.anl.gov/otc/Guide/faq/linear-programming-faq.html#free.

Another common application for linear programming in an energy context is to pick energy sources that will minimize the cost of supplying energy services. For example, suppose you are a power generator supplying electricity to a particular service area. Linear programming (or the more complicated nonlinear programming, in which all the functions in the model are not linear) can help determine whether coal, natural gas, oil, or wind is your cheapest way of satisfying power demands.

Summary

Crude oil is seldom used directly, but is more valuable when refined into a whole slate of products ranging from coke and resid at the bottom of the barrel up to refinery gases at the top end. Distillation divides the barrel into a number of products—gases, gasoline, kerosene, light gas oil, heavy gas oil, and resid—depending on the original composition of the crude oil. These products can be further processed to make more valuable products. Alkylation, polymerization, and isomerization make lighter products into heavier products; thermal cracking, catalytic cracking, visbreaking, and coking make lighter products from heavier products, but leave an even heavier residue. Hydrocracking is cracking in the presence of hydrogen, which leaves no heavier residue, while hydrotreating is used to remove sulfur and other impurities.

RVP and octane are the most important characteristics of gasoline, while cetane is an important characteristic of diesel. Refiners blend various products to meet the appropriate values for these characteristics to ensure good engine performance while meeting environmental regulations. In certain areas at certain times, U.S. government regulations require refiners to raise the oxygen content of fuels to reduce CO production. The most common oxygenates are ethanol and MTBE.

Oil companies run refineries to maximize profits. To do so, they should choose optimal refinery location depending on tax and transport costs while choosing crude and product slate depending on market requirements and constraints. Linear programming is a flexible tool that helps make these decisions by optimizing a linear objective function subject to numerous constraints.

A second popular use of linear programming is in solving transportation problems. Energy is often transported over long distances and often there is a choice among transit routes or modes. Electricity always travels by wire but voltage and current need to be chosen. Coal travels by rail, barge, tanker, conveyor belt, and truck. Oil and oil products travel by pipeline, tanker, barge, rail and truck. Gas travels by pipeline or can be liquefied and sent by tanker or truck. In addition, there is the choice of which producer is to satisfy which consumer. Transport costs should be minimized for all these choices subject to all capacity and demand requirements.

Often a given energy service can be supplied by a different energy product. Truck freight transport can be fueled by gasoline or diesel, cooking can be fueled by electricity or gas, and electricity can be made from fossil fuels, renewables, or nuclear sources. Linear and non-linear programming can be useful in deciding which energy product will be used to supply which energy service in the energy problems noted here.

15 Energy Futures and Options Markets for Managing Risk

The only certainty is uncertainty.

—Pliny the Elder

Introduction

Energy is often thought to be a risky business—a chance of gain balanced with a chance of loss. Energy-related personal risks include the possibility of accidents that have safety and health implications—a nuclear power plant melt down, an oil spill, an LNG explosion, air and water pollution. Energy economic risks include possible losses in real assets from falling crude oil prices, rising drilling rig costs, expropriation of a coal mine by a foreign government, a refinery fire, increasing environmental regulations on gasoline. Possible losses could also be financial, rather than from real assets.

To help pay for real assets, energy firms issue claims on the profits from them. For example, claims for Exxon-Mobil include stocks, bonds, and other financial agreements, which get their value from the value of Exxon-Mobil's underlying assets—oil leases, refineries, tankers, pipelines, and so forth.

Energy financial risk relates to possible losses from changes in the values of these financial assets issued by energy companies. (Brealy and Meyers, 1996)

Jorion (1997) cites five types of financial risks that energy companies face.

1. market risk relates to price changes of financial assets and liabilities
2. credit risk relates to defaults on contractual obligations
3. liquidity risk relates to the lack of market activity or to a failure to meet a cash flow obligation
4. operational risk relates to technical problems with financial trading systems and fraud
5. legal risk relates to losses from failures to comply with the law or adverse regulatory changes

Risk in an energy investment context relates not just to losses but also to the volatility of a return, usually defined as the variance. The popular notion of risk as losses under this definition would be downside risk. Because people tend to be risk averse, they often require a higher rate of return to compensate them for taking more risk, and they may be willing to pay to eliminate some risk. For example, an individual may prefer a sure $100 dollars invested in an asset with a 10% chance of paying $1000 (and a 90% chance of paying nothing). Although the expected values of the assets are equal ($100 and 0.10*$1000 + 0.9*$0= $100), a risk-averse person prefers the sure thing to a riskier venture (higher variance asset) with the same expected value. A risk-neutral person would be indifferent between the sure thing and the risky asset, while a risk-taker would value the risky asset more.

High volatility in energy prices since 1973 means there has been a desire on the part of some energy firms to reduce risk like never before. High volatility, coupled with developments in information technology, financial theory, and a political climate favoring market over government solutions, have led to the development of financial derivative markets. *Financial derivatives* are financial assets that derive their value from an underlying asset and represent a way of transferring risk from parties who want less risk to those who are willing to take on the risk—for a price. (Jorion 1997)

Some companies in the Power Marketing Association trade energy financial derivatives as seen at http://www.powermarketers.com. For other links on energy derivatives, see http://ourworld.compuserve.com/homepages/JWeinstein/energyde.htm.

Thus, an energy financial derivative is a financial instrument with a value based on some underlying energy asset. Siems (1997) notes that most energy derivatives are built on the foundation of three basic instruments:

- futures
- forwards
- options

An *energy futures contract* is an agreement to buy or sell a specific energy asset at some future point in time. The contract is purchased through an organized exchange with a standardized contract that can be resold on the exchange. The contract specifies the exact day that trading is closed and delivery. If you buy a June crude oil futures contract on the NYMEX for $30 per barrel, you are agreeing to buy 1000 barrels of crude oil at $30 per barrel in June. You pay a small transaction fee and put up a margin of typically less than 5% of the value of the contract.

A *forward contract* resembles a futures contract in that it is an agreement to purchase some asset in the future; however, the contract is not purchased on an exchange, nor can the contract typically be resold without the agreement of both parties. Because it is a bilateral agreement that is not standardized, it can be tailored to the individual customers needs. A 30-day forward contract to buy gas oil in Rotterdam would be a contract to buy gas oil in 30 days.

An *option* is the right to buy (call) or sell (put) an asset at an underlying price called the strike price. Energy options are usually written on futures contracts. If you own a call option to buy a natural gas future at $3 per Mcf on NYMEX, you have a right (but not the obligation) to buy natural gas at $3 per Mcf.

Energy Futures Contracts

Energy futures contracts stipulate that the buyer of the commodity has a long position and the seller has a short position. The contract date is designated by the delivery month; the exact delivery date is specified by the rules of a standard contract and varies by product.

For example, NYMEX oil futures stop trading three business days prior to the 25th of the month. On the 25th of the month, pipeline nominations are made for the next month. *Nominations* are the schedules for shipment for the next month. Thus, spot transactions for crude oil are really for delivery next month because of the time it takes to get in the pipeline queue. This means that spot and one-month futures price are almost synonymous, and the one-month futures is often used as a quote for the spot price or is designated as the spot price in contracts.

Other contracts have different last trading days, which vary from contract to contract. Samples of other contract information for energy futures and options can be can be found at www.NYMEX.com.

NYMEX accounts for an estimated 80% of the world's energy futures and options traded. Trading is done by open outcry in the trading pit and by electronic trading after hours on NYMEX Access, which began in June 1993.

A variety of energy futures contracts are traded on organized exchanges as shown in Table 15–1. Several additional contracts have been started but have been de-listed. Among the most recent such contracts are a variety of electricity contracts resulting from electricity market restructuring. NYMEX had six electricity contracts de-listed in February of 2002.

Table 15–1 Energy Futures Contracts

Product	Traded Since	Delivery	Exchange, Location	Web Page, http://
Electricity, Base	3/01	No Delivery	EEX, Germany	www.eex.de
Electricity, Peak	3/01	No Delivery	EEX, Germany	www.eex.de
Brent Crude	6/88	Sullom Voe	IPE, U.K.	www.ipe.uk.com
Gas oil	4/81	ARA	IPE, U.K.	www.ipe.uk.com
Natural Gas	1/97	NBP	IPE, U.K.	www.ipe.uk.com
Crude Oil, Light Sweet	6/02	No Delivery	Merchant Exchange, U.S.	www.merchants-exchange.net/
Crude Oil, Brent	6/02	No Delivery	Merchant Exchange, U.S.	www.merchants-exchange.net/
Natural Gas	5/02	No Delivery	Merchant Exchange, U.S.	www.merchants-exchange.net/
Gas Oil, European	1/02	No Delivery	Merchant Exchange, U.S.	www.merchants-exchange.net/
Gasoline Unleaded	6/02	No Delivery	Merchant Exchange, U.S.	www.merchants-exchange.net/
Heating Oil #2	1/02	No Delivery	Merchant Exchange, U.S.	www.merchants-exchange.net/
Electricity (forward)	93	No Delivery	NordPool (Scandinavia)	www.nordpool.com
Electricity	95	No Delivery	NordPool (Scandinavia)	www.nordpool.com
Coal, Central Appalachian	7/01	Ohio/Big Sandy Shoal Rivers	NYMEX, U.S.	www.nymex.com
Crack Spreads		NYH	NYMEX, U.S.	www.nymex.com
Gasoline, Unleaded	12/84	NYH	NYMEX, U.S.	www.nymex.com
Heating Oil #2	10/74	NYH	NYMEX, U.S.	www.nymex.com
Propane	8/87	TEPPCO	NYMEX, U.S.	www.nymex.com
Crude Oil, Light Sweet	3/83	Cushing, Oklahoma	NYMEX, U.S.	www.nymex.com

Table 15–1 Energy Futures Contracts (cont'd)

Product	Traded Since	Delivery	Exchange, Location	Web Page, http://
Crude Oil, Brent	4/01	No Delivery	NYMEX, U.S.	www.nymex.com
Natural Gas	4/90	Henry Hub, Louisiana	NYMEX, U.S.	www.nymex.com
Crude Oil, Lt Sweet EminNY	6/02	No Delivery	NYMEX, U.S.	www.nymex.com
Natural Gas EminNY	6/02	No Delivery	NYMEX, U.S.	www.nymex.com
Gasoline	7/99	Tokyo, Kanagawa, Chiba	TOCOM, Japan	www.tocom.or.jp/
Kerosene	7/99	Tokyo, Kanagawa, Chiba	TOCOM, Japan	www.tocom.or.jp/
Middle Eastern Crude	9/01	No Delivery	TOCOM, Japan	www.tocom.or.jp/
Electricity, NSW-peak	9/02	No Delivery	SFE, Sydney, Australia	www.sfe.com.au and http://www.d-cyphatrade.com.au/what_we_offer.html
Electricity, NSW-base	9/02	No Delivery	SFE, Sydney, Australia	www.sfe.com.au and http://www.d-cyphatrade.com.au/what_we_offer.html
Electricity, Vict-peak	9/02	No Delivery	SFE, Sydney, Australia	www.sfe.com.au and http://www.d-cyphatrade.com.au/what_we_offer.html
Electricity, Vict-base	9/02	No Delivery	SFE, Sydney, Australia	www.sfe.com.au and http://www.d-cyphatrade.com.au/what_we_offer.html
Electricity, SAus-peak	9/02	No Delivery	SFE, Sydney, Australia	www.sfe.com.au and http://www.d-cyphatrade.com.au/what_we_offer.html
Electricity, SAus-base	9/02	No Delivery	SFE, Sydney, Australia	www.sfe.com.au and http://www.d-cyphatrade.com.au/what_we_offer.html
Electricity, Queen-peak	9/02	No Delivery	SFE, Sydney, Australia	www.sfe.com.au and http://www.d-cyphatrade.com.au/what_we_offer.html

Table 15–1 Energy Futures Contracts (cont'd)

Product	Traded Since	Delivery	Exchange, Location	Web Page, http://
Electricity, Queen-base	9/02	No Delivery	SFE, Sydney, Australia	www.sfe.com.au and http://www.d-cyphatrade.com.au/what_we_offer.html
Electricity	05/01	Delivery point unknown	Gielda Energy SA, Poland	www.polpx.pl/news/230402.htm
Electricity, Green	05/01	Delivery point unknown	Gielda Energy SA, Poland	www.polpx.pl/news/230402.htm
Electricity, peak	05/01	Delivery point unknown	Gielda Energy SA, Poland	www.polpx.pl/news/230402.htm
Electricity, base	06/00		UKPX, England	www.ukpx.co.uk
Electricity, peak	06/00		UKPX, England	www.ukpx.co.uk
Heating Oil	04/02	No Delivery	Hannover Commodity Exchange, Germany	www.wtb-hannover.de/

All Contracts are futures contracts unless otherwise noted.

Notes: ARA = Amsterdam, Rotterdam, Antwerp; EEX = European Energy Exchange; EminNY = smaller contracts traded on the Chicago Mercantile Exchanges electronic system (Globex) but cleared on NYMEX; IPE = International Petroleum Exchange; NBP = Transco's National Balancing Point on U.K. Grid; NYMEX = New York Mercantile Exchange; NSW = New South Wales, Australia; NYH = New York Harbor; TEPPCO = Texas Eastern Product Pipeline Company; NordPool = the Nordic Power Pool between Denmark, Finland, Norway, and Sweden; Queen = Queensland, Australia; SAus = Southern Australia; SFE = Sydney Futures Exchange; TOCAM = Tokyo Commodity Exchange; Vict = Victoria, Australia;.
Source: Internet Search.

Asia has lagged behind Europe and North America in developing energy derivative markets. Fusara (1998) maintains that the greater price is due to greater regulation and state intervention in Asian markets that has limited price volatility and so the need for organized markets. Trading activity in China took off in 1993 and 1994 only to be banned by a suspicious government. The Singapore International Monetary Exchange (SIMEX), which recently merged with Stock Exchange of Singapore (SES) into the Singapore Exchange (SGX), began trading Brent Crude electronically in 1995, and the International Petroleum Exchange (IPE) and other energy derivatives with NYMEX in 1996. It has since de-listed all of its energy contracts.

An important feature of energy futures contracts is that they are *marked-to-market* every day: Contract gains and losses are settled at the end of each trading day and the contract is rewritten at the closing futures price.

For example, suppose you buy a crude oil futures contract for $30/bbl for June delivery and you have posted a margin of $3375. Under this contract you have agreed to buy crude oil at $30 a barrel in June. Some one else sells that contract for $30/bbl for June delivery and has also posted a margin of $3375.

Suppose then that tomorrow, the price of crude oil for next month delivery closes at $30.50. Since you have contracted to buy at $30, your contract gains value equal to $0.50 per barrel for 1000 barrels (a total of $500), whereas the contract that sells the crude for $30/bbl loses $500 in value. The $500 gain would be credited to your margin account and the $500 loss would be debited from the sellers' margin account. If your margin account goes below the daily minimum, you will have to bring it up to the required level or your position will be liquidated.

Such marking-to-market decreases the risk of default for derivative contracts and makes it possible to hold contracts on small margins (Hull, 2000).

In this example contract, if you closed out your contract on that day, you would have had the extra $500 exactly as though you had bought oil at $30 and sold it at $30.50 (minus a small transaction cost). Thus, any day you want to get out of the market, you can close out your position by taking the opposite position at the prevailing future's price and realize any gain or loss from the original contract.

Reviewing the history of U.S. oil prices (Fig. 15–1), we see periods of rather dramatic price volatility that resulted in the first oil futures contracts, in Pennsylvania, in 1860, which took the form of pipeline certificates. During the next 30 years, more than 10 exchanges in the United States, Canada, and Europe traded crude oil futures. With the Rockefeller monopoly—and, later, vertical integration and multinational control of the market—prices stabilized. (Weiner 1991)

It took a new round of volatility in energy prices that began with oil shocks in the 1970s, and continued on into deregulation in gas and electricity markets, to create a need for a market in risk management. Numerous energy futures contracts have been devised, as seen in Table 15–1.

- heating oil futures contracts started in 1979 at NYMEX and another started in 1981 at the IPE in London
- gasoline futures started trading on NYMEX in 1981, changed to unleaded gasoline in 1986
- contracts for West Texas Intermediate (WTI) followed in 1983 on the NYMEX and Brent Crude oil in 1988 on the IPE
- the 1990s saw successful futures contracts developed for natural gas, electricity, and, most recently, for coal at NYMEX
- Nord Pool had the first futures contract in electricity in 1993 with power click electronic trading commencing in 1996

2001 $ bbl

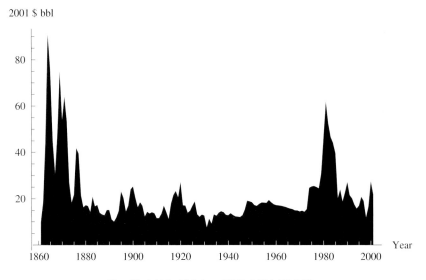

Fig. 15–1 U.S. Oil Prices 1859–2001 (2001$)

Source: 1861–1948, American Petroleum Institute, *Petroleum Facts and Figures* 1949–2001, EIA/DOE, *Annual Energy Review 2001*, http://www.eia.doe.gov/emeu/aer/txt/ptb0516.html, downloaded August 2003. Converted to real 2001 dollars using CPI from U.S. Department of Commerce, 1975, *Historical Statistics of The United States*, and U.S. Council of Economic Advisers, *Economic Report of the President 2003*, http://w3.access.gpo.gov/eop/, downloaded August 2003.

Futures exchanges are clearinghouses that act as intermediaries. They ensure performance by buying the contracts from the sellers and selling the contracts to the buyers, keeping buyers and sellers anonymous to one another. If one party in a contract fails to perform, the clearinghouse provides insurance by honoring the contract. Open contracts at the close of trading are matched, buyers to sellers, by the clearinghouse so deliveries can be made. Forward contracts generally take delivery; however, futures contracts generally take delivery on far fewer than 5% of contracts. Rather, these financial contracts are used to manage price risk: Instead of taking delivery, a futures contract holder will take the opposite position in the market so the contracts net out (e.g., a buyer of a crude futures contract [long position] sells a crude futures contract [short position]). Because so few deliveries are made, these futures contracts are sometimes referred to as paper barrels. The NYMEX petroleum futures market can be thought of as a Wall Street refinery.

Most exchanges provide information on current, as well as historical futures prices. Some of the more heavily traded energy futures are quoted in the popular press. For example, the *Wall Street Journal* lists price quotes for NYMEX futures, including crude oil, unleaded gasoline, heating oil, and natural gas; and for IPE

Brent crude and gas oil. Table 15–2 contains a sample futures quote for heating oil delivered to New York Harbor and traded on NYMEX. The contract size is 42,000 gallons and the price is in dollars per gallon.

Table 15–2 Sample Futures Quotes for Heating Oil on NYMEX

Futures Prices						Lifetime		Open
Heating Oil 1 (NYM) 42,000 gallons; $ per gal						High	Low	Interest
	Open	High	Low	Settle	Change	High	Low	Interest
June	0.7650	0.7720	0.7440	0.7504	-0.0137	0.9240	0.5550	22,011
July	0.7590	0.7660	0.7400	0.7451	-0.0135	0.8875	0.5625	30,876
Aug	0.7520	0.7630	0.7400	0.7466	-0.0115	0.8680	0.5705	11,756
Sept	0.7610	0.7625	0.7520	0.7486	-0.0110	0.8620	0.6215	8,223
Oct	0.7630	0.7640	0.7510	0.7526	-0.0105	0.8500	0.6290	4,903
Nov	0.7690	0.7690	0.7550	0.7566	-0.0100	0.8550	0.6450	6,837
Dec	0.7626	0.7740	0.7590	0.7606	-0.0095	0.8610	0.6500	15,788
Jan	0.7640	0.7700	0.7600	0.7621	-0.0090	0.8530	0.6540	4,994
Feb	0.7640	0.7650	0.7540	0.7551	-0.0090	0.8350	0.6500	4,269
Mar	0.7430	0.7430	0.7300	0.7321	-0.0090	0.7980	0.6370	4,821
Apr	0.7200	0.7200	0.7050	0.7086	-0.0090	0.7590	0.6275	2,722
May	0.6890	0.6890	0.6850	0.6856	-0.0090	0.7200	0.6140	555
Oct	0.7015	0.7015	0.7015	0.6906	-0.0095	0.7015	0.6655	107

Est. vol. 36,636; vol. Tues. 28,509; open int. 116,206; + 830.

Notes: Examples of other quotes can also be found on NYMEX's home pages at http://www.nymex.com
Source: *Wall Street Journal*, May 16, 2003:B7.

The first column is the month of the delivery date. The "open" is the first price of the day, "high" is the high price for the day, "low" notes the low price for the day, and "settle" is the last price of the day. The "change" is the difference in the settle price from yesterday to today. Since an April contract was down $0.0090 from yesterday, it must have closed yesterday at $0.7176. Note that all contracts beyond May were down $0.009. This is the maximum allowable daily change for months beyond the first two. (For more details on the maximum daily changes see, www.NYMEX.com, futures and options, heating oil, specifications.) Lifetime "high" and "low" represent the highest and lowest prices these contracts ever attained. "Open interest" is the number of contracts outstanding at the close of the day.

At the bottom of the quotes is "estimated volume," which tells the total number of futures contracts traded. The volume for Tuesday represents trading for the day before this quote. The open interest was the total number of contracts of all maturities that were open at the close of trading. The last number (+830) indicates that open interest was up 830 from the day before. A negative value would have indicated that open interest was down.

Another somewhat similar energy derivative is the forward contract, operating as over-the-counter (OTC) markets because they are not traded on organized exchanges but are bilateral—between two individual entities. They are typically not standardized but represent an agreement to buy or sell an energy product in the future at an agreed-upon price. A Brent crude oil forward market developed in the 1980s because there was no European crude oil futures market. (Brent forward contracts are unusual because the contracts *are* standardized.) Bilateral trades are made via telephone, telex, and fax. With no clearinghouse, all transactions and transacting parties must be tracked individually.

The series of bilateral agreements in this market (called daisy chains) are riskier than futures contracts because a default by one party can cause a whole series of defaults with no clearinghouse to provide insurance. Such a default happened in 1986, when crude oil prices fell from around $30 to under $10; some parties refused to take delivery and pay the higher contracted price. This refusal caused defaults down the rest of the chain. However, the Brent forward market survived.

There is less price transparency in the crude forward market than in the crude futures market, although *Platt's, Petroleum Argus,* and other news services survey participants and report prices daily. Delivery is at the Sulom Voe terminal in the North Sea. Since 15 days notice is required to schedule tankers to pick up the crude, contracts for the next month can be traded only up until the 15th day of the month before delivery. This is why the Brent forward market is sometimes called the *Brent 15-day market.* Cargoes nominated for delivery after the 15th of the month can still be traded but are traded on the spot market and are called *dated Brent.* (Slade et al., 1993, Weiner, 1988)

Hedging with Energy Futures

Energy futures contracts can be used to hedge (reduce the effects of) risk, to speculate and take on risk for an expected profit, and to plan cash flows for storage, transport, and processing. A *hedger* is a buyer or seller of a real commodity (commonly, an oil producer or refiner) who takes a position opposite of the forward or futures market. A producer holding crude is said to be long crude, so he sells, or shorts, a forward; a refiner who is short on crude buys a future; a speculator who is neither buyer nor seller of the product takes on risk for a profit.

To understand how this works, look at the following example. (We will ignore transaction and storage costs.) A trader has a barrel of crude in transit. He pays the current spot price ($S_t = \$18$) for the crude. Upon delivery at time T, he receives the spot price (S_T). If the price has risen to $19, he gains $1. Thus, he can lose or gain money depending on S_T. This is shown in three sample delivery prices in Table 15–3.

Table 15–3 Gains and Losses in the Spot Market at Various Prices

S_t	S_T	Gain or Loss (S_T - 18)
$18	$17	-$1
$18	$18	$0
$18	$19	$1

Now, if the trader wants to hedge, he sells a forward contract at t for delivery at T at a price of F_t^T. (Forward examples are used instead of futures because marking-to-market introduces some additional complexities that do little to change the value of F_t^T.) Suppose the contracted forward price is $F_t^T = \$18$ to deliver oil at time T. This means the trader has contracted to sell oil at $18 per barrel at time T. At T, the contract is worth (F_t^T - S_T = $18 - S_T) per barrel.

Thus, if the trader has contracted to sell oil at $18 but others are selling oil for only $17, the contract is worth $1; if the price rises to $19 and he has contracted to sell at $18, he will lose $1. Compare the value of the contract barrel with the value of a barrel of cargo (S_T = $18) at the same prices as above (Table 15–4).

Table 15–4 Gains and Losses in the Spot and Forward Markets at Various Prices

S_T	$S_T - S_t$ Spot Market	$F_t^T - S_T$ Forward market	Combined Market
$17	-$1	$1	0
$18	$0	$0	0
$19	$1	-$1	0

Note that what he gains or loses in the real market is offset in the futures market. Thus, he has been able to reduce the affective price volatility to himself. The cost has been his transaction cost.

The purchaser of the futures contract could have been another hedger, such as a refinery, or it could have been a speculator. If the buyer is a speculator, he experiences the full risk from price changes in the market; speculators take on risk, and hedgers shed risk. One can estimate the number of hedgers and speculators from the U.S. Commodity and Trading Commission (http://www.cftc.gov/) reports on commitment of traders (COT) by exchange and product. *Commercials*—those that deal in the derivative market and deal in the product—are considered hedgers. The *non-commercials* do not handle the physical product and are considered speculators. In July of 2003 more than half of the traders of crude oil on the Nymex were considered hedgers.

In the above example, the product for the spot and the futures market were the same. However, the two products do not have to be the same to use one to hedge the other; only the prices need be correlated.

What determines energy futures prices on financial assets?

An important phenomenon influencing futures prices is *arbitrage*, which is the simultaneous buying and selling of the same product to make a profit without any cash requirement or risk.

For example, if Deutsche marks are trading for $0.50 in one market and $0.51 in another market, you can buy them for $0.50 and resell them for $0.51 in the other and make a profit (unless transaction costs are more than $0.01). Arbitrage assures that in competitive *transparent markets* (one in which everyone knows the prices), the price of the same product should be the same across markets excluding transportation and transaction costs.

Arbitrageurs therefore help to promote market efficiency. It's easiest to see how using a diagram. (Fig. 15–2.)

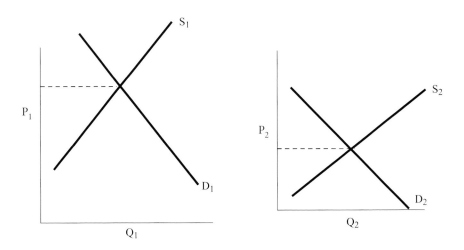

Fig. 15–2 Two Markets Before Trade

Suppose we have two markets before trade. Price is P_1 in market one and P_2 in market two. Now open the two markets to trade. Provided transaction and transportation costs are less than $P_1 - P_2$, trade should take place. To simplify our exposition, assume that transaction and transportation costs are zero. The good is cheaper in market two, so traders will buy in market two and resell the product in market one. As more product is purchased in market two, the price will increase in market two. As more product is sold in market one, the price will fall. The reallocation will continue until the prices are equal across markets as at P_T in Figure 15–3.

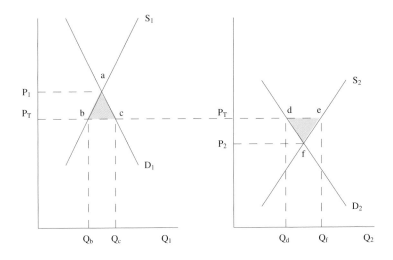

Fig. 15–3 Two Markets after Trade

Now market one consumes Q_b from the home market and imports $Q_c - Q_b$. Market two produces Q_f of which Q_d is consumed by the home market and $Q_f - Q_d$ is exported. For the market to be in equilibrium $Q_c - Q_b = Q_f - Q_d$.

We can also easily see the net welfare gains in the two markets. In market one, producers lose $P_T P_1 ab$ but consumers gain $P_1 acP_T$. Market one has a net gain of abc. In market two, the gains are the opposite. Consumers lose $P_2 P_T df$ but producers gain $P_2 P_T ef$ for a net gain in market two of def. Thus, the market is more efficient after the trade since there has been a net gain in welfare in both markets.

Now let's see how arbitrage and the underlying spot price influence a futures price. We start with the simplest case—the futures price of an asset sold at discount with no income. For example, you buy a U.S. Treasury bill (T-bill) at $9700. It redeems for $10,000 at maturity in 12 months. You receive no income from the bill and you get the difference between what you paid and the redemption value. The price of this security will vary over time as the interest rate changes until maturity, but will approach the redemption price as the asset approaches maturity.

Thus, if you hold the asset to maturity you have no price risk and know exactly what price you will receive. However, if you need cash and plan to sell the asset before maturity, you have price risk. One way of mitigating this price risk is to buy a futures contract. However, before you do so, you must know if the futures contract is properly priced.

Let's see what the futures price for such an asset should be. Suppose you will sell the T-bill at T, where T is some date before maturity of the bill. Take a futures contract for time T. S_T is the spot price of the bill at time T, which is unknown. S_t is the current spot price. F_t^T is the futures price at time t to be paid at T and r is the risk free rate of return considered here to be your cost of carry. Then:

$$F_t^T = S_t e^{r^*(T-t)}$$

The price for a futures contract should be equal to the principal and accrued interest over the time period (T − t). To see why, suppose that $F_t^T > S_t e^{r^*(T-t)}$. You will pay more for the asset at T by holding the futures contract than if you purchased the asset at time t and held it until T. Arbitrageurs would want to sell the futures contracts F_t^T and buy spot at S_t, thus lowering F_t^T and raising S_t. You can use the risk-free rate in this context to lock in a certain profit: You lock in the current price when you buy at S_t and you lock in the futures price when you sell F_t^T, as well.

Suppose you pay $930 for a discounted bond that you will sell in six months. If the annual risk-free rate is 6%, its futures price should be F = $930e^{0.06*0.5}$ = $958.3. But suppose F = $950. Since the futures contract is cheaper than the security at T, you should buy the futures for $950 and sell the bond for $930 (if you don't own the bond, sell it short). Put the $930 into the market at 0.06 percent yielding $930e^{0.06*0.5}$ = $958.3 at time T. Then buy the bond at the contracted $950 for a profit of $8.30. However, as arbitrageurs buy the futures, its price will rise and as they sell the bond, its price will fall until no money can be made from arbitrage of F = $S_t e^{0.06*0.5}$. Hull (2000, p.38).

What determines energy future prices on financial assets?

Modeling futures prices for energy commodities is slightly different than for energy stocks and bonds because commodities incur storage costs in addition to interest costs.

Suppose we have a barrel of oil today at S_t. The cost to delivery at T would be $[(S_t + U_t)^*e^{(r)^*(T-t)}]$, where U_t is the unit storage cost at time t, which we assume is paid up front for the whole time period. Alternatively, storage could be paid out over the storage period—perhaps once a month. In such a case, U_t would be the present value of storage costs at time t. Initially, we would expect the forward price at time t for delivery at T would be:

$$F_t^T = (S_t + U_t)^*e^{(r)^*(T-t)}$$

Often the convenient assumption is made that storage costs are some constant percent of the spot price (e^μ). Then we would expect the futures price at time t to be:

$$F_t^T = (S_t)e^{(r+\mu)*(T-t)}$$

For commodities bought and sold for actual consumption instead of just investment, there may be some additional benefits from holding inventories. This additional benefit is called a *convenience yield* (δ). Inventories can stabilize the production process by filling in during shortages or when there is higher-than-anticipated demand. In such periods, prices are likely to be higher; if you are holding stocks during these periods, you can benefit from the higher prices. Alternatively, in periods of weak demand or supply surpluses, prices may fall and inventory holders incur a cost or negative benefit of having stocks. The net benefits that result from holding inventories do not accrue to those who only hold futures contracts. If there are additional net benefits to the holder of stocks (δ), we can subtract this benefit from the costs of holding the inventory. The formula for the futures price then becomes:

$$F_t^T = S_t e^{(r+\mu-\delta)*(T-t)}$$

If $r + \mu - \delta > 0$, then $r + \mu > \delta$. This shows that the convenience yield is smaller than carrying costs, which are interest and storage. Such a market is called a *normal* or *contango market*, and F_t^T (for further out contracts) increases. (Fig. 15–4.)

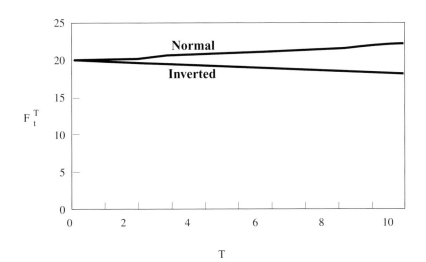

Fig. 15–4 Futures Prices Today by Maturity Date

For example, if r = 1%, μ = 1%, δ = 1%, and S_t = 20, then by substituting into the formula, we obtain:

$$F_t^T = S_t e^{(r + \mu - \delta)*T} = S_t e^{(0.01 + 0.01 - 0.01)*T}$$

For T = 5, we have:

$$F_t^T (T = 5) = \$21.025$$

For T = 10, we have:

$$F_t^T (T=10) = \$22.103$$

If $r + \mu - \delta < 0$, then $r + \mu < \delta$, and the convenience yield is larger than carrying costs (interest and storage). Such a market is called a *backward* or *inverted market* and further-out futures prices are lower. If there is a supply or demand shock with low inventories, we expect δ to be high and the market is more likely to be in *backwardation*. With high inventories, δ is more likely to be low or even negative and the market would be normal or contango.

With information on spot prices, future prices, and storage costs, you can easily compute the convenience yield. If storage is a percentage of the spot price, then:

$$F_t^T = S_t e^{(r + \mu - \delta)*T}$$

By taking the natural log, we obtain:

$$\ln F_t^T = \ln S_t + (r + \mu - \delta)*T$$

Solving for δ, we obtain:

$$\delta = r + \mu + (\ln S_t - \ln F_t^T)/T$$

Alternately, if storage is a fixed fee U_t, then convenience yield can be solved from:

$$F_t^T = (S_t + U_t)e^{(r - \delta)*T}$$

Taking the natural log again, we obtain:

$$\ln F_t^T = \ln(S_t + U_t) + (r - \delta)*T$$

Solving for δ, we get:

$$\delta = r + [\ln(S_t + U_t) - \ln F_t^T]/T$$

Convenience yields for Brent Crude are shown in Figure 15–5.

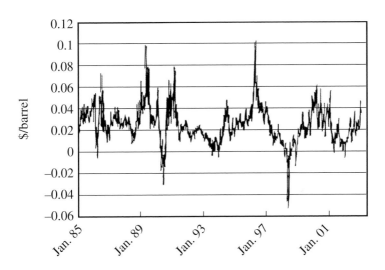

Fig. 15–5 Three-Month Convenience Yield for U.S. Light Sweet Crude Oil, January 1985 to January 2003.

Source: Three month convenience yields created from NYMEX Futures Data Reported at EIA/DOE, World Market Crude Oil Price Data, Daily NYMEX Light Sweet Crude Oil Futures Prices (U.S. dollars per barrel), April 4, 1983 to Present, http://www.eia.doe.gov/emeu/international/petroleu.html#IntlPrices, downloaded August 2003 and U.S. AAA Corporate Bond interest rates reported at http://www.federalreserve.gov/releases/h15/data/b/aaa.txt, downloaded August 2003. Monthly per barrel storage costs are assumed to be $0.30 per barrel paid at the beginning of each month, personal communication with Thorsten Viertel, Shell Group).

Convenience yields averaged $0.037 per barrel in 1985. However, Saudi netback pricing instituted in August of that year—followed by production increases—caused prices to spiral down at the beginning of 1986. Convenience yields fell and became negative briefly in March 1986. They rebounded and spiked in June. With OPEC's failure to reach a production agreement, they fell again, averaging around $0.03 per barrel from 1986 to 1988. They had been a bit higher in 1987 when prices averaged near $19 per barrel but a bit lower in 1986 and 1988, when price averaged between $15 and $16 per barrel. In late 1988, OPEC reached a production agreement and markets tightened. Oil prices—and convenience yield—increased, averaging more than $19 and $0.043 per barrel.

To determine whether the market was in backwardation, compare the one-month and four-month futures prices in Figure 15–6.

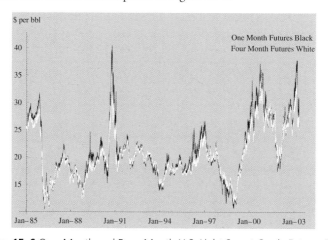

Fig. 15–6 One–Month and Four–Month U.S. Light Sweet Crude Futures Price

Source: EIA/DOE, World Market Crude Oil Price Data, Daily NYMEX Light Sweet Crude Oil Futures Prices (U.S. dollars per barrel), April 4, 1983 to Present, http://www.eia.doe.gov/emeu/international/petroleu.html#IntlPrices, downloaded August 2003.

The one-month futures is a good proxy for the spot price: When the futures price is lower than the spot, the market is in backwardation. When the futures is higher than spot, the market is in contango. The market was in backwardation during the gluts of 1985 and in contango during the beginning of 1986. Although price was falling, the market must have expected a rebound.

Prices generally trended up through 1989, but markets started to weaken in March 1990. Convenience yields fell and remained very low or negative from May until August 2, 1990 when Iraq invaded Kuwait. They rebounded, reaching a peak in February 1991, when it was clear that Saddam Hussein's forces would be routed. Convenience yields then trended down with a weak economy and increasing production from OPEC and the North Sea, becoming negative briefly in December 1993. The markets were in backwardation throughout the Gulf crisis until May of 1991.

Oil prices fluctuated around $20 per barrel throughout 1991 to 1993. Iraq was out of the market; Kuwait tried to regain prewar production. Turmoil in the FSU cut its oil exports. Convenience yields were high but fell as production began to recover. By 1993, OPEC and North Sea production increases were again putting downward pressure on oil prices. The market was in contango throughout 1993 as oil prices and convenience yields drifted down. Through 1994 and 1995, OPEC did not increase its quota and oil prices and convenience yields edged upward.

Through 1996, a strengthening world economy improved prices and convenience yields. The market was in backwardation, as is common when markets are tighter. Prices and convenience yields continued to fall through 1997 and most of 1998 as the Asian economy sank into deep recession, Iraq sold oil for humanitarian revenue, and OPEC produced over quota. The market again went into contango. In March, 1999, OPEC agreed to cut production; Norway, Mexico and Russia agreed to cuts as well. With these cuts and a recovering Asian economy, prices and convenience yields began to rise and the market went into backwardation.

With the terrorist attacks on the U.S. World Trade Center on September 11, 2001 and the ensuing weakened U.S. economy, the market again went into contango and convenience yields fell. By March 2002, oil production cuts, a strengthening U.S. economy, and the U.S.-Iraqi sparring over weapons inspections raised oil prices, increased convenience yields, and again put the market into backwardation. For greater detail of recent oil market history, see DOE's *Oil Price Chronicles* at http://www.eia.doe.gov/cabs/chron.html

Efficient Market Hypothesis

One of the oft-cited advantages of energy futures markets is that they provide price transparency and reveal information on energy price expectations. This efficient market hypothesis suggests that the futures price (F_t^T) plus any necessary risk premium (RP) is a good predictor of the spot price. Therefore, the expected spot price for electricity at PJM (the Pennsylvania, New Jersey, Massachusetts ISO) in an efficient market would be:

$$E(S_T) = F_t^T + RP_t$$

Absence of a risk premium would suggest that hedgers dominate the market on both sides in roughly equal numbers with no need for speculators. Significant speculators in the market would require an expected return and the risk premium would then not be zero. A statistical test of the efficient market hypothesis under the assumption of no risk premium could be done with the following function:

$$S_T = \alpha + \beta F_t^T$$

The null hypothesis of no-risk premium and market efficiency against the alternative of an inefficient market and/or a risk premium would be:

$$H_o: \alpha = 0 \text{ and } \beta = 1$$

Against:

$$H_1: \alpha \neq 0 \text{ and/or } \beta \neq 1$$

Herbert (1993) performed this test for the U.S. natural gas futures market and was able to reject the null hypothesis (that $\alpha = 0$ and $\beta = 1$) for November 1992 through February 1993. He concluded that the gas market was inefficient and also noted that other studies found such inefficiency in the early years of the U.S. crude oil futures markets. What is more likely is that the risk premium is not equal to zero; since, if markets were inefficient, there would be ways to systematically make profits. For example:

$$E(S_T) > F_t^T + RP_t$$

If so, then you should buy the futures since it would go up in value as you approached the end of trading. As all players tried to make profits, the profits would be dissipated. Indeed, Deaves and Krinsky (1992) find a risk premium in the crude oil market that varies over time.

Crack and Spark Spreads

Various derivatives can be combined into trading strategies. One such popular strategy is a crack spread: A refiner buying crude oil and selling products makes money on price differentials and is more interested in the difference between the crude and product prices than in the absolute price level of each. To lock in a spread, a hedger can simultaneously buy crude futures and sell product futures. To illustrate a crack spread, consider U.S. refinery output on February 25, 2000, for the four most important products. (Fig. 15–7.) Prices and actual quantities of these products are shown in Table 15–5.

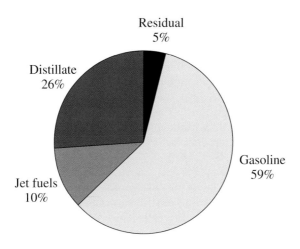

Fig. 15–7 U.S. Refinery Mix for Four Most Important Products, April 2003

Source: Computed from data in *OGJ* 4/28/03:98

Table 15–5 U.S. Refinery Products and Prices, April 2003

	1000 b/d	$/bbl
Gasoline	8,474	$35.57
Jet fuel	1,420	*$35.00
Distillate	3,787	$35.00
Residual	708	$24.88
Refinery Inputs	16,316	
Crude		$28.10

Note: *Estimated from distillate price.
Source: Computed from data in *OGJ*, 5/5/2003: 6, 98, 100

The weighted average value for products in this example would be:

0.59*35.57 + 0.10*35.00 + 0.26*35.00 + 0.05*24.88 = $34.84

The *crack spread*—the weighted value of the products minus the price of the crude oil—equals:

$34.84 - $28.10 = $6.74

In reality, the crack spread is slightly different from the above value because all the products from a barrel have not been accounted for. In the futures market, a derivative crack spread will ignore an even larger share of the barrel.

A typical crack spread will be a 3-2-1, with three barrels of crude for every two barrels of gasoline and one barrel of heating oil (distillate). Because price variations on spreads are typically less than on individual contracts, margins per contract will be smaller with a spread. (See http://www.NYMEX.com under futures and option crack spreads for typical margins.) A refinery seeking to hedge would sell a crack spread to buy crude oil and sell product futures. If you hedge for a refinery, you sell the spread closest to your product slate.

A newer trading strategy, the spark spread, and is intended to simulate the profits from a power plant. It was possible from 1996 to 2002 to hedge or sell such a spread on NYMEX by shorting electric power and buying the fuel used for generation (fuel oil, natural gas, or coal). However, in May 2002, the electricity contracts on NYMEX became OTC and so spark spreads must be bought and sold that way. Spark spreads have also started trading OTC in Europe.

As discussed previously, hedging in both futures and forward markets stabilizes prices for the hedger. They minimize downside risk and also upside profits. The profits and losses can be spectacular for speculators without the offsetting assets in the cash market. In 1992, Showa Shell, a Japanese refiner and distributor 50% owned by Shell oil, lost more than $1 billion in foreign exchange markets. Traders bought billions of unauthorized dollars forward in 1989 at an average exchange rate of ¥145. The traders rolled losses over from year to year without reporting them and were not found out until 1992. By the end, the dollar was trading at ¥125. (See: http://www.stern.nyu.edu/~igiddy/gfmup2.htm) Kashima oil, another Japanese company, also lost more than $1 billion speculating in dollar forward markets.

In a more complicated trading strategy, MG Refining and Marketing (MGRM)—a subsidiary of Metallgesellschaft A.G., Germany's 14th largest industrial firm in 1993 and 1994—contracted to supply gasoline and heating oil at fixed prices for 10 years. It then hedged these forward contracts with futures and other OTC assets. So far, so good. But MGRM had a problem. The hedging was in short-term assets, but the forward contracts were long term. Thus, the short-term assets had to be continuously rolled over. Such a strategy can work when markets are in backwardation or prices are falling but not when they are in contango or prices are rising, as they were through 1993 and the beginning of 1994 causing MGRM to lose about $1.5 billion.

Energy Futures Options

In both futures and forwards derivatives, owners are obligated to buy or sell an energy product at a set price; the derivatives effectively set prices for the given product at some point in the future. However, sometimes market participants only want to protect themselves from (or take advantage of) price increases or price decreases. For example, an electric generator that uses gas as a fuel may want to put an upper limit on its fuel price but a lower limit on the price it receives for electricity. In such cases, the power generator would want to turn to options markets.

An option allows (but does not obligate) the contract holder to buy or sell an asset at a set price (known as the *strike* or *exercise price*) by a certain date. For energy futures options, the underlying asset is a futures contract rather than the physical commodity itself. A *call option* gives the holder the right to buy a futures contract; a *put option* gives the holder the right to sell the futures contract.

For example, suppose an electricity generator holds a NYMEX June call option on a futures contract for natural gas at Henry Hub with a strike price of $2.60 per MMBTU. This option gives the generator the right to buy 10,000 MMBTUs for $2.60 per MMBTU any time up to four business days prior to the delivery month. Thus, the generator will not have to pay more than $2.60 for natural gas. Buying the call option effectively locks in a maximum price. If the same power generator bought a put option on an electricity futures contract for $50 per MWh, it has the right to sell its power for $50 per MWh. Buying a put option locks in a minimum price.

Options are not new; tulip options were traded as long ago as the 1600s in Holland, stock options on the London Stock Exchange in the 1820s, and options were traded OTC on commodities in the 1860s in the U.S. Exchange. Trading of U.S. stock options started in 1973 on the Chicago Board Options Exchange. The first energy futures option was for light sweet crude oil on the NYMEX in 1986. Option contracts and when they began can be seen in Table 15–6.

In February 2002, a number of electricity options were de-listed on the NYMEX and then re-introduced as OTC instruments in May of that year. (http://www.NYMEX.com, click on OTC Services) The newest options to be listed are calendar spreads for various products, introduced in June 2002.

Table 15–6 Option Contracts Listed as of July 1, 2002

Product	Traded Since	Delivery	Exchange	http://
Electricity-base (European)	9/89	No Delivery	Nordpool	www.nordpool.com
Crack Spread	10/94	NYH & Cushing	NYMEX	www.nymex.com
Natural Gas	10/92	Henry Hub	NYMEX	www.nymex.com
Brent Crude	9/01	No Delivery	NYMEX	www.nymex.com
Crude Oil Light	11/86	Cushing	NYMEX	www.nymex.com
Brent Crude Oil Calendar Spread	6/02	No Delivery	NYMEX	www.nymex.com
Brent/WTI Crude Oil Spread	9/01	No Delivery	NYMEX	www.nymex.com
Heating Oil	6/87	NYH	NYMEX	www.nymex.com
Heating Oil Calendar Spread	6/02	NYH	NYMEX	www.nymex.com
Natural Gas Calendar Spread	6/02	NYH	NYMEX	www.nymex.com
Light, Sweet Crude Oil Calendar Spread	6/02	Cushing	NYMEX	www.nymex.com
Gasoline Unleaded	3/89	NYH	NYMEX	www.nymex.com
Gasoline Unleaded Calendar Spread	6/02	NYH	NYMEX	www.nymex.com
Brent Crude	5/89	Sullom Voe	IPE	www.ipe.uk.com
Gasoil	7/87	ARA	IPE	www.ipe.uk.com

Notes: ARA = Amsterdam, Rotterdam, or Antwerp Harbor; NYH = New York Harbor.
Source: Exchange homepages and other Internet resources.

Options are not marked-to-market but, as with futures, are traded three ways:

- on organized exchanges with open outcry
- OTC using telephone, fax, and telex
- electronically

The buyer does not need to put up a margin since he owns the option outright, but the seller must post margin if the option is written on an exchange.

There are two types of basic put and call options. An American put or call option can be exercised any time up to expiration, but a European put or call option can only be exercised on the expiration date. Whether the option is American or European depends on the rules of the exchange, and not whether the exchange is in the Americas or Europe. American options dominate exchanges worldwide, but since European options are much simpler to value, they are the usual starting point for a discussion of options.

Most OTC options are European. These basic put and call options are called *plain vanilla* options while more complicated options (*exotics*) trade OTC rather than on organized exchanges. An example of an exotic is an Asian option, in which the value of the option depends on the average price of the underlying asset over some period of time. (Hull, 2000)

Pricing options

To help us understand options, Kolb (1994) begins with a European option, which can only be exercised at the expiration date. Since the call option gives the owner the right to buy the underlying asset at price K, the value of a European call at expiration depends on the spot price at expiration (S_T) of the underlying asset and the strike price K. If the price of the underlying asset exceeds K, the call owner can buy the asset for K and resell it for S_T making a profit of $S_T - K$. (Fig. 15–8) Below K the option has no value and will not be exercised.

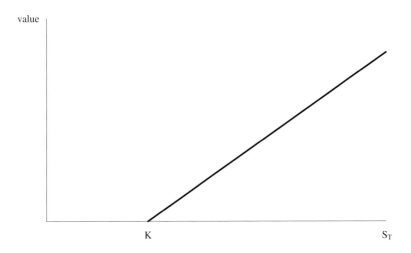

Fig. 15–8 Value of a European Call Option at Expiration

Options, whether they can only be exercised at time T or not, may have value at other times. A call is said to be "in the money" at time t if $S_t > K$; "at the money" if $S_t = K$, and "out of the money" if $S_t < K$. If S_t is much higher than K, the option is said to be "deep in the money;" if S_t is much less than K, the option is said to be "deep out of the money."

A put option offers the right to sell the underlying commodity at price K. The value of a put at expiration also depends on S_T and K. If the price of the underlying asset falls below K, the put owner can buy the asset for S_t and resell it for K making a profit of $K - S_T$. (Fig. 15–9.)

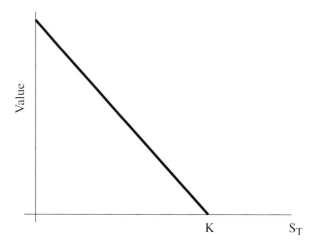

Fig. 15–9 Value of a European Put Option at Expiration

At prices for the underlying asset above K, the put has no value and will be allowed to expire. A put is in the money at time t if $S_t < K$, at the money if $S_t = K$, and out of the money if $S_t > K$. Selling an option is the same as shorting or writing an option; buying an option is the same as going long.

European options may assume four positions and each option's payoff depends on the price of the underlying asset at expiration. These positions and their payoff formulas are as follows:

- long call with payoff = max $[S_T - K, 0]$
- long put with payoff = max $[K - S_T, 0]$
- short call with payoff = -max $[S_T - K, 0]$
- short put with payoff = -max $[K - S_T, 0]$

Notice that the short position is the negative of the corresponding long position. Also, since S_T is not bounded, possible payoffs are infinite with a long call, and the corresponding possible losses are infinite for a short call. Thus, call writers may put themselves at considerable risk and are required to post margins. Typically, only large players write options; these include oil trading companies and large banks.

The formulas we've thus far considered show the payoff of the option at various spot prices; however, since we do not know what the spot price will be at S_T, we do not know the value of the option or what we should pay for it. Suppose we pay C_t for the call and P_t for the put at time t. Let $C_T = (1+r)C_t$ and $P_T = (1+r)P_t$, where r is the interest rate for the time period (T-t). Then the net payoff at the expiration of the above puts and calls at various spot prices are:

- long call with payoff $= \max [S_T - K - C_T, - C_T]$
- long put with payoff $= \max [K - S_T - P_T, - P_T]$
- short call with payoff $= -\max [S_T - K - C_T, - C_T]$
- short put with payoff $= -\max [K - S_T - P_T, - P_T]$

Options quotes

The price of an option is what it costs to buy it (the C_t and P_t from the previous section). Prices of some of the more popular options are quoted regularly in the financial press. For example, the option quote in Table 15–7 for natural gas at Henry Hub, traded on the NYMEX, is from the *Wall Street Journal*.

Table 15–7 Energy Futures and Options Quotes, May 15, 2003

Futures Option Prices

Natural Gas (NYM); 10,000 MMBtu; $ per MMBtu.

Strike Price	Calls-Settle			Puts-Settle		
	Jun	Jul	Aug	Jun	Jul	Aug
605	0.269	0.511	0.666	0.188	0.340	0.451
610	0.244	0.486	0.643	0.213	0.365	0.477
615	0.222	0.463	0.620	0.241	0.392	0.504
620	0.201	0.440	0.598	0.270	0.419	0.532
625	0.181	0.419	0.576	0.300	0.448	0.560
630	0.164	0.400	0.556	0.333	0.479	0.590

Notes: Est. vol. 47357 WD 21,277 calls; 11,703 puts
Op. int. Wed 506,310 calls; 440,510 puts.
Source: Wall Street Journal, 5/16/2003:B7.

The contract size is 10,000 MMBTU, measured in dollars per MMBTU. The first column is the strike price measured in cents per MMBTU. The next six columns are the price of puts and calls measured in dollars per MMBTU.

To discover the total option cost, multiply the option price times the contract size. For example, the right to buy 10,000 MMBTU in June for $6.05 per MMBTU would cost $0.269*10,000 = $2690. The buyer is obliged to pay the full cost of the option and cannot buy an option on margin. The last trading day is three business days before the first day of the next month. The seller of the option always gets to keep the cost of the option, whether the buyer exercises the option or lets it expire.

These market quotes tell us how the market values various puts and calls at a specific time. In the next sections, we will use the binomial pricing model to learn how to compute values for C_t and P_t.

Valuing Options

To use financial derivatives efficiently for hedging and speculation, it is important to know their values. To learn how to value options, we will start with a one-period binomial pricing model from Kolb (1994).

Suppose an underlying asset is worth $100 this period at time t. We assume the price of the asset can go up to $110 or fall to $90 next period T when the option expires. If we have a call option on this asset with a strike price of $100, the option will be worth either $10 or $0 next period. (Fig. 15–10.)

Fig. 15–10 Valuing a Call from an Underlying Stock Price

To learn the value of the call option today (C_t) we come up with a portfolio that is equivalent to the call option; arbitrage assures that portfolios with the same payoff will have the same value. To begin, we will look at such a portfolio and then see how to derive one. First buy one half of the above stock (It will be equal to $55 or $45 after one period.) (Fig. 15–11.)

Next, sell a bond worth $42.45 at the risk-free rate, which is 6%. It is worth –$42.45 now. Next period T you will have to pay back –(1 + 0.06)*42.45 = –$45.00 as shown in Figure 15–12.

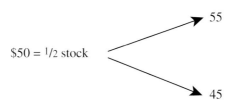

Fig. 15–11 Value of One-Half of a Stock In One Period

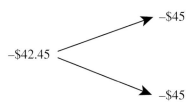

Fig. 15–12 Value of a Borrowed Bond in One Period

After a year, if the stock goes up, you will have $55 – $45 = $10. If the stock goes down, you will have $45 – $45 = 0. These payoffs are equivalent to the payoffs for the call option. So this portfolio must indeed have the same value as the call, or else there would be an arbitrage opportunity. The nice thing about this portfolio is that we know its value right now:

$$0.5S_t - 42.45 = \$50 - \$42.45 = \$7.55$$

We now know the value of the above call option to be $7.55. Since we can always find a replicating formula composed of the underlying asset and a risk-free bond, we can always value the option. It is quite easy to find a replicating portfolio (port) at time t.

Let N equal the number of shares of stock; B_t equal the value of the bond purchased, and r equal the risk-free interest rate. The portfolio now is equal to:

$$\text{Port} = N^*S_t + B_t. \qquad (15.1)$$

At time T, the debt equals the amount borrowed plus the interest or $B_T = (1 + r)^*B_t$. Assume the stock price goes up or down by the fraction n. Let $U = 1 + n$, $D = 1 - n$, and $R = 1 + r$. The portfolio value at expiration, if the stock price goes up, is:

$$\text{Port}_{u,T} = N^*U^*S_t + R^*B_t$$

The portfolio value at expiration, if the stock prices goes down is:

$$\text{Port}_{d,T} = N^*D^*S_t + R^*B_t$$

Designate the two values of the call option (10 and 0 in the previous example) to be c_u and c_d. Thus, c_u is the value of the call when the stock goes up, and c_d is the value of the call when the stock price goes down. To make them equal to the portfolio, set:

$$\text{Port}_{uT} = N*U*S_t + R*B_t = c_u = S_T - K = 10 \qquad (15.2)$$

$$\text{Port}_{dT} = N*D*S_t + R*B_t = c_d = 0 \qquad (15.3)$$

Solving for N and B_t tells you how many shares of the stock or underlying asset to buy and the value of the bonds you must buy.

$$N = (c_u - c_d)/[(U - D)*S_t], \qquad (15.4)$$

$$B_t = [c_u*(D) - c_d*(U)]/[(U - D)*(-R)] \qquad (15.5)$$

Once we know how many stocks and bonds to buy or sell, we can value the portfolio and, hence, the call option. In the above example:

$$N = (10 - 0)/[(1.1 - 0.9)*100] = 0.5$$

$$B_t = [(10*0.9) - (0*1.1)]/[(1.1 - 0.90)*(-1.06)] = -42.45$$

The solution tells us to buy half a stock and sell $42.45 worth of bonds. The value of the portfolio is, as before:

$$N*S_t + B_t = 0.5S_t - 42.45 = \$50 - \$42.45 = \$7.55$$

Puts can be valued in a similar way. What is interesting about these problems is that we do not need to know the probability of the stock price going up or down to value the option, nor do we need to know the investor's risk preferences. Whether the investor is risk averse, risk neutral, or risk experienced never enters the computation.

However, if we assume risk neutrality, we can convert the above value into probabilities. We will find such a conversion useful when we move to the multi-period binomial model. Further, since the valuation is not affected by the risk preferences of the investor, it does no harm to assume risk neutrality, but it gives us some valuable results.

To compute such probabilities, let p equal the probability that the stock goes up to 110 and $1 - p$ equal the probability that the stock price goes down to $90. The expected value of the stock in one year is $(p)*110 + (1 - p)*90$. A bond at the risk-free rate would be equal to 106 with certainty. If an investor is risk-neutral, he would find the stock and the bond portfolio equal in value; otherwise, prices would change to make them equal in value. Hence, we can estimate a probability p that would make these two portfolios equal in value or:

$$(p)*110 + (1 - p)*(90) = (1 + r)*100 = (1.06)*100 \qquad (15.6)$$

Solving for p:

$$110*p - 90*p = 106 - 90$$

$$p = 16/0.20 = 0.8$$

So the probability that the stock price goes up can be represented by 80% and the probability that the stock price goes down, 20%. Using these values, we can also value the option as follows:

$$[0.8*(10) + 0.2*(0)]/(1.06) = \$7.55$$

The numerator is the expected value of the stock and the denominator discounts that value of the stock back to the present. Note that this trick (which will prove useful in the multi-period valuation) yields the same value as earlier. Similarly, the general formula for probability under risk neutrality can be derived as follows:

$$(p)*US_t + (1 - p)*DS_t = (1 + r)*S_t = (R)*S_t$$

Solving, we get:

$$p = (R - D)/(U - D) \qquad (15.7)$$

What if there are two periods to maturity? To see what happens in this case, use a European put option, which expires after two periods. Let the spot price of the stock be 100 and the strike price be 101. The price increases/decreases are 10% and the risk free rate is 5%. The problem seems more complicated, but we can use the tools already developed to value the put option.

First, set up the lattice to view the various possible spot prices for the underlying asset shown below. The lattice has two nodes in period t+1. B is the node when the underlying asset goes up ($S_{t+1} = (1 + 0.10)*100 = 110$) and C is the price when the underlying asset goes down ($S_{t+1} = (1 - 0.10)*100 = 90$). There are three nodes in t+2. D is the node when the price goes up in t+1 and t+2 ($S_{t+2} = 1.1*1.1*100 = 121$). E is the node when the price has gone up in t+l period and down in t+2 or down in t+1 and up in t+2 ($S_{t+2} = 1.1*0.9*100 = 99$). F is the node where price has fallen in t+1 and t+2 ($S_{t+2} = 0.9*0.9*100 = 81$). (Fig. 15–13.)

These nodes also have implied values for our put option. For example, at node D, the stock value is 121; we have the right to sell the stock value at 101, and our put option is worth nothing. At node E, we have the right to sell our option at 101 and the price is 99. Our put option is worth $101 – $99 = $2. At F, our put is worth $101–81 = 20$. If we could find a replicating portfolio that gives us 0 when the stock price is 121 and 2 when the stock price is 99 and 20 when the stock price is 81, then we could value the put option. However, that is more difficult now than in the one-period case.

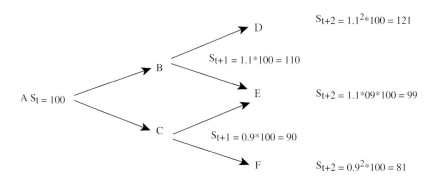

$S_{t+2} = 1.1^2*100 = 121$

$S_{t+1} = 1.1*100 = 110$

A $S_t = 100$

$S_{t+2} = 1.1*09*100 = 99$

$S_{t+1} = 0.9*100 = 90$

$S_{t+2} = 0.9^2*100 = 81$

Fig. 15–13 Value of an Underlying Asset in a Binomial Lattice

At node C, the situation is a bit more complicated. At first we might guess that the stock option is worth 101 – 90. However, this is a European option and we cannot exercise it at C; we can only hold it until the stock goes up to 99 or down to 81, or we can sell it to someone else. But a buyer cannot exercise the option until t+2, either. But if we know the probabilities of the stock price going up to 99 (p) or down to 81 (1–p) it is easy to value the option at node C:

$$P_C = (p*2 + (1-p)*20)/(1+r)$$

Similarly, we can easily price the option at node B.

$$P_B = (p*0+ (1-p)*2)/(1+r)$$

Now, to get the present value of the put at time t (represented by node P_A in Fig. 15–14), we follow the same procedure:

$$P_A = (pP_B + (1-p)P_C)/(1+r)$$

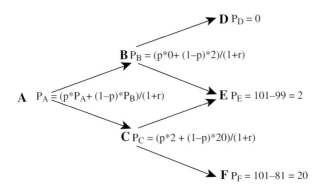

D $P_D = 0$

B $P_B = (p*0+ (1-p)*2)/(1+r)$

A $P_A = (p*P_A+ (1-p)*P_B)/(1+r)$

E $P_E = 101-99 = 2$

C $P_C = (p*2 + (1-p)*20)/(1+r)$

F $P_F = 101-81 = 20$

Fig. 15–14 Value of a Put Option in a Binomial Lattice

We have now successfully computed the value of the European put at each node in the lattice. What remains is to compute the p values as above, using equation 15.2. Since the price increases and decreases are 10%, then U = 1.1 and D = 0.9. Since the risk-free rate is 5%, R = 1.05 and the probability of a price increase is:

$$p = (R - D)/(U - D) = (1.05 - 0.9)/(1.1 - 0.9) = 0.75$$

The probability of a price decrease is:

$$(1-p) = 1 - 0.75 = 0.25$$

With these tools, we can compute the probability of the underlying asset being at each node, the probability of the put at each node, and the value of the put at each node:

- If the price rises from now until the first period (from node A to node B), then S = 1.1*100 = 110. The probability of a price increase is 0.75.
- To go from node B to node D, the price would have to increase twice, so the stock value would be 1.1*1.1*100 = 121; the probability would be equal to 0.75*0.75 = 0.5625.
- To go from node C to node F, the stock is worth 0.9*0.9*100 = 81. The probability of going from C to F would be 0.25*0.25 = 0.0625.
- Since there are two ways to get to E from A, you would add together the probabilities or 0.75*0.25 + 0.25*0.75 = 0.375.

Value of the stock at nodes of a two-period lattice and the likelihood of being at each node are shown below in Figure 15–15.

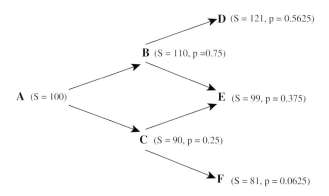

Fig. 15–15 Lattice with the Underlying Asset Value and Probability of Each Node

We can now also fill in the values for the above put as shown in Figure 15–16.

To value a European put (which can only be exercised at maturity), we find the value of the put at each node by staring at the end period.

- At D, if the stock price is 121 and exercise price is 101, the put is worth nothing
- At E, if the stock price is 99 and the option is to sell at 101, the option is worth $2
- At nodes A, B, and C, the value of the put is the discounted present value of the option at maturity, the option cannot be exercised

Thus, if you are at B, the only two possibilities would be for the put to go to D with probability 0.75 or to value E with probability 0.25.

- The value of the put at B would be (0.75*0 + 0.25*2)/(1.05) = $0.476
- The value at node C would be (0.75*2 + 0.25*20)/(1.05) = $6.19
- From A, all possible end nodes could be reached and the value would be (0.5625*0 + 0.375*2 + 0.0625*20)/(1.05)² = $1.81
- Alternatively, get the value by discounting back from the values at B and C as follows. (0.75*0.476 + 0.25*6.19)/1.05 = $1.81

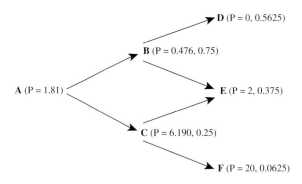

Fig. 15–16 Valuing a European Option with a Two-Period Binomial Lattice

Thus, the current value of a European put for the above stock is $1.81.

For an American option, the expected value of the put at points D, E, and F would be the same as for the European option (or the max [0, K – S_T]). Points A, B, and C might vary because you exercise the put at B and C if it is more valuable than to hold it to maturity. Thus, the problem is a bit more complicated.

Suppose you are at point B; if you hold the stock to maturity your discounted present value of the put is the same as for the European put ($0.476). The value of the put, if you exercise, is 0. You are better off holding, so the value of the put is the same as for the European put. At C, however, the value of your put, if you hold it to maturity, is [(0.75*2 + 0.25*20)/1.05 = $6.190], but if you exercise it, the value is $101 – $90 = $11. You are better off exercising your put, and so the value at C becomes 11. The value of the option at point A equals (0.75*$0.48 + 0.25*$11.00)/(1.05) = $2.83. (Fig. 15–17.)

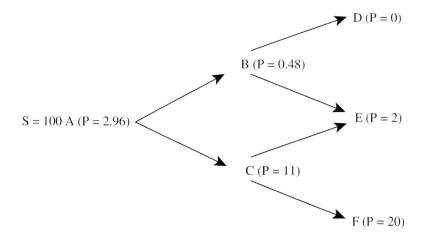

Fig. 15–17: Valuing an American Option with a Two-Period Binomial Lattice

With more time periods, you extend the model to more lattices and use the same procedure, starting at the expiration date and working backward.

Until now we have assumed that we know how much the price goes up or down in a future period, which we do not know for an asset. However, under some reasonable assumptions about how price changes are distributed, we can estimate a discrete price change approximation from historical data on price changes. (Kolb 1994) To understand such an approximation, we will take daily crude oil spot prices for Brent from 1991 to 2000.

First we translate price changes into rates of return. Remember, the rate of return on oil for a day is any capital gains or losses from one day to the next divided by the original value of the asset $[(S_{t+1} - S_t)/S_t = \Delta S_t/S_t]$. Thus if oil on Tuesday is 25 and oil on Wednesday is 25.50, the rate of return from Tuesday to Wednesday is $(25.50 - 25)/25 = 0.02$ or 2%.

Next, we approximate price changes by exponential functions for easier computation. Let $S_t = e^{\mu t}S_0$, where μ shows us how price changes from period 0 to t. If μ is positive, price increases; if μ is negative, price decreases. It is easy to see that μ is the continuous rate of return from period 0 to t. The proof is as follows: For very short time periods, we can approximate ΔS_t by its derivate $dS_t/dt = \mu_t e^{\mu t}S_0$.

The continuous rate of return is then:

$$(dS_t/dt)/S_t = \mu e^{\mu t}S_0/e^{\mu t}S_0 = \mu$$

Taking logs of the formula $S_t = e^{\mu t}S_0$, we get $\ln S_t = \mu t + \ln S_0$. Then $\mu t = \ln S_t - \ln S_0$. When t=1 then the continuous rate of return $\mu = \ln S_1 - \ln S_0$. Since μ can vary daily we can write the daily rate of return as $\mu_t = \ln S_t - \ln S_{t-1}$. The variance of μ_t is:

$$\hat{\sigma}^2 = \sum_{i=1}^{n} (\mu_t - \bar{\mu}_t)^2/(n-1)$$

Suppose you find that the variance for the daily Brent crude oil rate-of-return is $\hat{\sigma}^2 = 0.00052$ and the annual risk-free rate from three-month T-bills is 0.05. If your lattice has a daily period, then you can compute your D and U as follows:

$$U = \exp[(\hat{\sigma}^2)^{0.5}] = \exp[(0.00052)^{0.5}] = 1.02307 \qquad (15.8)$$

$$D = 1/U = 0.97745 \qquad (15.9)$$

$$R = 1 + r/365 = 1.00014 \qquad (15.10)$$

The risk-free probabilities can be computed from equation 15.7:

$$S_t{}^*U^*p + S_t{}^*D^*(1-p) = B_t{}^*(R)$$

If the current spot price for oil is $S_t = 30$, you can buy an equal value bond for $B_t = 30$. The investor is risk-neutral, so:

$$p = (R-D)/(U-D) = (1.00014 - 0.97745)/(1.02307 - 0.97745) = 0.497$$

Once you have U, D, r, and p, you can then use the binomial lattice method to compute the value of European and American puts and calls that expire any number of trading days out using the methodology discussed.

However, with approximately 250 trading days in a year, using a daily lattice method for one option for one year out would require a 250-period lattice. This can be cumbersome to compute, since the number of nodes at the end of the year would be 2^{250}. So, often lattices are computed using longer time periods, such as a week or a month. If your lattice period is a week, convert your variance to weekly data by multiplying by five—the number of trading days in a week—and use the weekly interest rate $= r/52$. If your lattice period is a month, convert your variance to monthly data by multiplying by 20—the average number of trading days per month—and use the monthly interest rate $= r/12$.

To complete our example using weekly data, first convert your variance to weekly data:

$$\hat{\sigma}^2_w = 5{*}\hat{\sigma}^2 = 5{*}0.00052 = 0.0026$$

Next, apply equations 15.8 and 15.9 to compute U and D:

$$U = \exp[(\hat{\sigma}^2_w)^{0.5}] = \exp[(0.0026)^{0.5}] = 1.05231$$

$$D = 1/U = 1/1.05231 = 0.95029$$

Next, compute the risk-free probabilities from equation 15.7. Suppose the risk-free annual rate taken from U.S. three-month T-bills is 5%. To get a weekly interest rate, divide the annual rate by 52 to get r = 0.05/52 = 0.00096.

$$p = (R–D)/(U–D) = (1.00096 – 0.95029)/(1.05231 – 0.95029) = 0.497$$

Now apply the lattice technique. To sum up the procedure for valuing options:

- use historical data to calculate the variance of returns for the underlying asset. For energy options it would be a futures price
- choose the division for your lattice
- convert your variance to correspond to the unit period of your lattice if necessary
- compute U and D using equations 15.8 and 15.9
- find the risk free interest rate for the periodicity of your lattice
- compute p using equation 15.7
- with U, D, and p, set up the lattice for the underlying asset
- using the underlying asset compute the value of the option at each expiration node
- for a European option, compute nodes prior to expiration by taking the discounted present value of the option at the next nodes
- for an American option, compute nodes prior to expiration by choosing the higher of the discounted present value of holding the option with the value of exercising

Variables that Affect Option Prices

Kolb (1994) discusses a number of variables that should affect the value of an energy option. These effects are summarized in Table 15–8 for American options.

As the underlying asset price increases, the call value increases because the likelihood of its being in the money increases. The reverse is true for a put. At a higher exercise price, the in-the-money region is smaller for a call and larger for a put, lowering the value for the former and raising the value of the latter. More risk or volatility for the underlying asset means more chance that the underlying asset will take on extreme values or more chance that the option will be deep in or out of the money. However, the downside is limited to zero so both puts and calls increase in value. If expiration is more distant, there is more time and more possibility to be "in the money" and so both options increase in value.

Table 15–8 Variables that Affect American Option Values before Expiration

Variable	Value of Call	Value of Put
1. Underlying Asset Price ↑	Up	Down
2. Exercise Price ↑	Down	Up
3. Asset Risk ↑	Up	Up
4. Time until expiration ↑	Up	Up
5. Interest rate ↑	Up	Down

Source: Kolb (1994).

If interest rates increase, Kolb's argument is a bit more complicated; you can think of a call as a potential liability that you would have to pay when exercising the option. The higher the interest rate, the lower the value of this future liability and the higher the call price. The opposite argument is made for a put: The put represents an asset or a payment when exercised at some future point. When discounted back at a higher interest rate, the value of this asset becomes less, reducing the value of the put. For more detail and arbitrage examples to demonstrate these principles in the no-dividend case, see Kolb (1994).

Option Trading Strategies

As with futures contracts, you can assemble option contracts into trading strategies. The contracts can involve a real asset and an option such as a covered call (in which you are long in product and you short a call). Alternatively, strategies may involve more than one option.

To examine the value of combining options at different strike prices, we focus on the value of European options at expiration. Remember: net profits for the buyers of a call and a put at expiration are:

$$\pi^{C}_{T} = \max(-C_t, S_T - K - C_T) \qquad (15.11)$$

$$\pi^{P}_{T} = \max(-P_t, K - S_T - P_T) \qquad (15.12)$$

Where K is the strike price, S_T is the spot price at expiration, C_T is the cost of the call and P_T is the cost of the put, both ncluding the interests costs until expiration. The costs or values of the calls and puts are a function of the spot and strike price at expiration, T.

Now, suppose you buy a put with P_T = $2.63 and a call with C_T = $0.78. Both have strike price 31. You want to value this trading strategy at the underlying asset prices S_T. To do so, value them separately and add together the values of the separate options. This is called a *long straddle*—buying a put and a call at the same strike price. You calculate the value of the straddle by adding the values of the put and call. Graphing the values of the put and call into two columns shows you the value of the

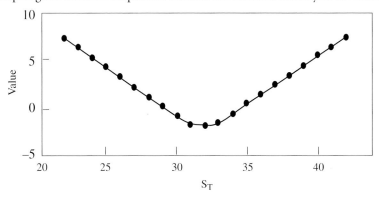

straddle. (Fig. 15–18.)

Fig. 15–18 Valuing a European Straddle at Expiration

You can see that such a strategy straddles the strike price—hence, its name. If you expect lots of volatility but don't know whether it will be above or below the strike price, this might be a good trading strategy. Examples of other spreads and a file for modeling them are available at http://dahl.mines.edu. Click on trading spreads.

Energy Swaps

Energy swaps are the most recent derivatives in financial markets, dating from the early 1980s. A swap is an agreement to exchange cash flows in the future according to some agreed upon formula; as with forward markets, these are bilateral OTC agreements.

Often the swap is an exchange of cash flows with one at a fixed rate and the other at a floating rate—a plain vanilla swap. For example, a U.S. independent energy company swaps a fixed natural gas price for a floating price with J. P. Morgan; Morgan accepts the differential from a fixed price of $2.35 per Mcf for five years. Under this agreement, if the price falls below $2.35, Morgan pays the independent the difference between $2.35 and the market price; if the market price goes above $2.35, the independent pays Morgan the differential. (*Oil and Gas Investor*, Vol. 15, No. 4, April, p. 28) In this way, the independent enjoys a fixed price of $2.35 for gas, while Morgan bears the result of the price differentials.

The agreement, which does not require up-front payments, stipulates the amount of the commodity covered by the swap, the length of the agreement, the price index that is the basis for the financial swap, and the frequency of payment. Fewer than three months is considered short term, while long term is six months to 30 years. Thus, swaps can provide much longer-term protection than futures contracts.

Swap agreements are bilateral agreements and are usually not publicly disclosed outside of some of the financial news services such as Reuters, Dow Jones, Bridge News, and Bloomberg. Swaps have not traditionally traded on exchanges until NYMEX introduced swaps trading for 25 common products on May 31, 2002. Although NYMEX swaps remain bilateral and provisions are confidential, the exchange provides default insurance by guaranteeing both sides of the transactions. Parties must maintain margins and the contracts are marked-to-market.

For more information on these contracts, go to http://www.NYMEX.com and click on OTC Services, then click on Product Slate. For a list of companies that belong to the International Swaps and Derivatives Association go to http://www.isda.org/. You will note that the majority of the members are large banks or other financial intermediaries. However, a few notable energy companies involved in the swap market are Duke Energy, Exxon-Mobil, El Paso Energy, and Elf Trading.

Summary

Market risk—volatility in energy prices and returns—is a fact of life for the corporate manager. Success requires that risk be properly managed. Sometimes companies may want to shed risk; at other times they may want to limit themselves to commercial risk; at still other times, they may take on more risk than what is considered normal.

Energy financial derivatives—futures, options, forwards, and swaps—can be used to manage energy market risk. They increase market efficiency by breaking up risk into pieces and transferring the pieces to those who will accept them at least cost. A corporation or other entity can accept the risks its wants and transfer the remainder to others. Thus, those who have a comparative advantage in dealing with a particular form of risk will take it on, and—as in any trading situation—such a trade will tend to make both parties better off.

A hedger deals in the real commodity and uses the financial markets to lock in a price and transfer risk; a speculator does not deal in the commodity itself but trades derivatives to try to make a profit and, in the process, provides liquidity to the market. Unwise speculators can put themselves at great risk; the landscape is littered with energy company driven billion-dollar mistakes in the derivative markets.

Energy price derivative schemes have come and gone over the past 150 years as price volatility has waxed and waned. With higher energy price volatility since 1973, a number of futures and options contracts on crude oil, oil products, natural gas, electricity, and coal have been developed and are traded on organized exchanges including NYMEX and the IPE.

A modern futures contract locks in a future price on an energy commodity. Going long in a futures contract locks in a future price to buy the underlying commodity while going short locks in a future price to sell it. Most futures contacts are not held until delivery but are resold and used to lock in the price of a future transaction. A clearinghouse—an intermediary for derivatives sold on organized exchanges—guarantees contract performance by buying contracts from sellers and selling contracts to buyers with buyers and sellers anonymous to each other. The clearinghouse concept, and the fact that futures contracts are marked-to-market every day, keeps transaction costs and default risk low.

To use futures to increase risk-management efficiency, it is important to know what a futures price should be. The futures price of a financial asset that does not pay dividends depends on the current financial asset price and the carrying costs according to the formula:

$$F_t^T = S_t e^{r\,*(T-t)}$$

The futures price of a commodity depends on the current commodity price, the discount rate, storage costs, and any convenience yield that results from holding the commodity according to:

$$F_t^T = S_t e^{(r + \mu - \delta)*(T - t)}$$

A convenience yield that is smaller than carrying costs means the market is normal, also called in contango. Here, futures prices are higher than the current spot price. The opposite is called a backward or inverted market; here, futures prices are lower than the current spot price.

Advantages of futures markets are that they provide price transparency and reveal information about price expectations. If futures markets are efficient, the expected spot price is equal to the futures price plus a risk premium. If the market is predominantly composed of hedgers on different sides of the market, the risk premium may be very small.

Spreads are trading strategies that include more than one financial asset. Selling a crack spread—buying a crude future and selling product futures—allows a refinery to hedge its refinery margin. Selling a spark spread—selling electricity futures and buying fuel futures—allows an electric utility to lock in a profit margin.

Futures options are another way to manage financial risk in energy markets. A futures option gives the holder the right to either buy or sell a futures contact on an energy commodity at a specified price. A call option allows the purchase of a futures contract; a put option allows its sale. An American option can be exercised anytime up to its expiration date, while a European option can only be exercised at expiration. An option price depends on the underlying asset price, the exercise price, the asset risk, the time until the expiration, and the interest rate.

An option can be priced by finding a portfolio consisting of the underlying asset and risk-free bonds carrying the same payout. Arbitrage arguments suggest that the option should then have the same price as the portfolio. This price does not depend on the probability that the underlying asset price goes up or down or on the investor's risk preferences, so we can assume that the investor is risk free and create probabilities that the underlying asset prices will go up or down. Using the variance of the underlying asset, a binomial lattice model, and computed probabilities, we can compute the value of an option for discrete time periods. The shorter the discrete time periods and the longer time until expiration, the more complicated these computations become. Companies who write options and make a living by managing risk use computer programs to help compute option values.

Options can be used to hedge and speculate and can be combined into trading strategies. Depending on how you think prices will evolve, various spreads may help you to manage risks. These include the straddle, strangle, bull, bear, ratio vertical, back, butterfly, and condor spreads.

The newest derivative is a swap; as with forward markets, swaps are usually bilateral OTC agreements not traded on exchanges. They can cover much longer periods than futures and options with time frames up to 30 years. They often involve financial transactions that allow parties to swap fixed for floating prices or interest rates.

16 Energy and Information Technologies

Technology changes, economic laws do not.

—Hal Varian, Dean of the School of Information
Management, University of California, Berkeley

Introduction

Technical changes in energy production and in the nature of their end-use products and services have profoundly affected the quality of life throughout recorded history. Technical changes—and the rate of these changes—have varied over the course of history, with acceleration since the industrial revolution.

Long-wave theory suggests that periods of accelerated technical change and groups of inventions spur economic growth and create cycles; for example, textiles provided change in the late 1700s and early 1800s, as did coal and steel in the late 1800s, electricity in the early 1900s, and petrochemicals in the 1950s. The information revolution of the 1990s was spurred by development of telecommunication protocols, electronic improvement of network automation, the transition from analog to digital, and growth in bandwidth.

Information technologies are not new; they evolved hand-in-hand with computer technology. In the early 1960s the technology began on mainframe computers with electronic fund transfer (EFT) and electronic data interchange (EDI). Originally transactions were carried on bilateral connections; by the 1970s, they were being conducted on value added networks (VAN) as banks and other large corporations needed a cheaper, safer, and faster way to track and transfer funds and information. Transaction standards were proprietary to the specific network. At the same time, the first business packages were used for accounting and others soon followed. First-generation office information systems in the late 1970s included Digital Equipment's Decmail, IBM's Display Writer, and Wang's Office Information System.

Supervisory control and data acquisition (SCADA) systems, which remotely control processes for pipelines, offshore oil, and gas production and electric utility production, transmission, and distribution, were early energy applications of information systems. *Relays*—electro-mechanical devices to turn current on and off—were used as early as the 1930s to control remote power stations in Sweden. Through the 1950s and beyond, systems were transformed from relays to *transistors*, which had no moving parts and were faster and more reliable. Custom-built SCADA systems remotely measure and collect data on pressures, pump status, compressor status, temperatures, tank levels, valve status, possible leaks, and current levels, among other assignments. SCADA systems can also be used to control processes through starting and stopping equipment and opening and closing valves.

Telephone lines, microwaves, and radio waves are also used to transmit data back to a central control station. Central command-and-control stations—with banks of computer screens and dials—allow the control of an entire system from a central location. Early applications were run on mainframes, then mini-computers, and finally microcomputers, beginning in the 1980s.

The proliferation of disparate computer systems meant that communication between and among them became more and more complex. As a result, software companies arose to provide customized business software to run on these various systems. Packages included accounting, provisioning, manufacturing resource planning (MRP), enterprise resource planning (ERP), and customer relationship management (CRM).

The development and mass acceptance of the personal computer (PC)—the Apple II in 1977 and IBM units in 1981—meant that disparate PC systems emerged, requiring inexpensive, off-the-shelf operating systems and standard applications such as word processing, spreadsheets, and databases. Moore's Law, with computing power doubling every 18 months, accentuated the problem.

This led to the rise of software companies like Microsoft, which was launched in 1975 to provide off-the-shelf business software to run on PCs. Sun Microsytems, launched in 1982, provided workstation replacements for mainframes by using a modular framework that could grow with its company clients. These powerful

Unix-based workstations could be connected to different classes of server depending on the users' computing needs. Landmark Graphics, founded in 1982, built the first workstation for geoscientists to analyze seismic data, which had been done on very large mainframes such as Cray supercomputers. Also during the 1980s, computer-aided design (CAD), engineering (CAE), and manufacturing (CAM) became quite common.

The second-generation mainframe office systems of the early 1980s evolved into third-generation systems by the end of the decade. Digital Equipment's All-in-One became All-in-One Phase II and IBM Profs became Office Vision; both moved to a client/server mode with PCs hooked to a centralized server. In this common model (still prominent today), the server that provides basic services and stores data for the client might be located and maintained at the vendor's site. The client processes the data locally and may be connected to the server by a private network or by the Internet.

Clients with a very limited service are called *thin clients;* a server that provides applications, data, and computing power is called an application service provider (ASP). Coffman (2000) lists the following ASP advantages:

- data integration and interpretation
- security
- wideband network access
- messaging and directories
- web servers
- document management
- shared applications
- network monitoring
- data management, storage, and retrieval

An oil industry example is Geonet Services (www.geonet.com), started in 2000 and offering almost 300 applications on its server for a range of vendors and clients who only pay for the time they use on an application.

Networks evolved in parallel with computers and provided powerful tools for connecting users to each other. Networks became ever more powerful as the number of connections increased with their value increasing as the square of the number of connections (Metcalfe's Law). The Internet, with a burgeoning number of connections, was initially sponsored by the U.S. military; later, other government branches developed it to maintain communication during a nuclear attack. It was designed to connect military, research, and educational institutions; commercial access was allowed beginning in 1991. The development of the worldwide web (www) in 1989 at CERN in Geneva allowed people to access documents over the Internet.

CERN's first version of Hypertext Markup Language (HTML) was released in 1991 as well. This language, which included tags to define data in the file and allowed links to other documents, developed out of the General Markup Language

(GML) from 1979. It was released by the American National Standards Institute (ANSI) in early 1983. The International Standards Organization (ISO) developed its version—the Standardized Generalized Markup Language (SGML)—in 1986. It is also referenced as ISO8879:1986.

Mosaic, developed at the University of Illinois in 1991, became the first commercial-grade Internet browser when it was made available in 1993. By 1994, there were an estimated 3 million Internet users, mostly in the United States. With its appealing graphical interface, the Internet became so popular that the government privatized it in 1995. Its use has mushroomed as a communication tool for business, consumers, and the government. By 2000, just over half of U.S. households had a computer and just over 40% of them had Internet access. By 2001, more than 60% of the U.S. population had Internet access and more than 400 million people worldwide used the Internet. (Table 16–1.)

Over time, many different applications had been implemented at the enterprise level to solve many different problems—procurement, logistics, accounting, and so forth. J.D. Edwards estimates that more than half of Fortune 500 companies still have more than two computer platforms that need to be linked together and to outside trading partners. Making all these applications communicate with each other is called Enterprise Application Integration (EAI). One of the key events that triggered EAI was the 1996 Telecom Act: the Baby Bells were forced to open their systems and to provide gateway solutions to enable access. The companies that required access (competitive local exchange carriers) also needed new tools to access customer and "telephony" usage data. Companies such as Vitria, Tibco, and BEA were instrumental in providing these EAI software tools.

Parallel changes occurred in energy industries. Grinpelc and Siegfried (2000) outline how the transition toward information technology has evolved in the oil and gas industry. Originally mainframe computers analyzed data and field samples. Special customized engineering applications developed for mainframe platforms were followed by customized applications for back-office activities, including financial, human resource, and distribution functions. Later desktop PCs and portable field computers allowed work independent of any central platform, and even in the field. Customized software gave way to packaged software while stand-alone applications became increasingly networked via intranets or attached to client-server technologies. More recently, integration has occurred across enterprise, data and technical platforms.

In the front office—sales, marketing, and core business activities—advances include seismic, engineering, geological tools, and e-commerce activities, while back-office enterprise resource planning (ERP) develops enterprise-wide information systems that productively network front-office, back-office, customers, and suppliers together. ERP allows real-time integration, analysis, and reporting of all enterprise activities, data, and transactions.

Standardized information business packages, with versions focused on the energy industry, have been developed for information applications including ERP,

Table 16–1 Population and Estimated Internet Users for Selected Countries

Country	Population in Millions	Internet Users in Millions	Percent Internet Users
Argentina	37.4	2.0	5.3%
Australia	19.4	5.0	25.8%
Austria	8.2	2.7	32.9%
Belgium	10.3	2.7	26.2%
Brazil	174.5	6.1	3.5%
Canada	31.6	14.2	44.9%
China	1,300.0	22.5	1.7%
Colombia	40.3	0.7	1.7%
Denmark	5.4	1.6	29.6%
Egypt	70.0	0.5	0.7%
France	60.0	11.0	18.3%
Germany	83.0	26.0	31.3%
Iceland	0.3	0.2	60.1%
India	1,000.0	5.0	0.5%
Italy	57.7	11.0	19.1%
Japan	126.8	22.0	17.4%
Malaysia	22.2	2.0	9.0%
Mexico	101.8	2.3	2.3%
Netherlands	16	6.8	42.5%
Philippines	82.8	2.0	2.4%
Romania	22.4	0.6	2.8%
Russia	145.0	7.5	5.2%
Saudi Arabia	22.8	0.3	1.3%
South Africa	43.6	1.5	3.4%
South Korea	47.9	16.7	34.9%
Spain	40.0	7.0	17.5%
Sweden	8.9	4.5	50.6%
Switzerland	7.3	3.4	46.6%
Taiwan	22.3	6.4	28.7%
Thailand	61.8	4.6	7.4%
Turkey	66.5	3.7	5.6%
Ukraine	48.8	0.8	1.5%
United Kingdom	59.6	33.0	55.4%
U.S. (2001)	278.0	168.0	60.4%
U.S. (1998)*			26.2%
Sum 66 countries#	**4,459.5**	**421.0**	**9.4%**

Notes: #Estimated to have 90% of Internet users.
Sources: http://www.isp-planet.com/research/2001/census.html, downloaded 3/9/02,
Statistical Abstract of the United States.

CRM, human resource management (HRM), data warehousing (DW)—sometimes called business intelligence (BI)—and supply-chain management (SCM), which provides links between the internal systems using ERP and outside suppliers and customers along the whole supply chain.

As energy (and other industries) engage in deregulation, and as the Internet becomes more accepted and pervasive in enterprises, EAI is becoming even more powerful through next-generation EDI. EDI has been renamed business-to-business (B2B). B2B is powerful, but still a bilateral relationship. Therefore, EAI offers another level of transaction management, through trading partner networks (TPN). TPN uses a hub or brain to connect partners (businesses) to each other through the Internet. Only the best EAI tools can provide such an advanced infrastructure. ANX began by connecting auto part suppliers and industrial users but has been extended into chemical, logistics, manufacturing and other industries. RosettaNet connects computer part manufacturers and builders to each other. Using these TPN services, rather than the earlier dedicated VANs, allow businesses to reduce transaction costs and inventories.

As electronic data transfer has evolved, so have standards for the data transfer. The oldest standard, X12, evolved out of proprietary EDI standards from the 1960s. In 1979, ANSI's Accredited Standards Committee (ASC) was asked to devise an EDI standard for the U.S. That standard, ASC X12, first published in 1984, has been continually updated and expanded and has become the U.S. EDI standard. Around this same time, a second standard emerged in Europe—the Guidelines for Trade Data Interchange (GTDI). The two standards caused confusion; some companies requested an international standard. This led the United Nations Economic Commission to Europe (UN/ECE) to develop yet another standard, the Electronic Data Interchange for Administration, Commerce, and Transportation (UN/EDIFACT). Since 1987, it has been accepted by the International Standards Organization as the world standard. (http://www.iso.org)

Although ASC X12 was to converge with UN/EDIFACT to one world standard by 1997, both standards remain, with EDIFACT more predominantly used by Europe and ASC X12 more predominantly used by the United States. A sample, comparing the two formats, can be found on page nine of the Electronics Industry Data Exchange Association's file http://www.eidx.org/publications/classes/EIDX-EDIFACT-Intro.pdf.

Moving EDI from private VANs and TPNs to the Internet is the task of the EDI over-the-Internet (EDI-INT) working group of the Internet Engineering Task Force (IETF), formed in 1996. Their applicability statement (AS1), which began testing in 1997, uses Simple Mail Transfer Protocol (SMTP) and HTML. SMTP sends messages in ASCII text. The AS2, which began testing in 2000, uses the Multipurpose Internet Mail Extensions (MIME) protocol and HTTP. MIME sends messages in binary code and can send attachments in ASCII text as well as other medias such as pictures, audio, or video. The EDI-INT standards cover the packaging and sending of ASC X12, EDIFACT, or information in any other format over the Internet, ensuring compatibility and security. Essentially, it is the envelope for the data and does not concern itself with the contents.

The non-profit GISB, renamed the North American Energy Standard Board (NAESB) and found at www.naesb.org, in January 2000, has been at the forefront in developing EDI Internet standards for the natural gas industry. GISB was formed in 1993 in response to federal deregulation of pipelines in the United States. In 1995 and 1996, it developed its electronic delivery mechanism (EDM) to provide a standard for Internet data delivery in the wholesale gas industry. FERC endorsed GISB standards in 1996. Originally GISB/NAESB standards were based on X12 and HTTP but more recently, NAESB standards converged with those of the Automotive Industry Action Group (www.aiag.org) into EDI-INT AS2, which was developed by the Internet Engineering Task Force. In January 2002, NAESB expanded into developing standards for the wholesale and retail electricity markets and the retail gas market. Its standards are now endorsed and used by many in the gas, automotive, electricity, and health care industries. They are thought to be the most widely used EDI standard in the United States. Group 8760 (www.8760.com) implements NAESB standards through its software, InsideAgent. In January 2003, the North American Electricity Reliability Council (NERC) and NAESB began a collaboration to coordinate their business standards and reliability efforts.

Another major EDI development came with Extensible Markup Language (XML) in 1996 with its introduction to commerce by Ariba and CommerceOne in 1997. This *meta-language*, a language to create a language, was specifically designed for the Internet. Although it uses tags like HTML, it's more flexible because you create your own data tags. And these tags do more than define how the text looks on a page, which is HTML's main mission: In XML, tags define the data on the page. The Electronics Industry Data Exchange Association, at http://www.eidx.org/publications/classes/EIDX-XMLIntro.pdf, illustrates this difference.

XML data can be converted to HTML through the use of style sheets for display purposes (such as a catalog), or can be left as is if display is not needed.

XML is much more cumbersome that EDI. However, XML is rapidly gaining ground because it provides more information and is especially suitable for cheaper, web-based information transfer. For example, access to a VAN may cost $10,000 to $30,000 per month; Internet access typically costs a fraction of this. Currently, many initiatives in XML are being developed along various lines.

The World Wide Web Consortium (W3C), at http://www.w3.org, is responsible for the syntax (indicating the basic structure of the language without any attention to meaning). For example, that tags need an open and closing bracket [<data>xxx</data>] is a syntax rule. A second area of development is the semantics of the language, which relates to the meaning of the various tags. Various organizations are working on semantics.

The third area of development is called the architecture of the language. This has to do with registry of businesses and processes, storage, messaging, and routing and data transport. At least three groups are working in this area. The United Nations Centre for Trade Facilitation and Electronic Business (UN/CEFACT), along with the Organization for the Advancement of Structured Information Standards (OASIS), are sponsoring open access ebXML. (http://www.ebxml.org/). Microsoft is sponsoring Biztalk. IBM, Ariba, and Microsoft began Universal Description, Discovery, and Integration of Web Services (UDDI) which has recently been folded into OASIS. For more discussion and tutorials on standards, see the Electronic Industry Data Exchange Association classes at *http://www.eidx.org/publications/eidxClasses.html.*

Beginning in June of 2002, the Chemical Industry Data Exchange (www.cidx.org), the Petroleum Industry Data Exchange (www.pidx.org), and agri-business trade group Rapid, Inc. (www.rapidnet.org) are cooperating to develop XML standards for their industries.

In addition to inter-application communication standards, a good EAI tool will provide a brain at the enterprise level to capture all necessary business processes by controlling all software applications. For example, Exxon-Mobil hires a new geologist. The brain contains a rule-based business process for new hires. It will instruct each application (e.g., accounting, human resources, etc.) to perform sub-processes to incorporate this employee's user data and needs into the system. Applications then communicate with each other through the brain.

The brain and its communication software are off-the-shelf applications designed to securely control the flow of information. Connectors, which interface between the brain and each application, translate data between the brain and the various application languages. All applications communicate through the brain. Most connectors can also be obtained off-the-shelf; non-mainstream applications need to be custom designed.

These applications—which began with the telecommunications companies—are becoming more and more popular in energy industries, especially because of energy deregulation. So, how are these technologies evolving and changing the way we do business?

Schumpeterian notions of creative destruction suggest that the old will give way to the new. Almost 75% of *Fortune's* 500 companies in 1955 no longer existed 40 years later. The same thing will happen with technologies as the old is absorbed, destroyed, and replaced with the new. Old information technologies required writing, typing, printing, mailing and telephones with low (or no) bandwidth capacity. New technologies require typing, electronic publishing, transfer, and customizing of products for users. They rely on the current telecommunication infrastructure—a mix of fiber optics, coaxial cable, copper wires, satellites, and microwave and cellular spectrum with increasing moves to wider bandwidths.

How will these technologies be used? How will they and their infrastructure evolve and diffuse? How will they affect business structure in the energy industries? Technological determinism suggests that such groups of inventions influence many aspects of daily life, including social change, income distribution, individual and social rights, employment, migration, privacy, sense (or lack) of community, and appropriate management styles. Some of the human dimension of the changes from the information revolution can be illustrated by the evolution of the Internet.

Steps of Internet Use

Siegel (1999) discusses nine steps of Internet use. First are the technical problems of setting up and getting connected, generally through an internet service provider (ISP). Siegel's second step is Internet use for electronic mail (e-mail), which he recommends over voice mail, since e-mail is fast, retrievable, skimmable, archivable, and can be annotated. ISPs typically offer e-mail service.

E-mail is not really new. It can be traced to telegraph messages more than a century ago. Telex machines—still used today to transmit on independent telex lines—were used extensively to send electronic messages from the 1920s to the 1980s. Mainframes often included e-mail systems beginning in the 1960s. The first e-mail on Arpanet (the military precursor to the Internet) was sent in 1971. With the advent of personal computers, proprietary dial-up mail services allow subscribers to e-mail while bulletin board systems allow users to post and exchange information. Local area networks (LAN) also provided e-mail services. Informal queries suggest that many energy companies began using e-mail in the mid-to-late 1980s; by 1995, e-mail migrated to the Internet in ever-increasing numbers.

Siegel's third step in Internet use is to search for information, either by search engines, directories, or links. Bookmarking sites, browsing, and links from site to site, can be supplemented by market research companies for harder-to-find information. Net research may help track the five competitive barriers that Porter discusses as being important:

1. threat of new entrants
2. bargaining power of customers
3. threat of substitutes
4. bargaining power of suppliers
5. rivalry among existing competitors

Awareness of your competitors, potential competitors, and suppliers' web sites—as well as sites that appeal to your customers—might provide important information relating to these five forces. Factors that may contribute to these five barriers include economies of scale, product, differentiation, product technologies and patents, along with distribution networks and other network effects. Browsing also suggests how best to develop your own Internet home page. The earliest home pages simply provided company news and information, but they have become sophisticated and interactive ways to seize that one chance to make a good first impression.

Siegel's fourth step in Internet use is to develop a web presence in buying and selling online, termed *e-commerce*. This requires communication and transaction tools so that you can provide sales and product information on line and e-market your wares. As with any marketing, it is important to measure your site's performance, determine cost per customer, and learn how to encourage repeat purchases. The four P's of marketing—price, product, place, and promotion—are as important as ever, but how they are implemented and how they translate into sales will vary.

Pricing is a particularly interesting issue to consider when providing information services. Information services have a high fixed cost but low variable costs; if one more person downloads a piece of information from your homepage, your variable cost could be zero. The old rule for a competitive market (price equal to marginal costs) will not likely cover your costs in such a market as this, so you must decide how to price to cover total costs. Radio and television evolved with the same cost structure; both media developed through the use of advertising. Having one more person tune into a program costs the networks nothing. Consumers were charged nothing up front but paid indirectly in the form of the products they bought.

We see some of the same patterns evolving on the Internet. Information is often provided free to the consumer, in a service supported by advertising. Advertisers may promote sales directly or collect information to target sales promotion. Whether this will continue depends upon how effective advertising on the Internet is.

Information—even if produced by the private sector—has some aspects of a pure public good. Private goods are depletable and excludable; pure public goods are not. Oil is a private good. If you consume a barrel of oil, it is depleted and not available. Information is non-depletable (sometimes referred to as non-rivalrous): If you consume information, you do not deplete it; others can consume it. There is no rivalry over the product. However, just as the owner of the oil can exclude you from using the oil if you do not pay for it, so information can be excludable, although exclusion may be more difficult than for a private good. Since theft of information does not deplete it, such theft tends to be more difficult to detect and prevent.

Information non-depletability suggests a role for government in its provisioning. Further, our earlier analysis—that we optimize social welfare by charging price equal to marginal cost—suggests that governments should not charge for online information, since the marginal cost of one more person using the information is zero. We already see energy information posted on the Internet by governments—at no cost. The EIA/DOE contains links to numerous such sites at http://www.eia.doe.gov/links.html.

In a non-competitive market (a market where information providers have some market power) providers might charge where marginal revenue equals marginal cost. In such a case, you may be able to turn a profit even if marginal cost is zero.

For example, suppose you provide seismic services and have some monopoly power in the market. Your fixed cost is 1500 and your marginal cost is zero. You face demand of $P = 2000 - Q$. If you can only charge one price, you would maximize profits:

$$\pi = PQ - 1500 = (2000 - Q)Q - 1500$$

First- and second-order conditions are:

$$\partial\pi/\partial Q = (\partial P/\partial Q)*Q + P = \textbf{Marginal Revenue} = -1*Q + 2000 - Q$$

$$= 2000 - 2Q = 0 => Q = 1000$$

$$\partial^2\pi/\partial Q^2 = \partial^2(\textbf{Marginal Revenue})/\partial Q^2 = -2 < 0.$$

Or charge where marginal revenue equals zero, provided that marginal revenue slopes down and you are able to cover your costs.

At a $Q = 1000$, your price would be 1000, your revenues would be $1000*1000 = 1,000,000$, so you would more than cover your costs.

Suppose you are able to segregate this market into a high-end (Q_1) and a low-end (Q_2). You sell Q_1 and charge P_1 in the high-end market and sell Q_2 and charge P_2 in the low-end market. Your profits in the high-end market are:

$$P_1Q_1 = (2000 - Q_1)Q_1.$$

Once you sell Q_1 at P_1, the rest of the market includes only those who are willing to pay less than P_1. Their demand would be $P_1 - Q_2$. Revenues in market two would be:

$$P_2 Q_2 = (P_1 - Q_2)Q_2 = (2000 - Q_1 - Q_2)Q_2$$

Total revenues in the two markets would be:

$$P_1 Q_1 + P_2 Q_2 = (2000 - Q_1)Q_1 + (2000 - Q_1 - Q_2)Q_2$$

Profits in the two markets would be:

$$(2000 - Q_1)Q_1 + (2000 - Q_1 - Q_2)Q_2 - 1500$$

First-order conditions for a profit maximum are:

$$\partial \pi / \partial Q_1 = 2000 - 2Q_1 - Q_2 = 0$$

$$\partial \pi / \partial Q_2 = 2000 - Q_1 - 2Q_2 = 0$$

Solving $Q_1 = 666.67$ and $Q_2 = 666.67$

$$P_1 = (2000 - Q_1) = (2000 - 666.67) = \$1333.33$$

$$P_2 = (P_1 - Q_2) = (1333.33 - 666.67) = \$666.67$$

Revenues in market one $= 1333.33 * 666.67 = \$888,888.89$

Revenues in market two $= 666.67 * 666.67 = \$444,444.44$

Total profits in the two markets:

$$\$888,888.89 + \$444,444.44 - 1500 = \$1,331,833.33$$

Second-order conditions ensure a maximum since:

$$\partial^2 \pi / \partial Q_1{}^2 = \partial(\textbf{Marginal Revenue}) / \partial Q_1 = -2 < 0$$

$$\partial^2 \pi / \partial Q_2{}^2 = \partial(\textbf{Marginal Revenue}) / \partial Q_1 = -2 < 0$$

$$\partial^2 \pi / \partial Q_1 {}^* \partial^2 \pi / \partial Q_2 - (\partial^2 \pi / \partial Q_1 \partial Q_2)^2 = (-2)^*(-2) - (-1)^2 > 0$$

By price discriminating, you are able to earn more profits than in the non-discriminating case. But if you discriminate, what is to keep people from buying in the low-priced market and reselling in the high-priced market, driving down the price? Varian notes a number of ways you can degrade your product to generate a high-end and a low-end product—maybe even a free product.

For example, the cheaper downscale product may:

- be released with a time delay
- have a poorer interface
- be less user-friendly
- have lower image resolution
- be slower
- be less flexible
- be less capable
- have less features and functions
- have less or no technical support
- have what Varian calls "nagware" that interrupts service and encourages customers to buy the better version

Pricing strategy may also vary depending on whether it is your basic price or part of a product promotion. It depends on the five C's of pricing—cost, customer, channel of distribution, competition, and compatibility with corporate goals such as image, market share, profits, and other product lines. Markup pricing is among the easiest to implement but may not maximize profits. If your markup is 20%, simply multiply your costs by 1.2 to determine the price. Breakeven pricing requires that you estimate costs and forecast sales and price to equalize them. Economic breakeven is where you make a normal rate of return.

For example, suppose your total cost function (including a normal rate of return) is TC = 6 + Q, and you face a demand curve Q = 15 − 2P. You break even where your revenues equal your costs, or where:

$$PQ - TC(Q) = PQ - 6Q$$

Substituting in for demand:

$$P(15 - 2P) - 6 - (15 - 2P) = -2P^2 + 7P - 21$$

Using the quadratic formula, you find two solutions (P = 1.5, Q = 12 and P = 7, Q = 1.) Another pricing strategy to consider is bundling goods for sale. To see how this might raise profits, suppose that you are selling computers and seismic software to oil and gas companies. The demand for computers is $P_1 = 15 - 3Q_1$ and the demand for software is $P_2 = 10 - 2Q_2$ with total cost $TC_1 = 3Q_1$ and $TC_2 = 6Q_2$. If you maximize profits separately, profit functions are:

$$\pi = P_1{}^*Q_1 - 3Q_1 = (15 - 3Q_1)Q_1 - 3Q_1$$

$$\pi = P_2{}^*Q_2 - 6Q_2 = (10 - 2Q_2)Q_2 - 6Q_2$$

First-order conditions are:

$$\partial\pi/\partial Q_1 = 15 - 6Q_1 - 3 = 0 => Q_1 = 2 \text{ and } P_1 = 9$$

$$\partial\pi/\partial Q_2 = 10 - 4Q_2 - 6 = 0 => Q_2 = 1 \text{ and } P_2 = 8$$

Profits are:

$$\pi_1 = 9^*2 - 3^*2 = 12$$

$$\pi_2 = 8^*1 - 6^*1 = 2$$

Total profits of $12 + 2 = 14$. Consumer surplus is shown in Figure 16–1.

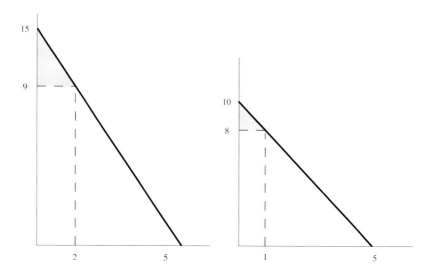

Fig.16–1 Consumer Surplus for Computer and Software Market

For each market we can compute, consumer surplus as:

$$CS_1 = \int_0^2 (15 - 3Q_1)dQ_1 - 2*9 = 24 - 18 = 6$$
$$CS_2 = \int_0^1 (10 - 2Q_2)dQ_2 - 8*1 = 9 - 8 = 1$$

The total consumer surplus is $6 + 1 = 7$.

Now package the computers and software together with $Q_1 = Q_2$ and charge $17 for the package. Consumers now cannot choose to individually buy $Q_1 = 2$ and $Q_2 = 1$. With these discrete choices, consumers must decide whether it is better to buy the bundled product or not. If they decide to buy the bundled product, they need to decide which bundle—the bundle with the largest consumer surplus, provided that the total consumer surplus is greater than zero. If the consumer surplus of all bundles is negative, the consumer should not buy any of the bundles. (Table 16–2.)

Table 16-2 Consumer Surplus for Bundled Products

$Q_1 = Q_2$	P =	profit =	CS
1	17	8	5.5
2	34	16	6
3	51	24	1.5

The consumer surplus for each bundle:

$$\int_0^{Q1}(15 - 3Q_1)dQ_1 + \int_0^{Q2}(10 - 2Q_2)dQ_2 - P$$

The consumer should choose the bundle, which maximizes consumer surplus at six. Although the buyer does not have as much consumer surplus as for the non-bundled groups, he is better off than if he buys no bundles or any other number of bundles. The producer profits for the bundled sales are:

$$\pi = 34 - 3*2 - 6*2 = 16$$

This is larger than the profits under the unbundled sales of 14.

Pricing is just one aspect of marketing. We also must identify needs that individuals and organizations have and satisfy these needs better than competitors. This requires planning, promoting, and distributing products, whether those products are ideas (information goods), physical goods, or services. Other components of marketing include buying, selling, transporting, storing, financing, risk taking, standardizing, and grading products. Market strategy may focus on the production of goods, selling, or otherwise satisfying customer needs. It may take on various perspectives—selling into a global market, developing customer relationships, product benefits to the customer, ethical behavior, providing the desired quality at best price, productivity of marketing, use of the latest marketing technology, focusing on the environmental aspects of products, or entrepreneurial, innovative marketing.

Place is usually another important part of marketing, but the Internet and e-commerce mean that where you sell your wares becomes much less critical. Transportation and transaction costs are lowered for finding and purchasing a good. E-commerce has been growing as consistently as the Internet; connections have increased. E-commerce trade relationships include:

- business-to-consumer (B2C). An early example is Amazon.com, launched in 1996 to sell books. Used product auctions facilitated by companies such as eBay, launched in 1999, are another example.
- business to business (B2B) evolutions of the EDI framework. For example, Grainger's electronic sales of maintenance, repair, and operation supplies (www.grainger.com) was launched in February 1999.
- business-to-government (B2G) has been increasing for the U.S. federal government since President Clinton in 1993 required EDI and electronic commerce for federal procurement.
- peer-to-peer (P2P) connects end-users directly to each other for exchange with no intermediary. Bilateral arrangements, such as energy swaps, benefit from such technology.

Tapscott et al. (2000) notes five types of participants in these e-commerce trade relationships:

1. customers
2. context providers, which organize the rules of the transactions
3. suppliers (also called content providers) produce the goods, services, and information provided to consumers over the web
4. commerce service providers help with financial management, security, data management, and goods distribution
5. infrastructure providers maintain the physical and electronic network for the commerce

Tapscott et al. also identify five types of business webs from their research: These are all trilateral, with context providers helping to facilitate the process.

- *Agoras*, such as e-Bay and the former Utility.com, serve to bring buyers and sellers together to trade with each other.
- *Aggregations*, which select products from various suppliers for customers, set prices, and ensure that contracts are fulfilled. Traditional brick-and-mortar aggregations such as Wal-Mart and Target have evolved into web-based clicks-and-mortar aggregations.
- *Value chains*, which are structured by the supplier to produce customized products. Cisco and Dell orchestrate and assemble custom-made products by controlling the whole process, from manufacture to end-user delivery. Renewable, distributed electricity services—in which a company builds, installs and services your PV equipment and bills you for electricity—would also be a value chain.
- *Alliances* integrates producers without the hierarchical control of value chains. Pantellos is comprised of a number of utilities and provides trading- and supply-chain management to the power industry.
- *Distributive networks* move goods, services, and information and allow tracking over the web. Classic examples include UPS and FedEX and more specialized energy logistics applications such as long-distance power transmission, pipelines, and tankers.

Some early e-commerce business webs took the form of agoras, which provide liquidity, price discovery, and include one-to-one negotiating, multiparty auctions, and exchanges. E-Bay, founded in 1995, is one of the pioneers for an online agora. Monster.com, with origins dating to 1993, brings together job openings with job seekers. Aucnet, launched in Japan in 1995, is an early example of an automobile auction. PennWell's OGJ Exchanges launched in March of 2000 brings together buyers and sellers of used and surplus oil, gas, and power generation equipment as well as buyers and sellers of oil and gas properties.

Auctions vary; a *sell-side auction* typically has one seller for a particular product with many buyers bidding. PennWell's OJG Property Exchange posts properties for which the owner takes bids. The English auction system starts with the lowest acceptable bid or reservation price of the seller; if it's not met, the item will not be sold. Successive buyer bids are made with the highest bidder winning the good. A Dutch auction begins at a high price, which is lowered until the buyer accepts the price. If there are multiple units, then the price is lowered to additional buyers until all units are sold. Auctions sell more than just items—South Africa's power pool allows sellers to supply hourly power using a Dutch auction.

In *buy-side auctions*, one buyer typically issues a request for quotation, receiving quotes from many sellers. Uranium.online.com is an example of a buy-side auction.

In a *sealed bid auction*, bidding is in secret, with all bid amounts only known to the supplier, who sells to highest bidder. The U.S. government uses sealed bids to auction offshore areas for oil and gas exploration. A Vickrey auction is a sealed bid auction in which the supplier sells to the highest bidder, but at the second-highest price. Although not as common, it is sometimes used in financial markets.

Exchanges are *double auctions* that match up many buyers and sellers using open or sealed bids from buyers and sellers. The New York Stock Exchange (NYSE) is a classic double auction in which both sides bid. Electronic power exchanges have become common; they include APX and the Scandinavian power pool. Numerous e-trading energy exchanges developed in the late 1990s, such as Dynegy, DukePower, and others. However, as of 2000, Julian King estimated 90% of energy trading was still done by phone or fax. (*Computer World*, April 14, 2000)

Although e-commerce started with B2C, early on it became apparent that the B2B market held greater promise, and it's estimated that B2B commerce is four to five times that of B2C. Web based e-commerce started in the energy industry in the mid-1990s; many e-commerce examples of agoras and other information technology companies in the energy industry can be seen at http://dahl.mines.edu.

B2B started with two e-commerce strategies. Some entities originated by combining e-commerce with non-virtual activities. Media examples of this include *OGJ*, the *Economist*, and the *Wall Street Journal*, where both paper and/or web-based alternatives exist. Others began life as virtual beings and are purely electronic. They typically are brokers or aggregators of information or web experience including Amazon, AOL, and Pantellos.

Many of the combined examples moved online in response to virtual competition in what Tapscott et al. (2000) calls the "Empire Strikes Back"— Barnes & Noble went online as the result of competition from Amazon.com. Bloomberg's Powermatch was the first to trade wholesale power beginning in 1998, but was soon followed by industry companies or consortiums such as Enron, Dynegy, and Tradespark.

Spears & Associates interviewed about 100 participants in the oil field services and equipment industry in 2000 about e-commerce experiences. They noted a rapid build-up of platforms that seemed to plateau in 2001. The expectation of the participants included time saving, cost saving, better control of business relationships, more information available, better selection of items, and cheaper unit costs. Their expectations were often not met and participants expressed concerns over a lack of security and privacy, too many relationships (creating confusion), utilization levels of staff and equipment, legal issues, high start-up costs, and mismatched orders. (*OGJ*, 3/12/2001:32)

Siegel's fifth level of Internet use is e-business, which is more focused and comprehensive than e-commerce. It gives customers the choice of what, when, where, and how to obtain goods, services, and information. In business, the customer is said to shape the corporation; this is likely to be even more so in the e-business world. Most sites offer ways to contact a company via e-mail for customer feedback. Accurate, up-to-date information ties compensation to performance, quality, and customer satisfaction. New customer services can be tried first on a small scale. When people want to participate, businesses can build a customer community. For example, Valvoline's webpage has information about car racing, downloadable car racing screensavers, and even greeting cards.

In the energy world, Enercom (http://www.enercomU.S.A.com) provides Internet-based customer relationship management to help energy companies attract, sell, and manage customers to keep them coming back. They provide home energy audit software, an energy calculator, and an energy library, and customer billing services.

Value chains fit under the e-business rubric and Cisco is the classic example. It orchestrates suppliers, itself, and its distributors to provide an end product. Dell also organizes its value chain to minimize inventories and provide the computer customers want, when they want it. ERP utilizes software to facilitate operation of value chains by gathering information from across the whole supply chain to monitor materials, orders, schedules, inventories, and transactions. SAP, Oracle, Peoplesoft, J.D. Edwards, and Baan are among leaders of ERP.

Although ERP grew 30 to 40% per year in the mid-to-late 1990s, it did not provide much analytical support, which lead to the development of SCM. SCM takes information from legacy and ERP systems and adds optimization models. SCM leaders are i2 Technologies and Manugistics. Others are moving to SCM through in-house development, alliances, and acquisition of other firms.

Alliances would also fall under e-business. These nonhierarchical groupings produce goods, services, information and experiences. InterContinentalExchange is an alliance of BP, Shell, TotalFinaElf, Societe General, Goldman Sachs, Morgan Stanley Dean Witter, and Deutsch Bank to trade oil, gas, and physical and financial electric power. Other energy e-commerce initiatives ally energy companies providing customers and products, with computer or software companies providing information technology. MySAP partnered with Statoil to provide an online marketplace for the oil and gas industry, and Shell partnered with CommerceOne for energy trading; neither alliance endured beyond the planning stage, however.

Distribution is also part of the supply chain. Distributive networks move goods, services, information, and experiences to where they are needed. They include roads, the power grid, the postal service, pipelines, and the Internet. UPS and FedEx provide classic examples of services for sending and e-tracking packages. Deregulated gas pipelines are required to post bulletin boards to transact business, which more recently has been moved to the Internet.

Siegel's sixth level is e-culture, in which people create personal Internet home pages and grow consumer communities. As horizontal linkages of similar interests develop, these communities get to know who is credible and who is not. Truth, rather than size, is an advantage as consumers more easily band together for more market power.

Siegel's seventh level is that of group collaboration, where everyone is on a network. This can be recreational (chatrooms and games) or professional (group projects and decision-making). Collaboration could be synchronous (everyone on at the same time as in a chatroom) or asynchronous (members participate on their own schedule in a threaded discussion). It could be internal to a company (intranet) or maintained with suppliers and partners.

A team project could put all players on the same page with the same goals and objectives. All the required information should be on the network, but the knowledge and data for collaboration may be managed by an outside firm. The team should be able to build on previous knowledge and everyone should use and contribute to the information. A well-designed collaboration should give a team the cohesion and focus of a well-motivated individual. An early example of software to enable team collaboration and data sharing was Lotus Notes developed in 1990 and purchased by IBM in 1994. Such software is coming to be called *groupware*. Geoquest, Schlumberger's software division, offers Mindshare, which allows oil and gas exploration and project teams to share information and collaborate online. Schlumberger also offers other information management programs.

Siegel's eighth level is a large-scale collaboration in which agents assist in the collaboration. Agents could set standards, match needs, pass on information, and be reimbursed from advertising, subscriptions, or fees for service. They could include *spiders*—programs that automatically search the Internet—as well as *bots*, which are programs that perform tasks on their owner's behalf. For example, http://www.pickasupplier.co.uk, finds the cheapest supplier for residential electricity and gas in the United Kingdom.

Agents can also filter customer information from previous purchases or site visits, chart indicated likes and dislikes, and track other observed behavior to match people with other people, groups, services, and products. Online clearinghouses match buyers and sellers and their agents for a commission. However, it is not yet clear whether a few large site managers (such as Yahoo and AOL Time Warner) will funnel the massive amount of information to end-consumers, giving these sites undue market power.

Siegel's ninth and final level is called living online. With such a deluge of information, we need filters to sift, process, and edit information. By sharing our personal identities, firms can customize products and services to suit our needs but the costs may be potential loss of privacy and the challenge of keeping track of various online identities, while the benefit will be more suitable and useful products and services. For more information from Siegel on using the information highway, see Siegel (1999) or http://Futurizenow.com. For a list of the 50 most Internet-savvy companies in 2000, see *Smart Business Magazine*, November, 2000.

As society and business move through these nine stages, the Internet changes business boundaries by allowing more competition and access. It puts Adam Smith's ideal of the invisible hand (friction-free capitalism) closer to a reality. However, in such an environment, only a few will succeed with the lowest price; the rest will need a customer service strategy. The Internet also allows companies to reshape relationships with customers, work seamlessly with colleagues, better deal with unpredictable demand, and appoint and track special teams for projects. It all requires that you excel in core competencies and selectively outsource where appropriate. It dissolves geographical boundaries and allows virtual companies to do larger projects. By allowing virtual real-time integration, we can collapse time, improve quality, and maintain time-to-market with increasing complexity. Constraints in such systems are more often cultural than technical.

Gates (1999) argues that you should strive to make data easy to get and customize. This requires fast corporate reflexes, which includes collecting bad news and acting upon it to turn it into good news. He cites the story of IBM losing market share to the smaller, nimbler DEC, which in turn was upstaged by the personal computer. IBM and DEC paid too much attention to each other and not enough attention to their customers.

Optimization Subject to Constraints

Often the best comments are from customers—particularly unhappy customers. Thus, pay close attention to complaints, recognize the problem, and tie the complaint to a fast solution. Once you establish the problems, prioritize them and act.

To prioritize, suppose your objective function is $O(P_1, P_2, P_3)$, where P_1, P_2, and P_3 are resources devoted to reengineering your company to solve problems one, two, and three, respectively. For business, O might be profits or costs related to your efforts at solving problems one, two or three. For a consumer, O might be utility or satisfaction gained from efforts at solving problems one, two, and three. Calculus guides us to how much effort P_1, P_2 and P_3 undertake. With no constraints, first take the derivative of our objective function with respect to each of the choice variables P_i and set them equal to zero or:

$$\partial O/\partial P_1 = 0$$

$$\partial O/\partial P_2 = 0$$

$$\partial O/\partial P_3 = 0$$

In these expressions, $\partial O/\partial P_i$ represents the marginal benefit of the last unit of effort spent on problem i. The solution to this system is a candidate for an optimum solution.

These first-order conditions tell us that you should increase efforts to solve problem i until there is no further change in O from the addition of more effort toward problem i. If we want to maximize O, we also need $\partial O/\partial P_i$ to be positive but decreasing. In other words, before the optimal level of P_i, adding another unit of P_i increases our benefits but the benefits continually decrease towards zero as we increase our efforts at solving problem i. This second-order condition is mathematically represented by $\partial^2 O/\partial P_i^2 < 0$ and helps assure that we have a maximum amount of O from our problem solving efforts. For a more complete discussion of economic optimization, see the classic text by Chiang (1984).

In the above example, we assumed no time constraints for your company; you had unlimited time to spend on solving these problems. This is unlikely to be the case. So, suppose O is profit received from time spent reengineering your company. Again, P_i is the re-engineering effort devoted to solving problems. However, your budget constraint is B, which in this case is your time budget ($B = P_1 + P_2 + P_3$). Now, when you optimize, you must make sure that your solution fits within your time constraint. This is easy to do using a Lagrangean multiplier technique: Rewrite your budget constraint as an implicit function (i.e., solve so that the equation has a zero on one side and all the variables on the other ($B - P_1 - P_2 - P_3 = 0$). Then, introduce a new variable (λ), called a Lagrangean multiplier. Multiply the budget constraint times the Lagrangean multiplier and add it to your objective function (L). This becomes our new objective function (L):

$$L = O(P_1, P_2, P_3) + \lambda (B - P_1 - P_2 - P_3)$$

Treat your Lagrangian multiplier the same as other choice variables. That is: take the derivative with respect to each of your choice variables including λ. This gives first-order conditions as follows:

$$L_1 = \partial O/\partial P_1 - \lambda = 0$$

$$L_2 = \partial O/\partial P_2 - \lambda = 0$$

$$L_3 = \partial O/\partial P_3 - \lambda = 0$$

$$L_\lambda = B - P_1 - P_2 - P_3 = 0$$

Notice that the last condition forces the solution to be along the constraint. Solving the initial three first-order conditions for λ, and setting them equal to each other gives us:

$$\lambda = \partial O/\partial P_1 = \partial O/\partial P_2 = \partial O/\partial P_3$$

The P_is that satisfy the above condition are candidates for an optimum. Again, diminishing marginal profits ($\partial^2 O/\partial P_i^2 < 0$) ensures that you have maximum solution. For a more complete discussion of economic optimization under constraints, see Chiang (1984).

To implement our optimization rule note that ($\partial O/\partial P_i$) is the marginal profit from the last hour worked on solving problem i. Then to prioritize, rank problems by marginal profits per hour spent. Suppose you are trying to save time entering and processing data to increase profits in your highly successful natural gas marketing company. You have 20 hours (H) to devote to re-engineering your company. You can:

- teach employees to use off the shelf software
- custom-design software to streamline your current system
- work with your customers to eliminate redundant data entry

Your chief information technology officer estimates annual profits from various hours spent on the three projects in Table 16–3. To make the problem tractable, we assume that the projects are independent of each other.

Which activity or combination of activities should you undertake to maximize profits, given your 20 hours? Components of the tasks in this case are discrete; assume that completing part of a component yields no benefits. The first component of task one takes one hour and yields a savings of 300 hours a year. The second task takes two hours and yields an additional 380-hour savings or 190 savings per hour for a total saving of 680 hours per year.

Table 16–3 Optimal Allocation of Resources

		Total New Profits			
Total Hours P_1	Total Profits O	Total Hours P_2	Total Profits O	Total Hours P_3	Total Profits O
0	0	0	0	0	0
1	300	2	590	3	1,500
3	680	4	1,100	4	1,900
4	805	5	1,300	6	2,450
5	850	6	1,400	8	2,900
7	900	8	1,500	9	3,050
8	910	9	1,530	10	3,120

		Marginal Increase in Profits/Change in Hours			
Total Hours P_1	Marginal Profits $\Delta O/\Delta P_1$	Total Hours P_2	Marginal Profits $\Delta O/\Delta P_2$	Total Hours P_3	Marginal Profits $\Delta O/\Delta P_3$
1	300	2	295	3	500
3	190	4	255	4	400
4	125	5	200	6	275
5	45	6	100	8	225
7	25	8	50	9	150
8	10	9	30	10	70

Using the above formula, O is profits and total hours is P. Replace the partial sign ∂ with a discrete change represented by Δ. The first order condition becomes:

$$\Delta O/\Delta P_1 = \Delta O/\Delta P_2 = \Delta O/\Delta P_3$$

Now, ΔO for the first component of task one is:

$$\Delta O = (300 - 0) = 300$$

ΔP_1 for the first component of task one is:

$$\Delta P_1 = (1 - 0) = 1$$

Then, for the first component, $\Delta O/\Delta P_1 = 300/1 = 300$. For the second component of task one, ΔO is:

$$\Delta O = (680 - 300) = 380$$

ΔP_1 for the second component of task one is:

$$\Delta O = (3 - 1) = 2$$

Then, for the second component, $\Delta O/\Delta P_1 = 380/2 = 190$, and so on.

Now, allocate your time across tasks. You achieve the highest time savings per hour from task three for the first four hours. You should spend an hour on task one and two hours on task two thereafter. Keep allocating your time until you have run out of hours.

Every investment in information technology has physical, human, and organizational costs. Physical costs are the hardware and software. Human costs are training and other adjustment costs. In neoclassical economics, we assume that consumers maximize utility and producers minimize cost and maximize profits. A complex-systems approach also considers the psychological, social, and institutional factors that go into decision-making, but new information technology users may not be able to make the psychological adjustment in the same amount of time that technology has changed. Human psychological costs include stress— feelings of helplessness, never getting anything done, always being busy, suffering a lack of control, being acted on by the system, and responding to rather than initiating activity.

The new information technologies may require reengineering of other processes, which will incur organizational costs. You may need to re-examine your processes; ask yourself, "Are we solving the right question? Can our processes be simplified?" If processes are mapped into too many pieces, no one sees the big picture. Too much delegation may result in too many potential failure points. Conversely, if processes are broken into too few pieces, effective specialization may be lost; you may not be able to take advantage of parallel rather than sequential tasking.

Can information be better used at any point in the process chain? Since opportunity cost is still an essential piece of information, you will need to under-stand tradeoffs at all levels. For more information on re-engineering your business in the information age, see http://www.speed-of-thought.com.

Management Styles

Choosing the optimal factor mix is only one decision for a manager. Classical management theory recommends well-defined roles and activities with a rather hierarchical organizational structure. To control and coordinate these activities, a manager must do a variety of things:

- plan processes
- collect and analyze information
- develop financial objectives and controls
- hire, fire, train, and motivate workers
- develop innovative marketing
- promote good customer and public relations
- obey laws and regulations
- upgrade and expand successful operations
- restructure and close failing divisions
- procure supplies—raw materials, energy, equipment
- design, produce, market, and sell goods and services
- control inventories
- transport and distribute goods and services
- control quality
- measure performance
- oversee research and development efforts
- choose technology

They must do so for day-to-day operations, planning the coming months, and strategic planning for the coming years. Each manager needs to determine how information technologies can assist in the above functions.

A behavioral science approach to management requires the same activities but the emphasis is on attracting, managing, and motivating people. Investment in human capital and attention to employee enhancement and satisfaction are paramount. Again, information technologies can help; boring repetitive work can be performed by machines, leaving the more interesting and challenging work to humans. Rewards can be tied quickly and easily to performance. Online knowledge bases and classes can ensure that employees continue to learn and develop their expertise. For example, Schlumberger, the world's largest oil services company (http://www.slb.com/Hub/index.cfm) has an extensive online database and links to numerous e-learning sites.

A management science approach focuses on mathematics, statistics, and modeling to optimize and manage production and operations. This approach is clearly complementary to new information technologies, since most of its data can be used in such modeling. Digital technologies have made data increasingly cheaper and more profuse. Sources include data collected by scanners when transactions are made, case studies, lab experiments, survey results, census, and data gathered over the web. Additionally, simulations can provide data and model uncertainty via Monte Carlo studies, in which random errors are generated by computer and added into the data.

Bounded rationality suggests that to prevent all data from becoming "pollution," you must process and make sense of it. Collecting and analyzing data can provide statistical information to back up management decisions but the less time spent on data processing, the more time is available for analysis and decision-making. Data mining can help data processing generate useful relationships. Data mining utilizes computer algorithms to find useful patterns in large amounts of data. It essentially consists of four techniques—market basket analysis, classification techniques, clustering techniques, and forecasting.

Market basket analysis tries to find relationships within a given product or service group—the market basket. If new homeowners often buy new appliances, target appliance ads to new homeowners. If upper-middle-class homeowners are more likely to buy green power, then Green Mountain Power can target marketing toward them. Classification techniques relate behavior to background, answering such questions as "What type of traveler is likely to take mass transit?" Clustering techniques try to break observations into groups with similar behavioral patterns. You might find that a cluster has certain similarities such as age, income level, race, or sex. Data mining may help you better understand customers, better personalize products and services, better understand customer needs, and better target advertising. For more information on data mining and links to programs, see, National Center for Data Mining's homepage http://www.ncdm.uic.edu/ and http://www.van-maanen.com/.

A systems approach to management focuses on organizing and coordinating interrelated parts for a single purpose. In legacy systems, one platform may be used for accounting, another for knowledge management, and yet a third for CRM, billing, or marketing. Information gathered in one system should be readily available if it is needed in another. Here again, EAI can help tie all the systems together.

One way of providing linkages is through a nonhierarchical network. This lattice structure of organization is ideal for information flow. Metcalfe's Law suggests that the value of a network equals the square of the number of nodes; thus, when critical mass is obtained, the value of the network increases faster than its cost. A good strategy in such a world is to reach a critical mass early. For instance, by the end of 1998, half of all U.S. households had PCs, and half of them were connected to the web. The rest of the world is also being attached to the web at a rapid rate. This lattice-type structure also seems to influence organizational structure: Structure is becoming more horizontal, with employees motivated more by cohesion than coercion.

Each of the listed management styles insists that its single approach provides good management theory. Contingency management maintains there is no one best way to plan, organize, and control, and that different techniques work in different contexts. For example, clearly defined jobs with rigid plans may be best enforced with autocratic leadership and tight controls; vaguely defined jobs with vague plans may be best enhanced with democratic leadership and loose controls. An organization may change with increased globalization; more emphasis on ethical, social, and environmental responsibility; changing demographic and skill requirements; increased emphasis on employee needs; and new information technologies.

Transaction costs suggest that the governance system that evolves in each case will be that which minimizes transaction costs. Each organization should strive to adopt the management system that minimizes total costs and maximizes the probability that it will achieve management goals.

Information and Mission

More attention is being paid to information management, but a firm retains an activity or supply chain that adds value to products and/or services. Thus, because each supply chain can also be considered a value chain, information should be used to make sure that each link in the chain adds value. As in earlier management approaches, a strategic plan is important. It starts with a vision—a clear image of what you want for your business or department. Focus on what you want to achieve and use the image to organize your activity. Collins and Porras (1994) investigated 18 companies and compared them to similar but less-successful competitors. They found the majority of the best companies have a strong vision of what they want to be with core values around which everything is organized. Once you have an overriding vision of what you want your company to be—its core set of values—devise a mission statement to provide information about how to realize the vision.

For example, the California Energy Commission's vision and mission statement:

> *It is the vision of the California Energy Commission for Californians to have energy choices that are affordable, reliable, diverse, safe and environmentally acceptable. It is the California Energy Commission's mission to assess, advocate and act through public/private partnerships to improve energy systems that promote a strong economy and a healthy environment. (http://www.energy.ca.gov/commission/mission_statement.html)*

The mission statement begets specific objectives, which can be further reduced into tasks and strategies that will accomplish the mission and realize the vision. Managing tasks in the classical approach is often hierarchical, with three levels of management or authority: operations managed by the first level, technical choices managed by the middle level, and company strategy choice reserved for the top level. Management in the information revolution may be more de-centralized, with management from the structure of tasks and three-level management blurred together.

Management is still required to perform the multiple functions of an average firm. For each of these functions, you still need to set objectives, forecast results, plan budgets, develop strategies and programs, and set policies. But for each function you will now also need to consider how information can best be used to add more value and reduce transaction costs.

Gates (1999) argues that information is the lifeblood of the modern company; that by allowing information to flow down the chain of command, you empower employees all along the line to be able to think, act, and adapt more quickly. Moving toward a paperless office with digital information flow is a first step. Ford has done away with paper invoices, for instance, while Microsoft has cut down from more than 1,000 paper forms to less than 100—all available electronically. Electronic forms, passed along digitally, give everyone easy access through a local network, e-mail, and web pages. Electronic forms allow feedback on the forms themselves as well as making it almost effortless to transfer information across the forms. Information entered only once at its point of origin takes fewer resources and errors are minimized. Electronic forms allow a self-service approach to routine transactions among and between businesses, consumers, and governments. Businesses can provide faster turnaround, lower cost, and lower prices. Although decisions may still be best made face to face, information may be best passed digitally.

Digital transactions also allow routine, one-dimensional, repetitive work to be computerized, leaving people to handle exceptions and focus on tasks with high "value-addeds." Increasingly, task workers will go away or become knowledge workers. Digital information allows companies to build a knowledge management system and institutionalize learning within the company. A corporate digital repository of information can preserve and augment knowledge and foster knowledge sharing.

Companies used to make money collecting and organizing information. The Internet means we need fewer layers of distributors and resellers. For example, airline ticket processing costs $8 with a travel agent but only $1 on the Internet; a bank transaction costs $1.07 at a bank branch, $0.52 by telephone, $0.27 by ATM, but only $0.01 on the Internet. Thus, intermediaries that formerly transferred goods and information will have to add value or die, since the Internet makes these transfers so much cheaper and faster. Personalized customer service will become the primary value-added. Digital transaction's other advantages are that they are less subject to distortion, easier to correct, able to include high-quality video/audio, provide more interactivity, and send more information at a time. Obstacles to digital transmission include a need for wider bandwidth and compatible encryption.

Transaction Costs

Technical change will influence transaction costs by changing asset specificity, frequency of transactions, speed of transactions, uncertainty, economies of scale, and economies of scope. For example, oil and gas exploration use of 3D seismic and real-time data transference to determine productivity of drill sites is a use of information technology that might reduce asset specificity. Analysis capabilities can be tied to many more drill sites than once was possible. In distribution and marketing, technology can make real-time energy information available to buyers and sellers through energy news services like Bloomberg's, Energy Intelligence Group, and Platts to reduce uncertainty. These new technologies may change the size and scope of firms along with transaction governance and the need for regulation; however, you will still need to organize transactions to make optimal use of bounded rationality while protecting against opportunism.

Some forces may lead to more informal forms of governance. Cheaper transaction costs may make some markets larger, reducing asset specificity and causing more purchases to be conducted in the spot market. For example, Rio Tinto sold more than 20% of its coal in the spot market in 2001, up from nearly zero in 1996. The new electronic coal-trading platform (www.globalcoal.com, launched in May, 2001) may have contributed to this shift. Cheaper transaction costs may increase the frequency of transactions, leading again to more informal governance and just-in-time (JIT) inventory systems. If competition increases, firms may focus more on core competencies and buy non-core goods and services from others, leading to less vertical integration.

Increasing information flows may eventually decrease uncertainty requiring less vertical integration and more trilateral, bilateral, and spot-market governance. Trusted third parties are emerging to provide authentication of cyber businesses' reputations and quality. E-Bay's feedback forum is one such a mechanism that helps build trust and reduces risk of loss. It helped to make the used goods market to take off. VeriSign (http://www.verisign.com/) and Cybertrust both provide authentification services. Companies can be certified for privacy and reliability by Truste (http://www.truste.com) or the Better Business Bureau (http://www.bbbonline.com). You can also file complaints with BBB online.

Decreasing transaction costs may make it cheaper to provide more idiosyncratic purchases, increasing customer choice. For large idiosyncratic purchases, more formal governance may still be required as increasing choice and increasing information may increase uncertainty because of bounded rationality. Although increasing uncertainty shouldn't matter so much for spot purchases, for more idiosyncratic goods governance again may become more formal. Newer types of governance—neither totally vertically integrated nor under long-term contract—may become more prominent. Extranets may cause the line between firms to become blurred. Pieces of the supply chain may become vertically integrated across firms. For very idiosyncratic purchases, teams working across firms may be able to deliver with information technologies allowing coordination. Procuring firms can be directly linked to suppliers and directly order; suppliers can be tied to inventory information for their customers so they can expeditiously fill orders. Wal-Mart and Cisco provide examples of managing the supply chain across enterprises.

Partnership and joint ventures across firms become easier to manage and may increase. These seem to be very common in the new information technology companies; SAP had more than 500 partners in eight kinds of partnerships at this writing:

1. **software**, including Dun and Bradstreet and Veritas
2. **consulting services,** including IBM Global Services, PWC Consulting
3. **technology**, including Oracle and Storage Tech
4. **support**, including Real Technology
5. **hosting**, including HP Outsourcing
6. **channels** for small- and medium-sized enterprises, including Hitachi
7. **content**, including Hay Group, Inc.
8. **education**, for which they had no partners listed

For a more complete discussion of the services that Sap's partners provide and a searchable database of partners, see http://www.sap.com/partners.

Changes Wrought by the Information Revolution

The Internet offers an enhanced sense of community. It is more sensory, more seamless, more engaging, and, if well-designed, allows complete immersion and focus on interaction with little distinction between the self and one's environment, between stimulus and response, and among past, present, and future. As the web gets bigger, the world gets smaller; the web allows integration of video, audio, and text along with the opportunity for more sophisticated and systematic visual experimentation.

There are also a number of worries about the Internet. As it changes the boundaries between one's public and private life, a loss of privacy could result. The Internet can be an addicting technology, and there is a possibility that society will so depend on entertainment that it will suffer a loss of community or become too distracted to solve societal problems. There is the fear of being overwhelmed by complexity, left behind, and displaced. Security is a concern and we need protection against cyber-terrorists and industrial espionage.

Ultimately, the changes wrought by the information revolution are new tradeoffs—inventory may tradeoff with information, telecommunication may tradeoff with transport. Competition for consumers' discretionary time will increase. We may see land use patterns change to clusters of residential, commercial, and recreational opportunities linked to employment by telecommunications. Economies of scale become less important as economies of scope and innovation ascend.

Some have questioned whether firms as we know them will even continue to exist. Coase's Theorem on organizational structure suggests that the organization structure that will evolve will minimize transaction costs. In a rapidly changing world, how will we know what structure that is? One way is to see what works and what does not in a sort-of Darwinian process. Or, as Porter describes it, "Ready, fire, aim!" The Internet accelerates this process by reducing transaction costs, which allows more experimenting. "If you are not making mistakes, you are probably not learning; if you are comfortable, you are probably falling behind or not gaining ground as fast as you might." Schumpeter thus suggests that we move forward or innovate by destroying and changing the old to move on to the new.

To be useful, information requires storage, transmission, and diffusion; however, information is not enough: We still need theory and analysis, or information may be more pollution than resource. Knowledge and information may have short life spans, whereas the principles that provide an analytical framework to help us think about changing situations in a structured manner may be timeless.

Moore noted in 1965 that the number of components on a chip doubled every 18 months. This change has gone on for more than 35 years, although the doubling time has been expanded to two years. Moore's Law has helped to define increasing technical change and spawned the popular quote, "Intel giveth and Microsoft taketh away." Hardware prices have fallen by a factor of 2700. Software has only fallen by a factor of two to three, which demonstrates that human constraints may be more binding than technological constraints.

Smart business magazine defines a firm's organizational IQ as "its ability to adapt to such change." This requires encoding change into the production process. Since human constraints are often the limiting factor, people must be trained with general skill sets that can be applied in diverse areas. For example, strong math training helps develop thinking skills and the kind of versatility needed to succeed in today's fast-paced world.

Technology encodes a way of thinking, giving advantages to some and disadvantages to others. Young countries may have advantages over old ones; the old may need to be retrofitted. It may require business process re-engineering to develop the appropriate organization structure for information flows with internal flows on an intranet and external flows on the Internet.

Summary

Information technologies trace to mainframe computers. They were joined more recently by personal computers, workstations, and networks. Privatization of the Internet in 1995 and, more recently, deregulation, have enabled information technologies to proliferate. Internet business users begin by getting connected, then move on to e-mail, browsing for information, establishing a web presence, e-commerce, e-business, and group collaboration. Five market models established for the Internet have been agoras, aggregations, value chains, alliances, and distributive networks.

Many companies provide hardware and software required for the new information services. Applications manage accounting, group collaboration, human resources, operations, customer relations, warehouse data, as well as procure supplies and trade. Software ties together legacy applications—to each other and to new systems both within and across firms. They have taken the form of EAI. EAI provides information flows while the newer SCM provides analysis of the data to facilitate more long term strategic planning.

The so-called dot-com crash and the meltdown of the NASDAQ in June of 2000 led to more level-headed thinking. Although it is too soon to tell how the technologies will sort out, remember that information is a factor of production just as any other and basic principles should be considered in making economic decisions. Moore's Law suggests that computer power doubles every 18 months or so; Metcalfe's Law suggests that the value of a network increases with the square of the number of users. Coase's law on organization suggests that market governance will be that which minimizes transactions costs. Users must consider physical, human, and organizational costs, along with the benefits of information, in deciding how much to use. Benefits include lowering costs by changing asset specificity, frequency of transactions, speed of transactions, uncertainty, and taking advantage of economies of scale and scope.

Pricing for information services is not entirely straightforward. Although the truism stating that price equals marginal cost may provide the socially optimal allocation, marginal cost for information services, which are non-rivalrous, may be almost zero. However, a zero price is not commercially viable unless another source of funding is present, such as advertising, government subsidy, or government provision.

Managers manage people and resources—including information—to design, produce, transport, and distribute goods and services at a profit. Each task requires setting objectives, forecasting results, planning budgets, and developing programs. Classical management undertakes these tasks using well-defined roles, tasks, and chains of command; behavioral management emphasizes the human dimension of attracting, managing and motivating people; and management science uses information along with mathematics, statistics, and modeling to optimize and manage production and operations. Systems management focuses on coordinating interrelated parts for a single purpose, while contingency management tries to apply the best management approach for each situation.

The old way of conducting business—bricks and mortar—will never be totally abandoned. Goods and services will still be produced using real goods and services. But better, faster, cheaper, or more customized products may be obtained by increasing information flow. This new way of doing business—clicks and mortar—uses information technologies to enhance customer loyalty, reach new markets, create new products and services, achieve market leadership, optimize business processes, enhance human capital, harness technology, and manage risk and regulation compliance.

Determining these changes and adapting to them—quickly—can give management a competitive edge. Numerous benefits to adopting information technologies are balanced by certain risks. Strategic and technological risks include picking the wrong technology; implementation and organizational risks include a poor adaptation of the technology or the possibility that the organization will not buy into the technology to its optimum. Timing risk relates to adopting the technology either too soon or too late.

17 Managing in the Multicultural World of Energy

We see things not as they are but as we are.

—Talmud

Introduction

Multinational oil companies are big and getting bigger. National oil companies are reorganizing and going global. Many of these large energy companies participate internationally through exports and imports, licensing and franchising of technologies and products, direct foreign investment, and joint ventures. Information and technology are pervasive and bringing us closer together. In this 21st century environment, multicultural communication and interaction are increasing, whether the culture is technical, corporate, or national. Business success requires the ability to operate effectively across diverse cultures and such effectiveness requires an understanding of and appreciation for numerous aspects of culture.

In this chapter, we consider the various aspects of intercultural differences across nations, how these differences can cause problems, and how these differences can be turned to competitive advantage.

Managing in global industries, such as energy, requires a wide skill set. A good manager must plan, organize, and control by maintaining financial control, building enthusiasm, developing innovative marketing, training personnel, measuring personnel performance, and controlling product quality. Enhancing corporate performance requires closing or modifying failing operations into new, more promising ones.

Often these more promising areas involve an international component. This has been made easier as privatization and deregulation of energy markets have caused major flows of international capital. This process is matched by increasing activity of state energy companies outside their national borders, either starting their own operations or setting up joint ventures with foreign partners. (Table 17–1.)

Table 17–1 Sample Large Energy Companies International Operations

Companies	Number of Countries Operated in
Multinational Oil	
Exxon Mobil	almost 200
BP Amoco	>100
ChevronTexaco	>150
ConocoPhillips	>40
Shell Oil	>130
Occidental Petroleum	9
TotalFinaElf	40
National Oil	
Saudi Aramco	6
Petroleos de Venezuela	3
Statoil	23
Coal Mining and Related	
BHP Billiton	>15
RAG Group	>200
Peabody Coal	18
State Electricity Company	
Électricité de France	35

Note: > indicates more than.
Source: Company homepages.

Increased globalization, increasing attention to ethical social responsibility, changing demographic and skill requirements, and consideration of employee needs are important elements in such management. The manager must not only manage work, organization, production, operations, and technology, but the human dimension, including employees and customers. It is this latter dimension that requires cultural and social skills when managing across national cultures.

Culture

A culture is the shared values, attitudes, and behaviors of a group—their customary ways of perceiving and doing things to satisfy needs. Maslow organizes needs into a four-category hierarchy beginning from the most basic:

- physiological needs like hunger and sex
- safety needs
- esteems for self and others
- need for self-fulfillment

Cultures satisfy these needs in different ways depending on religion, language, economic and political philosophy, educational system, physical environment and settlement pattern, and social organization, including family structure, literature, civil organizations, government organization, and law. Cultures evolve and their tenets are typically passed on through the family, education, work place, religion, and/or the media.

Hooker (1998) likens culture to a group ecosystem. The group may be a nation, in which case its culture includes language, ethics, religion, and customs. The group may also be a profession—engineering, geology, or economics—in which case its culture includes jargon, common methodologies, and analytical frameworks. It may be a corporation, with culture that includes decision-making processes, which might be bureaucratic, centralized, or entrepreneurial. It may be a piece of an organization such as a foreign division, a world headquarters, a refinery, or a research and development division. In each of these contexts, there is a prevailing culture. Understanding its norms and how the parts work together can lead to greater success in the given environment and a stronger chance of survival. Though the focus in this chapter is on national cultures, many of the concepts have wider application to the professional and corporate world.

Culture is learned, and national culture is currently accepted to be relative, rather than right or wrong when compared to some global absolute. However, various cultures have dominated across history (e.g., the ancient Romans, the 19th century British, and the 20th century Americans). Within national cultures, we find a wide variation in individual values and behavior. For example, suppose the culture trait is the value placed on individualism. Let this trait be measured by an index that goes from 1 to 20 with higher values indicating a greater preference for individualism. Suppose in Figure 17–1 the left-hand probability distribution with a mean of 51 represents Japan and the right hand distribution with a mean of 100 represents the United States.

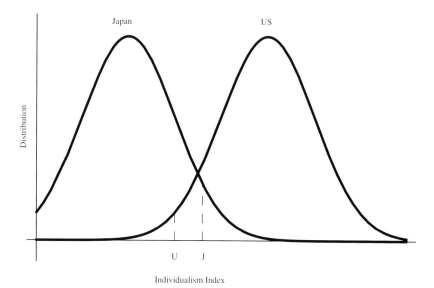

Fig. 17–1 Cultural Preferences for Individualism

From this figure, we see that the United States puts a higher value on individualism, on average, than the more group-oriented Japanese. Knowing this can be useful when trying to decide how to motivate personnel, market and sell products, or organize work assignments across individuals and teams in various cultures. It allows managers to avoid misunderstanding and to use the differences to their competitive advantage. Nevertheless, care must also be taken to not stereotype individuals, since wide differences exist within as well as across cultures. (For example, in the previous figure, the Japanese individual represented by J values individualism more than the American represented by U.)

The two most oft-cited authors classifying cultural differences—particularly relating them to the corporate world—are Hofstede (1984, 1994) and Trompenaars (1993). Hofstede notes four cultural elements in work-related activities:

- power distance (PD)
- uncertainty avoidance (UNC)
- individualism/collectivism (IDV)
- masculinity/femininity (MAS)

Hofstede conducted a huge survey of IBM employees in 50 countries and ranked their cultures based on these criteria. (Table 17–2.)

Table 17–2 Cultural Differences

Country or Region	PD 100%= high PD	UA 100%= high UA	IDV 100% = high IDV	MAS/FEM 100%= More MAS	UNI/PAR 100%= More UNI	NEU/AFF 100%= More NEU	SPE/DIF 100%= More SPE	ACH/ASC 100%= More ACH	IN/OUT 100%= More IN	C.Dyn. 100%= More L.Term
Arab Countries	77	61	42	56						
Argentina	47	77	51	59	57			60	68	
Australia	35	46	99	64	84		98	90	96	26
Austria	0	63	60	60	74		79	47	54	
Belgium	63	84	82	57	80		97	67	63	
Brazil	66	68	42	52	83			67	74	55
Bulgaria					58			29	36	
Burkina Faso							63			
Canada	38	43	88	55	91		87	95	73	19
Czechoslovakia			90			26	0	39		
Chile	61	77	25	29						
China					54		25	68	46	100
Colombia	64	71	14	67						
Costa Rica	34	77	16	22						
Denmark	17	21	81	17	82		95	96	63	
East Africa	62	46	30	43						
East Germany					58		76	31	42	
Egypt					37		68	56	36	
Ecuador	75	60	9	66						
Ethiopia							77	44	76	
Finland	32	53	69	27	86		82	76	60	
France	65	77	78	45	76	41	89	73	67	
Greece	58	100	38	60	64		77	74	63	
Guatemala	91	90	0	39						
Hong Kong	65	26	27	60	53	66	81	71	63	81
Hungary					70		19	64	55	
India	74	36	53	59	66		67	90	65	52
Indonesia	75	43	15	48	50	90	44	51	87	
Iran	56	53	45	45						
Ireland	27	31	77	72	100		96	88	70	
Israel	13	72	59	49						
Italy	48	67	84	74	70	0	88	72	60	
Jamaica	43	12	43	72						
Japan	52	82	51	100	82	100	70	41	39	68
Kuwait					68		77		44	
Malaysia	100	32	29	53	52		77		43	
Mexico	78	73	33	73	67		77	74	43	
Nepal							56	34		
Netherlands	37	47	88	15	77	71	97		64	37
New Zealand	21	44	87	61						25

Table 17–2 Cultural Differences (cont'd)

Country or Region	PD 100%= high PD	UA 100%= high UA	IDV 100% = high IDV	MAS /FEM 100%= More MAS	UNI /PAR 100%= More UNI	NEU /AFF 100%= More NEU	SPE /DIF 100%= More SPE	ACH /ASC 100%= More ACH	IN /OUT 100%= More IN	C.Dyn. 100%= More L. Term
Nigeria					70		62	71	62	14
Norway	30	45	76	8	86	73	88	100	69	
Oman					27		75			
Pakistan	53	63	15	53	70		77	88	100	0
Panama	91	77	12	46						
Peru	62	78	18	44						
Philippines	90	39	35	67	69		79	81		16
Poland					82		81		74	27
Portugal	61	93	30	33	72		93	57	68	
Romania					49			68	83	
Russia					43		24	57	50	
Salvador	63	84	21	42						
Singapore	71	0	22	51	60	51	70	50	46	41
South Africa	47	44	71	66						
South Korea	58	76	20	41	39		38	41	51	64
Spain	55	77	56	44	61		78	65	74	
Sweden	30	26	78	0	77		100	85	55	28
Switzerland	33	52	75	74	94		97	76	65	
Taiwan	56	62	19	47						74
Thailand	62	57	22	36	63		66	78	57	47
Turkey	63	76	41	47	72		86	57	58	
UAE					74		65		69	
U.K.	34	31	98	69	77	86	96	91	65	21
Uruguay	59	89	40	40	63		93	60		
U.S.	38	41	100	66	90	48	96	97	75	25
Venezuela	78	68	13	77	38		43			
West Africa	74	48	22	48						
West Germany	34	58	74	69	81		90	76	73	26
Yugoslavia	73	79	30	22	0		0		0	

Notes: PD = power distance; UA =uncertainty avoidance; IDV = individualism; MAS = masculine; FEM = feminine, UNI = universalism; PAR = particularism; NEU = Neutral; AFF = Affect; SPE = Specific; DIF = Diffuse; ACH = Achievement; ASC = Ascription; OUT = Outer; IN = Inner. Con D = Confucian Dynamism, L. Term = long term. All scores have been normalized from the originals to go from 0–100. Blank cells indicate missing data.
Sources: Hoecklin (1998), Hofstede (2001), Trompenaars (1994).

Power distance

Power distance represents the degree of equality in a group. Cultures vary by how authority is distributed within groups. The more hierarchical and centralized the management of the group, the larger the power distance and the higher the score in the table. Power distance is higher if the boss's decision is accepted—right or wrong.

In high power-distance contexts, the manager is viewed as an expert; in low power-distance contexts, the manager is viewed as a problem-solver in conjunction with the group. Egalitarian managers in high power-distance contexts may be viewed as weak and incompetent or employees may interpret the manager's help as a signal that employees are doing poorly. Authoritarian managers in a low power-distance context may be viewed as dictatorial.

Thus, managers with a more egalitarian approach may not work as well in Latin America, Arab countries, and Indonesia, which tend to maintain more power distance, as in the more egalitarian Northern Europe, United States, and Canada. Even within Europe we see differences. In a BP finance office, Germans tended to be more hierarchical; the Dutch, Scandinavians, and British were more likely to challenge authority, and the French accepted management authority more or less as a right and obligation. (Hoecklin, 1995)

Uncertainty avoidance

Uncertainty avoidance represents attitudes toward risk. Regions with high uncertainty avoidance (and larger scores in the table) include Japan, Southern European countries that have traditionally been more predominantly Roman Catholic or Orthodox, and South America; they are more uncomfortable with ambiguity, dislike conflict in organizations, and may prefer formal rules. They may be fairly conformist, with originality neither rewarded nor valued. Those with low uncertainty avoidance (Singapore, Scandinavia, Canada, the United States, and the United Kingdom) deal better with ambiguity and change and are more likely to take risks for commensurate rewards. Long-term job security tends to be important in high uncertainty-avoidance cultures. Jobs-for-life in the Japanese context reflect high risk-avoidance preferences. Managers are more likely to be chosen by seniority. Rules should not be broken, even for good reasons. In low uncertainty-avoidance cultures, job mobility is higher. Managers are more likely chosen by merit. There is more flexibility and judgment in interpreting and breaking rules.

Cultures have four ways of dealing with uncertainty:

- technology
- rules and law
- religion and ritual
- relationships

Technology (often favored in the West) may be used to deal with uncertainty resulting from nature. It can help provide food, improve material comfort, and conquer disease. Rules and law (or relationships) may be used to deal with uncertainty resulting from other people. We will see this aspect of culture discussed below. Religion and ritual may often help us cope with uncertainties beyond our understanding and to provide a basic value system.

Individualism/Collectivism

In the most individualistic cultures (higher IDV scores) in Hofstede's survey—the United States, Australia, and the United Kingdom—individual initiative and leadership are most valued. People are permitted (and expected) to have their own opinions; promotion is more likely to be based on merit and individual accomplishment. In collective societies, which are in the majority worldwide, the group is more highly valued and the individual receives value from being a member of the group. In return, the group is responsible for taking care of its individual members. Promotion is from within the group and tends to be based on seniority. Socialist countries in the past were very group-oriented, as are many East Asian and Latin American countries in Hofstede's sample. Thus, a brash individualistic American management style may fall flat in Asia or tribal Africa, where the group defines the individual and consensus is important.

Adler (1997) suggests that groups tend to be better at establishing objectives and evaluating and choosing alternatives to meet those objectives, whereas the individual tends to be better at coming up with objectives. The effectiveness of the orientation also depends upon the individual's cultural background. For example, Earley (1989) found that a Chinese working anonymously in a group performed administrative tasks better, while Americans performed the same administrative tasks better when working separately with personal attribution of the tasks.

Masculinity/Femininity

Masculinity/femininity relates to how important masculine values such as assertiveness and success are relative to feminine values such as relationships and physical environment. Higher values in the table reflect more masculine cultures and lower values reflect more feminine cultures. Cultures with an aging population also tend to shift somewhat to more feminine values.

These traits also indicate how important gender is in the business world. More masculine societies tend to have tighter specifications of gender-specific activities, more industrial conflict, and higher stress levels. Business women in masculine OPEC countries face special sets of problems not as prevalent in the more feminine cultures of Scandinavia; Gustavsson (1995) notes that feminine orientation towards human values is one of the important aspects of the Scandinavian management style. This style includes not only humanitarian values but also consensus decision-making and a commitment to equality. This commitment is across gender as well as socio-economic classes and discourages braggadocio and self-promotion. Equality also requires a less hierarchical structure with management more by vision and values and less by giving orders. For example, the Swedes were early leaders in moving from assembly line production to work teams at Volvo.

Hines (1992), in a somewhat similar vein, uses an Eastern framework featuring yin (creation) and yang (completion). Each is thought to have components of the other within it, with the dominance of the two forces changing and cycling through time. Yin (feminine) values are sharing, relatedness and kinship; cultures with a more yin orientation are more relaxed, responsive, open, flexible, and passive. Aboriginal cultures may have a yin framework toward land and work. Yang (masculine) values are quantification, objectivity, efficiency, productivity, reason, and logic; cultures with more of a yang orientation are more excitable, commanding, outgoing, decisive, and active. Western nations' accounting and accountability rules reflect a Yang orientation. (Greer and Patel, circa 1999)

Confucian Dynamism

In addition to the previous list of cultural indicators, Hofstede and Bond (1988) add an indicator called *Confucian Dynamism,* which is particularly important in understanding and functioning in Asian cultures and relates to a culture's orientation across time. Confucian values place a high importance on long-term commitments, respect for tradition, and a work ethic that favors thrift and persistence, delaying current gratification for longer-term gain. Business takes longer to develop in this type of society and change generally takes place more slowly than cultures with low long-term time orientation.

A longer-term focus also suggests that the individual may be more likely to submit to the group and its hierarchy and have a sense of shame. Shame in this context is outer based and relates to group approval; you bring shame if you make the group look bad, but you are only shamed if the group knows about it. Related to the concept of shame is the notion of face; *having face* means enjoying a high standing with one's peers. Being shamed causes one to *lose face.* One loses face through another's criticism, insults, or failure to show proper respect.

Group-oriented cultures that are shame-based often do not say "no" directly, for instance; they do not want to cause others embarrassment or loss of face. Westerners must take care to understand that something as seemingly simple as an affirmative response of "yes" may not really mean the individual is agreeing to something. In Japan it means, "I heard you." In China, answers can be evasive: something that is "inconvenient," is "under consideration," or "would be difficult" typically means "no." A "yes" said with air sucked in through the teeth also means "no." In India, too, evasive answers typically mean "no."

In more individualistic cultures with a shorter-term orientation, social control and incentives may be more guilt-based. Here, the obligation is to the self, and self-approval is important. In a guilt-based system of control, pressure is internalized: Your failures do not bring shame to the whole group and guilt is to be felt whether others know about it or not.

Time

Trompenaar suggests another way that cultures view time: Events may be considered sequential or synchronous. In *sequential* cultures, things are done one at a time in sequence; appointments and plans are closely adhered to. Someone working out of sequence may cause a whole plan to fail. In *synchronous* cultures, many things may be done at once—appointments and plans change; relationships are important. Turbulent cultures may be synchronous since many paths to the same end may increase the probability of ultimate success. However, a sequential person from the United Kingdom may be a bit disoriented in a meeting with a synchronous Arab or Latin American, who will stop the meeting for many interruptions.

Four out of five of Trompenaar's concepts deal with relationships with people, and his scores for these attributes are also shown in Table 17–2.

Universalism and Particularism

Universalists (UNI) believe that there are norms, values, and behavior patterns that are valid everywhere; particularists believe that circumstances and relationships determine ideas and practices. Universalist cultures score higher numbers in Table 17–2, while particularists score lower numbers.

In universal cultures (United States, United Kingdom, Australia and Germany), more focus is placed on rules and formal procedures, such as detailed contracts. Hooker (1998) argues that Western rule-based cultures (which he calls "rude") are influenced by the notions of justice rooted in Judaism, Islam, and the Greek notion of rationality.

Laws based on justice and reason are trusted to create social harmony and resolve conflict.

In particularist cultures (China, Japan, Korea, Indonesia, FSU, and Venezuela), relationships are more important and authority, group solidarity, and sensitivity to others are used to create harmony. Hooker calls these "polite" cultures since more attention is often paid to the feelings of others.

In parts of Asia, a strong influence of Confucius and respect for authority within families and within organizations prevails. In China, relationships between families and organizations (*gūanxì*) are developed through mutual obligations based on gifts and favors. Over time, trust is built and forms the basis for their interactions. Koreans are somewhat similar, but hierarchy is stronger than in China with gifts and favors larger and more important. Although the Japanese also yield to authority, they place more emphasis on the group than the other two countries. Group harmony and social ritual are extremely important to them.

Although Latin America evolved out of the Western tradition, Hooker (1998) argues that its repressive and turbulent past has contributed to its being particularist rather than universalist and rule-based. In a violent society with erratic and repressive rulers, family and friend were a source of safety and survival; only they could be trusted and great care was taken to not offend others.

Particularist culture's small talk and socializing are part of the familiarization and trust-building process. In a let's-get-down-to-business universalist culture, such activities might be considered a waste of time. Contracts can obviate the need for trust to a universalist, whereas the detailed contracts of a universalist might signal a lack of trust to a particularist, who expects that contracts and relationships will be modified over time.

McWorld/Jihad

Along somewhat similar lines, Barber (1996) looks at a social confrontation he calls "McWorld versus Jihad."

The McWorld point of view sees the world as one large market connected by information networks moving toward automation and homogenization. Centralized multinational companies with a headquarters office (or country) and more polycentric, transnational corporations use large amounts of natural resources to serve a global market. The headquarters office plays a leading role, coordinating activities of the various subsidiaries, while each production center specializes where it adds the most value with a key role to knowledge. McWorld is associated with occidental (particularly American) culture.

Jihad represents the point of view that opposes modern capitalism and clings to religious beliefs, ethnic traditions, and local and national communities. Jihad elements in a culture increase the risk for capitalists doing business in them; 24% of the world's oil reserves are in areas where Jihad beliefs are prevalent.

McWorld values and promotes economic well-being but not necessarily social and political well-being, while Jihad promotes community but is often intolerant. Barber suggests taking the best from McWorld while maintaining a cultural identity and sense of community from Jihad. He believes that Japan and China have been reasonably successful at doing just that. Alternately, McWorld managers in Jihad cultures need to pay special attention to indigenous groups and cultures.

Neutral/Affective

The neutral/affective trait indicates whether emotions are expressed or not. In neutral cultures (high numbers in Table 17–2) such as Japan, the United Kingdom, Singapore, and Indonesia, expressing emotions, particularly intense emotions, is viewed with disfavor and is considered unprofessional. More affective cultures (lower numbers in the table) such as Mexico, the Netherlands, China, and Russia are much more comfortable expressing emotions in public and may view people from neutral cultures as cold or deceitful.

A further division within these categories is whether emotion should be exhibited and whether emotions should be separated from reasoning processes for business decisions. Scandinavians tend to not exhibit their emotions and feel that emotions should be separated from business decisions. Southern Europeans tend to exhibit their emotions and not separate them from rationality in decision-making; Americans tend to exhibit but separate.

Specific/Diffuse

Specific/diffuse relates to how a culture views private and public relationships. An individual presents a public space to everyone and keeps a private space that is shared with selected individuals. In the specific cultures of Australia, the United Kingdom, and the United States, an individual has a small private space, which is compartmentalized from the public space. The public space is easily entered but is very restricted and compartmentalized.

In a diffuse culture such as China, the private space is larger and less compartmentalized, so it is harder to enter someone's public space in a diffuse culture because it allows easier entrance into the private space. Diffuse cultures may at first seem cold to those from a warmer culture; specific cultures may be viewed as shallow and superficial by their more diffuse neighbors. Specific cultures may find it very time consuming to work in diffuse cultures. For people from specific cultures, the requisite social activities may seem not only time consuming but perhaps even an invasion of privacy.

Achievement/Ascription

Hofstede explores how power and authority vary across a group. In Trompenaars category, and achievement/ascription (ACH/ASC), he explores how power and status are attributed to members of the group. In an achievement culture such as Australia, the United States, Switzerland, and the United Kingdom, one's status is determined by how well one performs desirable functions for the group; the emphasis is on task. Status and power in an ascriptive culture is more who you are than what you are. Status and power are conferred by things often ascribed at birth—gender, family, and social connections.

Ascriptive cultures include Venezuela, Indonesia, and China, where the emphasis is more on relationships than achievements. However, ascriptive status and power may enable leaders to get things done just as well as in an achievement culture that is likely to be more rule based.

Our relationship to our environment may also vary by the degree of control we feel we have over our destinies. Trompenaars designates cultures whose members feel that they are in control of their fates as *inner-directed* (IN) while those that feel they are merely "pawns in the game," controlled by fate, are *outer-directed* (OUT). Higher numbers in Table 17–2 indicate more inner-directedness, while lower numbers indicate more outer-directedness. North Americans and Europeans tend to be more inner-directed, while the Arab's "Inshallah," which means God willing and is often spoken after statements of coming events, suggests a more outer-directed view of the world. Native Americans would also fall more in the category of believing in fate.

Cognitive Styles

Cognitive style relates to how a culture organizes and processes sensory information—what we absorb and what we filter out. Coyne (2001) refers to two cognitive styles—open-minded versus closed-minded. A more open-minded culture examines external information and considers all points of view; a more closed-minded culture filters out a wider range of external information, particularly if it does not agree with preconceived notions.

The United States is an example of a more closed-minded culture. Theocratic societies, ruled by religion, tend to be closed-minded. Indeed, Coyne contends that most cultures are closed-minded if things are going well. Japan began to modernize only when threatened by foreign encroachment in the 1860s; U.S. complacency about American management techniques from the 1950s and 1960s began to break down in the 1980s and early 1990s as the Japanese took center stage. With this threat to national pride, American corporations began to adopt or consider many of the tenets of Japanese management, including total quality management, lean manufacturing, JIT inventories, an incremental approach to reducing waste and inefficiency by empowerment of people at all levels of the company, consensus decision-making, and a more paternal attitude towards labor to improve long-term loyalty.

Data that makes it through the filter is processed and assimilated in various ways. An associative individual tries to associate new data with personal experience. An abstract individual analyzes (breaks things into pieces) and tries to develop theories about processes and relationships. Whether someone is associative or abstract is heavily influenced by the educational system: Teaching by rote develops associative thinkers while teaching by problem solving produces more abstract thinkers, who are better able to deal with things that are completely new.

Life Values

Social cultures value people; economic cultures value acquiring wealth and satisfying physical needs. Theoretical systematic cultures value the acquisition of knowledge with little deference to beauty or usefulness. Power cultures value the acquisition of power and control over others, while religious cultures value unity with the cosmos. Truth is typically established by faith, fact, or feelings, with feelings being the most common.

Business Protocols

Coyne (2001) indicates a number of items of business protocol that vary considerably across cultures and should be mastered before doing business in another culture.

They include personal space, greetings, expectations about punctuality, necessity for making appointments, pace of business, value of personal contacts, delivery performance, business cards, when business discussions can take place, forms of greeting, use of titles, eye contact, gift expectations, and appropriate business dress.

Personal space

Hall and Hall (1984) note that personal space and territory vary across cultures. Japanese stand further apart from one another than do North Americans, who in turn stand further apart than Middle Easterners and Latin Americans. Latin Americans touch more frequently than either North Americans or Japanese. Greetings vary, as well. Learning and respecting personal space and greetings pay cultural dividends in business dealings.

Ritual

Ritual varies across cultures as well. Asia tends to have high ritual cultures where behavior tends to be more structured and to follow set rules.

For example, in Japan, rules govern gift giving, including the gift, the manner of presentation, the manner of acceptance, and how the gift receiver reciprocates. Another example is that of business cards in Asia: The card is presented with ceremony and is not to be shoved in the pocket after a glance.

Human nature

Adler (1997) notes various cultural conceptions of human nature. Cultures that view people as basically good tend to trust people until they are proven untrustworthy; cultures that view people as basically untrustworthy tend to use safeguards to protect themselves from people until they are proven trustworthy. Some cultures may be neutral or believe that each individual varies in his or her moral character. Such character is believed to be changeable by some and fixed by other cultures.

If humans are changeable—as the Chinese believe—they will spend more time and effort on training and encouraging personal improvement. If personalities and qualities are more immutable, more resources will be spent on selection and screening, as is done in the United States.

Humans and nature

Cultures vary in how they interact with the world and nature. They may feel they dominate, are in harmony with, or are subjugated by nature. Some cultures may view the world as stable and predictable while others view it as random and turbulent. Western cultures are more likely to feel they dominate nature whereas Eastern cultures may want to be in harmony with nature.

For example, the Chinese practice of Feng Shui (derived from Taoism) believes that there are natural laws and cycles whose energies you can harness as it flows through all things to be in harmony with nature. Form, shape, and, particularly, spatial alignment are used to bring the environment into alignment with natural energy flows. Thus, in a Far Eastern environment, office furniture alignment and location are important considerations for a smoothly flowing office and should not be left to chance.

Relations to work

Another aspect of the human relationship to nature, according to Kluckholn and Strodbeck (1961), is the orientation toward activity or the purpose of work. They establish three culture types—doing, being, or becoming. Doing cultures, such as the United States, focus on outward accomplishments for tangible rewards; being cultures, such as Latin America, enjoy the here and now and tend to be more spontaneous. They are more likely to accept circumstances and try to make the best of them, rather than changing circumstances. Becoming cultures focus more on the inner rewards of personal growth and self-actualization often associated with meditation and spiritual growth, featured in Buddhism and Hinduism.

Understanding a culture's relationship to nature and work often helps in motivating employees. Two management theories are associated with these concepts.

Theory X suggests that people dislike work but are motivated by basic needs of safety and security. In this doing context, a manager directs, controls, and coerces employees to get the job done. Theory Y maintains that people are motivated by achievement and self-actualization. In this becoming context, employees will work toward things to which they have a commitment. Managers should seek to motivate and then allow employees to grow and develop as they move toward their goals.

Adler (1997) notes advantages and disadvantages of the more decentralized Theory Y. Decentralization encourages decision-making and problem-solving skills, and improves creativity and job satisfaction. It can, however, require more expensive training, higher quality employees, increased information flows, and a need to develop accountability measures.

Communications

Communication is another area where misunderstandings and problems can arise across cultures. There are a number of aspects to communication. At the verbal level there are three components:

1. what you say
2. what you mean
3. what the listener understands

What you say may be interpreted differently in two cultures because of differences in meanings across cultures.

Cultures have their own icons in the form of symbols, heroes, and rituals that represent underlying values. Idioms, similes, and metaphors that represent these icons may convey meanings and emotions that do not translate across boundaries. Cowboy images may not be meaningful to a Japanese person; Samurai images may not translate from East to West. Telling an Egyptian, "Don't throw the baby out with the bath water," will not seem to be an appropriate ritual.

Words may have different meanings in different contexts. For example, the statement "Bill Clinton was born in Hope and grew up in Hot Springs," translated into Italian (and back into English) by Altavista's Machine Translation service, reads: "The invoice Clinton has been taken in the hope and it has been developed in warm motivating forces." Chevrolet Novas did not sell well in Mexico in part because *no va* in Spanish means doesn't go. One does not expect that the Iranian laundry soap Barf would sell well in the United States.

Low/High Context

Hall and Hall (1990) refer to low-context and high-context situations and cultures.

In a low-context situation, both parties know little about the context and nothing can be taken for granted. Everything must be spelled out. For example, the following sentence would not make sense in a low-context situation: "This book describes step-by-step procedures for setting up a DHCP server, securing your intranet with a firewall, running on an alpha system, and configuring your kernel." However, an advanced Linux operator would know exactly what is meant.

In a high-context situation, two parties understand context and very little needs to be spelled out. Cultures which are more homogenous and well connected (such as the Japanese, Arabs, and Mediterraneans) are typically high-context cultures. Cultures that are more individualistic and have more compartmentalized lives (North Americans and northern Europeans) are typically lower-context.

Explaining too much in a high-context culture may be taken as condescension; explaining too little in a low-context culture may lead to lack of understanding.

Body language

Adler (1997) suggests that words communicate 7% of meaning, tone of voice gives 39%, and the rest is conveyed through nonverbal means such as gesture, posture, and facial expression. Nonverbal communication may reinforce, contradict, or help clarify the verbal portion. If nonverbal actions contradict the verbal, the nonverbal is more likely to be the true signal. But nonverbal actions will only help clarify matters if the nonverbal signal means the same thing in other cultures. In some cases, nonverbal signals are identical across cultures—a smile is a greeting, a frown a signal of displeasure—but at other times, they are not.

Nodding one's head up and down means "no" to a Bulgarian, "yes" to an American, and "I'm listening" to a Japanese person. A North American may feel that someone who will not look you in the eye is shifty but may find an Arab's long eye contact aggressive. A Chinese or Japanese person, however, feels that direct eye contact is rude and aggressive. When nonverbal signals are contradictory, the most believable (in order of reliability) are: autonomic (involuntary) signals such as weeping; leg, foot, trunk, and hand gestures; facial expressions; and verbal communication. Someone who is lying often decreases the number of hand movements, increases the number of hand shrugs, increases the number of body shifts, and increases the frequency of hand-to-face contacts—particularly nose-touching, a sign of tension, and mouth covering. Slight facial changes are also caught and suppressed that can be picked up on slow-motion cameras, even if they are typically difficult to detect with the naked eye.

Nonverbal communication typically takes the form of some sort of action that may be inherited, discovered, absorbed, or learned. Morris (1988) considers the whole gamut of gestures in a business setting. *Baton signals* are used while speaking and tend to give rhythm and emphasis to spoken thoughts. Often they are hand movements but can include the head and body or even the feet. Hands can be palms up (supplication), palms forward (a barrier), palms down (calming or suppressing effect), palms wide (welcoming), fingers together to a point (emphasizing detail), hands pounding (a point), or a fist raised (warning). Such gestures vary across individuals, cultures, and occasions. Italians gesticulate a lot; Japanese, very little. Lower classes gesture more than upper classes, and the inarticulate gesticulate more than the articulate.

Finger pointing—or, where this is rude or taboo, a whole hand or even the head—may indicate a direction. Beckoning may take the form of the whole hand waving with the palm down (as in parts of Asia, Africa, Italy, Spain, and South America) or the palm up for most of rest of the world. Using just one finger is riskier as it may be teasing, sexual, sarcastic, or rude; a slight head jerk may also have a sexual connotation.

Salutation displays for greetings, good-byes, and other life transformations are universal but take various forms in various cultures. The amount of body and eye contact vary by how well the parties know each other, how long they have been separated, the privacy of the meeting, and local cultural display rules. Handshakes and bows are more formal; embraces and kissing, less so. Ritual talk shows concern and pleasure.

Cultures universally have ways of establishing and showing the dominance-submissive ordering. This varies from culture to culture but may be indicated by the depth of the bow, the seating at the table, who dominates the conversation, who is introduced first, and so forth. It is a good idea to learn these cues before dealing with a new culture. When friends of equal status are interacting, often they echo each other's gestures and posture and may synchronize their movements as they talk. You may want to try this to put a subordinate or equal at ease; however, it may be an aggressive act with a dominant person.

Even clothing acts as a display, with each article transmitting a signal. Knowing the appropriate dress code for each culture you deal with is useful. Inappropriate or overly revealing clothing may violate local taboos and put you at a severe commercial disadvantage, as can violating areas of the body that are not be touched. Each culture has body areas that are public zones and others that are private or taboo zones that vary by relationship and gender. These zones may not exist for babies and those that are most intimate but for most other relationships they do. For example, one should never touch the head of a Buddhist and males should be careful to avoid body contact with females in devout Muslim cultures.

Most cultures eat a few large meals over the course of the day, despite the fact that smaller meals are better physiologically. Morris (1988) argues that this custom evolves from our hunting past, where you feasted and shared food after the kill. This tendency is re-enforced by human sociability. However, table manners and food customs vary considerably. A belch that may be a sign of pleasure in one culture is rude and boorish in another. Many cultures use the fork in the left hand and the knife in the right, except the United States, or where fingers or chopsticks are used. Food and drink taboos, often of religious origin, include pork for Jews and Muslims, alcohol for Muslims, and beef for Hindus. Toasting rituals vary; when and if business is conducted at a meal varies, as well.

Paying attention to verbal and non-verbal nuances and shared cultural traits can be especially important to a successful advertising campaign. Observing advertising from another culture can also provide useful information on that culture's values.

Political culture

Democratic, market-based industrial economies typically function under rules of law with the generally accepted notion that if everyone acted within the law, the society would perform reasonably well.

Centrally planned command economies tackle the complex task of trying to produce and allocate goods and services to millions of people; strict central planning and adherence to the plan became their accepted norm. Economic incentives are not built into the system, leading to weak motivation for work, shoddy products, shortages, and queues. Controlling the economy becomes harder as products become more complex and consumers more sophisticated. In such settings, those who sidestepped the legal channels helped make an impossible system possible. Getting around the system, rather than working within it, becomes an accepted activity.

With the fall of the USSR, some western economists naively thought that privatization, liberalized prices, and market-based economies would fix the problems of the planned economies. Instead, powerful elites took control of the government and economic resources. The mafia's corruption became pervasive in the economy. Western laws were transplanted without the institutions or political will to enforce them. In the absence of the checks and balances developed over centuries in the West, cronyism, rather than liberal capitalism, evolved much like the age of the robber barons in the United States. Interpersonal relationships and connections become especially important in dealing with these and other corrupt cultures.

Company culture

As we have seen, companies have cultures not unlike nations. Recent mergers, privatizations, and a number of national companies going international are forcing many of these disparate corporate cultures to adapt to one other. Trompenaars (1993) lists three important aspects of corporate cultures:

1. the relationship between employees and their organization, or how employees view the organization and their place in it
2. the relationship between superiors and subordinates
3. whether the organization is person- or task-oriented

These relationships affect how the organization thinks, learns, and changes and how it motivates, rewards, and resolves conflicts. Trompenaar considers four different types of corporate structure:

- family
- Eiffel Tower
- guided missile
- incubator

These types vary by their vertical hierarchy and by whether they are task/person oriented (Fig. 17–2).

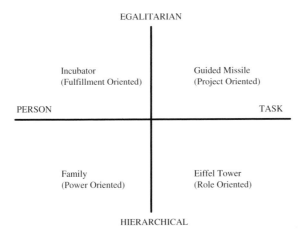

Fig. 17–2 Vertical Structure and Orientation for Four Corporate Structures

Source: Trompenaars, 1993

The Family Culture, prevalent in Japan, China, Venezuela, and India, is people-oriented but very hierarchical. It maintains control through loss of affection or place in the family and motivates with praise and appreciation. It is more prevalent in high-context, diffuse cultures that are more comfortable with intuitive than with rational knowledge. Development of people is a high priority and may be accomplished through training, mentoring, coaching, and apprenticeships. Change and conflict resolution come from evolving personal relationships.

The Eiffel Tower Culture, prevalent in Western industrial countries, is also very hierarchical but its orientation is toward the task rather than the person. There is a bureaucratic division of labor, a preference for order and stability, and conflict is considered irrational. Each level in the hierarchy has a clear function. Relationships are specific, status is ascribed by role and professional qualifications are important. The organization has a purpose that is outside and separate from personal needs for power or affection. Salary is influenced by difficulty, complexity, and responsibility of the assigned job role. Learning is to acquire the skills required for advancement. Organizational change is accomplished by changing the rules (which can be a slow process), while conflict is resolved by applying the rules. It is important to follow the rules and means are as important as the end.

The Guided Missile Culture is also impersonal and task-focused but is more egalitarian. Here, the end is what is important, and companies that follow this culture are often peopled by professionals who are cross-disciplinary. This culture is expensive because professionals tend to be expensive. Groups are formed for projects and dissolved when the project is completed. It is a neutral rather than an affective culture. Status derives from a member's contribution to problem solving for the task at hand. Members are evaluated by their peers, but it is harder to quantify individual contribution than in the Eiffel Tower Model. Members tend to be practical rather than theoretical and the group is organized around a problem rather than a discipline. Change is accomplished as projects come and go, along with the people involved in them. People are more loyal to their profession or projects than to the company. Motivating is intrinsic with management-by-objective and pay-for-performance.

Incubator Cultures—Silicon Valley-type firms—are egalitarian, people-oriented and are often founded by a creative team or entrepreneur. They may be motivated by hope and idealism with the organization existing for self-expression and fulfillment. The goal in such companies is to minimize routine tasks to free time for creative pursuits. Management confirms, criticizes, and provides resources for the creative process. Authority comes from the individual's ideas or inspiring vision. Individuals are motivated intrinsically and are committed more to work than to people. Change in such companies can be fast and spontaneous. Selfish power plays do not move the group forward and are anathema to it. Working for such companies can be intense and all absorbing but can lead to burnout. Conflict is handled by breaking apart and going separate ways and by experimenting to find the best course of action.

Summary

Culture is an ecosystem of shared values and customary ways of thinking, doing things, and reacting to each other and to our environment. It is passed on at home, at school, at work, and at play and determines how basic human needs for sustenance, safety, esteem, and self-fulfillment are satisfied. Despite individual variation within a culture, there is often a great deal of similarity, as well. Understanding and using these similarities, while allowing for the differences, can help one flourish in any culture, whether national, professional, or corporate.

People's attitudes vary towards authority, risk, and uncertainty. Confucion and Catholic cultures tend to have more hierarchy and a lower tolerance for risk than Protestant cultures; the Family and Eiffel Tower models of corporate governance are hierarchical, as well. Uncertainty may be minimized through technology, rules, law, religion and ritual, and relationships.

The relationship of the individual to the group is an important aspect of culture. The individual is especially important to Anglo cultures; the group tends to be more important in the Orient and tribal cultures. In individualistic cultures leadership and individual accomplishments are valued, and a private life and private opinions are acceptable. Guilt and intrinsic or internal motivation are important for social control. Collective cultures value the group more highly, with members more likely to hold the group opinion and to expect to be taken care of by the group. Bringing shame to the group or losing face within the group, and extrinsic or external motivation, are important for social control.

More masculine cultures value assertiveness and success; more feminine cultures value relationships and the physical environment, and allow more latitude in gender-specific activities. Time values also vary across cultures: Confucian values put a premium on long-term commitments and tradition; western cultures, particularly the United States, have a much shorter-term orientation. Cultures may view events as sequential or synchronous. The more sequential the orientation, the more important planning and timing are. The more synchronous the culture, the looser the plans and the more tolerance for interruptions.

Universalists believe in universal values and norms; particularists believe in relative values and norms that are particular to the circumstances. Universalist western cultures want detailed contracts and go by the book. Trust comes from having rules and obeying them. Particularist, Eastern-developing cultures focus on relationships, harmony, and individual feelings. Trust comes from the relationship not from the rules.

Neutral cultures do not display emotions; affective ones do. More diffuse cultures have a large private space that is hard to enter, but once in, you have access to much of that person's life. Different aspects of an individual's life are not as compartmentalized. Specific cultures tend to have a small private space that is compartmentalized from larger public space. The public space may be compartmentalized and easy to enter, whereas the private space is much harder to enter.

Few groups are completely egalitarian, so every group needs a way to allocate power. In achievement cultures, you earn power and status by what you do or by your contribution to the tasks at hand and group goals. In ascription cultures, you earn status and power by who you are, which may be associated with family, gender, or social connections.

Inner-directed cultures feel they have personal control over their fates and may feel that they dominate nature. More fatalistic, outer-directed cultures feel that they are controlled externally and may feel that they are dominated by nature.

We organize and process information in different ways. A more open-minded culture considers more information from a wider point of view; a more closed-minded culture considers less information from a narrower point of view. Cultures at threat are more likely to be open-minded than those for whom things are going well. An associative culture (more likely taught by rote) tries to associate new data with old experience and categories. An abstract culture (more likely taught by problem solving) tries to develop theories about processes and relationships that will allow one to understand and better cope with completely new things.

Values differ, truth is affirmed by various means, and perceptions of people are not universal. Aesthetic cultures value beauty and life experiences; social cultures strive for people. Economic cultures value wealth and physical comfort. Theoretical, systematic cultures value knowledge for knowledge's sake. Power cultures value power and control over others. Religious cultures value unity with the cosmos. Truth is verified by faith, fact, or feelings. Some cultures view people as trustworthy; others view them as untrustworthy. Some view people's personalities as immutable; others view them as changeable. Some view people as working to satisfy physical needs, others view them as working to achieve and become self-fulfilled.

Business protocols include personal space, greetings, expectations about punctuality, necessity for making appointments, pace of business, value of personal contacts, delivery performance, business cards, when business discussions can take place, forms of greeting, use of titles, eye contact, gift expectations, taboo zones, table manners, food taboos, and appropriate business dress.

Verbal communication has three levels—what you say, what you mean, and what the listener understands. Communication can run awry at each level. Idioms vary across cultures and may be misinterpreted. The emotional character of idioms and symbols may not translate across time and space. Low-context cultures require one to be more explicit than high-context cultures, which are more homogenous with many shared values and experiences.

More than 50% of communication may be nonverbal, in the form of gestures, posture, and facial expression, which may be inherited, discovered, absorbed, or learned. Baton signals give rhythm and emphasis to spoken words. Guide signs indicate direction. Salutation displays are for hellos, good byes, and life transformations. Signs of dominance and submission signal the social hierarchy. Echo postures are often observed among friends and can be used to put strangers and subordinates at ease.

How corporate cultures think, learn, change, motivate, reward, and resolve conflicts is determined by the relationship between employees and their organization, the relationship between superiors and subordinates, and whether the organization is person- or task-oriented.

The four corporate structures are the family, the Eiffel Tower, the guided missile, and the incubator. The family culture is hierarchical and people-oriented; the Eiffel Tower is hierarchical and task-oriented; the guided missile is egalitarian and task-oriented, and the incubator is egalitarian and people-oriented.

Cultural and corporate differences discussed in this chapter have implications on corporate behavior in various cultures. Adler (1997) indicates that they help determine the following:

- who makes decisions
- speed of decisions
- acceptable risk levels
- how problems are viewed and solved

A westerner is likely to view life as a series of problems to be solved using scientific and analytical thought. An American might be more likely to use induction and trial-and-error; a French person may be more likely to use deduction and a linear conceptual approach. An Easterner might be more likely to view life as a series of situations to be accepted and synthesized rather than analyzed, and multiple truths are accepted.

An Oriental would be more likely to take a more holistic approach that considers all the alternatives. An occidental from the United States or Germany would be more likely to take a sequential approach and make incremental decisions.

An important implication of how decisions are implemented depends on the ethical, institutional, and legal framework in the operating country. Environmental standards vary across countries. A gift that may be viewed as a bribe in the United States may be a normal part of business in Korea. Labor unions may negotiate national contracts in some countries, but not in others. Cartels may be illegal some places but encouraged in others.

Cultural differences also impact negotiations. The style may vary with the underlying values and assumptions of the culture and might be based on fact and logic, emotion, or ideals. Ritual may influence the opening offer, the amount of conflict, the size and timing of concessions, and the response to concessions. The autonomy and number of the negotiators is often related to the power structure and individualist tendencies of the culture.

Cross-cultural joint ventures, mergers, and teams must learn to move forward together. Some ingredients in the recipe for success are:

- clearly identify the end goal
- contrast and compare the way each culture or company would approach the goal
- assume differences until similarity is proved
- look at what is said and done rather than interpreting it
- choose the best approach or some better amalgam of the various approaches
- monitor feedback and continue to adapt

Appendix A: Glossary and Abbreviator

3-D Seismic – Three-dimensional underground images created by bouncing sound waves from various angles into the earth to measure potential for finding hydrocarbons.

4 P's of Marketing – Price, product, place, promotion.

5 C's of Pricing – Cost, customer, channel of distribution, competition, and compatibility with corporate goals.

Abatement of pollution – Reducing or eliminating pollution.

Abatement Subsidy – A payment from the government to induce firms to reduce pollution.

Achievement Culture – A culture that awards status by what an individual achieves or contributes to the group.

Ad Valorem Tax – A tax that is a percentage of the price of a good or service.

Additive Cost – If it costs the same to produce two goods together than to produce them separately, costs are additive. If it costs less to produce two goods together than to produce each separately, costs are sub-additive.

AER – Annual Energy Review

Aesthetic Culture – A culture that values beauty and harmony.

Affective Culture – A culture that displays emotions in public.

Aframax – Tankers from 75,000 deadweight tons to 115,000 that are not too large to enter African ports.

Aggregators – Markets that aggregate goods from many different producers and offer them for sale. For example, a supermarket is an aggregator.

Agoras – From the ancient Greek marketplace bring buyers and sellers together.

Alkylation – A chemical process involving alkyls that combines shorter hydrocarbons into longer ones. High-octane gasoline can be created by reacting alkanes and alkenes.

Alliances – A nonhierarchical association of businesses to buy or sell products or services.

American Option – An option is the right to buy (call) or sell (put) an underlying asset at a given price (strike price) that expires on a specific date. An American option can be exercised any time up to expiration.

Amortization – Allocating the cost of intangible assets over their legal life as specified in the tax code.

Amp – Abbreviation for ampere is a measure of electrical current or electron flow. A volt pushes one amp of current through a medium with a resistance of one ohm.

Analog data – Data that is continuously measurable such as sound or light waves or electrical current as opposed to digital data, which is measured as zeros and ones.

Annual Rate of Return – The annual interest rate that makes the stream of net revenues for a project equal to zero. Also called the internal rate of return.

Annual Yield – Another way of saying annual rate of return.

API – American Petroleum Institute

API Gravity – A measure of the weight of crude oil equal to (141.5/specific gravity) – 131.5. Specific gravity is the weight of a compound divided by the weight of water.

Application Service Provider (ASP) – A computer server that provides data, software applications, and computing power for clients.

Arbitrage – An investment strategy that ensures a profit with no net investment, such as buying a product in one market at a lower price and simultaneously selling it in another market at a higher price. Arbitrage helps markets allocate goods and services efficiently.

Arbitrator – A person who settles disputes between parties by appraising the facts, trying to get the parties to agree, and coming to a resolution. In binding arbitration, the disputing parties must accept the resolution.

Arms Length Transaction – A transaction between two unrelated parties in which each is acting on its own behalf independently of the other.

Ascription Culture – A culture that bases status and power on characteristics or qualities often ascribed at birth such as family or tribe.

Asian Option – A complicated option with a price based on the average price of the underlying assets over some period of time.

Asphalt – A solid petroleum product made of heavy long hydrocarbon molecules. It is used for roads, roofs, and water proofing. It is produced from solid natural accumulations as well as a refinery byproduct.

Asset Specificity – An asset is something of value that can be used to offset liabilities on a balance sheet. It might be physical capital, human capital, cash, or property. Asset specificity measures how particular the good is to specific transactions. For example, a pipeline that can only carry gas from one gas field to a particular market is a very specific asset, whereas a general purpose truck has all sorts of alternate uses and is a very general asset. The more specific the asset, the more the owner is subject to hold-up by the other side of the market.

At the Money – When the underlying asset for an option is at the strike price of the option.

Average Revenue – The money received per unit of sales equal to total revenue divided by sales. For a whole market where there is no price discrimination, the average revenue is the demand equation $P(Q)$ times sales Q divided by Q equal to $P(Q)*Q)/Q$, which is $P(Q)$ the demand equation.

Aversch Johnson (AJ) Effect – A higher level of capital stock than is socially optimal as the result of rate of return regulation that only allows a return on capital and not on other inputs.

Avoided Cost – The amount avoided for the incremental purchase or production of a good. In the United States, utilities were required to buy incremental power from qualifying independent power facilities (QF) if the utility's avoided electricity costs were higher than the prices of the qualifying facility.

b/d – Barrels per day

b/cd – Barrels per calendar

b/sd – Barrels per stream day

B2B – Business-to-business

B2C – Business-to-consumer

B2G – Business-to-government

Back Office Activities – Activities within a firm that support but do not deal directly with customers or the production activities of the firm. They include financial, human resources, and distribution activities.

Back Spread – A spread is buying/selling more than one derivative in a trading strategy. A back spread is going long (buying) more options than shorts (selling) all with the same expiration date. With a put back spread, buy at a lower strike price and sell at a higher strike price. With a call back spread, buy at a higher strike price and sell at a lower strike price.

Backstop Fuel – A higher priced fuel with high availability that we can transition to as currently cheaper fuels run out or become too expensive. Solar and other renewable energy sources are backstop fuels.

Backward Market – A market in which the futures prices are lower than the current spot prices. A backward market typically indicates that a market has a short-run shortage. Also referred to as a market in backwardation.

Barriers to Entry – Factors that prevent other firms from entering a market. They include cost and size advantages of existing firms, product differentiation and brand names, and some types of government regulation.

Baseload Electricity Production – The minimum amount of electricity that is produced all of the time.

Basis Differential – The difference between the current futures price and the spot price.

Baton Signals – Body movements, particularly with the hands, that give rhythm and emphasis to speech.

Bayesian Estimation – A methodology for estimating model parameters that combines data with knowledge of the probability distributions of the estimated parameters.

bbl – Barrel

BC – Before the current era or before the year zero.

bcf – Billion cubic feet

bcm – Billion cubic meters

Bear Market – A weak market in which prices are falling. Named such because a bear typically makes a downward movement with its head.

Bear Spread – A spread is buying/selling more than one derivative in a trading strategy. A bear spread is buying one option with strike price above the current spot market price and selling another one with strike price below the current spot market price. With a bear spread call, you buy and sell a call and with a bear spread put, you buy and sell a put.

Benefits of Pollution – Are any costs you forego by being able to pollute rather than having to abate. Benefits of pollution are then equal to the costs of abatement.

Bertrand Duopoly – A market with two producers in which each has market power and maximizes profits by setting price, taking the other producer's price as given. It is expected that this market will degenerate into competitive solutions with price equal to marginal cost.

Best Available Control Technology (BACT) – The current technology that eliminates the most pollution. Some pollution laws require that firms use BACT irrespective of the costs.

BI – Business intelligence.

Big Bang – A violent explosion that is thought to have created the universe.

Big Crunch – If there is enough matter in the universe so that gravity can counteract the current expansion of the universe, the universe will collapse in on itself in the Big Crunch. The other hypothesis is that the universe will keep expanding until the stars burn out, contract into black holes, and all matter will eventually evaporate into protons, electrons, neutrinos, and photons.

Bilateral Governance – Governance relates to how transactions are organized. Bilateral governance is controlling transactions by long-term contracts between two transactors.

Bilateral Monopoly – A market characterized by one buyer (monopsonist) buying from one seller (monopolist).

Binomial Pricing Model – A model in which the probability that an underlying asset will increase or decrease in a given period and the amount of change are computed from historical data and used to price options.

Biomass – Fuel made from biological or organic material. Examples are wood and animal dung.

Blackouts – A non-isolated power loss over an extended period of time due to a capacity shortage. It may result from peak loads higher than available capacity or from equipment failure.

Black and Scholes Model – A mathematical model for valuing financial options.

Bonds – A certificate of corporate or government debt that stipulates payment of interest and repayment of principal and interest at specified future dates.

Bonus Bidding – A bidding auction with upfront payment for the right to explore for crude oil or natural gas. Economists believe that competitive bonus bidding is typically the best way for owners to acquire the rents from their petroleum resources.

Bots – From the word robots, these are programs that run in the background of your computer and perform repetitive services such as searching the Internet, posting newsgroup messages, or comparing prices. Usually they have some decision-making ability. Examples are spiders that download web pages.

Bottleneck – An area of congestion that slows a process, such as in a pipeline or a refinery process.

Bounded Rationality – Making rational choices or optimizing one's objective function given one's cognitive limits and the information available.

Brainstorming – A problem solving technique where group participants shout out possible solutions, which are noted down for a specified period of time. Then, the group indicates the solution criteria, ranks the possible solutions, and picks the best.

Breakeven Pricing – Charging a price for which revenues exactly equal all costs including opportunity cost.

Brent Forward Market – The over the counter market for buying Brent crude oil at some future date.

Bricks and Mortar – Conventional retail and business establishments as opposed to online or e-commercial establishments.

British Thermal Unit (BTU) – The amount of energy needed to increase one pound of water one degree Fahrenheit at sea level. One BTU equals 0.252 kilocalories or 1.055 kilojoules.

Bronze Age – The age between the stone age and the iron age when bronze was discovered and used as a basic material. It varied by region but was roughly 4000 to 1200 BC.

Brownouts – An extended voltage drop over a significant region because of a power shortage or equipment failure.

Bull Market – A strong market in which prices are rising. Named after a bull because it tosses its head up.

Bull Spread – A spread is buying/selling more than one derivative in a trading strategy. A bull spread is selling one option with strike price above the current spot market price and buying another one with strike price below the current spot market selling price. With a bull spread call, you buy and sell a call. With a bull spread put, you buy and sell a put.

Business Intelligence (BI) – Software that enables a company to acquire, access, and use large amounts of data, also called data warehousing.

Business-to-Business (B2B) – E-commerce transactions between businesses.

Business-to-Customer (B2C) – E-commerce transactions with businesses selling to consumers.

Business-to-Government (B2G) – E-commerce transactions with businesses selling to government.

Butane – C_4H_{10} is a gaseous hydrocarbon extracted from natural gas, or a product from an oil refinery.

Butterfly Spread – A spread is buying/selling more than one derivative in a trading strategy. A butterfly spread is buying one option at a high strike price and one at a low strike price, and selling two options at an intermediate price. If the options are calls, it is called a call butterfly spread. If the options are puts, it is a put butterfly spread.

°C – Degrees Celsius

C_2H_6 – Ethane

C_3H_8 – Propane

C_4H_{10} – Butane

C_5H_{12} – Pentane

CAD – Computer-aided design

CAE – Computer engineering

Call Option – The right, but not the obligation, to buy an underlying asset at a strike price with a fixed expiration date.

CAM – Computer-aided manufacturing

Canvey LNG Terminal – The first liquid natural gas terminal (LNG) on Canvey Island, United Kingdom. It received experimental shipments of LNG from Louisiana in 1954 and regular commercial shipments from Algeria in 1964.

Capacity Constraint – The maximum amount of goods or services that a piece of equipment or a firm can produce.

Capacity Costs – The cost of putting in more equipment to produce an energy product or service.

Capacity Turnback – In the U.S. natural gas industry, long run transportation capacity contracts that were not renewed.

Cartel – Agreement between nations or producers producing similar energy products to influence the market, such as the OPEC cartel.

Catalytic Cracking – Heating oil or oil products under pressure in the presence of catalysts to break larger molecules into smaller molecules. It is an important refinery process for increasing the amount of gasoline produced from a barrel of oil.

CC – Capacity charge

CCGT – Combined-cycle gas turbine

CEA – U.S. Council of Economic Advisors

CEGB – U.K. Central Electric Generating Board

Cenozoic – The age of mammals starting 65 million years ago and continuing to the present.

CEO – Chief Executive Officer

Cetane – A clear liquid, $C_{16}H_{34}$. Cetane ignites well in diesel engines. A cetane rating is a measure of relative ignitability with cetane having a rating of 100. Common diesel fuels typically have a rating of 45 to 55.

Ceteris Paribus – The technique in economics of holding all exogenous variables constant except the one under analysis.

cf – Cubic feet

CFC – Chlorofluorocarbon

CH_4 – Methane

Change In Demand – A movement in the whole demand function that occurs because of a change in a variable other than the own price.

Change In Quantity Demanded – A movement along the demand curve as the result of a change in the own price caused by a change in supply.

Change in Quantity Supplied – A movement along the supply curve as the result of a change in own price caused by a change in the demand curve.

Change In Supply – A movement in the whole supply function that occurs because of a change in a variable other than the own price.

Chemical Energy – Energy produced as the result of a chemical reaction, such as burning fossil fuels.

Clean Cargo – Oil product cargoes, also called white cargoes, that have a narrower product specification requirement and lower tolerance for contamination, such as gasoline and kerosene. Pipelines and tankers may need to be cleaned when changing from one white cargo to another or from a dirty cargo to a white cargo.

Clearinghouse – An institution that is part of an organized exchange that guarantees each transaction and matches buyers to sellers when contracts come due.

Clicks and Mortar – Retail establishments that provide services by traditional retailing and wholesaling along with e-commerce.

Chlorofluorcarbons – Compounds once used as refrigerants and in aerosol sprays. They were banned in the 1990s in industrialized countries and are increasingly being banned in developing countries because of their damage to the ozone layer.

CIA – U.S. Central Intelligence Agency

CIO – Chief Information Officer

CO – Carbon monoxide

CO_2 – Carbon dioxide

Coases's Theorem on Externalities – In the absence of transaction costs and market power, that private markets will arrive at an optimal allocation in the presence of market externalities no matter how property rights are originally distributed.

Coases's Theorem on Transaction Costs – This theorem maintains that the likely form of market governance to evolve is one that minimizes transaction cost.

Cogeneration – Producing electricity and heat together.

Coking Coal – Low ash, low sulfur bituminous coal that can be used to make coke for iron and steel production. It is baked at high temperatures to eliminate the volatile elements. It is used as a fuel and to reduce the oxygen content in iron oxide to make iron.

Collectivist culture – A culture in which the group is more important than any individual member. The individual receives value from being a member of the group.

Command and Control Pollution Policies – Policies that order reductions in pollution and sometimes even mandate the technology to be used. They differ from market based policies which offer economic incentives by increasing the economic cost of pollution or increasing the economic benefit of abatement.

Commodity Futures Trading Commission (CFTC) – A U.S. regulatory agency created in 1974 to regulate futures and options markets. (http://www.cftc.gov/)

Common Carrier – A business that transports energy products and services, allowing equal access to all clients. This access is also called open access and third party access. In a regulated industry, common carriage may be mandated by law. Electricity and pipeline transmission services are increasingly open access as these markets are restructured.

Common Stocks – Financial assets that represent equity ownership in a business. They provide voting rights, a share in dividends and capital appreciation, and a share of liquidation assets after bond holders have been paid.

Commonwealth of Independent States (CIS) – A political federation formed in 1991 from eleven states of the former Soviet Union. It includes all former Soviet Republics except Estonia, Georgia, Latvia, and Lithuania.

Competitive Fringe – In a market where one firm has market power and a number of smaller firms do not, the group of smaller firms that competes is called the competitive fringe.

Compounded Interest – Interest paid on interest already earned. If interest is compounded annually, you receive interest on your interest payments after a year. If interest is compounded monthly, you receive interest on your interest in a month. If interest is compounded continuously you receive interest on your interest immediately as it accrues. Computing the value of an asset worth A dollars after t years with interest compounding continuously at rate t is Ae^{rt}.

Computer-Aided Design (CAD) – Using computer programs and imaging to design products.

Computer-Aided Engineering (CAE) – Using computer resources, mathematics, and scientific principles to solve practical problems such as designing equipment and facilities to produce and transport energy.

Computer-Aided Manufacturing (CAM) – Using computer programs to manufacture products.

Concessionary Agreement – Privilege to explore for petroleum and other mineral resources made by a government or private owner of the mineral. They stipulate the requirements for the privilege and any required payments.

Condor Spread – A spread is buying/selling more than one derivative in a trading strategy. Buying one option at a low price and one at a high price and selling two options at two intermediate prices. If the options are calls, it is a condor spread with calls and if the options are puts, it is a condor spread with puts.

Confucian Dynamism – A cultural trait that takes a long-run view and values tradition, thrift, and group values.

Constant Tax Per Unit – The same tax is charged on each unit sold.

Constrained Optimization – Finding the choice variables in a constraint set that maximize or minimize an objective function.

Consumer Surplus – The excess value a consumer obtains from a good equal to the area below the demand and above cost.

Consumption Per Capita – Average consumption per person, equal to total consumption divided by population.

Contango Market – A market in which the futures price is greater than the current spot price of the underlying asset. Also called a normal market.

Contestable Market – Market that allows other firms to freely enter or one that has low barriers to entry.

Context Providers – A computer program providing the infrastructure to build Internet content in the form of text, graphics, and audiovisual material.

Contingent Valuation – A technique for valuing non-market goods and services, such as better health and clean water, by surveying users of these goods and services.

Continuous Compounding – If interest is compounded continuously, you receive interest on your interest immediately as it accrues. Computing the value of an asset worth A dollars after t years with interest compounding continuously at rate t is Ae^{rt}.

Convenience Yield – The value received from holding an inventory of a product. This can be positive if the market is strong and prices are increasing, or it can be negative if the market is weak and prices are falling.

COO – Chief Operating Officer

Cooperative – A legal business form owned by its members, who receive its products and services rather than profits.

Corporate Tax – Taxes the government places on corporations. A corporation is a legal entity that has been granted a charter distinct from the individuals of which it is comprised. Owners of corporations have liability that is limited to their stock ownership but have to pay taxes on top of the taxes of the individual owners of the corporation.

Cost of Carry – Is the cost of holding a commodity or asset over time and includes any costs for storage, insurance, and financing.

Cost of Pollution – Any damage to humans and physical property as the result of pollution.

Cost, Fixed – A cost incurred that is not related to output. Fixed costs have to be paid whether the firm produces or not. Also called sunk cost. In the long run, there are no fixed costs.

Cost, Total – What someone has to pay for something. Total cost for a firm is the payment for all factors of production needed to produce its output, including opportunity cost. Total cost for a firm equals fixed plus variable cost.

Cost, Unit – The average cost to produce one unit of good. The total cost divided by the quantity produced.

Cost, Variable – A cost that is related to output. If you only pay for electricity that you use to run your production line, the cost will stop if you stop production.

COT – Commitment of traders

Cournot Duopoly – A market with two producers, each which has some market power and maximizes profits assuming that the other producer holds its quantity constant.

Covered Call – Writing or selling a call option while holding the underlying asset.

Crack Spread – A spread is buying/selling more than one derivative in a trading strategy. A crack spread is buying a crude oil future and selling gasoline and distillate futures to lock in a refinery margin. A common crack spread is 3-2-1, buying oil and selling gasoline and distillate in the ratio of 3-2-1, respectively.

Credit Risk – The hazard that a party to a financial contract may default. For example, there is a possibility that a party buying a Brent future may fail to make payment.

Cross Price Elasticity – The percentage change in quantity of one good that results from the percentage change in price of another good. If the quantity is the supply, it is a cross elasticity of supply; if the quantity is demand it is the cross price elasticity of demand. A positive cross price elasticity of demand suggests that goods are substitutes in demand, and a negative cross price elasticity of demand suggests that goods are complements in demand. A positive cross price elasticity of supply suggests that goods are complements in supply or are produced together. A negative cross price elasticity of supply suggests that goods are substitutes in supply.

Cross Subsidization – Charging a higher price in one market to be able to subsidize or charge a lower price in another market. For example, in some electricity markets business customers subsidized the residential market.

Crude Assay – An analysis of crude oil to determine its component parts. It typically includes API gravity, percent sulfur, percent nitrogen, pour point, and the percentages of various products defined by their boiling points, along with other information.

Culture – Shared attitudes, values, and customary ways of doing things for a group.

Cumulative Production – Adding up the total amount of production over time.

Current – Electron flow through a wire or appliance. It is measured in amps.

Customer Relationship Management (CRM) – All the activities used to attract and retain satisfied customers. With new information technologies, this is done by keeping 24X7 access, maintaining a two-way dialogue between the company and the customer, centralizing and remembering all information for a customer, and presenting one customer interface to deal with all interactions.

Data Mining – Techniques for extracting information from large databases.

Data Warehousing (DW) – Software that enables a company to acquire, access, and use large amounts of data, also called business intelligence.

Dated Brent – Brent crude oil that has been purchased forward with a specific loading date, usually within 15 days. Such Brent is considered to be on the spot market and its price is used as a benchmark in numerous oil contracts worldwide.

DCF – Discounted cash flow

Dead Weight Tons (DWT) – Ship carrying capacity including cargo, fuel, and provisions.

Deadweight Loss – The social optimum in a market is the amount of output that maximizes social welfare (total social benefits minus total social costs). If a market is producing at a sub-optimal output because of market failures such as monopoly power, externalities, or market-distorting government policies (taxes, subsidies, and price controls), the deadweight loss is the difference between social welfare at the optimum and social welfare at the sub-optimum. Deadweight loss is also called social loss.

Decline Rate – The percentage decrease in production each period. Production with a constant decline rate can be represented by $Q_t = Q_o e^{-at}$. Where Q_t is production in period t, Q_o is initial production, and a is the decline rate.

Decommissioning – Permanent shutdown of utility plants in a safe and systematic manner.

Deep In/Out of the Money – When the spot price for an underlying asset is way below the strike price for a put, the option is worth a lot and is deep in the money. When the spot price is way above the strike price for a put, the put is deep out of the money. When the spot price for an underlying asset is way above the strike price for a call, the call option is worth a lot and is deep in the money. When the spot price is way below the strike price for a call, the call is deep out of the money.

Degree Celsius – A metric measure of temperature. Water freezes at 0° Celsius and water at sea level boils at 100° Celsius.

Degree Fahrenheit – An English measure of temperature equal to 5/9° Celsius (C). Water freezes at 32° Fahrenheit (F) and water at sea level boils at 212° F. To convert a temperature from C to F use the formula F = 32 + 9/5C.

Degree Kelvin – A metric measure of temperature. One degree Kelvin equals 1° Celsius. Zero degrees Kelvin is absolute zero, the temperature at which all molecular activity ceases. Zero degrees Kelvin equals –273° Celsius.

Demand-Side Management (DSM) – Programs electric utilities use to manage the demand for power, often in the form of peak load reduction to avoid having to put in new capacity. Examples include peak load pricing and subsidizing energy efficient appliances.

Depletable – Something that is finite, that does not regenerate and can be used up. Fossil fuels are depletable, whereas wood plantations, if properly managed, are renewable.

Deregulation – Removing government regulations.

Diffuse Culture – A culture in which an individual's public space is small and private space is larger and not compartmentalized. It is harder to enter someone's public space in a diffuse culture because it allows easier entrance into his private space. It is the opposite of a specific culture where individuals have an easily entered public space that is quite compartmentalized from their private space.

Digital Information – Information that is stored and transferred as the digits zero and one.

Direct Tax – A tax on a person or other legal entity, as opposed to an indirect tax on goods and services.

Dirty Cargoes – Ship cargoes that leave residues in a tanker, which must be cleaned before a clean cargo can be transported. Residual fuel oil and crude oil are dirty cargoes.

Dirty Tricks In Negotiating – Unethical behavior intended to gain the upper hand in a negotiation. They include limited agendas, bait and switch, delaying tactics, escalating demands, zone defense, low-ball gambit, high-ball gambit, good cop/bad cop routine, verbal and nonverbal attacks, guilt trip, take it or leave it, and reneging on an agreement.

Discounted Cash Flow (DCF) – The present value of future flows of income. To compute discounted cash flow, discount each future income back to the present and add up the present values.

Discount Rate – The interest rate for converting or discounting future cash values to present values.

Dispatch – Controlling production and distribution in an energy system. For example, electricity dispatch would include deciding which generating units produce when, along with scheduling transmission and other electricity transactions.

Distillates – Petroleum products in the mid-point boiling range including kerosene, heating oil and diesel fuel. The boiling range is around 350–662 degrees Fahrenheit or 175–350 Celsius.

Distillation – Heating crude oil in a tall column to separate out products with different boiling ranges. At the top of the column, the gases are taken off, while heavier products with higher boiling points are taken off lower down.

Distribution Pipelines – Smaller pipelines that distribute gas locally to smaller customers.

Distributive Games – In game theory, players interact to optimize objective functions. In a distributive game, players typically negotiate over the distribution of a fixed sum.

Distributive Networks – A network is a system of interconnected channels. Distributive networks, such as a pipeline system or the Internet, move goods, services, and information.

Dividends – The profits paid out to owners of a corporation.

DOC – U.S. Department of Commerce

DOE – U.S. Department of Energy.

Dominance Submissions Signs – Signals, often body language, that indicate which members of a group are dominant and which members are submissive.

Dominant Firm – A firm in an industry that has more market power, while the other firms may be competitive.

Double Dividend – A tax policy that corrects two market inefficiencies. (e.g. reducing taxes on labor where they cause distortion and increasing taxes on energy to offset negative externalities.)

Double-sided market – Both sides of the market are bidding.

Downside Risk – In finance, risk is the variability of investment returns. Downside risk is the probability and size of negative returns on an investment.

Dry Natural Gas – Natural gas that does not contain any water or natural gas liquids, such as propane, butane, or natural gasoline.

DSM – Demand-side management

DW – Data warehousing

dwt – Dead weight tons

Duopoly – A market with two producers.

Duopsony – A market in which there are two producers and two buyers.

Dutch Auction – An auction in which the price is successively lowered until a buyer bids. The first bidder will be the high bidder who wins the bid.

E-Business – Electronic business in which the Internet is used for buying and selling and also for the whole supply chain with inter- and intra-firm connectivity.

E-Commerce – Electronic commerce, which is buying and selling products online.

EAI – Enterprise application integration

EBRD – European Bank for Reconstruction and Development

ECNZ – Electricity Corporation of New Zealand

Econometric Models – Economic models that have been estimated by fitting the functions to real world data, which is often historical.

Economic Cultures – Cultures that value wealth and satisfying economic needs.

Economic Profit – Total revenues minus total costs, including a normal rate of return. An economic profit is an amount above that required to keep the firm producing goods and services.

Economies of Scale – A firm has economies of scale if its average cost falls as its production increases. A firm has diseconomies of scale if its average cost increases as production increases. A firm has constant returns to scale if its average cost is constant as production increases.

Economies of Scope – A firm has economies of scope, if it is cheaper to produce more than one product together than for separate firms to each produce one product. When costs are sub-additive there are economies of scope.

EdF – Eléctricité de France

EDI – Electronic data interchange

EDI-INT – Electronic data interchange on the Internet

Efficiency in Investments – Paying the lowest cost for required investments in productive assets.

Efficiency in Pricing – Pricing at marginal social cost.

EFT – Electronic fund transfer

EIA/DOE – United States Energy Information Administration/Department of Energy

Eiffel Tower Culture – A task-oriented, rule-based hierarchical business culture with a bureaucratic division of labor. Tasks at each level are clearly defined, and rewards and advancement proceed from accomplishments and learning new skills.

Ekofisk Oil Field – First Norwegian oilfield discovered by Phillips Petroleum in 1969.

Elastic – An elasticity is elastic, if it is greater than one in absolute value.

Electrical Energy – The attracting force between electrons and protons and the repelling force between electrons and protons. It causes current to flow through wires, creating electricity.

Electric Power Grid – The network of electric power lines and substations for delivering electricity to final users.

Electromagnetic Radiation – Energy moved between electric and magnetic fields. Its basic component is the photon and it includes radio waves, infrared, light, ultraviolet radiation, microwaves, x-rays, and gamma rays.

Electron – Subatomic particle that has a negative charge and circles the nucleus of an atom.

Electronic Data Interchange (EDI) – The earliest form of electronic data transfer, it started with computer-to-computer exchanges for large companies on private networks using a nonproprietary standard format.

Electronic Fund Transfer (EFT) – Fund transfers that originate from electronic terminals, telephones, and computers.

Eminent Domain – A government or government-granted legal right to acquire property for public use at prices determined by the court. Pipeline, electricity, and rail rights-of-way have at times been acquired under eminent domain.

Emission – An unwanted substance discharged into the environment as the result of human activity.

Empowerment Decision-Making – Giving employees down the chain of command the right to make decisions.

End-Use Models – Models that compute energy consumption by summing up the energy using equipment times energy use per unit of equipment.

Energy Balances – Models that estimate total energy demand and supply and balance the two by changing scenarios or using some sort of backup energy source.

Energy Conservation – Decreasing the amount of energy used in a given economic activity.

Energy Engineering or Process Model – A model that represents some sort of energy processing, a refinery, or electricity generation.

Energy Forward Contracts – Bilateral over-the-counter contracts to buy or sell an energy product in the future.

Energy Futures – A standardized contract offered and guaranteed on an organized exchange to buy or sell an energy product in the future. Such contracts are used to lock in future prices and normally do not take delivery.

Energy Market – Where demanders and suppliers of energy products and services make exchanges.

Energy Subsidy – A government payment for the production or use of an energy product.

English Auction – A public sale in which bidding starts from a low price and continues until the item is sold to the highest bidder.

Enterprise Application Integration (EAI) – Information technologies that facilitate information flows between entities within a firm and across firms.

Enterprise Resource Planning (ERP) – Ties the different information systems within a firm together to gather information from across the entire enterprise to better keep track of and manage materials, orders, inventories, deliveries, and the whole production process. An ERP system provides for one user interface between the firm's entire data infrastructure.

EPA – U.S. Environmental Protection Agency

Equity Cost of Capital – Firms can finance activity by borrowing or by selling ownership rights or equity. The equity cost of capital is the rate of return required to attract equity financing.

ERCOT – Electricity Reliability Council of Texas

ERP – Enterprise Resource Planning ties the different information systems within a firm together to gather information from across the entire enterprise to better keep track of and manage materials, orders, inventories, deliveries, and the whole production process. An ERP system provides for one user interface between the firm's entire data infrastructure.

ESA – New Zealand Electricity Supply Authorities

ESI – Electricity supply industry

Ethanol – Ethyl alcohol with chemical composition C_2H_5OH is created from fermentation of corn or other sugars and starches. It is used as an oxygenate in gasoline in smoggy cities that do not met U.S. federal emission standards.

EU – European Union

European Economic Community (EEC) – The precursor to the European Union, developed to promote economic and political cooperation among its members.

European Energy Charter Treaty – A binding treaty signed in 1994 to ensure energy reforms and safe energy supplies from former Eastern Block countries.

European Gas Directive – A ruling passed in 1998 by the European Union to promote the free movement of gas across countries and gas security. It opens up the markets to third party access, which must be up to a third by around 2008.

European Option – An option is the right to buy (call) or sell (put) an underlying asset at a given price (strike price) that expires on a specific date. A European option can only be exercised at expiration.

European Single Market – Legislation passed in 1992 to create a single market amongst the member states of the European Union in which goods, services, capital, and persons pass freely between countries. Economic rules and regulations are also to be standardized.

European Union (EU) – An organization to provide economic and political cooperation between its 15 member states: Austria, Belgium, Denmark, Finland, France, Germany, Greece, Ireland, Italy, Luxembourg, The Netherlands, Portugal, Spain, Sweden, and the United Kingdom. It evolved out of the European Community and was renamed the European Union with the Mastricht treaty, which called for monetary union and gave members of the then-12 members of the European Community right to European citizenship and freedom to live, work, and vote in any of the 12 countries.

Excel Solver – Algorithm in Microsoft Excel to optimize functions subject to constraints.

Excess Supply – If quantity supplied is greater than quantity demanded at a given price, the unsold goods are called excess supply.

Exchange – A double auction that matches up buyers and sellers.

Excise Tax – A unit tax placed on a good or service.

Excludable in Consumption – Excludability makes it possible to prevent someone from consuming a good. Pure private goods are excludable in consumption, whereas pure public goods are not.

Exercise Price – The strike price or the price at which an option allows you to buy or sell the underlying asset.

Expected Value – The average value. For a random variable, the expected value is computed by weighting each value of the variable by its probability and adding together all the weighted values.

Expected Value of A Random Variable – The average value you would expect to get if you sampled over and over from the variable equal to $\sum_{i=1}^{n} X_i P(X_i)$, where X_i is value assigned to an event and $P(X_i)$ is the probability of the event occurring, n is the number of events that can occur, and $\sum_{i=1}^{n} P(X_i) = 1$.

Expiration Date – The date after which a financial option can no longer be exercised. The date after which an agreement or offer is no longer valid.

Extrapolating Historical Trends – Forecasting a variable by assuming the changes over time in the future will be the same as those in the past. For example, if electricity has been growing at 7% in the past, we assume it will grow at 7% in the future.

°F – Degrees Fahrenheit

Face – The cultural aspect that is one's outward appearance to the group. To perform poorly and make the group look bad brings shame and causes one to lose face if the group knows about it.

Facilitator – Someone who brings parties together for a negotiation.

Fair Return – The legally allowed rate or return for a regulated public utility company.

Family Culture – A people-oriented corporate culture that is very hierarchical. It motivates, resolves conflicts, and effects change through personal relationships.

Feedback Effects – When some outputs of a model or process are fed back as inputs and affect future outputs.

Feminine Culture – A more relationship-oriented culture with more flexibility in gender roles.

FERC – U.S. Federal Energy Regulatory Commission

FFL – Fossil fuel levy

Financial Assets – Assets are things of value. Financial assets are non-physical assets or debt instruments that facilitate the transfer of funds from lenders to borrowers. They include cash, checking accounts, bonds, stocks, and insurance policies.

Financial Derivatives – Financial assets that derive their value from an underlying asset upon which they are based. They include futures, options, forwards, and swaps.

Financial Risk – In finance, risk is the variability of investment returns.

Firm Transportation – Transportation that is contracted to be available on demand and can't be interrupted. A category of natural gas transportation in the U.S. natural gas industry.

First Law of Thermodynamics – The total amount of energy in an isolated system will always remain the same.

First Mover Advantage – The competitive advantage gained by a company by being the first to establish itself in a market.

Fission – Breaking atoms apart.

Flag of Convenience – A ship's flag is the country's flag where it is registered. Usually the flag is the country where the ship owner's company is incorporated. Sometimes another country is chosen because the country has lower taxes and weaker regulation. Such a flag is called a flag of convenience. Liberia and Panama are the countries most often chosen.

Forecast Feedback – When some outputs of a forecast influence what is being forecasted.

Foreign Exchange Rate – The price of one currency in terms of another currency.

Former Soviet Union (FSU) – The 15 countries that were once part of the Soviet Union. They are Armenia, Azerbaijan, Belarus, Estonia, Georgia, Kazakhstan, Kyrgyzstan, Latvia, Lithuania, Moldova, Russia, Tajikistan, Turkmenistan, Ukraine, and Uzbekistan.

FPC – Federal Power Commission

Franchise – The right to produce or distribute a good or service. In the past, governments have often given exclusive franchises to electricity utilities to produce, transport, and distribute electricity in a given area. Businesses may sell franchises to local companies to sell their product, such as a franchise that Shell might sell to a local gasoline station allowing it to sell the Shell brand.

Free Rider – An entity that receives benefits from a pure public good without paying.

Front Office Activities – Activities that deal directly with consumers of a product or service.

FSU – Former Soviet Union

ft^3 – Cubic feet

FTC – U.S. Federal Trade Commission

Fusion – Smashing atoms together to make a bigger atom.

G&A – General and administration costs

Game Theory Model – An interactive situation between a number of players who try to optimize their objective functions. The model includes the players, the set of possible actions, and their payoffs.

Gasification Plant – A plant to regasify liquid natural gas.

Gasoil – A middle distillate with boiling range around 260–340 degrees Celsius (500–644 degrees Fahrenheit), used for diesel and heating oil. Also called number two distillate.

Gathering Pipelines – Small pipelines used to gather oil and gas from wells in the field and transport them to larger, longer distance transportation pipelines.

GDP – Gross domestic product

Geothermal energy – Heat energy derived from the heat of the earth. It can be used to provide heat, or the heat can be used to produce electricity.

Gigawatt – A billion watts. A watt is a measure of electric power equal to one ampere under the pressure of one volt. Watts = volts times amps.

GISB – U.S. Gas Industry Standard Board

Global Pollutant – Pollutant that affects the whole globe such as excess CO_2, as opposed to a more restricted regional pollutant such as smog.

Global Warming – The rise in temperature resulting from gases such as CO_2 that trap heat in the earth's atmosphere, reducing the amount of heat that is reflected back to space.

Gold Plating – Unnecessary extravagance built into a project, such as gold-plated bathroom fixtures. Often done when someone else is paying for the project or to artificially increase the profits from building the project.

Government Regulation – Law created by a government to control an activity.

Government Revenues from a Tax – The total amount of money collected from a tax.

Government Share of the Take – The percent of profits from an energy product that the government receives in taxes.

Greenfield Project – A project that is totally new and is not an addition to a previously operating project.

Greenhouse Gases – Gases that increase the heat trapping capacity of the earth's atmosphere. According to EPA, they include CO_2, Methane, Nitrous Oxide, hydrofluorocarbons, perfluorocarbons, and sulfur hexafluoride.

Groningen Gas Field – The largest gas field in the Netherlands, discovered in 1961.

Gross Energy Production – The gross amount of energy needed to produce products. Under this definition, primary electricity consumption is converted to an equivalent amount of fossil fuel using some sort of heat rate or efficiency measure.

Groupware – Software that allows groups to transfer information and collaborate through electronic rather than personal contact.

GTL – Gas-to-liquids

Guide Signs – Body movements used to indicate a direction such as pointing a finger.

Guided Missile Culture – Task-oriented, egalitarian, impersonal cultures often peopled by professionals from across different disciplines. Status comes from performance and evaluation by peers about contributions to the project. Work is organized around projects and change arises as projects come and go and groups regroup in response.

Guilt-Based Culture – A culture that controls by internalizing bad feeling when someone has violated culture norms. This is opposed to a shame-based culture where bad feelings are only felt when one loses face or when the group knows an individual has violated cultural norms.

GW – Gigawatt

H_2O – Water

Heat Rate – The number of BTUs a utility plant requires to produce a kilowatt-hour of electricity.

Hedge Ratio – The percent of a product that is hedged.

Hedging – Taking the opposite position in the real market as in the derivative market to lock in a price. Thus, if you are long crude, you would hedge by selling a future.

Hedonic Pricing – Pricing where the total price reflects the sum of the prices of the different attributes of a good. Thus, an automobile would cost more the more comfortable, the better mileage, the higher the performance, etc., with total value determined by the value of each of the individual attributes.

Henry Hub – Gas delivery point in Louisiana for NYMEX gas futures and option contracts.

Herfindahl Index – An index that measures how concentrated an industry is. It is equal to the sum of the squared market shares and varies from monopoly with an index of one to perfect competition with an index of zero.

Hertz – The frequency or the number of times an electromagnetic wave cycles per second. For example, electricity in the United States is 60 megahertz, cycling 60,000,000 times per second, while in Europe it is 50 megahertz.

High Absorbers – OPEC countries with lower oil reserves and higher populations that have a high short-run need for current revenues.

High Context Culture – A culture in which there is a lot of shared knowledge and common understanding.

HNO_2 – Nitrous acid

HNO_3 – Nitric acid

Hold-up – Unethically taking advantage of someone in a business transaction by reneging on an agreement where high sunk costs limit the other party's options.

Horizontal Drilling – Drilling wells at an angle to increase the well bore and decrease drilling costs per unit of hydrocarbons found and produced.

Horizontal Equity – A criteria of fairness for taxation. Horizontally equitable taxes have people with similar incomes paying similar amounts of taxes.

Horizontal Integration – When a firm produces more than one good. Often the goods are similar so the firm may be able to take advantage of economies of scope.

Hotelling Rent – Rent is reimbursement for the use of something of economic value, which includes labor, land, capital, energy, ideas, and money. Rent for labor is usually called wages or salaries, rent for capital and land is usually called rent, rent for energy and ideas may be called royalties, and rent for money is called interest. Economic rent occurs when the rent payment is larger than necessary to entice the product into the market. The amount of the economic rent on a unit is price minus marginal cost. Rent caused by a fixed resource that is not expandable is called Hotelling rent. Hotelling rent serves to efficiently allocate a depletable resource across time. Hotelling rent is also called user cost.

HTML – Hypertext markup language

Hubbert Curve – A logistic curve of cumulative production first fit by the geologist Hubbert that is used to predict the total reserves of a depletable resource.

Human Resource Management (HRM) – All activities related to personnel management including job analysis, hiring, firing , disciplining, training, job classification, and motivating. A management philosophy that treats employees as individuals and emphasizes employee motivation and performance to achieve the objectives of the firm. Information technologies are useful in this management philosophy by providing self-service applications for employees, online training, real-time monitoring of performance and increasing information to employees so that they can be empowered to make decisions. It also allows routine repetitive operations to be automated so that employees can do more interesting and valuable work.

HVAC – High voltage alternating current

HVDC – High voltage direct current

Hydrocracking – Refinery process that heats heavy oil products under pressure in the presence of hydrogen to remove sulfur and increase lighter product yields.

Hydropower Flow – The amount of water flowing under a dam to generate hydroelectricity per unit of time.

Hydropower Head – Distance from the surface of the water to the turbine generating the hydroelectricity.

Identified Reserves – Fossil fuel reserves that are known to exist and be producible under current economic conditions.

IEA – International Energy Agency

IEAn – International Energy Annual

IEO – International Energy Outlook

INGAA – U.S. Interstate Natural Gas Association of America

In Situ – Mining a resource from its original place, such as underground leaching of uranium.

In the Money – When the strike price for a put is above the spot price for an underlying asset, the put is said to be in the money. When the strike price for a call is below the spot price for an underlying asset, the call is said to be in the money.

Income Elasticity of Demand – The percentage change in quantity of a good demanded that results from the percentage change in demander's income.

Income Tax – Tax paid on an individual's annual income.

Incubator Cultures - Egalitarian, people-oriented corporate culture often founded by a creative team or entrepreneur. Creativity is encouraged and leads to status. Conflict is dealt with by breaking apart, going separate ways, and experimenting to find the best course of action.

Independent Power Producer (IPP) – A wholesale electric power producer that is not owned by a regulated electric utility.

Independent System Operator (ISO) – An entity that coordinates regional electricity transmission. It is often regulated and is not controlled by the players in the market, nor is it allowed to discriminate amongst the players.

Indirect Tax – A tax on a good or service rather than on a legal entity.

Individualistic Culture – A culture where individual initiative and leadership are valued.

Inelastic – An elasticity is inelastic if it is less than one in absolute value.

Information asymmetry – When two sides of a negotiation do not have access to the same information.

Inner Directed Culture – A culture whose members believe they have control of their own lives and what happens to them.

Input-Output Models – A linear system of equations that represents a company, region, nation, or even the entire world. The equation coefficients represent the required inputs to produce each output including outputs that are inputs to themselves and/or other products. For example, electricity is an end-use demand, an input into generating electricity, and an input to a host of other products. The model keeps track of all end-use and intermediate uses as well. If you enter end-use demand to the model, it will compute the required total output for each good, which includes all end-use demands and intermediate goods.

Integrated Resource Planning – Public planning that considers both demand reduction and supply increase to satisfy end-use demand for energy services along with other societal objectives. It chooses the option that best meets total societal objectives. For example, a government utility would consider putting in compact fluorescent lights and building new generation capacity. Cost as well as environment and perhaps even income distribution might be taken into account when choosing the best option.

Interest Rate – The rate paid for borrowing money over a period of time.

Interest Rate Risk – The risk from increasing interest rates reducing an investments market value.

Internal Pricing Within an Integrated Firm – The prices different parts of a company charge each other for goods and services. Also called transfer pricing.

Internal Rate of Return – The interest rate that makes the stream of net revenues for a project equal to zero.

International Petroleum Exchange (IPE) – A futures and options exchange in London for oil and gas products. It is owned by Atlanta-based Inter-continental Exchange.

Internet Service Provider (ISP) – A company that provides a link to the Internet.

Interruptible Transportation – Transportation that can be interrupted and given to another customer, who has contracted for firm transportation. A category of natural gas transportation in the U.S. natural gas industry, it is cheaper than firm transportation.

INTERTANKO – International Association of Independent Tanker Owners

Inverted Market – A market in which the futures prices are lower than the current spot prices. An inverted market typically indicates that a market has a short-run shortage. Also referred to as a backward market or a market in backwardation.

Investor Owned Utility (IOU) – Public utilities that are privately owned. The private investor's goal is earning a rate of return on the investment.

IPE – International Petroleum Exchange

IPP – Independent power producer

Iron Age – The age in which humans have used iron—roughly 1200 B.C. to present. It started in different areas at somewhat different times.

IRP – Integrated resource planning

IRR - Internal rate of return

ISO – Independent system operator

Isomerization – A refinery process that converts straight-chained hydrocarbons into branched-chain hydrocarbons. It is used in the production of gasoline.

ISP – Internet service provider

Japan's MITI – Japan's Ministry of Trade and Industry. It has been very influential in promoting industry and exports in Japan. MITI was reorganized in 2001 and has been renamed the Ministry of Economy, Trade, and Industry (METI).

Jihad Culture – A culture that resists modern capitalism and values religious beliefs, ethnic traditions, and local and national communities.

Judgmental Models – Informal models that are used to forecast based on the considered opinion of experts in the area.

Just-In-Time (JIT) Inventories – Acquiring inventories only as they are needed to minimize inventory costs.

Just-In-Time (JIT) Manufacturing – Making the right product, at the right time, in the right amount.

Kilocalorie (kcal) –The amount of energy needed to raise a kilogram of water one degree Centigrade, which is 1000 calories. A calorie is the amount of energy needed to raise 1 gram of water by 1 degree Centigrade. A kilocalorie is the unit for the calories reported for food. One kilocalorie equals 4.187 kilojoules or 3.968 BTUs.

Kilojoule –A joule is the energy of one watt of power for one second. A kilojoule is 1000 joules and is equal to 0.239 kilocalories or 0.948 BTUs.

Kilowatt –A watt is a measure of electric power equal to one ampere under the pressure of one volt. A kilowatt is 1000 watts. Watt = volts times amps.

Kilowatt-hour (kWh) – A kilowatt operating for one hour.

km – Kilometer

KM – Knowledge management

l. ton – Long ton

LAN – Local area networks

LCP – Least-cost planning

LDC – Local distribution company

Lean Manufacturing – A manufacturing philosophy that emphasizes teamwork, empowering employees, mistake proofing processes (Poka Yoke), continuous incremental improvement (Kaizen), reducing waste (not producing a product ahead of time, not waiting for inputs, no unnecessary transport, no over processing, not too many inventories, no unnecessary movement, no defective product, and just-in-time manufacturing.

Least-Cost Planning – Considers demand reduction and capacity increase to supply an energy need. It is narrower than integrated resource planning because it only considers cost and not wider societal objectives.

Legal Risk – Legal risk relates to losses from failures to comply with the law or adverse regulatory changes.

Leontief Production Function – A function where output is related to inputs, and inputs are required to be used in certain fixed proportions to produce output. Thus, increasing one input without increasing all others in the same proportion will not increase output.

Levelizing Costs – Allocating capital and operating costs over output production. This cost will reflect the cost per unit produced at the time it is produced.

Limit Pricing Model – A model in which the price charged is the highest price that could be charged without attracting new entrants into the model. It would be a price and quantity such that an entering firm would drive the price down so much they could not cover their costs.

Linear Algebra – A branch of mathematics used to compactly write and solve systems of linear equations.

Linear Programming – An optimization model in which the objective function and the constraints are all linear.

Liquefied Natural Gas (LNG) – Natural gas that has been changed to liquid by cooling to minus 161.5° Celsius or minus 258.7° Fahrenheit.

Liquid Petroleum Gases (LPG) – Propane and butane, which are gases at normal atmospheric temperature, but are bottled under pressure as liquids.

Liquidity Risk – Liquidity risk relates to the lack of market activity or to a failure to meet a cash flow obligation.

LNG Vessel – A specially designed tanker that maintains a constant temperature for LNG.

Load Curve – A graph that shows the amount of power consumed at different times over a specified period. A daily load curve would show power consumption over a 24-hour period, perhaps by increments of an hour or less. Annual load curves might show consumption by day, week or month.

Load Following – A generating plant that changes output as loads vary.

Local Pollutants – Pollutants that do not travel over long distances.

LOLP – Loss of load probability

Long Position – With a long position you own an asset. The opposite of a short position in which you have sold a borrowed asset and, hence, owe it. Going long is to take a long position.

Long-Term Contracts – Contracts that hold for a long period of time, Usually more than a year.

Long Ton – Non-metric unit of weight equal to 2240 pounds or 1.016 metric tons.

Long Wave Theory – The theory that technical inventions spur economic change and create cycles.

LOOP – Louisiana Offshore Oil Port

Low Absorbers – OPEC countries that have high reserves and low populations. They can absorb smaller revenues for development than high absorbers and have a longer-term interest in their oil reserves.

Low-Context Culture – A culture in which there is little shared knowledge and common understanding.

LPG – Liquid petroleum gases

Lurgi Process – A chemical process for gasifying coal.

M – Thousand

m.ton – Metric ton

m^3 – Cubic meters

Maastricht Treaty – The 1992 European treaty that created the European Single Market and the European Monetary Union. With this treaty the EEC came to be called the European Community.

Magnetometer – An instrument used for measuring a magnetic field used to help locate oil and gas reserves.

Mainframe Computer – Computers are machines that accept, process, and output data using programs called software. In the past, computers were divided into three sizes: mainframe computers were the largest, minicomputers were in between and microcomputers or personal computers were the smallest. These distinctions have been blurred as computing power has gotten cheaper, but main frames are still the largest computers. Usually they are centralized computers accessed by multiple users.

Make-or-Buy Decision – If you need a manufactured item you can go to the market and buy it or you can vertically integrate and make the product yourself. The decision should be to do whichever is cheaper.

Management Styles – Different philosophies for organizing and administering a work place. They vary by whether the focus is on workers or on the task, how centralized the decision-making is, and how change is effected.

Manufacturing Resource Planning – A methodology or software that is a bit more advanced than Material Requirements Planning. It efficiently keeps track of not just materials, but all of the resources required in the manufacturing process. It links together business planning, sales and operations, capacity planning, scheduling, and material requirements. It has more analytical capability and allows hypothetical simulations. It is sometimes called MRP II.

Margin Account – Money required to be deposited in an account to protect a clearinghouse from default on financial derivatives or stocks bought with borrowed money.

Marginal Efficiency of Investment – The rate of return on the last unit of investment.

Marginal Production Cost – The cost of the last unit of production. It is represented by the derivative $\partial C/\partial Q$, where C is cost and Q is production.

Marginal Revenue – The money earned on the sale of the last unit. Can be presented by the partial derivative $\partial TR/\partial Q$.

Market Distortion – Externalities, market power, or government policies that distort the true costs and benefits in the market or prevent the market from reaching a social optimum.

Market Governance – The customary form of transactions including a spot market, long-term contracts, and vertical integration.

Market Power – When any players in the market are non-competitive or have the ability to influence the price.

Market Risk – Uncertainty from price changes.

Marketable Permits – Permits to pollute that can be bought and sold in the market place.

Marketed-Oriented Environmental Policies – Policies such as subsidies, taxes, charges and saleable permits that require economic transfers for the right to pollute or to reduce pollution.

Marking-To-Market – The daily changes in a margin account to reflect the daily gains or losses on futures or options contracts.

Markup Pricing – Charging a price that is a constant percent over economic costs. For example, if the markup is 10% and economic cost is C, then the price is 1.1C.

Masculine Culture – A culture in which assertiveness, power, and success are valued and the male and female roles are narrowly defined.

Maslow's Hierarchy of Needs – The most basic needs for every human being from most basic to higher needs they are: (1) physiological needs, (2) safety needs, (3) esteem for self and others, (4) need for self fulfillment.

Materials Requirements Planning – A methodology or software for efficiently keeping track of and managing all the materials required in a manufacturing process. It can be used to manage inventories, predict production lead times once orders have been received, and discover bottle-necks in the production process.

Maturity Date – Day when a futures contract must make arrangement for delivery or the day by which an option contract must be exercised or it will expire.

MC – Marginal cost

Mcf – Thousand cubic feet

McWorld Culture – A culture that considers the world as one large market connected by information networks moving toward automation and homogenization.

Mean – The theoretical mean of a random variable, x, which equals the value obtained by multiplying each value of x by the probability (or probability density) of x and then summing (or integrating) over the range of x. It is also called the expected value. It corresponds to the value you would expect to get on average if you sampled over and over from the random variable. A sample mean equals the sum of the sample values divided by the sample size.

Mechanical Energy – Energy of motion such as wind or water.

Mediator – One who helps in a negotiation.

Megawatt – One million watts. A watt is a measure of electric power equal to one ampere under the pressure of one volt. Watts = volts times amps.

MER – Monthly Energy Review

Mesozoic – The age of dinosaurs from 245 million to 65 million years ago.

Metcalfe's Law – A network's value increases as the square of the number of connections.

Methane – The gaseous hydrocarbon CH_4, which is the most common component of natural gas.

Methyl Tertiary Butyl Ether (MTBE) – A transparent, flammable liquid made from a reaction of methanol and isobutylene. Its chemical formula is $C_4H_9OCH_3$ and it is used to oxygenate gasoline.

METI – Japan's Ministry of Economy, Trade, and Industry. Formerly the Ministry of Trade and Industry (MITI).

Metric Ton – A metric unit of weight equal to 1000 kilograms or 0.9842 long tons.

Mill – One-tenth of one cent.

Minimax Regrets – A game theoretic criteria for policy choice when there is uncertainty about future states of the world. First, compute the regrets or loses for each policy under each state of the world. Next, consider the maximum regrets for each policy. Then, pick the policy that has the smallest maximum regrets.

MITI – Japan's Ministry of Trade and Industry. It has been very influential in promoting industry and exports in Japan. MITI was reorganized in 2001 and has been renamed the Ministry of Economy, Trade, and Industry (METI).

Mixed Oxide Fuel – Nuclear power plant fuel that contains uranium as well as recycled plutonium.

MM – Million.

MMBTU/s.ton – Million British Thermal Units per short ton

MMC – U.K. Monopolies and Mergers Commission

MMm.ton – Million metric tons

Model of Competition – A model of a market in which there is a homogenous product, many buyers and sellers with none having market pricing power, and each member of the market pursuing his own self interest. If it is a perfectly competitive market model, each player has perfect information on relevant economic aspects of the market.

Monopsony – A market in which there is one buyer of the good.

Moore's Law – States that computer power doubles every 18 months.

MOX – Mixed oxide nuclear fuel

MR – Marginal revenue

MRP – Manufacturing resource planning

MRP – Marginal revenue product

MTBE – Methyl tertiary butyl ether

Multi-Period Dynamic Model – A model of a fixed resource in which the objective function is the net present value of profits. This model allocates production over more than two periods.

Multiplant Monopoly – One producer and seller in a market that produces in more than one plant.

Multivariate Time Series – A statistical forecasting technique in which a variable is forecast by using historical values of itself and other related variables.

MW – Megawatt

MWh – Megawatt-hour

N_2O – Nitrous oxide

NAESB – North American Energy Standards Board

Nagware – Software that is sold more cheaply but that repeatedly nags you to buy the higher quality version when you use it.

Naphtha – A hydrocarbon derived from the refining of crude oil. Its boiling range is roughly 33° C to 204° C (91° F to 400° F). It is composed of pentane (C_5H_{12}), hexane (C_6H_{14}), heptane (C_7H_{16}), and other products. Its boiling range is sometimes designated as 5° C to 400° F.

National Ambient Air Quality Standards (NAAQS) – U.S. national standards on criteria pollutants. These are common pollutants whose control is deemed necessary for the overall air quality. They include: sulfur dioxide (SO_2), nitrogen dioxide (NO_2), Volatile Organic Compounds (VOC), particulate matter, carbon monoxide (CO), and lead (Pb).

Natural Gas – Gaseous mixture of hydrocarbons and nonhydrocarbons found in underground source rock. The most important component is usually methane (CH_4), but it may contain ethane (C_2H_6), propane (C_3H_8), butane (C_4H_{10}), and pentane (C_5H_{12}). The last three, called natural gas liquids (NGL), are typically removed and sold separately. Propane and butane are also called liquid petroleum gases (LPG).

Natural Gas Liquids – Liquids stripped out of natural gas and sold separately— propane (C_3H_8), butane (C_4H_{10}), and pentane (C_5H_{12}).

Natural Gasoline – Liquids derived from natural gas and composed of pentane, hexane, and heptane. Some references also include propane and butane. It can be used as blending stock for gasoline.

Natural Monopoly – An industry in which average costs fall as the firm gets larger. In such a market, it is more economical for there to be only one producer.

Nautical Mile – A unit of distance for water travel. One nautical mile, called a knot, is equal to 1.151 land miles.

Negative Externalities – An externality is an effect from an economic activity that involves someone not directly involved in the economic activity. The externality is negative if the effect imposes a cost on the external party.

Negotiating Style – The manner in which a negotiation is conducted. It can include whether concessions are made as the negotiation proceeds and whether the strategy is cooperative or competitive.

NEPOOL – New England Power Pool

NERC – National Electricity Reliability Council

Net Change – The difference in price from one day's closing price for a futures or option contract to the next.

Net Energy Production – The actual amount of electric power produced. Primary energy production is measured as the number of kilowatt-hours of electricity, not the amount of energy in the fossil fuels that would be required to produce the electricity.

Net Present Value – The amount of money you would need today to be able to replicate a future stream of income at the given interest rate.

Netback Pricing – Setting a resource price by taking end price and deducting costs of getting it to market. If the product were crude oil, it would mean setting the crude oil price per barrel by taking the weighted average product price per barrel and subtracting transportation costs, refinery margins, and taxes.

Network – A system of channels that interconnect. The interconnection points are called nodes. Often networks are for transportation or communication.

Network Model – A simplified mathematical representation of a system of interconnected channels with the interconnection points (nodes). The channels often represent transportation links. The nodes may represent energy transformation processes such as refineries or electricity generation, energy consumption, or energy production.

Neutral Culture – A culture that does not display emotions in public.

Neutron – A subatomic particle of neutral charge residing in the nucleus of an atom and consisting of an electron and a proton.

New York Mercantile Exchange (NYMEX) – The largest commodity exchange in the world.

NFFO – U.K. non-fossil fuel obligation

NGA – U.S. Natural Gas Act of 1938

NGM – Natural Gas Monthly

NGPA – U.S. Natural Gas Policy Act of 1978

NO – Nitric oxide

NO$_2$ – Nitrogen dioxide

NO_x – Nitrogen oxides

No-Regrets Policy – If we are uncertain about whether a negative state of the world such as global warming will occur or not, we may not want to undertake policies to offset the global warming. However, if we can design a policy that corrects a second problem, such as local pollution, that we know exists, that would also help offset global warming, that policy would be called a no-regrets policy.

Nonattainment Area – A region that does not meet the U.S. federal air pollution standards for criteria pollutants.

Non-excludable in Consumption – Goods for which it is not possible to prevent someone from consuming them. Pure public goods are non-excludable in consumption, whereas private goods are not.

Non-Linear Programming – Optimization subject to constraints where some or all of the functions are not linear.

Non-Rivalry in Consumption – One person's consumption of a good does not reduce the amount available to another person. I can consume information but it does not reduce the amount of information available for another to consume. A pure public good has this quality and is said to be non-rivalrous in consumption. A pure public good also has the quality of being non-excludable. However, private goods are rivalrous and excludable.

Nonverbal Communication – The exchange of information through body language and other means that do not use words.

North American Electricity Reliability Council (NERC) – A nonprofit voluntary organization formed in 1968 to promote secure electricity service on the wholesale power market. http://www.nerc.com/

Not in My Back Yard (NIMBY) – Individual's preferences to not want things built near them, particularly construction that is potentially unpleasant or dangerous. (e.g. power plants and waste disposal areas.)

NPP – Norwegian Power Pool

NPV – Net present value

Nuclear Energy – The force that holds the nucleus of an atom together. Energy may be emitted when an atom is split as in fission, or when atoms are smashed together as in fusion.

Nuclear Reactor – The mechanism in a nuclear power plant where the chain reaction takes place to heat the steam to produce power.

Nuclear Regulatory Commission (NRC) – The federal agency that regulates and inspects nuclear power plants to producing heat.

Nuke – Slang for nuclear power plant.

NYMEX – New York Mercantile Exchange

NYMEX Access – NYMEX's after hours trading platform.

NYPP – New York Power Pool

O_3 – Ozone

Objective Function – The function to be maximized or minimized in an optimization model.

Ocean Thermal Energy Conversion (OTEC) – An energy technology that uses the difference in temperatures between different layers of the ocean to produce electricity.

Octane – A petroleum product (C_8H_{18}), which has very good combustion qualities in 4-cycle gasoline engines. It boils at 124.6° C.

Octane Rating – A measure of the antiknock property (premature ignition) of gasoline. Iso-octane has a rating of 100 and heptane has a rating of zero. An octane rating of 90 would have the same knock characteristics as a mixture of 90% iso-octane and 10% heptane.

OECD – Organization for Economic Cooperation and Development

OFFER – U.K. Office of Electricity Regulation

Off-system Natural Gas – Natural gas that was outside of the regulated pipeline system in the United States. Hence, pipeline companies did not take ownership of this gas.

OGJ – *Oil & Gas Journal*

Ohms – A measure of electrical resistance in a conductor where one volt will create an electric current of one amp.

Oil Above-Ground Costs – Distributing oil and gas finding, developing, and operating costs over the production of the well. It includes the cost of waiting for the oil to be produced.

Oil and Gas Reserves – The amount of oil and gas that is known to be economically producible at current prices. Also called proven or known reserves.

Oil and Gas Resources – The total amount of oil and gas in the earth's crust. All of these resources will never be found and produced.

Oil In-Ground Costs – The total cost of finding oil reserves divided over all the reserves found.

Oil Sands – Heavy oil deposits in which much of the lighter products have evaporated. Also called tar sands.

Oil Spill – An accident in which oil escapes containment and leaks onto the ground or into a waterway.

Oligopoly – A market characterized by a few large sellers that have market power.

On-System Natural Gas – Natural gas that was purchased and transported by pipelines and so was inside of the regulated pipeline system in the United States. Hence, pipeline companies took ownership of this gas.

OPEC Price Elasticity of Demand – The percent change in quantity of OPEC oil bought as the result of a percent change in price of OPEC oil. In a dominant firm model, it is equal to $\varepsilon_w Q_w/Q_o - \varepsilon_f Q_f/Q_o$, where ε_w equals the world's demand elasticity, Q_w equals world production, Q_o equals OPEC production, ε_f is the supply elasticity of the competitive fringe and Q_f is the oil production of the competitive fringe.

Open Access – Allowing non-owners of a facility its use on a nondiscriminatory basis. Also called third party access. Open access facilities are called common carriers.

Open Outcry (OO) – A method of bidding by verbal signal for financial assets and commodities on organized exchanges.

Opening Price – The price of the first trade of the day on an organized exchange.

Operational Risk – Technical problems related to financial trading systems including computer failures and fraud.

Opportunism – Taking advantage of an opportunity without considering the ethical aspects of the consequence.

Opportunity Cost – What you forgo by undertaking an economic activity. The value of a resource in its next best alternative.

Opposite Position – In a futures market, if you are long in the cash market, you short a future, and if you are short in the cash market, you buy a future.

Optimal Level of Pollution – That level of pollution that maximizes the net benefits of pollution (total benefits minus total costs). Under normal circumstances the optimal level of pollution is that amount where the marginal benefits of pollution equal the marginal cost of pollution.

Optimization Models – Models in which the outputs are choice variables that give your objective function the most favorable value.

Option – The right to buy (call) or sell (put) an underlying asset at a given price (strike price) that expires on a specific date.

Option Quote – The highest bid or the highest price someone is willing to pay and the lowest offer or the lowest price someone is willing to sell for.

Organization for the Advancement of Structured Information Standards (OASIS) – A nonprofit organization with more than 500 corporations in more than 100 countries as members. The organization started in 1993 as SGML Open. The name changed to OASIS in 1998 and the organization is working with UN/CEFACT on open access ebXML. http://www.ebxml.org/

Organizational IQ – An organization's ability to adjust to change.

OTC – Over-the-counter

OTEC – Ocean thermal energy conversion

Outage – A temporary loss of power from isolated electricity transmission, generation, or distribution failures.

Out of the Money – When the spot price of the underlying asset is above the strike price for a put, it is out of the money. When the spot price of the underlying asset is below the strike price for a call, it is out of the money.

Outer-Directed Culture – Cultures that believe members have no control of their own lives but something external to them is in control.

Outsourcing – Paying another company to make a product or perform a service for you.

Over-the-Counter Market (OTC) – A market where transactions are privately arranged by phone, fax, and other means rather than on an organized exchange.

Own Price Elasticity – Percent change in quantity of a good divided by the percentage change in its own price. If it's a supply elasticity, the quantity is the change in production, and if it's a demand elasticity, the quantity change is the change in quantity purchased.

Paleozoic Era – Spans from 544 to 245 million years ago. The period when most fossil fuel resources were formed.

Panamax – A class of ship from 55,000–80,000 DWT that carries most of the oil products. It is the largest size class that can go through the Panama Canal.

Paper Barrel – A crude oil futures contract as opposed to an actual barrel of oil, which is sometimes called a wet barrel.

Partial Derivative – A mathematical term that represents the change in the dependent variable (y) as the result of a change in one of the independent variables (x_i) designated by $\partial y/\partial x_i$.

Particularist Culture – A culture that believes that norms, values and behavior patterns are determined by the particular circumstances as opposed to a universalist culture that believes norms, values and behavior patterns are valid everywhere at all times.

Passive Solar Energy – Designing buildings to minimize the amount of energy needed to heat and cool. (e.g. Southern facing windows with appropriately designed eaves will let in heat in the winter, but not in the summer when the sun is higher.)

Payroll Tax – A tax on wages and salaries. In the United States, it is used for social security payments.

PDNP – Proved developed non-producing reserves

PDP – Proved developed producing reserves

Peak load pricing – Charging higher prices during peak hours than off-peak hours. With straight fixed variable rates, peak users pay for capital or capacity costs whereas off-peak only pays for the variable costs.

Peak/Off-Peak Demand – Peak demand, also called peak load is the highest level of demand over a given time period. Off-peak is demand the rest of the time.

Photosynthesize – The chemical process within plants that creates carbohydrates from carbon dioxide, water, and light.

Photovoltaic (PV) – A mechanism that can convert sunlight to electricity.

Pipeline – Large metal conduits that carry crude oil, oil products, and natural gas under pressure. Liquid pipelines have pumping stations to move the product, whereas gas pipelines have compressors.

PGA – Purchased gas adjustment rules

PJM – Pennsylvania, New Jersey, Maryland power pool

Policy – A procedure to influence an outcome.

Polluter Pays Principle – Charging or making a polluters pay to pollute or pay for clean up rather than subsidizing them not to pollute. Economists believe that the polluter pays principle is more likely to give an efficient outcome than subsidization.

Pollution Permits – Legal authorization to pollute. If it is marketable, it can be bought and sold.

Pollution Tax – A payment of tax to the government for the right to pollute.

Polymerization – Chemical process that bonds monomers together to make polymers. In a refinery, it can be used to make gasoline from refinery gases.

Positive Externality – An externality is an effect from an economic activity that involves someone not directly involved in the economic activity. The externality is positive if the effect bestows a benefit on the external party.

Power Culture – A culture that values the control over others.

Power Distance – The degree of equality in a group.

Power Marketers – Economic players that purchase and re-sell electricity but do not have any generation or transmission facilities of their own.

Power Pool – An organization that operates an electric utility system in the short term. It economically dispatches power from various generating units and facilitates transactions in the wholesale market. It may or may not own the transportation system.

Precambrian – The period from 4.5 to 0.455 billion years ago during which life formed on earth.

Preferred Stock – A financial asset that represents equity interest in a company. It gives a right to share in the profits of the company and a right to a share of the assets if the company has to be liquidated. Preferred stock does not have to be paid dividends, but it must be paid dividends if common stock is paid any dividends. It pays a maximum dividend rate.

Price Anderson Bill – A U.S. bill that limits the liability for nuclear power accidents.

Price Discrimination – Selling goods to different buyers at different prices.

Price Elasticity of Demand – Percentage change in quantity demanded of a good divided by the percentage change in its own price. It is a measure of how responsive quantity demanded is to price.

Price Elasticity of Supply – Percent change in quantity supplied of a good divided by the percentage change in its own price. It is a measure of how responsive quantity supplied is to price.

Price Regulation – Government regulation that limits the price that can be charged for a good or service. This regulation includes rate of return, RPI-X, light-handed, and yardstick regulation.

Primary Electricity – Electricity not produced from fossil fuels, it includes nuclear, hydro, and power from other renewables.

Primary Energy – The energy contained in fossil fuels, uranium, and renewable energy sources that has not been changed into another form. Secondary energy is the result of the conversion of primary energy such as oil products from refineries.

Private Interest Rate – The rate paid to borrow money. A private interest rate is the rate paid on the private market.

Producer Surplus – An amount over and above what a producer needs to continue producing at the same level. In a competitive market, it is the area of above the supply curve and below the price. Also referred to as Ricardian rents.

Production Profile – How production changes over time.

Production Sharing Agreements – A legal contract in which a company produces oil for the owner and gets a percent of the production in payment.

Profit Tax – Usually a tax on accounting profits or on total revenues minus accounting costs, which do not include opportunity cost. A tax on economic profits would be on total revenues minus economic costs, which includes opportunity cost. A tax on economic profits is seldom passed since it is difficult to measure economic profits.

Propane – Hydrocarbon gas with formula C_3H_8. It is liquid under pressure and is sold as a liquid petroleum gas.

Property Right – A legal claim to a defined use of a good.

Prorationing – Government regulations on how much can be produced from a given oil well or a pipeline allocation of line space to shippers.

Proton – Subatomic particle that has a positive charge and resides in the nucleus of an atom.

Proven Oil Reserve – Known oil reserve that can be economically produced at current prices.

Public Good – A good that is non-rivalrous and non-excludable. That is, one person's consumption of it does not reduce the quantity for another and no one can be excluded from its use.

Public Utility Commission (PUC) – State regulators of public utilities.

Put Option – The right, but not the obligation, to sell an underlying asset at a strike price with a fixed expiration date.

PUC – Public Utility Commission

PUD – Proved undeveloped reserves

PUHCA – U.S. Public Utilities Holding Company Act

PURPA – U.S. Public Utilities Regulatory Policy Act

PV – Photovoltaic solar cell or present value.

Quad – Quadrillion BTUs

Qualifying Facility (QF) – A small producer or cogenerator that is allowed to sell electricity to public utilities under the auspices of the Public Utilities Regulatory Policies Act of 1978.

Quasi-Rent – Rent is reimbursement for the use of something of economic value, which includes labor, land, capital, energy, ideas, and money. Rent for labor is usually called wages or salaries, rent for capital and land is usually called rent, rent for energy and ideas may be called royalties, and rent for money is called interest. Economic rent occurs when the rent payment is larger than necessary to keep the producer in the market. Quasi-rent is excess payment that is larger than necessary in the short run to entice the product into the market. It is equal to price minus variable cost, since in the short run it is only necessary to cover variable costs. Any fixed cost is a quasi-rent in the short run. However, in the long run all costs must be covered and fixed costs become variable and are no longer quasi-rents.

Quaternary – The age of humans from roughly 1.8 million years ago to today.

Quota – A fixed limit on the amount of a product that may be imported.

R/P – Reserves over production

Radiant Energy – Energy in the form of electromagnetic radiation including light, television, radio, infrared and X-rays.

Rate Base – In rate of return regulation, the rate base is the value of the capital stock upon which you earn the legal rate of return.

Rate of Return – The interest rate that makes the stream of net revenues for a project equal to zero. Also called the internal rate of return.

Rate Order – A regulation setting a regulated enterprise's allowed prices or rates.

Ratio Vertical Spread – A spread is buying/selling more than one derivative in a trading strategy. Ratio vertical spreads are selling more options than you buy all with the same expiration. For a put ratio vertical spread you buy at the higher strike price and sell at the lower, whereas for a call ratio vertical spread, you buy at the lower strike price and sell at the higher.

Real Assets – Physical or tangible assets such as buildings, capital stock, and patents as opposed to financial assets, which represent debt.

Rebound Effect – When an energy-using piece of equipment becomes more efficient, less energy is used to produce the same energy service. However, energy cost for the energy service falls, which might increase the amount of energy service demanded. This increase in energy service demand is called the rebound effect.

REC – U.K. Regional Electricity Companies

Reengineering – Reorganizing production or other processes within a firm to make the firm more efficient and profitable.

Reforming – A process in a refinery that uses heat and pressure in the presence of a catalyst to raise the octane of gasoline.

Regasification Plant – A plant that changes liquefied natural gas (LNG) back to a gas.

Regional Pollutant – Pollutants that are restricted to a local region such as smog, which typically exists over a city. As opposed to a global pollutant that effects the whole globe such as excess CO_2.

Regulatory Stability – When regulations are not changed often or in unpredictable ways.

Reid Vapor Pressure – A measure of how easily a liquid, particularly gasoline, evaporates.

Religious Cultures – A culture that values unity with the cosmos.

Renewable Energy Sources – Energy sources that are not fixed but rejuvenate or continue to be produced over time such as sunshine and wind.

Rent – Reimbursement for the use of something of economic value, which includes labor, land, capital, energy, ideas, and money. Rent for labor is usually called wages or salaries, rent for capital and land is usually called rent, rent for energy and ideas may be called royalties, and rent for money is called interest. Economic rent occurs when the rent payment is larger than necessary to entice the product into the market. The amount of the economic rent on a unit is price minus marginal cost.

Reservation Price – The price at which an economic entity is willing to make a transaction. For a buyer, it is the highest price he will pay, and for a seller, it is the lowest price he will accept.

Reserve Over Production Ratio - Current proven reserves divided by current production. It is a measure of how long current reserves would last at the current rate of production.

Residual Oil – Heavy hydrocarbon product with sulfur and metal in it that is left after the lighter more valuable products have been boiled off from crude oil.

Ricardian Rent – Rent is reimbursement for the use of something of economic value, which includes labor, land, capital, energy, ideas, and money. Rent for labor is usually called wages or salaries, rent for capital and land is usually called rent, rent for energy and ideas may be called royalties, and rent for money is called interest. Economic rent occurs when the rent payment is larger than necessary to entice the product into the market. The amount of the economic rent on a unit is price minus marginal cost. Ricardian rent arises when some producers have lower cost than others but receive the marginal cost of the marginal producer. Ricardian rent helps allocate fixed quantities of low cost resources over their most valuable uses.

Ring Fenced – Keeping the accounting books strictly separate for a non-regulated and a regulated division of a company. This is to prevent the regulated segment from subsidizing the non-regulated segment.

Risk – Uncertainty or unknown variability in expected economic outcomes.

Risk Averse – A preference for a sure outcome to an uncertain outcome with the same expected value.

Risk-Free Interest Rate – The interest rate on an asset in which there is no possibility of default such as a bond from a totally reliable government.

Risk Lover – A person who prefers an uncertain outcome with the same expected value to a certain outcome of equal value.

Risk Neutral – An indifference between a sure outcome to an uncertain outcome with the same expected value.

Risk Premium – The amount you have to compensate someone over the risk free rate to take on an investment with a variable return.

Rivalry in Consumption – One person's consumption of a good precludes another person from consuming it. A pure private good has rivalry in consumption, whereas a pure public good does not. A pure private good is also excludable in consumption whereas a pure public good is not.

Royalty – When oil, gas, or other mineral is leased by the owner to another party that produces it, the royalty is the share of production or the share of the price that is paid by the lessee to the owner. A common royalty is 12.5% of the price.

Rules Manipulator – The person providing the rules for a negotiation.

Run of the River – A hydro power plant built on a river with no dam behind it.

RVP – Reid vapor pressure

s.ton – Short ton

Sales Tax – A tax based on a good when it is sold.

Salutation Displays – Cultural rules for greetings, good byes, and life transformations such as handshakes, bows, and kisses.

Satellite Images – Pictures taken from satellites circling the earth.

Say's Law – A macroeconomic idea that supply creates its own demand since enough income is generated in producing all goods to buy them all back.

Scenario Building – A way of analyzing or planning for the future by building alternative consistent possible future sequences of events and making decisions how to proceed in the case of each alternative.

Schumpeterian Creative Destruction – The notion put forth by Schumpeter that the creation of the new destroys the old as humans make economic progress.

SCM – supply chain management

Sealed Bid Auction – An auction in which bids are secret from other bidders.

Second Law of Thermodynamics – When energy is converted, it is reduced in quality and its ability to do work is decreased. This inability to do work is called entropy.

Secondary Electricity – Secondary electricity is the result of the conversion of fossil fuels into electricity.

Secondary Energy – Secondary energy is the result of the conversion of primary energy into another form such as the production of electricity from fossil fuels.

Self-Defeating Prophecy – A negative prophecy that causes people to react and prevent something from happening.

Self-Fulfilling Prophecy – A positive prophecy that causes people to react and cause something to happen.

Semiconductor – A crystal material, such as silicon, that conducts electricity better than an insulator but not as well as a conductor. It conducts poorly in a pure state but becomes a much better conductor when it has impurities. It is a key component in transistors.

Service Contract – An agreement to provide work for others. National oil companies may give service contracts to private companies to search for and develop oil. They may be similar to oil production sharing contracts but reimbursement is in money not in kind.

Settle – The last price of the trading day for a futures or option contract.

Severance Tax – A tax for taking a mineral out of the ground.

Shame-Based Culture – Cultures where it is important not to bring shame to the group. Causing shame to the group causes a loss of face.

Short Position – Having sold a borrowed asset.

Short Run – A period short enough so that some factors are fixed.

Short Ton – A non-metric unit of weight equal to 2000 pounds or 0.907 metric tons.

Shoulder Production – Electricity production between peak and base load.

Simulation Model – Mathematical model that approximates the behavior of an economic system or phenomenon. It can be used for planning and forecasting.

Single sided market – Only one side of the market is bidding.

SMP – special marketing program or system marginal cost

SO$_2$ – sulfur dioxide

SOE – state-owned entity

Social Culture – A culture that values people.

Social Interest Rate – The rate to be used to discount public investments. It may be lower than the market interest rate, if public investments are less risky, or higher than the market interest rate if public investments are more risky. It should be between consumers' rate of time preference, or how they will trade off future goods for present goods, and the gross rate of return on investment adjusted for risk.

Social Losses – For an economic situation, such as the production of a good, it is the difference between social welfare at an optimal level of production and social welfare at a sub-optimal level of production. Externalities, market power, and government taxation can result in sub-optimal production of a good. In a market with no externalities, social welfare is the sum of consumer and producer surplus.

Social Optimum – An economic outcome out of the feasible set of outcomes that maximizes social welfare.

Social Security Tax – A tax to pay for the U.S. government social security retirement program. It is a transfer payment in which the money is taken from those working and paying in and transferred to those eligible retirees.

Social Welfare – Social welfare for any economic situation is the difference between total social benefits and social costs. In a market with no externalities, it is the sum of consumer surplus and producer surplus.

Solar Energy – Energy based on sunshine in the form of either heat or electricity from photovoltaics.

Spark Spread – A spread is buying/selling more than one derivative in a trading strategy. A short spark spread simulates an electricity generator and is to sell electricity futures and buy the generator's fuel futures such as coal or gas.

Specific Cultures – A culture in which the public space and private space are not very compartmentalized. Because it is relatively easy to enter the private space from the public space, the public space is much more restricted to outsiders than in diffuse cultures.

Speculator – A person or institution that trades in the energy derivative markets without dealing in the cash market. They trade in order to take on risk in hopes of making a profit.

Spent Fuel Reprocessing – Taking the uranium and plutonium out of used nuclear power fuel in order to reuse it in mixed oxide fuel.

Spiders – A type of bot or robot software that searches the world wide web.

Spot Market – A place where a good or service is bought or sold by independent parties for immediate payment and delivery. Also called the cash market.

Stackleberg Duopoly – A market with two producers. The non-dominant producer maximizes profits given the dominant producer's production, while the dominant firm maximizes profits given the non-dominant firm's reaction function.

Stand-Alone Costs – The cost of producing a product when it is produced by itself with no other goods produced at the same time.

Statfjord Oil and Gas Field – The largest oil field in the North Sea discovered in 1974, which straddles the boundary between the Norwegian and British sectors of the North Sea.

Stone Age – Period of time from about 2 million BC to 2000 BC when humans used stone tools. Before the Bronze Age, it ended at different times in different regions.

Straddle Spread – A spread is buying more than one derivative in a trading strategy. A long straddle spread is buying a put and a call at the same strike price and expiration date. With a short straddle spread, you would sell instead of buy.

Straight-Line Depreciation - Using an annual depreciation charge for tax purposes equal to the value of the asset divided by its allowed depreciable life.

Straight-Fixed Variable Pricing – When peak users pay for capital or capacity costs and variable costs, and off-peak users only pay the variable costs.

Stranded Cost – A cost for an electric generation plant that was put in under regulation that becomes priced out of the market if restructuring allows new cheaper competitors to enter the market.

Strangle Spread – A spread is buying/selling more than one derivative in a trading strategy. A long strangle is buying a call with a strike price above the market price and the put strike price is below the market price. A short strangle would be selling these assets.

Strategic Petroleum Reserve (SPR) - A U.S. government stockpile of petroleum stored in salt domes along the Gulf of Mexico to be used in times of oil disruption.

Strict, Joint, and Several Liability – A property of the U.S. Superfund bill in which any one who has contributed to a toxic waste site can be billed for the whole mess, if the other contributors cannot be found.

Strike Price – The price at which a put or a call entitles you to sell or buy the underlying asset.

Subadditive Cost – If it costs less to produce two goods together than to produce each separately, costs are subadditive. If it costs the same to produce two goods together than to produce them separately, costs are additive.

Submarine Pipeline – A pipeline that is deep under water.

Subsidies – Government payments to encourage some economic activity.

Suezmax- A class of ship from 120,000–160,000 DWT. It is the largest class size that can go through the Suez Canal.

Supervisory Control and Data Acquisition Systems (SCADA) – A computerized system that remotely monitors and controls some energy system such as a pipeline system or power plant.

Supply Chain Management (SCM) – The supply chain is the set of processes that take a product from raw material procurement through to sales and delivery of the end product. Supply chain management is the set of procedures developed to organize and coordinate this process, often with the help of computer programs that provide information across the chain.

Survey – Questionnaire used to solicit information on planned activities for help in economic forecasting and planning.

Swap – An over-the-counter financial instrument that exchanges one set of cash flows for another. The most common type of swap is called a plain vanilla swap and is the exchange of a fixed for a floating rate.

System Dynamics Model – A set of mathematical equations with feedback loops that simulates a complex economic system over time.

Taboo Zones – Areas of the body that are not to be touched by certain segments of a culture. Often these areas have sexual or religious significance.

Tar Sands – Heavy oil deposits in which much of the lighter products have evaporated. Also called oil sands.

Target Revenue Model – A model of a resource exporting country that has as its goal the amount of revenue needed for economic development. Such a model has a downward sloping supply function, since a higher price will require lower sales to meet the target revenue.

Tariff – A tax on imports.

Tax Depletion Allowances – A percent of revenues that can be deducted from the sales price of a mineral to reduce taxable income.

Tax Equity – Whether a tax is distributed fairly across the taxable population. This depends on what is considered fair. It could be to tax entities in proportion to the government benefits they receive or to tax them in an equitable way. Horizontal equity has people having similar incomes paying similar amounts and vertical equity has people having dissimilar incomes paying dissimilar amounts.

Tax Free Bonds – Bonds in which the interest payments are not taxable.

Taxes on Products – A government assessed amount on a product to help support government spending.

Technological Determinism – The notion that technology has a determining influence on how economic and social systems evolve.

Terawatt – One trillion watts (10^{12} watts). A watt is a measure of electric power equal to one ampere under the pressure of one volt.

Theoretical Systematic Culture – A culture that values the acquisition of knowledge.

Theory X – A management theory based on the premise that people dislike work and must be coerced to work to satisfy their basic needs for economic security.

Theory Y – A management theory based on the premise that people want to develop and improve themselves and will willingly work if motivated by an interesting and challenging job.

Thermal Cracking – A refinery process that breaks larger hydrocarbons into smaller ones using heat.

Thermal Energy – Heat energy.

Third-Party Access – Allowing non-owners of a facility its use on a nondiscriminatory basis. Also called open access. Open access facilities are called common carriers.

Total Quality Management (TQM) – A business philosophy that focuses on continuous improvement by paying attention to customers, quantitatively measuring quality, and having all employees, not just management, contribute to quality improvement.

Town gas – Gas manufactured from coal.

Toxic Wastes – An unusable byproduct of consumption or production that causes death or disease.

TPA – Third-party access

Trading Partner Networks (TPN) - A network that uses a hub or brain to connect the partners (businesses) to each other through the Internet.

Trading Strategies – Buying more than one asset at a time.

Transaction Cost Economics – Maintains that the market governance that will prevail (spot market, bilateral contracts, vertical integration) is that which minimizes transaction costs.

Transfer Prices – The prices different parts of a company charge each other for goods and services. Such purchases are not arms-length purchases.

Transmed Pipeline – A submarine pipeline from Tunisia to Sicily that passes under the Mediterranean Sea.

Transmission Pipelines – Large pipelines that transport oil or gas over long distances.

Transmission System – The network of high voltage power lines that transports bulk power from the generator to the local distribution system.

Treaty of Rome – The treaty that created the European Economic Community.

Troll Gas Field – Norway's largest oil and gas field.

Turbine – A machine in which the flow of a gas or liquid turns blades that spin a shaft to produce some sort of work. If the shaft is connected to an electricity generator, the mechanical energy is converted into electrical energy.

Turnkey Plant – Plant that is totally built by a contractor with limited owner involvement. When it is turned over the owner, it is ready to go with just a turn of the key.

TW – Terawatt

Two Period Dynamic Model – A model of a fixed resource in which the objective function is the net present value of profits. This model allocates production over two periods.

U. S. Federal Energy Regulatory Commission (FERC) – An independent U.S. federal regulatory agency created in 1977 that regulates energy transmission involved in interstate commerce.

U.S. Federal Power Commission (FPC) – FERC's predecessor, created in 1920. The FPC regulated electricity and gas transmission involved in interstate commerce. Its functions were broken up between DOE and FERC.

U_{235} – Uranium isotope 235

U_3O_8 – Uranium oxide

UF_6 – Uranium hexafluoride

Ultra Large Crude Carriers (ULCC) – Ships measuring more than 320,000 DWT.

Unbundling – Breaking separate processes in the supply chain into separate products. For example, pipelines used to provide all the services of getting gas supplies to distributors. Now the steps in this process such as transportation, storage, and title transfer are required to be unbundled, so they can be purchased separately from different suppliers.

Uncertainty – Not knowing the exact outcome.

Uncertainty Avoidance – A cultural trait of a group in which uncertainty and change make members uncomfortable and are avoided.

Under-The-Boiler Use – Burning hydrocarbons to create hot water or steam.

Unified Governance – When transactions are governed by vertical integration.

Unit Capital Costs – The costs obtained by dividing capital costs over all units of production. Also called levelized capital costs.

Unit Operating Costs – Total operating costs divided by production. Also called average variable cost.

Unit tax – A tax on each unit sold. The tax is the same no matter what the price as opposed to an ad valorem tax in which the tax is a percent of the price.

Unitized Production – When a pool of oil is optimized and produced as one unit even if there are many owners of the pool. This procedure avoids the overproduction encouraged by the law of capture.

Univariate Time Series – A statistical forecasting technique in which a variable is forecast by using historical values of itself.

Universalist Culture – A culture that believes there are norms, values, and behavior patterns that are valid everywhere at all times.

UO_2 – Uranium dioxide

Upside Profits – In finance, risk is the variability of investment returns. Downside risk is the probability and size of negative returns on an investment.

Upside Risk – In finance, risk is the variability of investment returns. Upside risk is the probability and size of positive returns on an investment.

Urengoi Gas Field – Russian gas field that is the largest in the world.

USGS – U.S. Geological Survey

User Cost – The difference between price and marginal cost. A measure of Hotelling rent in a dynamically optimized market.

Utility Theory – A branch of microeconomics in which consumers are assumed to have utility functions that represent their preferences. Rational behavior assumes that they will undertake economic activity to maximize these functions subject to constraints. Although it is not strictly true that consumers typically have utility functions, under some fairly reasonable assumptions consumer preferences can be represented by such functions. Thus, they provide a convenient and powerful tool for analyzing consumer behavior.

V – Volt

Valdez Principle – Set of 10 environmental principles that corporations can voluntarily endorse and commit their company to. Endorsing companies fill out annual environmental reports and are committed to less emissions, waste reduction, and more sustainable operations. Also called the Ceres Principle.

Value Added Networks (VAN) – A service that provides communication channels between subscribers and may also provide security, error checking, message arrival confirmation, and other services.

Value Added Tax – A tax in which a producer does not pay a tax on goods bought from other firms but only on the value added from labor and primary material produced by the firm.

Value Chains – A series of sequential processes that create profits for a company.

Variance – The square of the standard deviation.

Vertical Equity – A criteria of fairness for taxation. Vertical equity has people with dissimilar incomes paying dissimilar amounts of taxes.

Vertical Integration – A market structure in which a firm handles more than one process in the supply chain. Thus, if an oil producer produces, transports, and refines oil it is a vertically integrated company.

Very Large Crude Carriers (VLCC) – Ships sized from 200,000 to 320,000 DWT.

Vickrey Auction – An auction in which the highest bidder wins but pays the second highest bid price.

Virtual Reality – Computer generated reality.

VLCC – Very large crude carrier

VOLL – Value of the lost load

Voltage – A measure of electromotive force or how hard electrons are being pushed through a conducting medium.

Wash Trading – Buying and selling the same product so that it appears that exchanges have been made but in reality there has been no real transaction of the product. Such trades might be conducted to make it appear that there is more activity in a stock or to artificially change the price of the product. Wash trading is illegal under amendments to the U.S. Commodity Exchange Act of 1936.

Watt – A measure of electric power equal to one ampere under the pressure of one volt.

Well-Defined Property Right – Exclusive right to clearly specified aspects of an economic good. A common area that everyone has access to does not have well-defined property rights.

West Texas Intermediate (WTI) – A light sweet crude produced in West Texas with API gravity of around 40. It is one of the crude oils specified in NYMEX crude futures and options contracts, and its price is an index used in numerous oil contracts.

Wet Natural Gas – Natural gas without the gas liquids removed.

Wildcatter – Someone drilling for oil or gas on a previously unexplored area.

Wind Energy – Energy that comes from the wind pushing blades to create mechanical energy. The mechanical energy may in turn be converted into electrical energy.

Winner's Curse – The winner of a bid for an oil concession may be the one who is most optimistic about the property. If they are overly optimistic, the curse is that they may win the concession but lose money in the process.

Work Bidding – A concession system for oil leases in which the bid is not in money but is a work program. Work bidding is often designed to hasten the development of the concession. The winning bid typically is the one that bids the most work or soonest work.

WTI – West Texas Intermediate (crude oil)

X-Inefficiency – Higher costs for government-owned facilities from lack of competitive discipline or having not only economic but other political and social objectives.

XML – Extensible Markup Language

Yamburg Gas Field – Second largest gas field in Western Siberia.

Yin/Yang – The female and male force in the Taoist religion. Each force is thought to have some of the other force within it.

For more business glossary terms, see http://www.investorwords.com/ or www.small-business-dictionary.org

Appendix B: Conversion Charts

International energy comparisons are fraught with difficulties. Not only are there the difficulties of currency conversions but fossil fuels come in a variety of metric and non-metric units including barrels, gallons, liters, metric tons, short tons, long tons, cubic feet, cubic meters and energy units. Energy units include kilocalories, British Thermal Units, kilowatt-hours, kilojoules, and tons of oil or coal equivalent. In addition, fossil fuels are not homogeneous but rather vary by energy content and impurities. I have deliberately used a variety of units throughout the book with conversions to familiarize the reader with the various units used. This brief appendix summarizes some of the more common conversions. There are numerous resources on the Internet for the metric to non-metric conversions. For example:

- http://allmeasures.com/Fullconversion.asp automatically converts into numerous other units when you enter a number and click on the table. It has been used for some of the conversions in this appendix.
- http://n93.cs.fiu.edu/measures/ from Florida International University is fairly complete, including printer measures and standard international units.

- http://www.wsdot.wa.gov/Metrics/factors.htm from the Washington State Department of Transportation contains an explanation of standard international units, numerous conversions, and a conversion program that can be downloaded.

Other prominent sources for conversions that include values for fossil fuels by country include the EIA/DOE *International Energy Annual*, Conversions and Heat Contents, http://www.eia.doe.gov/iea/convheat.html, the Organization of Oil Exporting Countries (nondated) *Oil Industry Conversion Factors*, and British Petroleum's *Statistical Review of World Energy* at http://www.bp.com/centres/energy2002/downloads/index.asp—all of which have been consulted for this appendix. The United Nation's *Energy Statistics Yearbook* contains numerous such conversions as well.

Energy Conversions

Metric prefixes include:

kilo = 10^3

mega = 10^6

giga = 10^9

tera = 10^{12}

Length

Metric equivalences:

1 meter = 100 centimeters = 1000 millimeters = 0.001 kilometers

It is easy to convert between these equivalences. For example, if you want to know what 1 centimeter equals in terms of the other units divide each value by 100. That is

0.01 meter = 1 centimeter = 10 millimeters = 0.00001 kilometers

Non-metric equivalences:

1 mile = 1760 yards = 5280 feet = 0.869 nautical mile

1 foot = 12 inches = 1/3 yard

To convert lengths from non-metric to metric multiply by value in the table below.

To convert lengths from metric to non-metric divide by value in the table below.

Non-metric ↓	Metric→ Millimeter	Centimeter	Meter	Kilometer
Inch	25.4	2.54	25.4×10^{-3}	25.4×10^{-6}
Foot	304.8	30.48	0.3048	304.8×10^{-6}
Yard	914.4	91.44	0.9144	914.4×10^{-6}
Mile	1.6093×10^{6}	1.6093×10^{5}	1.6093×10^{3}	1.6093
Nautical mile	1852×10^{3}	1852×10^{2}	1852	1.852

Area

Metric equivalences

1 sq. kilometer = 1×10^{6} meter = 100 hectares

Non-metric equivalences

1 square mile = 27.8784×10^{6} sq. feet = 3.0976×10^{6} sq. yards = 640 acres

To convert from non-metric to metric, multiply by the value in the table below.

To convert from metric to non-metric divide by the value in the table below.

Non-metric ↓	Metric→ Sq. meter	Sq. kilometer	Hectare
Sq. foot	92.9×10^{-3}	92.9×10^{-9}	9.29×10^{-6}
Sq. yard	0.8361	836.1×10^{-9}	83.61×10^{-6}
Sq. mile	2.59×10^{6}	2.59	259
Acre	4047	4.047×10^{-3}	0.4047

Volume

Metric equivalences

1 cubic meter = 1000 liters = 1 kiloliter = 10^{6} cubic centimeters

Non-metric equivalences

1 U.S. gallon = 4 quarts = 8 pints = 231 cubic inches = 0.833 Imperial gallons

1 U.S. barrel = 42 U.S. gallons = 5.615 cubic feet

To convert from non-metric to metric, multiply by value in table below.

To convert from metric to non-metric divide by value in the table below.

Non-metric ↓	Metric→ Liter	Cubic meter = Kiloliter
Quart	1.011	1.101×10^{-3}
Cubic foot	28.317	28.317×10^{-3}
U.S. Gallon	3.785	3.785×10^{-3}
Barrel	159	0.159

Weight

Metric equivalences

1 metric ton = 1000 kilograms = 1,000,000 grams

Non-metric equivalences

1 long ton = 2240 pounds = 1.12 short ton

1 pound = 16 ounces

To convert from non-metric to metric, multiply by value in table below.

To convert from metric to non-metric, divide by value in the table below.

Non-metric ↓	Metric→ Gram	Kilogram	Metric ton
Ounce	28.35	28.35×10^{-3}	28.35×10^{-6}
Pound	453.6	0.4536	453.6×10^{-6}
Short ton	907.2×10^{3}	907.2	0.9072
Long ton	1.016×10^{6}	1016	1.016

Temperature

Metric equivalences

Degrees Celsius (Centigrade) (C) = 273.5 + degrees Kelvin (K)

Non-metric equivalences

Degrees Fahrenheit (F)

Conversion of Metric to Non-metric

C = 9/5*F + 32

F = 5/9(C − 32)

F = 5/9(K +273.15 − 32)

Energy or Heat Values

Metric equivalences

1000 calories = 1 kilocalorie (also called a Calorie) = 4.184 kilojoules

1 kilowatt hour = 859.85×10^3 kilocalories

Non-metric equivalences

Horsepower Hour = 2544.3 BTU

1 quad = 10^{15} BTU

1 Therm = 100,000 BTU

To convert from non-metric to metric, multiply by value in table below.

To convert from metric to non-metric, divide by value in the table below.

| Non-metric ↓ | Metric→ | | |
	Calorie = Kilocalorie	Kilojoule	KWh
BTU	0.2519	1.055	293.07×10^{-6}

Approximate Heat Values and Barrels per Metric Ton for U.S. Energy Products

	BTU/unit	Unit	Barrels/m.ton
Coal	21,072,000	short ton	na
Oil	5,800,000	barrel	7.33
Dry Natural Gas	1,025	cubic foot	na
Natural Gas Liquids	3,800,000	barrel	10.40
Gasoline	5,253,000	barrel	8.53
Jet Fuel/Kerosene	5,670,000	barrel	7.93
Naphtha Jet Fuel	5,355,000	barrel	8.27
Distillate	5,825,000	barrel	7.46
Residual	6,287,000	barrel	6.66
Lubricant	6,065,000	barrel	7.00

Source: EIA/DOE, downloaded from http://www.eia.doe.gov/iea/convheat.html, *Monthly Energy Review June 2003.*

TOE is one metric ton of oil equivalent, often considered to be 10 million kilocalories.

TCE is one metric ton of coal equivalent, about 2/3 of a ton of oil equivalent.

LNG – 1 metric ton of LNG = 1.23 tons of oil equivalent = 1400 cubic meters of natural gas.

Appendix C: Bibliography

Adelman, M. 1972. *World Petroleum Market.* Washington D.C.: Resources for the Future, Inc.

Adelman, Morris. 1993. *The Economics of Petroleum Supply.* Cambridge, Mass.: Massachusetts Institute of Technology.

Adler, N. J. 1997. *International Dimensions of Organizational Behavior.* Cincinnati, Ohio: South-Western.

Ahuja, Ravindar K., Thomas L. Magnanti, and James B. Orlin. 1993. *Network Flows: Theory, Algorithms, and Applications.* Englewood Cliffs, N.J.: Prentice Hall.

Anderson, Robert O. 1984. *Fundamentals of the Petroleum Industry.* Norman, Okla.: University of Oklahoma.

Appenzeller, Tim. 2001. "The Force is With Us: Einstein is Vindicated." *U.S. News and World Report,* April 16, 2001.

Association for the Promotion and Advancement of Science Education (APASE). Energy http://www.swifty.com/apase/charlotte/energy.html. Downloaded 05/01.

Bacon, R. W. 1995. "Privatization and Reform in the Global Electricity Supply Industry." *Annual Review of Energy and the Environment*. 20: 119–43.

Barber, Benjamin R. 1996. *JIHAD vs. McWorld*, New York: Ballantine Books.

Bardhan, Pranab. 1997. "Corruption and Development: A Review of Issues," *Journal of Economic Literature*, XXXV (September): 1320–1346.

Barrett, Barbara. "Impact of Culture on Business Behavior." Asian Studies Module– Outline. http://lama.kcc.hawaii.edu/asdp/econ/asian/BARRETT3.html March 26, 2001.

Bergen Country Technical Schools. "Introduction to Technology." http://www.bergen.org/technology/ Downloaded 05/01.

Bergen Energy Brokers. Norway: http://www.bergen-energi.no/

Berger, Bill D and Kenneth E. Anderson. 1992. *Petroleum: A Modern Primer of the Industry*. Tulsa, OK: PennWell Press, 3rd Edition.

Best information of the Web. http://www.lkjassociates.com/nigeria.html.

Bjerkholdt, Olav, Eystein Gjelsvik, and Øystein Olsen. 1990. *The Western European Gas Market: Deregulation and Supply Competition*: In Bjerkholdt et al. 1990. 3–28.

Bjerkholdt, Olav, Øystein Olsen, and Jon Vislie. 1990. *Recent Modelling Approaches in Applied Energy Economics*. London; New York: Chapman and Hall.

Björkman, Karl Erik. 1999. "Driving Forces in the Technology Development of Control." Stockholm University. http://www.stacken.kth.se/!bjoptkmsn/kt/control.html Downloaded Feb 2002.

Bopp, Anthony E. and Neri, John A. 1978. "The Price of Gasoline: Forecasting Comparisons." *Quarterly Review of Economics and Business* 18 (Winter): 23–31.

Bourcier, D. V. and Kazin, C. A. 1993. *Utility Survey Results on Forecasting Methods and Assumptions*. New England Power Planning.

Box, George E. P. and Gwilym M. Jenkins. 1970. *Time Series Analysis: Forecasting and Control*. San Francisco: Holden-Day.

BP Statistical Review of World Energy. Various issues. http://www.bp.com/centres/energy2002/

Brain, Marshall. "How Stuff Works." http://www.howstuffworks.com

Brathwaite, Leon D. and Cheryl Bradley. 1997. "Analysis of Petroleum Product Prices (1992–1997)" and "The Feasibility of a California Petroleum Product Reserve." California Energy Commission, Energy Information and Analysis Division, Fuel Resources Office.

Brealy, Richard A. and Stewart C. Myers. 1996. *Principles of Corporate Finance.* New York: McGraw-Hill Companies, Inc.

Brinkman, Emile and Rabinovitch, Ramon. 1995. "Regional Limitations on the Hedging Effectiveness of Natural Gas Futures." *The Energy Journal* 16(3): 113–124.

Bronowski, Jacob. 1973. *The Ascent of Man.* Boston: Little Brown and Company.

Brooks, C. E. P. 1951. "Geological and Historical Aspects of Climate Change." In Malone, Thomas. *Compendium of Meteorology.* Boston, Massachusetts: American Meteorological Society, 1007.

Brynjolfsson, Erik and Brian Kahin. 2000. *Understanding the Digital Economy: Data, Tools, and Research.* Cambridge, Mass.: MIT Press.

Buccigross, James H. 2000. "The Gas Industry Leads the Way in Adopting the Internet for Electronic Commerce," Natural Gas (July): 15–20.

Burstein, Daniel and David Kline. 1995. *Road Warriors: Dreams and Nightmares Along the Information Highway.* New York: Dutton.

Cairncross, Frances. 1997. *Death of Distance: How the Communications Revolution Will Change Our Lives.* Boston, Mass.: Harvard Business School Press.

California Energy Commission. 2002. *2002–2012 Electricity Outlook Report.* (February) Report P700-01-004F. http://www.energy.ca.gov/reports/2002-02-14_700-01-004F. Downloaded May 5, 2002.

Capen, E. C., Clapp, R. V., and Campbell, W. M. 1971. "Competitive Bidding in High-Risk Situations." *Journal of Petroleum Technology* (June): 641–653.

Carley, Kathleen M. 2000. *Organizational Change and the Digital Economy: A Computational Organization Science Perspective.* In Brynjolfsson and Kahin: 325–351.

Carson, Rachel. 1962. *Silent Spring;* drawings by Lois and Louis Darling. Boston: Houghton Mifflin; Cambridge, Mass: Riverside Press.

Chambers, Ann; Schnoor, Barry; and Hamilton, Stephanie. 2001. *Distributed Generation: A Nontechnical Guide.* Tulsa: PennWell.

Chiang, A. C. 1992. *Elements of Dynamic Optimization.* New York: McGraw-Hill.

Chiang, A. C. 1984. *Fundamental Methods of Mathematical Economics.* New York: McGraw-Hill.

Choi, Chong Ju and Kelemen, Mihaela. 1995. *Cultural Competences: Managing Co-Operatively Across Cultures.* Aldershot, Hants, England; Brookfield, Vt.: Dartmouth.

Chown, Marcus. 1996. *Afterglow of Creation,* Sausalito, California: University Science Books.

Cleveland, Cutler and Robert Kaufmann. 1991. "Forecasting Ultimate Oil Recovery and Its Rate of Production: Incorporating Economic Forces into the Models of M. King Hubbert." *The Energy Journal* 12(2): 17–46.

Clô, Alberto. 2000. *Oil Economics and Policy.* Boston, Dordrecht, London: Kluwer Academic Press.

Coffman, Peter. 2000. "ASP's Ascendent." *The New Energy Economy.* (Fall): 30–31.

Cohen, Barry, Peabody, Gerald, Rodekohr, Mark, and Shaw, Susan. Circa 1995. *A History of Mid-Term Energy Projections: A Review of the Annual Energy Outlook Projections.* Washington D.C.: U.S. Energy Information Administration.

Collins, James C. and Jerry I. Porras. 1994. *Built To Last: Successful Habits of Visionary Companies.* New York: Harper Business.

Columbus Foundation. British Virgin Islands. http://www.thenina.com/. Downloaded 05/01.

Cookenboo, Leslie (1980) "Production Functions and Cost Functions: A Case Study." Reprinted in *Managerial Economics and Operations Research: Techniques Applications, Cases,* edited by Edwin Mansfield, New York: W.W. Norton & Company, 52-75.

Couper, Heather and Nigel Henbest. 1997. *Big Bang: The Story of the Universe.* New York: DK Publishing Inc.

Coyne Sr., Edward J. Syllabus and course material for BUSA 470, Business in the International Environment. Stanford University. Spring 2001. http://faculty.samford.edu/~ejcoyne/busa470.htm

Cremer, J. and S. Salehi-Isfahani. 1980. "A Theory of Competitive Pricing in the Oil Market: What Does OPEC Really Do?" CARESS, Philadelphia: University of Pennsylvania, Working Paper #80-4.

Crose, Wilbur. 1983. *Petroleum.* Chicago: Childrens Press

Dahl, Carol A. 1993. "A Survey of Energy Demand Elasticities in Support of the Development of the NEMS." Golden, Colorado: Department of Mineral Economics, Colorado School of Mines. October 19, 1993. Prepared for the U.S. Department of Energy.

Dahl, Carol A. and Daniel Celta. 1999. "Export and Domestic Pricing Decisions that Maximize OPEC Social Welfare." Draft. Golden, Colo.: Division of Economics and Business, Colorado School of Mines.

Dahl, Carol A. and Karlygash Kuralbayeva. 2001. "Energy and the Environment in Kazakhstan." *Energy Policy,* 29(6): 429–440.

Dahl, Carol A. and Thomas K Matson. 1998. "Evolution of the U.S. Natural Gas Industry in Response to Changes in Transaction Costs." *Land Economics* 74(3): 390–408.

Dahl, Carol A. and Balázs Nagy. 2004. "Leading Edge Information Technologies for Energy Industries." *Energy Newsletter,* International Association for Energy Economics, 3rd quarter, 7–13.

Davis, J. D. 1984. Blue Gold: *The Political Economy of Natural Gas.* London; Boston: Allen & Unwin.

Deam, R. J. 1981. "Understanding Energy" and "Long Range Pricing of Crude Oil" in *Mathematical Modeling of Energy Systems,* ed. Ibrahim Kavrakoglu, 211–246.

Deaves, Richard and Krinsky, Itzhak. 1992. "Risk Premiums and Efficiency in the Market for Crude Oil Futures." *The Energy Journal* 13(2): 93–118.

Debanne, J. G. 1973. "A Pollution- and Technology-Sensitive Model for Energy Supply-Distribution Studies" in *Energy Modeling,* ed. Milton F. Searl, 372–409.

Debanne, J. G. 1980. "Network Based Regional Energy Planning Models: An Evolutionary Expose." in *Energy Policy Modeling: Vol II,* ed. W. T. Ziemba and S.L. Schwartz, 155–184.

Debanne, J. G. 1981a. "Application of Generalized Trans-Shipment and Integer Programming Algorithms. in *Modeling of Large-Scale Energy Systems,* ed. W. Hafele and L. K. Kirchmayer, 401–409.

Debanne, J. G. 1981b. "Regional Network Based Modeling as a Tool in Energy Planning: An Evolutionary Expose" *Mathematical Modeling of Energy Systems,* ed. Ibrahim Kavrakoglu, Ph.D., 343–378.

Dixit, Avinash K. and Pindyck, Robert S. 1994. *Investment Under Uncertainty.* Princeton, N.J.: Princeton University Press.

Dowling, Edward T. *Introduction to Mathematical Economics.* Schaum's Outline Series (ME). New York: McGraw-Hill.

Dunn, Leroy Dr. and Jane Gravelle. 1975. *An Analysis of the Federal Tax Treatment of Oil and Gas and some Policy Alternative*, in U.S. House of Representatives. 1975: 357–407.

Petroleum History. Earth and Mineral Science, Pennsylvania State University. http://www.ems.psu.edu/~radovic/petroleum_history.html. Downloaded 05/01.

"Geologic Time Scale." *Encyclopedia Britannica.* Enchanted Learning Software. http://www.zoomdinosaurs.com/subjects/geologictime.html Downloaded 05/01.

Engine: Energy, Information, Exchange. http://www.gasandoil.com/ March 26, 2001.

European Commission, Directorate General for Energy and Transport. 2001. Annual Energy Review 2000, http://europa.eu.int/comm/energy/library/summary.pdf

Faruqui, Ahmad, Kuczmowski, Thomas and Lilienthal, Peter. 1990. "Demand Forecasting Methodologies: An Overview for Electric Utilities." *Energy* 15(3/4): 285–296.

Feng Shui. http://www.c-com.net/~aquarian/fengshui.htm. March 26, 2001.

Forrester, Jay. 2002. *Road Maps, A Guide to Learning System Dynamics.* Developed by the System Dynamics in Education Project at MIT under the direction of Professor Jay Forrester. http://sysdyn.mit.edu/road-maps/home.html

Fox, William F. 1983. *Federal Regulation of Energy*, Colorado Springs, Colo.: Shepard's/McGraw-Hill.

Frankel, Paul. 1969. *Essentials of Petroleum: A Key to Oil Economics.* New York, A. M. Kelley.

Freed, Daniel. 1997. "An Analysis of the Deregulation of the Electricity Industries of New Zealand, Norway, Sweden and the United Kingdom." Draft. Colorado School of Mines.

Gardner, Roy. 2003. *Games for Business and Economics*, New York: John Wiley and Sons.

Gates, Bill. 1999. *Business at the Speed of Thought.* Newport Beach, CA: Books On Tape.

Georgescu-Roegen, Nicholas. 1979. "Energy Analysis and Economic Valuation," *Southern Economic Journal,* 45(4): 1023–1058.

Giovanni, B. and A. Baranzini, editors. 1997. *Energy Modelling Beyond Economics and Technology.* Genève, Switzerland: Centre Universitaire d'Étude des problèmes de l'Énergié, Université de Genève.

Goodstein, Eban S. 1999. *Economics and the Environment.* Upper Saddle River, N.J.: Prentice Hall. 2nd Edition.

Gordon, Richard L. 1975. *U.S. Coal and the Electric Power Industry.* Baltimore: Resources for the Future. Johns Hopkins University Press.

Gordon, Richard L. 1987. *World Coal: Economics, Policies, and Prospects.* Cambridge (England); New York: Cambridge University Press.

Gordon, Richard, Jacoby, Henry and Zimmerman, Martin. 1987. *Energy Markets and Regulation: essays in honor of M.A. Adelman.* Cambridge, Mass.: MIT Press.

Gray, John. 1992. *Men are from Mars, Women are from Venus: A Practical Guide for Improving Communication and Getting What You Want in Your Relationships.* HarperCollins.

Green, R. 1995. "Lessons from electricity privatization in U.K., Pacific, and Asia." *Journal of Energy,* 5 (2): 235–247.

Green, R. 1996. "Reform of the electricity supply industry in the UK." *The Journal of Energy Literature,* II (1): 3–24.

Green, R. and Newbery, D. M. 1992. "Competition in the British Electricity Spot Market." *Journal of Political Economy,* 100(5): 929–953.

Greene, William H. 2000. *Econometric Analysis, 4th Edition.* Upper Saddle River, N.J.: Prentice Hall.

Greenstein, Shane. 2000. "The Evolving Structure of Commercial Internet Markets." in Brynjolfsson, Erik and Brian Kahin.

Griffin, James and Steele, Henry. 1986. *Energy Economics and Policy.* New York: Academic Press, 2nd Edition.

Grinpelc, Jorge and Richard Siegfried. Circa 2000. "Information Technology in the Oil and Gas Industry in Latin America." PricewaterhouseCoopers. http://www.pwcglobal.com/gx/eng/about/ind/energy/itog.pdf

Grove, Cornelius and Hallowell, Willa. 1994. "Global Patterns: Culture's Influence on Managerial Behavior." *Worldwide Business Practices Report.* Deerfield, Ill: International Cultural Enterprises (series of eight articles, January–September).

http://businessmajors.about.com/education/businessmajors/gi/dynamic/offsite. htm?site=http://www.grovewell.com/pub%2Dcultural%2Dinfluence.html. March 26, 2001.

Grübler, Arnulf. 1998. *Technology and Global Change.* Cambridge University Press.

Gustavsson, Bengt. 1995. "The Human Values of Swedish Management." *Journal of Human Values,* 1(2): 153-172. New Delhi: Sage Press. http://www.fek.su.se/home/gus/Papers\Swedval.htm March 26, 2001.

Guth, Alan. 1997. "Was Cosmic Inflation The 'Bang' Of The Big Bang?" *The Beamline,* 27 (14). http://nedwww.ipac.caltech.edu/level5/Guth/.

Hall, Edward T. and Reed Hall, Mildred. 1990. *Understanding Cultural Differences.* Yarmouth, Maine: Intercultural Press.

Haltiwanger, John and Ron S. Jarmin. "Measuring the Digital Economy." in Brynjolfsson and Kahin 2000. pp. 13–33.

Hamilton, James. 1994. *Time Series Analysis.* Princeton, NJ: Princeton University Press.

Hannesson, Rögnvaldur. 1998. *Petroleum Economics: Issues and Strategies of Oil and Natural Gas Production.* Westport, Conn., London: Quorum Books.

Hannesson, Rögnvaldur. 2001. *Investing for Sustainability: The Management of Mineral Wealth.* Boston/Dordrecht/London: Kluwer Academic Publishers.

Hartwick, John M. and Nancy D. Olewiler. 1998. *The Economics of Natural Resource Use.* New York: Harper and Row Publishers, Inc.

Hawking, Stephen W. 1988. *A Brief History of Time: From the Big Bang to Black Holes.* New York: Bantam Books.

Hearn, Greg, Mandeville, Tom and Anthony, David. 1998. *The Communication Superhighway: Social and Economic Change in the Digital Age.* St. Leonards, N.S.W.: Allen & Unwin.

Helm, D. 1995. "British utility regulation: theory, practice, and reform." *Oxford Review of Economic Policy,* 10 (3): 17–39.

Herbert, John H. 1993. "The Relations of Monthly Spot to Futures Prices for Natural Gas." *Energy*, 18(11): 1119–1124.

Hines, R.D. 1989. "The Sociopolitical Paradigm in Financial Accounting Research." *Accounting Auditing & Accountability*, Vol.2. No.1: 52–76.

Hinrichs, Roger A. 1996. *Energy: Its Use and the Environment*. New York: Saunders College Publishing, Harcourt Brace College Publishers.

Hjalmarsson, L. and Veiderpass, A. 1988. *The Swedish Electricity Market: A Survey of Market Behaviour and Mode of Functioning*. Monograph. Sweden: Department of Economics, University of Gothenburg.

Hjalmarsson, L. 1992. *The Market for Electricity in Scandinavia: Regulation and Performance*. Sweden: Department of Economics, Gothenburg University.

Hoecklin, Lisa. 1998. *Managing Cultural Differences: Strategies for Competitive Advantage*. New York: Addison Wesley.

Hoel, Michael, Holtsmark, Bjart and Vislie, Jon. 1990. "The European Gas Market as a Bargaining Game." in Bjerkholdt, Øystein and Vislie. *Recent Modelling Approaches in Applied Energy*, 49–65. London; New York: Chapman and Hall.

Hofstede, G., and Bond, M. H. (1988) "Confucius & Economic Growth: New trends in Culture's Consequences," *Organizational Dynamics* 16 (4), pp. 4–21.

Hofstede, Geert. 1991. *Cultures and Organizations: Software of the Mind*. New York: McGraw-Hill Book Company.

Hooker, J. N. 1998. "The polite and the rude." Shorter version published as "The polite and the rude: Etiquette abroad," Monash Mt. Eliza, *Business Review*, 3: 40–49.

http://ba.gsia.cmu.edu/jnh/courtesy.doc March 26, 2001.

http://caltex.com.au/prods/glossaryl.html

http://eiainfo.eia.doe.gov/emeu/cabs/lng.html

http://inseine.ifmt.nf.ca/~cms/ships/lng.jpg

http://news.bbc.co.uk/1/hi/in_depth/europe/euro-glossary/1216873.stm

http://royal.okanagan.bc.ca/mpidwirn/atmosphereandclimate/greenhouse.html#d

http://sbm-nt-1.tees.ac.uk/pcm/ccd_block3.htm March 26, 2001.

http://www.ashland.com/education/oil/refining/

http://www.bp.com/centres/energy/world_stat_rev/natural_gas/reserves.asp

http://www.cooplife.com/greene/glossary.html "Coming to Terms with Renewable Energy."

http://www.cre8tivetraining.com/lean/lean-terms.htm#bench

http://www.dictionary.com

http://www.edf.org/want2hlp/b-gw20steps.html

http://www.epa.gov/swerust1/mtbe/index.htm

http://www.shinnova.com/part/99-japa/abj17-e.htm "Non-verbal Communication." based on *Times Square Travel's: A Guide to Japan.* Downloaded 7/30/02.

http://www.thesupplychain.com/eng/resources/glossary/edi.asp

http://www.tsin.com/gloss.html. FERC glossary

http://www.wgc.org/roundtable/commj/101/

http://www.woodside.com.au/anws/index.html

Hull, John. 2000. *Options, Futures, and Other Derivative Securities.* Upper Saddle River, N.J.: Prentice Hall International, Inc.

Hunt, S. and Shuttleworth, G. 1996. *Competition and Choice in Electricity.* New York: John Wiley & Sons.

Huss, William R. 1986. "Forecasting in the Electric Utility Industry." *The Changing World Economy.* IAEE Eighth Annual Conference Proceedings. Cambridge, Mass.: November 19–21: 239–242.

Informa Publishing Group Ltd. 2001. *Lloyd's List Ports of the World, 2001.* London: Informa Publishing Group Ltd.

Institute for Global Policy Research, University of Virginia. *A Brief History Of Major Oil Companies In The Gulf Region With Corporate Contact Information* http://www.virginia.edu/igpr/apagoilhistory.html. Downloaded 05/01.

International Energy Agency. 1998. *Mapping the Energy Future : Energy Modelling and Climate Change Policy.* Paris, France: International Energy Agency. Referenced from http://www.iea.org/pubs/studies/files/mapping/mapping.htm. July, 2001.

Jaffe, Adam B., Steven R. Peterson and Portney, Paul R. 1995. "Environmental Regulation and the Competitiveness of U.S. Manufacturing: What Does the Evidence Tell Us?" *Journal of Economic Literature,* XXXIII. (March): 132–163.

Jenkins, Gilbert. 1989. *Oil Economists' Handbook.* New York: Elsevier Applied Science.

Jensen Associated, Inc. Presented at the United States/International Association for Energy Economics 21st Annual North American Meeting. Philadelphia, PA. September 24–27, 2000.

Jevons, William Stanley. 1965. *"The Coal Question: An Inquiry Concerning the Progress of the Nation, and the Probable Exhaustion of Our Coal Mines."* Reprints of the Classics. August M. Kelly: New York.

Jorion, Philippe. 1997. *Value at Risk: The New Benchmark for Controlling Market Risk.* New York: McGraw-Hill Companies, Inc.

Joskow, Paul L. 1987. "Asset Specificity and the Structure of Vertical Relationships: Emperical Evidence." *Journal of Law, Economics and Organization,* Spring 1988.

Joskow, Paul L. 1987. "Contract Duration and Relationship-Specific Investments: Empirical Evidence from Coal Markets." *American Economic Review,* 77(1): 169–185.

Joskow, Paul L. and Schmalensee, Richard. 1983. *Markets for Power: An Analysis of Electric Utility Deregulation.* Cambridge, Mass.: MIT Press.

Julius, DeAnne and Mashayekhi, Afsaneh. 1990. *The Economics of Natural Gas: Pricing, Planning and Policy.* Oxford, England: Oxford University Press.

Kahn, Herman, William Brown and Leon Martel with the assistance of the Staff of the Hudson Institute. 1976. *The Next 200 Years: A Scenario for America and the World.* Quill, N.Y.: Hudson Institute.

Karass, Chester L. 1968. "A Study of the Relationship of Negotiator Skill and Power as Determinants of Negotiation Outcome." Ph.D. Dissertation, University of S. California, Los Angeles.

Kennedy, Michael. 1974. "An Economic Model of the World Oil Market." *Bell Journal of Economics and Management Science* 5 (Autumn): 540–577.

Khartukov, Eugene M. 2000. "Russia's Oil Business: Any Niche for a National Oil Company." *Journal of Energy and Development,* 25(2): 217–238.

Kleindorfer, P.R. and Crew, Michael A. 1986. *The Economics of Public Utility Regulation.* Cambridge, Mass.: MIT Press.

Kluckhohn, Florence and Strodtbeck, Fred. 1961. *Variations in Value Orientations.* Evanston, Illinois: Row. Peterson & Co.

Kneese, Allen V. and Sweeney, James L. 1985. *Handbook of Natural Resource and Energy Economics,* Vol. I. Amsterdam; New York: North-Holland; New York, N.Y., U.S.A.: Sole distributors for the United States and Canada, Elsevier Science Pub. Co.

Kneese, Allen V. and Sweeney, James L. 1993. *Handbook of Natural Resources and Energy Economics, Vol. 3.* New York: Elsevier.

Koing, Rob and Roberta Lamb. 2000. *IT and Organizational Change in Digital Economics: A Sociotechnical Approach,* in Brynjolfsson and Kahin, 295–324.

Kolb, Robert. 1994. *Options: An Introduction,* 2nd. Edition. Miami, Fla.: Kolb Publishing.

Koren, Leonard and Goodman, Peter. 1992. *The Haggler's Handbook: One Hour to Negotiating Power.* Norton, W. W. & Company Incorporated.

Ku, Anne. Nov 2000. "The future of European energy brokerage." http://www.analyticalq.com/energy/online/

Kydes, Andy S. 1980. "The Brookhaven Energy System Optimization Model: Its Variant and Uses." *Energy Policy Modeling,* Vol. II. ed. W. T. Ziemba and S. L. Schwartz. 110–136.

Labys, W.C.; Paik, S.; and Liebenthal, A. M. 1979. "An Econometric Simulation Model of the U.S. Market for Steam Coal." *Energy Economics,* 1(1): 19–26.

Leffler, William L. 2000. *Petroleum Refining for the Non-technical Person,* 3rd Edition. Tulsa, Okla.: PennWell Books.

Littlechild, S. C. 1996. "Privatization, competition and regulation in the Scottish electricity industry." *Scottish Journal of Political Economy,* 43(1): 1–15.

Lohani, Prem R. 1996. "A Linear Programming Approach to Integrated Power Planning in Nepal: Optimizing the Electric Authority's Long-Term Portfolio of Demand and Supply-Side Resources," Ph.D. Thesis. Mineral Economics Program, Division of Economic and Business, Colorado School of Mines.

Lutkepohl, Helmut. 1993. *Introduction to Multiple Time Series Analysis,* 2nd Edition, Springer Verlag New York.

Lynch, Michael C. 1999. *Economics and Geology, not Economists vs. Geologists Understanding Oil Supply Trends.* For the 1999 BIEE Conference, MIT, September.

Ma, Cindy and Edwards, Franklin R. 1992. Futures & Options. New York: McGraw-Hill, Inc.

MacAvoy, Paul W. 1992. *Industry Regulation and the Performance of the American Economy.* New York: W.W Norton.

Manne, Alan S. and Leo Schrattenholzer with the assistance of Tola F. Minkhoff. 1988. *International Energy Workshop: Overview of Poll Responses.* Stanford, Calif: Stanford University, July.

Margherio, Lynn. 1998. *The Emerging Digital Economy.* Washington, D.C.: U.S. Department of Commerce.

Mariners Museum, http://www.mariner.org/age/menu.html. Downloaded 05/01.

Mariner-Volpe, Barbara. 2000. "The Evolution of Gas Markets in the United States," I & II, Presentation to the Bangladesh Ministry of Energy and Mineral Resources from the U.S. Energy Information Agency, Department of Energy and U.S. AID. (May) Washington, D.C.: http://eia.doe.gov/emeu/presentations/natgas.htm November 2001.

Mariner-Volpe, Barbara. 2001a. "Natural Gas Conveyance and Rates." Presentation to the Bangladesh Ministry of Energy and Mineral Resources from the U.S. Energy Information Agency, Department of Energy and U.S. AID. (Feb.) Washington, D.C.: http://eia.doe.gov/emeu/presentations/natgas.htm November 2001.

Mariner-Volpe, Barbara. 2001b. "U.S. Natural Gas Markets, Developments and Outlook," Presentation to the Bangladesh Ministry of Energy and Mineral Resources from the U.S. Energy Information Agency, Department of Energy and U.S. AID. (Feb.) Washington, D.C.: http://eia.doe.gov/emeu/presentations/natgas.htm November 2001.

Mariner-Volpe, Barbara. 2001c. "Natural Gas Conveyance and Restructuring." Presentation to the Bangladesh Ministry of Energy and Mineral Resources from the U.S. Energy Information Agency, Department of Energy and U.S. AID. (Feb.) Washington, D.C.: http://eia.doe.gov/emeu/presentations/natgas.htm November 2001.

Maslow, Abraham H. 1970. *Motivation and Personality.* New York: Harper & Row.

Masseron, J.D. 1990. *Petroleum Economics.* Paris: Editions Technip.

Mbendi. "Information for Africa, world's top mining, energy and international trade websites." http://mbendi.co.za/indy/oilg/gas_af.htm.

Mathews, Stephen, William Nix, and Evan Berlack. 2001. "Internet Privacy, Security is Next Hurdle for Oil and Gas Industry." *Oil and Gas Journal.* June 18: 79–81.

McCabe, Peter J. 1998. "Energy Resources—Cornucopia of Empty Barrels." *AAPG Bulletin*, 82(11): 2110–2134.

McFadyen, Stuart, Colin Hoskins, and Adam Finn. 1998. "The Effect of Cultural Differences on the International Co-production of Television Programs and Feature Films." *Canadian Journal of Communication*, 23(4). http://www.wlu.ca/~wwwpress/jrls/cjc/BackIssues/23.4/mcfadyen.html Downloaded 7/21/2002.

McGregor, Douglas. 1967. *The Professional Manager,* Edited by Caroline McGregor and Warren G. Bennis. New York: McGraw-Hill.

McKim, Robert. 2000. *Five "Do's" For Customer Relationship Management in the Digital World*, http://www.msdbm.com/Article.cfm?PageID=150 Downloaded 7/7/2002.

McMullin, Dennis M. 2001. "Managing Oil and Gas Asset Life-Cycle Projects with Private Exchanges." *Oil and Gas Journal.* June 18: 79–81.

Mead, Walter. 1994. "Towards and Optimal Oil and Gas Leasing System." *Conference Proceedings of the 17th Annual International Association for Energy Economics Annual Meeting.* Stavanger, Norway: May 25–27.

Meadows, Donella, Dennis Meadows, and Jorgen Randers. 1992. *Beyond the Limits.* Chelsea Vermont: Green Publishing Company.

Meadows, Donella, Dennis Meadows, Jorgen Randers, and William W. Behrens. 1972. *The Limits to Growth.* New York: Universe Books.

Mendonaça, Augusto and Dahl, Carol. 1999. "The Brazilian Electrical System Reform." *Energy Policy.* 27: 73–83.

Meritet, Sophie. 1999. "Why New Distributed Generation Units Might Transform Power Industry's Organization: The Case of Gas Microturbines." *Conference Proceedings of United States Association For Energy Economics, International Association for Energy Economics: The Structure of the Energy Industries: The Only Constant is Change.* 20th Annual North American Conference. August 29–September 1: 83–92. Orlando, Fla.

Michaels, R. J. 1989. "Reorganizing electricity supply in New Zealand: Lessons for the United States." *Contemporary Policy Issues* VII: 73–90.

Micklethwait, John and Wooldridge, Adrian. 1997. "The Art and Practice of Japanese Management, Strategy and Business." Booz Allen Hamilton. http://www.strategy-business.com/strategy/97107 Downloaded 3/28/2001.

Mitchell, John and Vrolijk, Christiaan. 1998. "Closing Asia's Energy Gaps." The Royal Institute of International Affairs. http://www.riia.org/briefingpapers/bp41.html#west. Downloaded 3/26/2001.

Mork, Erling, and Knut Anton Mork. 1999. "Macro and Regulatory Environment of Energy markets: A European Perspective." *Conference Proceedings of United States Association For Energy Economics, International Association for Energy Economics: The Structure of the Energy Industries: The Only Constant is Change.* 20th Annual North American Conference. August 29–September 1: 345–353. Orlando, Fla.

Morris, Richard. 1999. *The Universe, the Eleventh Dimension, and Everything: What We Know and How We Know It.* New York: Four Walls Eight Windows

Morrison, Terri, Conaway, Wayne A., Borden, George A., and Koehler, Hans. 1994. *Kiss, Bow, or Shake Hands: How to Do Business in 60 Countries.* Holbrook, Mass.: Adams Media Corporation.

Mostert, Noël. 1974. *Supership.* New York: Knopf (distributed by Random House).

Musgrave, Richard and Musgrave, Peggy. 1989. *Public Finance in Theory and Practice.* New York: McGraw-Hill.

Mushrush, George W. and Speight, James G. 1995. *Petroleum Products: Instability and Incompatibility.* Pennsylvania: Taylor & Francis: Bristol.

National Petroleum Council. 1972. *U.S. Energy Outlook.* Washington, D.C.

Neff, Thomas L. 1984. *The International Uranium Market,* Cambridge, Mass.: Ballinger Pub. Co.

Nei, Hisanori. 2000. "The Transformation of Japanese Energy Policy," *The Journal of Energy and Development.* 25(2): 173–185.

New Zealand Ministry of Economic Development. 2001. *Chronology of New Zealand Electricity Reform.* Energy Markets Policy Group. http://www.med.govt.nz/ers/electric/chronology/ Downloaded 5/5/2002.

Newcom, Richard and Rieber, Michael. 1985. "The Economics of Coal and Nuclear Energy" in Vogely 1985.

Noreng, Oystein. 2000. "The New Balance of Private and Public Interests in the Restructuring of the Petroleum Industry." A European Perspective, *The Journal of Energy and Development.* 25(2): 187–202.

Oil and Gas Journal. 2001. *Petroleum Software Technology Guide.* Tulsa, Okla.: PennWell Press.

Organization for Economic Cooperation and Development. 1977. *World Energy Outlook.* OECD.

Organization of Petroleum Exporting Countries. 2000. OPEC *Annual Statistical Bulletin.* Vienna: OPEC Secretariate. http://www.opec.org, click on publications, click on Annual Statistical Bulletin.

Orlikowski, Wand J. and C. Suzanne Iacono. 2000. *The Truth Is Not Out There: An Enacted View of the "Digital Economy."* in Brynjolfsson and Kahin, 352–380.

Paisie, John E. 2001. "'E-transformation' of Oil Companies." *Oil and Gas Journal,* June 18, 66–77.

Pearce, David W. and R. Kerry Turner. 1990. *Economics of Natural Resources and the Environment,* Baltimore: The Johns Hopkins University Press.

Pertamina. Indonesia's State Oil & Gas Company. http://www.pertamina.co.id Downloaded 3/26/2001.

Pindyck Robert S. and Daniel Reubenfeld. 1997. E*conometric Models and Economic Forecasts,* 4th edition. New York: McGraw-Hill.

Pisani, Michael J. 1992. "Japanese Management: Colorado Style." http://ppl.nhmccd.cc.tx.us/~mikep/Links/Management/JapaneseMgt.html Downloaded 03/01.

Porter, Michael E. 1990. *Competitive Advantage of Nations.* New York: The Free Press.

Portney, Paul R. and Robert N. Stavins. 2000. *Public Policies for Environmental Protection.* Washington, D.C.: Resources for the Future.

Prast, William and Lax, Howard L. 1983. *Oil Futures Markets: An Introduction.* Lexington, Mass.: LexingtonBooks.

Qatar Petroleum. "4th Doha Conference on Natural Gas." http://www.qgpc.com.qa/. Downloaded 3/26/2001.

Radetsky. 2001. *The Green Myth—Economic Growth and the Quality of the Environment.* Essex,UK: Multi-Science Publishing Co. Ltd.

Raiffa, Howard. 1982. *The Art and Science of Negotiation.* Cambridge, Mass.: Harvard University Press.

Ramsey, Frank P. 1927. "A Contribution to the Theory of Taxation" *Economic Journal,* March, 37:47–61.

Ray, G. F. 1979. "Energy Economics—a Random Walk in History," *Energy Economic,* 1(3): 139–143.

Richter, Roxane. 2000. "New Threats—Rivals Stampede into Online Energy." *The New Energy Economy,* 67–70.

Riva, Joseph P. 1995. "World Oil Production After Year 2000: Business As Usual or Crises?" Congressional Research Service Issue Brief made available by The National Council for Science and the Environment, August 18. http://www.cnie.org/nle/eng-3.html. Downloaded 05/01.

Robinson, Colin. 1992. "The Demand for Electricity: a Critical Analysis of Producer Forecasts." in David Hawdon, *Energy Demand: Evidence and Expectations,* London: Surrey University Press, 215–234.

Sampson, Anthony. 1975. *The Seven Sisters: The Great Oil Companies and the World They Shaped.* New York: Viking Press.

Sawhill, John C. and Cotton, Richard. 1986. *Energy Conservation Successes and Failures.* Washington, D.C.: Brookings Institution.

Schwartz, Peter. 1991. *The Art of the Long View.* New York: Doubleday.

Scotese, Christopher R. "Paleomap Project," University of Texas, Arlington. http://www.scotese.com/climate.htm. Downloaded 05/01.

Selley, Richard. 1997. *Elements of Petroleum Geology.* New York: W.H. Freeman and Company.

Siegel, David. 1999. *Futurize Your Enterprise: Business Strategy in the Age of the E-Customer.* John Wiley and Sons.

Siems, Thomas. 1997. *10 Myths About Financial Derivatives,* Washington, D.C.: Cato Institute, Cato Policy Analysis No. 283. http://www.cato.org/pubs/

Simkin, William. 1971. *Mediation and the Dynamics of Collective Bargaining.* Washington, D.C.: Bureau of National Affairs.

Skov, Arlie. 1995. *An Analysis of Forecasts of Energy Supply, Demand, and Oil Prices.* Society of Petroleum Engineers, SPE Hydrocarbon Economics and Evaluation Symposium, Dallas Texas: 239–253.

Slade, Margaret E., Kolstad, Charles D., and Weiner, Robert J. 1993. "Buying Energy and Nonfuel Minerals: Final Derived, and Speculative Demand." in Kneese and Sweeney. 1993. Chapter 20: 935–1009.

Small, John. 2002. *Hedge Markets for Electric Power in New Zealand.* A Report to the Ministry of Economic Development. (March) http://www.med.govt.nz/ers/electric/hedgemarkets/index.html. Downloaded 5/5/2002.

Smartbusiness Magazine. October 2000: 78–88.

Smith, Michael D., Joseph Bailey, and Erik Brynjolfsson. 2000. "Understanding Digital Markets: Review and Assessment." in Brynjolfsson, Erik and Brian Kahin: 99–136.

Speigel, Murray R. 1995. *College Algebra.* New York: McGraw-Hill:.

Staglioni, Vito A. 2001. *A Policy of Discontent: The Making of a National Energy Strategy:* Tulsa, Okla.: PennWell Press.

Steinberg, Don. 2002. "The Ultimate Technology Survival Guide." *Smart Business Magazine.* (February): 37–49.

Stermole, Franklin J and Stermole, John M. 2000. *Economic Evaluation and Investment Decision Methods.* Golden, Colorado: Investment Evaluations Corporations.

Stern, Jonathan. 1984. *International Gas Trade in Europe. The Policies of Exporting and Importing Countries.* London: Heinemann Educational Books.

Stern, Jonathan. 1985. *Natural gas trade in North America and Asia.* Aldershot, Hants, England; Brookfield, Vt., U.S.: Gower.

Stern, Jonathan. 1987. *Soviet Oil and Gas Exports to the West: Commercial Transaction or Security Threat.* London: Gower.

Stern, Jonathan. 1990. *European gas markets: challenge and opportunity in the 1990s.* London: Royal Institute of International Affairs; Aldershot, Hants, England; Brookfield, Vt., U.S.: Dartmouth.

Stern, Jonathan. 1995. *Russian Natural Gas 'Bubble': Consequences For European Gas Markets.*

Sterner, Thomas. 1992. *International Energy Economics.* London: Chapman & Hall.

Strauss, Otto P. and Elizabeth M. Lown. 1978. *Oil Sand and Oil Shale Chemistry.* Verlag Chemie, New York: Westheim.

Sweetser, Al. 1998. "An Empirical Analysis of a Dominant Firm's Market Power in a Restructured Electricity Market: A Case Study of Colorado." Ph.D. Thesis. Mineral Economics Program, Division of Economic and Business, Colorado School of Mines.

Symonds, G. H. 1955. "Linear Programming: The Solution of Refinery Problems." Esso Standard Oil Co., New York.

Tapscott, Don. 1996. *The Digital Economy: Promise and Peril in the Age of Networked Intelligence.* New York: McGraw-Hill.

Tapscott, Don. 1998. *Growing up Digital.* New York: McGraw-Hill.

Tapscott, Don, David Ticoll, and Alex Lowy. 2000. *Digital Capital: Harnessing the Power of Business Webs.* Cambridge, Mass.: Harvard Business School Press.

Taylor, Paul. 1997. *Behavioural Modelling, Messy Problems, and Pragmatism: A Consulting Approach to the Modelling Process.* in Giovanni and Baranzini: 35–51, 107–119.

Tenenbaum, B., Lock, R., and Barker, J. 1992. "Electricity privatization: structural, competitive and regulatory options." *Energy Policy.* (December): 1134–1160.

The New Palgrave: A Dictionary of Economics. edited by John Eatwell, Murray Milgate and Peter Newman. London: McMillan Press, Ltd. New York: Stockton Press. Tokyo: Maruzen Company Limited.

The Russia Journal. News and Analysis Online. http://www.russiajournal.com/start/business/article_43_2047.htm

Tietenberg, Tom, 1992. E*nvironmental and Natural Resource Economics.* New York: HarperCollins Publishers.

Tirole, Jean. 1989. *The Theory of Industrial Organization.* Cambridge, Mass.: MIT Press.

Tissot, B.P. and D.H. Welte. 1984. *Petroleum Formation and Occurrence.* New York: Springer-Verlag.

Todaro, James. 2001. "Natural Gas Futures Market." Presentation to the Bangladesh Ministry of Energy and Mineral Resources from the U.S. Energy Information Agency, Department of Energy and U.S. AID. Washington, D.C. http://eia.doe.gov/emeu/presentations/natgas.htm, Downloaded 11/2001.

Torvanger, Asbjorn. 1995. "Sources of Energy and the Environment." in Siamack Shojai. *The New Global Oil Market: understanding energy issues in the world economy.* Westport, Conn.: Praeger: 147–157.

Trompenaars, Fons. 1993. *Riding the Waves of Culture: Understanding Cultural Diversity in Business.* London: Nichols-Brealey.

Trompenaars, Fons. "Pisces, Cultural Background." University of Teesside.

Tussing, Arlon R. and Barlow, Connie C. 1984. *The Natural Gas Industry: Evolution, Structure, and Economics.* Cambridge, Mass.: Ballinger Pub. Co.

U.K. Department of Trade and Industry. *Digest of United Kingdom Energy Statistics 2000.* http://www.dti.gov.uk/EPA/digest.htm

U.K. Electricity Association. 2002. *Electricity Companies in the United Kingdom— A Brief Chronology.* http://www.electricity.org.uk/inds_fr.html. Downloaded 4/27/02.

U.S. Central Intelligence Agency. 1977. *The International Energy Situation Outlook to 1985.* ER77-10270 U. Washington, D.C.

U.S. Department of Commerce. 1998. *The Emerging Digital Economy.* Washington, D.C.: U.S. Government Printing Office. http://www.ecommerce.gov/danc1.htm Downloaded 12/28/2001.

U.S. Department of Energy, Energy Information Administration. 1996. *Coal Data: A Reference.* Washington, D.C.: U.S. Government Printing Office.

U.S. Department of Energy, Energy Information Administration. 1997. *U.S. State Energy Severance Taxes, 1985–1993.* http://www.eia.doe.gov/emeu/sevtax/ Downloaded 3/28/2001.

U.S. Department of Energy, Energy Information Administration. 2001. *Natural Gas Transportation — Infrastructure Issues and Operational Trends.* http://www.eia.doe.gov/pub/oil_gas/natural_gas/analysis_publications/ natural_gas_infrastructure_issue/pdf/nginfrais.pdf Downloaded 11/5/2001.

U.S. Energy Information Administration, Department of Energy. 2003a. *Country Analysis Briefs.* http://www.eia.doe.gov/emeu/cabs/content.html Last accessed 08/03.

U.S. Energy Information Administration. Department of Energy. 2003b. "Energy in the United States: 1635– 2000," *Annual Energy Review 2002.* Washington D.C.: U.S. Government Printing Office. http://www.eia.doe.gov/emeu/aer/ contents.html

U.S. Energy Information Administration. Department of Energy. 2003c. *International Energy Outlook.* http://www.eia.doe.gov/oiaf/ieo/index.html. Last accessed 08/03.

U.S. Energy Information Administration. Department of Energy. 2003d. *International Energy Annual,* Washington D.C.: U.S. Government Printing Office. http://www.eia.doe.gov/emeu/idea/contents.html

U.S. House of Representatives. 1975. *Background Reading on Energy Policy.* Washington, D.C.: U.S. Government Printing Office

U.S. Federal Energy Administration. 1974. *Project Independence Report.* Washington, D.C.: U.S. Government Printing Office.

Van der Leeuw, Charles. 2000. *Oil and Gas in the Caucasus and Caspian, A History.* Surrey, U.K.: Curzon Press.

Van Dyke, Kate. 1997. *Fundamentals of Petroleum.* Austin, Texas: University of Texas, Austin.

Vanscoy, Kayte. 2000. "Unconventional Wisdom." *Smart Business Magazine,* 11(10): 78–88.

Varian, Hal. 2000. "Market Structure in the Network Age." in Brynjolfsson and Kahin, pp. 137–150.

Verleger, Philip K. 1993. *Adjusting to Volatile Energy Prices.* Washington, D.C.: Institute for International Economics.

Viscusi W. K., John Vernon, and J. Harrington Jr. 1996. *Economics of Regulation and Antitrust.* 2nd edition, Cambridge, Mass.: MIT Press.

Vogelsang, Ingo and Benjamin M. Compaine. 2000. *The Internet Upheaval.* Cambridge, Mass.: MIT Press.

Vogely, W.A. 1985. *Economics of the Mineral Industries.* in Seeley W. Mudd Series, New York: American Institute of Mining, Metallurgical, and Petroleum Engineers, Inc.

Von Neuman, John and Morgenstern, Oscar. 1944. *Theory of Games and Economic Behavior.* Princeton: Princeton University Press.

Wälde, Thomas W. and Lubbers, Ruud. 1996. *The Energy Charter Treaty: An East–West Gateway for Investment and Trade.* London, Boston: Kluwer Law International.

Walls, W. David. 1995. "An Econometric Analysis of the Market for Natural Gas Futures." *The Energy Journal,* 16(1): 71–83.

Weiner, Robert J. 1991. "Origins of Future Trading: The Oil Exchanges in the 19th Century." *Working Paper.* Waltham, Mass.: Department of Economics, Brandeis University.

Welfens, P.J., B. Meyer, W. Pfaffenberger, P. Jasinski, and A. Jungmittag. 2001. *Energy Policies in the European Union: Germany's Econological Tax Reform.* New York: Springer.

Wilhite, Harold. 1997. *Framing the Socio-cultural Context for Analyzing Energy Consumption.* in Giovanni and Baranzini: 35–51.

Williamson, Oliver E. 1985. *The Economic Institutions of Capitalism.* New York: Free Press. London: Collier Macmillan.

Williamson, Oliver E. 1986. *Economic Organization: Firms, Markets and Policy Control.* New York: New York University Press.

Williamson, Oliver E. 1993. "Transaction Cost Economics Meets Posnerian Law and Economics." *Journal of Institutional and Theoretical Economics,* 149(1): 99–118.

Workshop on Alternative Energy Strategies. 1977. *Global Prospects 1985–2000.* (WAES) New York: McGraw-Hill.

World Energy Conference. 1978. *Study Group Report on Oil and Gas Resources.* Guildford, U.K.: IPC Science and Technology Press.

Wright, Tim. 1984. *Coal Mining in China's Economy and Society 1895–1937.* Cambridge, England: Cambridge University Press.

Yergin, Daniel. 1991. *The Prize: The Epic Quest for Oil, Money, and Power.* New York: Simon and Schuster.

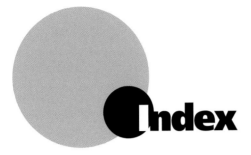

Index

M

O

obligation to supply, 118, 121
Occidental, 147
octane, 368
octane number, 350–351
Office of Electricity Regulation (Offer), 117
off-peak demand, 106, 108
off-system consumers, 190
OGJ Exchanges, 431
oil
    capital costs for extracting oil, 334
    historical use of, 16–17
    history of, 136
    production and prices, 147–151
    substitutions for, 255
oil and gas, 12
Oil and Gas Journal, 32
oil and gas reserves, 342
oil company mergers, 166
oil crisis (1973), 30
oil embargo (1973), 255
oil futures contracts, 377
oil market, 146
oil market history, 388
oil pipelines, 361
oil product consumption, 344
oil production in Europe, 257
oil reserves, 165, 179, 337
oil shale, 14–15
oil shipments, 358
oil shocks (1970s), 377
Oil Springs, Ontario, 18
oil substitutes, 165
oil tankers, 358–359
oil wells, 18
oligopoly, 6
oligopsony, 6
one-period binomial pricing model, 398
online clearinghouses, 434
on-sided dispatching algorithm, 116
on-system consumers, 190
OPEC, 136
    demand curve and marginal revenue curve for, 156–160

demand curve for, 152
formation of, 147
high absorbers within, 162
history of, 146–151
low absorbers within, 162
marginal costs for, 152
oil price management, 147
optimal production for, 152
and price elasticity of demand, 160–162
production allocation for, 152
total revenue maximization for, 167
open access, 113, 131
    for independent power producers (IPPs), 115
    of natural gas, 191
open-minded culture, 461
operating costs, 334
operational risk, 372
opportunism, 178
opportunity cost of capital as discount rate, 300
opportunity costs, 86, 177, 210, 308
optimal allocation, 43
optimal consumption, 296
optimal level of pollution, 204–206
optimal production for OPEC, 152
optimization, 435–439
optimization techniques, 31
option prices, 409
option purchases, 396
option quotes, 397
options, 7, 372, 373
    net payoff of, 397
    procedure for valuing, 408
    trading methods for, 394
option sales, 396
option trading strategies, 409–410
option valuation, 398–408, 413
Organization of Petroleum Exporting Countries (OPEC), 5
organized exchanges, 374
outer-directed cultures, 461
out-of-pocket costs, 86
out of the money, 395
outsourcing, 182

V